A Tutorial Guide to PT/Modeler™ 2.0 and Pro/ENGINEER®

Richard F. Ferraro

 **ADDISON-WESLEY**

An imprint of Addison Wesley Longman, Inc.

Reading, Massachusetts • Harlow, England • Menlo Park, California
Berkeley, California • Don Mills, Ontario • Sydney • Bonn • Amsterdam
Tokyo • Mexico City

Vice President, Publisher: Robert Woodbury
Senior Producer: Denise Olson
Project Manager: Phoebe Ling
Production Manager: Karen Wernholm
Producer's Assistant: Morgan Baker

Cover Designer: Alwyn Velásquez
Senior Manufacturing Coordinator: Judy Sullivan
Copy Editor: Adrienne Rebello
Compositor: Mike Wile
Proofreader: PC&F

Visit the Addison-Wesley CAD series site on the World Wide Web at http://www.awl.com/cseng/cad/ptc for additional information, technical tips, and to send e-mail to technical support.

Parametric Technology Corporation makes no endorsement of the text or user manuals accompanying this product. PTC assumes no responsibility for the performance of the software or for errors in this manual.

Information described in this manual is furnished for information only, is subject to change without notice, and should not be construed as a commitment by Parametric Technology Corporation (PTC). PTC assumes no responsibility or liability for errors or inaccuracies that may appear in this manual.

Parametric Technology Corporation and Pro/ENGINEER are registered trademarks of Parametric Technology Corporation in the United States and other countries. Parametric Technology, PTC, the PTC logos and PT/Products, PT/Modeler, PT/Render, PT/Library, PT/Library Access, PT/Basic Library, the PT/Products logo and all product names in the PT/Products line are trademarks of Parametric Technology Corporation in the United States and other countries. All other company and product names are trademarks or registered trademarks of their respective owners.

ISBN 0-201-35651-1

1 2 3 4 5 6 7 8 9 10 CRS 01009998

Preface

You hold in your hands a guide to a powerful design and production tool. PT/Modeler™ is a robust subset of Pro/ENGINEER®, the premier feature-based parametric modeling package from Parametric Technology Corporation (PTC), the CAD/CAM/CAE industry's leading supplier of software tools used to automate the mechanical development of a product from its conceptual design through production. Worldwide, more than 15,000 companies employ PTC's integrated software technologies to reduce time to market, improve engineering processes, and optimize product quality. Because the PT/Modeler and Pro/ENGINEER interfaces are virtually identical, this book can be used to learn the basics of both products, though throughout this text PT/Modeler commands are referenced.

If you are new to PT/Modeler or Pro/ENGINEER, this manual presents basic concepts and procedures in an efficient, accessible way, allowing you to get up and running quickly. Information about PT/Modeler—ranging from getting started basics to advanced assemblies—is presented in a need-to-know fashion that makes it easy to remember. Numerous figures illustrate the techniques and the step-by-step tutorials. The book is organized so it is useful during the tutorial phase, during review, and later as a reference. This manual may be used independently for self-study, or in conjunction with a basic engineering graphics course or introductory engineering and/or design courses.

This manual may be used in conjunction with a basic engineering graphics course, with introductory engineering design courses, or independently for self study.

Organization

The chapters proceed in a logical fashion to guide you from the basics to more advanced techniques:

Chapter 1 covers important basics to get you up and running, including interacting with the PT/Modeler environment, directories, saving files, and working with menus.

Chapter 2 describes how to work in a three-dimensional modeling environment including orienting, manipulating, zooming and panning, and the use of datum planes.

Chapter 3 presents a first look at features. In 3D modeling, parts are made of features. This chapter describes what features are, how they are used to build parts, and provides a first pass at building protrusions, holes, cuts, and rounds. Discussions also include how to suppress features, hierarchical relationships, and the feature order list.

Chapter 4 covers the powerful PT/Modeler Sketcher, including proper sketching philosophy, basic shapes, aligning, dimensioning, sketching in 3D, and feature regeneration.

Chapter 5 shows you how to create an engineering drawing, including placing views, orienting views, printing, and dimensioning. Different types of views include 2D and 3D, projections, full, broken, partial, and section views.

Chapter 6 builds a deeper understanding of the features touched upon earlier, including protrusion, holes, rounds, edge chamfers, and cuts. This chapter also describes chamfers, shells, revolved features, using feature groups, and the powerful patterning capability.

Chapter 7 provides extensive information on modifying, redefining, and reordering the features within a part.

Chapter 8 shows you how to use layers, including organizing a part, creating layers, placing features onto layers, showing and hiding layers, and how to determine what features are on a layer.

Chapter 9 provides important information on troubleshooting your model.

Chapter 10 shows you how to create assemblies out of individual parts. Included are the techniques for 3D orienting parts in the assembly, creating subassemblies, viewing parts in different colors, using assembly layers, and creating exploded assemblies.

Chapter 11 introduces the more advanced capability called relations. Relations allow the designer to "program" the part, using equations to describe dimensional relationships within the part. Several examples are provided.

In addition, the text includes 62 individual tutorials presented in an easy-to-follow table format, and important background information on topics such as parametric design, 3D solid modeling, hierarchical design, and creating engineering drawings. In this text you will also find information on accessing and using the data files that accompany the text. Finally, overview material is presented on PT/Render and PT/Library.

Acknowledgments

I would like to acknowledge the individuals who contributed to the development and implementation of these tutorials by reviewing the manuscript and making many suggestions to improve this book. They include:

Brett Baraclough
United States Military Academy
West Point, NY

Kevin Beard
Central Lakes College
Staples, MN

Dave Heaton
Parametric Technology Corporation
Waltham, MA

Mark Marenghi
New Technology Solutions, Inc.
Tewksbury, MA

Mike Paskerian
Parametric Technology Corporation
Seattle, WA

Marie Planchard
Massachusetts Bay Community College
Wellesley, MA

Donald Roth
Gannon University
Erie, PA

A special thanks to Rollin Dix of the Illinois Institute of Technology and to his students for their review and for technical validation of the tutorial steps.

Editing, testing, and producing step-by-step tutorials requires a tremendous amount of publishing expertise, and I would be remiss if I did not acknowledge those who worked on this guide, without whose diligence and hard work this book could not have been published: Karen Wernholm, Morgan Baker, and especially project manager Phoebe Ling.

Lastly, thanks to Paula Lowe, for her editing, support, and a million other things that assisted in the writing of this book.

Richard F. Ferraro

Note

We at Addison Wesley Longman would like to thank our friends and colleagues at Parametric Technology Corporation for their support and good advice: Jane O'Sullivan, Manager of Sales Operations PT/Products Group; Dave Pettine, Educational Sales Manager, Eastern Region; Larry Fire, Educational Sales Manager, Western Region; Brian Barnes, Product Manager; Blake Courter, Associate Application Engineer; Jim Sperry, Group Leader, Quality Assurance; Jeff Eaton, Vice President & General Manager of PT/Products; and John Inman, Director of Inside Sales.

Addison Wesley Longman

Contents

Chapter 1   Working with PT/Modeler   11

Chapter 2   Viewing the Model   37

Chapter 3   A First Look at Features   95

Chapter 4   Working in Sketcher   135

Chapter 6   Understanding Features   257

Chapter 9   Troubleshooting Your Model   365

Chapter 11   Working with Relations   463

Introduction

PT/Modeler™ and Pro/ENGINEER® are powerful software packages that offer parametric, feature-based modeling, design, and assembly capabilities. This tutorial guide will take you step-by-step from the basics to the more advanced features of the software. Because the interfaces of the two products are virtually identical, you can use this text to learn both programs even though throughout this text PT/Modeler is the product referenced. At the same time, you will learn about parametric solid modeling.

It is best to start at the beginning of this book and work your way through chapter by chapter. A wide range of topics are presented and many of them are interrelated. To optimize your experience with the tutorials in this text, in some instances a topic is introduced briefly in one chapter and then discussed in detail in a later chapter. For example, in the Features chapter, you will be using some techniques that will be taught thoroughly in the following Sketching chapter. In other chapters, there are forward references to material that will be covered in later chapters.

This book provides an important balance of step-by-step tutorials—essential when learning complex software—and supportive text. The tutorials reinforce what you have learned from the text portion of the book and get you up and running quickly. The tutorials are small projects as opposed to one big project. As a result, you can work with a tutorial and its accompanying data file without worrying about the file's usage later in the book. (See the inside front cover for important information on accessing the data files that accompany the tutorials.) You can also skip a section if you cannot complete it and return to it when you have a better understanding.

Take the time to understand each step in the tutorials. It is possible to parrot each entry without thinking about what you are doing. For optimal learning, however, follow the instructions, then improvise, try things a different way, and finally, try it again without the tutorial.

It is important that you understand the many options the software presents. A variety of techniques for achieving the same goal (e.g., drawing a circle or selecting an object) are presented. In addition, the book is organized so it is easy to refer back to a section to refresh yourself on a particular technique.

Parametric Technology Corporation

Parametric Technology Corporation (PTC) is the CAD/CAM/CAE industry's leading supplier of software tools used to automate the mechanical development of a product from conceptual design through production.

The PT/Products™ family, a division of PTC, includes a fully associative suite of mechanical design, analysis, documentation, and manufacturing applications. Based on the proven technology of Pro/ENGINEER®, the core module, **PT/Modeler**™, is a robust, 3D parametric, feature-based, solid modeling system for part and assembly design, detailing, and documentation.

This book concentrates on solid modeling and the program refers to itself as PT/Products both in its introduction and within its title bar. The icon is titled **PT/Modeler.** From this point on, we will refer to this software as **PT/Modeler.** Below, we walk through short descriptions of PT/Modeler and some of its popular add-ons. If you are working with additional PT/Products add-ons or with Pro/ENGINEER and its wide variety of add-ons, please refer to the product user manuals that came with your software for descriptions.

PT/Modeler

PT/Modeler is the design development software. This program helps you perform the actual 3D modeling. You can start from scratch or work from existing files to create parts, assemblies, and drawings. It is possible to view the results in a number of ways, including wireframe, hidden line, and shaded versions. You can even manipulate lights for your final rendered version.

The focus of this book is **PT/Modeler.** Some discussion is provided on PT/Render and PT/Library.

PT/Render

If you are running on Windows NT, you can access the powerful PT/Render. Additional menu items will appear in **PT/Modeler** allowing you to create photo-realistic renderings of your model. Special effects including complex lighting, shadows, reflections, transparencies, and texture mapping are available. The PT/Render options are not discussed in this book.

Note that you can create shading 3D views of an object with **PT/Modeler** using the *shade* mode. **PT/Modeler** produces 3D views, which may include wireframe, hidden line, no hidden line, and shaded.

PT/Library

PT/Library allows you to bring standard parts, that is, nuts, screws, bolts, brackets, into your model. An extensive database is provided. PT/Library is not discussed in this book.

3D Solid Modeling

You will be working in a three-dimensional (3D) space. At times, you will pop into a two-dimensional (2D) space to work on a sketch or to view a projection. The key point is that you do your design and construction in the three-dimensional space (3-space).

This is different from traditional CAD software where you typically work on views of a 3D object projected onto various 2D planes. This 3D solid modeling software is clearly the future and unquestionably, **PT/Modeler** is the pioneer of this new wave.

Solid modeling represents an object as a defined region of space, not merely by a set of surfaces. The term *solid* connotes that information on the inside of the object is also provided in the model. In addition, because it is dealing with solids, the software can calculate things such as mass and center of gravity.

Solid modeling is similar to sculpting with clay. You start with a blob, maybe form it into a cube, cut out some parts, stick some shapes on, round a corner or two, drill a hole, and cut out a shape. Stand back and voilà. You have a 3D solid model.

Feature-Based Design

All of these Parametric Technology products are feature-based. What does that mean? A feature is a building block. A part is described by a sequence of features.

Look at the solid model in Figure 1. As you can see, the part consists of a number of features. The base plate is an extruded protrusion feature based on a rectangular section. It has a chamfer feature that bevels its top edge. The base plate also has a cut feature that removes some material from the base plate. Connected to the base plate is a shaft. This shaft is represented by another extruded protrusion feature. This time the protrusion is based on a circular section. The shaft has a hole feature extending through the shaft and a cut feature making a slot in the top of the shaft. The shaft is connected to the base plate using a round feature. Near the top of the shaft is another shaft extending sideways. This second shaft is also an extruded protrusion based on a circular section. In summary, the part, as seen in Figure 1, is described by a sequence of features.

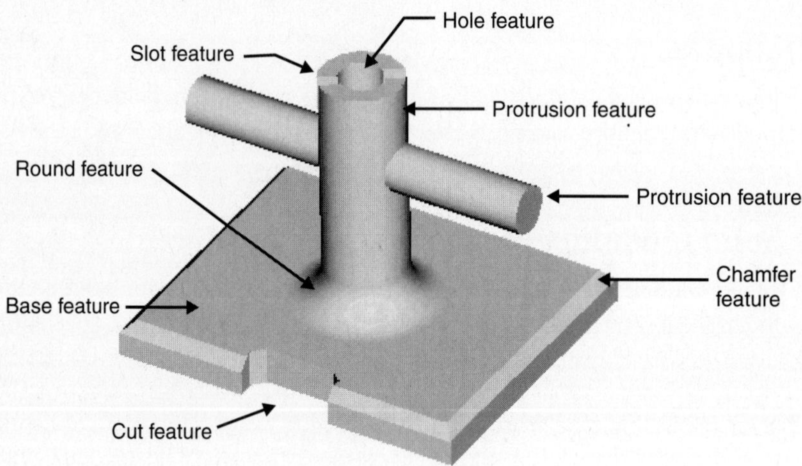

Figure 1 A 3D model.

Feature Construction Lists

Features are ordered in a construction list. Parts are built one feature at a time, starting with the base feature. In Figure 1, the base plate is constructed followed by the shaft, slot, chamfer, and finally the rounded edge. Does it matter what the order is? Certainly, a feature A that is located on or by a feature B cannot be constructed before B. In other words, a child of A cannot proceed A in the feature list.

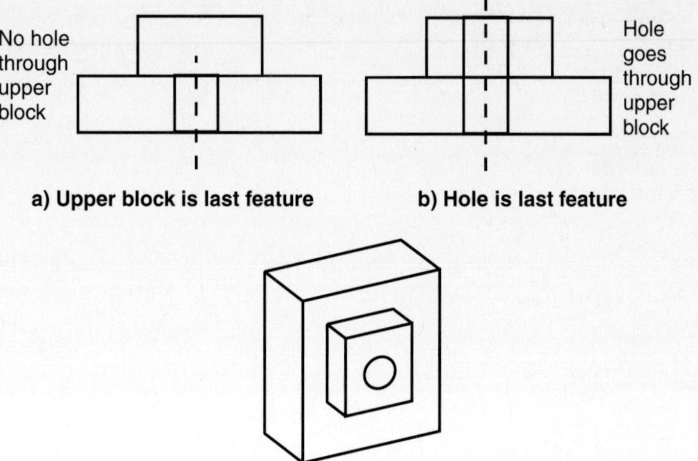

Figure 2 Placing a hole in different locations of the feature construction list.

In Figure 2, for example, there are three features. The first feature is the base; the second feature is a block integral to and located on the surface of the base. The third feature is a hole that extends from the top of the block downward. It is defined to go all the way through the part. In Figure 2(a), we see that the hole does not extend through the smaller block. The reason is the feature list constructs first the base, next the hole, and last the smaller block. In Figure 2(b), the hole extends through the smaller block. Can you guess why? It is because the hole is defined last of all.

Base Feature

The first feature constructed, in our case the base plate, is called the base feature. All other features are *based* on this base feature. Another way of saying this is "the base feature is parent to all other features." Move the base feature, and all other features move with it. As a result, selection of the base feature is an important step in the model building process.

> **TIP:** Choose the block of solid most like the solid blank from which you would make the part by machining and attaching other features.

Parametric Design

During the creation of features it is necessary to provide locating and sizing dimensions. These dimensions are parameters that control the feature. The features are *parameter-driven*. Parameters can be either assigned fixed values or they can be calculated from other parameters.

Consider the rectangles in Figure 3. The length of the sides are declared explicitly in Figure 3(a), but they are declared as symbols in Figure 3(b). An equation can be set up that describes the relationship between these two symbols. For example:

$$A = 100$$
$$B = A / 2$$

Using these parametric relations, it is always possible to insure that the height will be one-half the width. The equations that you set up can be quite complicated, including many mathematical operators. In **PT/Modeler**, these equations are called *relations*. This is illustrated in Figure 3.

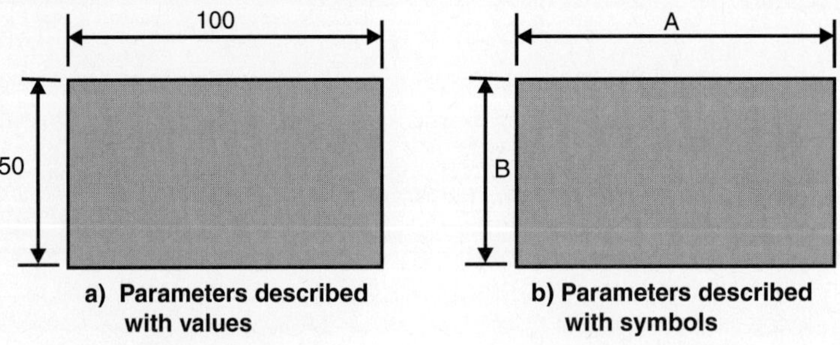

Figure 3   Parametric representation of dimensions.

Hierarchical Design

Your designs may get quite complex, with hundreds of parts, each part consisting of many features. The parts might be organized into assemblies. An assembly could consist of multiple subassemblies. Getting at a particular feature of a particular part in a particular subassembly of a particular assembly could be a daunting task were it not for the hierarchical elements designed into **PT/Modeler**.

Good organization is critical to a successful design. This takes some forethought, but it is well worth the effort. It is possible to change the hierarchical relationships later in the design, but it can be difficult depending on *how much* and *what* has to change. Consider an automobile. There are thousands of parts in the auto. The manufacturer making the engine would not need the specifications for the radio. The organization of the design clearly affects the usability of the model.

Figure 4 illustrates a hierarchical design of a lamp. Note that the lamp assembly is the parent of a base, head, pole, and light bulb subassemblies. The head subassembly is the parent of the shade and electrical subassemblies and a bracket part. The electrical subassembly is the parent of the bulb socket and wiring subassemblies and the switch arm and switch nut parts. The switch arm part consists of the base Feature 1 that is the parent of Features 2, 5, 6, and 7. Feature 2 is the parent of Features 3, 4, 8, and 9. Who is the parent of Feature 8? You can follow up the chart to find the answer. All of the grandparents are also parents. Move the head assembly and you can bet that Feature 8 will move along with it.

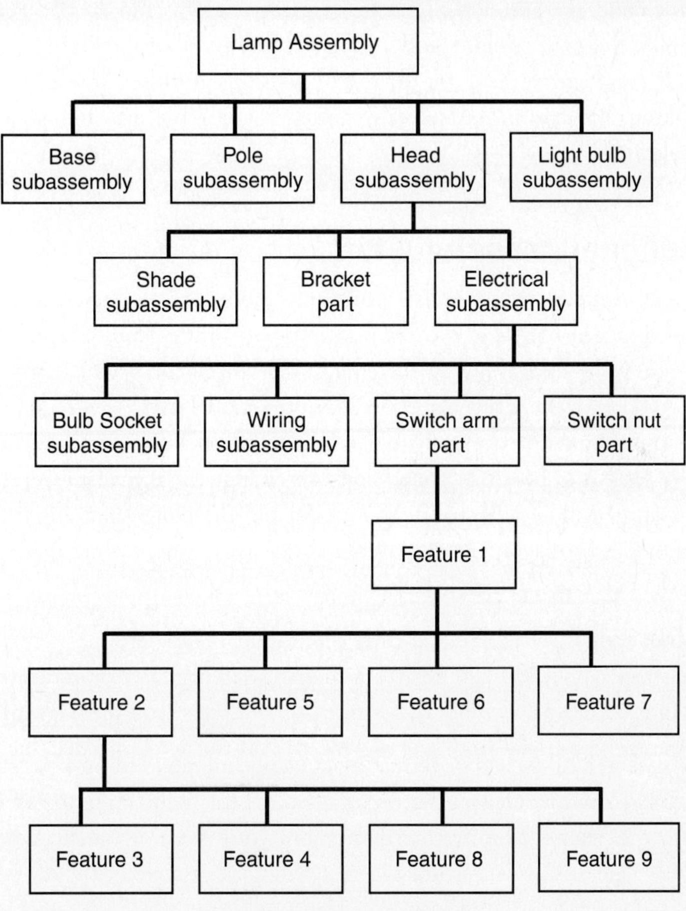

Figure 4 Hierarchical design.

A child can have multiple parents and a parent can have multiple children. The rule to remember is that no child can be a parent to its parent or vice versa.

Creating Engineering Drawings

A special mode is dedicated to the making of engineering drawings. It is called the *drawing* mode. The drawing mode is a powerful and flexible tool. You will be surprised how easy it is to create drawings once your part or assemblies are designed. It is as if you have your model and an x-ray camera. Just point and shoot. You can place 3D views of your model, taken from any angle, on the drawings. It is possible to place standard front, top, or side projected views, or projected views from any angle. In addition, you can create sectional views, detailed views, and auxilliary views. You can also draw on drawings, add annotation, notes, and powerful tables. You can reference actual part dimensions in the tables such that if you change the value in the table, the part actually changes automatically. And do not worry about dimensioning these views. The model already contains all of the dimensional information. All you have to do is ask for the dimensions and then move them around to your liking. All in all, you are really going to enjoy the drawing capabilities of **PT/Modeler.**

Bidirectional Associativity

This large term means that you can work on a model (part or assembly) from any number of different places. You can work on a part in the Main Graphics window, a child window, an assembly, the sketcher, a drawing, or in a table. Any time you modify a parameter, the result will show up in the model itself. Consequently, if you are polishing a drawing at a final stage of the design process, and you realize that you want a length to be a bit longer, you can change the dimension on the drawing. The change will be reflected in the model and therefore, viewable from any of the other modes of display. If you change a radius of a part while in an assembly that uses the part, the part itself will change.

Said another way, there is one and only one model. There are many ways to *view* the model. You can view the model from many different 3D viewpoints, from a flat 2D drawing, or in an assembly. Regardless of the view, you are viewing a single model. Change the model from any viewpoint and the actual model changes.

Many software products take a picture of a model for such things as assemblies or drawings or 3D views. Modify the picture and you have not touched the original model. This type of software is not bidirectionally associative.

Consider the case where one designer makes a widget part. Many other designers use this part in their assemblies. Suppose that one of the assembly designers, not on a first-name basis with the widget designer, changes the widget's length. The widget changes. What happens to all of the other assemblies? Big problem, right? It could be if you are not careful. This is where database management, write protection, and version control systems come into play.

Conventions Used in this Book

You will be interacting with **PT/Modeler** in a number of ways. You will be clicking, moving, and dragging the mouse, typing keys on the keyboard, and selecting menu items. Often, an action on a figure or in a list of instructions is abbreviated. The following conventions are used in this book.

Mouse:

mLb	mouse left button click
mMb	mouse middle button click
mRb	mouse right button click
Ctrl-drag-mLb	hold Control key and drag left button
Ctrl-drag-mMb	hold Control key and drag middle button
Ctrl-drag-mRb	hold Control key and drag right button

Menu:

Select *xxx*

where *xxx* indicates a menu selection. This means you left click the mouse on the *xxx* menu item. For example, select Exit, select Protrusion.

xxx >yyy

where *xxx* and *yyy* indicate menu selections. Select *xxx* then select *yyy* in *xxx*'s submenu. See the following example.

xxx | yyy

Select *xxx* and then the *yyy* option. The *yyy* option is also a menu selection.

Feature >Protrusion | Extrude >Solid | Done

This complex chain indicates that you should select the **Feature** menu item, then the **Protrusion** menu item. At that point, you have options for the protrusion; select the **Extrude** and **Solid** options and then the **Done** option. Menu selection is described in detail in Chapter 1.

Dialogs:

Click *xxx*

Click a dialog button. For example, Click OK, or Click Preview.

Message Window:

Query

```
Enter object to save
[Default.prt]?
```

What's in Store?

PT/Modeler is about solid modeling. It helps you from conception through final documentation and testing. There are several distinct steps in this process. You will often bounce around between the steps. A solid model is rarely designed in a single pass. There are several modalities within **PT/Modeler** that you may use to get through these steps. These include feature creation, working with the model in 3-space, sketching in 2-space, creating drawings, and building assemblies.

Within each of these modalities there are simple as well as complicated techniques. A User's Guide might have individual chapters devoted to features, sketching, assemblies, and drawings. However, this is not necessarily the best way to learn. In this text we have chosen to present the simple aspects of features, sketching, assemblies, and drawings first to get you up and running, then revisit each topic in more depth, presenting the more powerful aspects.

Chapters 1 through 5 provide a first pass through the software. These will get you started by introducing you to some of the basic features and the sketcher. Considerable time is spent on viewing a model in 3D space, and setting up rendering modes including hidden line, no hidden line, and shading. We will end this first pass with a comprehensive look at how to produce a drawing.

Chapters 6 through 11 provide the second pass. You will get a more thorough look at the different features available to you. Here we present modifying a design, the importance of layers and how to use them, and troubleshooting your designs. In Chapter 10, we will dive into the Assembly mode and create several assemblies. Last, you will learn how to use Relations and will really see why parametric design is so powerful.

An Additional Thought or Two

There are many capabilities in **PT/Modeler** that are not covered here. You can use the help system to guide you through these other powerful features. You will find yourself asking the question "Can **PT/Modeler** do this?" Nearly always, the answer is "yes."

Chapter 1

Working with PT/Modeler

1.1 The PT/Modeler Environment

There is a lot to learn here. I know you are anxious to get modeling, and I will get you there as soon as possible.

PT/Modeler runs on many different computer platforms. The program itself does not look like other Windows programs; it does not have the standard menu items at the top of the page, the tool bars, or status bars to which you are accustomed. Rather, it has its own interface. The interface was designed to be fast, providing maximum information with minimum clutter. Once you get the hang of it, you will find the system quick, easy, and intuitive to use.

1.2 Memory Organization

The first thing that you will need to get used to is the memory organization. PT/Modeler anticipates that you will want to work on a number of parts at the same time, and anticipates the need to keep multiple parts in memory for quick access. This allows you to get parts onto and off of the screen rapidly. You can have several parts, assemblies, or drawings active in memory at a time, each displayed in their own graphics window. In addition, you can also have parts, assemblies, or drawings that are not actively displayed in a graphics window still resident in session memory. This allows you to load the part, assembly, or drawing back into active memory quickly.

It is critical that you understand this organization clearly. It keeps these parts in a memory cache. You can select to display certain parts while not displaying other parts. I refer to parts that are displayed as being in *active* memory. I refer to parts that are not displayed as being in *session* memory. This operation is unlike most Windows applications.

> **NOTE:** Closing a Window that displays a part using >Quit Window, does not remove the part from memory. It moves the part from active memory to system memory. This part is neither saved nor quit without saving. The part is still resident in system memory. Quit Window can be thought of as reducing a window to an icon. The part still resides in memory; however, it is not displayed in a window.

Figure 1.1 illustrates the memory organization of PT/Modeler. A part might be newly created or it might reside on a disk file. You can access a part from the disk by selecting the Retrieve or the Search/Retr menu items. Either way, we now have a part in active memory that is visible in a window on the screen. At this point, you could choose to create another part from scratch or load another part from disk using the same technique. You can work in multiple graphics windows, each with separate parts. In fact, you can have multiple windows, each with the same part.

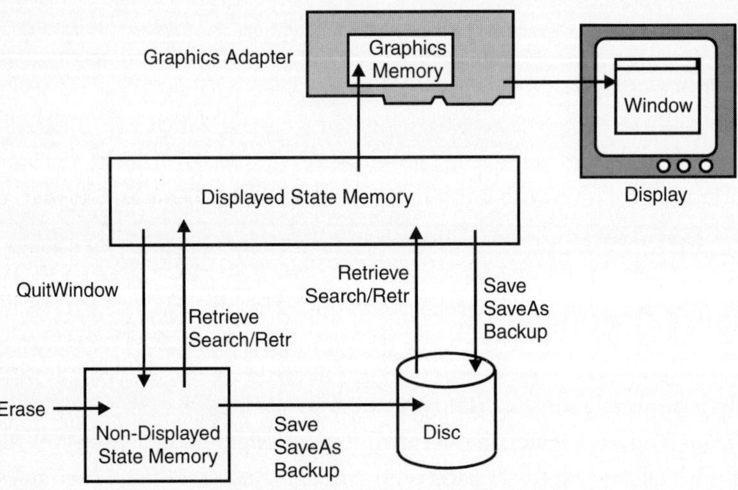

Figure 1.1   Memory organization.

Now, you will want to save this data. It is possible to do this using the Save, SaveAs, or Backup menu items. These copy the data from session memory to the disk. Suppose that we create two new parts and each resides in a window on the screen. First, we create part A and then part B. Part A resides in our main graphics window.

Part B resides in a second graphics window. We can resize either window any way we like. Let's save part A using the Save command. This creates a copy of part A on the disk.

Now suppose we want to get Part B off of the screen. We would select the Window associated with Part B (more on how to do this later) and use the QuitWindow command. This erases the window. No warning message that we have not saved Part B. Poof! It's gone. Well, not really. The QuitWindow command merely places Part B out of active memory and into session memory. We can bring it back up using the Retrieve or the Search/ Retr command. This time, it comes from the session memory.

You can save a file to disk regardless if the data is in active or session memory— no need to bring it into a window. Consequently, when data is removed from active memory, using QuitWindow, the data is still preserved and can be recalled. However, suppose that you modify a part, Part A. Further, suppose that you do not like the modifications and want to revert back to your original on disk. If you use QuitWindow to remove it from the screen, the modified Part A still resides in session memory. Subsequently, if you attempt to retrieve Part A, the modified version will be loaded back into active memory and the modified part will be displayed in a graphics window. You would need to Erase the modified Part A either from active or session memory. This is discussed in the next section.

1.3   Running and Exiting PT/Modeler

Run PT/Modeler by clicking on the icon or through the start menu. Perhaps you will want to place the PT/Modeler icon on your desktop. If you have a slower machine, the program may take a while to initialize so be patient. Once up and running, the program can be exited through the Exit command.

As mentioned previously, it is possible to have multiple parts open at a time. For example, you can have one part in the main graphics window and other parts in subwindows. Each of these parts is stored in session memory. Only one is active at a time, even though many might be displayed. It is necessary to actively switch between displayed windows in order to make a different part active. This is accomplished using the Change Window command.

1.4   Files

Numerous file types can be created with PT/Modeler. Some of these files are binary files and others are text files. Of course, text files can be read and modified using a text editor.

By far, the most common ones that will concern you are the part files, with the *.PRT extension. You will read and write these files during these tutorials. As you create drawings, you will save and restore them using the *.DRW file format. When you get into assemblies, you will be using the *.ASM file format. If you choose to define a part using *relations*, you will create a *.DAT data file. These files can be edited in a text editor. Sketches can be saved using the *.sec format. The most common data formats are provided in Table 1.1.

Extension	Description
*.PRT	Part files
*.DRW	Drawing files created in the Drawings Mode
*.ASM	Assembly files created in the Assembler Mode
*.SEC	Sketch files created in the sketcher

Table 1.1   Common Data File Formats

You may be interested in custom configuring PT/Modeler working with the CONFIG.PRO file. This file is loaded at start up and controls whether the display and plotter work and how. It also controls many other aspects of PT/Modeler. Several CONFIG.PRO files are read in sequence to complete the definition. As you shade parts (they do not have to be gray) you will create and read COLOR.MAP files. It is possible to configure the system colors, including the line colors, and window background colors using the *.SCL extension. You can customize the Menu using the MENU_DEF.PRO file. The most common configuration files are shown in Table 1.2.

Extension	Description
CONFIG.PRO	Configuration file created internally or externally with a text editor
COLOR.MAP	Color files created with View >Cosmetic >Appearances
*.SCL	System Color files created with Misc >System Colors
MENU_DEF.PRO	Menu configuration files created externally with a text editor

Table 1.2   Common Configuration File Formats

When you request information about a part or assembly through the Info menu, you generate an *.INF information file. This is shown in Table 1.3.

Extension	Description
*.INF	Information files generated by Info

Table 1.3   Common Information File Formats

Needless to say, there are many other file formats used in conjunction with PT/Modeler.

1.5 Directories

The PT/Modeler program reads several configuration files during startup. One such file is `config.pro`. I have provided a custom `config.pro` file that needs to reside in the same directory where the software is installed. This file sets up some default directories.

When you install the PT/Modeler software, you will need to create or enter a directory in which to install. After the installation, this <install dir> directory contains a `bin` directory where all of the binary executables are found. There are several other directories; of note is the `text` directory. You will be putting configuration files in this directory. You will need to put my custom `menu_def.pro` file in this directory, replacing the default file that comes with the standard installation. *Please read the inside front cover for downloading instructions.*

1.5.1 Working Directory

PT/Modeler considers one current directory to be open at a time. This is called the *working* directory. You can change the working directory through the >Misc >Change Dir menu item or access files in subdirectories of that active directory. All files saved will be written to the active directory.

1.5.2 Search Directories

By default, PT/Modeler will use the working directory as the search path. The simplest way to add directories to the search path is by adding commands to the `config.pro` file. PT/Modeler will look for files in the search path and will accept the first file with the desired name.

1.5.3 The Environment Submenu

It is possible to customize PT/Modeler through a number of configuration files. One such file is `config.pro` which is read and used at startup. It is convenient to change a setting or two quickly or temporarily during a session. This can be accomplished through the Environment submenu, shown in Figure 1.2. A section of the menu is dedicated to check boxes. These check boxes enable or disable commonly used parameters. Many are used to enable or disable the display of non-geometry objects such as reference planes, points, rotation references, and other items that might clutter the display. I turned off the display of many of these (by un-checking the respective boxes) when I created figures for this book.

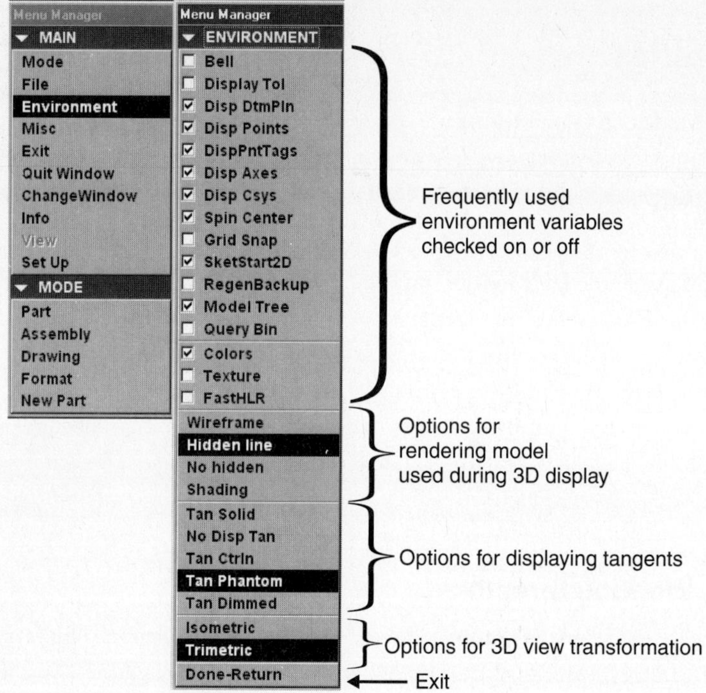

Figure 1.2   The Environment submenu.

Also included in this submenu are options for 3D display, displaying tangents, selecting the desired 3D view-transformation, and as expected, a Done-Return selection.

1.5.4   Configuration Files

There are several configuration files that PT/Modeler reads in at start up. These files help customize your system. I have used two configuration files to configure PT/Modeler. The first file, `config.pro`, will set system variables, set search paths, and create keyboard macros. The second file is a configuration file that adds items to the menu system. This file is called `menu_def.pro`. Both files are provided in Appendix A.

At startup, PT/Modeler reads in configuration files from the directories as shown in Table 1.4. Multiple `config.pro` files can be read into the program. PT/Modeler starts with a set of default conditions for all of its parameters. Parameters set in any of the `config.pro` files will overwrite these default settings. A parameter set in a `config.pro` file will be overwritten by the same parameter being written in a later `config.pro` file. Under certain circumstances it is possible to load a `config.pro` file when running in PT/Modeler.

Order	Location	Description
1st	Loadpoint	The directory where the PT/Modeler executable resides
2nd	Login	The home directory for your login ID.
3rd	Start-up directory	The working directory when PT/Modeler is started

Table 1.4   Reading in `config.pro`

1.6   Saving Files

The technique employed for saving files is at once straightforward and complicated. Active parts, drawing, sketches, and a number of other specific files can be saved. These are saved to the current directory. You will not be prompted for the directory. You will, however, be prompted for the object to save.

PT/Modeler does not overwrite files. Each time you save an object, it appends an incrementing number onto the end of the filename. For example, if you saved a part MY_PART.PRT, modified it, then saved it again, you would write a new file MY_PART.PRT.2. Modifying it and saving it again produces MY_PART.PRT.3. It is assumed that no number is equivalent to a .1.

1.6.1   File >Save

When you select the File >Save menu option, a query appears in the message window asking you for the part (or other object) to save.

```
Enter object to save [Default.prt]?
```

Keying Enter causes the file Default.prt to be saved to the current directory. PT/Modeler asks you for the file name. It places the expected file name as a default in the query. This occurs because you can save any object in memory, not just objects that are visible. More on that later. For now, just key Enter to save a file.

1.6.2   File >Save As

You can also save an object to the current directory with a different name. Be careful here. PT/Modeler does not follow the Microsoft conventions. Suppose you have a part named MY_PART. You could Save As using the name MY_AS_PART. A file, MY_AS_PART.PRT, is saved in the current directory. The object MY_PART is not saved. Now here's the kicker. You are still working on the part MY_PART. Make more changes, and you are changing MY_PART. You can work with the file MY_AS_PART by loading it into session memory. You can save MY_PART, and quit the window or erase the file, MY_PART, from memory.

1.6.3   File >Backup

You can save an object to another directory using the File >Backup menu selection. You will be prompted to enter a directory name and then the object name.

1.6.4   File >Erase

This command removes data from active or session memory. The data associated with a part can either be displayed or nondisplayed. A part that is displayed is associated with a window on the screen. When you use the QuitWindow menu command, you remove the part data from the screen. This data is not eliminated. Rather, it is now in the nondisplayed state. Nondisplayed memory can still be saved to disk or redisplayed without referring back to the disk file. This nondisplayed state is a cache for the part data. It allows you to set aside a part while you work on another part.

1.6.5   File >Purge

If you are working on a complicated part, you could end up generating several files along the way. One unique file is saved during each save operation. A naming sequence is created by appending a number on the end of the file name. For example, MY.PRT.1, MY.PRT.2, . . . MY.PRT.83. Once you are satisfied with the most recent version, you can select File >Purge to delete all files except MY.PRT.83.

1.7   The PT/Modeler Screen

PT/Modeler uses multiple windows. After startup, there are three windows displayed by this application as illustrated in Figure 1.3. These are the main Graphics Window, the Menu Window, and the Message Window. As you can see, the menus are drawn to the right of the Main Graphics Window. The Message Window is partially hidden beneath the Main Graphics Window. Three lines of the Message Window are visible as a default. You can scroll this window to see earlier queries and responses.

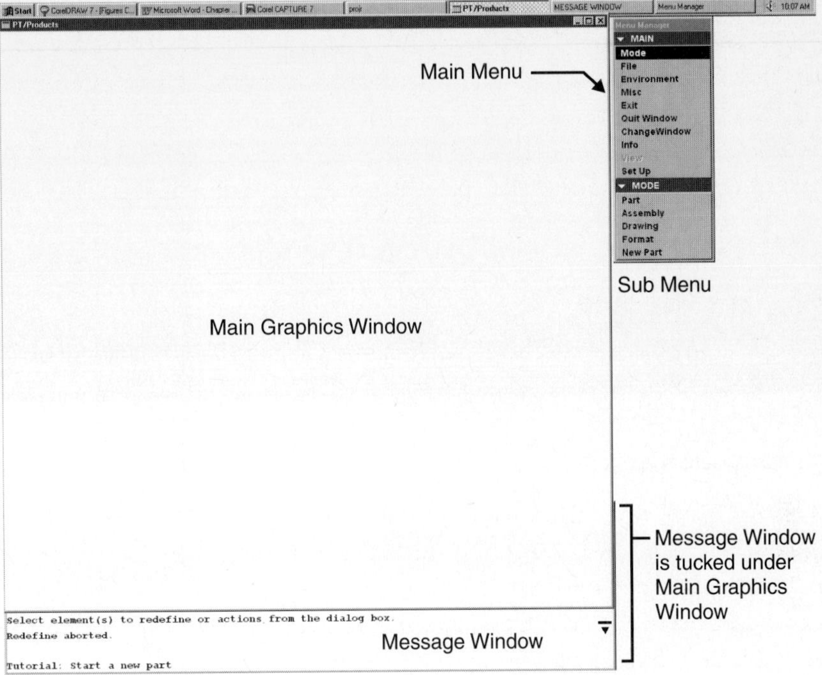

Figure 1.3   The application display windows at startup.

After a part is loaded, an additional window is displayed. This window is called the Model Tree window. It displays information about the part. The Model Tree window is displayed in the upper-left corner of the Main Graphics Window. The Model Tree is often placed beneath the Main Graphics Window unless needed. In addition, submenus will be displayed as you use the menu system. Both the Model Tree and some submenus are displayed in Figure 1.4.

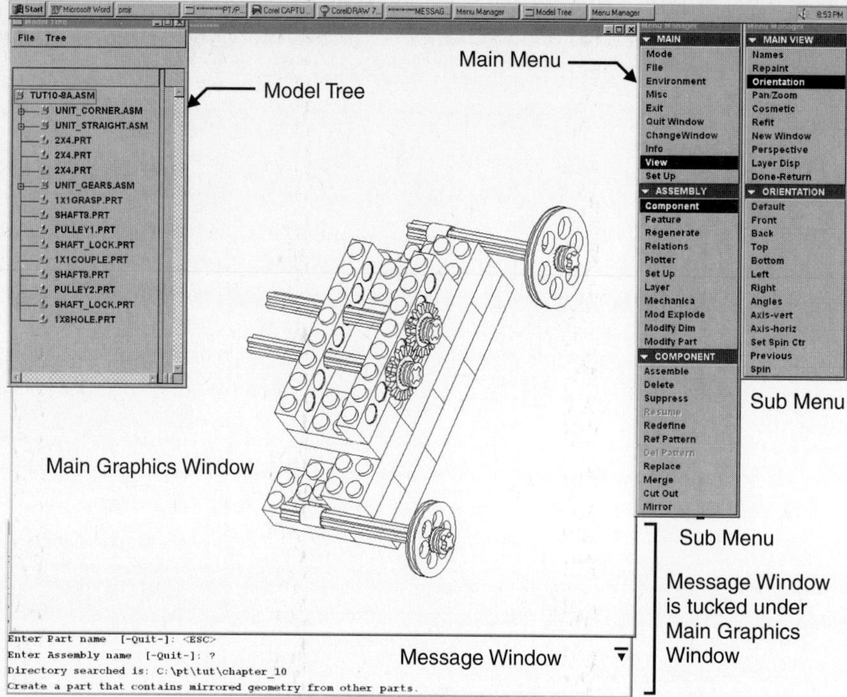

Figure 1.4   The application display windows after a part is loaded.

1.7.1   Main Graphics Window

This window is the parent of all other windows. As you design your part, 3D views of the part are displayed in this main graphics window. You manipulate the part within this graphics window. Sometimes you will perform other graphics operations, for example, sketching, that also take place in this window. The part might be drawn in 3D or 2D, wireframe, hidden line, or shaded formats. You can change the colors of the window, the colors of the lines, or the shading colors of the part. You will click in this window, rotate, pan, and zoom the part. The menus often direct you to pick some item from this window.

Child windows can also contain parts. You operate in a child window in the same way that you operate in the main graphics window. When you QuitWindow from a child window, the window itself is removed from the screen. The main graphics window is never removed from the screen.

1.7.2   Menu Window(s)

One or more Menu windows are always displayed on the screen. Your primary interaction with the software will be through these menus. These menus can drop additional submenus down or to the left or right depending on your settings.

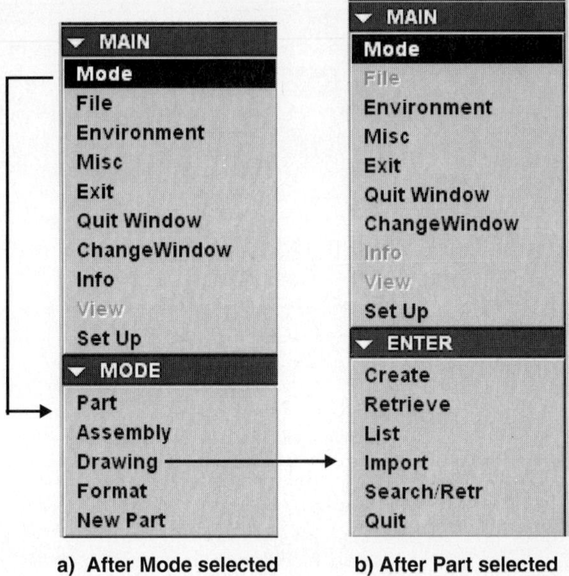

a) After Mode selected   b) After Part selected

Figure 1.7   The titles of submenus.

1.7.4   Working with Menus

You will become very proficient at using the menus after a few designs. At first, however, they may seem complicated. Figure 1.8 illustrates a common menu scenario. Here, we have a series of cascading menus moving down the screen. The

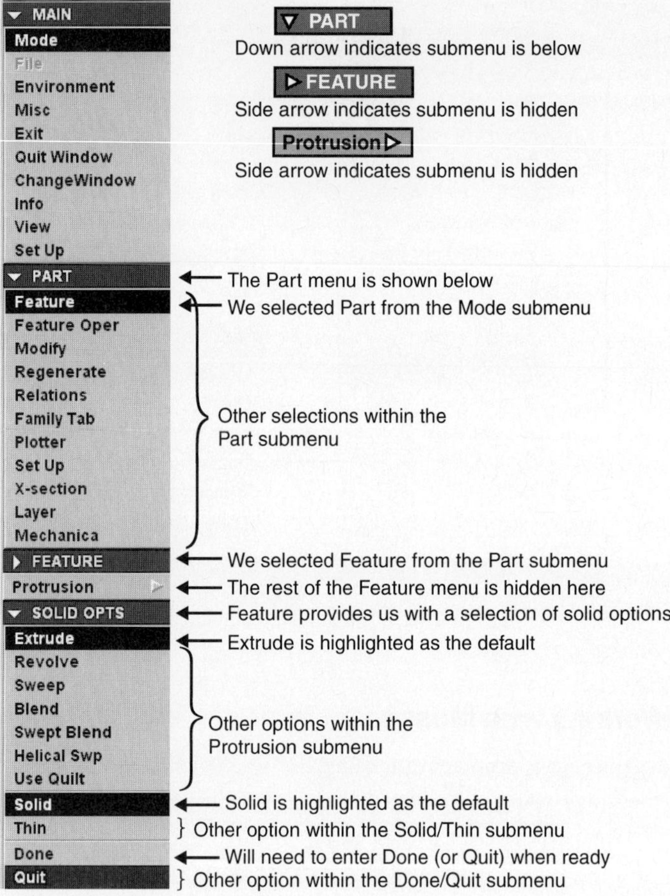

Figure 1.8 Menu definitions.

topmost menu is the Main menu. From this menu, the Part submenu has been selected. From the Part submenu we have selected the Feature item. From the Feature submenu we have selected the Protrusion item. In our terminology we have the following:

>Main >Part >Feature >Protrusion

This means select Main, select Part, select Feature, and select Protrusion. This is kind of long-winded since we are hitting Feature so many times from the Part submenu. Feature always stems from Part so we will simplify this to the following:

>Feature >Protrusion

From the Protrusion submenu we have options to select, called the Solid Opts. The initial set of options include Extrude, Revolve, . . . Use Quilt choices. The default is Extrude as indicated in black. Should we select Extrude, we have other options. The first is whether the extruded protrusion should be solid or thin. The Solid item is selected by default. If you like these selections, and you often will, it is possible to select from the last set of options: >Done or >Quit. Done will continue us on the merry path of building a solid extruded protrusion. >Quit will exit out of this path and return to an earlier state. Let's assume you just hit >Done.

Our terminology for this is as follows:

>Feature >Protrusion | Extrude | Solid | Done

> **TIP:** You do not need to select an option that is already indicated in black because it is the default selection. If you select an item, and the menu persists, you can reselect another item. All submenus will change automatically. If the menu disappears after selection, you are out of luck.

Menus, as you can see, can represent a lot of information and can ease the task of setting up multiply-dependent relationships. Figure 1.8 details most aspects of menus.

1.7.5   Model Tree Window

The Model Tree window provides information about a current part. This window shows all features in the part. The order of the features in the list indicates the order in which the features will be built to construct the model. The Model Tree can be customized to show other information about each feature.

You may configure the model tree as you wish. In Figure 1.9(a) the default Model Tree is displayed. This is the simplest Model Tree. Only the feature names for the active part are shown in the Model Tree list. Note the File and Tree menu items on the top of this window. These can be used to configure the system creating a custom Model Tree as shown in Figure 1.9(b). Here you will find a great amount of information regarding each feature. This can be very useful during the design and modification phase. You can save and restore Model Tree settings through the File Menu item.

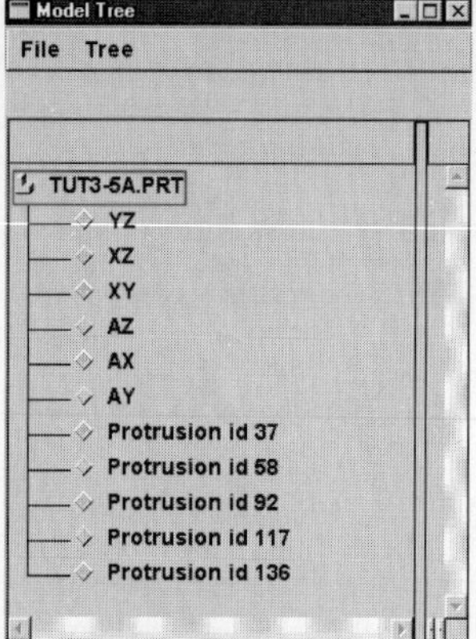

a) Simple Model Tree

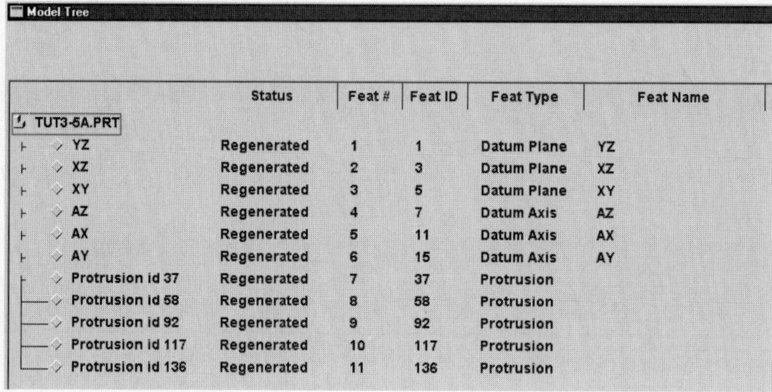

		Status	Feat #	Feat ID	Feat Type		Feat Name
TUT3-5A.PRT							
	YZ	Regenerated	1	1	Datum Plane	YZ	
	XZ	Regenerated	2	3	Datum Plane	XZ	
	XY	Regenerated	3	5	Datum Plane	XY	
	AZ	Regenerated	4	7	Datum Axis	AZ	
	AX	Regenerated	5	11	Datum Axis	AX	
	AY	Regenerated	6	15	Datum Axis	AY	
	Protrusion id 37	Regenerated	7	37	Protrusion		
	Protrusion id 58	Regenerated	8	58	Protrusion		
	Protrusion id 92	Regenerated	9	92	Protrusion		
	Protrusion id 117	Regenerated	10	117	Protrusion		
	Protrusion id 136	Regenerated	11	136	Protrusion		

b) Expanded Model Tree

Figure 1.9   The Model Tree.

It is possible to add and remove columns to the Model Tree using the Tree Menu item and the Add/Remove Columns dialog box as shown in Figure 1.10(a). In addition, you can format these columns to the desired width using the Format Dialog as shown in Figure 1.10(b).

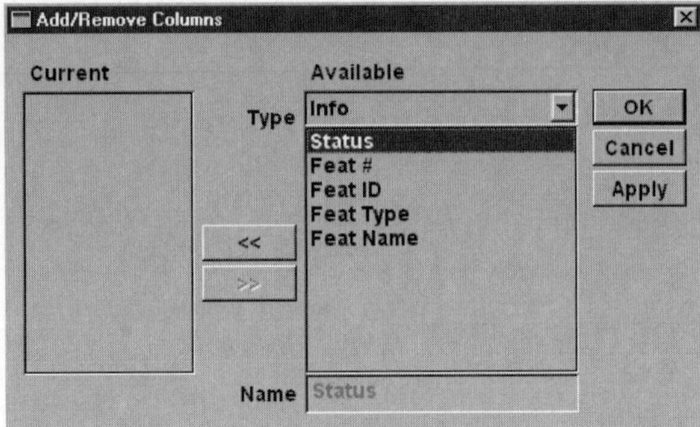

a) Add/Remove Columns Dialog

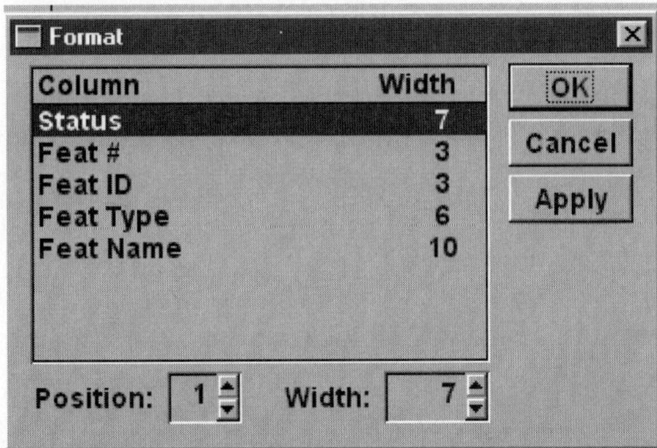

b) Format Columns Dialog

Figure 1.10   Model Tree dialog boxes.

1.7.6   Message Window

The Message window provides information, and queries and accepts responses from the user. The Message window is described in the user interaction section of the introduction. Messages are provided to the user to help describe the current state of the software. When the software requires interaction, the user is queried to enter information into the Message window. Most of this window is hidden beneath the Main Graphics Window. You can scroll through this window to see previous lines of text.

Command Prompt and Response

Although the great majority of actions will be through the menus, there are a good number of times when you will be asked to enter something from the keyboard. This might be the text of a file name, a number for a parameter value, or equations and comments entered into what are called *relations*. The command prompt appears in the message window. The software is configured such that the three bottom lines of the message window are visible beneath the main graphics window.

> **TIP:** Pay attention to the command prompts. The software will wait until you respond. If the system seems hung up, it may well be a query waiting for a response.

Command prompts are displayed on the second line from the bottom of the message window. You must type a response. The response that you type is displayed in red. You can ESC out of some commands, but others you must answer. If you realize an earlier error and want to go back, you will have to answer the query and then return to the earlier error using a feature called *redefine*. PT/Modeler provides excellent access to previous inputs. You are never trapped, and you rarely have to go back very far to change something that you have done. You cannot just bug out of a prompt.

There is no general Undo command; however, during some operations, specific undo commands are provided.

Notes and Tips

The last line of the Message window is a single-line help message similar in function to the status bar in many Windows applications. Placing the cursor over a menu item causes that item's hint to be displayed on this bottom line. The bottom line does not scroll with the rest of the message window. This line can be useful, since it often indicates what to do next. However, be careful, since you might be in one operation when you move the cursor over another unrelated menu item. Another hint will be displayed indicating the action for this unselected menu item.

1.8   Interacting with PT/Modeler

You will interact with PT/Modeler with the mouse (perhaps a 3D pointing device) and the keyboard.

1.8.1   The Mouse

It is highly recommended that you purchase a three-button mouse for use with this package. The software utilizes the middle button extensively. However, do not fret. You can always simulate the middle button with a Shift-Left-Button code. The Mouse is used for a number of different tasks. If you understand the function of the various mouse buttons, you can often use a mouse click to reduce the amount of time you spend moving the mouse over to the menu bar.

Some of you may desire to use a 3D pointing device like the Logitech Magellan. Popular 3D devices are supported by the software but are not covered in this book. Many feel that the 3D zoom-rotate-pan feature accomplished with a Ctrl-mouse combination alleviates the need for a 3D pointing device. The choice is yours.

1.8.1.1   Mouse Dragging

In many Windows graphics applications you drag the mouse. That is, you click and hold the Left button at the start of an operation; you move the mouse while holding down the Left button; and finally, you release the button at the destination. You will seldom drag in PT/Modeler. The same operation is accomplished by Left-button clicking the mouse at the start of an operation and then releasing the Left button before moving the mouse. After moving the mouse to the desired location, you click the Left mouse button again. There are some exceptions; one follows. A second exception is dragging a scroll bar.

1.8.1.2   Mouse Button Actions

It is possible to 3D zoom-rotate-pan the view of a part or assembly using the Ctrl-mouse actions. This is a very powerful feature that you will use extensively. In this case, you will drag the mouse. The mouse codes for these operations are shown in Table 1.5. More on 3D rotation can be found in Chapter 4.

Function	Operation	Action
Zoom	Ctrl-Left (mLc)	Drag up or down for **zoom out.** Drag down or right for **zoom in.**
Rotate	Ctrl-Middle (mMc)	Grab hold of an imaginary sphere surrounding the part and **rotate** the sphere by dragging the mouse.
Pan	Ctrl-Right (mRc)	Drag up for pan up. Drag down for **pan down.** Drag left for pan left. Drag right for **pan right.**

Table 1.5   3D Zoom-Rotate-Pan Mouse Button Actions

When drawing in the Sketcher, there are two modes of operation for sketching. You may want to draw lines, circles, and arcs. You can do this without selecting the Line, Circle, or Arc menu item for each. Rather, you can select the MouseSketch mode and use the mouse to draw lines, circles, and arcs commands. The mouse actions for these three operations in the MouseSketch Mode are shown in Table 1.6.

Alternatively, you can select the Line, Circle, or Arc menu items and draw exclusively with the Left button (mLc).

Function	Start	End	Interrupt
Line	Left (mLc)	Left (mLc)	Middle (mMc)
Circle	Middle (mMc)	Middle (mMc)	Left (mLc)
Arc	Right (mRc)	Right (mRc)	Middle (mMc)

Table 1.6 Sketcher MouseSketch Mode Mouse Button Actions

Often a middle button can be used to end an operation. Pay attention to the hints in the last line of the message box. If a mouse button can be used for a special shortcut, it will be indicated on this line.

Table 1.7 provides a concise look at mouse-button activity. You will rely on the mouse to do nearly all of your selecting, sketching, and dimensioning. It is well worth the effort to memorize and use these mouse shortcuts. Query selecting is a very useful tool. It can be very difficult to select a particular item, be it a face, edge, centerline, or vertex. Query select provides a method to insure you get the right pick. You pick on an item that may be your desired intent. PT/Modeler will go through the possible candidates one at a time. You respond by clicking Next if it is not the one you want. In this case, the next candidate will be highlighted. You can accept the desired item by clicking Accept. This is a very useful tool. I cannot tell you how many times I was sure I could pick the right item, only to be fooled and later regret that I did not use Query Select. The key is remembering the mouse shortcuts.

Mode	Left Button	Middle Button	Right Button
Regular	Pick	Done Select	Query Select
Query Select	Pick	Accept	Next
Sketcher	Line	Circle	Arc
Dimensioning	Pick	Place	

Table 1.7 Mouse Actions in Several Modes

1.8.2 The Keyboard

There is not much to say about the keyboard. You must get used to Ctrl-mouse dragging for the 3D manipulations. You will have to get used to Left-mouse and

Left-Ctrl-mouse dragging if you have a two-button mouse. Enter file names or values when requested. A query for information typically contains a default value contained in brackets. When this is the case, and when the default is satisfactory, a simple Enter from the keyboard will suffice. Often an ESC key will get you out of entering a response. Sometimes ESC-Enter-Enter is required. You may have to enter a value, even if you do not want to, just to get out of the query.

> **TIP:** Pay attention to the Queries. Read the question unless you are sure you know what the software is requesting. If the system seems hung, it is likely a query waiting for a response.

1.8.3   Dialog Boxes

Dialog boxes are not used extensively in PT/Modeler. In most cases, the dialogs perform as expected. Make selections and click on buttons. There is one very important dialog box that you will see and use repeatedly during the design and modification of features: the Element dialog box.

1.8.3.1   The Element List Dialog

The Element dialog box is shown in Figure 1.11. Note that there is a list of elements and a set of buttons. The buttons remain constant for each feature. The list changes depending on the number of steps in the feature. The elements are a kind of list of sequential operations that took place during the design of a feature. Most steps in the design process are represented by an element in this list. During design, the step that you are currently working on is indicated by the >highlight. During modification, you can select any of these elements by Left-mouse clicking on the element. That element will be highlighted with the >. You will then be able to return to that step and perform the desired operations.

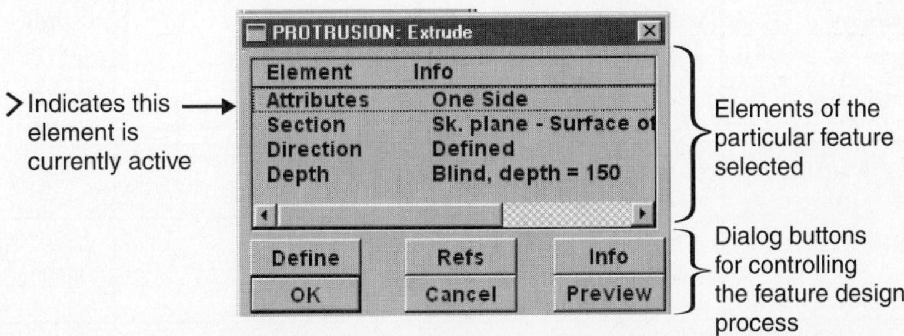

Figure 1.11   The Element dialog box.

In Tutorial 1.1 you will run PT/Modeler, create a file, save the file in a number of ways, manipulate windows, and exit the program. You should gain a working knowledge of the following:

- Executing and exiting PT/Modeler
- How parts in display mode memory relate to parts in non-display mode memory
- Saving, SaveAs, BackUp, Erasing Parts
- Working with multiple windows

Tutorial 1.1   Running PT/Modeler

No files opened

Files saved: Tut1-1a.prt
Tut1-1b.prt
..\backup\tut1-1b.prt

Step	Action	Description	Further Actions	Result
1	Click PT/Modeler Icon	Run PT/Modeler		After some time, PT/Modeler on screen
2	Mode >Misc >Show Dir	Show current directory		Message similar to "Directory searched is c:\ptc\ptprod\bin"
3	Change Dir	Change the current directory	Type **c:\proe\tutorial\ chapter_1**	
4	>Done-Return	Leave Misc menu		Misc menu removed
5	>New Part	Create a new part	Type **tut1-1a** then **Enter**	Datum planes displayed; Model Tree initiated
6	>File >Save	Save this part	**Enter** to accept [TUT1-1a.PRT]	File tut1-1a.prt saved to current directory
7	>Save As	Save this part with new name	**Enter** to accept [TUT1-1a.PRT] to be copied; type **tut1-1b.prt** then **Enter**	Accept part [TUT1-1a.PRT] as source; part tut1-1a.prt saved to tut1-1b.prt
8	>Backup	Save [TUT1-1a.PRT] to another directory	Type **c:\proe\temp,** **Enter** to accept [TUT1-1a.PRT]	Choose e:\proe\temp as new directory; accept part [TUT1-1a.PRT] as source
9	>Mode >Quit Window	Remove part from display		Graphics window is blanked
10	>File >Erase	Erase [TUT1-1a.PRT] from display-mode memory		Error! "No current object." Nothing is displayed in graphics window
11	>Mode >Part >Search/ Retr | In Session	Look at part files currently in non-display memory	Select TUT1-1a.PRT	Datum planes displayed

Tutorial 1.1   Running PT/Modeler (continued)

Step	Action	Description	Further Actions	Result
12	>File >Erase	Erase [TUT1-1a.PRT] from display-mode	Select Confirm	Part tut1-1a.prt cleared from memory
13	>Part >Search/Retr | Current Dir	Read part from current directory	Select tut1-1.prt from list	Datum planes displayed
14	>Mode >Part >Search/ Retr | Current Dir	Read another part from current directory	Select tut1-1b.prt from list	Child window displayed with Tut1-1b
15	>Ctrl-Drag-mLb	Zoom in child window	Ctrl and drag left button in Child window	Datums disappear and small coordinate system rotates in child window
16	Click inside Main Graphics window	Attempt to select Main window		Main window overwrites child window
17	Ctrl- Drag -mMb	Rotate in Main window	Ctrl and drag middle button in Main window	Error! Nothing happens; we haven't changed to that window
18	ChangeWindow (from Mode menu)	Change to Main window	Click in Main window	Main window now selected
19	Ctrl- Drag -mMb	Rotate in Main window	Ctrl and drag middle button in Main window	Datums disappear and small coordinate system rotates in main windows
20	>Quit Window	Remove tut1-1a.prt from Main window		Part tut1-1a.prt taken out of display mode memory into session memory
21	>ChangeWindow	Change to Child window	Click in Child window	Child window now selected
22	>Quit Window	Remove tut1-1b.prt from child window		Part tut1-1b.prt taken out of display mode memory into session memory—note: child window removed from screen
23	>File >EraseNotDisp	Erase nondisplayed parts in session memory	Confirm	An info window is displayed showing all parts in session memory; Confirm erases them all
24	Type **q**	Quit the information window		Information window is removed
25	>File >EraseNotDisp	Attempt again to erase nondisplayed parts in session memory		Error! No objects will be erased. All objects were erased in last operation
26	>Exit	Exit program	Click Yes to confirm	PT/Modeler exited

1.9   **Working the Menus**

I want to spend a little time on the menu structure. It is important to understand. The Main menu is at the top of the menu hierarchy. From the Main menu, you can assess Mode, File, Environment, etc., as seen in Figure 1.12(a). The first item in the Main menu is >Mode. From the Mode menu, you can access >Part, >Assembly, >Drawing, >Format, or my macro, >New Part. In this case, and as the default, the Mode item is highlighted and its submenu is displayed underneath the Main menu. From this submenu, you can enter into one of the Part, Assembly, . . . etc., modes as shown in Figure 1.12(b). You enter into one of these modes by Creating, Retrieving from disk, or importing. Suppose you accessed Part from the Mode menu and you choose to enter Part by retrieving a file. The Part menu is now displayed, as shown in Figure 1.12(c). From the Part menu, you can build, modify, or operate on a feature. Suppose you want to build a feature. You would use the Feature menu item to build a new feature. Feature is highlighted and its submenu is shown on the next page. From this menu, you can select to create a Protrusion, Round, Cut, . . . etc. Now further suppose you wanted to create a Protrusion. The Protrusion submenu is displayed, as shown in Figure 1.12(d). From this menu you can select to Extrude, Revolve, Sweep, . . . etc. Once one of these types of protrusions is selected, additional menus would appear, continuing to lead you through the design process.

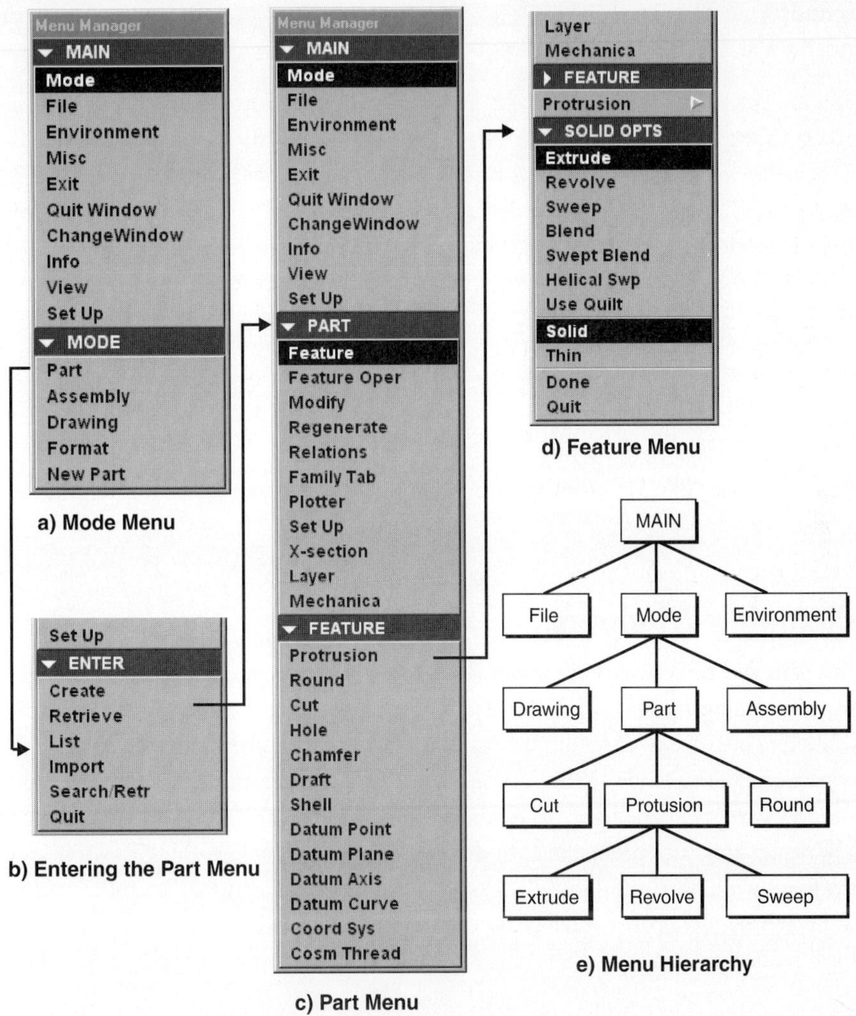

Figure 1.12   Menu structure.

A hierarchy of menus is shown in Figure 1.12(e). You move up and down this chain of menus as you do your work. Suppose that you are at the Part menu, and you want to change an environment variable. You could click on Environment and an Environment submenu would be displayed, leaving the rest of the Part menu still in place. You could change the Environment variable and then pop back to your work. In this case, the Environment submenu would be displayed to the right of the existing menu.

What happens if you are working on a part and you want to load in another part in a child window? Good question. You are in the menu of Figure 1.12(c), and there is no Part menu available. This is a very important issue, one that you will get confused on at some time. Let's try and clear it up now.

You are currently in the Part mode. You want to get back to the Mode mode to get access to the Part item as seen in Figure 1.12(a). To do this, you click on the Main item at the top of the menu. This brings you back to the Main mode where you can access the Part menu. Now, the process repeats itself and you work your way down the menu chain retrieving the second part into a child window. You see what you needed to see and now want to return back to your first part in the main window.

The Quit Window item can be used to remove the second part from the child window. Since this removes all data from the child window, the child window is itself removed, and you are left in no-man's-land. You are placed back into the Mode mode. How can you access the first part still displayed in the main window? All you have are the choices in Figure 1.12(a). The answer is using the ChangeWindow menu item, as discussed in the next section.

1.10   Changing Windows

You can, and often will, have multiple windows open. A single window is sufficient when designing a part. During the design process, you may want to view the part from a different orientation or see another part. You can accomplish this by requesting another part using the >Mode >Part >Retrieve command for example. This will open a child window with the requested part. A second common scenario occurs when working on a drawing. You can open a child window to see the part while keeping the drawing in the main window. A third popular example is when working in an assembly, and you want to bring up a part to change its view. Do not worry about the details here. All of these parts, drawings, and assemblies items will be discussed in later chapters.

To move from one window to the next you use the ChangeWindow command. Click the ChangeWindow item and then click inside the window that you want to become active.

> **NOTE:** Clicking on the title bar of a window brings that window to the top, but does not activate that window.

If there is no current active window, you are in no-man's-land as discussed in Section 1.9, using the ChangeWindow command will bring the selected window active. Thus, if you click ChangeWindow and then click in the main window, the menus associated with that main window will return.

Viewing the Model

A three-dimensional modeling software package, like PT/Modeler, helps you design and model in three dimensions (3D). Arguably, the most difficult aspect of working in 3D on a computer is the limitation that we are trapped on a 2D plane. We typically use a 2D mouse and almost always view the model on a 2D display.

Let's look at viewing the model first. We must constantly pan, zoom, and rotate the model around in order to produce a desirable view. Since we are using a 3D modeling tool, the model is built up in 3D piece by piece. We are constantly working in the 3D space. However, we are restricted to viewing the model on a 2D display. Consequently, we will have to become proficient with the 3D viewing tools available in PT/Modeler.

Second, we will look at picking. We will be constantly picking planes, edges, and surfaces from our 3D model. We might need to place a protrusion on a particular surface, align a feature to a display plane, or round an edge. We will need to specify which feature on our 3D model we intend for a given purpose. It is possible to select a feature from the Model Tree by name or by picking. Most often, we will use picking. Once again, we will have to pick our features from a 2D projection of our model as seen on the screen. This can be quite challenging.

Fortunately, PT/Modeler has excellent 3D viewing tools. This chapter will teach you how to use them.

2.1   3D Coordinate Systems

In a rectilinear 3D space, we will consider X, Y, and Z axes. First, consider the 2D case shown in Figure 2.1(a). Note that the origin is at the lower-left of the page. X goes out horizontally and Y goes out vertically. We are all used to this coordinate system. Now, lets add a third dimension, Z. This is shown in Figure 2.1(b). We see that Z extends out of the page towards you. It could have just as easily gone into the page. Both would be valid coordinate systems. We differentiate these two systems by what is called the right-hand rule, and the left-hand rule. The coordinate system of Figure 2.1(b) is called the right-hand rule. Take your right hand and point your index finger along the X axis and the second finger along the Y axis. The thumb always points towards the positive Z axis. PT/Modeler uses right-hand coordinate systems so you should commit this to memory.

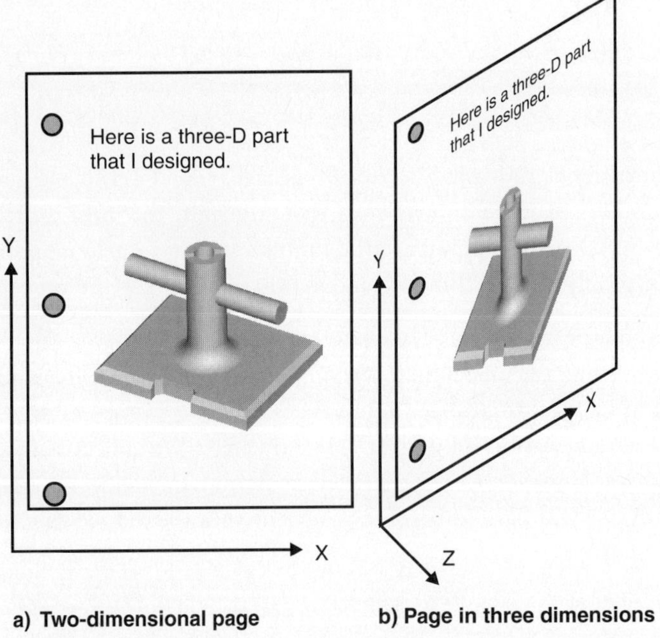

Figure 2.1   Two- and three-dimensional coordinate systems.

Now, in both the 2D and 3D coordinate systems, we have negative values. A point to the left of the page in Figure 2.1(a) would have a negative X coordinate. A point beneath the page would have a negative Y coordinate. The same holds in the 3D case shown in Figure 2.1(b). This directionality of the 3D system is important in 3D modeling.

The X, Y, and Z axes coordinates are denoted by the distance along the respective axes. If we are plotting a point, we might say it had an X=8, Y=10, Z=5 coordinate.

This would place it uniquely in our 3-space. This is shown in Figure 2.2. What if we specified the point X=8, Y=10 but gave no value to the Z coordinate? Where would this point be located in our 3-space? The answer is, these two coordinates do not uniquely define a point. The point is said to be *under-constrained.*

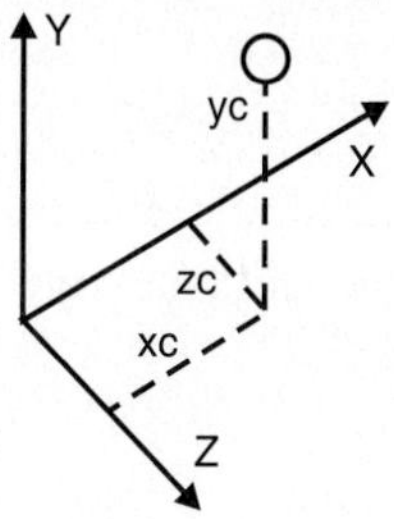

Figure 2.2   A point and a plane in 3D space.

Let's take a slightly different look at our 3D coordinate system as shown in Figure 2.3(a). Here, I have renamed the axes AX, AY, and AZ. Our viewpoint is up, to the right, and in front of our 3D axes origin. In Figure 2.3(b), three planes are added to the 3D space: the XY, the XZ, and the YZ planes. Note that the AX axis can be thought of as the intersection between the XY and the XZ planes. The AX axis is perpendicular or normal to the YZ plane. Similarly, the AY axis is the intersection between the XY and the YZ planes. It is perpendicular or normal to the XZ plane. Lastly, the AZ axis is the intersection between the XZ and the YZ planes. It is perpendicular or normal to the XY plane. From our vantage point, we are looking at the positive faces of each of the three planes. That is, we are looking at the positive YZ plane because the positive AX axis is extending towards us. We are looking at the positive XZ plane because the positive AY axis is extending towards us. We are looking at the positive XY plane because the positive AZ axis is extending towards us.

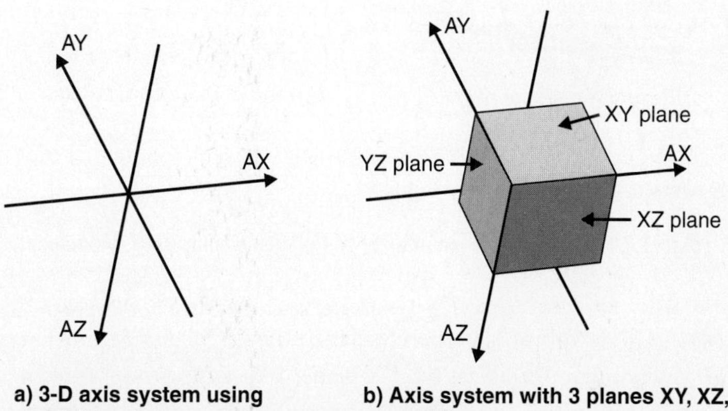

a) 3-D axis system using right-hand rule

b) Axis system with 3 planes XY, XZ, and YZ

Figure 2.3   Axes and planes in a three-dimensional space.

The three drawings in Figure 2.4 are very similar to what you will see in PT/Modeler. Note the three axes AX, AY, and AZ. Here we have the same three planes: XY, XZ, and YZ. This time, the plane extends through the origin of our coordinate system, as opposed to the neat corner shown in Figure 2.3(b). These are a little bit difficult to visualize. In Figure 2.4(a), the XY plane is highlighted in gray. In Figure 2.4(b), the XZ plane is highlighted and in Figure 2.4(c), the YZ plane is highlighted. In each case, we are still top-right-front of the origin.

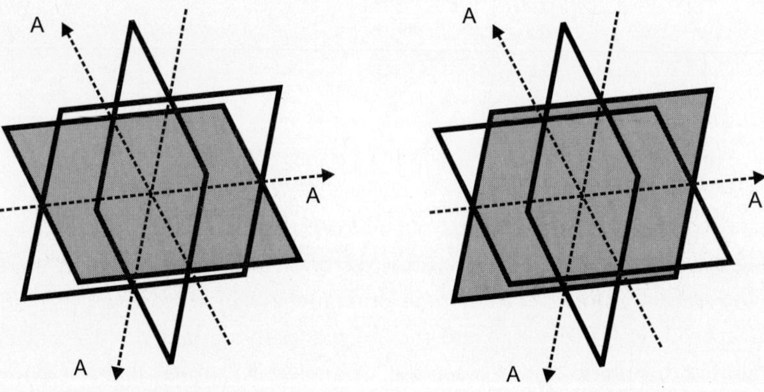

a) Axis system with XY plane highlighted   **b) Axis system with XZ plane highlighted**

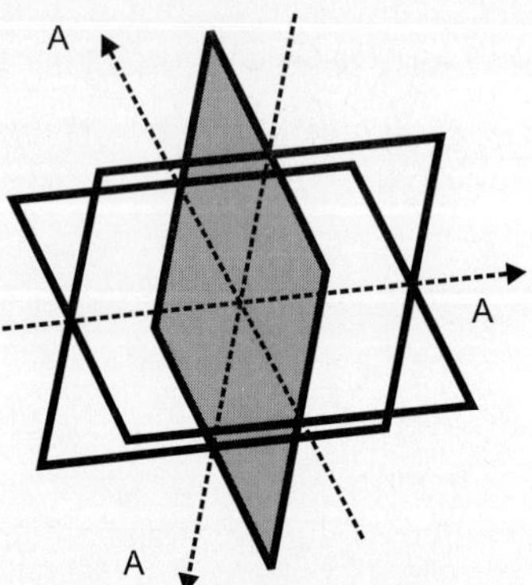

c) Axis system with YZ plane highlighted

Figure 2.4   Representation of axes and planes similar to PT/Modeler.

Suppose that our viewpoint is perpendicular to the XY plane. Another way to say this is our viewpoint is normal to the XY plane. The term *normal* more accurately describes a vector pointing away from a plane. Our viewpoint is along the Z axis. How does PT/Modeler display the Z axis? The Z axis, named AZ, points positively out of the page due to the right-handed coordinate system used exclusively in PT/Modeler.

At times, PT/Modeler will draw arrows during feature creation. If the arrow is not drawn perpendicular to the page, you will clearly see the head of the arrow. However, if the arrow is pointing perpendicular to the screen, symbols will be used to indicate whether the direction is into or out from the page. An arrow pointing out from the page is shown in Figure 2.5(a). The direction of the arrow is symbolized by two concentric circles. If it is pointing into the page, as seen in Figure 2.5(b), the vector is shown as a circle with perpendicular lines. The image is one of looking at an arrow. If you look at the arrow tip, you would see the point and cone of the arrow. If you looked at the back of the arrow, you would see the feathers and not the tip as shown in Figure 2.5(c).

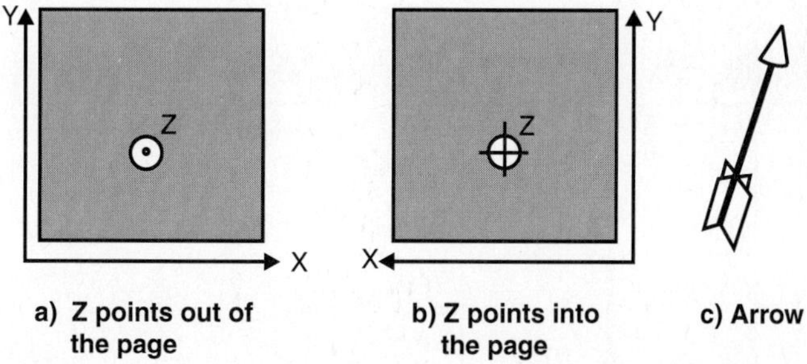

Figure 2.5   Axes representation when viewing normal to a plane.

2.2   Datum Planes

In PT/Modeler, the XY, XZ, and YZ planes are called the Datum Planes. Datum planes are infinite in size. They will be drawn to encompass the largest dimensions of your current model; however, they are in no way limited to this size. The Datum planes provide us with our frame of reference. Datum planes have a positive and negative side. Consider making a model. We will construct three cards such that they model the three datum planes. These cards will all be orthogonal planes. Two planes are orthogonal if they intersect at a right angle. We will make one side of the cards out of red stiff construction paper and the other side out of yellow construction paper.

> **NOTE:** PT/Modeler uses the color yellow to denote the positive face of a plane, and it uses the color red to denote the negative face of a plane.

Figure 2.6 illustrates such a system. Cut out two squares, 4" on a side, from yellow paper and two squares, 4" on a side, from red paper. Cut one square 5" on a side, from yellow paper, and one square, 5" on a side, from red paper. Glue the red and yellow sides together making three cards. Now make the cuts as indicated in Figure 2.6. The cuts in the 5" piece, as seen in Figure 2.6(c), should be 4" long, leaving a half inch on each side. Draw the plane names, XY, XZ, and YZ on both sides of the respective pieces. Draw in the axes, as shown.

Construct the datum planes by first connecting the XY and YZ planes together cut to cut, forming a cross such that the two cut sides intersect. Make sure the axes align properly and glue in place. Next, slide the XZ card over the connected XY and YZ planes, making sure, once again, that the axes line up. Glue in place. Now you have an excellent model. You won't believe how many times you will refer to this model when designing using PT/Modeler. I have found such a model invaluable.

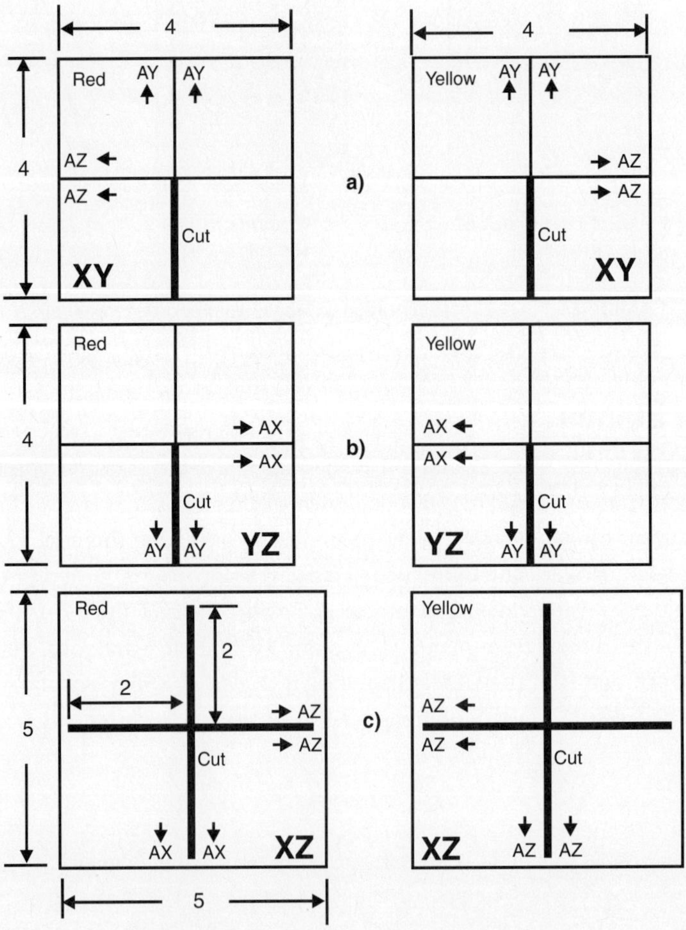

Figure 2.6   Datum Plane construction kit.

The finished model should look like the datum planes displayed in Figure 2.7. Note the positive and negative planes denoted with the yellow and red color, respectively. From the viewpoint shown in this picture, we would see only the yellow faces of the datum planes. This is the same view shown when the datum planes are displayed in the default orientation.

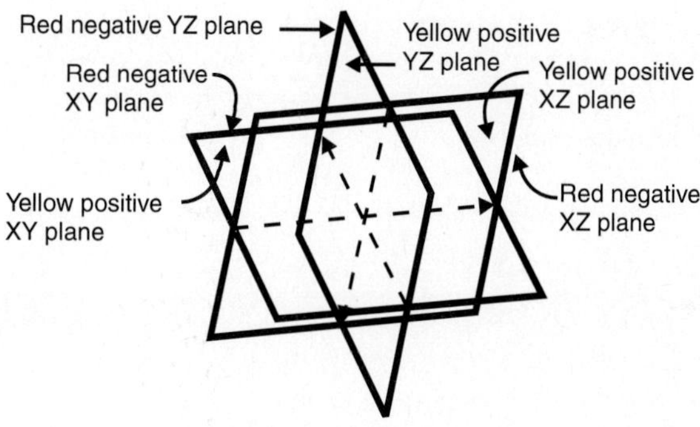

Figure 2.7   Positive and negative datum planes.

Now we get to the fun part. Let's rotate around our viewpoint of the datum planes in several different orientations as shown in Figure 2.8. The AX, AY, and AZ axes labels do not necessarily point in the positive orientations of the axis. In Figure 2.8(a), the triad at the spin center shows that the AZ axis positive direction is down and to the left (as oriented on the page). However, the AZ axis is seen towards the back of the figure. The triad points in the positive direction.

Note that the darker lines symbolize the positive yellow sides of the faces, and the lighter lines symbolize the negative red sides of the faces. Can you orient your construction paper model to match these orientations? Try it.

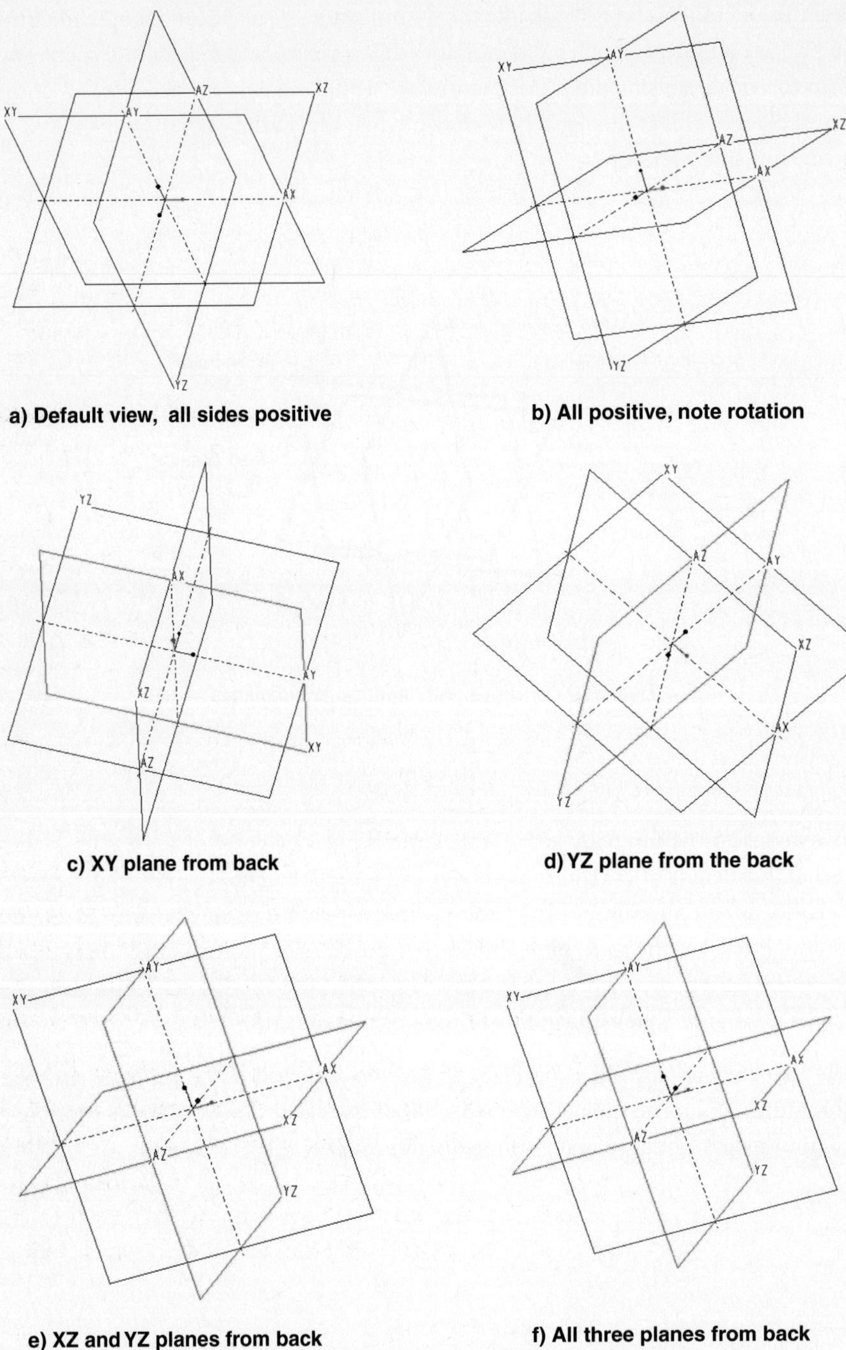

Figure 2.8   Datum Planes seen from several different viewpoints.

Believe me, this is a very important exercise. You will not believe how many times you design your model, only to find out that you put a feature in upside down, or on the wrong face due to a misunderstanding of the basic three-dimensional orientation.

2.2.1   Default Datum Planes

Default datum planes are very important. When we start a model, we will always begin with the first feature being a set of default datum planes. This provides us with a reference in our 3D space. We can use this to reference dimensions, orient our part, and provide easily accessible sketch planes (more on sketch planes in Chapters 3 and 4).

We are just about ready to build our first part. I have provided a menu item called New Part, in the Mode menu. When you select the New Part, a series of operations will take place. One of operations creates a set of default datum planes. It renames the planes to XY, XZ, and YZ. It also renames the three axes to AX, AY, and AZ. These three datum planes and three axes are the first six features of your model, present before any actual geometry is added. None of these features actually represent any solid material in the model.

> **TIP:** Always start a model with the Default Datum Planes. It is not required; however, you will likely regret skipping this step.

The first solid feature of a model has to be a protrusion that adds mass. After all, it would do us little good to add a hole to space. Before we add this first protrusion, we will create a set of default datum planes. We do this through the feature menu.

Figure 2.9 shows the Feature submenu with the Datum selection choices. You can select to create a datum plane, a datum axis, or a datum curve. We will be dealing later with datum curves and axes. If there is a blank model, and you select datum plane, PT/Modeler will create three datum planes called the *default datum planes*. It will name them DTM1, DTM2, and DTM3.

> **NOTE:** My New Part menu item renames the default datum plane names from DTM1, DTM2, and DTM3 to XY, XZ, and YZ, respectively.

The three default datum planes and the three axes provide our first six features in the model. All six are reference features. Thus far, we haven't added any geometry. We will use these datum planes and axes to align and reference our geometry.

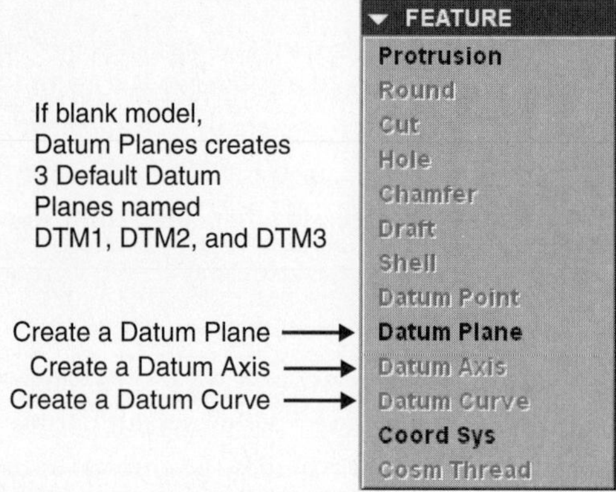

Figure 2.9   Creating datums from the Feature submenu.

2.3   Using Default Datum Planes

It is now time to add some geometry as we begin the model. A model doesn't strictly need any global reference. It could be constructed along any axis or oriented to any plane. Consider making a cylinder. It doesn't really matter whether the cylinder is aligned along the AX, AY, or AZ axes. It doesn't matter if it extends positively or negatively from the XY plane. When it is all said and done, it is just a cylinder.

However, there are times when it is convenient to use a standardized reference system. For example, PT/Modeler has a default view. This view always aligns the Y axis upwards, the X axis to the left, and the Z axis to the right. This default plane is shown in Figure 2.10. This is a great reference tool. Oftentimes, you will pan-zoom-rotate to some odd angle and rely on the Default View to bring you back to a known reference. It can be very useful to design your parts to be consistently oriented to this plane. For example, suppose you were designing ten toys that would sit on a table. It would be wise to design each such that up was along the positive AY axis. Perhaps it wouldn't matter which way the front or side was. Suppose you were designing stereo components. Again, up should be oriented along the AY axis. This time, it would be useful to have the front of the units point along the positive AZ axis. This forces the right direction to be aligned to the positive AX axis.

NOTE: In a right- or left-handed three-dimensional system, only two axes are independent. The third is dependent on the first two.

It is even more important to orient your parts consistently when designing parts that will fit into assemblies. You can always align and rotate parts around during the assembly process. However, this is time consuming and can be really annoying.

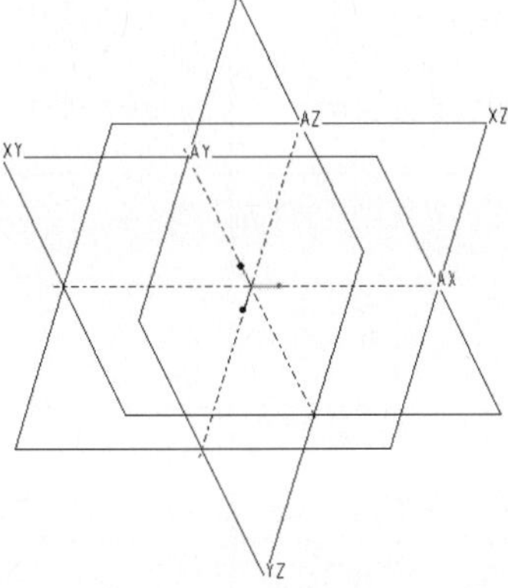

Figure 2.10   Default datum planes in Default View.

In Tutorial 2.1 we will experiment with the default datum planes. You will start up a new part, create default datum planes, and get used to rotating the datum planes around in the three-dimensional space.

Tutorial 2.1 Default Datum Planes

No files opened or saved.

Step	Action	Description	Further Actions	Result
1	Click PT/Modeler Icon	Run PT/Modeler		After some time, PT/Modeler on screen
2	>Mode >Misc >Show Dir	Show current directory		Message similar to "Directory searched is c:\ptc\ptprod\bin"
3	>Change Dir	Change the current directory	type **c:\proe\tutorial\ chapter_2**	
4	>Done-Return	Leave Misc menu		Misc menu removed
5	>Mode >New Part	Create a new part	Type **tut2-1a**	Default datum planes are constructed in Main window
6	>Mode >Part >Create	Create a new part	Type **tut2-1b**	New blank Child window is created
7	>Feature >Datum Plane	Create a set of default datum planes		Datum planes are created with axis names DTM1, DTM2, DTM3
8	>Feature >Setup >Dtm Name	Change a datum name		Query to select axis, csys, or planes
9	Click on >DTM1	Change the name of DTM1		DTM1 highlighted in cyan; query to Enter New Name [DTM1]
10	Type **XY**	Change DTM1 to XY		Name changed to XY
11	Click on >DTM2	Change the name of DTM2		DTM2 highlighted in cyan; query to Enter New Name [DTM2]
12	Type **XZ**	Change DTM1 to XZ		Name changed to XZ
13	Click on >DTM3	Change the name of DTM3		DTM3 highlighted in cyan; query to Enter New Name [DTM3]
14	Type **YZ**	Change DTM1 to YZ		Name changed to YZ
15	>Quit Window	>Exit this window		Window is removed
16	ChangeWindow	Change to the Main window	Click in the Main Graphics window	Back in Main Graphics window
17	Ctrl-Drag-mLb upward or to the right	Zoom out	Click in Main Graphics window; hold down the Ctrl key and drag the mouse Left button upward or right	Datums become smaller
18	Ctrl-Drag-mLb downward or to the left	Zoom in		Datums become larger

Tutorial 2.1 Default Datum Planes (continued)

Step	Action	Description	Further Actions	Result
19	Type **F1** (presumes mapkey is defined)	Go to default view		Macro brings us to default view
20	Ctrl-Drag-mMb around	Rotate	Click in Main Graphics window; hold down the Ctrl key and drag the mouse Middle button upward or right	Datums get rotated
21	>View >Orientation | Default	Go to default view		Menus bring us to default view
22	Repeat Ctrl-Drag-mLb and Ctrl-Drag-mMb	Practice zooming and rotating		
23	Ctrl-Drag-mRb around	Pan	Click in Main Graphics window; hold down the Ctrl key and drag the mouse Right button upward or right	Datums get panned
24	>Exit	Exit program	Click Yes to confirm	PT/Modeler exited

2.4   Placing Objects onto Datum Planes

You will rely on the default datum planes as references when you begin to build your geometry. The first feature that you place into a part is called the base feature. In our case, the base feature will always be a datum plane. The first solid feature has to be a protrusion. A protrusion adds mass. We could not select a feature that removes mass, since the model has no mass to remove.

The first step is to figure out a reference plane for placing the protrusion. This plane becomes the sketching plane. You always draw features within the sketcher (see Chapter 4). The sketcher always draws on a 2D surface called the *sketching plane*. You can pick any plane in 3-space to be a sketching plane. The sketching plane becomes the reference that connects the new feature to other features that already exist. If the new feature is the base feature, the sketching plane has to be a datum plane. It might be a default datum plane or a new datum plane that you create. If other geometric features already exist in the model, you could choose a datum plane, or any planar surface of the geometry. Geometric surfaces are called *faces*.

2.4.1   One-Sided or Two-Sided

As you proceed through the steps of designing a feature, you will be asked whether the new feature should be one-sided or two-sided. This menu is shown in Figure 2.11. The new feature will begin at the sketching plane and work its way outwards. If the feature is to be one-sided, it will extend in one direction from the sketching plane. If the feature is two-sided, it will extend in both directions. If the feature is one-sided, you will have to enter which of the two directions you desire.

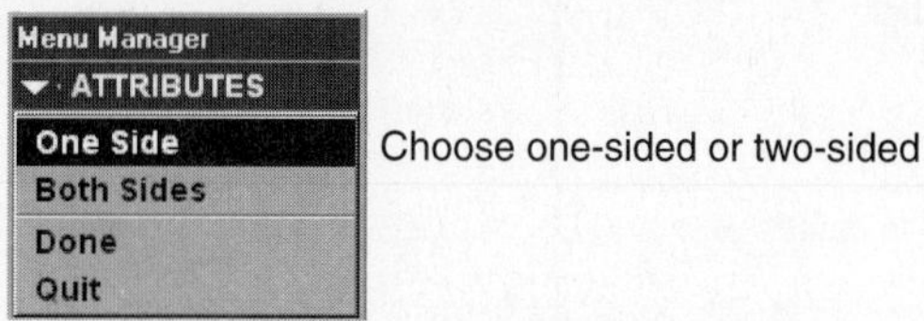

Figure 2.11   One-sided or two-sided feature.

2.4.2   Selecting a Sketching Plane

It is not always obvious which plane or surface should be the sketching plane. This is discussed more fully in Chapter 3. For now, let us suppose that you know the plane you want as the sketching plane. Perhaps you are going to add a hole using a cut feature into the top of the block. The sketching surface would be the top face of the block. Maybe the hole goes all the way through the block. In this case, you could choose either the top or the bottom of the box. Perhaps it doesn't make any difference whether you choose the top or the bottom of the box as the sketching surface. But, then again, maybe it does.

> **NOTE:** The face or plane that is selected as the sketching plane is a parent to the new feature. Move the face or plate later on and you move the feature. Delete the face or plane and you delete the feature.

A Setup Plane submenu is displayed as shown in Figure 2.12. You can select the sketching plane by picking a suitable plane directly, by query select, or by use of a menu. Picking datum planes is described more fully in Chapter 4. However, it is best to grasp the fundamentals now. Picking a plane is very risky business. It can be very difficult to select the desired plane in a 3D space when all you have is a 2D display. You have to be careful here. It is much safer to use Query Select. Just pick a feature in the area of the desired feature, and you can select the correct face when PT/Modeler highlights it. Picking a wrong plane can waste a lot of time. It requires considerable backtracking to select another.

Whatever way you choose, in most cases, you need to select a sketching plane before you can design your part.

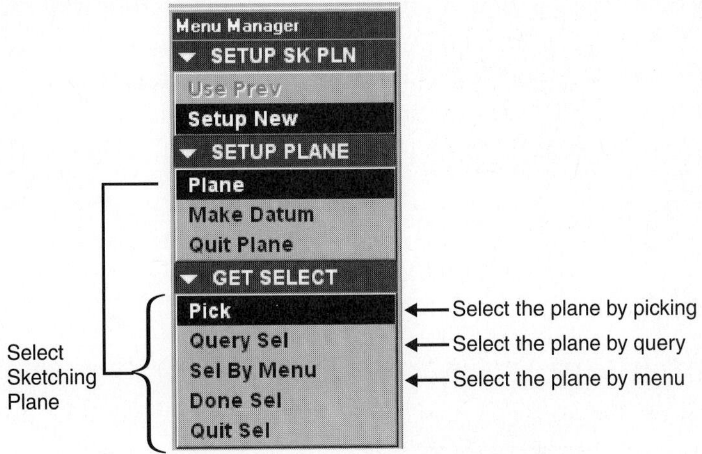

Figure 2.12   Picking a sketching plane.

2.4.3   Selecting a Reference

We are about ready to sketch onto our 2D sketching plane. After having selected the plane, it is now necessary to orient the plane on the display surface for our drawing. Consider the following analogy: A camera is positioned normal to the selected sketching plane and a picture is taken of the plane. We print the photo as a transparency. We now have a two-dimensional representation of the object. This print represents our sketching plane. We are going to sketch on the transparency. Did you ever work with a transparency overhead or a slide projector? There are eight possible orientations and it can be trying to get top-side-up and right-side-right, both at the same time. Our next task is to instruct PT/Modeler how to orient this picture on the screen.

The reference plane is used for this purpose. The reference plane does not figure into the design at all. It is only present to help us draw our feature. The reference plane orients the sketching plane on the screen. Refer again to our transparency analogy. It really wouldn't matter if you drew on an upside-down picture, as long as you knew that it was upside down. Similarly, it wouldn't matter if the picture was backwards or left-to-right reversed. The drawing would work out fine as long as you knew whatever transformation took place. Consequently, the reference plane is a convenience. But, oh what a convenience it can be if selected correctly. I can guarantee that you will, at some frequency, draw a feature upside down or left-side-right because you did not select the correct reference plane.

Figure 2.13 shows the Reference Plane menu. It always appears after selecting the sketching plane. The top submenu allows you to select one of Top, Bottom, Right, or Left. These choices refer to the four sides of the screen as shown in Figure 2.14. You can choose only one of these four. Your selection says, the plane that I am about to pick should be placed onto (one of) the top, bottom, right, or left of the screen. The reference doesn't have to be a plane—an edge will suffice. However, I prefer sticking with planes.

Once selected, you need to pick the desired edge, surface, or datum plane for your reference. Once again, you can pick or query select through the choices. Query select is the wise choice.

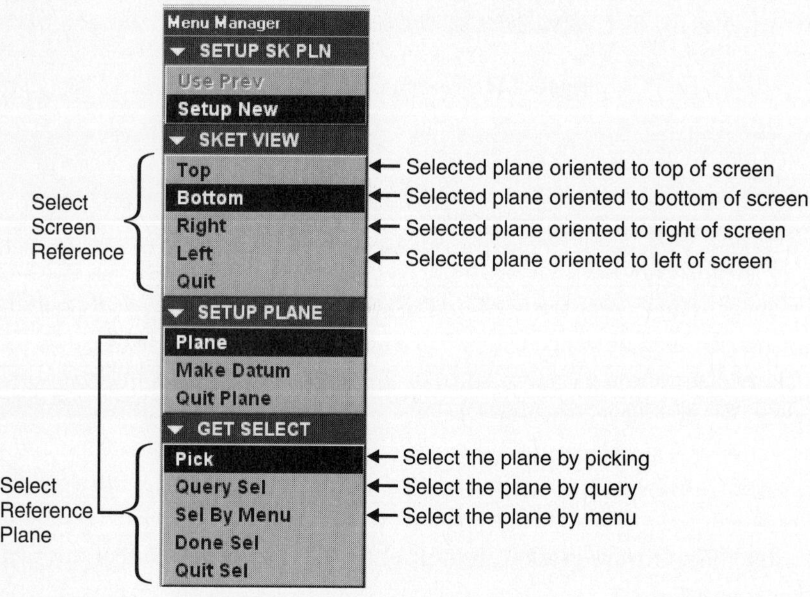

Figure 2.13   Picking a reference plane.

Orienting the sketching plane is tricky business. It is a good idea to practice after finishing Tutorial 2.2, selecting different faces and reference planes to hone your skills. Nearly every feature you build will require you to select a sketching plane and a reference.

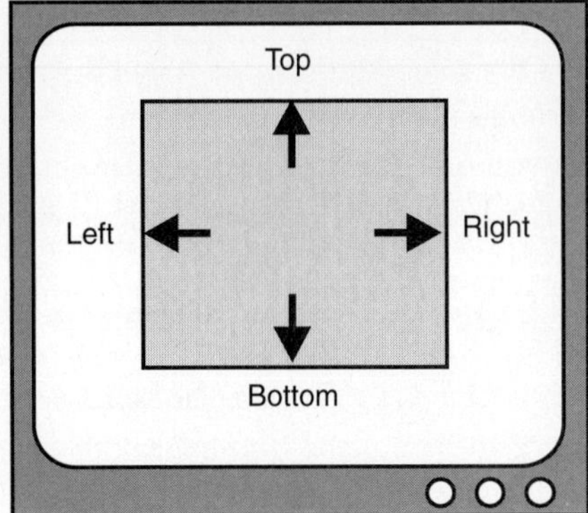

Figure 2.14   Orienting onto the display.

It is time for a tutorial on picking and orienting sketching planes. We will read a dice part and practice selecting sketching and reference planes. The dice is shown in Figure 2.15(a) as it is oriented in the default view. A shaded view, with axes superimposed, is shown in Figure 2.15(b). Additional shaded views are shown in Figure 2.15(c). By the end of the tutorial you should be able to predict the correct orientation for the sketching plane accurately. Let's hope you don't leave it up to a roll of the dice.

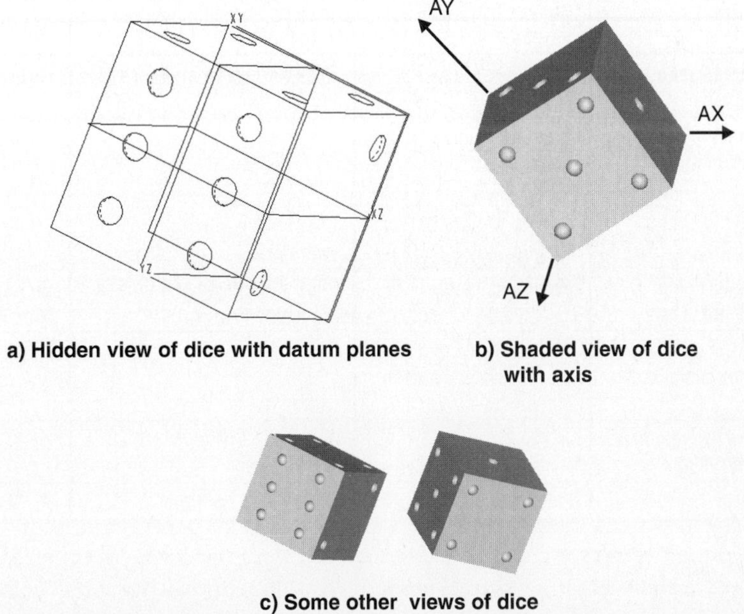

a) Hidden view of dice with datum planes   **b) Shaded view of dice with axis**

c) Some other views of dice

Figure 2.15   Dice part with datum planes and axes.

Tutorial 2.2 will begin your quest towards understanding how to select sketching and reference planes. I only take you through a single scenario. After selecting a sketching plane and reference plane, you will pop into the sketcher. Now is not the time to sketch so I have you quit the sketcher and cancel the operation. Try selecting bottom-left and right faces as your reference and see what happens.

Tutorial 2.2 Selecting Sketching and Reference Planes

Files opened: Tut-2.prt   **No files saved.**

Step	Action	Description	Further Actions	Result
1	Click PT/Modeler Icon	Run PT/Modeler		After some time, PT/Modeler on screen
2	>Mode >Misc >Show Dir	Show current directory		Message similar to "Directory searched is c:\ptc\ptprod\bin"
3	>Change Dir	Change the current directory	Type **c:\proe\tutorial\ chapter_2**	
4	>Done-Return	Leave Misc menu		Misc menu removed
5	>Part >Search/Retr	Read in a part	Select **Tut2-2**	Dice is displayed on screen
6	>Feature >Protrusion | Extrude | Solid | >Done	Add a solid extruded protrusion		Ready to select sketch plane; Attributes menu comes up
7	>One Side | >Done	Go into >Query Select >Mode	Click on the rightmost face with the 2	>Query Selects a face
8	>Query Sel	Go into >Query Select >Mode	Click on the rightmost face with the 2	>Query Selects a face
9	**Next** until 2 face highlighted in red	Selecting 2 face	Click **Accept** when 2 face is highlighted	Arrow comes out of 2 face
10	Okay if out of face; flip if into face then okay	Want protrusion to come out of face		Select reference plane sub-menu is displayed
11	>Query Sel	Go into >Query Select >Mode	Click on the topmost face with the 4	>Query Selects a face
12	**Next** until 4 face highlighted in red	Selecting 4 face	Click **Accept** when 4 face is highlighted	Go into sketch >Mode; see Note 1
13	>Quit | Confirm from Sketcher submenu	Abort out; we don't want to do any sketching yet		
14	>Cancel | Yes from Feature Dialog			
15	>Exit	Exit program	Click Yes to confirm	PT/Modeler exited

After successfully entering sketch mode, a two-dimensional view of our selected sketch plane is provided. Sketch mode allows you to draw onto this surface. The correct surface of the dice, with the 2 face, is shown in sketch mode in Figure 2.16.

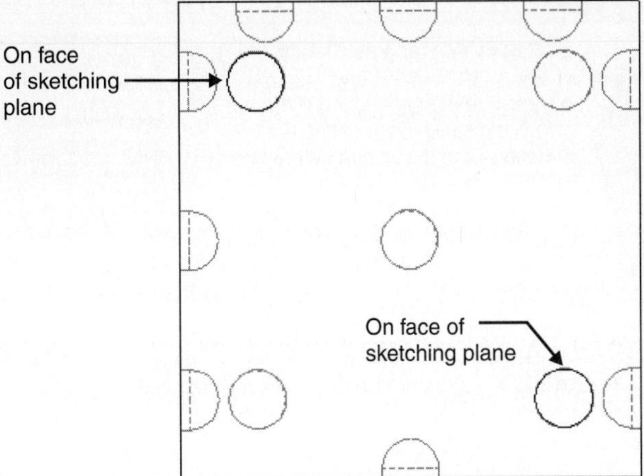

Figure 2.16   Resultant surface from Tutorial 2.2.

2.4.4 Specifying Direction

After you have selected the sketching plane and reference, you will need to indicate the direction of the new feature with respect to the sketching plane. Is the reference going into the sketching plane or coming out of the sketching plane?

We have one more degree of freedom to specify. In our transparency analogy, we mentioned placing the transparency backwards. How do we know what side of the transparency that we are drawing on? There are two factors that affect the answer to this question.

The first factor is the type of feature. Features can be thought of as either adding or removing material. If we add material, as in a protrusion, PT/Modeler will orient the part so the feature grows out towards us. If we subtract material, as in a cut, PT/Modeler will orient the part so the feature grows away from us. Therefore, you need to be mindful of your viewpoint and whether you are adding or subtracting material.

The second factor is user selected. A red arrow is drawn outward from the reference plane as shown in Figure 2.17(a). You are requested to either accept the direction of the arrow or flip the arrow. You accept the direction by selecting OK. You flip the arrow's direction and then select OK to change the direction. The menu is illustrated in Figure 2.17(b). No such menu selection is presented if the feature is to extend in both directions.

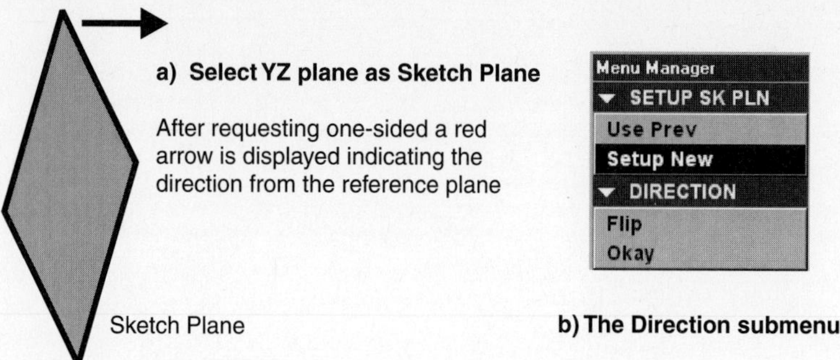

Figure 2.17   Selecting the direction with the Flip submenu.

Figure 2.18 illustrates all three cases. A cylindrical protrusion is extruded from the YZ plane in a positive yellow direction as shown in Figure 2.18(a), in a negative red direction as shown in Figure 2.18(b), and out both directions as shown in Figure 2.18(c).

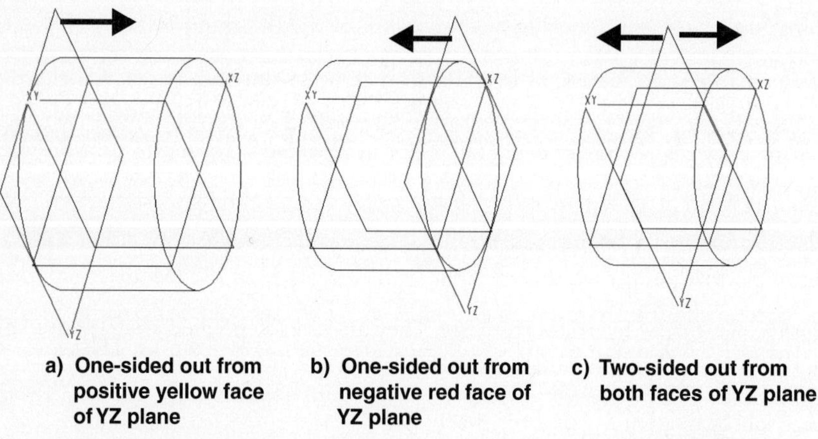

Figure 2.18   Examples of one-sided and two-sided cylinder protrusion feature.

At this point, you have entered everything necessary to begin your sketching. You will learn about sketching in the next two chapters.

2.5   Creating Datum Planes

Datum planes can be assigned as features to your model. There are a number of ways to specify where the plane should be placed and how it should be oriented. You create a datum plane from the Feature menu as shown in Figure 2.19.

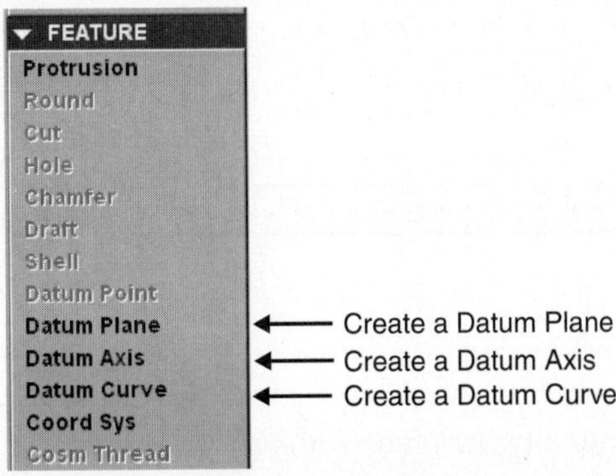

Figure 2.19   Creating a datum plane.

Once you have selected to create a datum plane, the fun really begins. It is necessary to specify where you want the plane. You can select a point that the plane will go through, be normal to, be parallel to, be offset from, at an angle to, or tangent to. These choices are shown in Figure 2.20(a). Once one of these is selected, you will be provided with a set of filters. These filters help you to select the aligning feature on your model. For example, if you select to create a plane offset from another plane, then the filters would only highlight Plane. In Figure 2.20(b), I have selected to create a datum plane *Through* something. The filters will allow you to select AxisEdgeCurve, Point/Vertex, Planes, or Cylinders since the datum plane could go through any of these.

Datum planes are themselves features. They are used to provide a reference to geometric features. Uses include:

- Specifying a sketching plane
- References for dimensions
- References for views
- References for assemblies

There are several ways to specify a plane. A plane is a two-dimensional object. Recall from your geometry memories that a plane can be defined by another plane (as

Offset), by a line and a point, or by three points. Constrain planes using the menu shown in Figure 2.20(a) as described in Table 2.1.

Menu Selection	The Datum plane
Through	Must pass through the specified point, edge, vertex, or cylinder
Normal	Is perpendicular to a specified axis, surface, or other plane
Parallel	Is parallel to a surface or another plane
Offset	Is parallel to a surface or another plane and located a specified distance away
Angle	Is at a specified angle from a surface or another plane
Tangent	Is tangent to a curved surface or the edge at an end point

Table 2.1   Constraining a Plane

It often takes two or more of these constraints to specify the location of the plane fully. *Parallel* to another plane and *Offset* from another plane both require a distance measure from the reference plane. *Normal* to a plane requires a specification indicating where the planes intersect. This could be an edge or two points. *Tangent* also requires a point indicating where the plane touches the curved surface.

A plane can be defined by three points (not in a straight line). Consequently, you can constrain a plane by providing three points *Through* which the plane passes. A plane can also be defined by a line and a point not on the line. Consequently, you could select a Through point and an axis.

Often, you will want to constrain a plane using the *Angle* constraint. This is the case when you want to define a radial pattern. You could specify that the new plane would be at an *Angle* to another plane in conjunction with the plane going *Through* an axis.

After selecting one of the constraint menu items, it is necessary to pick the reference associated with the constraint. For example: Through what? Parallel to what? Normal or Tangent to what? Offset from what?

The menu manager will anticipate selections for you. It will highlight in black all possible filters associated with your constraint choice. For example, if you select Parallel, the menu manager will highlight Plane, leaving the others un-highlighted. Figure 2.20(b) shows all four highlighted due to the *Through* selection. All items highlighted are ORed to the filter. That is, with all four highlighted, you are able to pick axis, edges, points, vertex, planes, or cylinders. You can further filter your data by clicking on the highlighted items to remove them from the filter. For example, if you know that you want to go through an axis, click on Point/Vertex, Plane, and

Cylinder to un-highlight them. This would leave only Axis and Edges highlighted. Therefore, you could pick only an axis or edges. This simplifies the picking and query select process by limiting the possible choices.

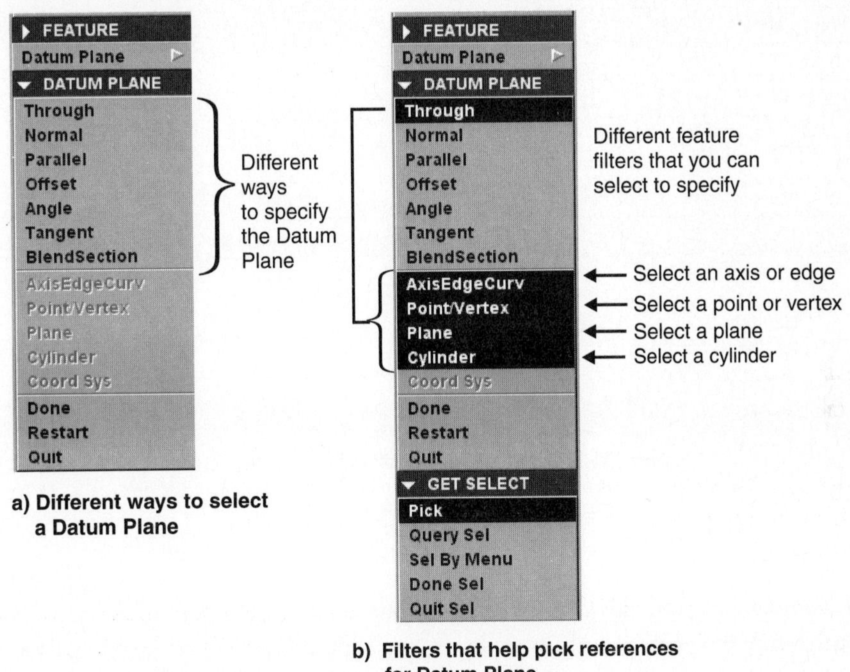

Figure 2.20   Specifying the location of the datum plane.

Figure 2.21(a) shows the model face that should be selected for the reference plane. The reference plane will be constructed parallel to this reference plane, and offset from this reference plane from a specified distance. I selected to enter a value for the offset rather than pick a feature to specify the offset. During the specification process, an arrow extended outward from the selected plane and I was queried to enter a value for the offset. Since I wanted the offset datum plane to be inside the model, I specified a negative value. This is perfectly legal, and in fact, the dimensional reference is oriented such that a positive number is used from that point on. Figure 2.21(b) illustrates the resultant datum plane.

> **NOTE:** When a datum plane is fully specified, all menu items are grayed and a message indicating that the plane is fully constrained is displayed in the message window.

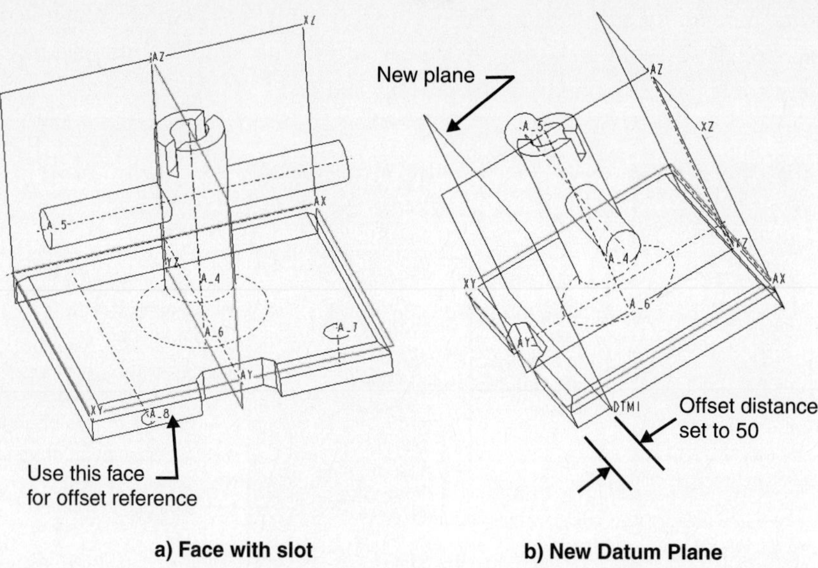

Figure 2.21   Specifying the location of the datum plane.

In Tutorial 2.3, you will create an offset datum plane. Offset datum planes are the easiest, so it is a good place to start. Later, in Chapter 3, we will revisit this part and add some hole features to points on this offset datum plane. We will not use this specific file again, so try creating other datum planes.

Also in Tutorial 2.3, a datum plane is constructed tangent to a cylinder and normal to the face of the notch. Figure 2.22(a) shows the cylinder and notch that will be selected. Figure 2.22(b) shows a top view of the new datum plane.

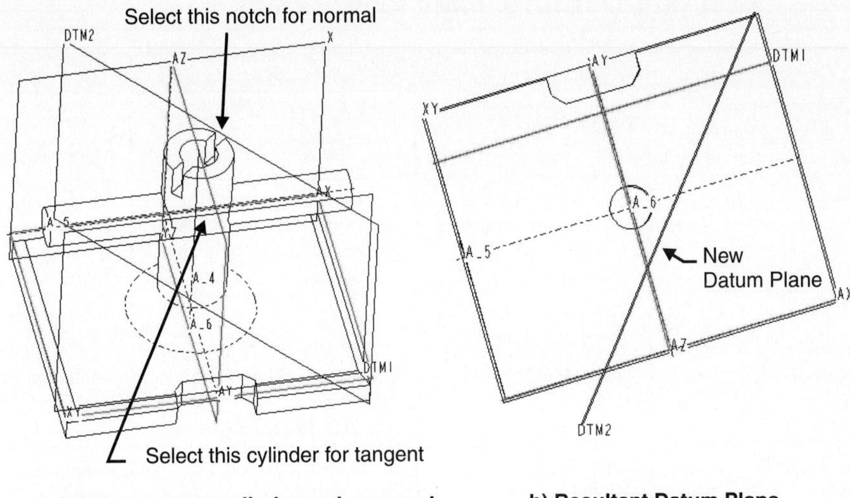

a) Select a tangent cylinder and a normal surface

b) Resultant Datum Plane

Figure 2.22   Specifying the location of the datum plane.

Tutorial 2.3   Creating Datum Planes

Files opened: Tut2-3a.prt

Files saved: Tut2-3b.prt
Tut2-3c.prt

Step	Action	Description	Further Actions	Result
1	Click PT/Modeler Icon	Run PT/Modeler		After some time, PT/Modeler on screen
2	>Mode >Misc >Show Dir	Show current directory		Message similar to "Directory searched is c:\ptc\ptprod\bin"
3	>Change Dir	Change the current directory	Type **c:\proe\tutorial\ chapter_2**	
4	>Done-Return	Leave Misc menu		Misc menu removed
5	>Part >Search/Retr	Read in a part	Select **Tut2-3a**	Part is displayed on screen
6	Ctrl-drag-mMb	Rotate part downward so we can see the top face		Part is rotated downward
7	>Feature >Datum Plane | Offset	Add a datum plane offset from a face		Ready to pick a plane
8	>Query Sel	Go into >Query Select mode	Click on the front-most face with the notch as in Fig 2.21(a)	>Query Sel selects a face

Tutorial 2.3   Creating Datum Planes (continued)

Step	Action	Description	Further Actions	Result
9	**Next** until desired face is highlighted in red	Selecting desired face as in Fig 2.21(a)	Click **Accept** when a face is highlighted	
10	>Enter Value	Enter Value; want offset to be into part: 40 if into part −40 if out of part	If arrow points away from part, enter negative value; if arrow points into face, enter positive value	Message indicating plane is fully constrained
11	>Done	Finished specifying offset datum plane		Datum plane seen as in Fig 2.21(b)
12	>File >SaveAs	Save file with new name	Enter to accept part [Tut2-3a] to save; type **Tut2-3b** for new name	Tut2-3b.prt saved to current directory
13	>File >Erase	Erase all parts in active memory		System is empty
14	>Part >Search/Retr	Read in a part again	Select Tut2-3b	Part is displayed on screen
15	>Feature >Datum Plane	Create another datum plane tangent to cylinder and normal to notch		Datum plane selection sub-menu is displayed
16	>Tangent | Cylinder	Create a tangent constraint to cylinder	Click on cylinder (use >Query Sel) as in Fig 2.22(a)	Cylinder selected
17	>Normal	Create a normal constraint to notch as in Fig 2.22(a)	Click on notch (use >Query Sel)	Notch selected; all options for selection are grayed and message indicates that plane is fully constrained
18	>Done	Finished specifying offset datum plane		New Datum seen as in Fig 2.22(b)
19	>File >SaveAs	Save file with new name	Enter to accept part [Tut2-3b] to save; type **Tut2-3c** for new name	Tut2-3f.prt saved to current directory
20	>Exit	Exit program	Click Yes to confirm	PT/Modeler exited

2.6   Creating a Datum Axis

From the feature menu in Figure 2.18, you can also create a datum axis feature for your model. Axes are very useful for referencing, especially when we have concentric circles, holes, cylinders, arcs, or revolved features. An axis is a one-dimensional object that, like a datum plane, is infinite in length. When you draw an axis, it will appear to have a beginning and end. However, an axis only has direction and location, not length. Consequently, the axis extends in both directions, regardless of how it is drawn.

In Tutorial 2.4, you will create three datum axes, AX, AY, and AZ. You will specify the axis location as the intersection between two planes; in this case, the datum planes. Note that the AX axis is located at the intersection of the XY and XZ planes. The AY axis is located at the intersection of the XY and YZ planes, and the AZ axis is located at the intersection of the XZ and YZ planes.

Tutorial 2.4   Creating a Datum Axis

Files opened: Tut2-4a.prt   **Files saved:** Tut2-4b.prt

Step	Action	Description	Further Actions	Result
1	Click PT/Modeler Icon	Run PT/Modeler		After some time, PT/Modeler on screen
2	>Mode >Misc >Show Dir	Show current directory		Message similar to "Directory searched is c:\ptc\ptprod\bin"
3	>Change Dir	Change the current directory	Type **c:\proe\tutorial\ chapter_2**	
4	>Done-Return	Leave Misc menu		Misc menu removed
5	>Part > Search/Retr	Read in a part	Select Tut2-4a	Dice is displayed on screen
6	Click on Model Tree	Bring Model Tree on top of Graphics window		
7	>Feature >Datum Axis | Two Planes	Create a datum axis through two planes	Requests you to select two planes	
8	Click on YZ and XZ in the Model Tree	Select intersection of YZ and XZ for axis		Axis created
9	Select >Two Planes again	Create a datum axis through two planes	Requests you to select two planes	
10	Click on YZ and XY in the Model Tree	Select intersection of YZ and XY for axis		Axis created
11	Select >Two Planes again	Create a datum axis through two planes	Requests you to select two planes	
12	Click on XZ and XY in the Model Tree	Select intersection of XZ and XY for axis		Axis created
13	>File >Save As	Save file to tut2-4a	**Enter** to accept [tut2-2a] as part to save; type **tut2-2b** as new name	File tut2-2a saved
14	>Exit	Exit program	Click Yes to confirm	PT/Modeler exited

2.7   Creating Temporary Datum Planes: MakeDatum

Lastly, we will deal with *temporary datum planes*. Sometimes, it is necessary to create a Datum Plane for a single feature. Suppose we wanted to sketch on a plane inside a part, as we did in Tutorial 2.3. Suppose that there would be only one feature on this plane. Now, with the default datum planes, and other datum planes, a model can get pretty cluttered. It would be nice to associate a datum plane with a feature. The datum plane could be hidden, unless the specific feature was selected for redefinition. Temporary datum planes are used for this exact purpose. You create temporary datum planes on-the-fly during feature creation. This operation is called MakeDatum.

Tutorial 2.5 covers some pretty complicated material. This is definitely an advanced topic. You will be requested to take actions inside the sketcher. I know that you have not been introduced to the sketcher yet so you can take the exercise all the way to the sketcher and then abort out, or you can follow the tutorial through to the end and actually create the default datum and its protrusion.

The goal of this tutorial is to create a ring around our part as shown in Figure 2.23(b). This ring is called a revolved protrusion. First, we are going to specify a temporary datum plane, with the MakeDatum command. This datum plane will be constrained to a polar coordinate system with an angular and radial dimension. The datum plane is shown in Figure 2.23(a). It is oriented at 45 degrees from the XZ plane. It goes through the center axis of the part.

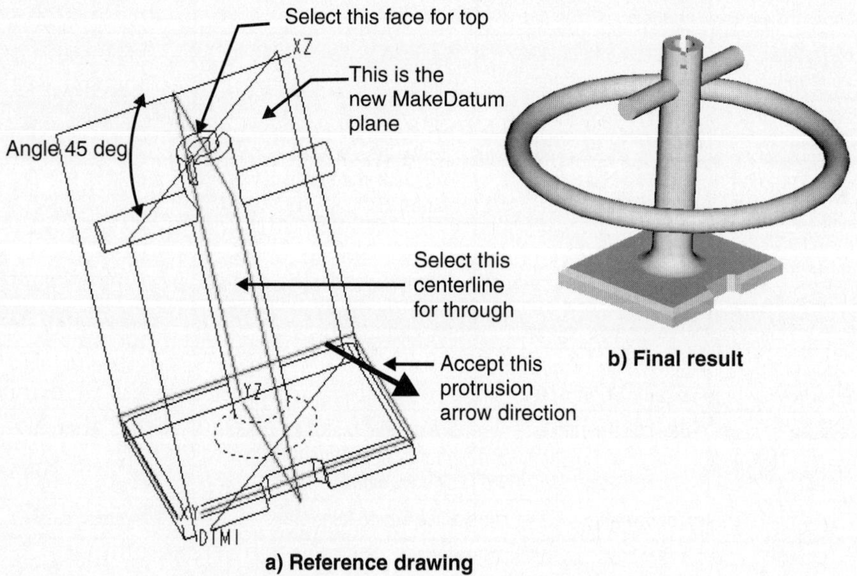

Figure 2.23   Adding a protrusion using MakeDatum.

We will do this by reading in our part and adding the protrusion feature. We will select a revolved protrusion instead of an extruded protrusion. Both of these will be described in later chapters. During the design phase, we will take a side trip to design the MakeDatum feature. After we request the Revolved Protrusion and indicate that one-sided will suffice, the dialog box shown in Figure 2.24 is displayed. If we accept the Plane default, we would specify our sketching plane. Instead, we want to create a temporary datum plane and use that plane for our sketching plane.

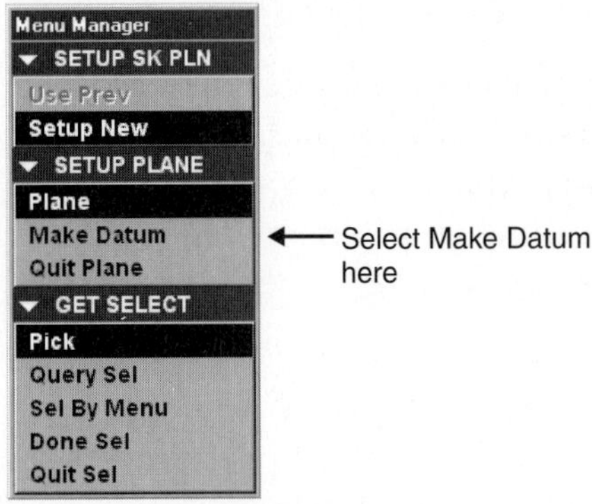

Figure 2.24   MakeDatum Dialog.

We create a MakeDatum plane exactly the same as we create any datum plane. The dialogs are identical to those in Figure 2.20. In this tutorial, we want to constrain the plane to go through the center axis of the part and to be angled 45 degrees from the XY plane. Once properly constrained, the datum plane is created and we are back to selecting our part. Figure 2.23(a) shows the arrow indicating the direction that PT/Modeler would like to protrude the feature. We accept this direction. Since we are going to rotate the part around 360 degrees, it wouldn't matter anyway. From here, we pop into the sketcher.

Now we are on uncharted territory. If you get lost here, don't worry. It will all be explained in Chapters 3 and 4. Try and get through the tutorial. It isn't that complicated, and you will gain valuable confidence when you take on the sketcher in the following chapters. We are going to revolve a circle around the 360 degrees. The cross-section of the ring is a circle. It wouldn't need to be, but that is our design goal.

To draw the circle in sketcher, select sketch and circle from the menus: Sketch >Circle. Click in the sketcher window about where the center of the circle is marked in Figure 2.25(a). It is indicated *with First mLb*. This means click the left mouse button here first. This sets the center of the circle. Now extend the circle a bit. Don't drag the mouse. The software is not intended for this. Get in the habit of simply clicking in the center and then click again after moving out to the circumference of the desired circle. Click again at *Second mLb*. A circle should be drawn as indicated in Figure 2.25(a).

Next draw a centerline along the part's vertical axis. You accomplish this by selecting >Sketch >Line >Centerline. You are already in the Sketch submenu so you don't have to select Sketch again. Simply click on Line and then Centerline. This centerline is also indicated in Figure 2.25(a). Don't worry if it is exactly straight or exactly on the line. We will align it next. Click the left mouse button, *Third mLb,* beneath the base plate and then above it at *Fourth mLb* as indicated in the figure. The dashed centerline should be drawn.

We are ready to align the centerline of our part to the coordinate system AY axis. Click on Align and then click on the centerline and on the AY axes. In places, these overlap so you could double-click at the same location. This tells the software to align our new centerline with the axis or plane beneath it. In the sketcher, close is good enough. The AY axis happens to be beneath our new centerline. You will get a message indicating –ALIGNED–.

Now click on AutoDimension. This command will perform an automatic dimensioning based on your drawing. This is a very useful tool! This command wants to know to which references you want the circle to refer. The diameter of the circle needs no reference. Both the height of the circle and the distance from the centerline have to be specified. So, click on the centerline and click on the base plate AX axis. It is always a good idea to use QuerySel when picking.

The AutoDimension operation should be happy now so click on Regenerate. A message should be displayed indicating that the regeneration was successful. This creates the dimensioned and constrained result. The dimensions will be shown in the sketcher view and they should be similar to Figure 2.25(b). You can easily change these dimensions to match the figure. Click on Modify and then click directly on the dimension that you want to change. You are queried for the desired value. Click on all three dimensions and enter the values as shown in the figure. Once again, it is time to regenerate the part. Click Regenerate. A message should be displayed indicating that the regeneration was successful.

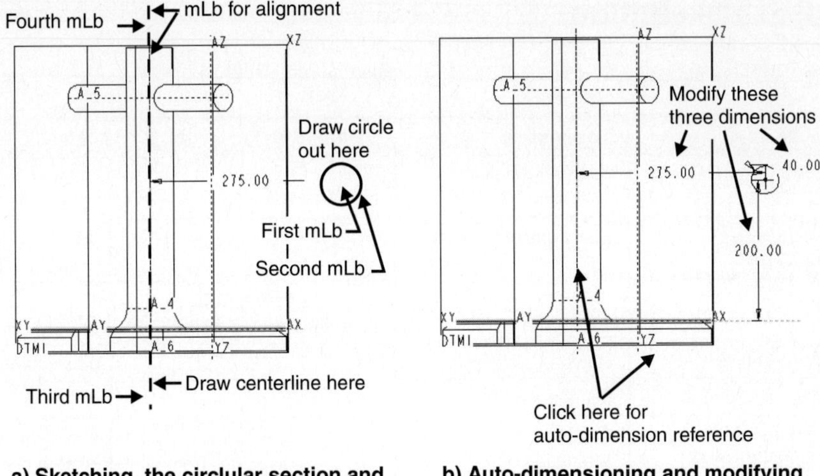

**a) Sketching the circlular section and
center line with alignment**

b) Auto-dimensioning and modifying

Figure 2.25   Placing a circular section in sketcher.

We are done with the sketcher now so click Done. This brings our focus to the
Dialog box. Click on OK and type F1 to get the default 3D view. Rotate the part
around a bit.

Tutorial 2.5 MakeDatum

Files opened: Tut2-5a.prt   **Files saved:** Tut2-5b.prt

Step	Action	Description	Further Actions	Result
1	Click PT/Modeler Icon	Run PT/Modeler		After some time, PT/Modeler on screen
2	>Mode >Misc >Show Dir	Show current directory		Message similar to "Directory searched is c:\ptc\ptprod\bin"
3	>Change Dir	Change the current directory	Type **c:\proe\tutorial\ chapter_2**	
4	>Done-Return	Leave Misc menu		Misc menu removed
5	>Part >Search/Retr	Read in a part	Select Tut2-5a	Part is displayed
6	>Feature >Protrusion | Extrude | Revolve | >Done	Add a solid revolved protrusion		Ready to select MakeDatum sketch plane
7	>One Side | >Done	Select one-sided protrusion		
8	> Make Datum >Through	Want to constrain plane to go through axis	>Query Sel to select the vertical center axis of our part	Center axis selected turns red
9	>Angle	Want to constrain plane to be at an angle with respect to the XZ plane	>Query Sel to select the XZ axis	Message indicating fully constrained; all constraint choices are grayed out
10	>Done	>Done with constraining datum plane		
11	>Enter Value	Want datum to be 45 degrees from XZ	Type **45**	Arrow is displayed pointing out from datum plane
12	Okay to direction arrow	Don't care what direction protrusion extends from		Select reference plane sub-menu is displayed
13	>Top	Want surface at top of shaft to be at the top of our 2D sketch	>Query Sel top face of shaft	2D sketch >Mode is entered (see Fig. 2.25)
14	>Sketch >Circle	Want to draw a circle that will be our ring section as in Fig. 2.25(a)	Click first mLb at center of circle and second mLb at diameter in Fig. 2.25(a)	Circle drawn
15	>Sketch >Line | Centerline	Want to draw a vertical centerline aligned to centerline of part	Click third mLb beneath part and fourth mLb above part in Fig. 2.25(a)	Centerline drawn in dashed line
16	>Align	Align new ring centerline to old part axis	Click twice, once on ring centerline and once on part axis; can double click at same point	---- ALIGNED ---- message

Tutorial 2.5 MakeDatum (continued)

Step	Action	Description	Further Actions	Result
17	>AutoDimension	Need to constrain the ring section to the part; let AutoDimension do it for us	Click once on aligned centerlines and once on top surface of plate in Fig. 2.25(b)	We instructed AutoDimension to use only these two features to align our circular section
18	>Done Sel > >Done	>Done providing references for AutoDimension	Regenerates after >Done Sel	Regeneration successful message
19	> 360 > >Done	Asked how many degrees in the rotation		Part is now generated
20	Click Preview button in Feature dialog	Want to see result before committing to it	Use F1 key and Ctrl-Drag to manipulate view of part in 3D	See result
21	Click Ok button in Feature dialog	Commit to new feature		
22	> Modify	Let's modify the dimensions	>Query Sel to select the ring as the feature to modify	Ring dimensions are shown in the view
23	Click on a dimension	Change a dimension	Change to value in Fig. 2.26	Repeat for all three dimensions
24	>Regenerate	Ready to rebuild part		Regeneration successful message
25	Should see part change			
26	>File >SaveAs	Save part	**Enter** for part to save [tut2-5a]; type **tut2-5b.prt**	
27	>Exit	Exit program	Click >Yes to confirm	PT/Modeler exited

Once you have a good view, click >Modify in the Part menu. The software needs to know what to modify. Click anywhere on the ring. Once again, use >QuerySel to insure making the correct pick. We see the final dimensions that we will use for this protrusion. Note the radial and angular dimensions as referenced from the centerline of the main shaft. This means that the ring is not constrained to the base in either of these two directions. The ring is still constrained to the base in the height direction. We can therefore readily change the size of the base (but not the height) without worrying about messing up the ring dimensions.

When we modify a feature, the dimensional parameters associated with that feature are displayed on the screen. Figure 2.26 illustrates the dimensions of our part after our request to modify the ring feature. We can click on any feature in the part. Dimensions associated with any feature can be modified from this menu item.

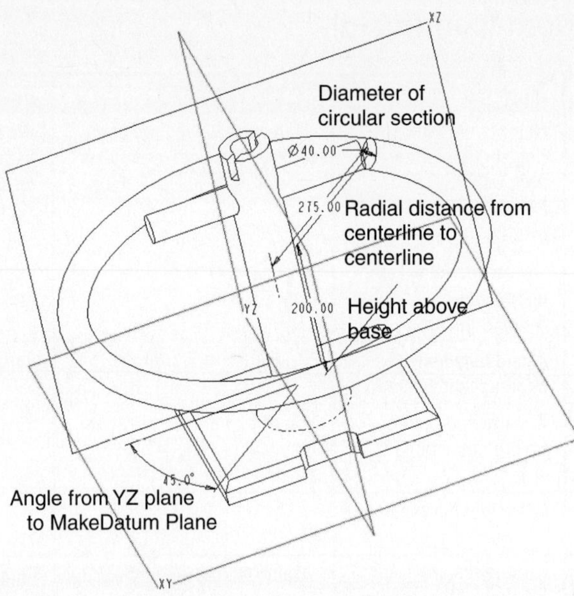

Figure 2.26   Modifying the ring.

2.8   Manipulating in 3D Space

Next, we will look at different ways to view the model. You should be starting to get used to the three mouse moves summarized again in Table 2.2.

Terminology	Action	Result
Ctrl-Drag mLb	Control Key down and drag the left mouse button	Zoom in and out
Ctrl-Drag mMb	Control Key down and drag the middle mouse button	Rotate in 3D space
Ctrl-Drag mRb	Control Key down and drag the right mouse button	Pan in 3D space

Table 2.2   Mouse Control of 3D Views

Rotating in 3D space can be thought of as fixing an object inside a transparent ball. The mouse rubs along the outer surface of the ball spinning it around. Spin up, sideways, or diagonally. Luckily, you can see the result of your rotation as you drag the mouse so you don't have to understand it empirically.

2.8.1   The Spin Center

The acute among you might ask the questions: Great, put the object inside the ball, but put it where? From what center are you rotating? If we put the center at the center of the Sun, and rotate the Earth, then the Earth moves around the sun. If we put the center at the center of the Earth, the Earth rotates about its own axis. There are times when we want to rotate about a specific center. We might want the center near the center of a part or we might want the center near some end of the part. Suppose we have a long shaft with two gears on either end. If the center of rotation is at the center of the rod, then the two gears are going to spin around a large radius. It would be difficult to see different views of the gears. If we position the center at the center of the axis, at the center of a gear, then rotating the part would keep the gear on-screen. A big difference, don't you agree?

PT/Modeler gives us a tool called the *spin center.* It is that little red, green, and blue job that is always at the intersection of the XY, XZ, and YZ planes (in other words, the origin). The red side corresponds to the positive AX axis. The green side corresponds to the positive AY axis and the blue side corresponds to the AZ axis. Get the connection? RGB . . . XYZ . . . ABC . . . VGA . . . CIA?

> **NOTE:** Datum planes are not displayed during 3D mouse dragging. If you start a part with the Default Datum Planes, at the start you will not see anything but the original XYZ triad of arrows rotate as you move the mouse.

We can choose to display or hide the spin center from a check box in the Environment menu. We can also position the spin center through the View >Orientation >Set Spin Center menu selection. This menu is shown in Figure 2.27. As you can see, you can specify the placement for the spin center to be the center of the screen or the center of mass of the part. Alternatively, you can position it on an axis, a point, or with respect to a coordinate system.

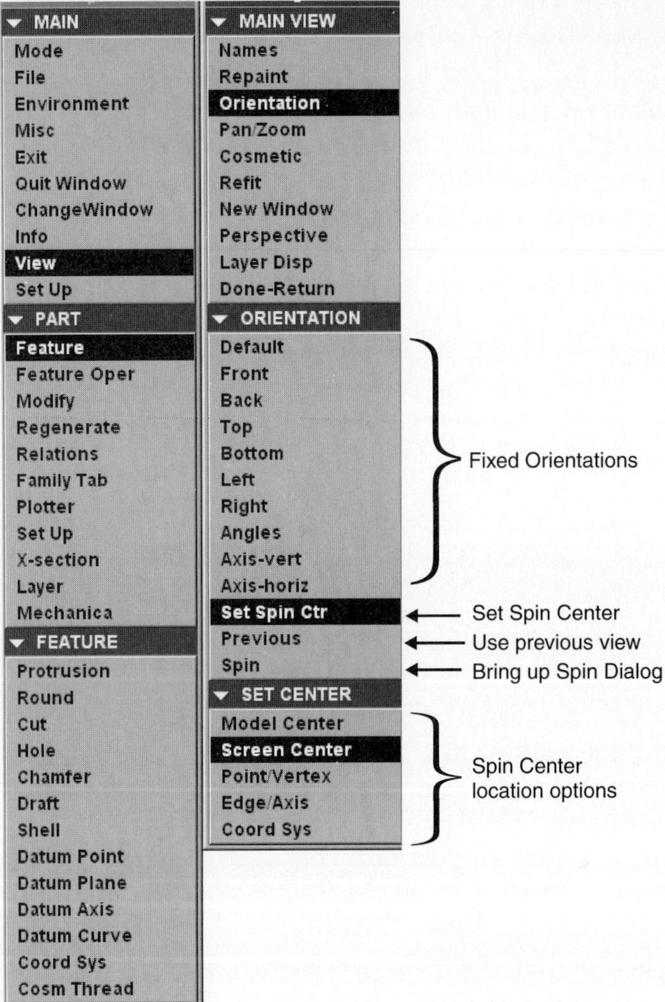

Figure 2.27   The View Menu with the Orientation submenu.

We will refer back to Figure 2.27 throughout the remainder of this chapter.

2.8.2 The Spin Dialog Box

You will use the mouse 90 percent of the time to orient your views. There will be occasions when you will want to specify actual values for pan, zoom, and rotate. A dialog box is provided for this purpose. The number of slider controls varies depending on the constraint placed on the spin center. If the spin center is aligned to an axis or edge, only one rotate control exists and this rotates the object about that axis or edge. This is shown in Figure 2.28(a). If the spin center is set to the center of the part, three controls are provided, one each for X, Y, and Z rotation. This is shown in Figure 2.28(b). In this second case, the rotation is with respect to the X, Y, and Z axis of the part itself. This should be contrasted to the case where the spin center is set to the center of the screen. In this later case, there are still three rotation spinners with respect to the X, Y, and Z axis. However, in this case, these are the X, Y, and Z axis of the screen. The Z axis is assumed to be coming out of the monitor towards you. There is a big difference between these two coordinate systems. If you spin the part, using Ctrl-Drag-mMb, then the part coordinate system will rotate along with the part. If you had selected the center of the part model as the spin center, the part would now rotate about a different set of part XYZ axis. The Z axis might point to the left, up, or at any angle, depending on the rotation. If, on the other hand, you had set the spin center to the center of the screen, then rotating the part would always be with respect to the monitor. You would have to rotate your monitor to get the angles to change. Both are very, very useful. Your degree of proficiency at manipulating the view of the part will directly affect your ability to design in 3D effectively.

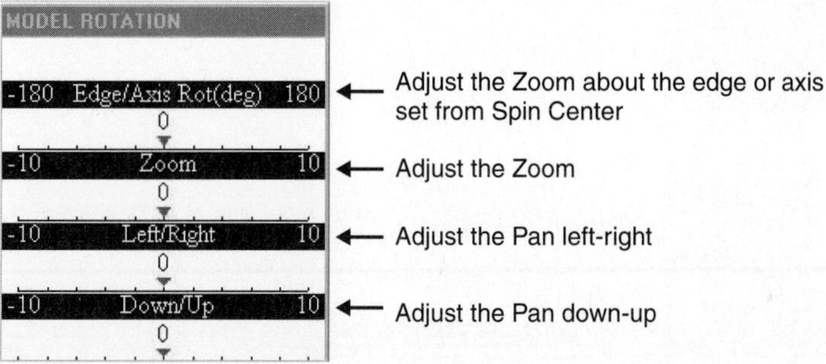

a) Menu after setting spin center to an axis

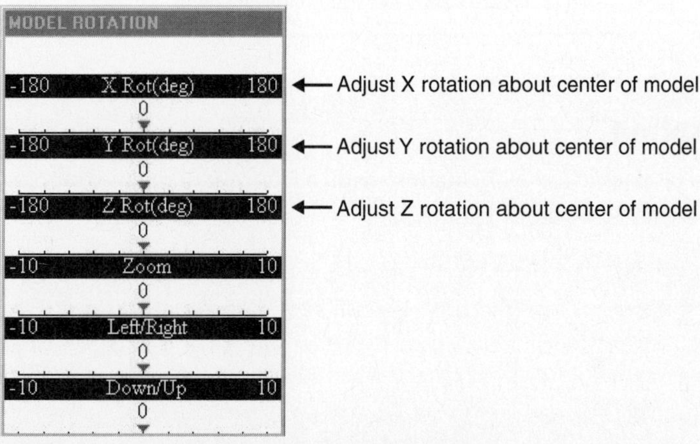

b) Menu after setting spin center to center of part

Figure 2.28   The Spin Dialog box.

2.9   Pan/Zoom

The Pan/Zoom control in the View menu provides an excellent method for moving about in two-dimensions on the screen. This menu is shown in Figure 2.29. You cannot change the rotational angle from this control. A Pan-Zoom submenu is displayed. This submenu also allows you to zoom in or out. Zoom In requests that you click twice to define a rectangular region. This region will be zoomed to fill the entire screen. Zoom Out pulls the camera farther away from the part. Panning is accomplished using the Pan item. Simply click on any location in the graphics window, and this point moves to the center of the display. You can back up one view with Previous. Lastly, you can return to the view present when you first clicked on the Pan/Zoom menu item using Reset.

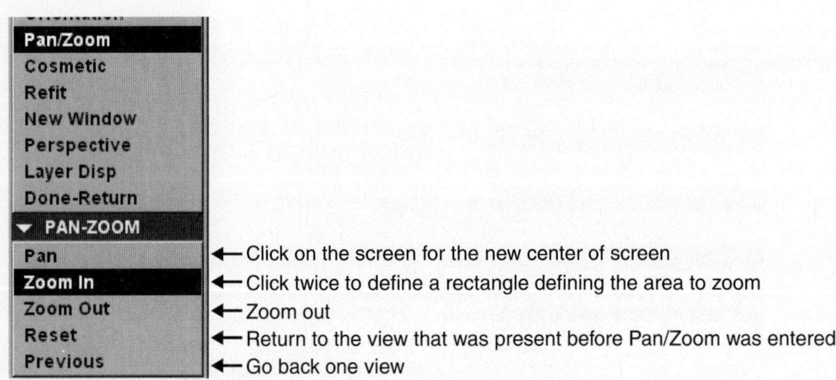

Figure 2.29   The Pan/Zoom submenu.

2.10   Orientation

As would be expected, the orientation menu allows you to orient your part. The orientation menu is shown in Figure 2.30.

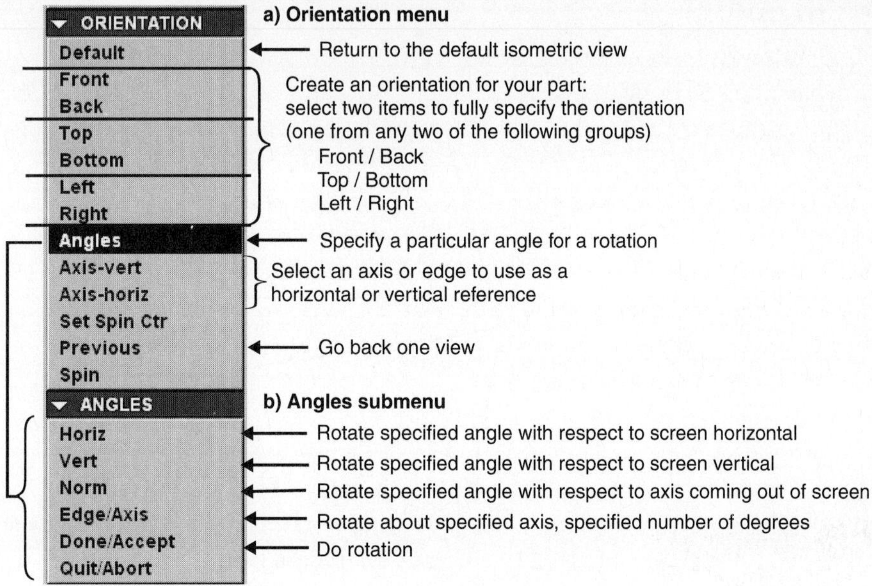

Figure 2.30   The Orientation and Angles submenus.

The most common control is the Default selection. This returns the view to a large isometric view of the entire part. This is a great way to return to a known state. I have included another look at the default view in Figure 2.31 for you to submit to memory. Note the direction of the axis. Towards the bottom of the menu is the Previous entry which takes you back one view. This is also very useful.

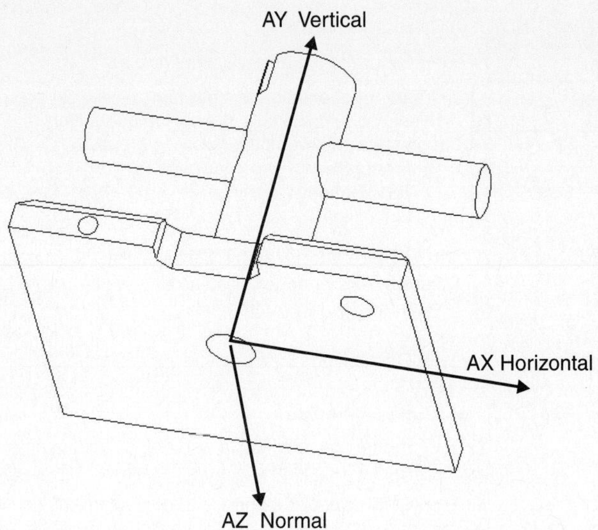

Figure 2.31   Default View revisited.

The top portion of the menu provides orientations with respect to the screen. These are grouped into Front/Back, Top/Bottom and Left/Right. It takes two picks to orient a part. For example, Top and Right would completely orient the part. After selecting Top, you would pick a face on your part that will be oriented parallel to the top of the screen. Similarly, after selecting Right, pick a face on your part that will be oriented parallel to the side of the screen and positioned on the right side of the screen. Alternately, you could select Front-Bottom, Front-Right, etc. After picking two, the view is automatically changed.

Next we have the angles menu selection. This brings up the Angles submenu as seen in Figure 2.30(b). This is pretty straightforward. The top three selections, Horizontal, Vertical, and Normal relate to the screen axis where Horizontal is across the screen, Vertical is up and down, and Normal is out of the screen. After selecting one of these, you are prompted to enter an angle. When you click Done/Accept, the part is rotated about the horizontal axis. Remember that this is the horizontal axis with respect to the screen. Similarly, you could select to rotate the part about the vertical or normal axis. In fact, you can set up multiple rotations before clicking the Done/Accept key. The screen rotations are illustrated in Figure 2.32(a).

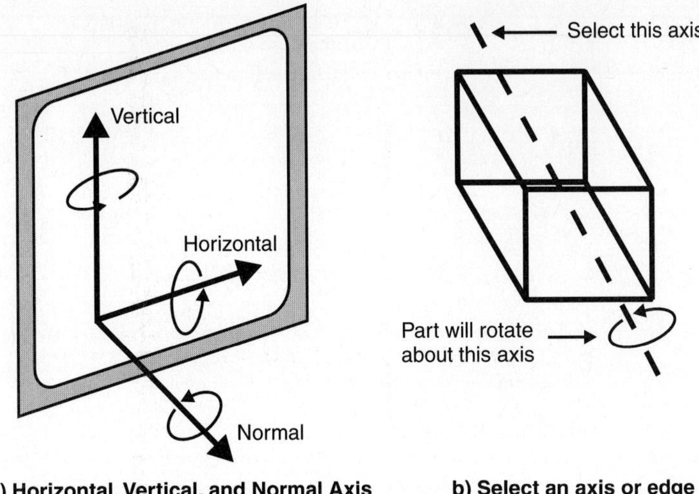

Figure 2.32   Rotations with respect to the screen and an arbitrary axis.

It is also possible to select an arbitrary edge or axis for the rotational axis. Once again you will need to provide the rotation angle after selecting the edge or axis. This rotation is shown in Figure 2.32(b).

2.11 Named Views

It is possible to spend considerable time setting up views, whether through Ctrl-Drag, Pan/Zoom or the Spin Dialog. Fortunately, you can save a view and recall it later by name. These are called *named views*. Named views are accessed through the Names menu option in the View menu as we saw in Figure 2.27. Any Named view can be selected by clicking on the menu item. You can also retrieve a Named view by clicking on Name and responding to the query by typing in the name. Saving a name is just as easy. Simply click on Save and type in the new name. Delete a name by clicking Delete and selecting the name to be deleted. The Names submenu is shown in Figure 2.33.

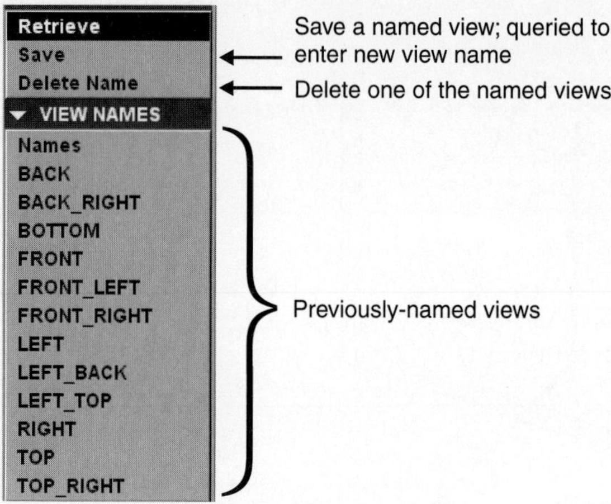

Figure 2.33   The Names menu.

Tutorial 2.6 will get you on the way to mastering the use of views. In the tutorial, you will create views using the Ctrl-Drag, Spin, and Pan/Zoom mouse methods as well as the Orientation menus. You will name views and see how you return to these views. You will also manipulate the spin center.

In Tutorial 2.6, you will practice using the techniques discussed earlier for rotating, panning, and zooming your model. You will get to look at several views. You will find that you create preferences for one technique over another. Clearly, the Ctrl-Drag-Mouse movement commands are the quickest. However, these can be difficult to control and you will benefit greatly from being comfortable with the other techniques. You will also name a view and recall that named view. This is very useful and can save a great deal of time. Having the right view often means creating the desired feature correctly.

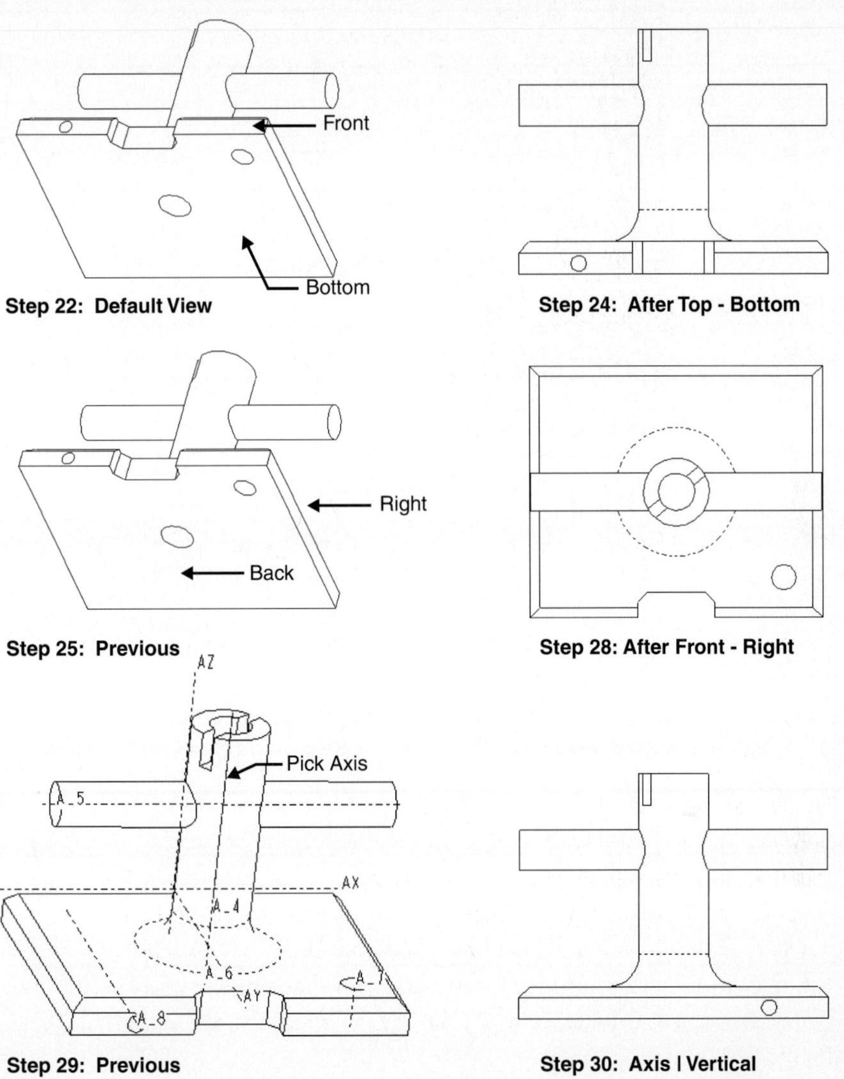

Figure 2.34   Tutorial orientation, part 1.

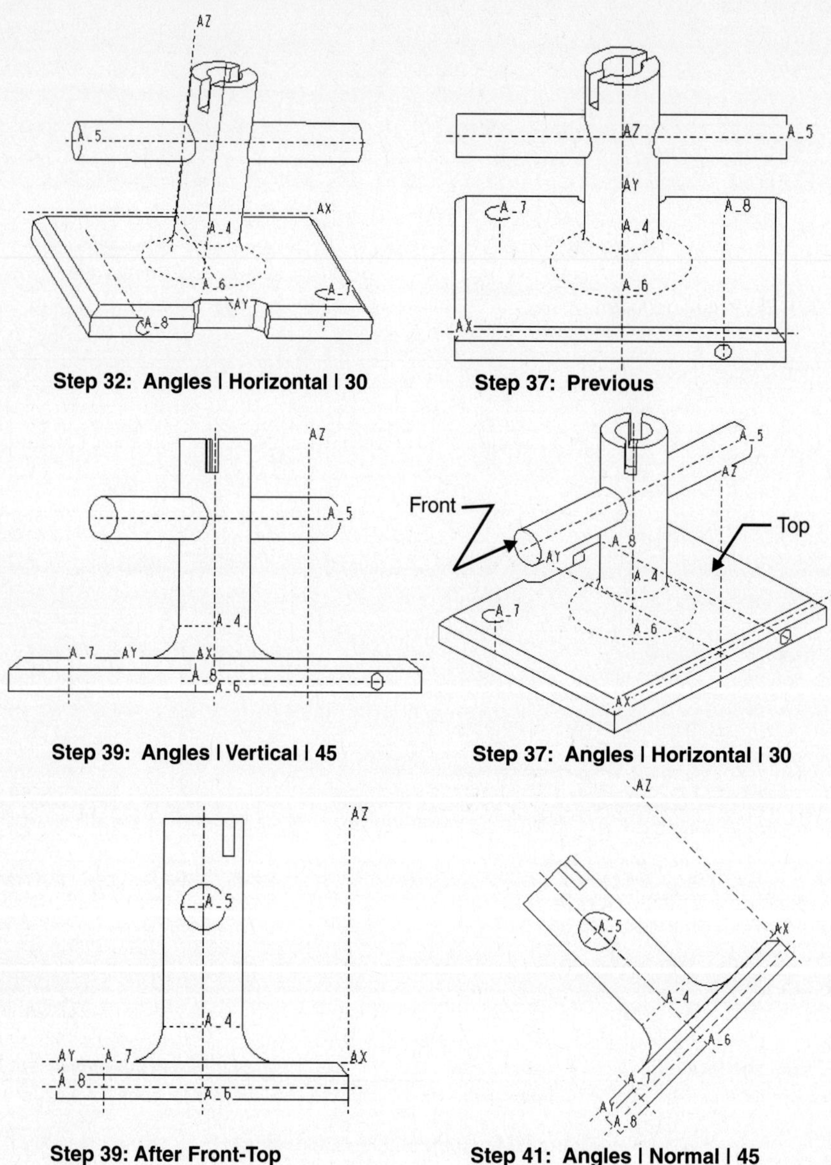

Figure 2.35 Tutorial orientation, part 2.

Tutorial 2.6 Orienting Your View in 3D

Files opened: Tut2-6a.prt   **No files saved.**

Step	Action	Description	Further Actions	Result
1	Click PT/Modeler Icon	Run PT/Modeler		After some time, PT/Modeler on screen
2	>Mode >Misc >Show Dir	Show current directory		Message similar to "Directory searched is c:\ptc\ptprod\bin"
3	>Change Dir	Change the current directory	Type **c:\proe\tutorial\ chapter_2**	
4	>Done-Return	Leave Misc menu		Misc menu removed
5	>Part >Search/Retr	Read in a part	**Tut2-6a**	Part is displayed
6	>Environment	Set up the environment	Set up checks as seen in Table T2.6; select No hidden	Part displayed with axis, spin center and no hidden lines shown
7	Ctrl-Drag-mMb	Rotate		Part rotates about spin center
8	>View >Orientation >Spin Center Ctr | Edge Axis	Move the position of the spin center to axis A_7 on hole	Click on axis A_7	Spin center moves
9	Ctrl-Drag-mMb	Rotate		Part rotates about hole; note rotation is constrained to a circular motion around axis
10	Ctrl-Drag-mLb up	Zoom out making part smaller		Part gets smaller
11	Ctrl-Drag-mRb up-right	Move part to upper-right quadrant of screen		Smaller part now sits in upper-right corner of screen
12	>Set Spin Ctr | Screen Center	Set spin center to screen center		Spin Center icon moves to center of Main Graphics window
13	Ctrl-Drag-mMb	Rotate		Part rotates about center; note rotation revolves part around center of screen and moves around the screen
14	>View >Default	Go back to default view		Part goes to default position
15	>View >Pan/Zoom | Pan	Use Pan >Mode	Click (mLb) around on the screen to select new center of view	Part is panned around screen
16	>View >Default	Go back to default view		Part goes to default position
17	>View >Pan/Zoom | Zoom Out	Zoom out		Part gets smaller

Tutorial 2.6 Orienting Your View in 3D (continued)

Step	Action	Description	Further Actions	Result
18	>View >Pan/Zoom | Zoom In	Zoom in	Click (mLb) top-left of shaft and bottom right of shaft to make a new zoom rectangle	See mostly shaft on screen
19	>View >Pan/Zoom | Previous	Back to Zoomed out from Step 17		
20	>View >Pan/Zoom | Reset	Back to view before entering Pan/Zoom		
21	>View >Orientation >Set Spin Ctr | >Model Center	Set Spin center to >Model center		
22	>View >Orientation | Default	Go back to default view		Part goes to default position as seen in Step 22 in Fig. 2.34
23	>View >Orientation | Bottom	Select bottom of plate as Bottom		
24	>View >Orientation | Front	Select face of plate with notch as Front		Part gets oriented as Step 24 in Fig. 2.34
25	>Previous	Back to default		Part gets oriented as Step 25 in Fig. 2.34
26	Ctrl-Draw-mMb	Rotate part up to see top plate of part		
27	>View >Orientation | Right	Right side of plate as Right		
28	>View >Orientation | Back	Select bottom face of plate as Back		Part gets oriented as Step 28 in Fig. 2.34
29	>Previous	Back to same view from Step 26		Part gets oriented as Step 29 in Fig. 2.34
30	>Axis-vert	Select an axis to orient for vertical	Pick Center axis A_4 using >Sel by Menu or >Query Sel	Part gets oriented as Step 30 in Fig. 2.34
31	>Angles | Horizontal	Rotate by 30 degrees horizontal	Type **30** after query	
32	>Done/Accept	>Done with angles		Part gets oriented as Step 32 in Fig. 2.35
33	>Previous	Back to same view from Step 30		Part gets oriented as Step 33 in Fig. 2.35
34	>Angles | Vertical	Rotate 45 degrees from vertical	Type **45** after query	
35	>Done/Accept	>Done with angles		Part gets oriented as Step 35 in Fig. 2.35
36	>Angles | Horizontal	Rotate by 30 degrees horizontal	Type **30** after query	

Tutorial 2.6 Orienting Your View in 3D (continued)

Step	Action	Description	Further Actions	Result
37	>Done/Accept	>Done with angles		Part gets oriented as Step 37 in Fig. 2.35
38	>View >Orientation | Top	Select top of plate as Top		
39	>View >Orientation | Front	Select end face of cross bar as Front	Use >Query Sel	Part gets oriented as Step 39 in Fig. 2.35
40	>Angles | Normal	Rotate by 45 degrees from screen normal	Type **45** after query	
41	>Done/Accept	>Done with angles		Part gets oriented as Step 41 in Fig. 2.35
42	>View >Names | Save	Save this view	Type **end_angle**	
43	>View >Default			Back to default view
44	>View >Names | Retrieve	Get the view	Click on end_angle	View from Step 41 returns
45	>Exit	Exit program	Click >Yes to confirm	PT/Modeler exited

Item	Selection
Bell	Checked
Disp Axes	Checked
Spin Center	Checked
SketStart2D	Checked
>ModelTree	Checked
Colors	Checked
No hidden	Selected
Tan Phantom	Selected
Trimetric	Selected

Table T2.6

Environment Settings

2.12 **Rendering Techniques**

There are a number of different ways to view your part. From the Environment menu you can select to enable or disable the display of datum planes, axes, as well as the spin center. At the bottom of the Environment menu you can select whether to display the part in wireframe, hidden line, no hidden line, or shading. Options are also available regarding the display of tangents. Lastly, you can choose to view the model in either an isometric or a trimetric view. I have provided a description and sample of many of these options in Table 2.3 and in Figures 2.34 and 2.35.

Menu Selection	Description
Wireframe	Display all hidden lines as well as visible lines with same line weight
Hidden line	Display hidden lines with a subdued gray color
No hidden	Hide all hidden lines
Shading	Use shading

Table 2.3   Rendering Options

Items such as datum planes, points, tags, axes, and coordinate systems can be quickly enabled or disabled using the Environment menu check boxes. Figure 2.36 illustrates many of these different options.

NOTE: In the shading mode, all axes, labels, and datum planes are turned off. The spin center can be displayed if checked in the Environment menu.

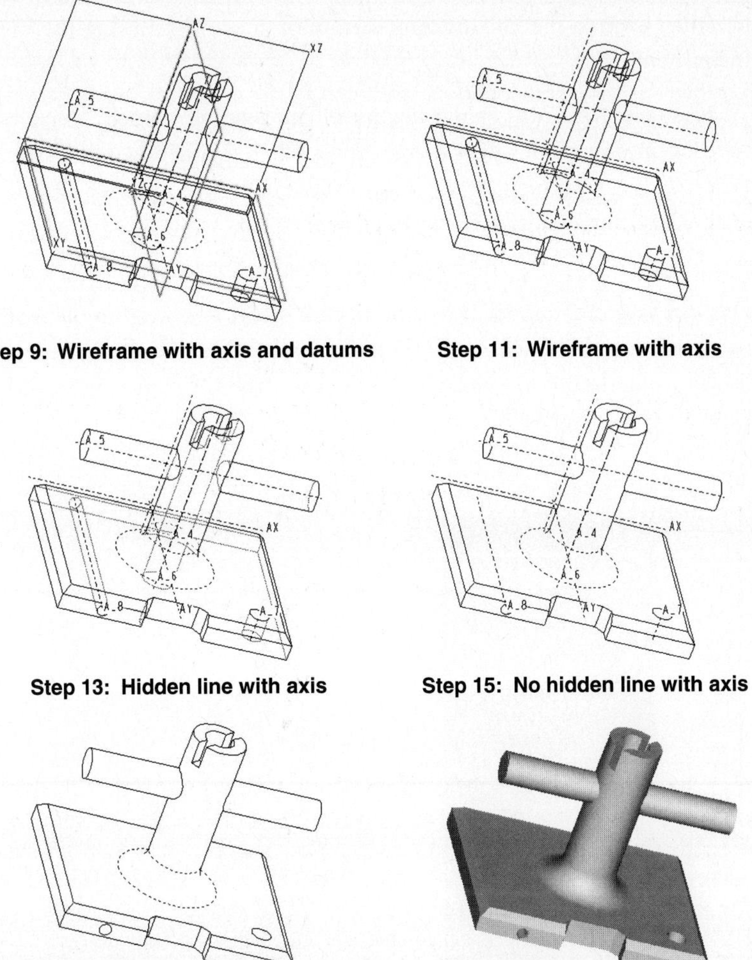

Figure 2.36   Examples of different rendering options.

The viewing options selected in the environment box force the system to always render the model using this technique. Often you might desire to shade an item temporarily. This can be accomplished using the View >Cosmetic >Shade menu option as shown in Figure 2.37. This brings up the shade submenu and from here you can select Display to see the shaded rendering of your model on the display. You can quickly return back to the line drawing version of your model using the View >Repaint menu item.

From the Shade menu you can set the quality of the shading model. I have not found any need to mess with this. If your system is really bogging down during rendering a complex part, you might want to turn this quality factor down. A query asks for the new rendring quality factor. The default is 3.0.

You can send the shaded view to the display using the Display menu item or to a disk file using the Save menu item. If saved to a disk file, it is written to the working directory and the shaded file has a .SHD file extension. This file can be restored onto the display using the Restore option. Simply enter the file name of the .SHD file that you would like displayed.

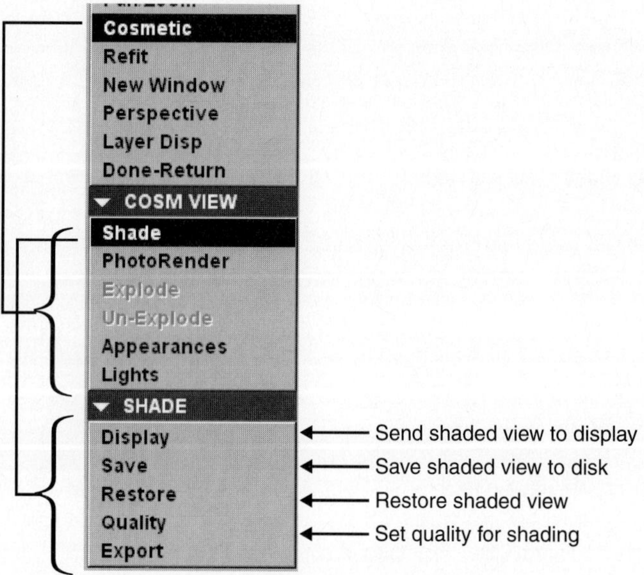

Figure 2.37   Shade menu.

2.13 Colors and Material Properties

Thus far, we have looked at only grayscale renderings. It is possible, through the Appearances submenu, to select other colors. You might want different colors for different parts in an assembly. A shaft can be shaded blue, a gear shaded green, and a block shaded cyan. You can even color different surfaces in a part with different colors.

At default, there is one color loaded into the system: white. When shading, this color is decreased in intensity from white to black to create the shading colors. If the color is set to brightest blue, the colors on the model range from brightest to darkest blue. You can also scale the brightness factor by choosing a color other than the brightest version.

Colors range in intensity from 0 (darkest) to 100 (lightest). All colors are composed of three components, red, green, and blue. A color at intensity 100 is called fully saturated. Table 2.4 provides some common colors. Note that the intensity of colors is nonlinear. Thus, a gray scale of 50 is not 50 percent as bright as a gray scale of 100. This is due to the logarithmic sensitivity of the eye. A gray scale of 80 is about 50 percent of 100.

Name	Red	Green	Blue
White	100	100	100
Gray	80	80	80
Black	0	0	0
Red	100	0	0
Green	0	0	100
Blue	0	0	100
Cyan	0	100	100
Magenta	100	0	100
Yellow	100	100	0
Orange	100	50	0

Table 2.4   Common Colors

The colors resident are stored in a Color Set. These colors can be displayed using the Show option in the Appearances menu as seen in Figure 2.38(a). You can define new colors by clicking on the Define option. The Define option brings up a Material Editor. We will return to the material editor in a second. A Color Set is shown in Figure 2.38(b).

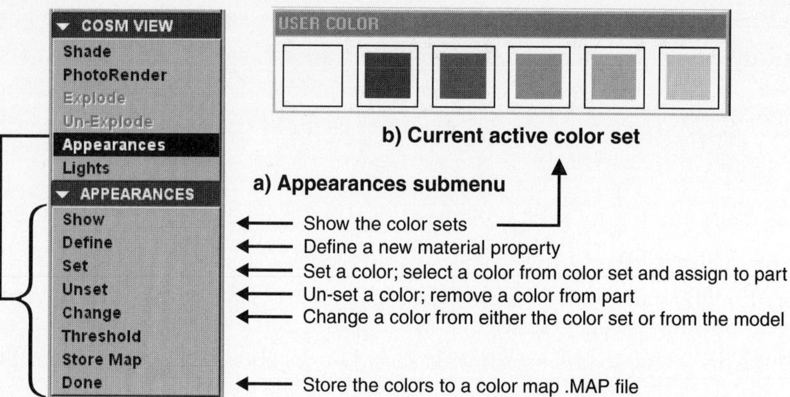

Figure 2.38   The Appearances menu and the Color Set window.

You can create additional colors in the Color Set using the Define option. You can modify colors in the color map using the Change option. If you select Change, another dialog appears asking you if you want to change a color that resides in the part or in the Color Set. Now, all colors in the part reside in the Color Set. The renderer will create a ramp of colors for shading purposes out of the single color in the Color Set. For example, you get all grays from a single color, white, in the color set.

This brings up an interesting point. You can set a color to either a surface or an entire part. If you click Set, then select a color from the color set, you can assign this color to the part. For example, clicking Set, then selecting the color blue from the Color Set, followed by clicking the part causes the part to be drawn in the selected color. All line drawings and shadings show up in blue (or shaded versions of blue). You can also unset a color using the Unset command. You must select the part whose color you want to unset.

2.14 The Material and Color Editor Dialog Boxes

During rendering, the colors associated with each pixel representing the part is determined by the parts material qualities. A part might have a shiny material like metal or a dull material like wood. A material also has a color assigned to it. A material might represent a red plastic case or a blue metal rod. For now, we will just deal with colors.

You can add colors to the Color Set using the Define menu item in the Appearances menu. A material editor dialog box comes up as shown in Figure 2.39. Note that there are two controls for the basic material quality, color and highlight. Both have two sliders, one for the ambient color and one for the diffuse color. Ambient colors are the colors that you see when there is not direct light shinning on an object. In a room with ambient light, there is brightness (of some intensity) but no distinct light source or direction to the light. Diffuse colors are the colors that you see when light is shining on them. Suppose you have a room with an overhead light creating indirect light and a lamp sitting on a table. Further suppose the table is plastic and is colored blue. You would see a circular pattern of light on the table where the light from the lamp is striking the surface. This area would be represented by the diffuse color component of the material. You would also see the rest of the table being illuminated by the indirect overhead light. The rest of the table would be represented by the ambient color component of the material.

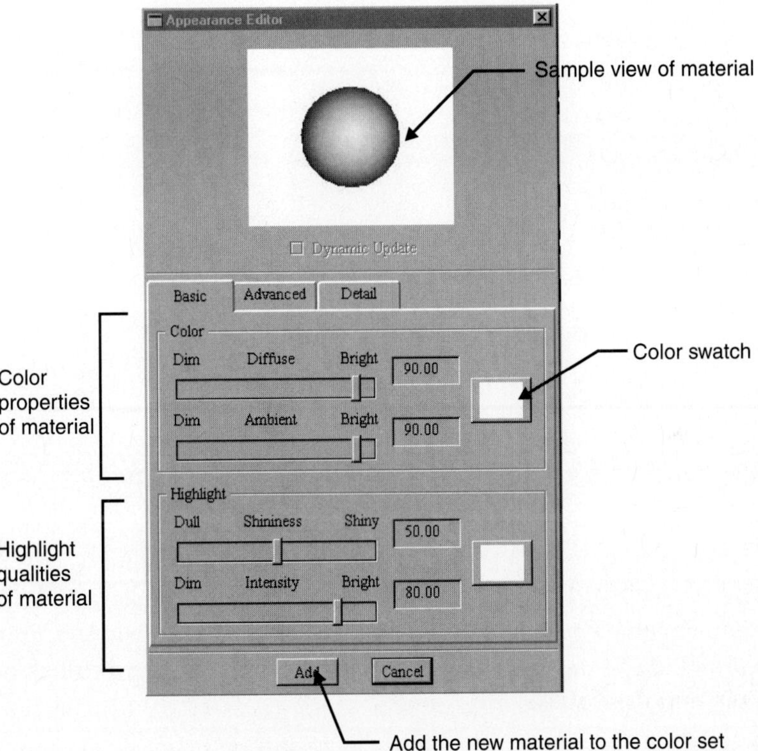

Figure 2.39   The Material dialog boxes.

For now, let's leave the Highlight sliders alone. Let's also leave the sliders in the color box alone. We will just deal with the color. If you click on the color swatch, the Color dialog box appears as shown in Figure 2.40. The color swatch indicates the current color setting for that material. From the Color dialog box, we can select the amount of red, green, and blue for our new color. Once the sliders are set, choose

OK. You will be returned to the material dialog box. Note that the color in the material color swatch has changed reflecting the change from the Color dialog. Choose Add to add this new color to the color dialog.

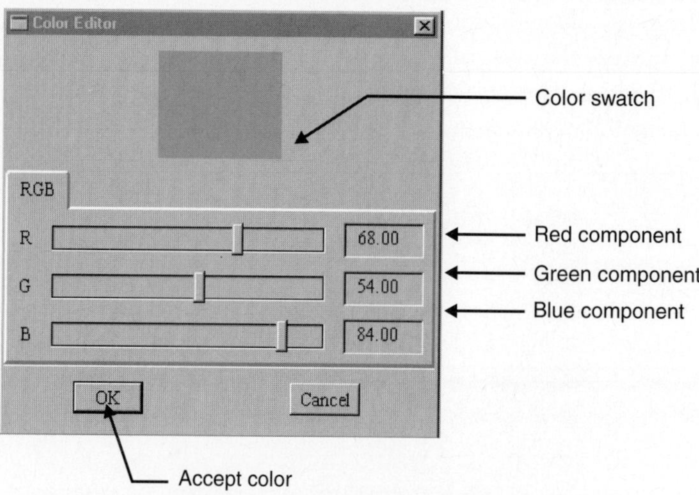

Figure 2.40   The Color Editor dialog boxes.

In Tutorial 2.7 you will be using all of the rendering options discussed in this chapter. You will create different renderings of the part. You will create new colors and assign a blue color to the part. From this point on, feel free to choose whatever rendering model that you desire. However, remember if you do not draw hidden lines, you might have to do a lot of rotations to get at an edge you need. Also, axes and datum planes can be very useful. It is easy to get at the Environment check boxes, so you can turn these off and on at will.

Tutorial 2.7   Rendering Options

Files opened: Tut2-7a.prt   **Files saved:** Tut2-7b.prt

Step	Action	Description	Further Actions	Result
1	Click PT/Modeler Icon	Run PT/Modeler		After some time, PT/Modeler on screen
2	>Mode >Misc >Show Dir	Show current directory		Message similar to "Directory searched is c:\ptc\ptprod\bin"
3	>Change Dir	Change the current directory	Type **c:\proe\tutorial\ chapter_2**	
4	>Done-Return	Leave Misc menu		Misc menu removed
5	>Part >Search/Retr	Read in a part	**Tut2-7a**	Part is displayed
6	>View >Orientation|Angles | Edge/Axis	Get a good orientation for our >Mode	Select A_5 axis running though upper bar	Ready to enter number of degrees
7	Enter 60 for 60 degrees rotation		>Done/Accept	Part displayed in good orientation
8	>View >Names >Save	Name this view	Type name: **For_Tutorial**	View is saved
9	>Environment	Set up the environment	Set up checks as seen in Table T2.7 Column Step 9	Part displayed as in Step 9 of Fig. 2.36
10	>Done-Return			
11	>Environment	Set up the environment	Set up checks as seen in Table T2.7 Column Step 11	Part displayed as in Step 11 of Fig. 2.36
12	>Done-Return			
13	>Environment	Set up the environment	Set up checks as seen in Table T2.7 Column Step 13	Part displayed as in Step 13 of Fig. 2.36
14	>Done-Return			
15	>Environment	Set up the environment	Set up checks as seen in Table T2.7 Column Step 15	Part displayed as in Step 15 of Fig. 2.36
16	>Done-Return			
17	>Environment	Set up the environment	Set up checks as seen in Table T2.7 Column Step 17	Part displayed as in Step 17 of Fig. 2.36
18	>Done-Return			
19	>Environment	Set up the environment	Set up checks as seen in Table T2.7 Column Step 19	Part displayed as in Step 19 of Fig. 2.36
20	>Done-Return			
21	>Environment	Set up the environment	Change render >Model back to hidden line	Part displayed as in Step 17 of Fig. 2.36 again
22	>Done-Return			
23	>View >Cosmetic >Appearances | Show	Look at current color set		Only see single white color in user color window

Tutorial 2.7   Rendering Options (continued)

Step	Action	Description	Further Actions	Result
24	Define	Bring up material editor		
25	Click on Color swatch (inside the border of color window in the color control region)	Ready to specify a color		
26	Red=100, Green=0, Blue=0	Define a full saturation red	Click on OK then click on Add in Appearance editor	Red shows up in color set
27	Click on Color swatch	Ready to specify a color		
28	Red=0, Green=100, Blue=0	Define a full saturation green	Click on OK then click on Add in Appearance editor	Green shows up in color set
29	Click on Color swatch	Ready to specify a color		
30	Red=0, Green=0, Blue=100	Define a full saturation blue	Click on OK then click on Add in Appearance editor	Blue shows up in color set
31	Click on Cancel	Ready to specify a color		
32	>Appearances >Show	Show colors in color set		White, red, green, and blue are displayed in User Color window
33	Set then Click on Blue color in Color >Set	Assign blue material to our part; object dialog appears	Click Part in Object dialog	Part outlined in blue
34	Cosmetic >Shade >Display	Shade the display		Part shaded in blue
35	File >Save As	Save with new name	Enter then **Tut2-7b**	File saved
36	>Exit	Exit program	Click Yes to confirm	PT/Modeler exited
37	Click PT/Modeler Icon	Run PT/Modeler		After some time, PT/Modeler on screen
38	>Mode >Misc >Show Dir	Show current directory		Message similar to "Directory searched is c:\ptc\ptprod\bin"
39	>Change Dir	Change the current directory	Type **c:\proe\tutorial\ chapter_2**	
40	>Done-Return	Leave Misc menu		Misc menu removed
41	>Part >Search/Retr	Read in a part	Type **Tut2-7b**	Part is displayed
42	>View >Cosmetic >Appearances >Show	Look at the color set		Color set only has white
43	>View >Cosmetic >Shade >Display	Display a blue shaded part		Part is blue
44	>Exit	Exit program	Click Yes to confirm	PT/Modeler exited

Item	Step 9	Step 11	Step 13	Step 15	Step 17	Step 19
Disp DtmPln	Checked	No	No	No	No	No
Spin Center	Checked	No	No	No	No	No
Disp Axes	Checked	Checked	Checked	Checked	No	No
Rendering	Wireframe	Wireframe	Hiddenline	No hidden line	No hidden line	Shaded

Note: You can have Bell, SketStart2D, >ModelTree, Colors checked throughout this tutorial. All other boxes (besides those in Table T2.7) can be unchecked. Both TanPhantom and Trimetric can be checked.

Table T2.7   Environment Settings

A First Look at Features

As discussed in the Introduction, Features are the building blocks of your design. When you design a part, you are building up the part feature by feature. Each feature consists of a set of specifications, dimensions, and instructions. A feature's specifications include the type of feature it is (hole, protrusion, round, etc.), references to parents and children, and details about the feature (straight hole, solid protrusion, number of sections, etc.).

3.1   What Is a Feature?

Dimensions provide specific values or relations as required by the specifications. A hole would need a diameter; a rectangle would need a width and height. These dimensions might be a numeric value (3.85) or a relation (x = y / 2). In addition, these dimensions would have references to other features. For example, this hole is 5.35 inches from the edge of the block. Lastly, a feature has intelligence. Each knows where to place and orient itself. Each knows how to draw itself. Figure 3.1 illustrates these definitions.

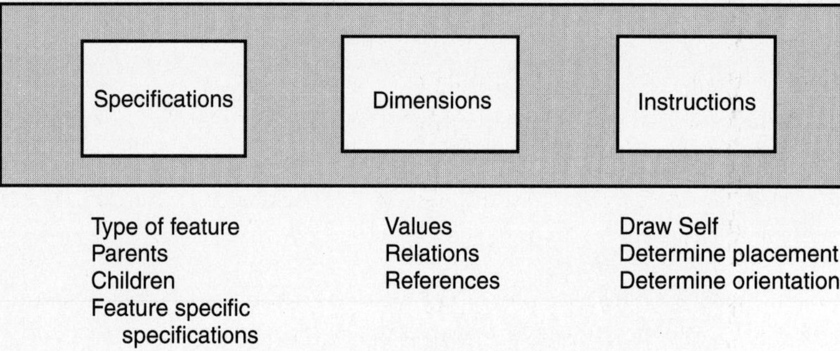

Figure 3.1   Components of a feature.

I have broken down features into a hierarchical chart as seen in Figure 3.2. This chart is not complete, but it does give you a rudimentary idea as to how different features relate to each other. There are two basic types of features: some involve geometry and others are only references. A part might have a base plate feature, which contains geometry. It has mass. Alternatively, a part could also have a datum plane that is used to reference a connecting plate. This plane has no mass.

Features can also be divided into those that add material and those that remove material. A feature cannot do both at the same time, although some features, namely the round, can do either. Protrusions (and sometimes rounds) are features that add material. Features that remove material include holes, cuts, (sometimes rounds), and chamfers.

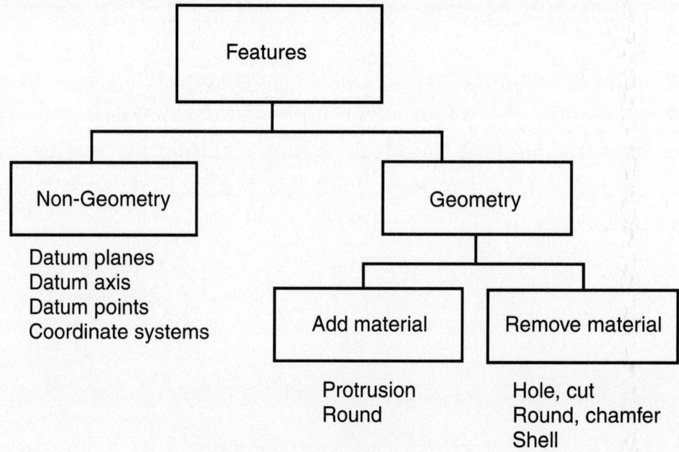

Figure 3.2   Types of features.

3.1.1   Feature Menus

During the feature design process, a number of menu selections will be provided to you in a sequential fashion. At times, selecting a menu item is all that is necessary. This is a specification; for example, you could indicate that you want a Solid Protrusion. Some menu items require you to type a value; for example, you might type a value indicating the diameter of a hole.

Some menu items require some picking on the screen. For example, you could reference other features in the part in order to constrain the new feature. These menu items provide the dimensions to the feature. Lastly, for sketched features, you need to provide a sketch. You will specify the feature in a step-by-step fashion. When you are finished with the specification process, the feature has all the information that it needs. It can then go ahead to place, orient, and draw itself. The >Feature menu is shown in Figure 3.3(a). The first item in the Feature submenu is >Protrusion. Once >Protrusion is selected, the Solid Opts submenu is displayed as shown in Figure 3.3(b). Various types of Protrusions including Extruded, Revolved, Swept, Blended, etc. are shown in this submenu.

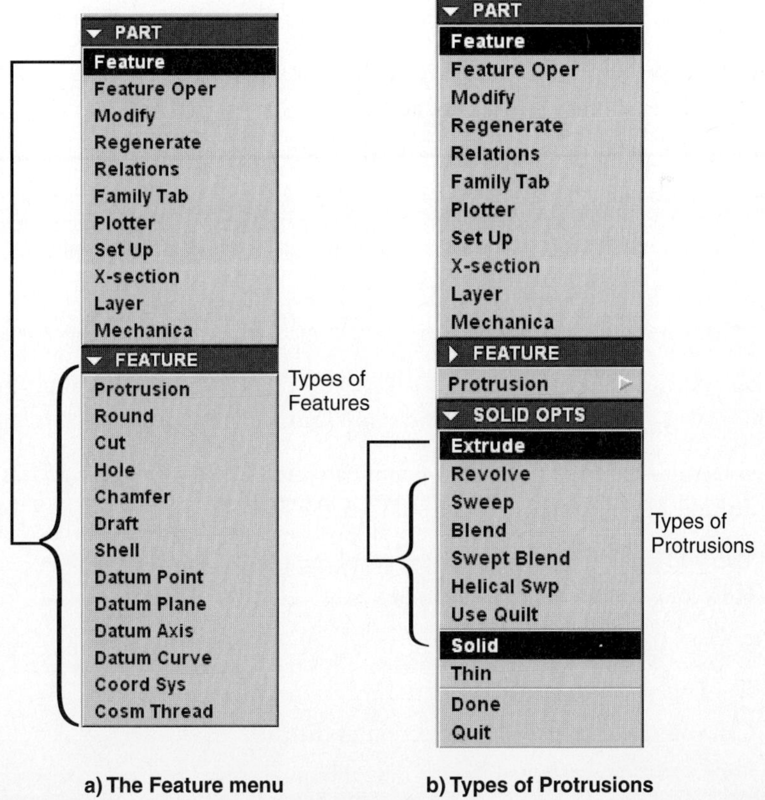

a) The Feature menu   b) Types of Protrusions

Figure 3.3   Feature and Protrusion menu.

3.1.2 **Pick-and-Place versus Sketched Features**

There are two ways to create features: *pick-and-place* and *sketched.* Pick-and-place features include holes, rounds, and chamfers. All of the other features are sketched features. The difference between pick-and-place and sketched features has to do with the way that they are specified. This is illustrated in Figure 3.4.

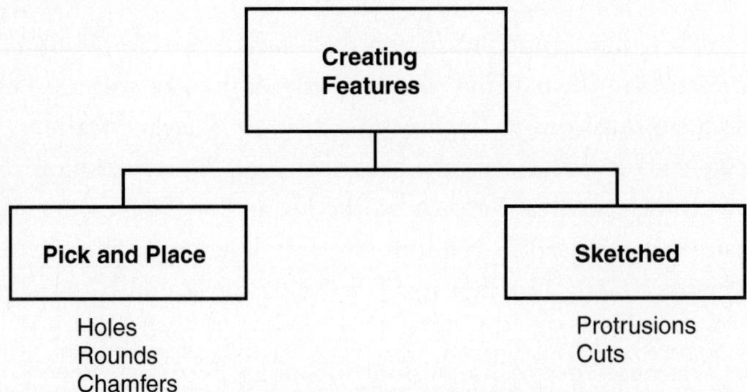

Figure 3.4   Creating features.

A pick-and-place feature is similar to a cut-and-paste feature. For example, if I asked you to drill a hole in a piece of wood, you would ask me the following:

> How big is the hole?
> Where is the hole placed?
> How deep is the hole?

Similarly, if I asked you to make a round, you would ask me the following:

> What is the radius of the round?
> What edge should I round?

In neither case would I have to provide a sketch of what the round or the hole looks like. This is why they are called pick-and-place features.

Sketched features, on the other hand, require a sketch, hence the name. If I asked you to extrude a piece of metal, you would ask the following:

> Can you give me a sketch of a section of the protrusion?
> How long should the protrusion be?

Similarly, if I asked you to make a cut in a piece of metal, you would ask the following:

> Can you give me a sketch of a section of the cut?
> How deep should the cut be?

Both require a sketch. To produce a sketch, PT/Modeler provides us with a Sketch mode. Everything we sketch will be on a 2D planar surface. Consequently, we sketch in two dimensions.

I have chosen to present this introductory chapter on features before the introduction to sketching in Chapter 4. This is a chicken-and-egg situation—both want to be first. My approach is to provide you with some definitions of features in this chapter and to allow you to begin work in the sketcher. In Chapter 4 you will gain a greater understanding of the sketcher.

Let's begin with looking at some simple features.

3.2   Which Feature First?

The first feature, the base feature, is very important. The base feature is the parent of all other features. The first feature should be a set of datum planes. As discussed in Chapter 2, these are called the default datum planes, and provide an absolute reference for the rest of the part.

Datum planes do not have any geometry. What should the first geometric feature be? First, it has to be a protrusion. You must add material before you can remove material. This is illustrated in the menu of Figure 3.5. Note that only the Protrusion selection, along with the Datums, is available for selection.

Second, the base feature should probably be the largest feature in your part. It should be the one that connects to the most other things in the part. As the parent, all other features in the part will depend on it. It is sometimes obvious which feature in a model should have this distinction. In a V-8 engine block, a V-shaped extruded protrusion might be a good choice as a base feature. Often, a base plate makes for a very good base feature.

> **TIP:** Choose the block of solid most like the solid blank from which you would make the part by machining and attaching other features.

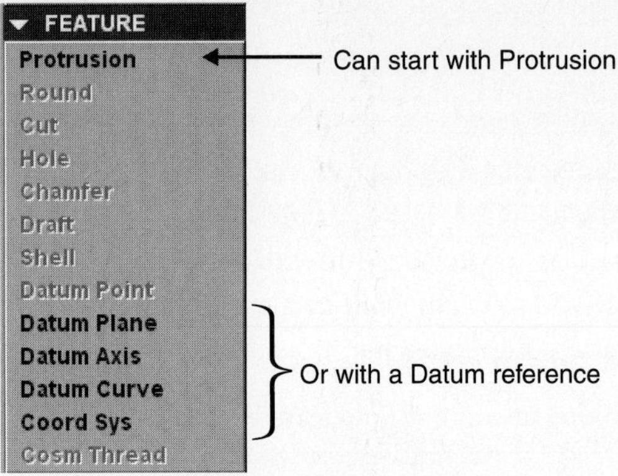

Figure 3.5   First feature.

3.3   Features that Add Material: The Protrusion

The first feature type that we will look at is the protrusion. A protrusion adds material to a model, and can be any shape. Figure 3.5 provides the Feature menu. Note that protrusion is one of the types of features. Both Geometric features, including protrusions, rounds, cuts, holes, chamfers, drafts, and shells, are present along with the non-geometric features, including datum planes, datum points, datum axis and datum curves. Clicking on the protrusion item brings up the Solid Opts submenu. Within this submenu are different types of protrusions including extrude, revolve, sweep, blend, and others.

3.3.1   The Extruded Protrusion

The first form of protrusion that we will look at is the extruded protrusion. An extruded protrusion is based on a single section that is extended in a single direction. A piece of railroad track is an excellent example. Using a playdough analogy, consider that the material is pliable and can be pressed through a form. The length of the protrusion is based on the length of material that extrudes out the form. The shape of the protrusion is based on the shape of the form. If the form is a circle, the shape that extrudes out the form is a cylinder. If the shape is an "I", the protrusion is an I-beam. The form must be closed.

Figure 3.6(a) illustrates some extruded protrusions based on the forms in Figure 3.6(b). With playdough we would use a form. In solid modeling, the form is called a section. Take a cross-*section* anywhere in the protrusion and you get the same *section*.

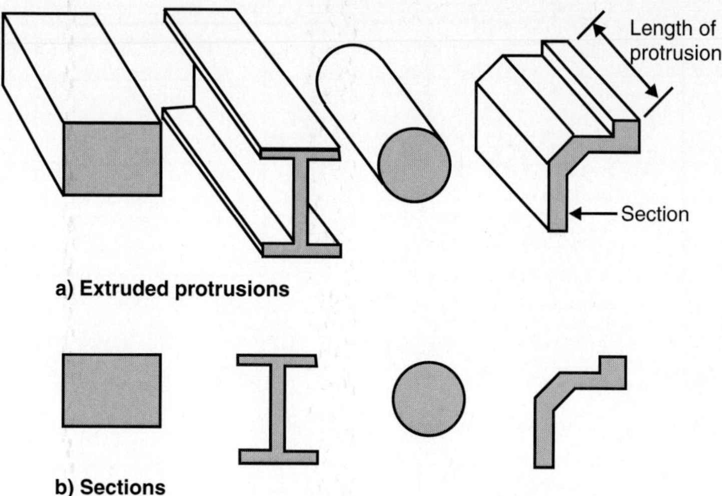

Figure 3.6   Extruded protrusions and corresponding sections.

Extruded protrusions have two faces, a start and an end. The section specifies the start face. The end face is the same as the start face. The shape is pulled through the defining face. This face has to be on a plane. Extruded protrusions are always pulled at a right angle, normal that is, to the defining section.

Extruded protrusions are sketched features because you have to provide a sketch of the section. You also have to provide a frame of reference for the section indicating where you want the section to be placed and how it should be oriented. If I asked you to add the cylindrical protrusion to the I-beam protrusion, you would ask the following:

> Where should I place the cylinder?
> How should the cylinder be facing?

We know that an extruded protrusion has a defining face. This is called the *section*. We also know that the extruded protrusion is at right angles to the section. Suppose we know the shape of the section and length of the protrusion. If we place the section plane somewhere on our part we completely specify where the protrusion will be placed. This is called *constraining* the protrusion. We are constraining the protrusion to be in a specific place and in a specific three-dimensional orientation. With the design of the section, the length of the protrusion and the set of constraints of the section plane, we completely specify the protrusion.

Figure 3.7 provides an example of constraints. In Figure 3.7(a) we have a two-dimensional system. We desire to constrain a circle to the rectangle. The circle is partially constrained because there is no constraint in the X direction tying down the circle. This is alleviated in Figure 3.7(b) with the addition of a second dimension.

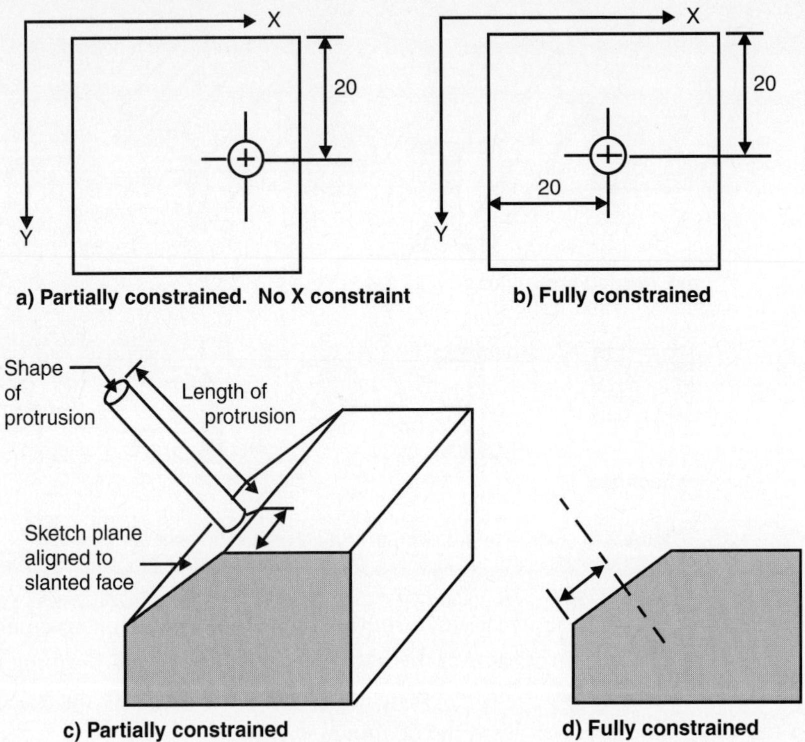

Figure 3.7   Constrained protrusion.

In three dimensions things really get interesting. Another simple example is provided in Figure 3.7(c). Here, we want to constrain a cylinder to a block. The block has an angled face. There are a great number of places where we could constrain this cylinder. The cylinder's section face could be placed parallel to any of the block's seven faces. In fact, it would not even have to be parallel to a face. It could just as well be at a weird angle extending from the block. Since the extruded protrusion is always normal to the section face, all we have to do is constrain the section face, and the protrusion is constrained along with it.

Let's pick the angled face to be the section plane. In order to build our extruded protrusion on this section plane, we need to provide the two dimensions that specify the center of the circular section of the protrusion. These are shown in Figure 3.7(c) and Figure 3.7(d). Our protrusion is now completely constrained. A typical extruded protrusion on a sketching plane is shown in Figure 3.8(a). The sketching planes and sections of the protrusions are shown in Figure 3.8(b).

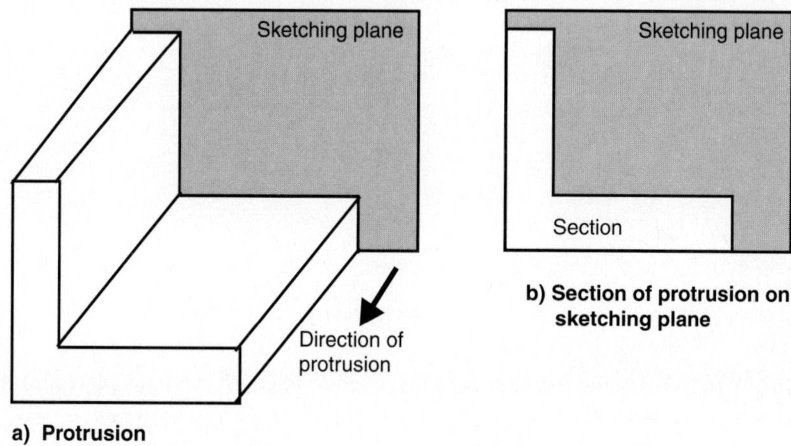

Figure 3.8   Typical protrusion and section on a sketching plane.

The very same constraints apply to other sketched features as well. The opposite of a protrusion is a cut. Cuts remove matter. Cuts are defined in the following sections.

In Tutorial 3.1 you will be entering into the unfamiliar realm of the sketcher. Do not get too bogged down. There is very little required in the sketcher. Just follow directions for now and have confidence that you will pick up the details in Chapter 4.

In this tutorial, you will design a part from scratch using the New Part menu item. This creates a set of default datum planes. Next, you will select the section plane for the protrusion. The section plane is the same as the sketch plane. Once inside the sketcher, you will design your part in two dimensions. The plane you are drawing on is the sketch plane. You will select the sketch plane and provide a reference for the sketch. Inside sketcher, you will use the Mouse Sketch function to create the vertices of your part.

When sketching, do not worry about being absolutely accurate. Sketcher will automatically make lines horizontal or vertical upon regeneration. That is, sketcher will change lines that are nearly horizontal or vertical into horizontal and vertical lines during the next regeneration. It will also assume you are connecting the first and last vertex so do not be nervous about drawing. Also, the exact shape is not critical, so draw it close to the illustrations shown in Figures 3.9 and 3.10.

> **NOTE:** In Mouse Sketch mode, the left mouse button, mLb, is used to draw rubber-banding line chains. It is only necessary to click on a vertex one time. A line automatically connects consecutive clicks. The mMb button is used to end a line chain.

The cut section can be open or closed depending on the geometry of the part. For example, the cut taken out of the base plate in the Introduction Figure 1, could be open. PT/Modeler understands that the outside edge of the base plate should be used as the open edge of the cut. Once the section is completely drawn, align two of the edges to the datum planes. We have to constrain our new part in the coordinate system set up by the default datum planes. We want the L bracket to align to the AX and AY axis.

Once aligned, it is time to let AutoDimension do its work. AutoDimension will create dimensions based on the scale of your drawing. You have not provided any absolute value, so it doesn't know if one grid mark indicates one inch or one mile. However, your drawing does provide all of the relative dimensions that it needs to dimension your feature. Do not worry about the actual values generated. These do not matter for now. We will look at dimensioning in Chapter 4.

> **TIP:** The digitized location on the sketch plane determines the dimension values created by the system.

In the following tutorials, I provide a set of suggestions for setting up your environment. The settings in the environment affect which items are displayed and whether the 2D or 3D view uses hidden lines or no hidden lines. You can experiment with your own settings. You can have Bell, SketStart2D, ModelTree, Colors checked throughout this tutorial. All other boxes, besides those in the table can be unchecked. Both TanPhantom and Trimetric can be checked.

Tutorial 3.1 Creating an Extruded Protrusion

Files opened: Tut3-1a.prt **Files saved:** Tut3-1b.prt

Step	Action	Description	Further Actions	Result
1	Click PT/Modeler Icon	Run PT/Modeler		After some time, PT/Modeler on screen
2	>Mode >Misc >Show Dir	Show current directory		Message similar to "Directory searched is c:\ptc\ptprod\bin"
3	>Change Dir	Change the current directory	Type **c:\proe\tutorial\ chapter_3**	
4	>Done-Return	Leave Misc menu		Misc menu removed
5	>Mode >New Part	Create a new part	Type **tut3-1a**	Default datum planes are constructed in Main window
6	>Environment	Set up the environment	Set up checks as seen in Table T3.1 Column Step 6	
7	>Done-Return			
8	>Feature >Protrusion | Extrude | Solid | Done	Create an extruded protrusion solid		
9	>One Side	Protrusion will extend one side out of the sketching plane	>Okay to protrusion direction	
10	Pick XY datum plane for sketching plane	Select XY datum in Fig. 3.9(a)		Pick face for protrusion; this is the sketching plane
11	>TOP	Pick XZ datum plane for TOP reference to sketching plane in Fig. 3.9(a)	Pick XZ datum	Go into sketcher mode in Fig. 3.9(b)
12	>Sketch >Mouse Sketch	Sketch the L bracket in Fig. 3.9(c)	7 mLb picks ending with 1 mMb pick to end section sketch	After last mMb, no longer drawing line
13	>Align	Align the vertical line Y1 with the AY axis	mLb on the Y1 line mLb on the AY axis as shown in Figure 3.9(d)	Message ---- ALIGNED ----
14	>Align	Align the horizontal line X1 with the AX axis	mLb on the X1 line mLb on the AX axis as shown in Figure 3.9(d)	Message ---- ALIGNED ----
15	>AutoDimension	Have sketcher do dimensions for you		Sketcher requests that you provide it with references
16	mLb on AY axis mLb on AX axis as shown in Figure 3.10(e)	Need to provide references to help auto dimensioning	>Done - Sel	Part gets dimensioned in Fig. 3.10(f); message ---Section regenerated successfully Select DIMENSION to be moved

Tutorial 3.1 Creating an Extruded Protrusion (continued)

Step	Action	Description	Further Actions	Result
17	>Done			
18	>Blind | Done	Arrow is showing direction of protrusion; accept this direction of protrusion in Fig. 3.10(g)	Type **300** for the blind depth of the protrusion, then **Enter**	Part is now ready to be previewed
19	Click Preview, type F1	View part in default view	Click OK to accept protrusion	Part should look like Figure 3.10(h)
20	>View >Environment		Set up checks as seen in Table T3.1 Column Step 20	
21	>File >SaveAs	Save file with new name	Enter to accept [tut1a.prt] then type **tut3-1b.prt**	Part saved
22	>QuitWindow			
23	>Exit	Exit program	Click Yes to confirm	PT/Modeler exited

Item	Step 6	Step 20
Disp DtmPln	Checked	No
Spin Center	Checked	No
Disp Axes	Checked	No
Rendering	Hidden line	No hidden line

Table T3.1   Environment Settings

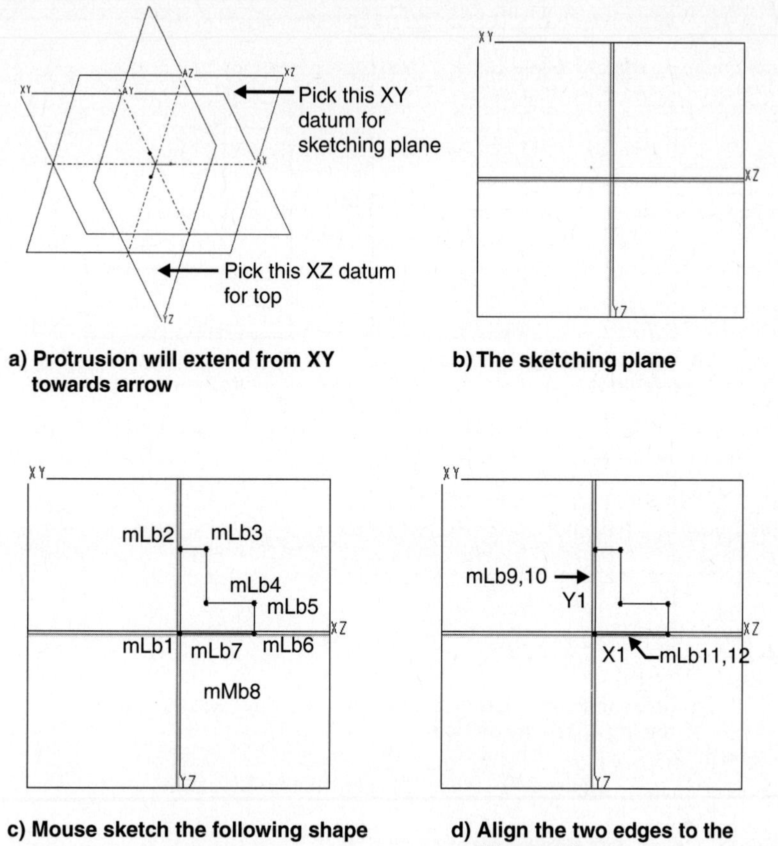

Figure 3.9   Illustrations for Tutorial 3.1, part 1.

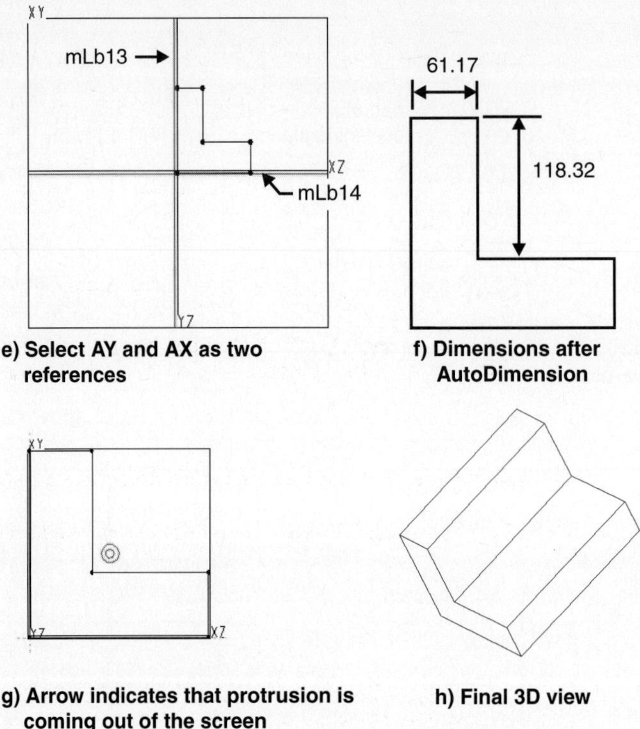

e) Select AY and AX as two
references

f) Dimensions after
AutoDimension

g) Arrow indicates that protrusion is
coming out of the screen

h) Final 3D view

Figure 3.10   Illustrations for Tutorial 3.1, part 2.

3.4   The Round

The round is a circular fillet or rounded corner. Rounds can add material, as illustrated in the inside round of Figure 3.11(a). Rounds can also remove material, as seen in the outside round in the same figure.

Figure 3.11(b) shows a block feature, perhaps created from an extruded rectangle. A round is added to an edge of this extruded rectangle feature as seen in Figure 3.11(c). The round is now a child feature of the extruded rectangle. It is referenced to the extruded rectangle by way of the particular selected edge. The round would have an associated radius.

An elbow is shown in Figure 3.11(d). This is also likely from an extruded L. A round is added to the inside corner of this feature as seen in Figure 3.11(e). This round adds material. Once again, the round feature is now a child feature of the extruded L, referenced by its edge.

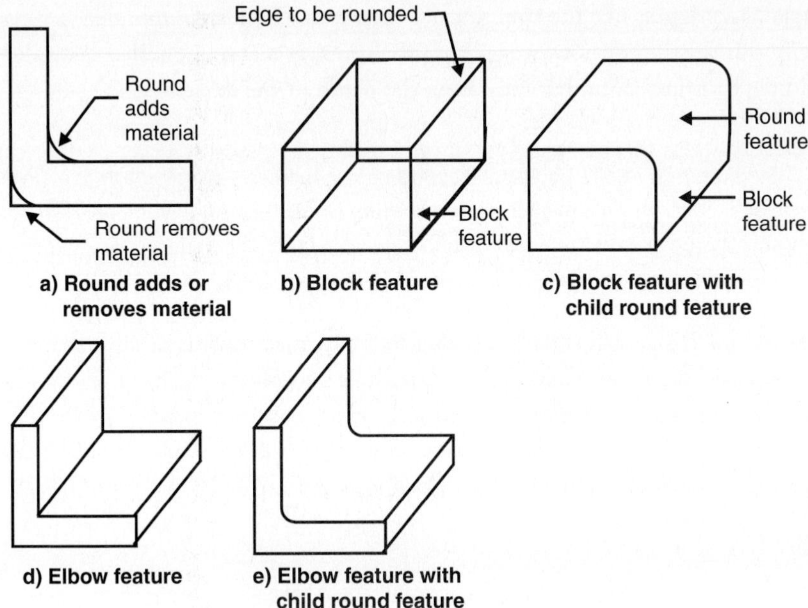

Figure 3.11 Rounding edges.

Rounds are very expensive little features. There are a considerable number of calculations involved in the generation of a round. It is a wise idea to suppress all rounds while the rest of the part is being built.

> **TIP:** Add your rounds at the end of a design. That way, they will not bog down the calculations during the generation of the part. Suppress rounds whenever possible to reduce calculation time.

3.5 Features that Remove Material

Removing material is just as fun. You can remove material using either the pick-and-place features or sketched features. Three simple pick-and-place features that remove material are holes, rounds, and chamfers.

3.6 The Hole

A hole is a protrusion with a circular section that removes matter. You can create a hole using a Hole feature or the Cut feature. The Hole feature is pick-and-place while the Cut feature is sketched. Because the Hole feature is a pick-and-place feature, you do not have to create a sketch. The shape is always a circular of some specified diameter (or radius). The circle is defined by a center point. The center point needs two reference edges or axis for its placement.

A hole has a depth, like the cylindrical protrusion. There are a number of ways to specify this depth. For now, we will use the simplest technique called *blind* depth. Blind depth is just a number indicating the depth of the circle.

> **TIP:** You can think of a hole as a mass-removing extruded protrusion with a circular section. You will need to select a sketch plane, that is the plane where the circle will be placed. You then need to constrain the circle and specify a depth.

In Tutorial 3.2, you will start by reading in a part that consists of an L shape. You will create a hole feature and position the hole on one of the faces of the block. Next, the hole has to be dimensioned and referenced to two edges of the block. Following the hole, you will select two of the edges and place rounds on the edges. Figure 3.12 provides guidance when selecting edges and faces for this tutorial.

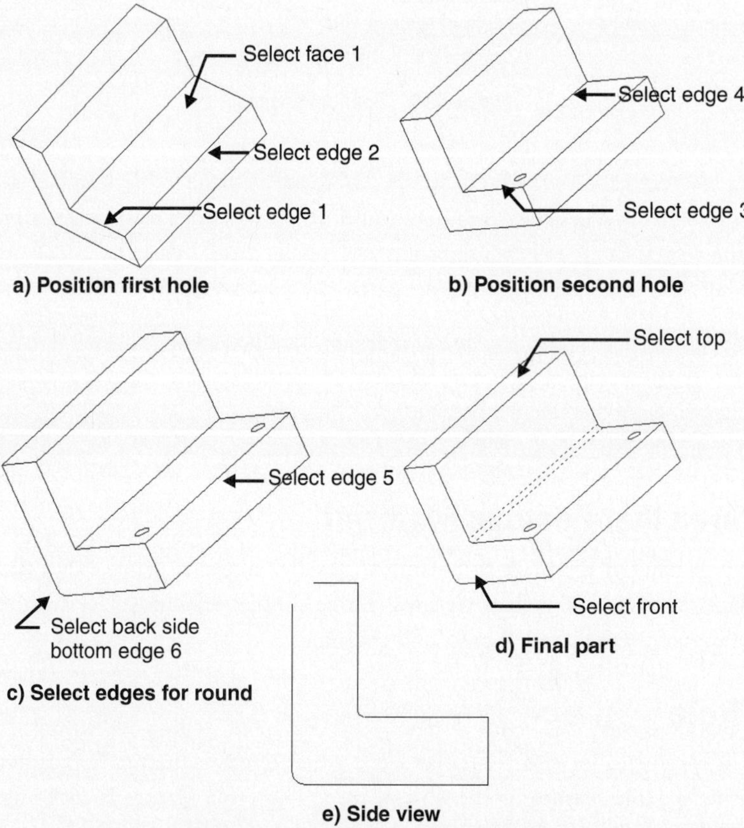

Figure 3.12   Illustrations for Tutorial 3.2.

Tutorial 3.2 Creating Holes and Rounds

Files opened: Tut3-2a.prt   **Files saved:** Tut3-2b.prt

Step	Action	Description	Further Actions	Result
1	Click PT/Modeler Icon	Run PT/Modeler		After some time, PT/Modeler on screen
2	>Mode >Misc >Show Dir	Show current directory		Message similar to "Directory searched is c:\ptc\ptprod\bin"
3	>Change Dir	Change the current directory	Type **c:\proe\tutorial\ chapter_3**	
4	>Done-Return	Leave Misc menu		Misc menu removed
5	>Part >Search/Retr	Read in a part	Select **tut3-2a**	Part is displayed
6	>Environment	Set up the environment	Set up checks as seen in Table T3.2 Column Step 6	
7	>Done-Return			
8	>Feature >Hole | Straight | Done	Create a hole feature that has a straight cross section	Select face 1 in Fig. 3.12(a)	Pick face for circle; can be thought of as sketching plane
9	>Linear | Done	Use linear dimensions to its references		
10	Click on edge 1	Select edge 1 for first reference in Fig. 3.12(a)	Type **50** for distance from this edge to center of circle	
11	Click on edge 2	Select edge 2 for first reference in Fig. 3.12(a)	Type **50** for distance from this edge to center of circle	
12	>One Side | Done	Want circle to extend in one dimension from this plane and to go through all geometry in part	>Through all | Done	Finished specifying the circle
13	Select edge 1 as in Fig 3.12(a)	Use edge 1 as one edge for dimension reference		
14	Select edge 2 as in Fig 3.12(a)	Use edge 2 as one edge for dimension reference		
15	Type **30**	Enter diameter		Finished specifying the circle
16	Click Preview	Look at resultant hole	Click OK	Hole is placed
17	>Feature >Hole | Straight | Linear	Create a hole feature that is straight and uses linear dimensions to its references	Select face 1 in Fig. 3.12(a)	Pick face for circle; can be thought of as sketching plane

Tutorial 3.2 Creating Holes and Rounds (continued)

Step	Action	Description	Further Actions	Result
18	Click on edge 3	Select edge 3 for first reference in Fig. 3.12(b)	Type **450** for distance from this edge to center of circle	
19	Click on edge 4	Select edge 4 for first reference in Fig. 3.12(b)	Type **150** for distance from this edge to center of circle	
20	>One sided | through all	Want circle to extend in one dimension from this plane and to go through all geometry in part	>Done	
21	Type **30**	Enter diameter		Finished specifying the circle
22	Click Preview	Look at resultant hole	Click OK	Hole is placed
23	>Feature >Round | Constant | Edge Chain | Done	Create a round	Select edge 5 in Fig. 3.12(c)	
24	Type 10 for radius of round	Enter radius of round	Click OK	Round created
25	>Feature >Round | Constant | Edge Chain | Done	Create a round	Select edge 6 in Fig. 3.12(c)	
26	Type **10** for radius of round	Enter radius of round	Click OK	Round created; part shown in Figure 3.12(d)
27	>View >Orientation	Get a side view	>Front then select side face >Top then select top face	Side view created in Fig. 3.12(e)
28	>Environment		Set up checks as seen in Table T3.2 Column Step 26	
29	>File >SaveAs	Save file with new name	Enter to accept [tut3-2a.prt] then type **tut3-2b.prt**	Part saved|
30	>QuitWindow			
31	>Exit	Exit program	Click Yes to confirm	PT/Modeler exited

Item	Step 6	Step 28
Disp DtmPln	Checked	No
Spin Center	Checked	No
Disp Axes	Checked	No
Rendering	Hidden line	Hidden line

Table T3.2 Environment Settings

In Tutorial 3.3, you will start by reading in a part that consists of an L shape. You will create a hole feature as you did in Tutorial 3.2. Position the hole on one face of the block. Next, the hole has to be dimensioned and referenced to two edges of the block. Following the hole, you will select two of the edges and place rounds on the edges. This hole is defined to a blind depth extending only partially through the lower portion of the L.

Once the first hole is complete, I will show you how to modify the diameter of the hole while you are still in the feature design process. This is important because we all make mistakes or change our minds. The Preview stage of the hole feature design is an excellent place to make changes. You can step through the design flow and change any of the parameters that you desire. The feature dialog, in this case named the HOLE: Straight dialog, is displayed in Figure 3.13(a). You can select any of the Elements in the list for modification. In this case, select the Diameter item in the Feature Dialog. You must scroll down the list to see the Diameter Element as seen in Figure 3.13(b). Next, click the Define button. This instructs the software to repeat the steps that defined that particular parameter.

Here is where the flexibility of parametric design really shines through. You will enter a new diameter value and it is reflected in the Dialog as seen in Figure 3.13(d). You can click on Preview to view the change or OK to accept the change.

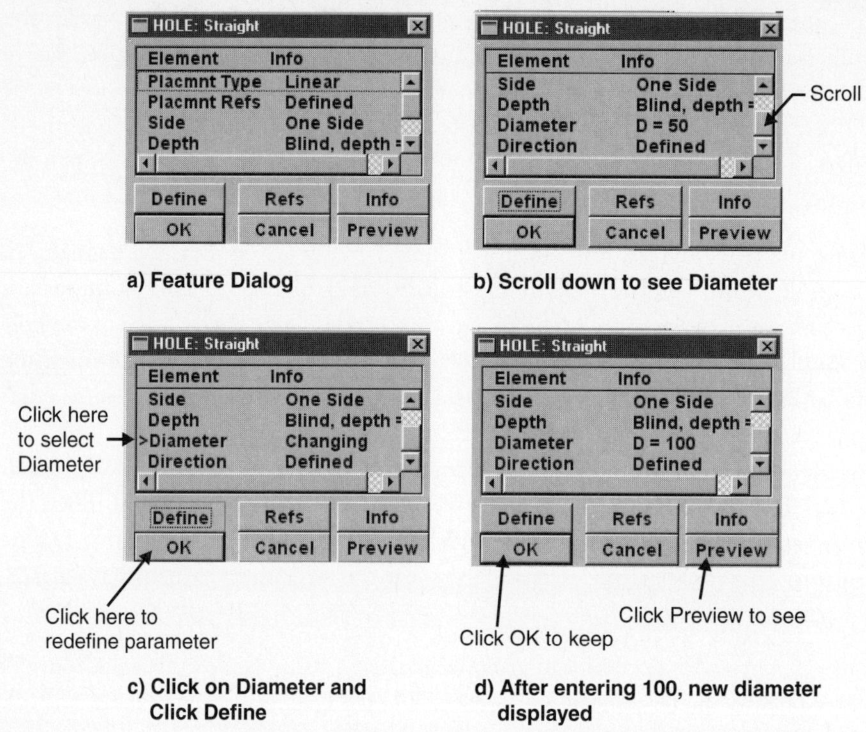

Figure 3.13   Redefining using the Feature Dialog.

Lastly, you will design a coaxial hole that starts at the lower surface of the first hole and shares the same axis. Figure 3.14 provides guidance when selecting edges and faces for this tutorial.

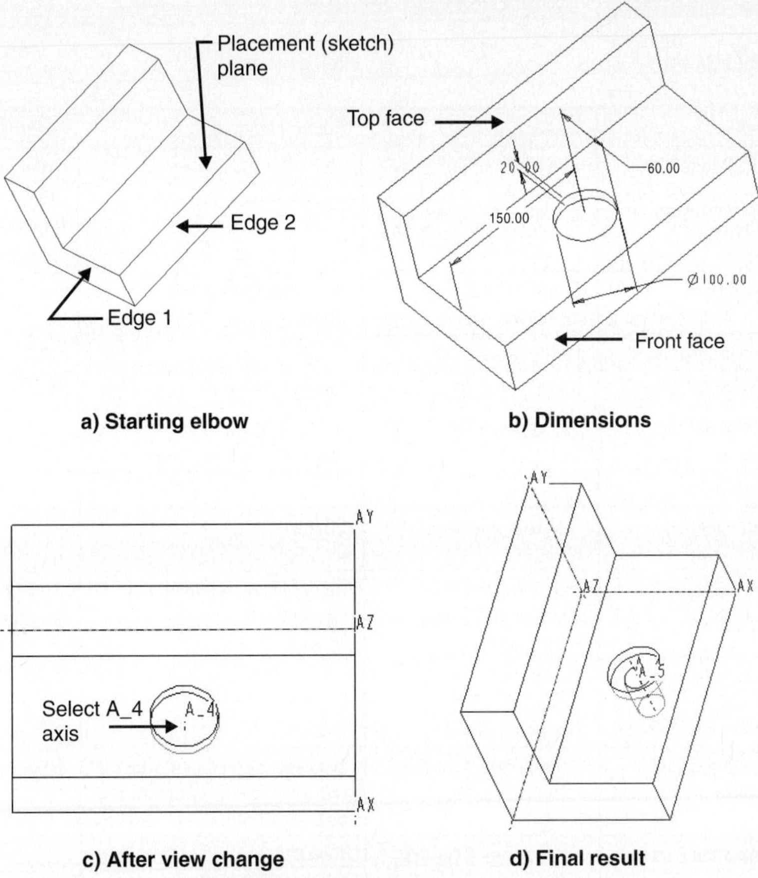

a) Starting elbow

b) Dimensions

c) After view change

d) Final result

Figure 3.14   Illustrations for Tutorial 3.3.

Tutorial 3.3 Creating Two Coaxial Holes

Files opened: Tut3-3a.prt   **Files saved:** Tut3-3b.prt

Step	Action	Description	Further Actions	Result
1	Click PT/Modeler Icon	Run PT/Modeler		After some time, PT/Modeler on screen
2	>Mode >Misc >Show Dir	Show current directory		Message similar to "Directory searched is c:\ptc\ptprod\bin"
3	>Change Dir	Change the current directory	Type **c:\proe\tutorial\chapter_3**	
4	>Done-Return	Leave Misc menu		Misc menu removed
5	>Part >Search/Retr	Read in a part	Select **tut3-3a**	Part is displayed
6	>Environment	Set up the environment	Set up checks as seen in Table T3.3 Column Step 6	
7	>Done-Return			
8	>Feature >Hole | Straight	Create a hole that is straight	>Done	
9	> Linear | Done	Hole uses linear dimensions to its references	Select placement plane in Fig. 3.14(a)	Pick face for circle; can be thought of as sketching plane
10	Click on face as in Fig. 3.14(a)	Pick face for circle; can be thought of as sketching plane		
11	Click on edge 1 as in Fig. 3.14(a)	Select edge 1 for first reference in Fig. 3.14(a)	Type **150** for distance from this edge to center of circle as in Fig. 3.14(b)	
12	Click on edge 2 as in Fig. 3.14(a)	Select edge 2 for first reference in Fig. 3.14(a)	Type **60** for distance from this edge to center of circle as in Fig. 3.14(b)	
13	>One Side | Done	Want circle to extend in one dimension from this plane and to go partially through geometry		
14	>Blind | Done	Want circle to go partially through geometry	Type **20** for depth as in Fig. 3.14(b)	
15	Type **50**	Enter diameter		Finished specifying the circle
16	Click Preview	Look at resultant hole		Hole is placed
17	Click on Diameter (may have to scroll down) in Feature dialog	Want to reselect Diameter parameter to make hole larger diameter	Click Define	See Figure 3.14 for illustration of the redefine process

Tutorial 3.3 Creating Two Coaxial Holes (continued)

Step	Action	Description	Further Actions	Reslut
18	Type **100**	Enter new diameter		
19	Preview	Accept this hole	OK	
20	>View >Orientation	Get a front view	As in Fig. 3.14(b), >Front then select front face >Top then select top face	Front view created
21	>View >Orientation >Angles | Horizontal	Tilt by 60 degrees	Type **60** and **Enter** then >Done/Accept	Resultant view in 3.14(c)
22	>Feature >Hole | Straight	Create a hole feature that is straight and uses a preexisting axis reference		
23	>Coaxial | Done	Create hole that uses a preexisting axis reference	Select axis A-4 for first reference as in Fig 3.14(c)	
24	Select lower surface of first hole as in Fig 3.14(c); use >QuerySel to insure that you get the lower surface	Select face for hole; can be thought of as sketching plane		
25	>One Side	Want circle to extend in one dimension from this plane	>Done	
26	>Thru all	Want circle to go through all geometry in part	>Done	
27	Type **100**	Enter diameter		Finished specifying the circle
28	Click Preview	Look at resultant hole	Click OK	
29	F1 for default orientation	Look at result		Hole is placed part seen in Fig. 3.14(d)
30	>File >SaveAs	Save file with new name	Enter to accept [tut3-2a.prt] then type **tut3-3b.prt**	Part saved
31	>QuitWindow			
32	>Exit	Exit program	Click Yes to confirm	PT/Modeler exited

Item	Step 6
Disp DtmPln	No
Spin Center	No
Disp Axes	Checked
Rendering	Hidden line

Table T3.3 Environment Settings

3.7   The Cut

A cut is similar to a hole, except the section is not restricted to being a circle. The sketch must define a closed contour. The sketch of a cut can be opened or closed. If the sketch is closed, the open section of the cut will have to be aligned to some other edge in the part creating the closed contour. The line and the section cannot cross each other. You will have to specify the sketching plane for the face of the cut and the depth of the cut. The protrusions of Figure 3.6 could be cuts except mass would be removed instead of added.

In Tutorial 3.4, you will design a cut feature into our L bracket. This is nearly identical to Tutorial 3.1 where you designed an extruded protrusion. You will once again pick a sketch and reference plane, sketch the cut and view the result. In sketcher, you will be using the AutoDimension feature. Although it is not a good idea to rely too heavily on AutoDimension, for now it will suit our purposes. The intent of this tutorial is not to teach dimensioning. Do not worry about the actual values generated. We will look at dimensioning in Chapter 4. Figure 3.15 provides guidance regarding Tutorial 3.4.

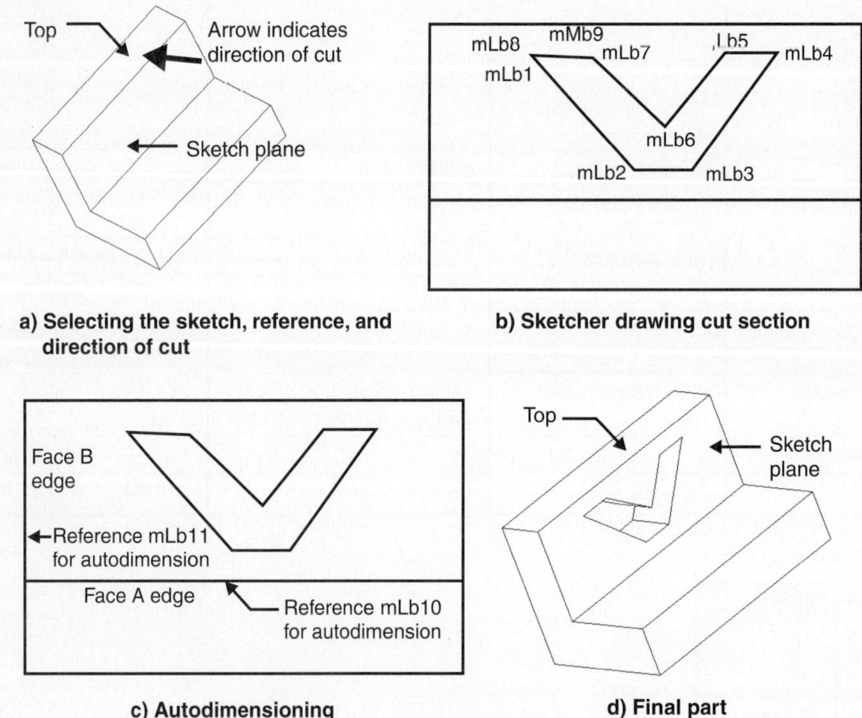

Figure 3.15   Illustrations for Tutorial 3.4.

Tutorial 3.4 Creating a Cut

Files opened: Tut3-4a.prt
(Elbow part)

Files saved: Tut3-4b.prt
(Elbow part with holes and rounds)

Step	Action	Description	Further Actions	Result
1	Click PT/Modeler Icon	Run PT/Modeler		After some time, PT/Modeler on screen
2	>Mode >Misc >Show Dir	Show current directory		Message similar to "Directory searched is c:\ptc\ptprod\bin"
3	>Change Dir	Change the current directory	Type **c:\proe\tutorial\ chapter_3**	
4	>Done-Return	Leave Misc menu		Misc menu removed
5	>Mode >New Part	Create a new part	Type **tut3-4a**	Default datum planes are constructed in Main window
6	>Environment	Set up the environment	Set up checks as seen in Table T3.4 Column Step 6	
7	>Done-Return			
8	>Feature >Cut | Extrude | Solid | Done	Create an extruded cut		
9	>One Side | Done	Cut will extend one side out of the sketching plane	>Okay to direction	
10	Pick face for sketching plane	Select face in Fig. 3.16(a)		Pick face for cut; this is the sketching plane
11	>TOP	Pick XZ datum plane for TOP reference to sketching plane in Fig. 3.16(a)	Pick XZ datum	Go into sketcher mode in Fig. 3.16(b)
12	>Sketch >Mouse Sketch	Sketch the V in Fig. 3.16(c)	8 mLb picks ending with 1 mMb pick to end section sketch	After last mMb, no longer drawing line
13	>AutoDimension	Have Sketcher do dimensions for you		Sketcher requests that you provide it with references
14	mLb on face A edge mLb on face B edge as shown in Figure 3.10(c)	Need to provide references to help auto dimensioning	>Done - Sel	Part gets dimensioned; you can ignore dimensions-- Message --- Section regenerated successfully—select DIMENSION to be moved
15	>Done			Done with Sketcher
16	>Blind | Thru all	Arrow is showing that material will be removed into the cut; accept this direction	>Done	Part is now ready to be previewed
17	Click Preview Type F1	View part in default view	Click OK to accept protrusion	Part should look like Figure 3.10(h)

Tutorial 3.4 Creating a Cut (continued)

Step	Action	Description	Further Actions	Result
18	>File >SaveAs	Save file with new name	Enter to accept [tut3a.prt] then type **tut3-4b.prt**	Part saved
19	>QuitWindow			
20	>Exit	Exit program	Click Yes to confirm	PT/Modeler exited

Item	Step 6
Disp DtmPln	Checked
Spin Center	No
Disp Axes	No
Rendering	Hidden line

Table T3.4   Environment Settings

There are many other types of cuts. We will look at others, including revolved cuts, in later chapters.

3.8   Direction of Removing Material

During the design of the cut, a very important arrow was displayed. It indicates the direction in which the material will be cut. Suppose a circle is drawn in the sketcher as the section for a cut. The question arises: Do you want to cut away everything on the inside of the circle or everything on the outside of the circle? This is illustrated in Figure 3.16. Make sure that you answer this query carefully. The arrow points in the direction that material will be removed. PT/Modeler chooses a direction that material will be removed. You can flip the arrow with the menu Flip command if this is not the desired direction.

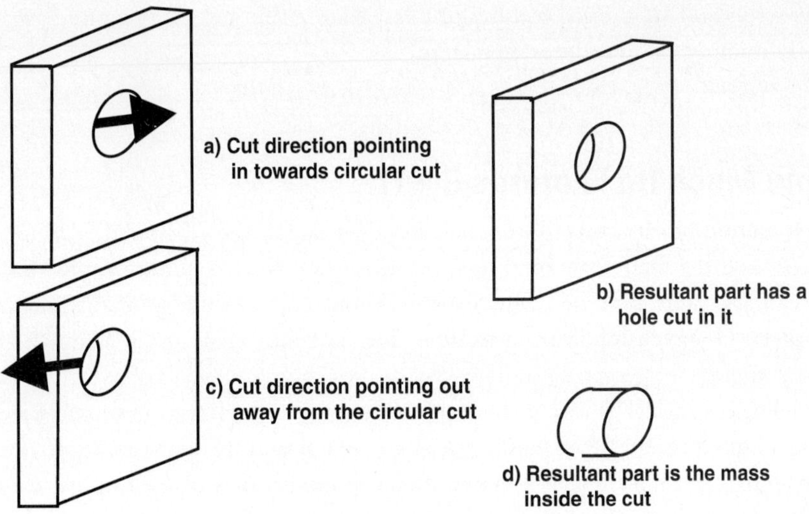

Figure 3.16   Removing material.

3.9   Suppressing Features

One very useful capability of PT/Modeler is the ability to suppress features. You can turn off a feature for a time while other features are being drawn. This can provide a nice way to reduce clutter or decrease regeneration and rendering times. Suppose you are only working on an area of a complex part. You could suppress those features that are unrelated to your section of the part. As another example, consider a complex part with many holes and rounds. There would be axes everywhere. It is possible to reduce the clutter on the display by suppressing the unrelated holes and rounds for a time. Once you are ready to have the suppressed features displayed again, you simply resume the features. Suppressing a feature causes all children of the suppressed feature also to be suppressed. A suppressed feature is removed from the Model Tree feature order. A suppressed feature does not add to the mass of a part.

Suppress features using the Suppress item in the Feature Operations menu. You are asked to pick the desired feature to suppress. You can suppress a single feature or a range of features, or all features on a layer. Note that we have not discussed layers yet; layers will be covered in later chapters. You can either click on the feature in the model, using QuerySel, or you can click on the feature in the model tree. Similarly, you resume a feature using the Resume item in the Feature Operations menu. You may resume all suppressed features, the last feature suppressed, a feature based on its ID number, or all features on a layer.

3.10   How Much Do Features Cost?

Each feature has its costs. The model files get larger, the regeneration times get longer, and the rendering times increase. It is often wise to minimize the number of features where possible. We will learn about effective use of features in later chapters. However, minimizing features does not mean cramming as much stuff into a single feature as possible. This goes against the design goals of a feature-based modeling package. The idea is to keep features simple. Each feature should have its own unique purpose. You should avoid the temptation to lump multiple operations into a single feature. It is very difficult to modify or separate out the features later on.

As an example, consider a bar with five holes in it. You could design a single feature consisting of five holes. Alternately, one feature could be designed for every hole. Consider the first case: If all holes were in a single feature (done in the same sketcher session), how would you display only three of the holes? You could suppress all holes, but not any of them individually.

As a second example, consider the rounded L shown Figure 3.12(d). During the construction of the part, we first extruded the L, added some holes, and then added the rounds. This was a good design. Alternately, we could have designed the L in the sketcher to already have the rounds included. This would be efficient, but it would eliminate the possibility of suppressing the rounds at a later time.

> **NOTE:** As a general rule, complex features are faster but less flexible. Simple features are slower yet more flexible.

3.10.1   General and Specific Features

You can design a circular hole in a part using a Hole feature or using a Cut feature. Which is better? Well, if you know that the hole is going to be circular, then you would be best to use the Hole feature. A cut is a general tool. It can have nearly any closed shape. The cut has a specific algorithm that it uses during regeneration to build itself. Its algorithm is far more complicated than the algorithm for the hole. Consequently, you would waste precious processor time using a cut where a hole would do. If at some point downstream you envision changing the circular hole to an elliptical one, you would be better suited to use the cut. It is simpler to change the sketch of a cut than to completely redesign a new cut feature. The sketch plane, reference plane, and reference dimensions are already in place.

> **NOTE:** A specific feature, like the hole, is faster but more inflexible than a more general feature, like the cut.

3.11   Selecting the Best Feature

There are a number of factors that determine a "best" feature. Each design might have a different set of constraints. One design might be specific to a single usage, and another might be used in a wide variety of applications requiring constant modification. The "best" model that you can build is one that satisfies the specifications of your design. This is called capturing your design intent. Understand your goals and design to meet them.

3.12   Parent-Child Relationships

Parts are made from features. Features have relationships with each other. One such relationship is the order in the Model Tree. This relationship indicates which feature will be constructed first. A second relationship relates to layers. Layers can be created to help organize features. Lastly, and most important, is the parent-child relationship of features.

As an example, an extruded feature A is extruded from a face of feature B. A hole feature C is placed in Feature A and a second hole is placed in Feature B. This is illustrated in Figure 3.17. The hierarchical relationship is shown in Figure 3.17(b). Arrows point from the child to the parent. This indicates that the child is dependent upon the parent. The hole C is dependent on the feature A. Now, since feature A is dependent on feature B, the hole C is also dependent on feature B. Hole D is dependent on Feature B. This is not too difficult to understand, at least not for simple parts. Trouble begins when you want to modify parts. Let's look at another example.

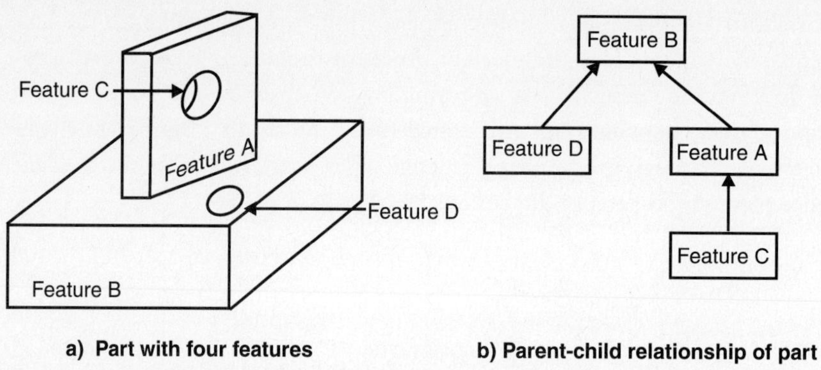

a) Part with four features   **b) Parent-child relationship of part**

Figure 3.17   Parent-child relationship of features in a part.

In Figure 3.18(a), once again we see our two blocks; this time the holes are aligned vertically as seen in Figure 3.18(b). It is our design intent to keep these holes aligned vertically due to some alignment that will occur at an assembly level. Let us suppose that we need to slide feature A over towards one end of the feature B as seen in Figure 3.18(c). The hierarchy is shown in Figure 3.18(d). Note that the hole, C, moved along with feature A. Now, the two holes are not aligned! Thus, our model did not satisfy the constraints of our design specification. We knew that the holes had to remain aligned. Suppose we design a new hierarchy as seen in Figure 3.18(e). This time, when we move the part, the hole C moves with respect to feature A, but it does NOT move with respect to Feature B or D. Our design intent is met.

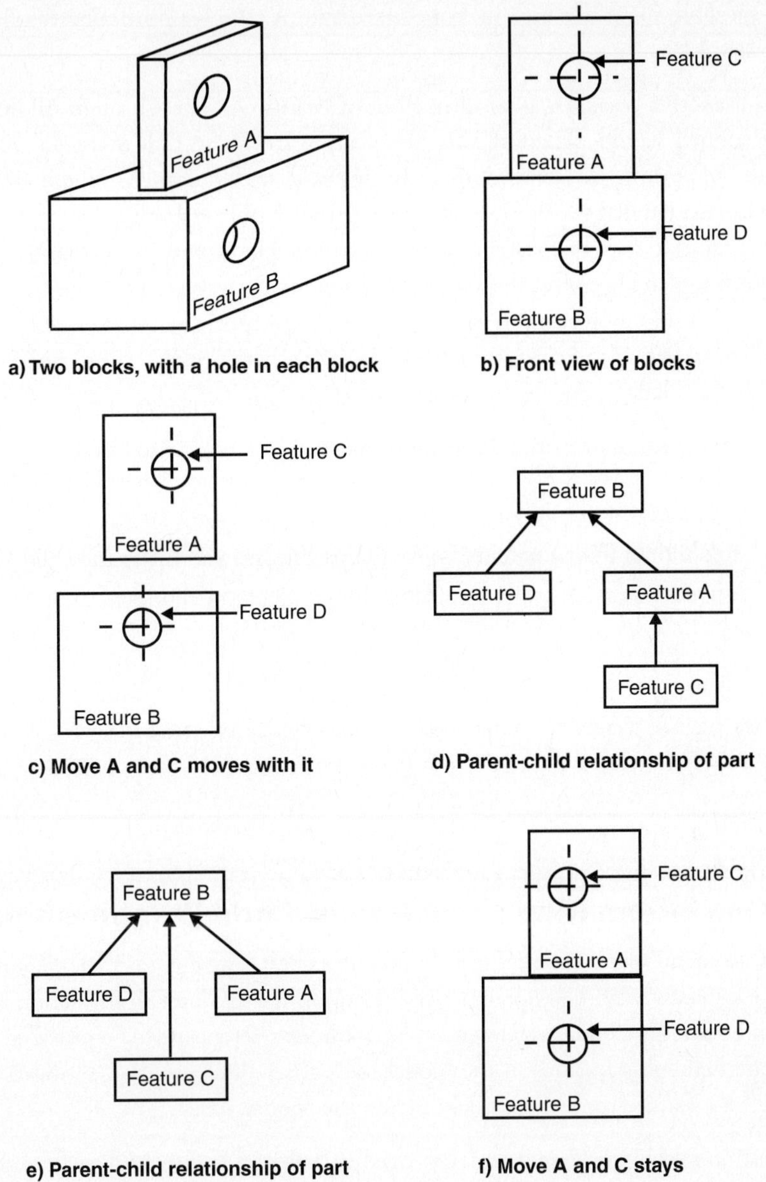

a) Two blocks, with a hole in each block

b) Front view of blocks

c) Move A and C moves with it

d) Parent-child relationship of part

e) Parent-child relationship of part

f) Move A and C stays

Figure 3.18   Parent-child relationships when a part is moved.

How would we design this part? We want Feature C hole to be constrained in all three dimensions to Feature B instead of Feature A. This is simple when looking at the front view. However, Feature A is set back from the face of Feature B. We could use the face of Feature C as the sketching plane for the hole Feature A. This would start the hole some distance in front of Feature A. We would define the hole as Through-All.

What if another feature was to sit in front of Feature A? The Through-All hole we just designed would penetrate this new feature since the hole starts in front of Feature A. This might not be desired. In this case, we would need to add an offset datum plane parallel to the front face of Feature D but set back to be coplanar to where Feature C is to be located. Feature C can then be aligned to the datum plane. The datum plane becomes the sketching plane for Feature C. This works, as long as Feature A does not move in forward or backward from the front face of Feature B. This works all of the time if the front face of Feature A is also constrained to the new Datum Plane.

The rules regarding parent-child relationships can be summarized as follows:

- Parents own children
- Children follow parents; move the parent and you move the child
- Delete a parent, you delete all children, including grandchildren

TIP: Always design your parent-child relationships to capture your design intent.

3.13   Getting Information about Parent-Child Relationships

The Info menu has a ParentChild submenu as shown in Figure 3.19. This menu provides an easy way to see parent-child relationships in a part. Information about a feature's parents, children, references, or children's references can be provided. The software highlights features in the model that satisfy these criteria. As always, you can select a feature from the model or from the Model Tree.

For example, clicking Parents queries that you select a feature. All parents of the selected feature are then highlighted on the model. Similarly children of the selected feature are highlighted by selecting Children.

A very useful tool is References. You can see all of the references that a particular feature uses as constraints. Unlike parents or children, references are shown one at a time. By selecting Next or Previous, you can view other references.

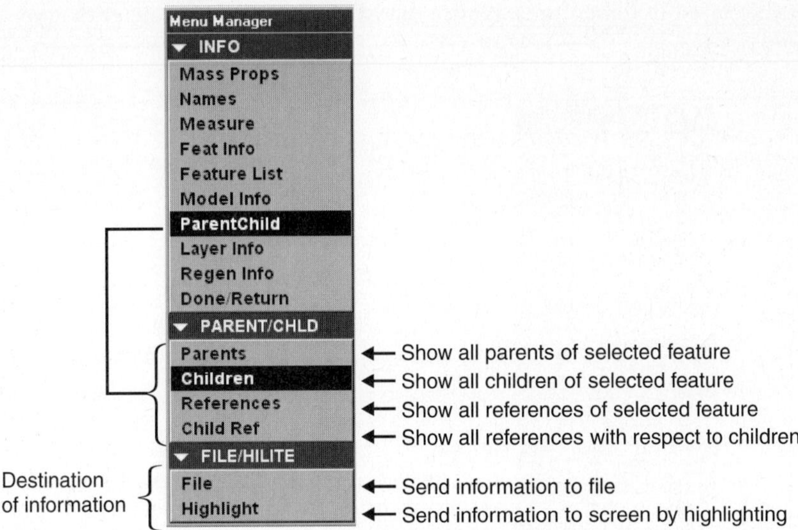

Figure 3.19   Info >ParentChild menu.

3.14 Modifying a Feature

In Tutorial 3.4 you got a first look at modifying a feature. You used the Define button in the feature dialog to modify a dimension during the feature creation stage of design. There is a simpler way to change a dimensional value. In the Part menu is a Modify item. The Modify submenu allows you to change the dimensional values associated with a feature. You cannot change references, planes, or sketches. When you select Modify, you are requested to select the feature that you would like to modify. You can select this feature by clicking on the feature in the graphics window or by selecting the feature from the model tree. After a feature is selected to modify, the dimensions associated with that feature are displayed on the part.

The Modify submenu is shown in Figure 3.20. The Value selection is highlighted during default. This allows you to select a feature (use querySel) and then simply click on whatever dimension you wish to modify. A query appears in the Message Window requesting the new value. The old value is always given as a default. You will not see the change after the new value is entered. The change is not reflected in the part until a regeneration. This allows you to make multiple changes before initiating a regeneration.

The Modify submenu also allows you to clean up the display. Sometimes dimensions will lay on top of each other cluttering the display and making picking very difficult. You can move a dimensioned value by clicking Move Dim and selecting the dimension to move. Select the dimension by clicking on the dimension. You can also select to move the name of a datum plane or change the number of significant digits displayed in dimensions. Notice that the only actual parameter that you can modify is a Value.

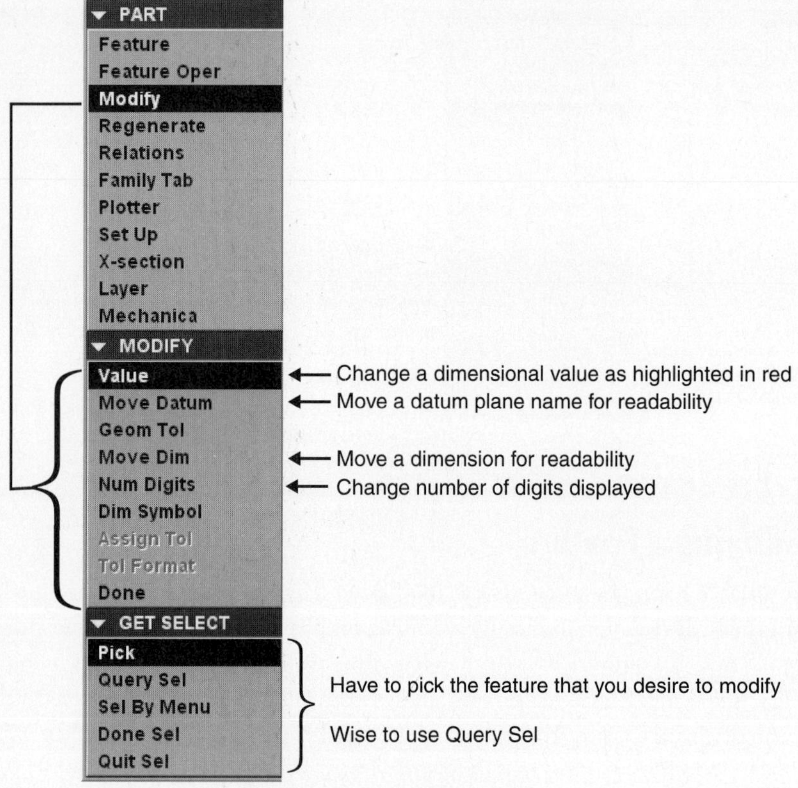

Figure 3.20   Modify submenu.

In Tutorial 3.5 we will use the Modify command to move around some poles in a part as shown in Figure 3.21(a). The part has a base plate, a left and right pole, and two plates on top of the poles. First, move the right pole. Notice that the right pole is referenced to the back and right side of the base plate. Remember that you must regenerate before you will see the resultant change. You will modify the dimension from 40.00 to 20.00 as noted. After regeneration, the part looks like Figure 3.21(b). Note that the plate on top of the bar moved with the bar—a clear indication that the plate is a child of the bar.

Next, modify the width of the base plate by changing the 100.00 dimension to 200.00. This changes the width of the base plate, and we get the peculiar result shown in Figure 3.21(c). Note first that the right pole did not move while the left pole moved. The left pole moved 100.00 units along with the front face of the base plate. That is because the back surface of the base plate is referenced to the XY datum plane. Consequently, when the width is increased by 100.00 units, the base plate extended from the XY

Datum plane (the back surface of the base plate). Thus, the front face of the plate moved 100 units. Since the right pole is referenced to the back pole, it did not move. However, the left pole did move. This would indicate that it is referenced to the front face of the base plate. Indeed, our suspicion is correct, as shown in Figure 3.21(d).

Now, the top plate that used to sit on the left pole did not move. We can assume that it is not a child of the left pole. It is, in fact, a child of the right pole.

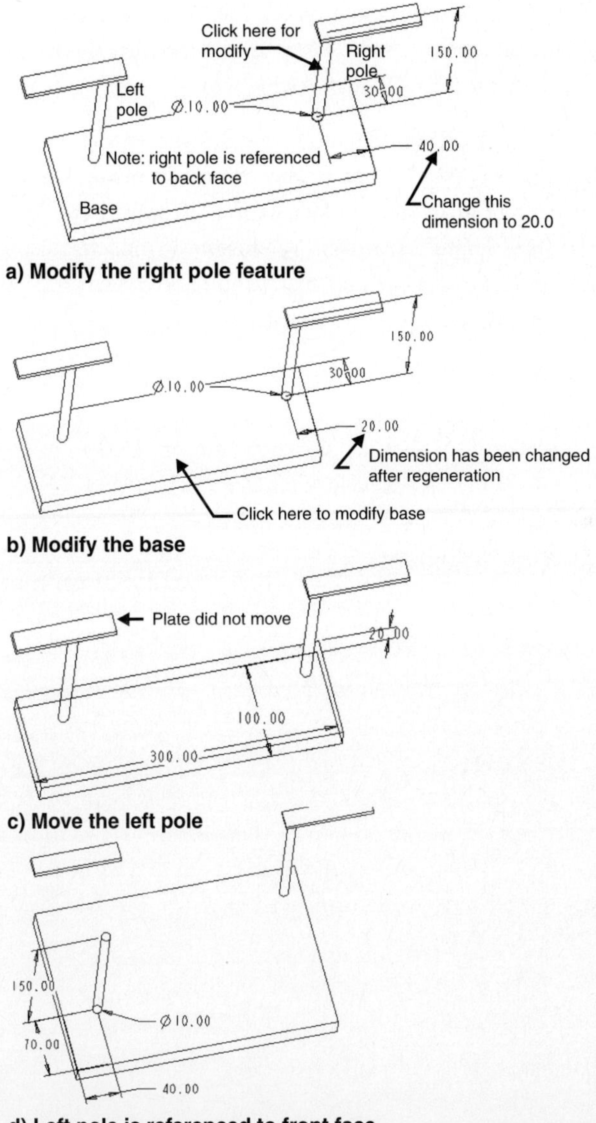

Figure 3.21   Illustrations associated with Tutorial 3.5.

During the later steps of this tutorial, we look at the Info menu's ParentChild item. From this menu we can highlight parents, children, or references to help us understand our model. I have created this model to be particularly complex in its parent and child relationships. We saw that the left-most plate did not move with the left-most bar. We assumed that it was referenced to the right-most bar. Is that the whole story?

Clicking on Info >ParentChild >Parents | Display, we select the left-most plate. The display highlights the base (as we would suspect since it is the parent of all features), the right-most bar (as we would also suspect), the plate over the right-most bar, and the left-most bar. I thought we had cleared up the fact that the left-most plate was not a child of the left-most bar. Well, we were wrong.

Next we go to the Info >ParentChild >Info >References and select the left-most plate. One reference is highlighted at a time. From this menu, we see that the left-most plate was referenced to the top face of the left-most bar. Consequently, the height of the left-most plate depends on the height of the left-most bar. Thus, the left-most plate is a child of the left-most bar (among other features). As you can see, parent child relationships can be very complex.

> **NOTE:** Any time a feature A relies on another feature B, even for one dimensional reference, feature A is a child of feature B.

Tutorial 3.5 Parent/Child Effect

Files opened: Tut3-5a.prt   **No files saved.**

Step	Action	Description	Further Actions	Result
1	Click PT/Modeler Icon	Run PT/Modeler		After some time, PT/Modeler on screen
2	>Mode >Misc >Show Dir	Show current directory		Message similar to "Directory searched is c:\ptc\ptprod\bin"
3	>Change Dir	Change the current directory	Type **c:\proe\tutorial\ chapter_3**	
4	>Done-Return	Leave Misc menu		Misc menu removed
5	>Part >Search/Retr	Read in a part	Select **tut3-5a**	Part is displayed
6	>Environment	Set up the environment	Set up checks as seen in Table T3.5 Column Step 6	
7	>Done-Return			
8	F1	Go to default display view to mess things up		
9	View >Angles | Horizontal	Change the view to something reasonable	Type **270**, then **Enter**, then >Done/Accept	Rotate the view about the display horizontal axis
10	>Feature >Modify	Modify the right pole	Select right pole in Fig. 3.21(a)	Right pole is selected, dimensions are shown
11	Click on the 40.00 dimension	Change the 40 to a 20	Type **20**	
12	Regenerate	See the change		New part is displayed as in Figure 3.21(b)
13	>Feature >Modify	Modify the base	Select the base in Fig. 3.21(a)	Base is selected, dimensions are shown
14	Click on the 100.00 dimension	Change the 100 to a 200	Type **200**	
15	Regenerate	See the change		New part is displayed as in Figure 3.21(c)
16	>Feature >Modify	Modify the left pole	Select the left pole in Fig. 3.21(a)	Left pole is selected, dimensions are shown in Fig. 3.21(d)
17	>Info >Parent Child | Children | Highlight	Show all children of selected feature	Select the right pole then >Done and F2 to repaint	Notice that both upper plates are children
18	>Info >Parent Child | Children | Highlight	Show all children of selected feature	Select the base plate then >Done and F2 to repaint	Notice that everything is a child of the base plate since it is the base feature
19	>Info >Parent Child | Parents | Highlight	Show the parent of selected feature	Select the left-most plate that is floating in space then >Done and F2 to repaint	Notice that all but the right pole are parents

Tutorial 3.5 Parent/Child Effect (continued)

Step	Action	Description	Further Actions	Result
20	>Info >Parent Child | Children | Highlight	Show the children of selected feature	Select the left-most bar that is moved forward then >Done and F2 to repaint	Notice that the left upper plate is a child of this bar
21	>Info >Parent Child | Children | File	Show the children of selected feature	Select the left-most bar that is moved forward then >Done and F2 to repaint	Check the feature numbers in the info window
22	>Info >Parent Child | References	Show the references of a selected feature	Select the left-most plate that is floating in space then >Done and F2 to repaint	First feature is top face of left-most bar
23	>Next	See >Next reference		Front face
24	>Next	See >Next reference		Left-most face of right-most bar
25	>Next	See >Next reference		Back face of right-most bar
26	>Next	See >Next reference		Front face of right-most bar
27	>QuitWindow			
28	>Exit	Exit program	Click Yes to confirm	PT/Modeler exited

Item	Step 6
Disp DtmPln	No
Spin Center	No
Disp Axes	No
Rendering	Hidden line

Table T3.5
Environment Settings

What have we learned from all this? Well, first, the Modify command is a very easy way to change dimensions in features. Second, parametric-based modeling makes changing parts very easy. Third, parent and children relationships can be very complex. A feature can be the child of many parents. If a Feature A is referenced to some edge or axis of another Feature B, then it is a child to that Feature B.

3.15 The Feature Order List

Parts are built one feature at a time. Features are ordered in a feature list. The feature list is displayed in the Model Tree window. Using the Model Tree was described in Chapter 1. The basic Model Tree contains just the ordered list of features. Other characteristics of these features can also be displayed in the Model Tree. Configuration dialogs are provided to help you customize the Model Tree display.

These dialogs are selected from the Model Tree window menu, and are discussed in Chapter 1.

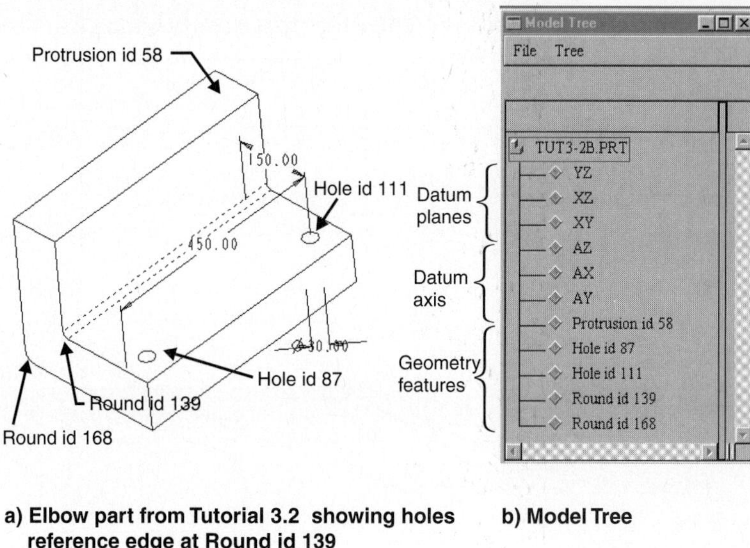

a) Elbow part from Tutorial 3.2 showing holes reference edge at Round id 139   **b) Model Tree**

Figure 3.22   Hole feature and Model Tree from Tutorial 3.2.

The part from Tutorial 3.2 is shown in Figure 3.22(a). Its Model Tree is shown in Figure 3.22(b). If you recall, we placed two hole features into the elbow as seen in Figure 3.23(a). When positioning Hole 1, the edge L1 and edge F1 were used as references for the dimensions. Consequently, the dimensions show up referenced to these features. Now, you dimensioned Hole 2 using different references. For this hole, you used Edge L1 and Edge B1. This all seems well and good until we added our round features as shown in Figure 3.23(b). As we can see, Hole 2 is now referenced to an edge that has been rounded. What gives?

The answer has to do with the order in which features are built. Recall that a part is constructed, one feature at a time, from Model Tree. One feature is executed at a time. Each feature knows how to construct and reference itself, based on its parameters. No feature can refer to a feature later in the list. No feature has any knowledge about any feature later in the list. Consequently, when the holes are drawn, they reference the three edges from the earlier protrusion feature. No edges were rounded at that time. Suppose that a machine shop could build this part, feature by feature, following the Model Tree order. They would make the L bracket, measure the dimensions of the three edges, and drill the holes.

In our model, the next feature is the round. It is this round that causes the concern. It would be a better idea to reference the hole off of a different, nonrounded surface. Perhaps a datum plane could be placed coplanar with the vertical face. This datum could then be used for the dimension.

The PT/Modeler part storage works differently from the machining described. Try to imagine inspecting the part with the rounded edge. It cannot be done because the edge is missing.

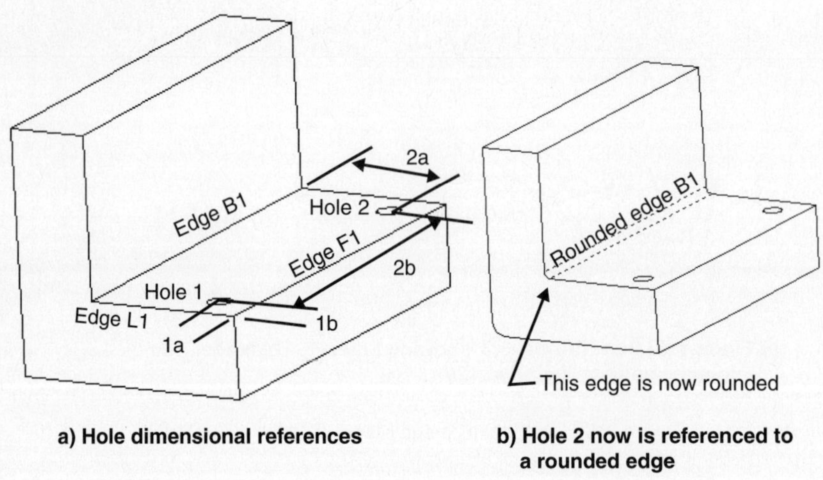

Figure 3.23   Dimensional references of holes from Tutorial 3.2.

Working in Sketcher

Sketcher is the two-dimensional drawing engine within PT/Modeler. Most of the features are sketched features that require a section drawing. You draw these section drawings in Sketcher. In this chapter we will draw sections for protrusions, cuts, and sketched holes. Troubleshooting section designs in Sketcher are covered in Chapter 9.

Sketcher is used to draw sections for features. Consequently, Sketcher and features are inseparable. Several sketching techniques have been previously introduced in Chapter 3; this chapter will describe a number of them further.

The first step to understand sketching is to know how to get into Sketcher. Getting into Sketcher is easy—getting into Sketcher and being oriented correctly is a little more challenging. We will work on getting into Sketcher before we tackle Sketcher itself.

4.1   Getting into Sketcher

As indicated, you will be sketching on a two-dimensional surface. The challenge is specifying the correct two-dimensional surface within the three-dimensional model space. At times you can select an existing face from your part. At other times, you will need to create a datum plane.

Before entering Sketcher, it is necessary to specify both a sketching (also called section) plane and a reference. Figure 4.1(a) provides the menu selections for selecting a sketching plane. You can either pick an existing plane from your model or create a temporary datum plane. If you pick an existing plane, the plane can be either a geometric face from the model or an existing datum plane. Alternatively, you can select to create a new temporary datum plane using MakeDatum.

> **NOTE:** MakeDatum creates a temporary datum plane associated with a specific feature. This plane is only visible and can be used only when you are working with that specific feature.

Once you select your sketching plane, you must provide an orientation reference for this plane. The two-dimensional sketching plane is infinite in size, but rectangular in shape. Consequently, like any two-dimensional rectangle, the two-dimensional sketching plane has a top, bottom, left side, and right side.

It is necessary to orient the sketching plane with respect to your model. One of these top, bottom, left, or right sides needs to be selected and provided a reference. For example, you could say "Align the top of my sketching plane to this top face of the part." Or "Align the left side of my sketching plane to this back side of my part." Similarly, you could say "Align the bottom side of my sketching plane to the XY datum plane." Lastly, you could say "Align the top side of my sketching plane to this new temporary datum plane that I am going to create right now using MakeDatum."

When you select a face of your part for a datum plane, the outside face is always selected. Remember that every face has one outward facing side. You always sketch onto the outward facing face. A datum plane faces in two directions: positive and negative. If you are using the default color scheme with a blue background, the positive-facing side (called the positive side) is drawn in yellow and the negative-facing side (called the negative side) is drawn in red. You can select either of these sides for the sketching plane.

Since the view of the datum plane is projected onto a two-dimensional plane (the screen), you can see only one side of a datum plane at a time. If you are looking at the positive face of a datum plane, the datum plane is drawn using yellow lines. If you are looking at the negative face of a datum plane, the datum plane is drawn using red lines. If you select a datum plane that is drawn in red, you are drawing on the negative-facing side. Alternately, if you select a datum plane that is drawn in yellow, you are drawing on the positive-facing side.

Two menus are provided before you can enter Sketcher. The first helps you select the sketching plane as shown in Figure 4.1(a). As expected, two selections are provided, one for selecting an existing plane (either face or datum) and one for creating a new temporary datum plane.

The second menu shown in Figure 4.1(b) is for selecting the reference. The reference does not have to be a reference plane; it can be a straight edge. It would be quite legal to say "Align the top of my sketching plane to this edge." From here, you can select one of Top, Bottom, Right, and Left. You need only specify one side since this is sufficient to constrain the sketching plane.

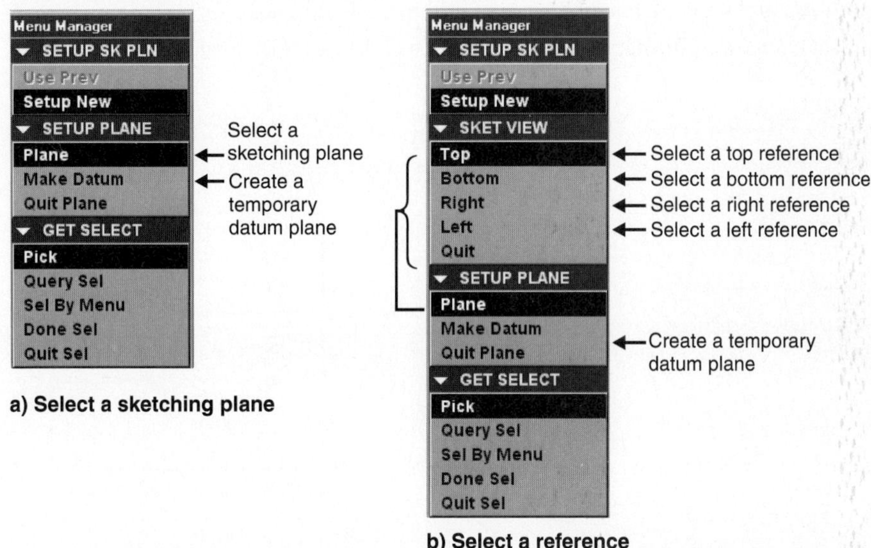

a) Select a sketching plane

b) Select a reference

Figure 4.1   Menus for selecting a sketching plane and reference.

Let's start with an example. Consider the part in Figure 4.2(a). Suppose we want to place a circular cut on the front face. We could select the front face as the sketching plane. Alternately, we could select a datum plane if one was coplanar with the front face, or we could use MakeDatum to create a temporary face there. For now, select the front face as the sketching plane. Next, we need to create a reference for this plane. Perhaps you like drawing upside down—you could select the bottom surface as the Top reference. Perhaps you prefer to draw sideways—you could select the side face as the Top reference. I prefer drawing right-side-up so I will select the top face as the Top. As indicated in this figure, I could also select the bottom face as Bottom or the side face as Right and achieve the same goal.

After selecting the reference plane, Sketcher comes up and takes over the main graphics window. Sketcher has a grid and displays all items currently selected for view in the Environment menu as shown in Figure 4.2(b). For example, in this case we have hidden lines and no datum planes displayed. Thus, we see hidden lines, as referenced by the display of the side cut and the fact that there are no datum planes displayed.

Since we are in Sketcher, we might as well draw our circular cut. I chose to use a circular cut, as opposed to a hole, because the point is to use the sketcher. Straight holes do not need to use the sketcher. I sketch the hole (more on that later), dimension, and regenerate. The regeneration process confirms that all went well with a "Regeneration successful message." You will come to love that message. I am now done with the sketcher. Thus, I select Done. After Preview and OK from the features dialog, we are left with the part shown in Figure 4.2(c). As desired, there is now a circular cut, otherwise known as a hole, on the front face.

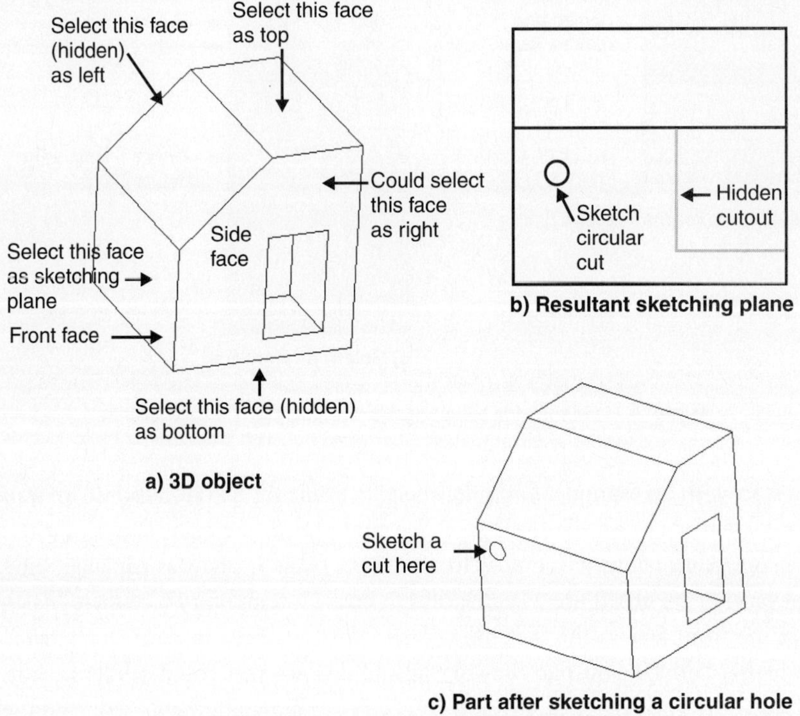

Figure 4.2   Picking a sketching plane and reference Part 1.

We will go through the sketch process another time; this time we will choose to view our model sideways. This isn't always a bad idea. Perhaps it is more natural to draw the feature sideways. Maybe the orientation of the feature has an up-down orientation but it happens to sit sideways on the part. We will define a rectangular cut on the front face. I select the front face as the sketching plane and this time choose the side face as the Top reference as shown in Figure 4.3(a). The sketcher brings up the view in Figure 4.3(b). Take a second or two to get oriented to this view. Note the hidden cutout is now towards the top-right of the part and the hole is displayed near the bottom of the sketch view. We are looking at the front face but we have tipped the part over on its side. We draw a rectangle in the sketcher, dimension it, and regenerate to get the resultant part shown in Figure 4.2(c). Note that the rectangle's long axis was pointed vertically in the sketcher. This translates into horizontally when we see our standard view of our part again. Actually the part has no top or bottom; we are just choosing one.

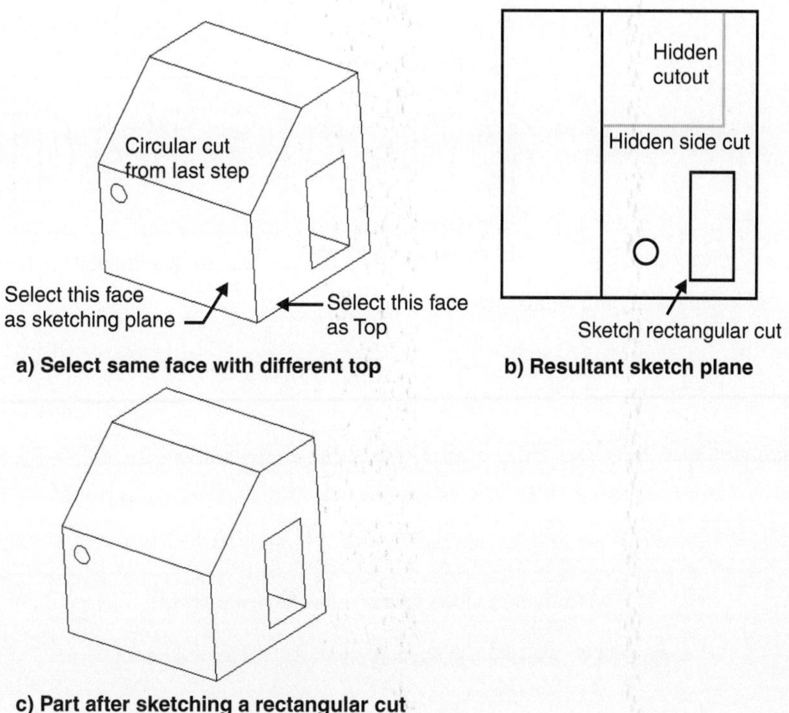

a) Select same face with different top   **b) Resultant sketch plane**

c) Part after sketching a rectangular cut

Figure 4.3   Picking a sketching plane and reference Part 2.

We will make one more cut in our part. Let's choose the back-facing face inside the cutout as shown in Figure 4.4 as the sketching plane. Let's also select the side face as Right. This brings up the sketcher with our part seen from its front. However, we have x-ray vision here, and we are actually not at the front of the part. We are on the face midway through the part. We still see the circular and rectangular cuts.

However, these are drawn as hidden lines since they are in back of us. It is as if we crawled into that cutout and are looking towards the back of the part.

This time, I sketch a key way onto that surface, dimension, and regenerate. Two views of the resultant key way cut are shown in Figure 4.4(c). In this case, I defined the cut to be Thru-Next so that it proceeds through the next surface. This means the cut goes through the back face of the part. The circular and rectangular cuts were defined as Blind dimensions and did not extend through the part.

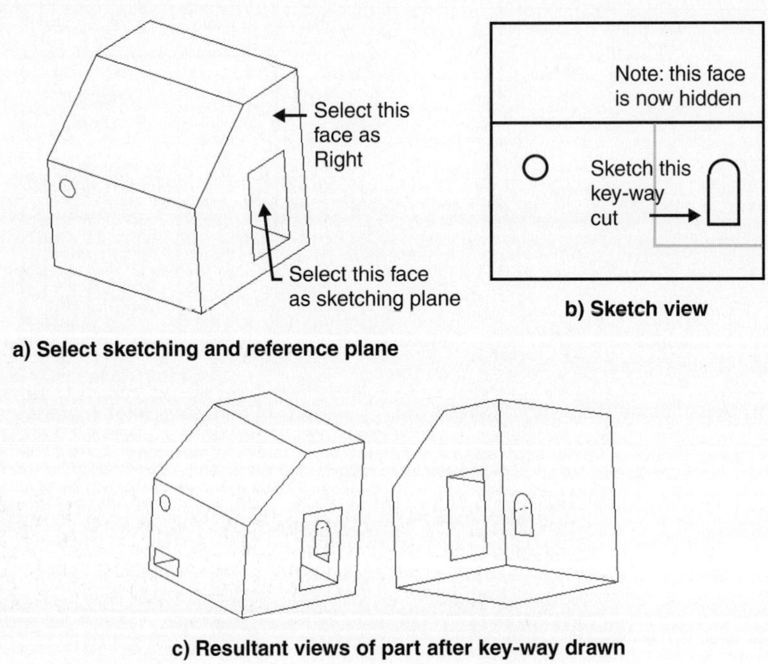

a) Select sketching and reference plane

b) Sketch view

c) Resultant views of part after key-way drawn

Figure 4.4   Picking a sketching plane and reference Part 3.

Next, let's select a datum plane as the sketching surface. Recall that datum planes have two sides. Take extra care when selecting a datum plane as either a sketching plane or a reference plane. There is nothing worse than a two-faced datum plane! Datum planes have zero width. They are analogous to a playing card with the numbers and symbols on one side and the back of the card on another. Since the card is on a plane, we can see one side or the other, but never both at the same time. I enable the display of the datum planes in the Environment menu.

Two views of the part are shown from different perspectives in Figure 4.5. The first, in Figure 4.5(a), positions our viewpoint such that we are looking at the positive face of the datum plane. The datum plane is displayed in yellow. This indicates that we are seeing the positive face. Rotating the part a bit, as seen in Figure 4.5(b), shows the negative side of the datum plane. It is displayed in red.

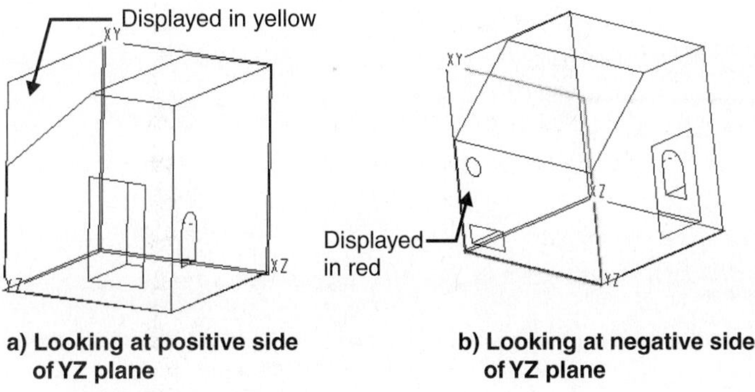

**a) Looking at positive side
of YZ plane**

**b) Looking at negative side
of YZ plane**

Figure 4.5   Positive and negative sides of a datum plane.

Suppose we want to make a protrusion from this datum plane. Select the YZ datum plane as the sketching plane. We could define the top face of the Part as Top. This leaves us with a partially constrained sketching plane. Are we looking from the front of the part into the part? Are we looking from inside the part outwards? This ambiguity is handled by the software. A red arrow is displayed asking if this is the desired direction of protrusion. If it is, we click OK. If it is not the correct direction, we click Flip and then OK. It can only be one of the two directions corresponding to the two sides of the datum plane. These arrows are shown in Figure 4.6(a).

> **NOTE:** Sometimes it is very confusing to tell the datum planes apart. The placement of the name of the datums XY, XZ, and YZ can often be deceiving. It is safest to use QuerySel or to select the desired datum from the Model Tree.

Continuing on, we want the protrusion to extend out from the front face of the part. Had we selected the front face as the sketching plane, it would automatically come outward since that is the only allowed direction for a face. We sketch the circular protrusion, dimension, and regenerate to build the part as seen in Figure 4.6(b).

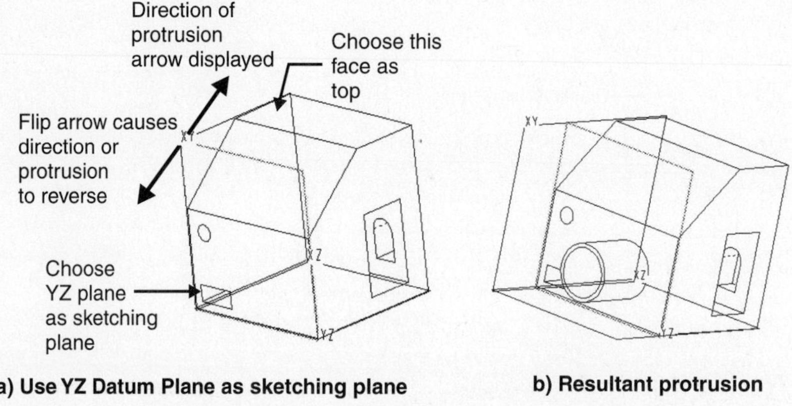

a) Use YZ Datum Plane as sketching plane   **b) Resultant protrusion**

Figure 4.6   Using a datum plane as a sketching plane.

4.2   Drawing in Sketcher

You can use some basic drawing tools in Sketcher. These include the point, line, circle, rectangle, and arc. The line and circle can be drawn from the MouseSketch mode or from the line and circle modes. The MouseSketch mode is provided as a simple way to draw lines and circles using just the mouse. There is only one way to draw a point and a rectangle. Consequently, these items do not bring up child menus. There are several ways to draw lines, circles, or arcs. These items bring up submenus. Each is discussed in detail in the following sections.

When would you want to use points in 3D Modeling? Most likely you will use points as references. You could place points at intersections or center points of circles or arcs. These points can later be referred to as geometric items.

It is important for you to realize that there are these various ways to draw items in Sketcher. You may prefer one or the other, but there will be times when an alternative technique solves the problem quickly and accurately. Each is simple to use so I encourage you to experiment.

4.2.1   Points

Points are easy to draw. Simply select point from the Sketcher menu and click where you would like to place a point.

4.2.2   Lines

Lines are straight segments that connect two points. There are two types of lines in Sketcher. The first is the geometric line. Perhaps you draw three geometric lines together to create a triangle. The second type of line is the centerline. The centerline is a reference used for circles and arcs. Centerlines are used when making revolved features and to show symmetry. Revolved features are discussed in Chapter 6. The type of line drawn is based on the menu selection as seen in Figure 4.7.

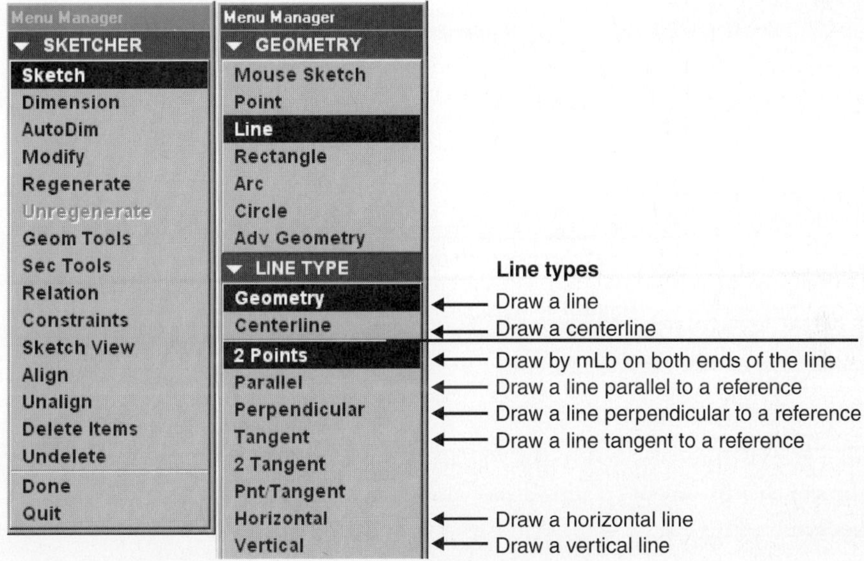

Figure 4.7   Line drawing menu.

Figure 4.8 illustrates some of the common line drawing methods. The first line, A, is drawn using the default two-point method. This is the same method used in MouseSketch mode. Note that this mode draws line chains. You click once at each vertex. This allows multiple connected lines to be drawn without worrying about connecting the endpoints. To end a line, it is necessary to middle-click, mMb, the mouse. Next, a parallel line is drawn. Before drawing the parallel line, select the line to which you want the new line to be parallel. Once selected, click on an endpoint for the new line. You are constrained to draw parallel to the selected line. This is the same for perpendicular lines.

Tangent lines require an arc or spline. You are requested to click on an endpoint of the arc or spline. Once selected, and it can be a little sensitive, you are constrained to draw the line tangent to this curve. Horizontal and Vertical draw horizontal and vertical lines, respectively. The interesting thing about these selections is that it chains alternating between the horizontal and vertical. To draw the shape in Figure 4.8, I merely clicked on each vertex. Each time I clicked it changed from horizontal to vertical. You end the chain using the mMb mouse middle button.

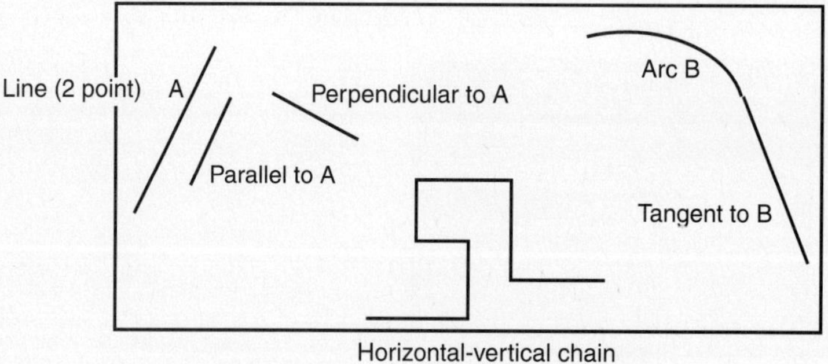

Figure 4.8   Typical lines drawn in Sketcher.

The goal of Tutorial 4.1 is to get you accustomed to drawing lines. You will enter the sketcher by way of creating a protrusion. In Sketcher you will draw a bunch of lines mimicking Figure 4.8. Do not worry about exactness. Just try and get it close. You will also practice deleting some lines and save the sketch file to a file named Tut4-1L.sec. You will then abort exit out of Sketcher. Note that we are not ready to finalize a sketch yet.

Tutorial 4.1 Drawing Straight Segments in Sketcher

Files opened: Tut4-1a.prt   **Files saved:** Tut4-1.sec

Step	Action	Description	Further Actions	Result
1	Click PT/Modeler Icon	Run PT/Modeler		After some time, PT/Modeler on screen
2	>Mode >Misc >Show Dir	Show current directory		Message similar to "Directory searched is c:\ptc\ptprod\bin"
3	>Change Dir	Change the current directory	Type **c:\proe\tutorial\ chapter_4**	
4	>Done-Return	Leave Misc menu		Misc menu removed
5	>Mode >Part >Retrieve	Read a part	Type **tut4-1a**	A rectangular block is displayed
6	>Environment	Set up the environment	Set up checks as seen in Table T4.1 Column Step 6	
7	>Done-Return			
8	>Feature >Protrusion | Extrude | Solid | Done	Create an extruded solid protrusion		
9	>One Side | Done	Protrusion will extend one side out of the sketching plane		
10	Pick XY datum plane for sketching plane	Select XY datum	>Flip then >Okay to accept protrusion direction arrow	Pick face for protrusion; this is the sketching plane
11	>TOP	Pick XZ datum plane for TOP reference to sketching plane	Pick XZ datum	Go into sketcher >Mode
12	>Sketch >Mouse Sketch	Draw some lines as in Figure 4.8	mLb around the screen to get used to drawing line chains; mMb to end line drawing	
13	>Line | 2 point	Draw a line as in Figure 4.8	mLb, mLb then mMb to end	Line drawn
14	>Line | Parallel	Draw a parallel line as in Figure 4.8	Select first line, then mLb mLb (note line ends automatically)	Parallel line drawn
15	>Line | Perpendicular	Draw a perpendicular line as in Figure 4.8	Select first line, then mLb mLb (note line ends automatically)	Perpendicular line drawn
16	>Delete Items	Delete the perpendicular line; use Done Sel to finish	mLb on the last line drawn (perpendicular); >Done Sel	Perpendicular line drawn is deleted
17	>Delete Items	Delete the parallel line Use mMb to finish delete	mLb on the parallel line drawn, then mMb to finish delete	Parallel line drawn is deleted

Tutorial 4.1 Drawing Straight Segments in Sketcher (continued)

Step	Action	Description	Further Actions	Result
18	Redo steps 14 and 15	Redraw parallel and perpendicular lines		
19	>Arc | 3-point	Draw an arc for tangent lines as in Figure 4.8	mLb for one end, mLb for a second end, move mouse to rubber-band arc, mLb to select centerpoint of arc	Arc drawn
20	>Line | Tangent	Draw a tangent line to the arc lines as in Figure 4.8	Select an endpoint of an arc, then mLb at end of tangent line	Tangent line drawn to arc
21	Rectangle	Draw rectangle lines as in Figure 4.8	mLb on one corner, mLB on opposite corner	Rectangle drawn
22	>File | Save As	Save the sketch as a tut4-1.SEC file	Type **Enter** to accept sketch, type **tut4-1** to save file	File saved
23	>Quit | Confirm	Abort out of sketcher		
24	Click Cancel	Abort out of protrusion	Click Yes	
25	>QuitWindow			
26	>Exit	Exit program	Click Yes to confirm	PT/Modeler exited

Item	Step 6
Disp DtmPln	Checked
Spin Center	No
Disp Axes	No
Rendering	No hidden line

Table T4.1   Environment Settings

4.2.3 Circles

The Circle menu is shown in Figure 4.9. The most common way to draw a circle, and in fact the default, is the Ctr/Point method. This method is used in MouseSketch as well as from the circle menu. An mLb click positions the center of the circle. From there, you move the mouse to the desired location where the circumference of the circle will be drawn. Another simple and frequently used technique is the Concentric circle option. Here, you click on a preexisting circle or arc. This defines the center of the new circle. Next, mLb click on the circumference of the old circle. A new circle follows the mouse. You should not drag the mouse. Simply move the mouse and the new circle will follow. When the new circle is correct, mLb again to end the process. Clicking again on the circumference brings out a new circle. Circles can also be drawn using the Fillet command. A fillet draws a circle between two objects. You are instructed to select two objects for the fillet. Once both are selected, the fillet is automatically drawn.

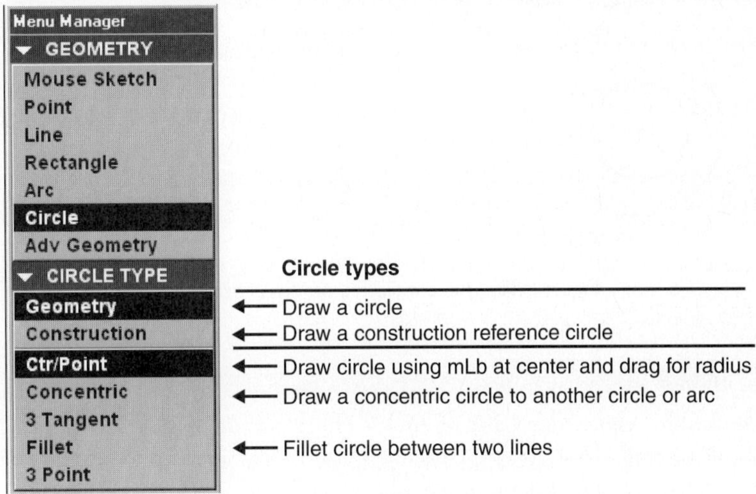

Figure 4.9   Circle menu in Sketcher.

Figure 4.10 provides an example of drawing circles in the sketcher. First, the Ctr/Point method is used to draw a circle. This circle is then used to draw a concentric circle. A construction circle is drawn using the Construction menu. The circle can be drawn using any of the circle drawing menu selections. Use the Line or MouseSketch menu item to draw two lines. Next, select the Fillet menu item. By selecting both lines, a fillet is automatically drawn. Lastly, an arc is drawn. This arc is drawn using the three-point method.

Arcs are covered in the next section. Simply mLb once for one end of the arc; mLb again for the second end; and move the mouse to move the center point of the arc. When properly positioned, mLb a third time to place the arc. The arc is drawn with a center point. Use the Concentric command to draw a circle concentric to the arc.

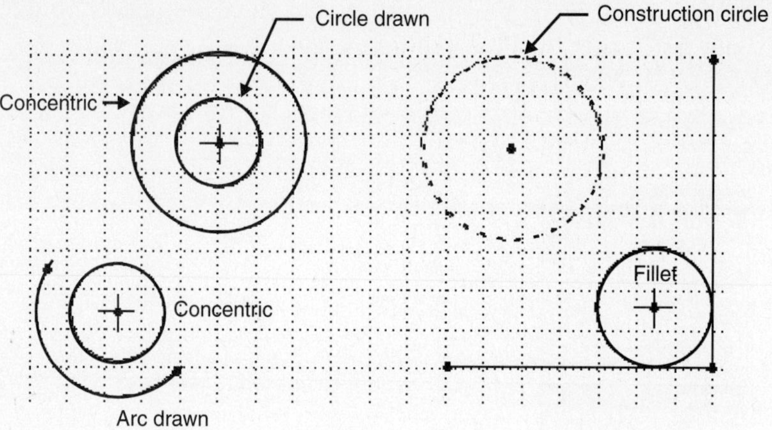

Figure 4.10   Typical circles drawn in Sketcher.

4.2.4 Arcs

Arcs are nothing more than parts of circles whose circumference does not necessarily extend the full 360 degrees. Drawing arcs is similar to drawing circles. The Arc menu is shown in Figure 4.11. Analogous to circles, concentric arcs are drawn by first selecting a preexisting circle or arc. Once selected, mLb click where you want the circumference of the new arc to be placed.

An arc is drawn with a radial sector line. Moving the mouse increases or decreases the angle defining the arc. When the correct angle is achieved, mLb click a last time to set the arc. Arcs, like circles, can form Fillets. The difference is the arc is open, and it will automatically connect to the end of the two items selected. In the process, it will adjust the two items so that the fillet can be tangent to both.

The Ctr/Ends arc is drawn by an mLb click on one end of the arc, and then an mLb click where the center of the arc is to reside. Moving the mouse drags the arc around. This either increases or decreases the angle of the arc. Click a last time when the desired angle is achieved. A three point arc is drawn by an mLb click on one end followed by an mLb click on the second end. Moving the mouse drags the arc around by its center point. When properly positioned, mLb click to set the arc.

A Tangent End arc is very useful for connecting an arc to another item such that the meeting points are tangent. The other item can be a line or arc. First, select the desired preexisting item by mLb clicking on an endpoint. Moving the mouse adjusts the size of the arc. The center is fixed based on the tangent constraint. Next mLb click when the arc is properly positioned. This is a two-click arc that is very fast and convenient.

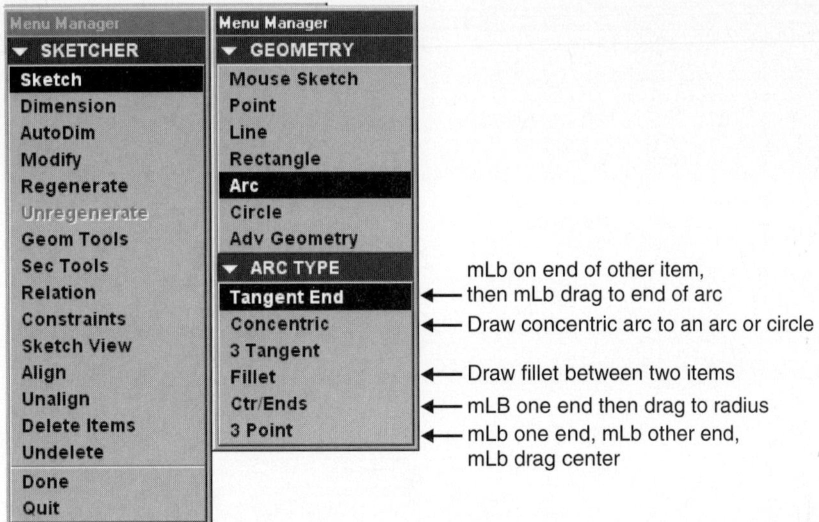

Figure 4.11   Arc menu in Sketcher.

The goal of Tutorial 4.2 is to get you accustomed to drawing arcs and circles. Once again, you will enter the sketcher by way of creating a protrusion. In Sketcher you will draw a bunch of circles mimicking Figure 4.12. As with Tutorial 4.1, just try and get it close to the arcs in the figure. You will save the circle sketch to a file named Tut4-2C.sec. You will use the Sel Many option to delete all arcs drawn using unselect to keep all lines but erase all circles. This time you will draw the arcs, save them to a file named Tut4-2A and then abort exit out of Sketcher. We are still not ready to finalize a sketch. Figure 4.12(a) illustrates Steps 12 through 18 of the tutorial. Figure 4.12(b) illustrates Steps 20 through 26.

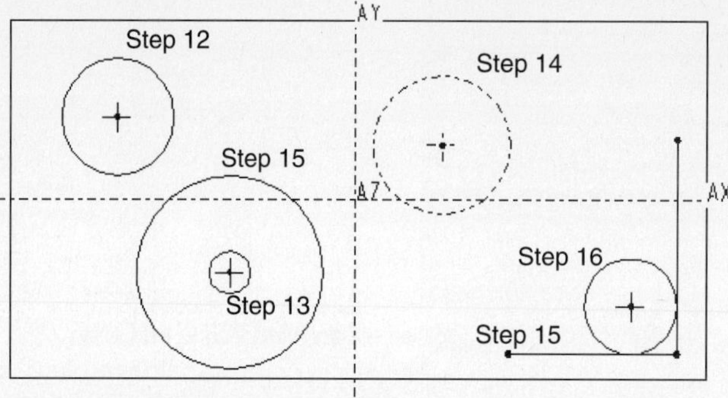

a) Tutorial 4.2 Steps 12 through 16

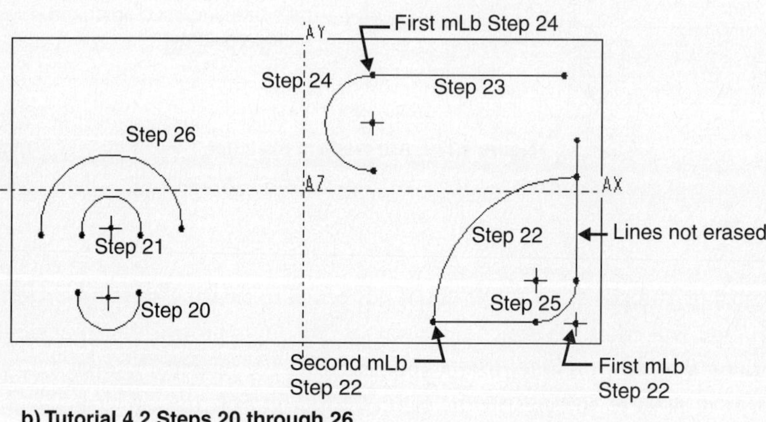

b) Tutorial 4.2 Steps 20 through 26

Figure 4.12   Illustrations for Tutorial 4.2.

Tutorial 4.2 Drawing Curves in Sketcher

Files opened: Tut4-2a.prt   **Files saved:** Tut4-2.sec

Step	Action	Description	Further Actions	Result
1	Click PT/Modeler Icon	Run PT/Modeler		After some time, PT/Modeler on screen
2	>Mode >Misc >Show Dir	Show current directory		Message similar to "Directory searched is c:\ptc\ptprod\bin"
3	>Change Dir	Change the current directory	Type **c:\proe\tutorial\ chapter_4**	
4	>Done-Return	Leave Misc menu		Misc menu removed
5	>Mode >Part >Retrieve	Read a part	Type **tut4-2a**	A rectangular block is displayed
6	>Environment	Set up the environment	Set up checks as seen in Table T4.2 Column Step 6	
7	>Done-Return			
8	>Feature >Protrusion | Extrude | Solid | Done	Create a extruded solid protrusion		
9	>One Side | Done	Protrusion will extend one side out of the sketching plane		
10	Pick XY datum plane for sketching plane	Select XY datum in Fig. 4.9(a)	>Okay to protrusion direction	Pick face for protrusion, this is the sketching plane
11	>TOP	Pick XZ datum plane for TOP reference to sketching plane	Pick XZ datum	Go into sketcher >Mode
12	>Sketch >Mouse Sketch	Draw a circle as in Fig. 4.12(a)	mMb to select the circle from Step 13, mLb drag to adjust the diameter of a concentric circle, and mLb to end adjustment and place circle	Circle drawn
13	>Circle | Geometry | Ctl/Pont	Draw a circle as in Fig. 4.12(a)	mLb to select the center of the circle; move mouse to end of radius and mLb to end	Circle drawn
14	>Circle | Construction | Ctl /Point	Draw a construction circle as in Fig. 4.12(a)	mLb to select the center of the circle; move mouse to end of radius and mLb to end	Circle drawn in dashed lines
15	>Circle | Geometry | Concentric	Draw a concentric circle as in Fig. 4.12(a)	mLb click on the circle from Step 13; click on the desired circumference of the new circle	

Tutorial 4.2 Drawing Curves in Sketcher (continued)

Step	Action	Description	Further Actions	Result
16	>Line | Horizontal	Draw two lines whose end points meet at right angles as in Fig. 4.12(a)	mLb click move mouse horizontally, mLb click move mouse vertically, mMb click to end line sketching	Corner drawn
17	>Circle | Fillet	Fillet between two lines as in Fig. 4.12a.	mLb on vertical line, mLb on horizontal line	Fillet circle drawn tangent to both lines
18	>Delete Items | Pick Many	Select everything drawn in Sketcher so far	Draw a rectangle around all items drawn; mLb on opposing corners	All items selected
19	>Unsel Item	Unselect the two lines	mLb on two lines to deselect then >Done Sel	All circles erased
20	>Sketch >Arc | 3-point	Draw an arc as in Fig. 4.12(b)	mLb twice for both end points, drag arc center, mLb to set	Arc drawn
21	>Sketch >Arc | 3-point	Draw another arc as in Fig. 4.12(b)	mLb twice for both end points, drag arc center, mLb to set	Arc drawn
22	>Sketch >Arc | Ctr/Ends	Draw an arc by specifying a center and two end points as in Fig. 4.12(b)	mLb on center of lines as in Fig. 4.12(b), mLb to place an end point, move mouse to drag arc and mLb to set	Arc drawn
23	>MouseSketch	Draw a line as in Fig. 4.12(b)	mLb to draw line both ends of line, mMb to end	Line drawn
24	>Arc | Tangent End	Draw an arc tangent to the new line as in Fig. 4.12(b)	mLb on end of line, move mouse to size arc, mLb to end	Arc drawn tangent to line
25	>Arc | Fillet	Draw a fillet at the right corner of the two lines as in Fig. 4.12(b)	mLb on horizontal line, mLb on vertical line	Fillet drawn
26	>Arc | Concentric	Draw a concentric arc as in Fig. 4.12(b)	mLb on arc from Step 20, move mouse to desired radius of new arc, mLb to set radius, move mouse to set angle, mLb to set	Draw concentric circle
27	>Quit | Confirm	Abort out of Sketcher		
28	Click Cancel	Abort out of protrusion	Click Yes	
29	>QuitWindow			
30	>Exit	Exit program	Click Yes to confirm	PT/Modeler exited

Item	Step 6
Disp DtmPln	Checked
Spin Center	No
Disp Axes	Checked
Rendering	No hidden line

Table T4.2   Environment Settings

4.3   **Picking and Deleting**

Throughout your designs, you will be doing a significant amount of picking. You will be picking from all aspects of the design from setting up, feature sketching, 3D viewing, to assemblies and drawings. It is a wise investment of your time to understand at least some of the more common ways to pick.

Sketching provides an excellent environment for learning about picking. The Pick menu, associated with Deleting items, is shown in Figure 4.13. The most common way to pick an item is to use the Pick menu selection, highlighted by default, and simply mLb on the desired item. Individual items in the sketcher are not reflected in the Model Tree so you will have to pick them with the mouse in the sketcher graphics window.

Picking an item in this manner selects one element at a time. For example, a line chain might have ten line segments. Picking one segment only selects that segment and not the rest of the chain. For that reason, it is very convenient to use the Pick Many command. With this command you can draw a bounding rectangle around all items in the sketcher that you desire to select. Draw the bounding rectangle, like any rectangle, by mLb clicking on opposing corners of the rectangle. All items completely within the bounding rectangle will be selected.

Often, you will include items in the Pick Many command that you did not intend. Use the Unsel Last menu item to deselect the last item selected. Use the Unsel Item to deselect a specified item. With the Unsel Item highlighted, all items that you click on in the sketcher will be unselected (if already selected).

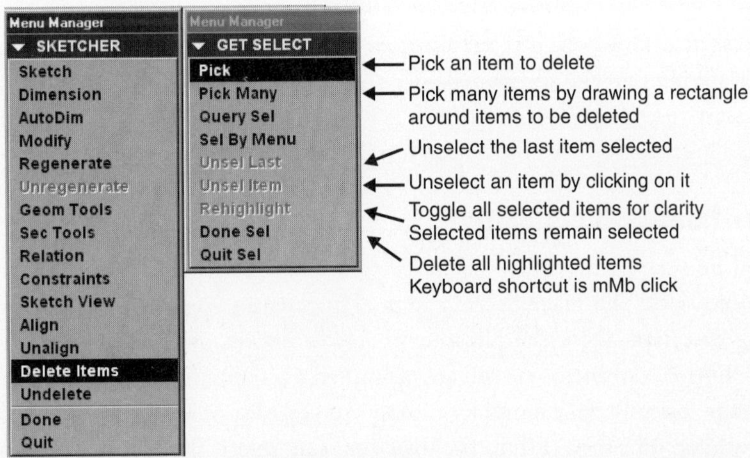

Figure 4.13   Picking menu.

You should already be very familiar with Query Sel. Unless your sketcher drawings are incredibly dense, you can probably pick your items directly without the use of Query Select. When you are satisfied with your selections, you can delete the items using Done Sel. If you want to abort exit, use Quit Sel. All selected items will become deselected.

> **TIP:** The mouse shortcut for Done Sel is mMb. It is much faster to rely completely on the mouse rather then bouncing back and forth from the mouse to the menu when selecting items. Use mLb to select the item. Then use mMb to accept the selection.

4.4   Reading and Writing Sketch Files

We are going to work in Sketcher creating our first actual feature in this chapter. Before we begin, I want to discuss how you read or write a sketch file. This can be very useful for all of those sections that you use repetitively.

4.4.1   Write a Sketch File

You have already written a sketch file in the previous tutorial. To write a sketch file from within Sketcher, simply click on the MAIN>File menu item from the main menu. This brings up the File submenu. Click on Save to save the current sketch. The sketcher automatically assigns a name to a sketch as you are building it. You can keep this name or you can rename it by selecting SaveAs. Remember when using SaveAs that the first response is to type Enter, thereby accepting the default sketcher name as the *input data to be saved*. Accepting this name means that you want to save the current sketch. Next, type in the new name that you want to use for the sketch. However, be careful to remember that you are still working in the original file and not the file named with the SaveAs. To work on the new sketch, it is necessary to erase the current sketch and read in the recently saved and renamed sketch. This is somewhat obtuse, but it is the way that the software works.

4.4.2   Read a Sketch File

To read in a sketch file, click on the Section Tools menu item from the Sketcher menu and select the Place Section item. This menu is provided in Figure 4.14. Placing a section alerts the Sketcher that you desire to read in a sketcher file (*.sec) from disk or memory. You are prompted to enter a file name. You can enter a file name directly, or respond by typing ? to get a list of available section files in the working directory. From the list you can select the desired section file (*.SEC).

Once you have selected a sketch, a child window is displayed showing the new sketch. It is necessary to place the sketch onto the sketching plane. This can be tricky, so bear with me. You will practice in the next Tutorial. You will be placing the sketch onto the sketcher plane. This means that you must constrain the new sketch onto the sketching plane.

The sketch that you are about to place has no reference whatsoever. During placement, you can scale, move, and rotate the sketch. You will be dragging the sketch onto the sketching plane so the new sketch will need two points of reference. These points are used only during the placement process. Neither of these points has to be on a line or arc; they are simply references. You will click somewhere in the child window that contains the sketch that you are about to place.

Scaling occurs about the first point, called the *scaling point.* If you choose a point on the left side of the sketch, the sketch will scale towards the right. If you choose a center point, the sketch will stretch (or compress) around the center. The second point is the drag point. You will place the sketch with the mouse. The drag point indicates what part of the new sketch lines directly under the pointer of the mouse. The scale point and drag point can be the same or different points.

Once these are selected, you have to enter a rotation and scaling value. The rotation angle determines the amount that the new sketch will be rotated counterclockwise. For now, let's assume that this will stay zero. However, you might want to rotate 90 degrees to change orientations. Lastly, enter the scale factor. You can accept the default scale factor of 1.0 and dynamically scale later during the placement.

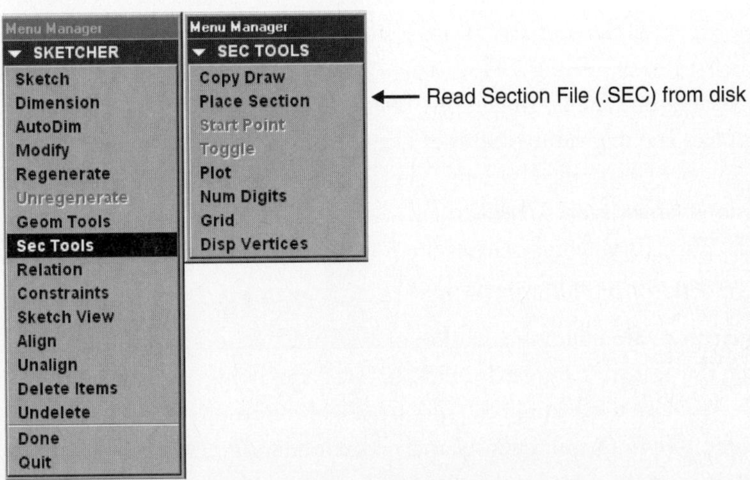

Figure 4.14 Section Tools menu.

You now have control of the new sketch, and it should follow the mouse about on the screen. You can dynamically scale the new sketch while you drag the sketch. The mouse buttons have the following function:

- Left button mLb: finish placing
- Middle button mMb: abort the placement
- Right button mRb: toggle the Scale/Drag

The first two are obvious. Once again, the convention in PT/Modeler is NOT to drag the mouse. Rather, you move the mouse around and click mLb when done. The Right mouse button is used to switch between dragging and scaling. Clicking the Right mouse button puts you into scale mode. Instead of dragging the new sketch, motions of the mouse scale it. Right click again to return to the dragging mode.

4.5   The Four Steps to Sketching (SADR)

Thus far, we have concerned ourselves with getting into Sketcher and with sketcher drawing tools. Now it is time to do some sketching. Roll up your sleeves and let's get to work. Recall that the goal of sketching is to produce a section drawing. In this chapter, we limit our use of these sections to protrusions and cuts.

A section has to be completely constrained for it to be useful. This means that the sketch has to be sufficiently dimensioned so that it can be built. No dimensions can be missing. Further, no additional dimensions can be present. Not having enough dimensions leads to ambiguity. This is called under-constrained. It is not enough to say that a rectangle is one inch wide. We need to specify the height as well.

If there are too many dimensions there is redundancy. This is called over-constrained. Too many dimensions can lead to errors downstream. Figure 4.15 illustrates an over-constrained system. The height of the object has one too many dimensions. Everything is correct and the part could be built, however, it is not allowed. What if someone changes the 8 to a 9. Now, the total height is no longer 30, requiring the 30 to be changed to 31.

In a sketch, we are building a section of a feature. We need to specify the dimensions of the feature completely without over specifying them. Still, that is not enough. We have to constrain the new item with respect to the rest of the part. We have to be able to unambiguously and nonredundantly place our new feature into the rest of the part. The sketching plane handles the orientation. We must dimension the feature such that the feature is constrained within the sketching plane.

Figure 4.15(a) illustrates a case where the horizontal dimensions are over-constrained and in Figure 4.15(b) the vertical dimensions are under-constrained. Once those problems are fixed, by removing and adding a dimension respectively, the new feature can be placed into the preexisting part. In Figure 4.15(c), the top horizontal line of the feature is constrained to be parallel to the top horizontal line of the part. Also, a set of dimensions constrains the left corner. In summary, we have provided an alignment by saying that the two horizontal lines are parallel. We then provided dimensions that tied down the left-top corner.

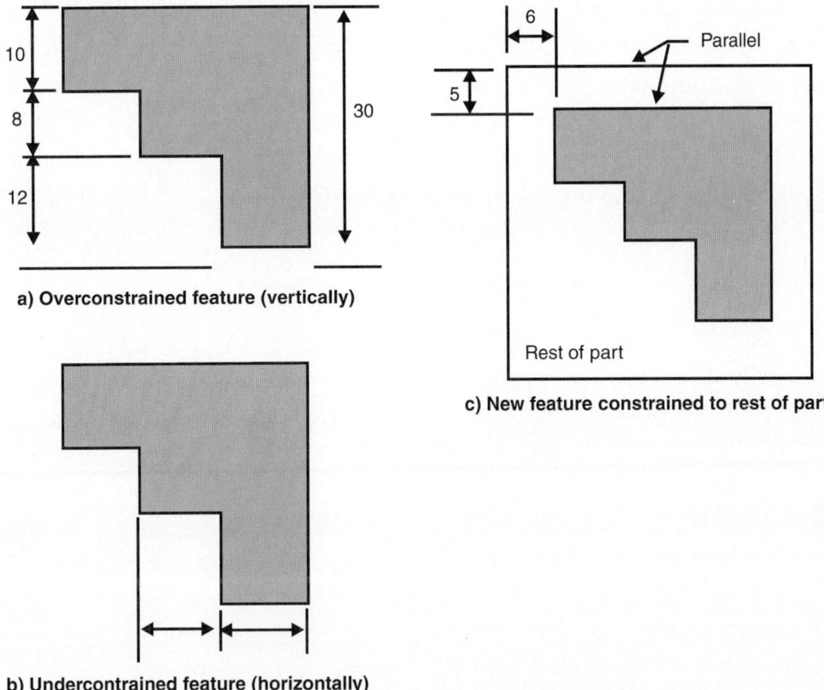

Figure 4.15   Over-constrained and under-constrained features.

We are about to create a sketch. But first, let's look at the sketching philosophy. PT/Modeler requests that you follow a technique called SADR. These letters stand for Sketch, Align, Dimension, and Regenerate. They indicate the order that you should use to design your sketches. This is an important design philosophy that should be followed. You may have to change some habits developed using CAD systems where you dimension lines as you draw them. This is not the case in Sketcher. The idea here is to rough sketch the section, align it to the datum planes, axes, or other features in the part, dimension it, then regenerate it. The dimensions that you enter are not built into the part until you regenerate the part. This way you can set up a number of sketch elements, alignments, and dimensions and then batch regenerate them together. Each of these four design steps is described next.

4.6   Sketching

The first step to constrain a feature is to provide the sketch. Draw the approximate shape of the desired feature section using the point, line, rectangle, arc, and circle tools as described in Section 4.2. You do not have to be exact here. You are *sketching* it in.

Sketcher is quite intelligent. This is no simplistic line-drawing module. It is quite effective at anticipating your desires. It makes a set of assumptions about your design intent. These assumptions ease your sketching task. You can make lines nearly horizontal or vertical. Lines can be almost parallel, almost perpendicular, or just about overlapping. Close is good enough for Sketcher. Sketcher will assume that you desired horizontal, vertical, parallel, perpendicular, or overlapping lines. It will fix them for you. These assumptions are described in Section 4.10.

> **TIP:** When closing features, make sure that the first and last points are close to each other. If you can see a space, then it is likely that PT/Modeler can see a space. This can cause a regeneration error.

Tutorial 4.3 provides some practice at sketching. You will read in a simple block part, rotate it to get access to the back face, select the back face as the sketching plane, and sketch four elements that use straight lines. Once completed, you will save the sketch and quit out of Sketcher.

In Figure 4.16(a), the part tut4-3a is shown after typing F1 to see the default view. You want to sketch on the backside for this tutorial. However, the backside of the face is not accessible. You could Ctrl-drag middle button to rotate the part. However, if you spin it around the horizontal axis, the top of the part would be oriented towards the bottom. Be careful. A more reliable way to view the backside is to rotate the part around the vertical by 180 degrees. This produces the view in Figure 4.16(b). Note that the AX axis now points towards the left. Now you can select the front face for the sketching plane. This flip has hidden the top surface so we can select the bottom face as the Bottom reference.

After selecting to create a One-sided solid extruded protrusion, you are brought into the sketcher as seen in Figure 4.16(c). Note the orientation of the AX axis. The direction of this axis indicates that we are looking at the back face of the part. Note also that AY axis is still pointing upward. This indicates that we have not turned our part upside down. We are ready to begin our sketching.

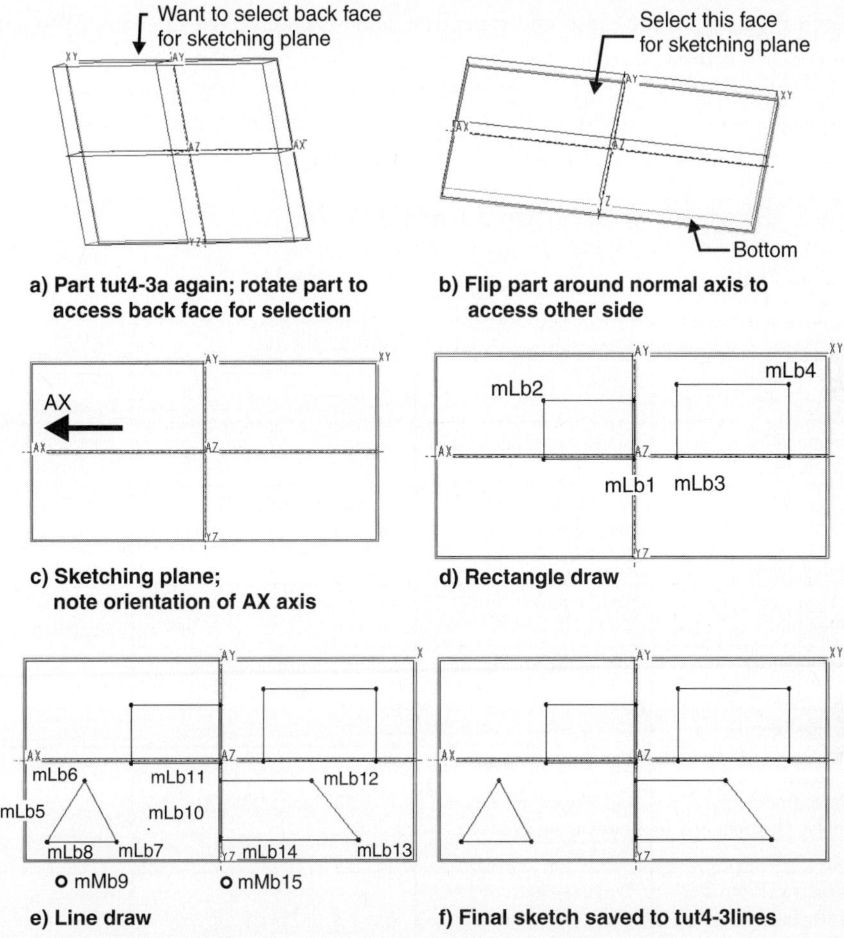

Figure 4.16   Illustrations associated with Tutorial 4.3.

First, draw the rectangles shown in Figure 4.16(d) using the Rectangle tool. Click on the center point at mLb1 to set the first point of the rectangle. Move the mouse to point mLb2 and click again to set the first rectangle. Repeat the process for mLb3 and mLb4 to draw the second rectangle. You do not have to worry about the position of the rectangles. You want to overlap the AX and AY axis as shown. Next, draw the triangle using the Line tool. Start at mLb5 and click at 6, 7 and close the figure by clicking over mLb5 again with mLb8. Note that mMb9 reminds you that it is necessary to middle-click the mouse to end the line chain. Last, draw the angled shape in the lower-right quadrant. Use the Line tool to draw the line chain. Start at mLb10 and click at the indicated points through mLb14. Use mMb15 to end the line chain. This concludes the sketch.

At this point we are ready to save the sketch. Use File | Save As. Accept the default sketch file name as the input and type Tut4-3lines as the sketch file name. You can abort exit out from Sketcher. This file will be used in Tutorial 4.4.

Tutorial 4.3 Sketching Straight Line Features

Files opened: Tut4-3a.prt   **No files saved.**

Step	Action	Description	Further Actions	Result
1	Click PT/Modeler Icon	Run PT/Modeler		After some time, PT/Modeler on screen
2	>Mode >Misc >Show Dir	Show current directory		Message similar to "Directory searched is c:\ptc\ptprod\bin"
3	>Change Dir	Change the current directory	Type **c:\proe\tutorial\ chapter_4**	
4	>Done-Return	Leave Misc menu		Misc menu removed
5	>Mode >Part >Retrieve	Read a part	Type **tut4-3a**	A rectangular block is displayed
6	>Environment	Set up the environment	Set up checks as seen in Table T4.3 Column Step 6	
7	>Done-Return			
8	Type F1	Go to default view		
9	View >Orientation | Angles | Vertical	Flip around the view to see the back face in Fig. 4.16(b)	Type **180** then **>Done/Accept**	
10	>Feature >Protrusion | Extrude | Solid | Done	Create an extruded solid protrusion		
11	>One Side | Done	Protrusion will extend one side out of the sketching plane		
12	Pick XY datum plane for sketching plane	Select XY datum in Fig. 4.16(b)	Okay to protrusion direction	Pick face for protrusion; this is the sketching plane
13	>Bottom	Pick Bottom face for Bottom reference to sketching plane	Pick Bottom face in Fig. 4.25(b)	Go into sketcher >Mode; note orientation of axis as in Fig 4.16(c)
14	>Sketch >Rectangle	Draw a rectangle in Fig. 4.16(d)	mLb1 and mLb2	Rectangle drawn

Tutorial 4.3 Sketching Straight Line Features

Step	Action	Description	Further Actions	Result
15	>Sketch >Rectangle	Draw a rectangle in Fig. 4.16(d)	mLb3 and mLb4	Rectangle drawn
16	>Sketch >Line	Draw a triangle in Fig. 4.16(e)	mLb5 to mLb8, mMb9 to end	Triangle drawn
17	>Sketch >Line	Draw a shape in Fig. 4.16(e)	mLb10 to mLb14, mMb15 to end	Shape drawn
18	>Quit | Confirm	Abort out of Sketcher		
19	Click Cancel	Abort out of protrusion	Click Yes	
20	>QuitWindow			
21	>Exit	Exit program	Click Yes to confirm	PT/Modeler exited

Item	Step 6
Disp DtmPln	Checked
Spin Center	No
Disp Axes	Checked
Rendering	No hidden line

Table T4.3   Environment Settings

Tutorial 4.4 provides some sketching practice. You will read in the same block part, select the front face as the sketching plane, and sketch three elements that use arcs and circles lines. Once completed, you save the sketch and abort out of Sketcher.

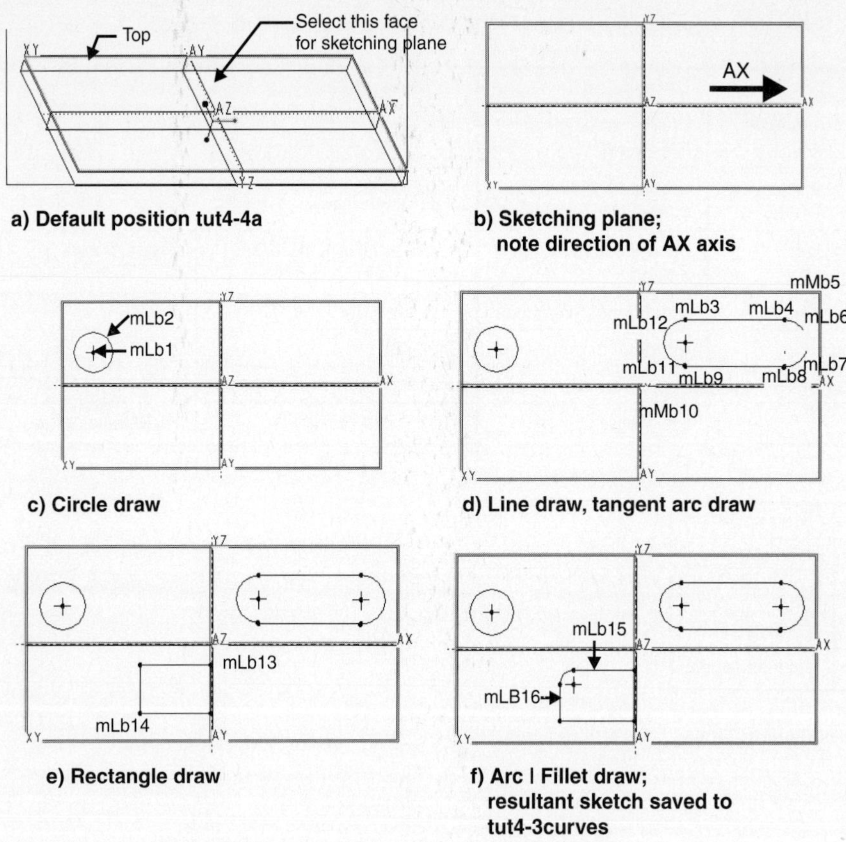

Figure 4.17 Illustrations associated with Tutorial 4.4.

First, draw the circle shown in Figure 4.17(d) using the Circle | Ctrl/Pnt tool. Click mLb1 to set the center of the circle. Move the mouse to the desired radius and mLb2 click to set the rectangle. Next, draw the line-arc feature. Once again, you do not have to worry about the exact position or size of these items. Draw this second feature by first using the line tool. Draw a line from mLb3 and mLb4. Note mMb5 ends the line chain.

Next, select Arc | Tangent and mLb6 click the first end of the arc onto the end of the line at mLb4. Now move the mouse downward to set the diameter of the arc and click mLb7. Note the arc is automatically constrained to be tangent to our line. Select the Line tool again and mLb8 click onto the free end of the arc at mLb7. Draw the line to mLb9 and end the line with an mMb10. This end point should be under mLb3. Finish up with an Arc | Tangent. MLbll click on the open end of

our line at mLb9 and move the mouse upwards until the free end of the arc intersects with mLb3 to close the figure.

We could have drawn this figure using the rectangle tool. In this case we would
draw the rectangle, delete the two vertical ends, and draw in the tangent arcs. Draw
the lower item last. Start with Rectangle and draw the rectangle as shown in Figure
4.17(e). Next, round the corner using the Arc | Fillet command. mLb click on the
horizontal edge and then mLb click on the vertical edge. The fillet is automatically
created. Both lines are cut back to meet the fillet.

> **TIP:** Try to avoid using Fillets. In normal part design, leave the corner square at
> the sketcher stage. Use an additional round feature to round the corner. This
> way, the round can be suppressed or modified easily.

At this point we are ready to save the sketch. Use File >Save As. Accept the default
sketch file name as the input and type Tut4-3curves as the sketch file name. You can
abort exit out from Sketcher. This file will be used in Tutorial 4.6.

Tutorial 4.4 Sketching Curved Features

Files opened: Tut4-4a.prt   **No files saved.**

Step	Action	Description	Further Actions	Result
1	Click PT/Modeler Icon	Run PT/Modeler		After some time, PT/Modeler on screen
2	>Mode >Misc >Show Dir	Show current directory		Message similar to "Directory searched is c:\ptc\ptprod\bin"
3	>Change Dir	Change the current directory	Type **c:\proe\tutorial\ chapter_4**	
4	>Done-Return	Leave Misc menu		Misc menu removed
5	>Mode >Part >Retrieve	Read a part	Type **tut4-4a**	A rectangular block is displayed
6	>Environment	Set up the environment	Set up checks as seen in Table T4.4 Column Step 6	
7	>Done-Return			
8	Type F1	Go to default view		
9	>Feature >Protrusion	Extrude	Solid	Done	Create an extruded solid Protrusion		

Tutorial 4.4 Sketching Curved Features (continued)

Step	Action	Description	Further Actions	Result
10	>One Side | Done	Protrusion will extend one side out of the sketching plane		
11	Pick XY datum plane for sketching plane	Select XY datum in Fig. 4.17(a)	Okay to protrusion direction	Pick face for protrusion; this is the sketching plane
12	>Top	Pick Top face for Top reference to sketching plane	Pick Top face in Fig. 4.27(b)	Go into sketcher >Mode; note orientation of AX axis in Fig. 4.17(b)
13	>Sketch >Circle	Draw a circle in Fig. 4.17(c)	mLb1 and mLb2	Rectangle drawn
14	>Sketch >Line	Draw the top line of rounded shape in Fig. 4.17(d)	mLb3 and mLb4, mMb5 to end	Line drawn
15	>Sketch >Arc | Tangent | End	Draw a tangent arc in Fig. 4.17(d)	mLb6 to mLb7	Arc drawn
16	>Sketch >Line	Draw the bottom line of rounded shape in Fig. 4.17(d)	mLb8 and mLb9, mMb10 to end	Line drawn
17	>Sketch >Arc | Tangent	Draw a tangent arc in Fig. 4.17(d)	mLb11 to mLb12	Arc drawn
18	>Sketch >Rectangle	Draw the rectangle in Fig. 4.17(e)	mLb13 and mLb14	Rectangle drawn
19	>Sketch >Arc | Fillet	Round a corner in Fig. 4.17(f)	mLb15 to mLb16 to select the two sides	Fillet drawn
20	>Quit | Confirm	Abort out of Sketcher		
21	Click Cancel	Abort out of protrusion	Click Yes	
22	>QuitWindow			
23	>Exit	Exit program	Click Yes to confirm	PT/Modeler exited

Item	Step 6
Disp DtmPln	Checked
Spin Center	No
Disp Axes	Checked
Rendering	No hidden line

Table T4.4   Environment Settings

4.7   Aligning

The second step toward constraining a feature is to align whatever elements in the feature's section should line up to preexisting elements of the part. This feature might be the first feature (the base feature) of a part or it might be a later feature added to an already complex part. Either way, we need to fix the placement of this feature onto the sketching plane. This is called alignment.

You make alignments by using the Align menu item. Something on a new feature is aligned to something on a preexisting feature. You cannot align sketch geometry to other sketch geometry. We have to align a new feature, be it a line, curve, or whatever, to a preexisting feature. Consequently, you need to pick a new feature and then pick an old feature. Often, the new and old will overlap. For example, a new axis being sketched might be drawn on top of an existing edge in the part. You can select the old and new by double clicking at a single location. PT/Modeler will first pick the sketched axis and secondly pick the underlying preexisting geometry.

If we are adding a first feature, all we have for alignment are the three datum planes and the three axes. If we are adding a feature to a part, we have all kinds of lines, arcs, and such from the part to use for alignment (as well as the datums and the axis). When we sketch, we sketch onto a transparency. We can see the part onto which we are sketching beneath the transparent sketching plane. We can align to the features of the preexisting part. We cannot change any of the preexisting part from the sketcher, but we can align to them.

4.7.1   Aligning Overlapping Elements

Consider the following examples. The first geometric feature that you add to a part is called the base feature. As always, the datum planes and axes proceed the first geometric feature as seen in Figure 4.18(a). Suppose we are making a rectangular extruded protrusion that wants to be 8 units wide by 4 units high. For some reason, or simply by convention, we want to place the feature to the right of the AY axis and above the AX axis as drawn. We sketch the rectangle as shown in Figure 4.18(b). We sketch the rectangle so that it looks wider than high. That's close enough for now. That's the "S" or sketch stage. Now, we need to align our new feature with the existing features in the part; this is the "A" stage. Looking at the rectangle, we can see that the left edge aligns to the AY axis and the bottom edge aligns to the AX axis. We instruct Sketcher to align the new (left edge of rectangle) to the old (AY axis). We instruct Sketcher to align the new (bottom edge of rectangle) to the old (AX axis). That's alignment.

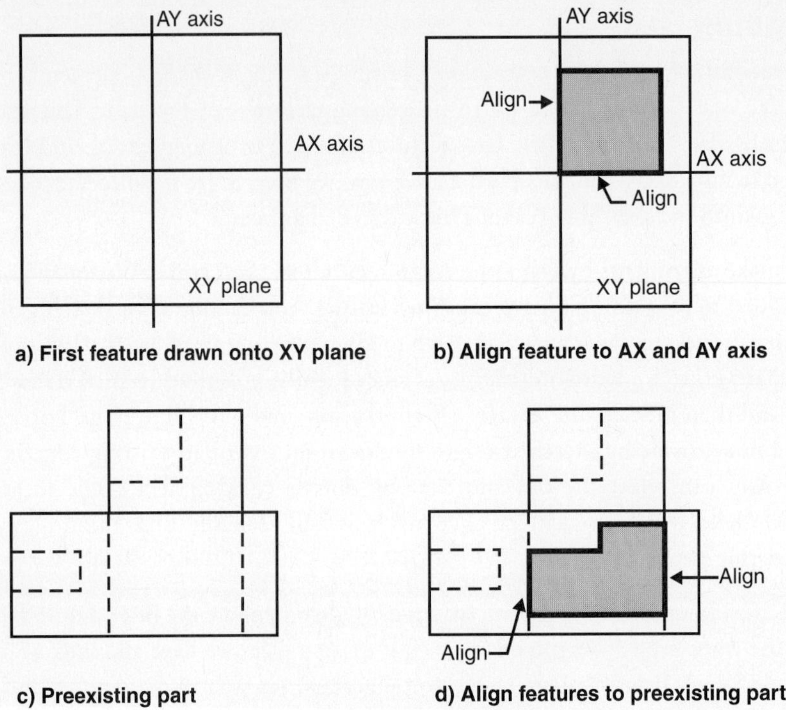

a) First feature drawn onto XY plane   **b) Align feature to AX and AY axis**

c) Preexisting part   **d) Align features to preexisting part**

Figure 4.18   Aligning a feature.

In Figure 4.18(c), a sketching plane is drawn on top of a preexisting part. This time we want to draw a more complicated feature as shown in Figure 4.18(d). We sketch the shape and align the left and right edges with the hidden edges from the preexisting part. We instruct Sketcher to align the new (left edge of new feature) to the old (hidden line). Again, we instruct Sketcher to align the new (left edge of new feature) to the old (hidden line). We have aligned our part to our best ability. We do not have any horizontal lines from the preexisting part that we can use for alignment. Or do we?

4.7.2   Aligning Nonoverlapping Elements

So far we have aligned overlapping lines. What about nonoverlapping lines? Let's look at this part more closely. Suppose it is our design intent that the lower-top horizontal line should be at the same height as the top hidden line to the left of the preexisting part. We would align this new edge with the old top edge of the hidden line as shown in Figure 4.19(a). Similarly, we could align the middle vertical edge on the top of our new feature to the right vertical hidden edge of the preexisting part. This completes the alignment phase of the sketch. The next stage in the design is dimensioning. In this example, only two dimensions remain unspecified before the part is fully constrained. These are shown in Figure 4.19(b).

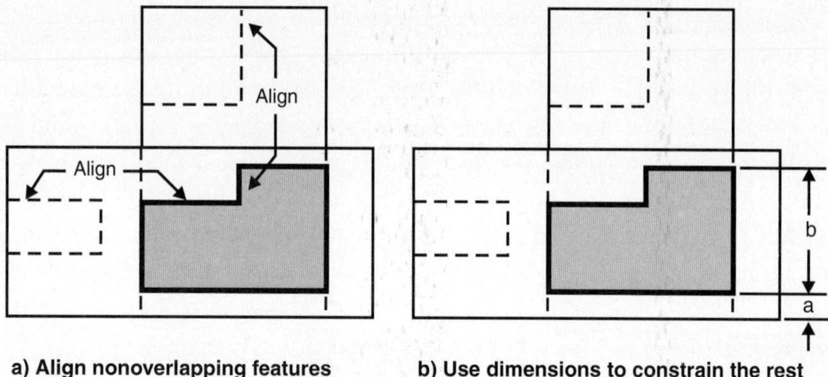

Figure 4.19 Aligning a feature to a nonoverlapping edge.

When an alignment is successful, an – ALIGNED – message is provided. If the alignment was unsuccessful, an "Entities cannot be aligned" message occurs. There is no other indication on the sketcher that an alignment is in place.

4.7.3 Breaking Alignments

You can break alignments using the Unalign menu item. This requires that you select the new item that you have aligned. Once selected, any existing alignment will be removed. A "Section entity has been unaligned" message is provided indicating success. If no alignment was in place for the new item, the unalign operation would be unsuccessful and the message "The entity or vertex is not aligned—cannot unalign" is provided.

You can align endpoints as well as lines and arcs. Take care when aligning a line. A line has two endpoints, and aligning the line itself is not the same as aligning one of the endpoints. Aligning the line automatically includes the alignment of endpoints; however, aligning an endpoint does not necessarily align the entire line.

4.8 Dimensioning

Thus far we have sketched and aligned the section. It is now time for dimensions. You should not have provided any dimensions until this point. This is very important because the sketcher will make assumptions about your section based on your sketch and alignments. Providing dimensions before alignments could affect the sketcher's assumptions.

There are two aspects to dimensions that we will consider. First, we need to sufficiently dimension the feature such that the feature can be added to the part. Second, we need to fulfill our design intent with the dimensions. Dimensions create parent-child relationships. The references that are chosen for the dimensions affect the design and manufacturing of the part. Consider the example part in Figure 4.20(a). The height of this part is sufficiently dimensioned. Similarly, the same part is sufficiently dimensioned in Figure 4.20(b). Both parts can be built but there are differences. One difference is in tolerances. The tolerances in Figure 4.20(a) would add together producing a greater tolerance for the total height of the part. In Figure 4.20(b), the tolerance of the total height is limited to one tolerance. However, the individual step height of the top-most stair would be subject to additive tolerances. There is no right or wrong answer. Perhaps one better satisfies your design intent.

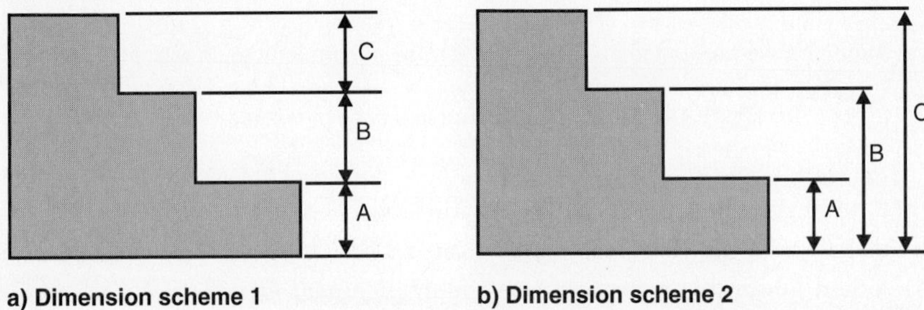

Figure 4.20   Aligning a feature.

More importantly, consider what happens if you change the height of the second stair in Figure 4.20(a). The total height of the part would also change. This would not be the case in Figure 4.20(b) where changing the height of the second stair would leave the total height unchanged but would affect the height of the top stair.

This issue of referencing is very important in parametric solid modeling. One would like to compartmentalize the dimensions of a part such that changing a feature in one place does not affect a feature in another place. Good dimensioning practice can reduce the cross-feature errors. This is a dangerous aspect of design. If someone changes a dimension on a feature on one side of a part, they might not take the time to look at the other side of the part. Perhaps, inadvertently, a feature in another area of the part referenced an edge that the change affected. This original change could ripple through the design, creating havoc.

> **TIP:** You can check all references made by a feature using the >Info >Parent >Child >References as discussed in the last chapter.

Dimensions are added to a sketch using the Dimension menu item in Sketcher. From Dimension, you are presented with the standard pick menu and requested to select the items that you desire to dimension. There are two aspects to creating dimensions. The first is the mechanics of placing the dimensions onto the sketch;

the second is understanding which dimensional references to use. This chapter will deal specifically with the mechanics of placing dimensions.

There are a number of ways to create dimensions. I will discuss some of these, and give you an opportunity to practice using them in the next tutorial.

You select the entities to be dimensioned with the left mouse button. You place dimensions with the middle mouse button. This is a two or three step process. First, select the item that you want to dimension, and second, place the dimension. You can place the dimension near the line or far from the line depending on the space available in your sketch.

4.8.1 Dimension the Length of a Line

You can dimension the length of a line. Perhaps the line is the width of a rectangle or a side of a triangle. First, mLb on the line to be dimensioned. Next, move the mouse to the position where you want to place the actual dimension. When in position, mMb click to place the dimension. Several examples are shown in Figure 4.21(a) with the resultant dimensions shown in Figure 4.21(b). Note there is one mLb to pick the line and a second mLb to place the dimension.

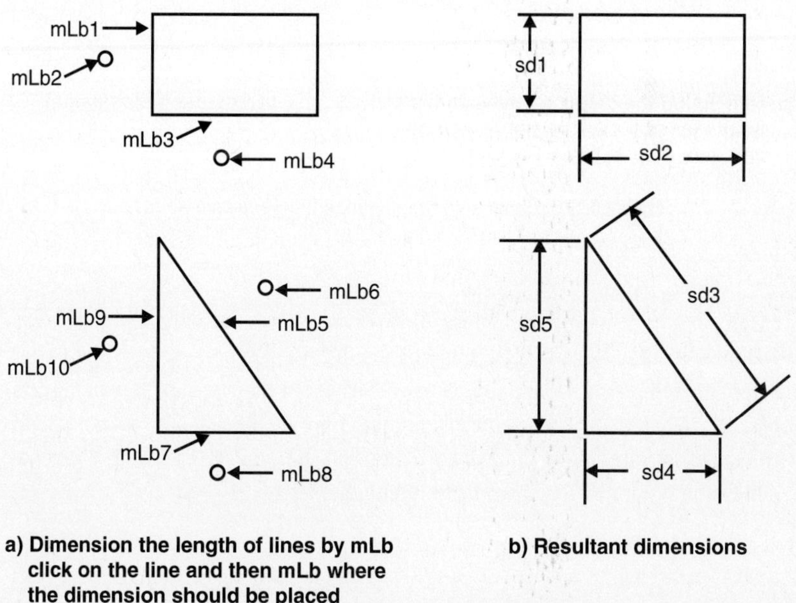

a) Dimension the length of lines by mLb click on the line and then mLb where the dimension should be placed

b) Resultant dimensions

Figure 4.21 Dimension the length of a line.

4.8.2   Dimension the Distance between Two Points

You can dimension the distance between two points. Perhaps you want the distance between two lines or the distance between an arc's center point and a line. You could find the distance between the end points of a line. This would give you the same result as dimensioning the line directly. Several examples are shown in Figure 4.22(a), with the resultant dimensions shown in Figure 4.22(b). Note there are two mLbs for every dimension to pick the points and an mMb to place the dimension.

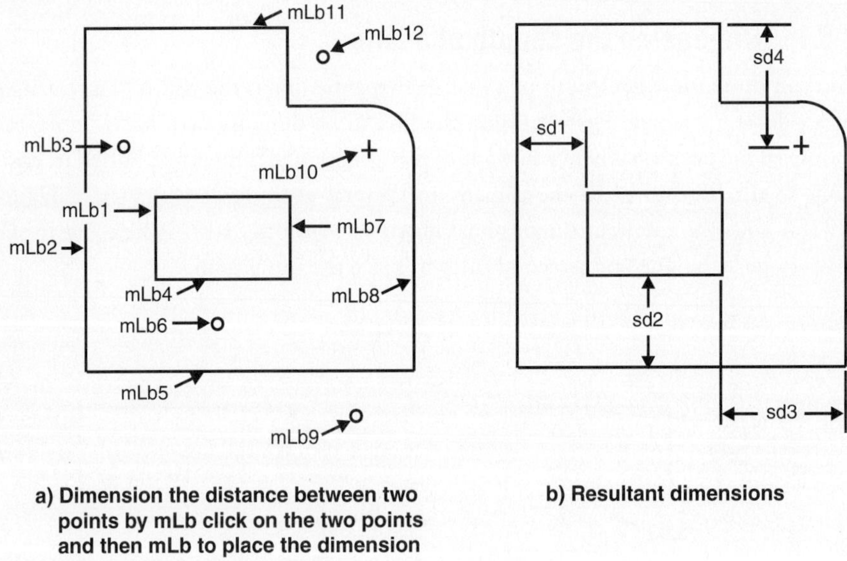

a) Dimension the distance between two points by mLb click on the two points and then mLb to place the dimension

b) Resultant dimensions

Figure 4.22   Dimension the distance between two points.

NOTE: At times, the dimensioning software might require additional input. You will have to keep a watchful eye on the menus. If the system seems hung after selecting two points for a measurement, look at the menus. A submenu may be present requesting further information about the dimension. You would select Horizontal if you want a horizontal dimension, Vertical if you want a vertical dimension or length, if you want the length of a line.

4.8.3   Dimension an Angle between Two Lines

Angular dimensions indicate the number of degrees of an angle between two lines. Make an angular dimension by mLb clicking on the two lines and then mMb clicking to place the dimension. A triangle is dimensioned in Figure 4.23(a). Note there are three picks: two for the lines and one to place the dimension. The result is shown in Figure 4.23(b).

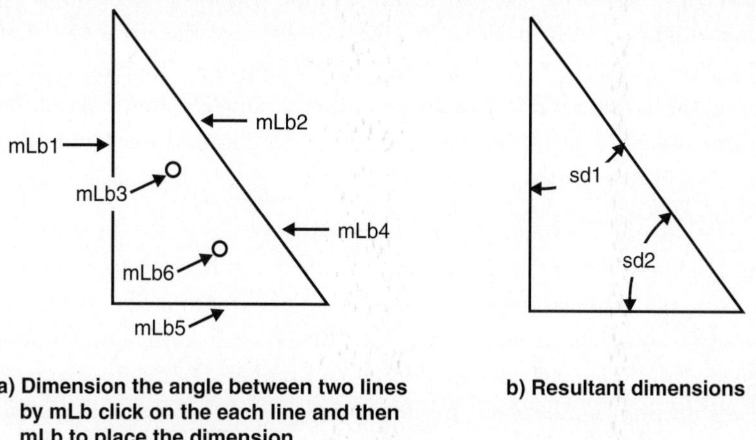

a) Dimension the angle between two lines by mLb click on the each line and then mLb to place the dimension

b) Resultant dimensions

Figure 4.23   Dimension an angle between two lines.

4.8.4   Dimension a Radius or Diameter

You can dimension the radius or diameter of an arc or circle by mLb clicking on the arc or circle and then moving the mouse to the desired position for the dimension before mMb clicking again. If you single click on the arc or circle, the dimension will be a radius. If you double click on the arc or circle, the dimension will be a diameter. Some examples are shown in Figure 4.24.

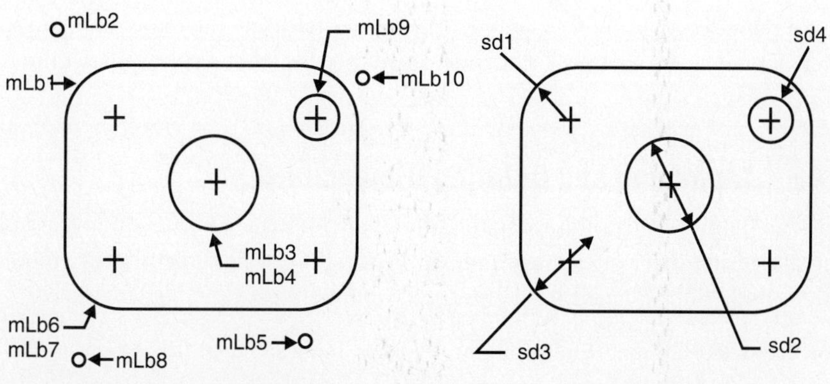

a) Dimension a radius or diameter by single or double mLb clicking on the arc or circle and then mLb to position the dimension

b) Resultant dimensions

Figure 4.24   Dimension a radius or diameter.

4.8.5   Dimensions and Values

The sketching plane has a default scaling. That is, every grid mark represents a certain number of units. The scale will change as you build your part. For example, a first base feature has only the datum planes with which to work. At no point has any indication been made as to the actual size of the part. At default, the numbers are quite large. A typical rectangle filling the sketching plane on the screen might be 400 by 200. If you draw a first rectangle onto the sketching plane and dimension it 4 by 2, the sketcher scale will change to accommodate your wishes. It will scale down the size of each grid mark to make a drawing surface applicable to your part.

In the last three figures, notice that the dimensions have the value sdN where N = an incrementing number as opposed to actual values like 22.4, or 135.0. These sdNs are symbolic dimensions used by Sketcher until actual numbers are provided. You do not have to provide actual numbers. You can regenerate without ever putting numbers on the dimensions. The sketcher will use whatever scale factor is currently active, and substitute values in the place of the symbols according to its scale factor. Alternately, you can modify the dimension and provide a value in the place of the symbol. Each dimension has a symbolic value and a dimensional value. When you assign a dimensional value to a dimension or when you perform a regeneration, the dimensional values are displayed. The symbolic values are still present and you will see how to use these to create relations in Chapter 11.

It is very convenient to keep symbols around as long as possible. Get your sketch to regenerate successfully before entering all the actual values. You might find out that there is a reference that is wrong or an assumption has been made that you do not desire. In these cases, you might have to delete the dimension and start over. This would waste all the time spent placing the actual values onto the dimensions.

4.8.6   Modifying and Deleting Dimensions

You can modify dimensions using the Modify menu item. Choose Modify and pick the dimension that you want to modify. Pick right on the dimensional symbol or value. You will be queried in the message window to provide the new value.

You can delete a dimension through the Delete Item menu choice. Selecting Delete brings up the pick submenu anticipating that you will want to delete more than one item. Select all desired dimensions and click Done Sel or alternately use the mMb to delete all selected items. After a regeneration, Sketcher automatically puts you in the Modify mode.

AY axis. mLb click on the left side of the rectangle followed by an mLb click on the AY axis. Move the mouse up and mMb click to set the dimension. The item in the lower right quadrant needs its top edge dimensioned to the AX axis. The triangle needs its bottom-right vertex aligned to the AY axis and its top vertex dimensioned to the AX axis. Your dimensions should look like those in Figure 4.26(b).

Notice that my "sd" numbers might not be the same as yours. Do not worry about discrepancies. Just get each dimension that is seen in Figure 4.26(b) in place. Regenerate the part. Oops! We get an error. We did not need the vertical most measure on the bottom-right item. In Figure 4.26(b), this is sd13. The Sketcher anticipated that you want to delete this item so it has selected the Delete menu item. You can mLb click right on the sd13 dimension to select it, and then mMb to accept the deletion. Regenerate again and you should get success. You are done in Sketcher so click Done and Preview to see the resultant protrusions. Type F1 to see the default view and end with OK. The part should look like Figure 4.26(c). Save this part as tut3-4b.

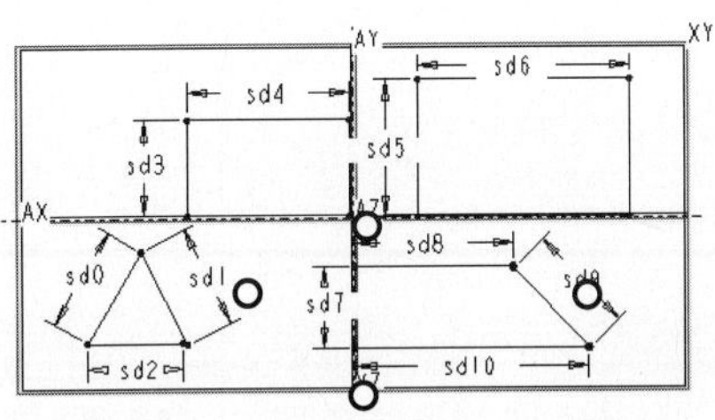

a) First place length dimenions: mLb click once on line, move off a bit, mLb to place dimension

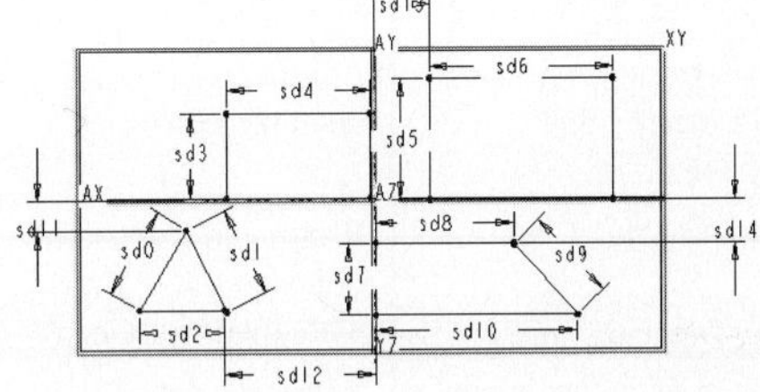

b) Second place reference dimensions: mLb click on edge of sketch, then mLb on axis reference, move mouse a bit and mLb to place dimension

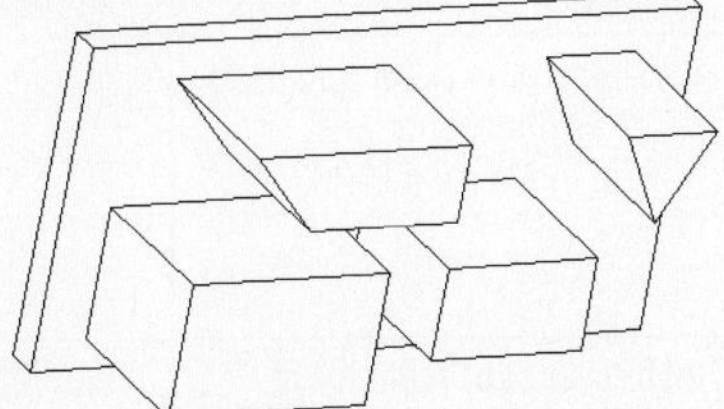

c) Resultant part: note that we have rotated from default view about normal axis to see this side

O = Align Point: double click to align new line with old axis

Figure 4.26   Illustrations associated with Tutorial 4.5, part 2.

Tutorial 4.5 Dimensioning Lines

Files opened: Tut4-5a.prt,   **Files saved:** Tut4-5b.prt
Tut4-3lines.sec

Step	Action	Description	Further Actions	Result
1	Click PT/Modeler Icon	Run PT/Modeler		After some time, PT/Modeler on screen
2	>Mode >Misc >Show Dir	Show current directory		Message similar to "Directory searched is c:\ptc\ptprod\bin"
3	>Change Dir	Change the current directory	Type **c:\proe\tutorial\ chapter_4**	
4	>Done-Return	Leave Misc menu		Misc menu removed
5	>Mode >Part >Retrieve	Read a part	Type **tut4-5a**	A rectangular block is displayed
6	>Environment	Set up the environment	Set up checks as seen in Table T4.5 Column Step 6	
7	>Done-Return			
8	Type F1	Go to default view		
9	View >Orientation | Angles | Vertical	Flip around the view to see the back face in Fig. 4.25(a)	Type **180** then >Done/Accept	
10	>Feature >Protrusion | Extrude | Solid | Done	Create an extruded solid protrusion		
11	>One Side | Done	Protrusion will extend one side out of the sketching plane		
12	Pick XY datum plane for sketching plane	Select XY datum in Fig. 4.25(a)	Okay to protrusion direction	Pick face for protrusion; this is the sketching plane
13	>Bottom	Pick Bottom face for Bottom reference to sketching plane	Pick Bottom face in Fig. 4.25(b)	Go into sketcher >Mode
14	>Sec. Tools >Place Section	Bring in the section saved from Tutorial 4.3	Type **tut4-3lines** or type **?** to get a list	Child window appears as in Figure 4.25(c)
15	Type **Enter** to accept 0.0 rotation angle or Type **0**	No rotation desired	Click on zoom point and drag point as instructed and shown in Figure 4.25(c)	
16	Type **Enter** to accept 1.0 scale or Type **1**	One-to-one scale desired		
17	Move mouse to below intersection of AX, AY axis	Position read sketch onto sketching plane in Fig. 4.25(d)	mLb to accept placement	Sketch locked down onto sketching plane

Tutorial 4.5 Dimensioning Lines (continued)

Step	Action	Description	Further Actions	Result
18	>Align	Align the four edges to datum planes in Fig. 4.26(a)	mLb twice on the edges in Fig. 4.26(a) selecting >Align between each set to assure that the "Aligned" message is not left over from a previous alignment	
19	>Dimension	Place all line length dimensions in Fig. 4.26(a)	mLb click to select line and mMb to position dimension on sd3 through sd12	Line lengths dimensioned
20	>Dimension	Place all reference dimensions in Fig. 4.26(b)	mLb click to select line, mLb to select reference, and mMb to position dimension; do for sd13 through sd17	Line references dimensioned
21	>Regenerate	Build the sketch		Error message; sd13 indicated as EXTRA DIMENSION
22	>Delete	Delete sd13	mLb on sd13 to select, mMb to accept sd13 for deletion	Sd13 deleted
23	>Regenerate	Build the sketch		Regeneration successful
24	>Done	Done with Sketcher		
25	>Blind | Done	Respond to request for protrusion length	Type **100**	
26	Click Preview	Preview the part	Type **F1** for default view then click OK to accept	
27	>File >Save As	Save file	Type **Enter** to accept input, type **tut4-5b** to accept new part	File tut4-5b.prt saved
28	>QuitWindow			
29	>Exit	Exit program	Click Yes to confirm	PT/Modeler exited

Item	Step 6
Disp DtmPln	Checked
Spin Center	No
Disp Axes	Checked
Rendering	No hidden line

Table T4.5   Environment Settings

Tutorial 4.6 is very similar to Tutorial 4.5. Here, you will read in the same block part from Tutorials 4.3, and 4.4, and 4.5, access the front face as the sketching plane, read the sketch file saved in Tutorial 4.4, and place that sketch onto the part's front face. From here, you will align and dimension the curved-based features, regenerate the part, and view the result.

This time we are going to dimension the sketch that we drew in Tutorial 4.4. Open the part file and take care to select the proper face and Top reference as shown in Figure 4.27(a). Create a one-sided solid extruded protrusion to get into Sketcher as shown in Figure 4.27(b). At this point, use Place Section to read in a section. Type in the name of the desired section, tut4-3curves. You could type "?" to see all possible sections that were saved in the current directory. This brings up the section in a child window. We want to place this section onto our sketch. To do this we select 0.0 rotation, 1.0 scaling, and pick a drag and zoom point in the child window as shown in Figure 4.27(c). We now have control of the sketched entities that we read in. These entities follow the mouse as we move around our Sketcher window. Position the mouse such that the cursor is at the intersection of the AX and AY axis (center of Sketcher). Click the mouse left button to place the sketch at this location.

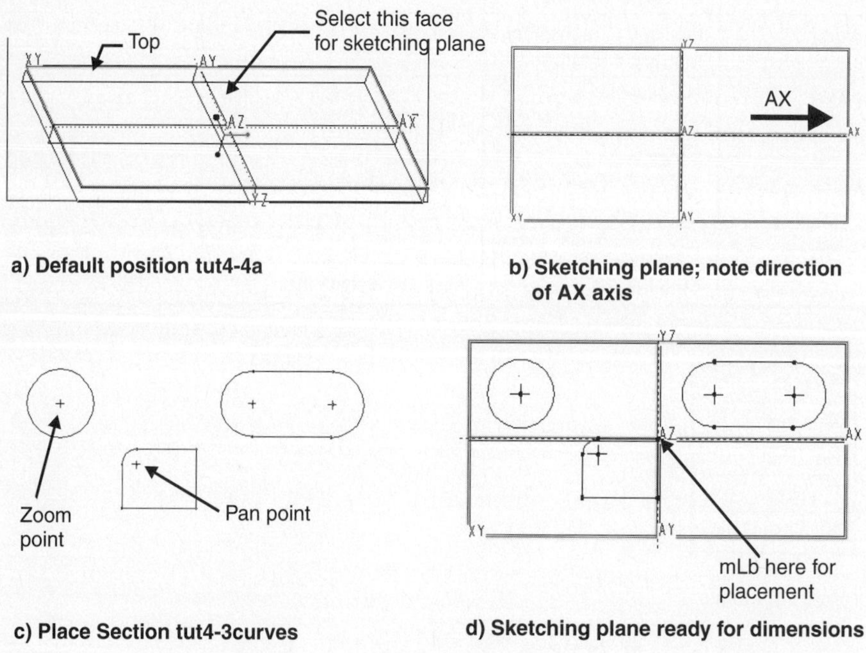

Figure 4.27   Illustrations associated with Tutorial 4.6, part 1.

Before we dimension, it is necessary to align whatever lines in the new feature that should be aligned. Select Align to align the two sides of the lower entity that overlaps the AX and AY axis as seen in Figure 4.28(a). We are ready to dimension these three items. Start by dimensioning the arcs and circles. Dimension the diameter of the circle. You do this by double mLb clicking on the circle to select a diameter measurement. Next, move off the circle to mMb click again thereby placing the dimension. Provide a radius dimension for each of the two round ends of the left-top item and the fillet of the lower item. mLb click once on the arc, move the mouse, and lastly, mMb click again to set the radius dimension.

Now, you will need to reference these items to the preexisting part. We want to reference to the AX and AY axis. The circle center point needs both a horizontal and vertical reference. Use the AX axis for the horizontal reference and the AY axis for the vertical reference. The rounded rectangle to the right also needs both a horizontal and vertical reference. I have chosen to provide a dimension between the centerpoints to constrain this distance. mLb click on each centerpoint; then mLB click in the center to set this dimension. mLb click on the left-center point, and mLb click on the AY axis to provide the horizontal reference dimension. mLb click on the right-center point, and mLb click on the AX axis to provide the vertical reference dimension. The lower figure needs some length dimensions so mLb click once on each of the three sides shown in Figure 4.28(b). Since it is already aligned, these dimensions will suffice.

Your dimensions should look like those in Figure 4.28(b). Once again, do not worry about any major discrepancies. Just get each dimension that is seen in Figure 4.28(b) in place. Regenerate the part and you should get success. You are done in Sketcher so click Done and Preview to see the resultant protrusions. Type F1 to see the default view and end with OK. The part should look like Figure 4.28(c). Save this part as tut3-4c.

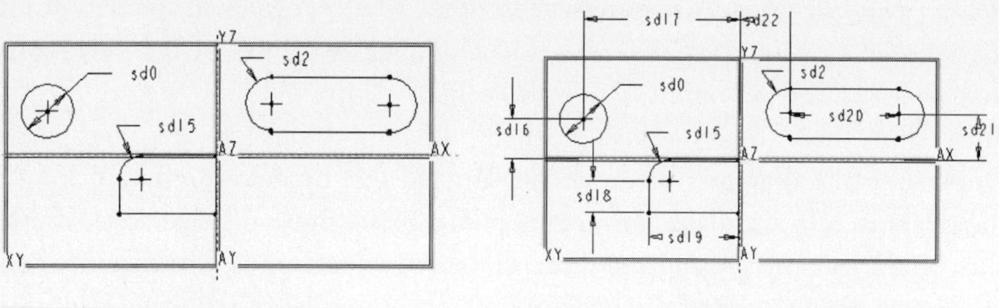

a) First dimension arcs   b) Second dimension references

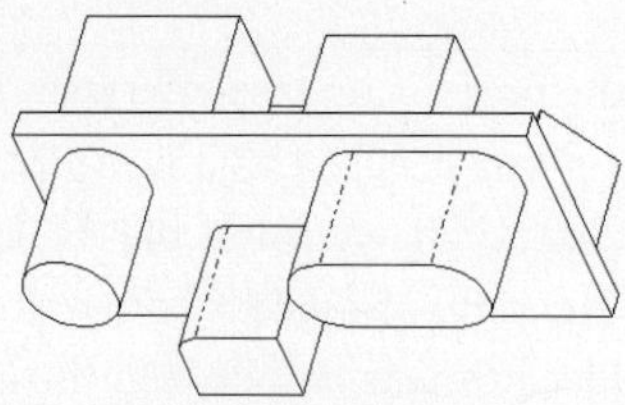

c) Resultant part

Figure 4.28   Illustrations associated with Tutorial 4.6, part 2.

Tutorial 4.6 Dimensioning Curves

Files opened: Tut4-6a.prt,   **Files saved:** Tut4-6b.prt
Tut4-4curves.sec

Step	Action	Description	Further Actions	Result
1	Click PT/Modeler Icon	Run PT/Modeler		After some time, PT/Modeler on screen
2	>Mode >Misc >Show Dir	Show current directory		Message similar to "Directory searched is c:\ptc\ptprod\bin"
3	>Change Dir	Change the current directory	Type **c:\proe\tutorial\chapter_4**	
4	>Done-Return	Leave Misc menu		Misc menu removed
5	>Mode >Part >Retrieve	Read a part	Type **tut4-6a**	A rectangular block is displayed with protrusions from Tutorial 4.5
6	>Environment	Set up the environment	Set up checks as seen in Table T4.6 Column Step 6	
7	>Done-Return			
8	Type F1	Go to default view		
9	>Feature >Protrusion | Extrude | Solid | Done	Create an extruded solid protrusion		
10	>One Side | Done	Protrusion will extend one side out of the sketching plane		
11	Pick XY datum plane for sketching plane	Select XY datum in Fig. 4.27(a)	Okay to protrusion direction	Pick face for protrusion; this is the sketching plane
12	>Top	Pick Top face for Top reference to sketching plane	Pick Top face in Fig. 4.27(a)	Go into Sketcher >Mode
13	>Sec Tools | Place Section	Bring in the section saved from Tutorial 4.3	Type **tut4-4curves** or type **?** to get a list	Child window appears as in Figure 4.27(c)
14	Type **Enter** to accept 0.0 rotation angle or type **0**	No rotation desired	Click on zoom point and drag point as instructed and shown in Figure 4.27(c)	
15	Type **Enter** to accept 1.0 scale or type **1**	One-to-one scale desired		
16	Move mouse to intersection of AX,AY axis	Position read sketch onto sketching plane in Fig. 4.27(d)	mLb to accept placement	Sketch locked down onto sketching plane
17	>Dimension	Dimension diameter on circle in Fig. 4.28(a)	mLb click twice to select circle for diameter dimension	Circle diameter dimensioned
18	>Dimension	Radius on arc in Fig. 4.28(a)	mLb click once to select arc for radius dimension on two arcs	Arc radius dimensioned

Tutorial 4.6 Dimensioning Curves (continued)

Step	Action	Description	Further Actions	Result
19	>Dimension	Place reference dimension in Fig. 4.28(b)	mLb click to select circle center, mLb click on AY, and mMb to horizontal position dimension for circle	Circle referenced horizontally
20	>Dimension	Place reference dimension in Fig. 4.28(b)	mLb click to select circle center, mLb click on AX, and mMb to vertical position dimension for circle	Circle referenced vertically
21	>Dimension	Dimension distance between center points on rounded rectangle in Fig. 4.28(b)	mLb click to select center of arc, mLb click to select center of other arc, mMb to position horizontal distance dimension, in response to message prompt click >Horizontal	Distance dimensioned
22	>Dimension	Reference dimension between left center point on rounded rectangle and AY axis in Fig. 4.28(b)	mLb click to select center of left arc, mLb click to select AY, mMb to position horizontal distance dimension	Distance dimensioned
23	>Dimension	Reference dimension between right center point on rounded rectangle and AX axis in Fig. 4.28(b)	mLb click to select center of right arc, mLb click to select AX, mMb to position vertical distance dimension	Distance dimensioned
24	>Dimension	Radius of corner of rectangle with one rounded corner	mLb click on radius then mMb near radius to place dimension	
25	>Dimension	Length and width of rectangle with one rounded edge	mLb click on horizontal line then mMb near horizontal line, mLb click on vertical line, mMb near vertical line	
26	>Regenerate	Build the sketch		Regeneration Error, one of the radii of the rounded end rectangle indicated as EXTRA DIMENSION
27	>Delete	Delete the highlighted dimension	mLb on highlighted dimension, mMb to accept dimension for deletion	
28	>Regenerate	Build the sketch		Regeneration successful
29	>Done	Done with Sketcher		
30	>Blind | Done	Respond to request for protrusion length	Type **100**	
31	Click Preview	Preview the part	Type **F1** for default view then click OK to accept	

Tutorial 4.6 Dimensioning Curves (continued)

Step	Action	Description	Further Actions	Result
32	>File >Save As	Save file	Type **Enter** to accept input, type **tut4-6b** to accept new part	File tut4-6b.prt saved
33	>QuitWindow			
34	>Exit	Exit program	Click Yes to confirm	PT/Modeler exited

Item	Step 6
Disp DtmPln	Checked
Spin Center	No
Disp Axes	Checked
Rendering	No hidden line

Table T4.6   Environment Settings

4.9   Regenerating

Once you have sketched, aligned, and dimensioned the section, you are ready for regeneration. Once you click Regenerate from the Sketcher menu, PT/Modeler will use all of the dimensions that you have provided and attempt to generate the fully constrained sketch. If you have fully constrained the sketch, you will be rewarded with a "Regeneration Successful" message. If the regeneration was not successful, you will get a rather cryptic message such as "Locate section with respect to part." In this case, the offending lines or points will be highlighted with a red marker, affectionately called the "red measles." This means that the part is not sufficiently constrained. You must take action. Perhaps a line, radius, or point are not dimensioned or not referenced to some preexisting item.

> **TIP:** Never leave the sketcher until a section regenerates thinking that you will complete the feature successfully.

4.9.1   A First Look at Troubleshooting Regeneration

Alternatively, you could get the message, "EXTRA DIMENSION FOUND" indicating just that. It will highlight what it thinks is the offending extra dimension in red. This is only its guess at what is "extra." You should look closely at your feature and its dimensions to determine why there is an extra dimension. Perhaps the assumptions have aligned the item in some way that makes the dimension unnecessary. Your intent might have been to use the dimension as opposed to the assumptive alignment. The alignment might not have been expected. In this case you will have to find the alignment and break it.

The topic of troubleshooting regeneration is a big one. It is discussed more fully in Chapter 9. You should be able to work out the problems that you encounter until then by paying close attention to the tutorial instructions.

> **TIP:** Regeneration is meant to be an iterative process. Build your feature a little at a time. Take the regeneration of a complicated feature in steps. Get a portion of a complex feature to regenerate before building the next portion of a feature. This makes troubleshooting far easier.

Two other error messages occasionally show up. These have to do with segments being too small or having zero length. What happens if, while drawing a line chain, you inadvertently double click on a point? A very small line segment would be created. During regeneration, this line segment might be too small for Sketcher to handle. It would type the "Segment too small" or the "Zero length segment" message in the Message window. You delete this segment or take some other action to fix the problem. You can zoom in and hunt this segment down or do a Select Many from the Delete menu item to create a rectangular region and see if the small bugger shows up highlighted as a red dot.

4.10   **The Sketcher Assumptions**

The sketcher earns its pay when you click Regenerate. At that time it has to attempt to fully constrain the section sketch. First, it will look at the alignments and dimensions that you have placed on the section. If it can fully constrain the part using these dimensions alone, it will successfully regenerate. If, on the other hand, it cannot fully constrain the section, it will do its best to understand your design intent. During its attempt to constrain, it will build a list of all of the elements in your sketch that it could not constrain. These might be an arc with no radius dimension, a line with no length, or a rectangle that has no horizontal reference. Its goal is to find a dimension or reference to each one of the items in its to-do list. In its process of trying to accomplish this noble goal, it will attempt to figure out your design intent.

Perhaps a line that has no length is one of the horizontal lines in a rectangle and the other horizontal line of that rectangle does have a length dimension. The sketcher can figure this one out easily. Perhaps the arc that has no radius is one of the four arcs that round the corner in a rectangle. Maybe one of the other three arcs has a dimension and all of the arcs are drawn with nearly the same radius. In this case, the sketcher would assume that you wanted all four arcs to be the same radius, and it would check that arc right off of its to-do list.

> **NOTE:** Sketcher will only align to entities that you have referenced in some way. For example, suppose an edge in the preexisting geometry lies directly beneath an edge in the newly sketched geometry. Sketcher will NOT align to this preexisting edge unless you direct it to do so.

Perhaps a top of a rectangle has no reference with respect to the preexisting part. Sketcher says, "No way, send an error message." When the to-do list is done, the user is given back control of the sketcher. It is up to the user to check the part to make sure that any assumptions that the sketcher might have made were correct. It is also up to the user to fix any problems that the sketcher could not fix.

4.10.1 Assumptions Are View-Centric

I know that you are just dying to ask the very pertinent question "How does Sketcher know if two lines are close enough to be considered coplanar?" The sketcher has a threshold meter. The neat thing about the sketcher is that it realizes that you are using a mouse on a screen to draw. You have had three cups of coffee and your mouse hand is shaking. That vertical line has a bit of angle to it. It also appreciates that you have better things to do with your time than sit there and try and draw that perfect vertical line. It wants to cut you some slack, but at the same time it knows that if it assumes too much, there are going to be problems.

The compromise solution is a good one. The sketcher looks at the sketched view to determine the decision threshold. This is called *view-centric*. If a vertical line varies from vertical by one or two pixels from the bottom to the top, it will likely assume "this is a vertical line." Now it would not matter if you were zoomed way in and the difference amounted to .001 microns or if you were zoomed way out and the difference amounted to 150 light years. It is the view that matters. How many pixels off?

One consequence of this view-centric philosophy is that different results occur based on your zoom factor. Suppose a line is off-vertical by a few pixels and regeneration fails to detect it as a vertical line. One solution is to zoom out. The process of zooming out will tend to straighten up the line. Regenerating at this zoomed out view will likely result in Sketcher assuming the line is vertical. This is an important concept, but please do not overuse this technique. A good design should not need it. Each time you zoom in or out, you could be affecting other assumptions in other areas of your section. This can be potentially dangerous.

> **TIP:** Pick a zoom factor that you are comfortable using. Perform all of your regenerations near to this zoomed out level. This will avoid inconsistent regeneration results.

4.10.2 Sketcher Assumptions

I have organized the sketcher assumptions into the ten assumptions provided in Table 4.1. The sketcher will use these assumptions in an attempt to constrain entities in a section that have not been specifically dimensioned or aligned. There are line assumptions, arc and circle assumptions, point assumptions, and centerline assumptions. While trying to constrain the section, Sketcher will look at all of the unresolved entities in its to-do list and check out each one against these assumptions. If it concludes that an assumption can be successfully deduced, such that the error is beneath a threshold, it will accept the assumption and take action. It will constrain, dimension, or modify the entity. Sketcher will then move on to the next unresolved item in its list.

Assumption	Description
Line Related Assumptions	
Horizontal and vertical lines	A line that is nearly horizontal or vertical will be converted to horizontal or vertical.
Parallel and perpendicular lines	A line that is nearly parallel and perpendicular to another sketched entity will be converted to parallel and perpendicular with respect to that other entity.
Collinearity	A line that is nearly collinear with another line will be made collinear.
Equal segment lengths	A line that has nearly the same length as another line will be assigned the length of the other line.
Arc and Circle Related Assumptions	
Equal radius/diameter	An arc that has nearly the same radius/diameter as another arc will be assigned the radius/diameter of the other arc. The same holds true for circles.
90, 180, and 270 degree arcs	If an arc is near 90, 180, or 270 degrees it will be set to 90, 180 or 270 degrees.
Centers lying on same horizontal or vertical	The centerline of an arc or circle that lies on nearly the same horizontal or vertical line as the centerline of another arc or circle will be set to that other arc or circle's centerline.
Tangency	An entity that is nearly tangent to the end of an arc will be set to be tangent to the end of that arc.
Point Related Assumptions	
Points lying on other entities	A point that lies near another entity will be set to lie on that entity.
Centerline Related Assumptions	
Symmetry	An entity that is drawn nearly symmetric about a centerline will become symmetric.

Table 4.1   Sketcher Assumptions

It is probably a good idea to look at some examples. You can use the sketcher assumptions to your advantage. However, use the sketcher drawing tools to their fullest extent before relying on the assumptions to bail you out. For example, if you need to connect an arc and a line such that the line is tangent, use the tangent arc or Tangent Line drawing command. This will create a perfect and dependable tangent junction. The fewer assumptions that the sketcher makes, the better. If you need to draw a line that is parallel or perpendicular to another line, use the Parallel or Perpendicular line drawing menu selections when you draw the line in the first place. It is faster to go to the menu than it is to try and estimate the correct orientation and then later find out that Sketcher does not agree with your estimate.

Sketcher cuts you some slack. Realize, however, that this is no excuse for getting sloppy. If you need a horizontal line, use the grid markings and do your best to get it horizontal. You do not have to be perfect, but get it close.

4.10.3 Working around the Assumptions

There will be times when you know that your intent will be misunderstood. In some cases, you can break an assumption. For example, you can easily break a line length assumption. Suppose the length of one line is assumed to be the same as the length of another line. You can resize the first line by providing a dimension or by modifying the sketched line. This will break the assumption. Other assumptions are not so simple to break. If a line is drawn nearly horizontal (or vertical) and it is assumed to be horizontal (or vertical) during a regeneration, it cannot be changed.

You can disable assumptions using the >Constraints>Disable menu command from within Sketcher. This is discussed in Section 9.10. You could enter Redefine to delete the line and redraw it. Alternatively, if you catch it, you can un-regenerate and change your design.

4.10.4 Exaggerating

In most places you should avoid exaggerating. The sketcher is not such a place. If you want a line to have a two-degree angle from vertical you should exaggerate the angle in the sketch. Draw the line such that it has a much larger angle. You might provide it with an angular dimension, say 10 degrees. After a successful regeneration, go back and change the angle to two degrees. This will keep Sketcher from trying to make it vertical.

Similarly, if you want two lines to have different but similar sizes, exaggerate the difference in the sketch. You can dimension them or regenerate and then dimension them to their similar sizes. Follow the same technique if you want two lines not to be coplanar or a line and an arc not to be tangent. Exaggerate, regenerate, and re-dimension. That is your ticket.

4.11 **Sketcher Indicators**

Sketcher provides symbolic notation on sketches after regeneration. These symbols indicate some of the assumptions that Sketcher made. A typical sketcher screen after regeneration is shown in Figure 4.29. Note the legend in this figure. You can readily see the assumptions made by Sketcher. It has assumed coplanar lines and that there are only two distinct dimensions.

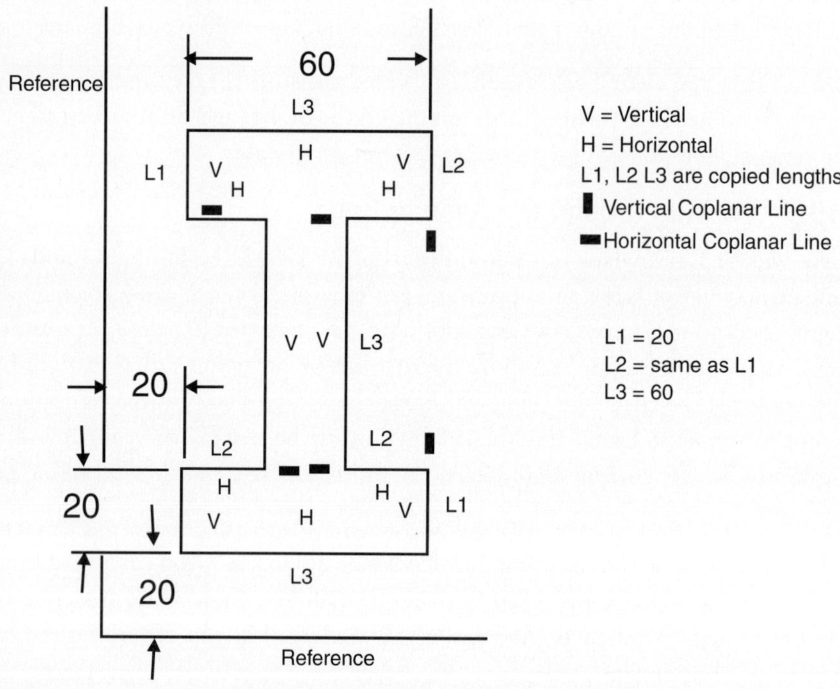

Figure 4.29   Sketcher assumption notations.

4.12 **Sketching in 3D**

Up until this point, we have seen the part in a two-dimensional view while in Sketcher. This is not a restriction. You can Control Drag the mouse or use any of the View controls to place the part in a three-dimensional view. This can be very useful when you need to reorient yourself. Sometimes the parts can be complex and difficult to visualize from a 2D perspective. This is seen in Figure 4.30(a). Sketcher is in a 2D orientation looking right at the sketching plane, but where is the sketching plane? Rotating the part slightly, as seen in Figure 4.30(b), the sketch becomes apparent. You can continue sketching when in 3D mode.

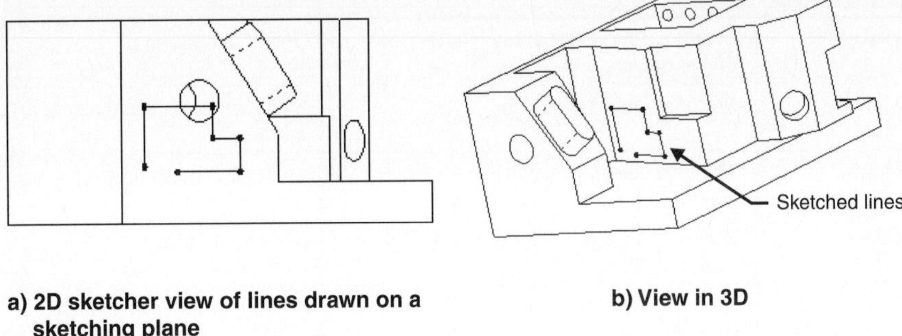

a) 2D sketcher view of lines drawn on a sketching plane

b) View in 3D

Figure 4.30   Sketcher 2D and 3D modes.

When in a 3D view, you can easily return to the 2D sketch view by selecting >Sketch View. The view when entering the sketcher is determined by a check box called SketStart2d in the Environment menu. When checked, Sketcher starts in 2D mode always with the sketching plane parallel with the screen. When unchecked, Sketcher does not change the view of the part. That is, the view is unchanged.

4.13   The Sketcher Grid

You can manipulate the grid in sketcher using the Section Tools, accessed by >Sec Tools. The Section Tools menu is shown in Figure 4.31. Selecting >Grid On/Off toggles the visual state of the grid. You can also change the origin, spacing, and angle of the grid from this menu.

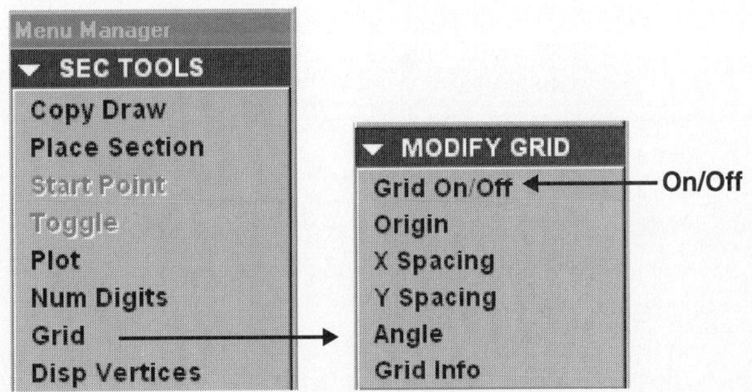

Figure 4.31   Turning on and off the sketcher grid.

4.14   Geometric Operators

There are several drawing tools that can be accessed through the >Geometry Oper item. The menu is shown in Figure 4.32 along with a description of several of the commands. Table 4.2 briefly describes each operation.

Operator	Description	Technique
Intersect	Create a new vertex at the intersection of two objects	Select the two lines
Mirror	Mirror object about a line	Select mirror line and object to mirror
Move	Move an object from one location to another	Select object to move
Trim	Connect two objects at their extended intersection	Select both objects
Divide	Divide an object into two at specified location	Click where break should occur

Table 4.2 Geometric Operators

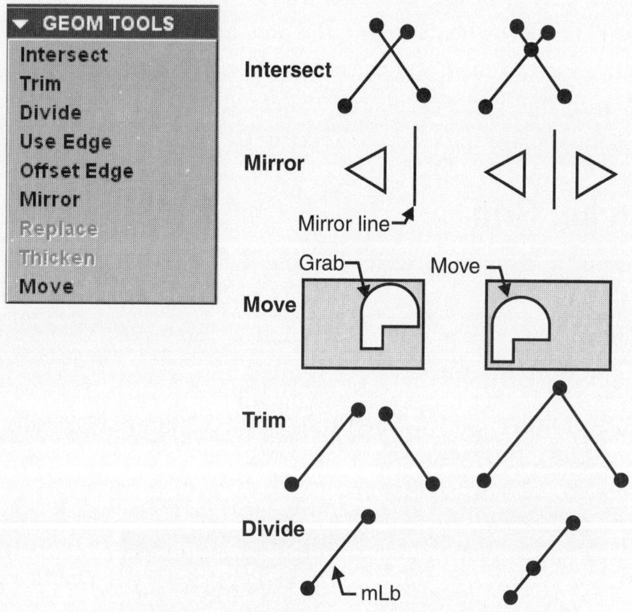

Figure 4.32 Geometric Operators.

The Basics of Drawings

Drawings provide a method of hardcopy for your designs. Unlike a CAD system, you are not meant to design your parts while making your drawings. Rather, you design your parts using solid modeling inside the Part mode. When the part is designed, and ready to be documented, you enter the Drawing mode. A Drawing can be thought of as a type of view used to display the part or assembly onto paper. Multiple views can be placed onto the same drawing. Drawings can import views directly from the Part mode. Thus, you can utilize all the techniques regarding the creation of views from Chapter 2.

Drawings also provide a set of new views including projection, sectioned, and detailed views. You can build full, half, broken, or partial views. Sectioned views can use a wide variety of cross sections. You can incorporate scaling and a different view of a part into your drawings.

You can select from a variety of standard-size paper formats with automatic border and title block. You can document your drawings with notes and annotations. Actual dimensions from the part can be incorporated right into notes. A powerful table editor allows you to build tables that can be used for hole charts, bill of materials, or to document other appropriate items in your part.

No drawing would be complete without dimensions. The great news is that you do not have to add any dimensions. You already completely dimensioned your part. All you have to do is enable them and, voilà, they are present on your drawing. You, of course, will want to dress them up a bit to best fit the drawing's intent. Sophisticated tools let you move dimensions around a view or between views.

Lastly, you can read, write, and modify drawings as you would expect.

5.1   Drawing Files

During the creation phase of a drawing, you will be asked to provide a drawing name. Drawings append the (.DRW) extension onto the file name. Each drawing has a sheet size or a drawing format. You save drawing files in the same way that you saved part and sketch files. Use either Save or SaveAs from the File menu.

Remember, if you use SaveAs it is necessary to first enter the drawing name that you want to save (typically the active drawing. Only then do you provide the new name for the drawing. I stress new name because you cannot overwrite a file with SaveAs. Recall, if you are in drawing FIRST_FILE.DRW and you save it using SaveAs to SECOND_FILE.DRW, you are still working on the FIRST_FILE.DRW drawing. If you make modifications and Save, the modifications are saved to FIRST_FILE.DRW and not to SECOND_FILE.DRW. Further, you cannot then do a SaveAs providing the name SECOND_FILE.DRW since this file already exists! The proper approach is to perform the SaveAs to SECOND_FILE.DRW, use the File>Erase menu to erase the FIRST_FILE.DRW from memory, and then Drawing >Retrieve to read SECOND_FILE.DRW. At this time, FIRST_FILE.DRW is safely put away onto disk and out of memory. We are working exclusively in SECOND_FILE.DRW.

> **TIP:** Name the drawing file with a similar name as the part file. This will make file management easier.

5.2   Drawing Windows and Part Windows

Both drawings and parts can reside in separate windows on the same screen. You can have a part in the main drawing window and add a drawing into a child window. Alternately, you can start with a drawing in the main window and open a part into a child window. You can then use ChangeWindow to switch between the two. This is quite useful, as you will see in Tutorial 1.1. It is very easy to change the view of a drawing while in the Part Mode. It is not so easy in the Drawing Mode. Consequently, you will often want to switch to the Part Mode window to change the view. This new view can then be named and imported into the drawing. This is a fast and effective way to create views for your drawings.

Multiple windows can be opened at the same time. You might have two different parts that you want to be manipulating while you are creating the drawing. Alternately, you could have different views of a part in separate windows while working on a drawing.

5.3   Scale Factors

Drawings are all made to scale. Consequently, each view in a drawing has a scale factor. Each drawing has a scale factor as indicated in a note at the bottom of the drawing. When a new view is created, you can select to enter a scale factor (detail Views require scale factors). If no additional scale factor is entered, the scale factor of the drawing is used as the scale factor of the view.

5.4   Creating a Drawing

You access the Drawing Mode through the Main menu as shown in Figure 5.1(a). Once selected, the Drawing submenu is displayed providing you with the options to create a new drawing or retrieve an existing drawing. Figure 5.1 provides the look at the Main drawing menus.

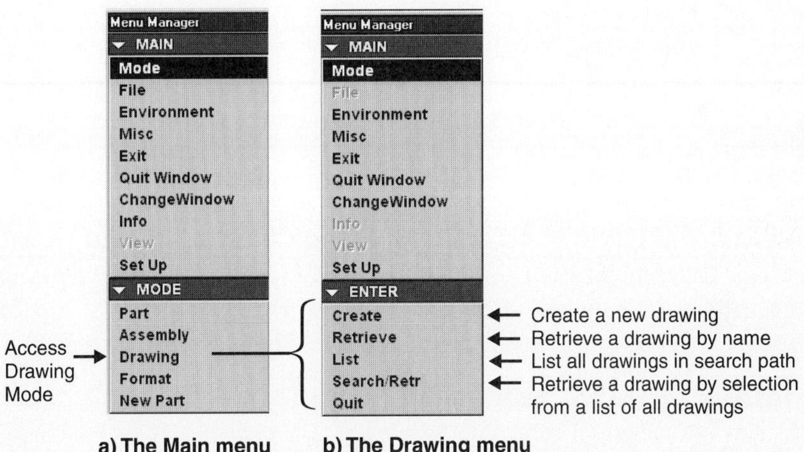

Figure 5.1   Main and Drawing menus.

5.5   Drawing Formats and Sizes

Drawings can be oriented in a Portrait or Landscape mode. Portrait mode drawings are taller than wide, and landscape mode drawings are wider than they are tall. Once the orientation is set, you can select from one of the standard drawing sizes available in a menu. Alternately, you could select to provide your own drawing size using the >Variable option. The Drawing Format menu is displayed in Figure 5.2.

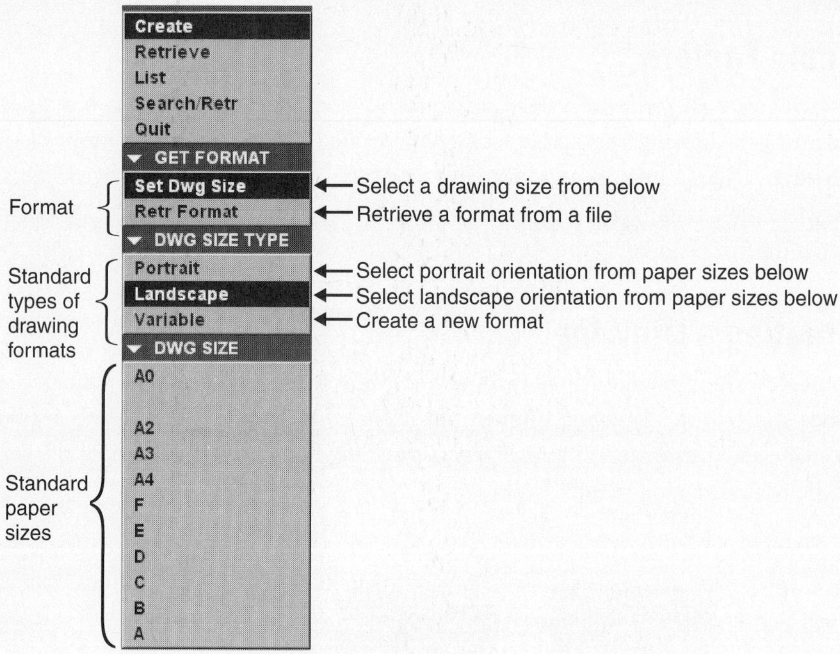

Figure 5.2   Drawing Format menu.

The format of the drawing can be changed later if you want a bigger or smaller page. This is accomplished by using the Sheets >DwgFormat >Add/Replace menu item. Changing the format is discussed later in this chapter.

5.6   Deleting, Erasing, and Resuming Views

You will undoubtedly create views that you don't want or that you just want to get off of the page for a while. You can use the Delete menu item to delete a view. This completely removes the view and any reference to it. Once deleted, it is gone. There is no undelete. On the other hand, you can erase a view using the Erase menu item. Erased views are simply hidden views. You can keep them hidden or bring them back to life using the Resume menu item. Perhaps the view is cluttering the drawing at this time and you want to get rid of it temporarily. Perhaps the view is for your reference and it is never intended to be displayed with the actual production drawings.

5.7 Moving Views

You will be placing views on the drawing using a click of the mouse. The position of the cursor indicates the center of the drawing. This can be very difficult to predict. The best approach is to position your new view such that it has a lot of room. You can always move views around on the page later using the Move item in the Views menu.

5.8 Views

There are several view types available for you to place into a drawing: General, Projected, Auxiliary, and Detailed. There are dependent views and independent views. The only independent view is the General View. You select the orientation for this view; it does not depend on any other view. All other views are dependent on another view. For example, a Projected view is based on a projection from another view, a Detailed view is a detail of a part of another view, and an Auxiliary view is projected off of an inclined surface from another view. Each of these four views is described next. You select drawing views from the Views menu as seen in Figure 5.3. From this menu, you are also required to select view options. These include the view portion, cross-sectioning, and scaling. You can select a full, half, broken, or partial view. You can select to have cross sectioning, or to disable cross sectioning, and you can select a scale independent from the rest of the drawing. These options are discussed in the next section.

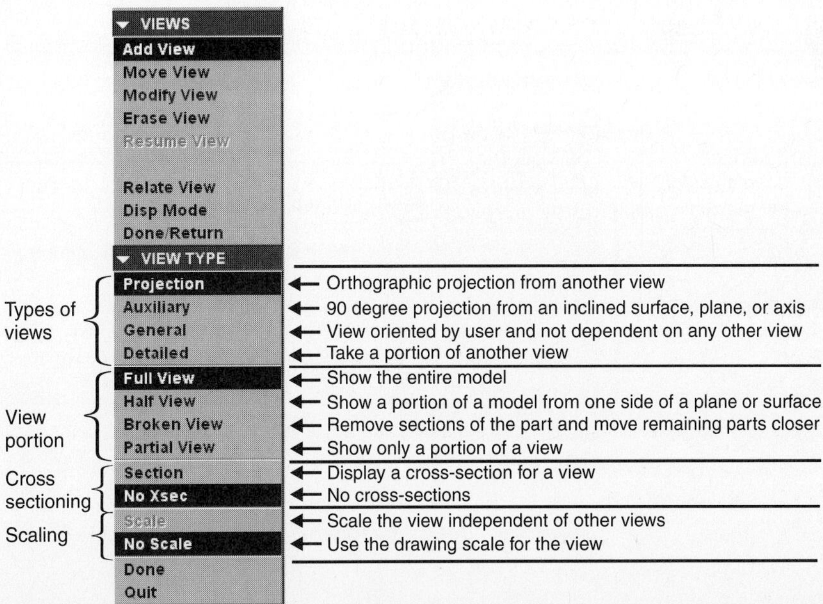

Figure 5.3 Adding a View submenu.

5.8.1   General Views

A General view can be any view that you select from a part. It is the only independent view. When you create a new drawing, the General view is the only selection possible. How could you create an independent view when there are no views to depend on? When you place a General view, you are asked for a part or assembly file to use. In this chapter, we are drawing parts. Selecting or providing a name for a part causes that part to be placed onto the drawing in a default view orientation. Remember the default view from the Part mode? This may or may not be the view that you had desired.

Your next task is to orient the part to your needs. You could, of course, keep the default view if desired. Otherwise, you will need to reorient the part. The part is displayed with datum planes. You might require these datum planes during the reorientation. These datum planes are only temporary and will be removed after you reorient the part. You can reorient the part using the commands from the Orientation menu in Figure 5.4. This menu should look very familiar since it is the same Orientation menu as described in Chapter 2. If the reorientation is simple then use this menu. You can select Top-Front, Bottom-Right combinations to orient the part. You can choose horizontal or vertical axis, or you can bring up the Angles submenu to describe how to orient the part.

> **NOTE:** In the following figures, I have disabled hidden lines, datum planes, and axis for clarity. These elements can be displayed if desired. This is by no means a limitation of Drawing mode.

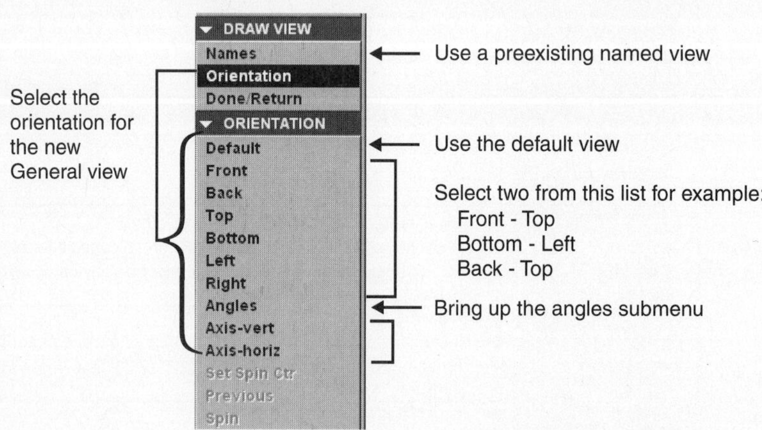

Figure 5.4   Orienting a General view.

Alternately, you can reorient the part from the Part Mode. Perhaps you planned ahead, and during the part creation you saved some Named views for your drawing. In this case, you can select one of these named views for the General view in the drawing. If not, do not fret. You can go back to the Mode menu and read the part into a child window. Use ChangeWindow to select that window. You are now in Part Mode in the child window, as well as Drawing Mode in the main window. From the Part Mode window create the desired view and save it as a named view. Use ChangeWindow to go back to the main window and select the Names option in the orientation menu.

Figure 5.5 provides several different General views. Each of these views is an independent General view. Each was created using the Views >Add View >General | Full View | No Xsec | No Scale menu selection. We could have created the top and right side views using a Projection from any of the other isometric views shown. This goes to show that a General view can be *any* view of a part. Some of these General views were Named views. Others were achieved using the Angles menu item, and still others were created using the Top-Right type selections.

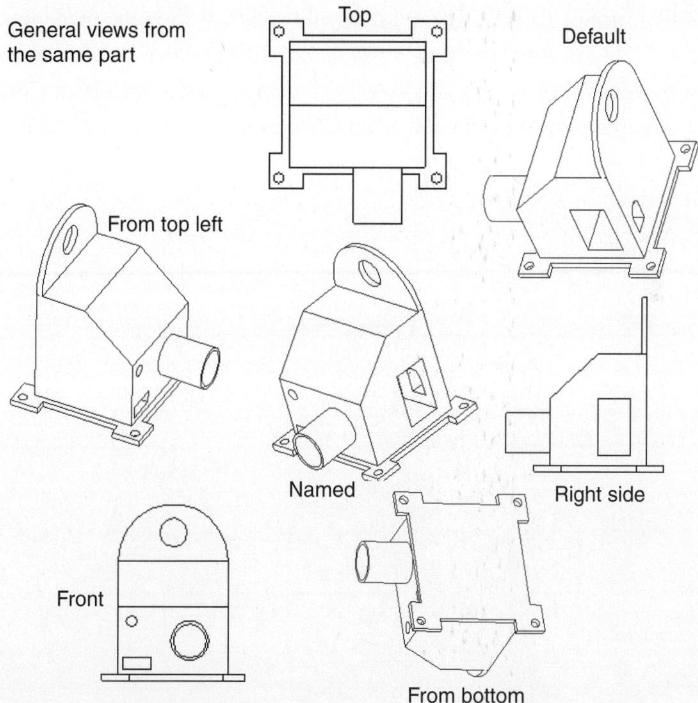

Figure 5.5   Several General views of the same part.

5.8.2   Projected Views

Projected views are dependent views. They provide an orthographic projection of a part as seen from one of its sides. Typical projected views are front, back, top, bottom, right, and left side. Projected Views are really simple to use. You would add a projected view by View >Add >Projected with whatever options are desired. From there, you are requested to click on the desired place in the drawing to place the view. In Figure 5.6, I am using the General view as the reference for the Projected views. This is not absolutely necessary—I could project off of one of the Projected views. More on that later.

In this case, the General view is set up to be a front view. This is not necessary—any view would work. If you click above the General view, you would automatically get a Top view from the perspective of the General view. If you click to the right of the General view, you would get a right-side view. If you click to the left of the General view, you would get a left-side view. If you click below the General view, you would get a bottom view.

Please remember, these names, top, left, side, bottom, etc., are always with respect to the referenced part. In this figure, the referenced part was a front view so it makes sense to call a project to the right a "right-side view." If the reference view was displayed upside down, then clicking a projected view above the upside-down reference view would still provide a top view with respect to the reference view orientation. We would normally call this resultant view a "bottom view." There are no absolutes.

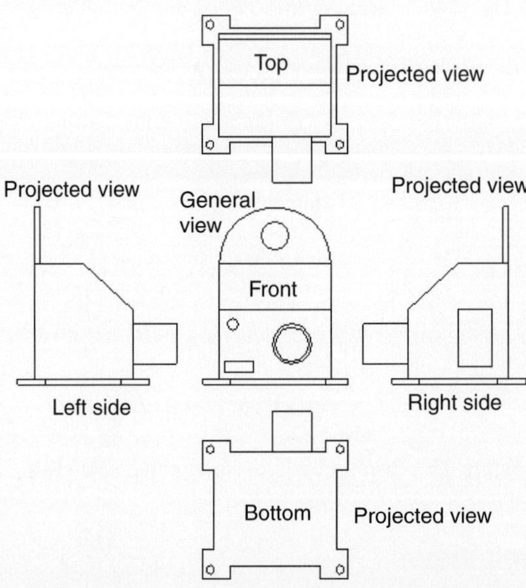

Figure 5.6   Projecting off of an orthographic.

In Figure 5.7 we see that the reference view does not have to be an orthographic view. In this case, the reference view is a General view, which is an isometric view. Clicking to the left, top, right, and bottom produces views of the General view from that perspective. Consider this analogy. We place a model of the part on a table in some orientation. It can sit in any orientation without falling. If we click to the right of the model, a camera is placed to the right of the model and a picture is taken. This becomes the Projected view. From Figure 5.7, we can see that we no longer have classic "right-side-view" or "top-view" projections.

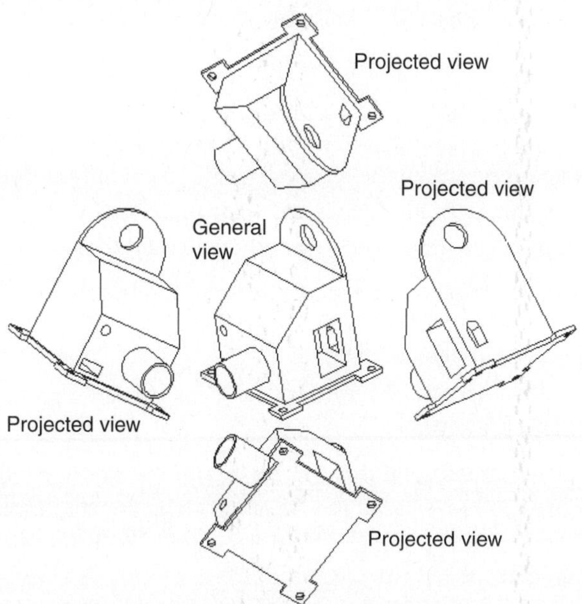

Figure 5.7   Projecting off an isometric.

When you click in a drawing to place a projected view, the software determines the correct orientation based on whether the click was to the top, right, bottom, or left of a reference view. It places the new projected view in line with the reference view. The position of the click is used to distance the projected view from the reference view. The lines in the projected views always line up with the lines in the reference view. You do not have to worry about alignment.

As mentioned, a projected view can be made off of any other view. In Figure 5.8, a General view is placed and oriented to be a front view of the part. A Projected view is clicked to the right of this part.

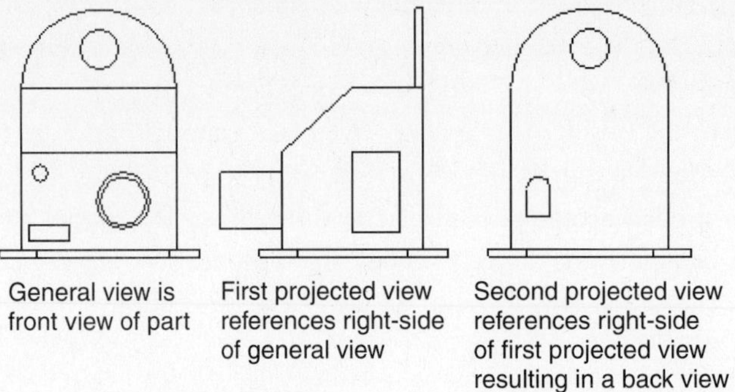

Figure 5.8   Projecting off of a projection.

During the process of creating a Projection view, at no time are you requested to provide information regarding the reference view. You simply click on the drawing and the software automatically figures out what projection you are after, based on the location of the click with respect to another view already on the drawing. What happens if there is ambiguity? Suppose you clicked between two views. How would the software know which view you are referencing? In these cases, you are queried to click on the desired reference view.

5.8.3   Auxiliary Views

Auxiliary views are projections that are made normal to an arbitrary surface or datum plane. Auxiliary views can also be made along an axis. Typically, Auxiliary views are made off of slanted surfaces. Auxiliary views are, in actuality, a generalized Projection view.

When placing an Auxiliary view, it is necessary to select the face, datum plane, edge, or axis from which the projection will be taken. Like a projection, you click in the drawing where you want the Auxiliary view to be placed. Once selected, a 90 degree projection is taken and displayed at a location in the drawing. Similar to the Projected view, the Auxiliary view is aligned to the Reference view. Only the distance between the selected face and the mouse click is used. This distance is then measured from the face along the face normal.

Figure 5.9 illustrates three Auxiliary views taken from a General view. The General view is a side view of the part. The top surface of this view is used as the projection surface to create the top view of the part. As you can see, this is identical to the top Projection view for this part. This is the same for the front view shown to the right of the part taken from the front edge of the part. Lastly, an angled Auxiliary view is taken from the slanted surface of the part. The resultant Auxiliary view is shown.

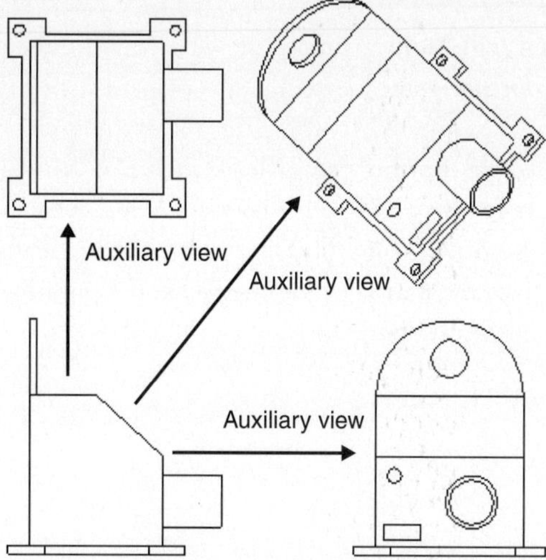

Figure 5.9   Auxiliary views.

A second part is shown in Figure 5.10(a). A General view of this part is displayed in Figure 5.10(b). The slanted surface is used to create an Auxiliary view. Notice how the Auxiliary view, combined with the General view, provides a clear description of the part. This view is far more instructive than the traditional top or side Projection views would provide.

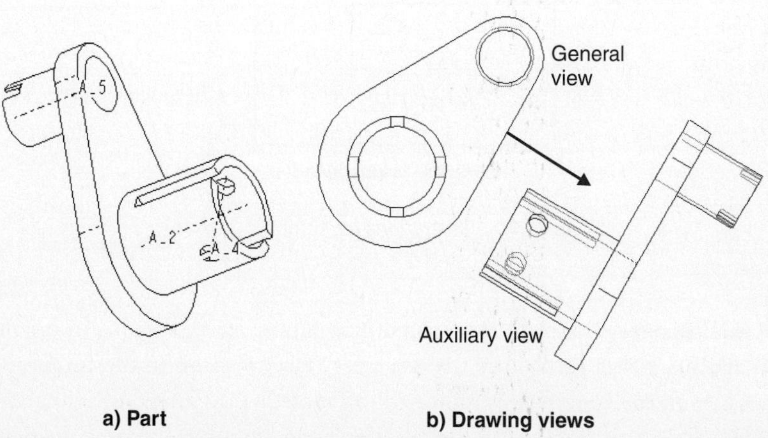

a) Part   **b) Drawing views**

Figure 5.10   A part and its Auxiliary view.

5.8.4   A Couple of Tutorials

In Tutorial 5.1, you will build a simple drawing. First, enter the drawing mode using the Mode >Drawing menu item. Next, create a new drawing using the >Create item. You are requested to enter the format and size. Select Dwg Size | Landscape | A. Enter the drawing name Tut5-1. A (.DWG) will be appended onto the filename. You are ready to add your first view. Select Add View >General | Full | View | No Xsec | No Scale Done. This creates a General view. Click on the center of the drawing to place the part. The part is placed temporarily with datum planes displayed. This is shown in Figure 5.11.

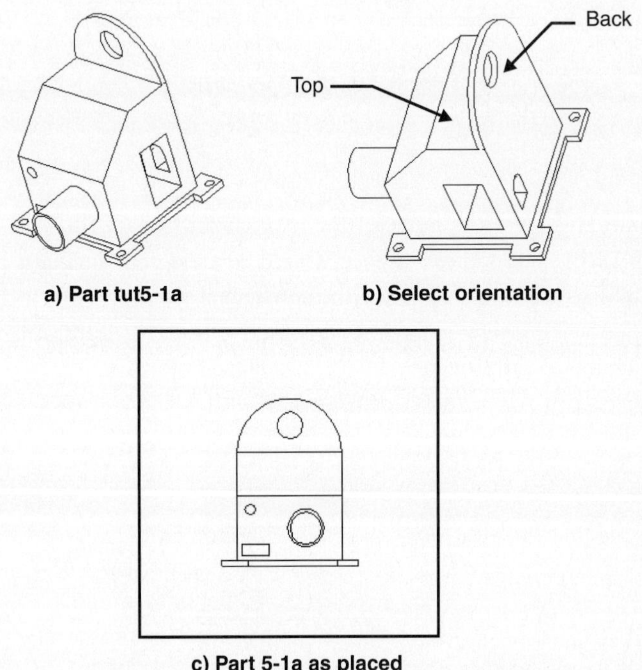

a) Part tut5-1a   b) Select orientation

c) Part 5-1a as placed

Figure 5.11   Illustrations for Tutorial 5.1, part 1.

Now it is necessary to create the desired orientation for this view. An orientation menu appears. Select Back since that is an easy face to access in the current default view. Click on the Back face as indicated in Figure 5.11. Click on Right and select the Right face as shown in the figure. The Orientation menu and the resultant drawings are shown in Figure 5.12.

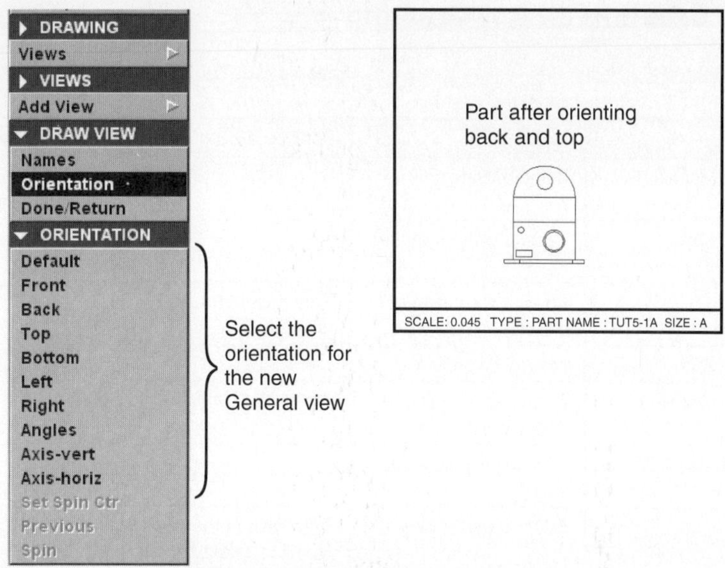

Figure 5.12   Illustrations for Tutorial 5.1, part 2.

Next, place two Projected views onto the drawing as seen in Figure 5.13. Select >Add View >Projected >Full View >No Xsec >No Scale | Done and simply click to the right of the General view to create a right side view. Repeat the process and click above the General view to create a Top view. The drawing should now be saved using >File >Save and accepting the default file name.

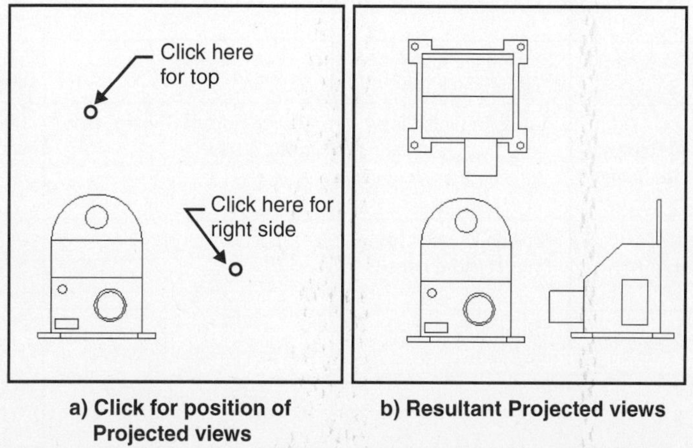

Figure 5.13   Illustrations for Tutorial 5.1, part 3.

Tutorial 5.1 Creating a First Drawing

Files opened: Tut5-1a.prt   **Files saved:** Tut5-1.dwg

Step	Action	Description	Further Actions	Result
1	Click PT/Modeler Icon	Run PT/Modeler		After some time, PT/Modeler on screen
2	>Mode >Misc >Show Dir	Show current directory		Message similar to "Directory searched is c:\ptc\ptprod\bin"
3	>Change Dir	Change the current directory	Type **c:\proe\tutorial\ chapter_5**	
4	>Done-Return	Leave Misc menu		Misc menu removed
5	>Mode > Drawing >Create	Create and name a drawing	Type **tut5-1**	
6	| Landscape | A	Drawing is landscape size A		
7	>Views	Add a General view	Type **Tut5-1a** then **Enter** or type **?** to select part from list	
8	>Add View | General | Full View | No Xsec | No Scale | Done	Preparation for adding the first view		
9	Click in center of drawing	Place new view onto drawing		Part is placed onto drawing with datum planes enabled temporarily until part is oriented
10	>Back	Select back surface in Fig. 5.11(c)		
11	>Top	Select top surface in Fig. 5.11(c)	>Done/Return	Part is oriented and displayed in Fig. 5.12
12	>Add View > Projection | Full View | No Xsec | No Scale | Done	Add a Projected view	Click to top of General view in Fig. 5.13(b)	Left side view displayed
13	Click to top of General view in Fig. 5.13(a)	Provide location for Projection on top		Top view displayed in Fig. 5.13(b)
14	>Add View >Projection | Full View | No Xsec | No Scale | Done	Add a Projected view	Click to right of General view in Fig. 5.13(b)	Right side view displayed
15	Click to right of General view in Fig. 5.13a	Provide location for Projection on right		Right view displayed in Fig. 5.13(b)
16	>Done-Return	>Done with environment		
17	>File >Save	Save drawing file	Type **Enter** to accept tut5-1	File tut5-1.dwg saved
18	>QuitWindow			
19	Exit	Exit program	Click Yes to confirm	PT/Modeler exited

In Tutorial 5.2, you will create a drawing and place a General view, a set of Projected views, and Auxiliary views onto this drawing. Start out by Selecting >Drawings from the Mode Menu. Create a new drawing with >Create selecting an A size Landscape orientation. You are asked to enter the name for the drawing; type Tut5-2. You are asked to enter the part to be used in the drawing; enter Tut5-2. A blank drawing page is provided. Select >Views >AddViews to create a new view. The first view has to be a General view, so select >General >Full >No Xsec | No Scale. You will have to enter the part name, TUT5-2. This creates a full view using the scale of the drawing. Click on the upper-left corner of the drawing to place this view. You now need to orient the view. To do this, select Names from the Orientation menu and select TUT5-1view1 from the list. Click >Done to accept the placement. Repeat this process, this time clicking on the upper-right corner of the drawing to place the same part. Note that once a single General view is placed, you can select among the other View types. Make sure to Select >General the second time around since Projected is highlighted as the default.

At this point we have the two General isometric views shown in the top corners of Figure 5.14. Now, place a third General view. This time, we will select the orientation by clicking on the front face as Front and the DTM2 place (not shown in the figure but shown on the screen) as Bottom. This places the orthographic front view in the lower center of the figure. From here, place two Projected views, again using the >Full >No Xsec >No Scale options. Place these views to the right and top of the front view. You will have to select the front view as the reference view since there is ambiguity in the drawing regarding which view you want to project from. Lastly, add an Auxiliary view using the same the >Full >No Xsec >No Scale options. Place this view in the lower-left corner. Click on the edge indicated in Figure 5.14 to select the projection edge. Use the Move Menu selection to drag the views around for proper placement on the drawing.

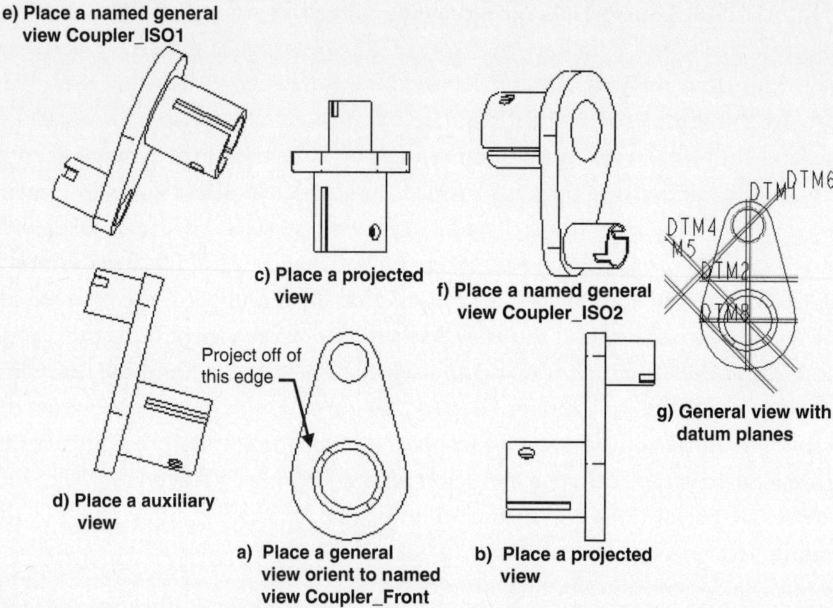

Figure 5.14 Illustrations for Tutorial 5.2.

Tutorial 5.2 Creating a Second Drawing

Files opened: Tut5-2a.prt   **Files saved:** Tut5-2.dwg

Step	Action	Description	Further Actions	Result
1	Click PT/Modeler Icon	Run PT/Modeler		After some time, PT/Modeler on screen
2	>Mode >Misc >Show Dir	Show current directory		Message similar to "Directory searched is c:\ptc\ptprod\bin"
3	>Change Dir	Change the current directory	Type **c:\proe\tutorial\ chapter_5**	
4	>Done-Return	Leave Misc menu		Misc menu removed
5	>Mode >Drawing >Create	Create and name a drawing	Type **tut5-2** then **Enter**	
6	>Set Dwg Size | Landscape | A	Drawing is landscape size A		
7	>Views	Add a General view	Type **Tut5-2a** then **Enter** or type **?** to select part from list	
8	>Add View | General | Full View | No Xsec | No Scale | Done	Preparation for adding the first view		
9	Click in center of drawing	Place new view onto drawing		Part is placed onto drawing with datum planes enabled temporarily until part is oriented
10	>Names	Want to use a named view	Click on COUPLER_FRONT then >Done/Return	Part displayed in front view in Fig. 5.14(a)
11	**F2** for >View >Repaint	Use F2 macro for repaint to see new view		
12	>Add View >Projection | Full View | No Xsec | No Scale | Done	Add a projected view		
13	Click to right of General View in Fig. 5.14(b)	Provide location for Projection on right		Right view displayed in Fig. 5.14(b)
14	>Add View >Projection | Full View | No Xsec | No Scale | Done	Add a projected view		
15	Click to top of General View in Fig. 5.14(c)	Provide location for Projection on top		Top view displayed in Fig. 5.14(c)
16	>Add View >Auxiliary | Full View | No Xsec | No Scale | Done	Add an auxiliary view		

Tutorial 5.2   Creating a Second Drawing (continued)

Step	Action	Description	Further Actions	Result
17	Click to left of General view in Fig. 5.14(d)	Provide location for Projection on side	Click on left side in Fig. 5.14(c)	Auxiliary view displayed in Fig. 5.14(d)
18	Click on DTM6 as in Fig 5.14(g)	Use DTM6 as axis of projection		
19	>Add View >General | Full View | No Xsec | Scale | Done	Add an isometric General view with independent view scaling		
20	Click to top-left of General view in Fig. 5.14(e)	Provide location for view on top left	Double default Scale; if [.004] then type **0.008** and **Enter**	Top-left view displayed in Fig. 5.14(e)
21	>Names	Want to use a named view	Click on COUPLER_ISO1 then >Done/Return	Part displayed in front view in Fig. 5.14(e)
22	>Add View >General | Full View | No Xsec | Scale | Done	Add an isometric General view		
23	Click to top-right of General View in Fig. 5.14(f)	Provide location for view on top right	Double default scale; if [.004] then type **0.008** and **Enter**	Top-right view displayed in Fig. 5.14(f)
24	>Names	Want to use a named view	Click on COUPLER_ISO2 then >Done/Return then **F2** to repaint	Part displayed in front view in Fig. 5.14(f)
25	>Done-Return	>Done with environment		
26	>File >Save	Save drawing file	Type **Enter** to accept tut5-2	File tut5-2.dwg saved
27	>QuitWindow			
28	Exit	Exit program	Click Yes to confirm	PT/Modeler exited

5.8.5   Detailed Views

Detail views provide a detailed look at a portion of a reference view. The Reference view can be any type of view. A Detail view of an orthographic view is shown in Figure 5.15(a). A Detail view of an isometric view is shown in Figure 5.15(b). Detail views are a bit complicated to construct. There are a number of parameters that you have to enter. After a while, you get used to the parameters and they become second nature. Detail views can be manipulated like any other view. There is no implied alignment between the Detail view and the Reference view.

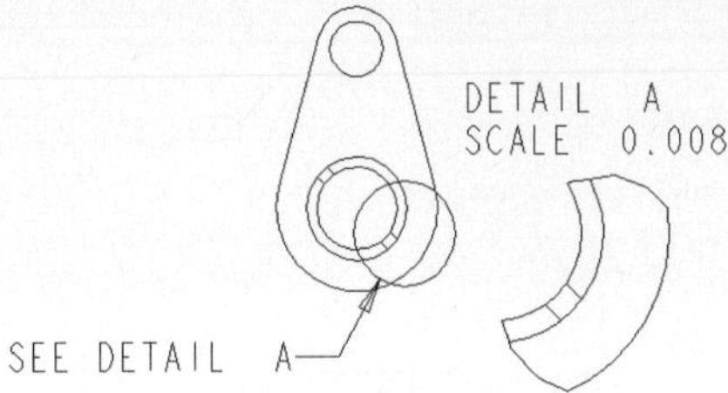

a) Detail A from top view

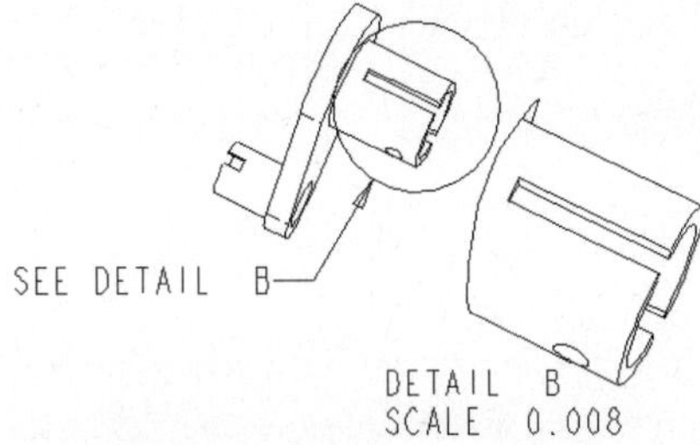

b) Detail B from isometric view

Figure 5.15   Two Detail views.

You can create only one type of Detailed view as seen in the menu options of Figure 5.16. Note that only Full view sections with no cross sections are allowed. You are able to scale the Detail view at a different scale factor from the reference view. It is common to select a scale factor for the Detail view to be greater than the scale factor of the Reference view. This provides a Zoom-In effect. You have to specify which portion of the Reference view should be zoomed and the amount of zoom. To specify the portion of the zoom you select a center of the zoom region on the reference part and draw an area around the portion of the view to be zoomed. You draw the portion using spline chains. I will describe how to use spline chains a little later.

You also need to specify a name for the Detail view and where the Detail view should be placed on the drawing. Next, you will replace the spline chain sketch of the boundary area with a circle, ellipse, horizontally and vertically aligned ellipse, or a spline as picked from a menu list.

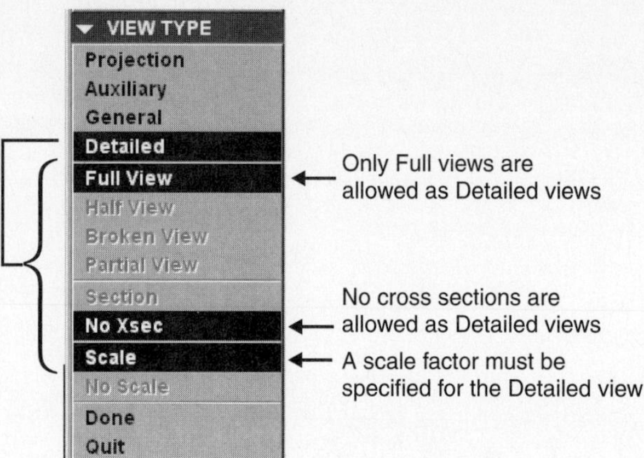

Figure 5.16   Menu selections for boundary types.

A note is included with each Detail view. The note is associated with the boundary of the detail in the reference view. It annotates the reference view indicating that a Detail view of specified name exists on the drawing. The note has an arrow that points to the boundary area (either the circle, ellipse, or spline). You have to indicate where you would like the arrow attached to the boundary line. A title is included with the Detail view indicating the name of the detail.

The steps to creating a Detail view are as follows:

1. Specify the type of Detailed view. No options here: View > Detailed >Full View >No Xsec >Scale | Done.
2. Select a location on the drawing where you want the Detail view to be located.
3. Enter the scale factor. A default value is provided in the query. This is the scale of the Reference view.
4. Select a center point on the reference view around which the detail will be taken.
5. Sketch a spline chain that defines the boundary area.
6. Name the Detail.
7. Select a shape that will encircle the area of replacing the spline chain.
8. Position where the Note arrow will touch the boundary area.

It is easy to mix up Steps 2 and 4, placing the Detail view on top of the Reference view. Move slowly at first and read the queries carefully, following the eight steps listed previously. Sometimes the queries aren't all that helpful. The eight steps are illustrated in Figures 5.17 and 5.18. Detail views will become clearer when we get into the tutorials. You will create a Detailed view in Tutorial 5.3. The steps of this tutorial are illustrated in Figures 5.17 and 5.18. The goal of this tutorial is to create the Detail view shown at the bottom of Figure 5.18.

Step 1: Pick Detailed view from menu

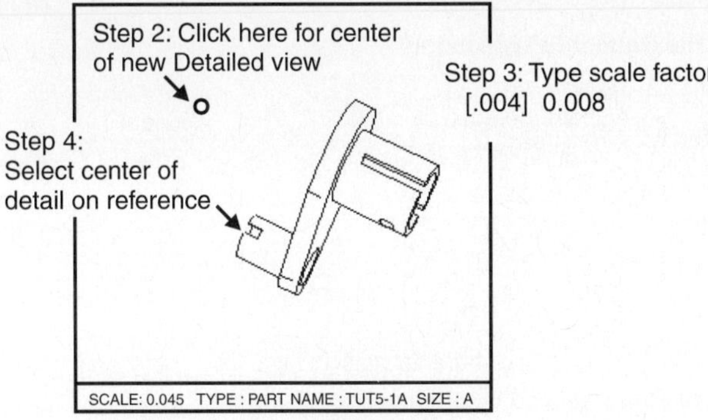

a) Setting up for the Detailed view

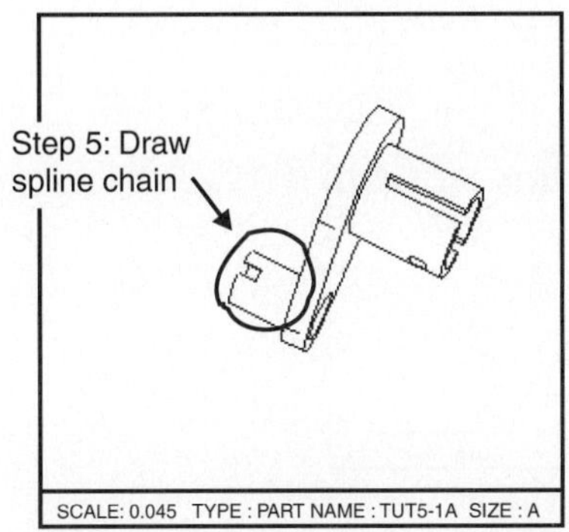

b) Drawing the boundary area sketch

Figure 5.17   Example of a Detail view for Tutorial 5.3.

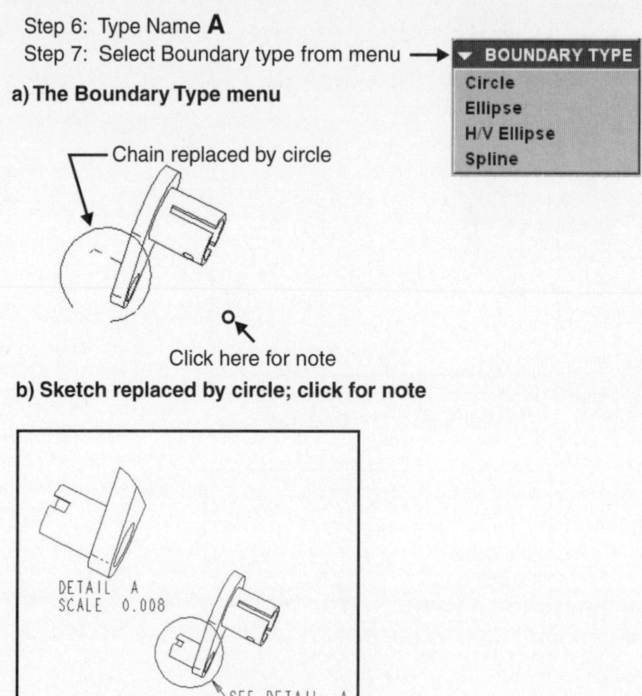

Figure 5.18   Example of a Detail view for Tutorial 5.3.

Tutorial 5.3   Creating a Detailed View

Files opened: Tut5-3a.prt   **Files saved:** Tut5-3.dwg

Step	Action	Description	Further Actions	Result
1	Click PT/Modeler Icon	Run PT/Modeler		After some time, PT/Modeler on screen
2	>Mode >Misc >Show Dir	Show current directory		Message similar to "Directory searched is c:\ptc\ptprod\bin"
3	>Change Dir	Change the current directory	Type **c:\proe\tutorial\ chapter_5**	
4	>Done-Return	Leave Misc menu		Misc menu removed
5	>Mode >Drawing >Create	Create and name a drawing	Type **tut5-3** then **Enter**	

Tutorial 5.3 Creating a Detailed View (continued)

Step	Action	Description	Further Actions	Result
6	>Set Dwg Size | Landscape | A	Drawing is landscape size A		
7	>Views	Initialization: Model selection for the drawing	Type **Tut5-3a** then **Enter** or type **?** to select part from list	
8	>Views >Add View | General | Full View | No Xsec | No Scale | Done	Add a General view		
9	Click in center of drawing	Place new view onto drawing		Part is placed onto drawing with datum planes enabled temporarily until part is oriented
10	>Names	Want to use a named view	Click on COUPLER_ISO1 then >Done then **F2** for view repaint	Part displayed in isometric view in Fig. 5.17
11	>Views >Add View >Detailed | Full View | No Xsec | Scale | Done	Add a Detailed view		
12	Click to top-left of General view in Fig. 5.17	Provide location for Detailed view above and to the left		
13	Type **0.008**	Query says scale is [0.004]; want double scale		
14	Click on center of area to be detailed in Fig. 5.17	Indicate where center of interest is on Reference view		
15	mLb click around area of interest; mMb closes and ends sketch in Fig. 5.17	Sketch a spline chain; spline does not have to be pretty since it will be replaced in later step	Spline circle sketched close enough to allow software to place a circle automatically	Sketch disappears as sketch is ended with mMb
16	Type **A**	Respond to query to name Detail view		Name will be "Detail A"
17	Select >Circle	Replace spline with a circle in Fig. 5.18		
18	Click to right and below reference view in Fig. 5.18	Indicate where you want note placed		Note is placed, detail view is drawn in Fig. 5.18
19	>Done-Return	>Done with environment		
20	>File >Save	Save drawing file	Type **Enter** to accept tut5-3	File tut5-3.dwg saved
21	>QuitWindow			
22	Exit	Exit program	Click Yes to confirm	PT/Modeler exited

5.8.6   Drawing a Spline Chain

Spline chains are drawn like line chains. Spline chains are line chains with the lines replaced by a spline curve. To draw a spline chain mLb click at the point where the spline chain should start. mLb click at a series of points approximating the curve that you desire. Each time you click, a straight line is drawn back to the last point. This line is converted to a curve as you provide the curvature. When you are ready to close the spline, middle button click, mMb. You don't need to click on the first point to close a spline. The software knows that it should be a closed shape.

5.9   View Options

These three option areas are within the View Menu when creating a view as seen in Figure 5.3. These options specify whether you want a full, half, broken, or partial view. They specify whether you want cross sections and whether separate scaling should be employed for the new view.

5.9.1   Full View

The Full view shows the entire model. All of the views in the figures thus far have been Full views. Detailed views must be Full views.

5.9.2   Half View

Half views show only a portion of the model. The model can be split by a planar face in the model or by a datum plane. When creating a Half view, special care has to be taken when selecting the orientation of the view. A planar face or datum plane will be used to separate the view. This face or plane must be parallel to the drawing surface. Therefore, if you choose a named view, make sure that such a face exists.

When creating a Half view, you first have to select the orientation of the view. This locks the view down on the page. Datum planes are still available for selection of the face; however, it is not possible to rotate the face around. Consequently, it can be very difficult to find the right face or datum plane. You must know the face name or datum plane name that you are going to use and select it from the model tree or Query Select. An example of a Half view is shown in Figure 5.19.

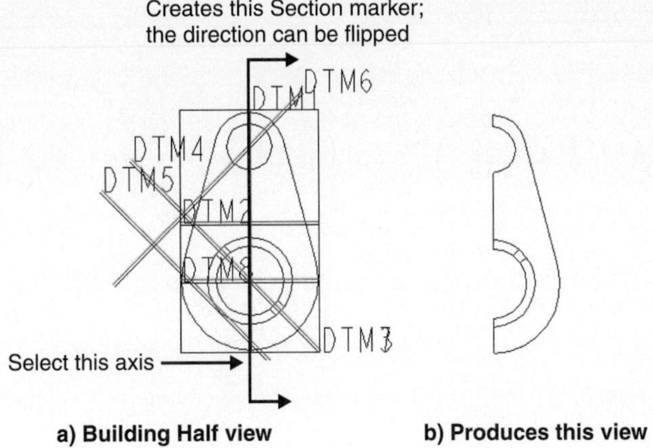

a) Building Half view   **b) Produces this view**

Figure 5.19   Example of a Half view.

In Tutorial 5.4 you will build a Half view. First, place a General view, in a side orientation. You can easily orient this view by selecting DTM1 as the Front reference and DTM2 as the Bottom reference. Alternately, you can select the Named view, COUPLER_SIDE. Next, select a Projected view, Half view, No Xsec, and No scale. Click to the right of the General view to place the new Projected view. From here select DTM1 as the cut plane. The steps are shown in Figure 5.20(a)–(c) and the resultant drawing is shown in Figure 5.20(d).

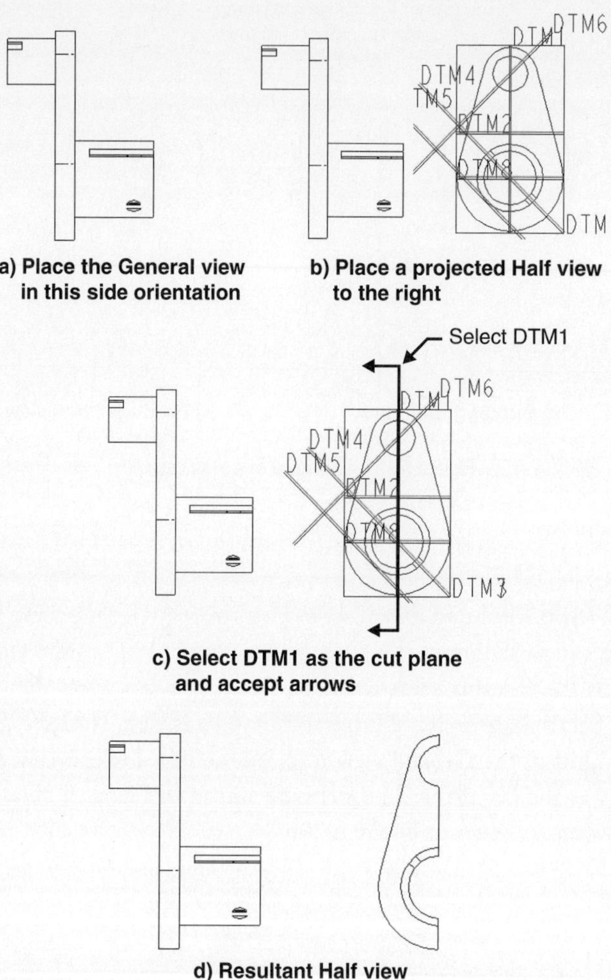

Figure 5.20 Build a Half view for Tutorial 5.4.

Tutorial 5.4　Creating a Half View

Files opened: Tut5-4a.prt　　　　　　　　**Files saved:** Tut5-4.dwg

Step	Action	Description	Further Actions	Result
1	Click PT/Modeler Icon	Run PT/Modeler		After some time, PT/Modeler on screen
2	>Mode >Misc >Show Dir	Show current directory		Message similar to "Directory searched is c:\ptc\ptprod\bin"
3	>Change Dir	Change the current directory	Type **c:\proe\tutorial\ chapter_5**	
4	>Mode >Drawing >Create	Create and name a drawing	Type **tut5-4** then **Enter**	
5	>Set Dwg Size | Landscape | A	Drawing is landscape size A		
6	>Views	Initialization: Model selection for the drawing	Type **Tut5-4a** then **Enter** or type **?** to select part from list	
7	>Add View | General | Full View | No Xsec | No Scale | Done	Add a General view		
8	Click in center of drawing	Place new view onto drawing		Part is placed onto drawing with datum planes enabled temporarily until part is oriented
9	>Names	Want to use a named view	Click on COUPLER_SIDE then >Done/Return	Part displayed in side view in Fig. 5.20(a)
10	>Views >Add View > Projection | Half View | No Xsec | No Scale | Done	Add a Projected view in Half view		
11	Click to right of General view in Fig. 5.20(b)	Provide location for Half view Projected view to the right		Projected view shown in Full view with datum planes in Fig. 5.20(b)
12	Click on DTM1	Select DTM1 as the cut plane in Fig. 5.20(c)		
13	Click OK	Accept Arrows for view direction		Half view shown in Fig. 5.20(d)
14	>Done-Return	>Done with environment		
15	>File >Save	Save drawing file	Type **Enter** to accept tut5-4	File tut5-4.prt saved
16	>QuitWindow			
17	Exit	Exit program	Click Yes to confirm	PT/Modeler exited

5.9.3 Broken View

Broken views are used to remove a center portion of a drawing showing both ends. Usually, this type of view is used when there are details of importance at the ends of a part but the part is long. The details would be lost due to scaling if the entire part was shown.

You create a Broken view by adding break lines to a Projected or General view. You can add horizontal break lines or vertical break lines. All lines associated with the region of the model between consecutive break lines will be removed. You can also delete break lines if they are no longer wanted. Once the break lines are placed, selecting Done will remove the material between them.

Tutorial 5.5 takes you through the steps of creating a Broken view. Create a drawing named Tut5-4. Next add a General view using the part tut5.4a. This General view should use the Broken view option. Use the named view COUPLER_LONG to orient this view as seen in Figure 5.21(a).

At this point a menu appears as shown in Figure 5.21. Start by Adding two vertical breaks as shown in Figure 5.22. All material between these two vertical lines will be deleted. Note that the vertical lines extend through the entire part.

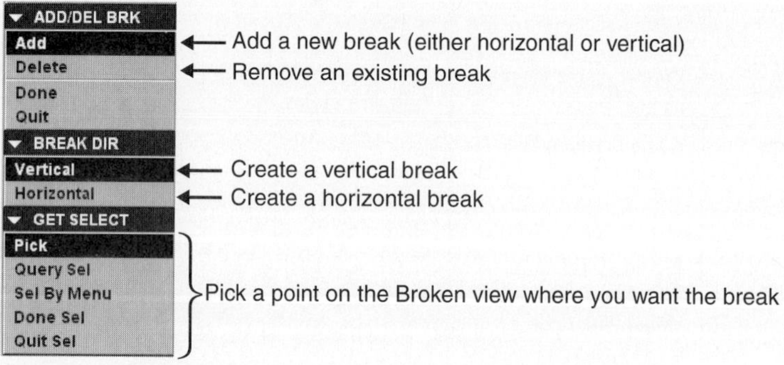

Figure 5.21   Broken view menu used to place breaks.

NOTE: You cannot add horizontal break lines on a horizontally projected Broken view, nor can you add vertical break lines to a vertically projected Broken view.

After placing the two vertical breaks, select Done. The model is now displayed with all material between the two breaks missing. The break is indicated by a vertical line. You can now choose to replace the vertical line with a spline. In this tutorial, simply click Done and ignore the spline option. The break will be shown with a single vertical line.

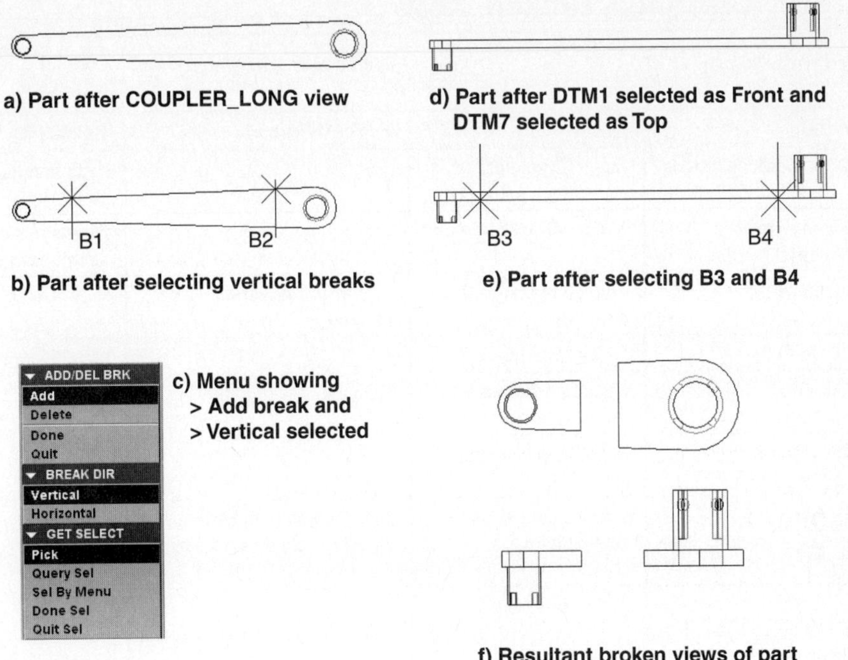

Figure 5.22   Build a Broken view for Tutorial 5.5.

The Broken view is completed. The two distinct portions of the Broken view are still part of the same view. One is independent and the other dependent. You can move the dependent view using the View >Move menu item. You can also move both portions of the Broken view by clicking on the independent view. As you select a view, highlights will show you which view is dependent and which is independent.

Tutorial 5.5   Creating a Broken View

Files opened: Tut5-5a.prt   **Files saved:** Tut5-5.dwg

Step	Action	Description	Further Actions	Result
1	Click PT/Modeler Icon	Run PT/Modeler		After some time, PT/Modeler on screen
2	>Mode >Misc >Show Dir	Show current directory		Message similar to "Directory searched is c:\ptc\ptprod\bin"
3	>Change Dir	Change the current directory	Type **c:\proe\tutorial\ chapter_5**	
4	>Done-Return	Leave Misc menu		Misc menu removed
5	>Mode >Drawing >Create	Create and name a drawing	Type **tut5-5** then **Enter**	
6	>Set Dwg Size | Landscape | A	Drawing is landscape size A		
7	>Views	Initialization: Model selection for the drawing	Type **Tut5-5a** then **Enter** or type **?** to select part from list.	
8	>Add View | General | Broken | No Xsec | No Scale | Done	Add a General view		
9	Click in center of drawing	Place new view onto drawing		Part is placed onto drawing with datum planes enabled temporarily until part is oriented
10	>Names	Want to use a named view	Click on COUPLER_LONG then >Done/Return	Part displayed in side view in Fig. 5.22(a)
11	>Add >Vertical are selected as defaults	Add a vertical break using menu in Fig 5.22(c)	Click on B1 in Fig. 5.22(b)	Vertical break mark shown
12	>Add >Vertical are selected as defaults	Add a vertical break using menu in Fig 5.22(c)	Click on B2 in Fig. 5.22(b)	Vertical break mark shown
13	>Done	>Done with positioning breaks		Middle region removed from part; two ends compressed together in Fig. 5.22(c)
14	>Done	>Done; don't want spline now		Middle region pulled apart in Fig. 5.22(d)
15	>Views >Move View	Move one end of view closer to other if desired		Resultant broken view shown in top portion of Fig. 5.22(e)
16	>Views >Add View | General | Broken | No Xsec | No Scale	Add a General view Broken	>Done	No need to enter part name; same part is assumed

Tutorial 5.5   Creating a Broken View (continued)

Step	Action	Description	Further Actions	Result
17	Click beneath other drawing	Place new view onto drawing		Part is placed onto drawing with datum planes enabled temporarily until part is oriented
18	>FRONT	Want a side view	Use Sel By Menu	Datum	Name	
19	Select DTM1			
20	>TOP	Want a side view	Use Sel By Menu	Datum	Name	
21	Select DTM7		>Done/Return	Side view displayed in Fig. 5.22(d)
22	>Add >Vertical are selected as defaults	Add a vertical break using menu in Fig 5.22(e)	Click on B3 in Fig. 5.22(e)	Vertical break mark shown
23	>Add >Vertical are selected as defaults	Add a vertical break using menu in Fig 5.22(e)	Click on B4 in Fig. 5.22(e)	Vertical break mark shown in Fig. 5.22(e)
24	>Done	>Done with positioning breaks		Middle region removed from part; two ends compressed together
25	>Done	>Done; don't want spline now		Middle region pulled apart
26	>Views >Move View	Move one end of view closer to other if desired		Resultant Broken view shown in Fig. 5.22(f)
27	>Done-Return	>Done with environment		
28	>File >Save	Save drawing file	Type **Enter** to accept tut5-5	File tut5-5.dwg saved
29	>QuitWindow			
30	Exit	Exit program	Click Yes to confirm	PT/Modeler exited

5.9.4   Partial View

A portion of the part is shown that resides inside a boundary. This is similar to a Detail view.

5.9.5   Section View

Section views are partial views taken through an arbitrary plane. A Section view lets you see inside a part. You will need two views to document a section view properly. These are the Section view itself and a Reference view that indicates where the section was taken. An example is shown in Figure 5.23. The front view of the part shows that a section, named EE was taken at the specified cut through the part. The Section view, named EE, is displayed showing a cut through the part. Cross section lines have been applied to this Section view.

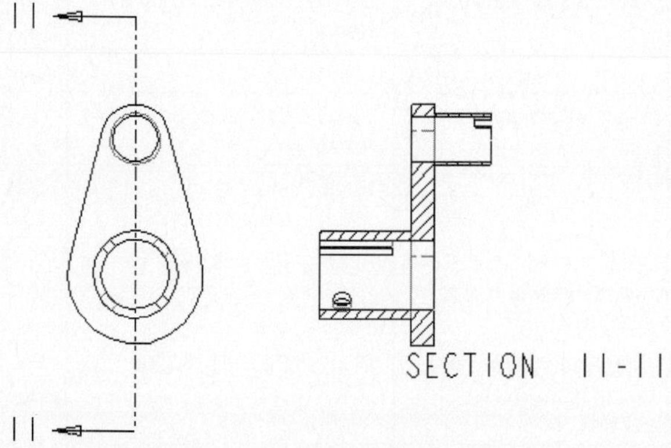

Figure 5.23   Example of a Section view.

Section views are really simple to create, however, you do have to answer a number of queries correctly. In addition, you do need to know the names of your datum planes before you begin. I refer you to Section 5.12 and Section 5.13 at this time. Section 5.12 provides you with a clear view of the part and the datum planes that you will be using in the next tutorial. Section 5.13 provides a description of how to select datum planes by name. In Tutorial 5.6, we will create a Section view. In the process, you will have to understand where the datum planes are in the model and how to select them from a menu by name. Please refer to these two sections now.

We are ready to start the tutorial. The first thing that you will do is open a new drawing. As a first step, onto this fresh drawing, you will place a General view of our part. Select the front face of the cylinder and the datum plane DTM2 as shown in Figure 5.24 to orient the part. Next create two Projected views, one to the left and one above the General view. These will be useful for reference.

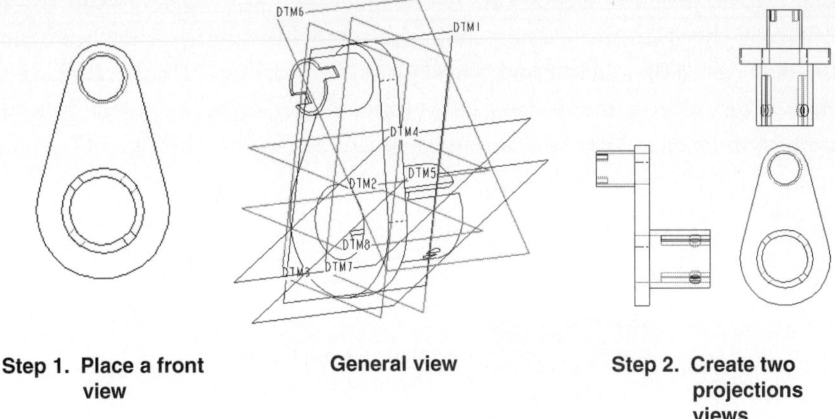

Figure 5.24　Placing a General view and two Projected views.

At this point, you are ready to add a Section view. To do this, select Add Views >Projection >Full View >Xsec | No Scale. Next, you are queried to provide the name of the cross section and to click on the location in the drawing where the Section view should be placed. Type FF as the name and click to the right of the part front view. A menu comes up requesting information about the type of cross section. This menu is shown in Figure 5.25. You will select the Full cross section with a total Xsec options. Other cross section types can be created and you can experiment with these at a later time. I prefer the Full, Total Xsec options.

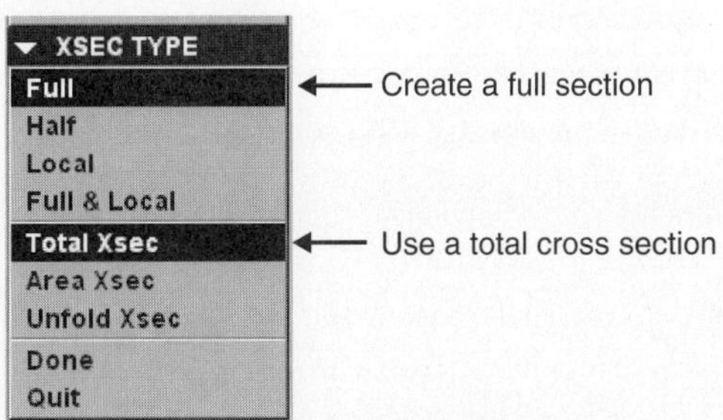

Figure 5.25　Cross Section type menu.

You are now ready to select where you want the part cut open. Once the cut is made, then you can select which side of the cut should represent the part in the Section view. There are two options here, as shown in Figure 5.26(a). The first option is to create a new section cut. The second option is to retrieve a preexisting cut. We will choose to create a new cut in this tutorial. From this Xsec Create submenu, you can select a Planar and Single plane cross section. Had you decided to retrieve a cross section, the available cross section names would be provided on the bottom of the menu. After selecting to create our section FF, the name FF would be added to this list, as shown in Figure 5.26(b).

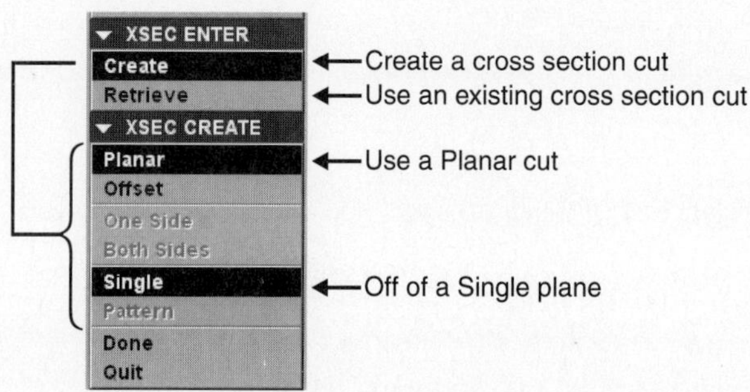

a) Create a new section cut

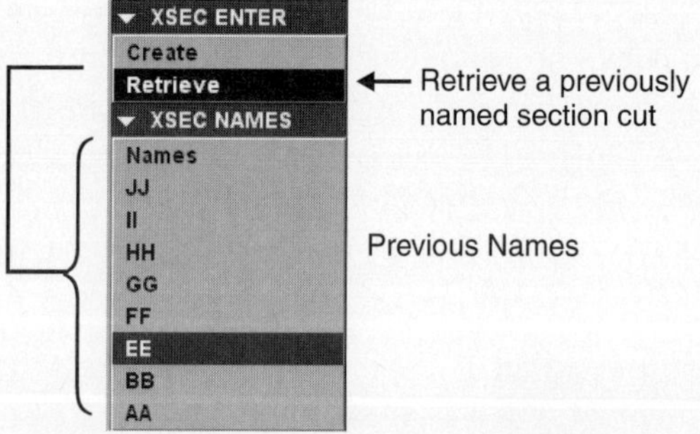

b) Retrieve a previous planar section cut

Figure 5.26   Creating a cut section menu and Retrieving a cut section menu.

You have selected to create a cut. It is now necessary to specify where that cut should be located on our part. We can choose an existing plane in the part or make a temporary datum plane to be used for this cut. We will choose to select an existing datum plane from the menu shown in Figure 5.27. Now, if display of datum planes is enabled in the Environment menu, you can pick or Query Select one of the faces or datum planes. You can easily select the datum planes from the Model Tree. Alternately, you can use the Sel By Menu option.

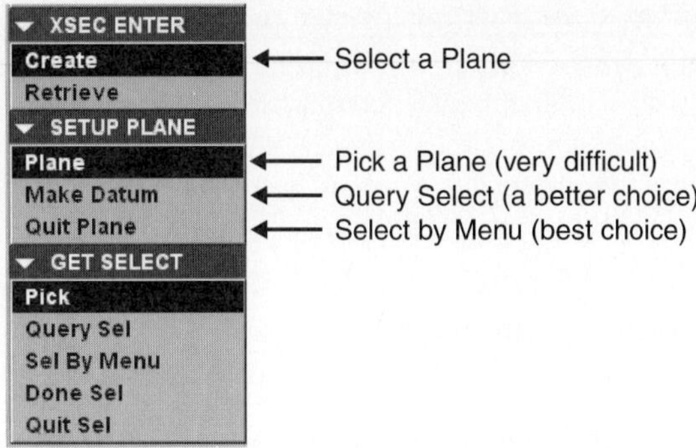

Figure 5.27 Creating a cut section submenu.

One last step and you're home free. You are requested to select a view where the reference arrows can reside. The reference arrows show the name of the cross section and the direction of the cut. A view has to be on the drawing that shows the cut plane such that it is oriented perpendicular to the drawing. This orientation is necessary, or else PT/Modeler could not draw the arrows indicating the direction of the cut. Select the top view, and accept the direction of the arrows. It really would not matter which direction that the arrows pointed since the part is symmetric about this axis. The resultant section view is placed on the drawing, along with the reference as seen in Figure 5.28.

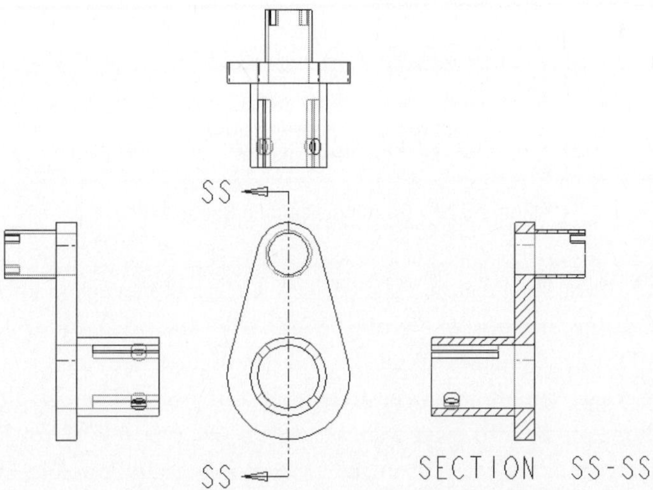

Figure 5.28 Drawing with a Section view.

There were a lot of steps, yet each one was simple. One piece of valuable experience that I hope you gained is that planning is essential when creating Section views.

Know your part, know your datum planes, place an appropriate view that will accept the reference arrows. This view is often the same view that the Projected view referenced.

You will now repeat these steps for a second section view as shown in Figure 5.29. We create a Projection, Xsec, NoScale view as before naming it HH and placing it below our front view. This time we are selecting the DTM8 plane as the cut surface. Everything else is done the same.

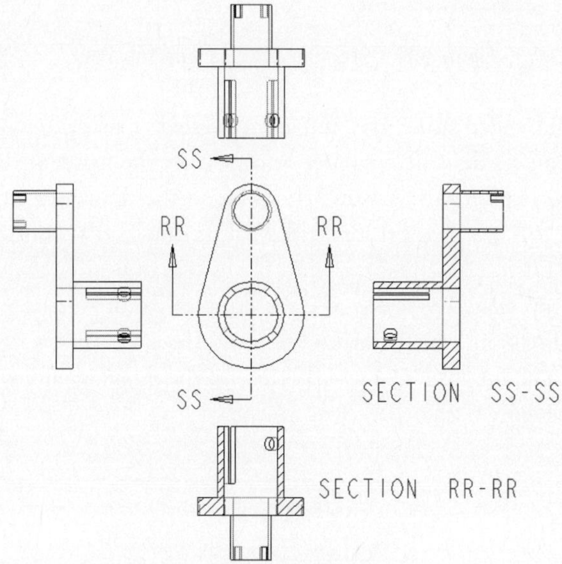

Final resultant drawing after
two section views placed

Figure 5.29   Creating a second Section view.

In Tutorial 5.6, you will create a Detailed View. Create a Drawing and place the part Tut5-3a onto the drawing as a general View. Note the orientation. Next, add a >Projected Detailed >Full >No Xsec >Scaled view. Click above and to the right of the General view. You are requested to enter a scale factor. The default [0.004] is provided in the prompt. To make a double scale detail, type 0.008. You should now click the center point of interest on the General view as indicated in Figure 5.30. Name the view A. The Note will include the word Detail followed by the selected name. In this case, the detail is Detail A. Do not add Detail to the name or it will be repeated. Draw a spline chain circle to the approximate shape of the circle shown in Figure 5.30. This will be replaced with an actual circle when you select Circle from the menu. A detail note is added to the drawing. Click to the right of the General view for the note placement.

You are now ready to touch up your drawing. Move the drawings using >Move >View to a desirable location. Move the dimensions using >Drawing >Detail >Move Text. Click on the text and move it to an appropriate location. Illustrations for Tutorial 5.6 are found in Figures 5.24 through 5.29.

Tutorial 5.6   Creating a Cross-Section View

Files opened: Tut5-6a.prt   **Files saved:** Tut5-6.dwg

Step	Action	Description	Further Actions	Result
1	Click PT/Modeler Icon	Run PT/Modeler		After some time, PT/Modeler on screen
2	>Mode >Misc >Show Dir	Show current directory		Message similar to "Directory searched is c:\ptc\ptprod\bin"
3	>Change Dir	Change the current directory	Type **c:\proe\tutorial\ chapter 5**	
4	>Done-Return	Leave Misc menu		Misc menu removed
5	>Mode >Drawing >Create	Create and name a drawing	Type **tut5-6** then **Enter**	
6	>Set Dwg Size | Landscape | A	Drawing is landscape size A		
7	>Views	Initialization: Model selection for the drawing	Type **Tut5-6a** then **Enter** or type **?** to select part from list	
8	>Add View | General | Full View | No Xsec | No Scale | Done	Add a General view		
9	Click in center of drawing	Place new view onto drawing		General view is drawn with datums
10	>Names	Want to use a named view	Click on COUPLER_FRONT then >Done/Return	Part displayed in front view in Fig. 5.24(a)
11	>Views >Add View >Projection | Full View | No Xsec | No Scale | Done	Add a projected view		
12	Click to top of Front View in Fig. 5.24(c)	Provide location for Projection on top		Top view displayed in Fig. 5.24(c)
13	>Views >Add View >Projection | Full View | No Xsec | No Scale | Done	Add a projected view		
14	Click to Left of Front View in Fig. 5.24	Provide location for Projection on Left		Left view displayed in Fig. 5.24(c)
15	>Views >Add View >Projection | Full View | Section | No Scale | Done	Add a projected Sectioned view		
16	>Full >Total Xsec | Done	Select Section Type from menu in Fig. 5.25		

Tutorial 5.6 Creating a Cross-Section View (continued)

Step	Action	Description	Further Actions	Result
17	Click to Right of Front View in Fig. 5.24(c)	Provide location for Projection on Right		Right view displayed in Fig. 5.28
18	>Create | Planar | Single | Done	Cross Section Type from Menu in Fig. 5.26(a)		
19	Type **SS** (or some section name not already used)	Create a new section		
20	Create | Plane | Sel by Menu | Name | DTM1	Select DTM1 as cut section from menu		See Fig. 5.33
21	Click on Center view	Want Center view to have section reference arrows in Fig. 5.28		Section is placed in Fig. 5.28
22	>Add View >Projection | Full View | Section | No Scale	Add a projected Sectioned view		
23	>Full >Total Xsec | Done	Select Section Type from menu in Fig. 5.25		
24	Click to Bottom of front View in Fig. 5.29	Provide location for Projection on Bottom		Bottom view displayed in Fig. 5.29
25	>Create | Planar | Single | Done	Cross Section Type from Menu in Fig. 5.26(a)		
26	Type **RR** (or some section name not already used)	Create a new section		
27	Create | Plane | Sel by Menu | Name | DTM8	Select DTM8 as cut section from menu		See Fig. 5.33
28	Click on Center view	Want center view to have section reference arrows in Fig. 5.29	>Done/Return	Section is placed in Fig. 5.29
29	Drawings | Modify | Xhatching |	Change cross hatching	Pick cross hatch in both new section views then >Done-Sel	
30	Spacing | Hatch | Overall | Half | Half	Halve the distance between cross hatch lines		Cross hatching gets denser
31	>Done	Finished, now repeat for a second time		
32	>File >Save	Save drawing file	Type **Enter** to accept tut5-6	File tut5-6.dwg saved
33	>QuitWindow			
34	Exit	Exit program	Click Yes to confirm	PT/Modeler exited

5.9.6   Scale

The scale factor can be entered independent of the drawing scale. Projected and Auxiliary views cannot be scaled. General views can be scaled, and Detailed views must be scaled.

5.10   Printing a Drawing

Print a drawing using the Plot command. A plot dialog appears. Click OK in this dialog. If you are connected to a printer, the Windows Printer Dialog appears as shown in Figure 5.30. Click OK and the selected sheets in the drawing will print. A title bar disclaimer indicates that this software is for educational purposes only.

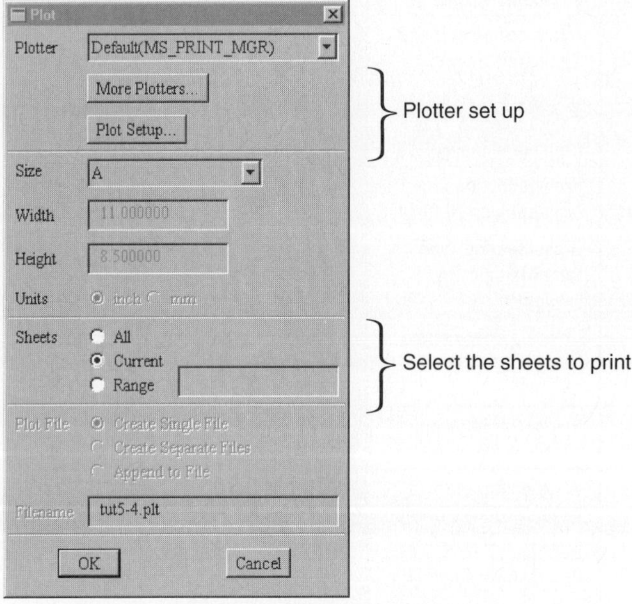

Figure 5.30   Plotter dialog.

5.11   Working with Multiple Sheets in a Drawing

A drawing starts with one sheet as a default. As you would suspect, this is sheet one. A drawing can have multiple sheets. This is a great way to organize your drawings as opposed to naming separate files for each sheet. The sheet menu is shown in Figure 5.31. From this menu you can add or delete new sheets to your drawing. You can reorder the sheet numbers. You can also move from sheet to sheet going directly to a numbered sheet, or going to the next or previous sheet.

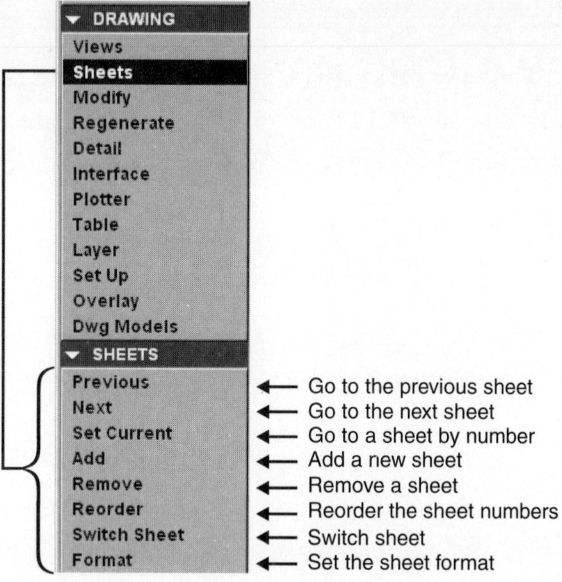

Figure 5.31   The Sheet menu.

We will be working with a drawing with multiple sheets during the dimensioning Tutorial 5.8.

5.12   Description of the Model

Throughout this chapter we have relied on a simple model. This model is relatively simple, as seen in Figure 5.32(a). However, when we enable the display of the datum planes through the Environment menu, the model gets pretty cluttered, as seen in Figure 5.32(b). It would be nice to work without datum planes to maintain an uncluttered view; however, in Drawings, you will often need datum planes displayed when picking Partial and Sectional separation planes.

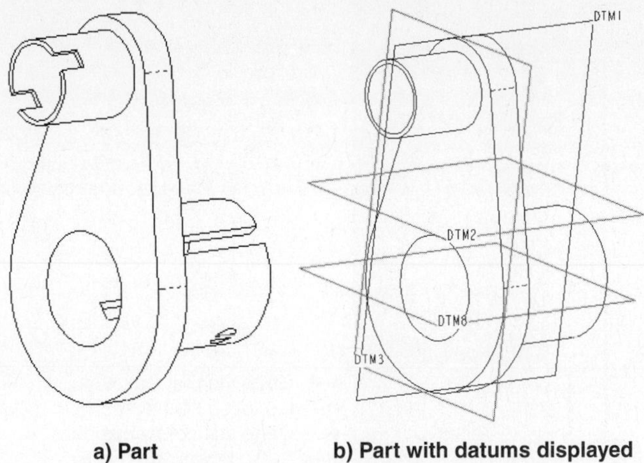

a) Part   **b) Part with datums displayed**

Figure 5.32 Model with and without datum planes.

I have provided a simplified view of the model in Figure 5.33 for your reference. I suppressed several of the unnecessary datum planes using the Suppress option of the Feature Operator menu. Notice that features were based upon these datum planes that I removed. Consequently, the datum planes were parents to these features. When I suppressed the datum planes, the child features were also suppressed. You can refer to this figure when working with this model in the drawing tutorials in this chapter. You can disable view of the datum planes from the Environment menu and refer to the datums by Name. I will show you how to do this in the next section.

As an additional note, I could have used MakeDatum planes for some of these features. This would help reduce the clutter. I wanted to keep the datum planes accessible for sections so I chose to create permanent datum planes instead.

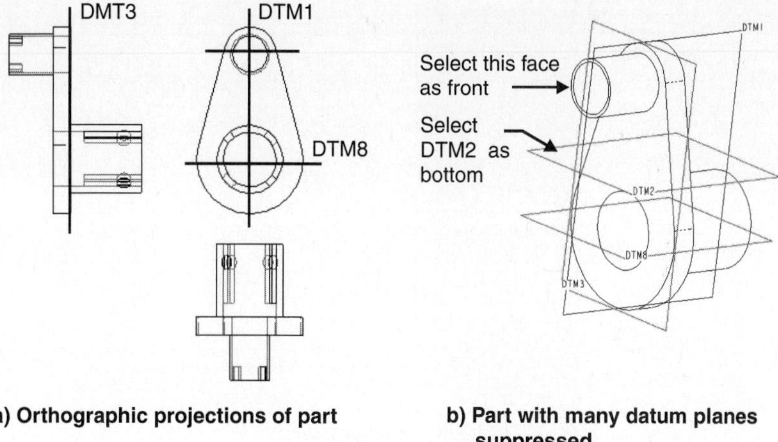

Figure 5.33   Simplified model with a few important datum planes.

5.13   Referring to Entities by Name

During the drawing process, you are constantly referring to datum planes. Unfortunately, while working in the Drawing mode, you cannot rotate around views to catch site of the desired datum plane for a pick. You could keep the part open in a separate window and refer back and forth from the Part mode in one window to the Drawing mode in the other window. You could rotate the part around in the Part mode and then jump back to the Drawing mode. This works, but it can be difficult to keep your place when you change modes. I recommend keeping datum planes off during Drawing. Refer to the figures in Section 5.13 to know which datum plane you want. Then, when asked to select a plane, follow the menus as seen in Figure 5.34 to refer to the datum plane by name.

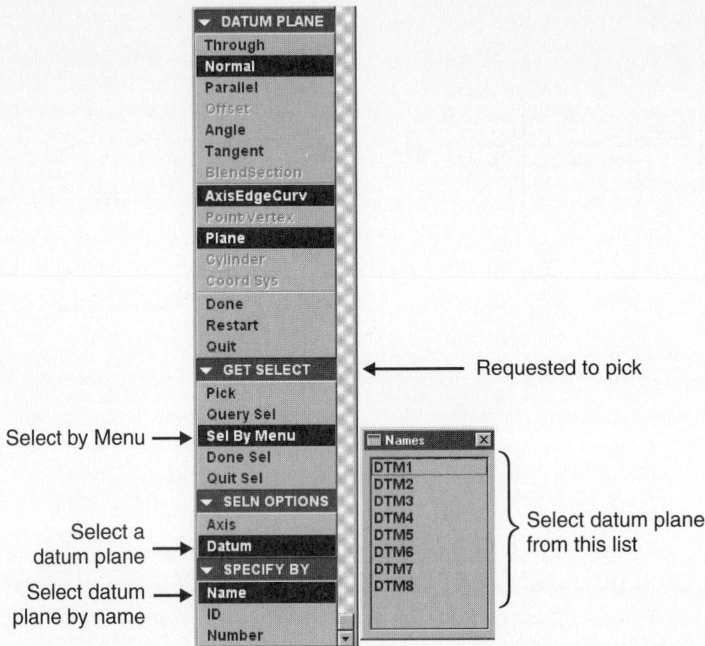

Figure 5.34   Simplified model with a few important datum planes.

5.14   Dimensioning a Drawing

Dimensioning of a part is accomplished during the design phase of solid modeling as features are created and modified. When you get to the Drawing stage, your dimensions should be in place. There are times when you will want to modify a part, based on a drawing. I suggest you go back into Part mode to accomplish this task. Since the part is fully constrained, all dimensions are available as you work in Drawing mode. All you have to do is show the dimensions on the drawing. However, this does not mean that your work is nearly done. Far from it. Creating a workable drawing is a bit of an art.

There are many ways to show the dimensions on a set of views. Choosing one technique might be difficult to understand and prone to errors. Dimensions relating to the same feature might be strewn across several views. Dimensions might be too close to each other, leaving ambiguity as to which edge a value, arrows, or witness lines references. You might actually find that creating views on the drawing and placing dimensions is an iterative process. You can start out with a set of views that seem sufficient, only to find that when dimensions are shown, the entire drawing looks like a spider web of lines, arrows, and text totally obscuring the drawing.

There are a great number of options available to you during the dimensioning process. I describe several of these in this chapter. You can experiment with the others as you master these techniques.

5.14.1   The Detail Menu

Dimensioning is accessed through the Detail menu item in the Drawing menu. The Drawing menu, shown in Figure 5.35(a), is reached through the Mode menu. During the course of this section, you will revert back to this Drawing menu many times as you switch Views, Sheets, and Details. We have already discussed the Views and Sheets menu. I will be discussing the following functions from within the Detail menu, shown in Figure 5.35(b).

- Choose which dimensions to show or erase
- Move dimensions within a view
- Move the text associated with a dimension
- Move dimensions across different views and flip arrows around for better readability

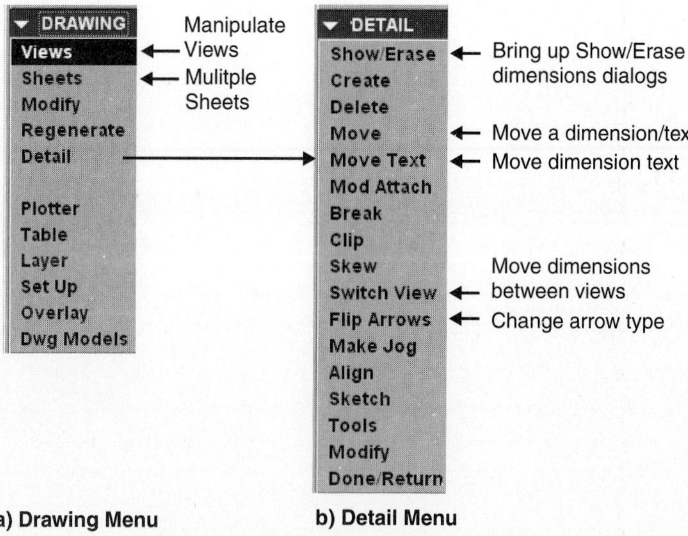

Figure 5.35   The Drawing and Detail menus.

5.14.2   Show/Erase Dialogs

Two dialogs are provided to assist you in showing dimensions, as well as reference dimensions, notes, symbols, and other items not discussed in this section. Figure 5.36(a) provides the Show dialog box. From here you can select the dimensions you wish to display. Note that I will only be showing dimensions so the first button should always be selected as indicated. You can select the dimensions by feature, part, view, or combinations thereof. I will discuss dimensions by feature exclusively in this section. The radio button at Show by . . . Feature should be checked throughout the next two tutorials. A button is provided to Show All dimensions. This is a pretty drastic step since everything shows up at once.

> **NOTE:** Erased dimensions are not deleted; they are merely removed from the view.

The Erase button at the top of the dialog accesses the Erase Dialog box as shown in Figure 5.36(b). As with the Show dialog, you should always have the Dimension button activated and the Feature radio button selected. An Erase All button allows you to erase all dimensions in one fell swoop.

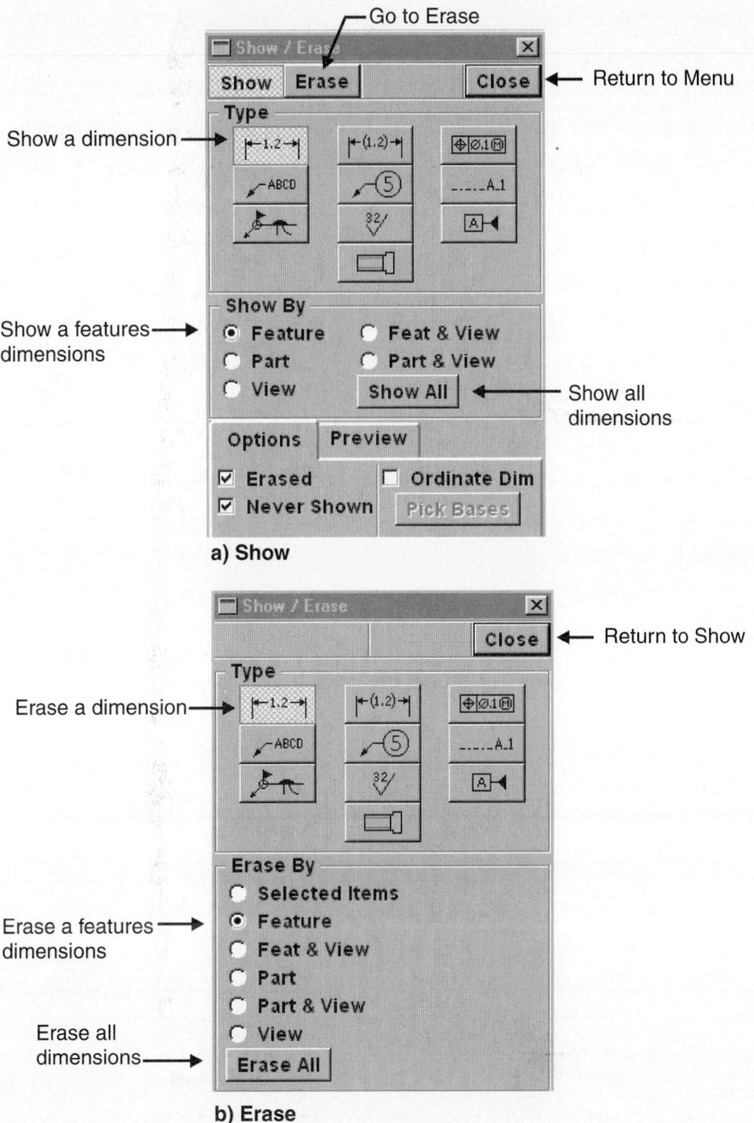

Figure 5.36   The Show and Erase dialog boxes.

5.14.3   Automatic Placement of Dimensions

The dimensioning software will place dimensions on the views provided in the drawing. It tries to do a good job, but it is up to you to finish the job. In reality, the software does all of the hard work. It remembers exactly which dimensions must be shown. You will not have to worry about under or over constraining the part with dimensions.

However, you will definitely have to touch up the placement of the dimensions. You will want to fuss with the dimensions to make the drawing more readable. As well, it is desirable to move your views around to provide sufficient room for the dimensions. It is likely that you will formulate new views to better display the dimensions.

5.14.4   Placing Dimensions a Feature at a Time

We will be working with dimensions feature by feature. Starting with a set of views, we will place the dimensions on the drawing by selecting a feature and then manipulating the dimensions for that specific feature. Once they are placed where we want them, we will select the next feature and position those. We will continue with this process until all dimensions are placed.

> **NOTE:** The dimensioning software remembers the position of dimensions. Suppose you position a set of dimensions to make them readable and then erase the dimensions. The next time you show the dimensions, they will appear in the same locations that you left them. This is true most of the time.

Dimensions consist of a text value and a line with an arrow at the end pointing to the referenced item. The arrow might touch the item directly or touch a line that is an extension of the item. These extension lines are called witness lines.

I suggest the following steps to use when dimensioning a drawing:

1. Lay out some preliminary views leaving plenty of space between views.
2. Decide if you want one sheet or multiple sheets organizing your views such that each sheet has a focus.
3. Start with the Show All button to see what you are up against. Look at the distribution of dimensions among views. Erase All to remove all dimensions and reposition or add new views to accommodate the dimension requirements. For example, if a side view is heavily loaded with dimensions, add other views that provide a side orientation.
4. Start with the base feature. Add dimensions one feature at a time, positioning the dimensions as you go.
5. Add Detail Views as necessary to accommodate the dimensions.
6. Distribute the dimensions among several views, keeping a focus for each view. Minimize the spread of dimensions relating to a single feature to two views if possible.
7. Keep each feature's dimensions shown while you add dimensions for other features. This way you will not position a dimension for a new feature on top of an older dimension that is now erased.

8. Save your work often using the SaveAs command. Choose a file name that ends in a number. Increment the number on every Save As. This way, you can easily revert back to a known state if your drawing goes amuck.

9. It is easy to select a feature, see the dimensions, and then hide the dimensions again. In this manner, you can determine which features still require dimensions. If you have already selected a feature, no new dimensions will appear. Make sure to check out all views.

10. When you think you have shown the dimensions for every feature, select Show All and see if any more dimensions appear. If so, you had not hit each feature. This last step insures that all dimensions are displayed and that the part is fully constrained in the drawing.

In Step 4, you will be positioning the dimensions for a given feature. I suggest that you follow the following steps during this cleaning up process.

1. Open the Show Dialog.

2. Select the desired feature.

3. Close the Show Dialog.

4. Use >Move to separate all dimensions so that you can both see each dimensional value and see whatever objects are referenced.

5. Use >Move Text to help clarify the dimensions.

6. Use >Flip Arrows to further clarify the dimensions.

7. Move dimensions to other views, creating new views if necessary.

8. Repeat Steps 4 through 7 until the feature is clearly dimensioned.

5.14.5   Selecting Items

When manipulating dimensions, you will select objects on the drawing surface. These objects might be reference faces or features. Rely on Query Sel to pick features. If you select the wrong feature, you may have a difficult time erasing the new unwanted dimensions.

When selecting during a >Move operation, you can select the text or the witness line. If you select the text, you can move the dimension on the surface. The witness lines will remain stuck to its reference feature. If you select the witness line, a small square appears on the witness line. As you drag the mouse, the small square follows up and down the witness line. This is the technique to use when positioning witness lines. If you select the end of the witness line, you can angle the witness lines creating a skew effect.

5.14.6   Witness Lines

Witness lines are extensions of the feature. A witness line is shown in Figure 5.37(a). You will have to clean up witness lines. This is accomplished by selecting the witness line and dragging a small box to position the end of the witness line.

In Figure 5.37(b), a witness line extends out the left side of an edge. Suppose that you want to position the text on the right side of the edge. The witness line is left running across the entire part. Clean up all witness lines as shown in Figure 5.37(c) by selecting the witness line and dragging the end to the desired location.

A second case often occurs where witness lines reference the center of a circle or arc, but do not extend long enough to cross the center. Extend the witness lines to cross the center for a more readable dimension. Do not try and select the end of the witness line if you want to move the end. Simply select anywhere on the line and drag to the end of the line.

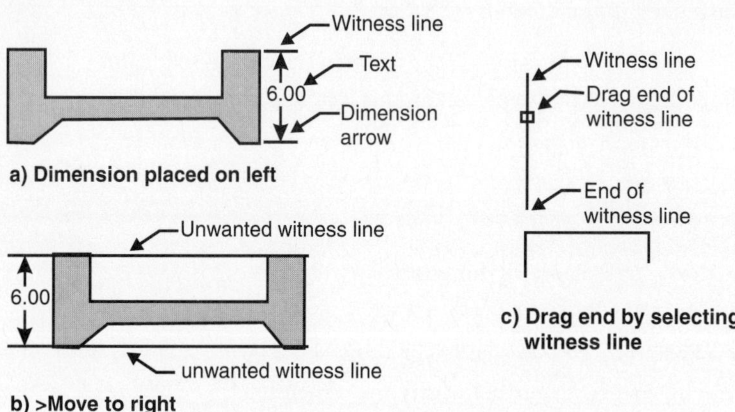

Figure 5.37   Placing the ends of witness lines.

5.14.7   Switch Views

The >Switch Views command is used to move dimensions from one view to another. After selecting >Switch Views, select the desired dimensions by clicking on the text associated with a dimension. You can select multiple dimensions: Select >Done-Sel (the short cut for this is mMb). Next, click on the desired view and the dimensions are moved.

5.14.8   Positioned Dimensions

Positioned dimensions are drawn in the highlighted color. As soon as you move the dimension, it changes to the standard line color. This provides you an easy way to determine the dimensions which you have already handled. You can simply use >Move and double click on any dimension to remove the highlight color.

5.14.9   A Dimensioning Exercise Tutorial

In Tutorial 5.7, you will create an A-sized drawing named Tut5-7. Place a General view of the part Tut5-7a near the center of the drawing. Use the >Names | FRONT orientation to achieve a front view as seen in Figure 5.38(a). Select the >Detail Menu and >Show/Erase to place some dimensions. Make sure that the Show Dialog has the dimension button and the Feature radio button selected as shown in Figure 5.38(a). Select the main body of the part as seen in Figure 5.38(a). The dimensions shown in Figure 5.38(b) are displayed. Select >Move and reposition the top-most 20 dimension as seen in Figure 5.38(c). Select >Move again and move the text to the other side of the arrow as in Figure 5.38(d). >Move the text to the center and this time select the ends of the witness lines to properly position the ends as seen in Figure 5.38(e). Choose >Show/Erase > Erase > Erase All to remove all dimensions.

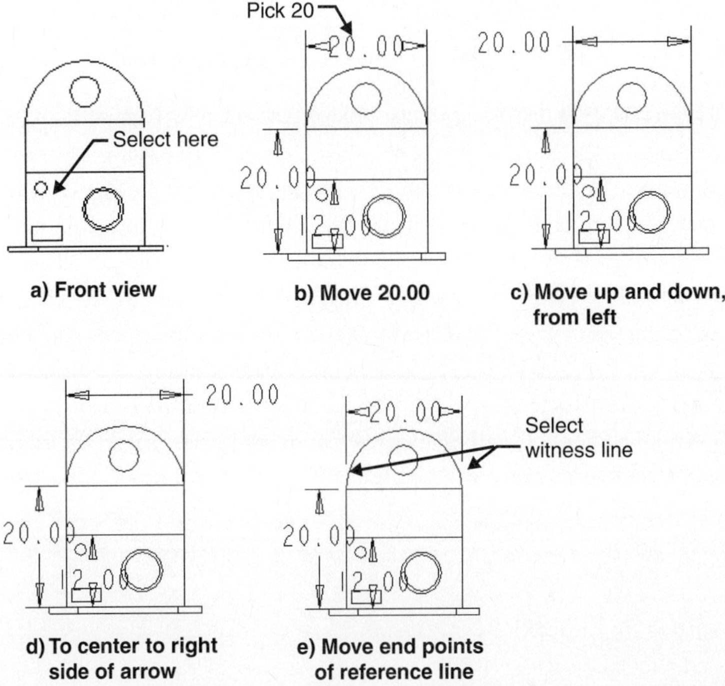

Figure 5.38   Manipulating dimensions using >Move and >Move Text.

Choose >Show/Erase again and select the cylinder protrusion out the front face of the part. Move the 6.00 dimension as seen in Figure 5.39(b). Now, use the >Move Text command to move the 6.00 over to the left of the arrow indicator. Select >Flip Arrows to create the arrows seen in Figure 5.39(d). Choose >Show/Erase > Erase > Erase All to remove all dimensions.

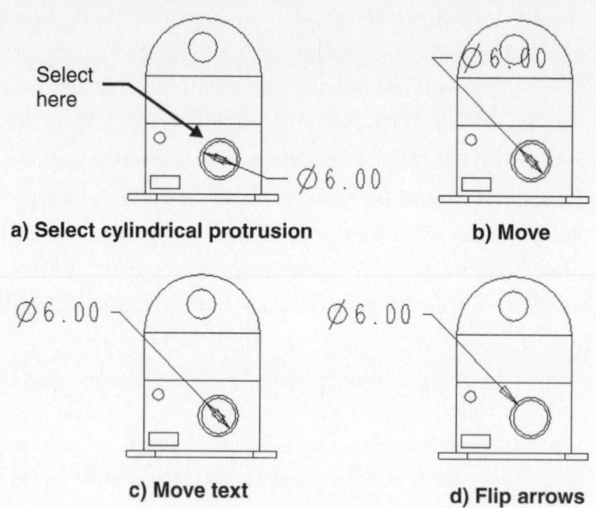

Figure 5.39   Practice using >Move, >Move Text, and >Flip Arrows.

Choose >Show/Erase again and select the base plate as shown in Figure 5.40(a). Make sure that Hidden Lines is selected in the Environment menu. Separate the dimensions using the >Move and >Move Text commands until they can all be seen. Do not worry about readability for now. We just want to be able to see what each dimension is trying to convey. Now, rearrange the dimensions as seen in Figure 5.40(b) using the >Move, >Move Text, and >Flip Arrows commands. Notice how all of the dimensions associated with the base plate are crammed into the single view. This is very objectionable and many dimensions are impossible to understand. Next, we will rectify this problem. Choose >Show/Erase >Erase >Erase All to remove all dimensions.

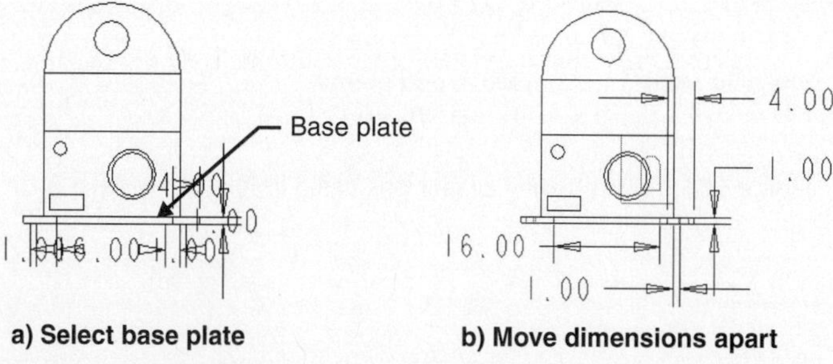

Figure 5.40   More practice using >Move, >Move Text, and >Flip Arrows.

At this time, add two new projected views using the >Views >Create >Projected menu selection clicking above and below the front view creating a top and bottom view. Now, choose >Show/Erase again and select the base plate as shown in Figure 5.41(a). Next, check No Hidden Lines in the Environment menu. We have enough views that we will not be needing hidden lines. Rearrange the dimensions as seen in Figure 5.41(b) using the >Move, >Move Text, and >Flip Arrows commands. This time you will also need the >Switch Views command.

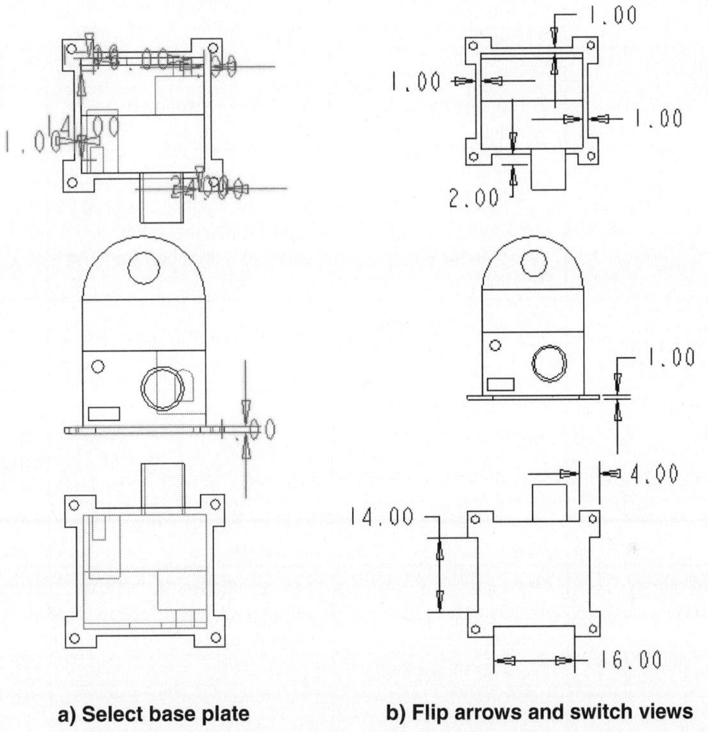

a) Select base plate   **b) Flip arrows and switch views**

Figure 5.41   Base plate dimensions using >Switch View.

Tutorial 5.7 Dimensioning Exercises

Files opened: Tut5-7a.prt   **Files saved:** Tut5-7.dwg

Step	Action	Description	Further Actions	Result
1	Click PT/Modeler Icon	Run PT/Modeler		After some time, PT/Modeler on screen
2	>Mode >Misc >Show Dir	Show current directory		Message similar to "Directory searched is c:\ptc\ptprod\bin"
3	>Change Dir	Change the current directory	Type **c:\proe\tutorial\ chapter_5**	
4	>Done-Return	Leave Misc menu		Misc menu removed
5	>Mode >Drawing >Create	Create and name a drawing	Type **tut5-7** then **Enter**	
6	>Set Dwg Size | Landscape | A	Drawing is landscape size A		
7	>Views	Initialization: Model selection for the drawing	Type **Tut5-7a** then **Enter** or type **?** to select part from list.	
8	>Add View | General | Full View | No Xsec | No Scale | Done	Add a General View		
9	Click in center of drawing	Place new view onto drawing		Part is placed onto drawing with datum planes enabled temporarily until part is oriented
10	>Names	Want to use a named view	Click on FRONT then >Done/Return	Part displayed in front view in Fig. 5.38(a)
11	>Drawing >Detail >Show/Erase	Show some dimensions	Select Dimensions, Features; select front-lower face as Fig 5.38(a)	Dimensions shown
12	Click Close button	Close the Show/Erase Dialog		Dialog closes, menu returns
13	>Move & Select top-most 20 dimension as Fig 5.38(b)	Experiment with Move	Move 20 to left as Fig 5.38(c)	Dimension changes
14	>Move & Select top-most 20 dimension as Fig 5.38(c)	Experiment with Move	Move 20 to center as Fig 5.38(d)	Dimension changes
15	> Move & Select witness lines	Move ends of witness line	Move end of witness line as in Fig 5.38(e)	Dimension changes
16	>Show/Erase, Select Erase, then Erase All	Erase all dimensions	Upon confirm click Yes	All dimensions erased
17	Click Close button	Close the Show/Erase Dialog		Dialog closes, menu returns

Tutorial 5.7   Dimensioning Exercises (continued)

Step	Action	Description	Further Actions	Result
18	Select Show & Select front cylinder protrusion	Dimension protrusion as Fig 5.39(a)	>Move Select diameter 6.00 and move to top left as Fig 5.39(b)	Dimension changes
19	>Move Text & Select 6.0 again	Move just the text to left of arrow line	Move text to left as Fig 5.39(c)	Dimension changes
20	>Flip Arrows	Change arrows from double in to single out	Click on 6.0 dimension	Arrows change to single arrow
21	>Show/Erase, Select Erase, then Erase All	Erase all dimensions	Upon confirm click Yes	All dimensions erased
22	Select Show & Select base plate	Dimension protrusion as Fig 5.40(a)		Dimension changes
23	Click Close button	Close the Show/Erase Dialog		Dialog closes, menu returns
24	>Move, >Move Text, >Flip arrows	Create the dimensions as Fig 5.40b.		
25	>Done/Return	Exit from >Detail menu		
26	>Views >Add View >Projection | Full View | No Xsec | No Scale	Add a projected view		
27	Click above of General view in Fig. 5.41(a)	Provide location for Projection on top		Top view displayed in Fig. 5.41(a)
28	>Add View >Projection | Full View | No Xsec | No Scale	Add a projected view		
29	Click below of General View in Fig. 5.41(a)	Provide location for Projection on Bottom		Bottom view displayed in Fig. 5.41(a)
30	Select Show & Select base plate as in Fig 5.41a.	Dimension protrusion as Fig 5.41(a)	>Move Select all dimensions and spread apart	
31	Click Close button	Close the Show/Erase Dialog		Dialog closes, menu returns
32	>Detail >Switch View	Move 14, 4, and 16 to bottom view	mLb on 14, 4, and 16; mMb to >Done-Sel, mLb on bottom view	Dimensions are moved to bottom view
33	>Move, >Move Text, >Flip Arrows	Organize dimension as Fig 5.41(b)		Dimensions organized
34	>File >Save	Save drawing file	Type **Enter** to accept tut5-7	File tut5-7.dwg saved
35	>QuitWindow			
36	Exit	Exit program	Click Yes to confirm	PT/Modeler exited

5.14.10   Dimensioning Patterns

Selecting the original gives you the dimensions associated with the original feature. You have to select one of the patterned instances to get the dimensions associated with the pattern. Selecting more than one patterned instance has no effect.

5.14.11   Moving Views from One Sheet to Another

As you build your drawings, it is very convenient to work on one sheet, as opposed to multiple sheets. It is difficult to move dimensions from one view to another if the two views are on separate sheets. Make the one sheet as large as necessary. Then, when you are done, add additional sheets to the drawing using the >Sheets>Add command. Determine the views that should reside on each page. Move the views to the other pages as necessary using the following procedure:

1. Go to the sheet that contains all of the views.
2. Select >Sheets>Switch Sheets.
3. Select all views that are to be moved to a separate page.
4. Select >Done-Sel indicating that all views have been picked.
5. Select >Done-Return indicating that nothing else needs to be picked.
6. Select >Next to get to the desired page.
7. Click on the sheet to place the view(s).
8. Change the paper size down to accommodate the views or paper specification.

5.14.12   Dimensioning a Part Tutorial

In Tutorial 5.8 we are going to completely dimension the same part, Tut5-8a, on a drawing with two sheets. If you want to see where we are going, the two final sheets are provided in Figures 5.48 and 5.49. You will be using the same commands as in Tutorial 5.7. This time you will be pressed to get all the dimensions correct. It is only through working with a complex example such as this that you gain a working understanding of dimensioning. After dimensioning a few parts, lock into a procedure that works for you.

The steps that we will be following, labeled "a" through "i" are shown in the three views of Figure 5.42. First, create a new drawing named Tut5-8. Place a General View as before using the >Names | Front view, and to its left place a side view using a full Projected view.

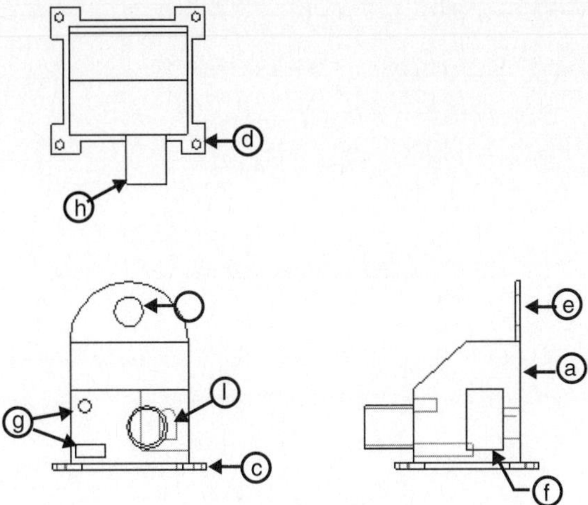

Figure 5.42   Feature pick list, "a" through "i."

Select the base feature marked "a" in Figure 5.42. Manipulate the dimensions to achieve the look in Figure 5.43(a). Select the hole feature marked "b" in Figure 5.42. Manipulate the dimensions to achieve the look in Figure 5.43(b).

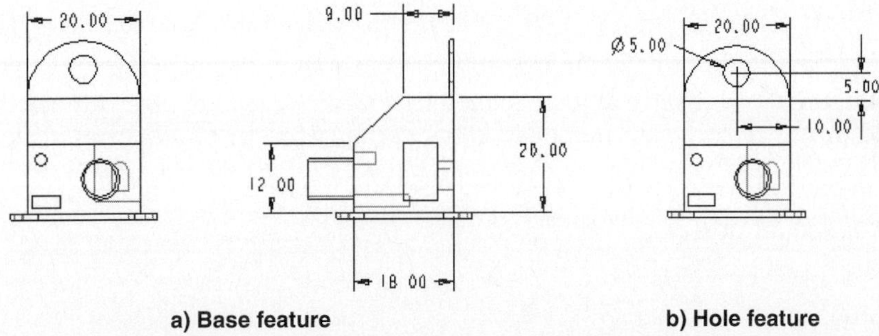

a) Base feature   **b) Hole feature**

Figure 5.43   Dimension base feature on front and right-side view.

We will need some more views before we can continue. Create a top view by adding a Full Projected view above the front view. Create a bottom view by adding a Full Projected view beneath the front view. Select the base plate feature marked "c" in Figure 5.42. Move the dimensions as shown in Figure 5.44(c).

Select a hole in the base plate marked "d" in Figure 5.42. Note that not all of the dimensions appear. These holes were patterned so you will have to select both the original and a pattern. Use >Switch View to get all of the dimensions associated with the holes on the bottom view as seen in Figure 5.44(d).

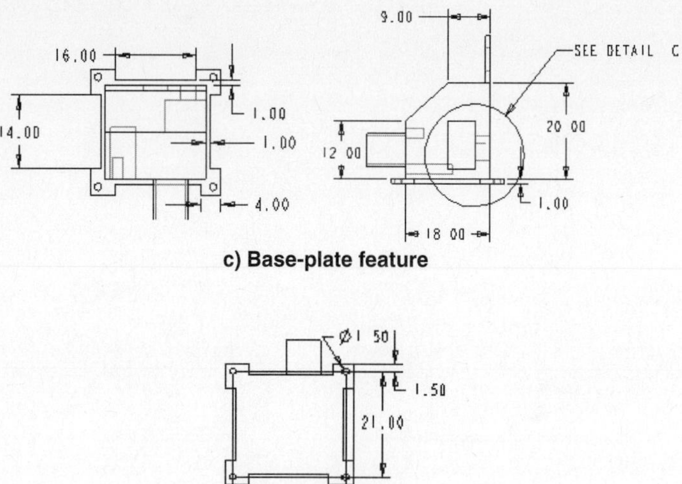

c) Base-plate feature

d) Base-plate holes

Figure 5.44   Dimension the base plate feature.

Select the Back plate marked "e" in Figure 5.42. Move the dimensions as seen in Figure 5.45(a). Next, we want to dimension the side cut as seen in Figure 5.45(a). The drawing will get very cluttered so we will create a Detailed view called "C." Give the Detailed view a scale of 0.142, twice the scale of the Projected view. Place it above and to the right of the right-side view as seen in Figure 5.45(f). The purpose of this view is to give us more room for the dimensions associated with the cut. Therefore, make sure that the spline outline includes the back portion of the base for dimensional references. Once the Detail view is created, select the cut and manipulate the dimensions as seen in Figure 5.45(f).

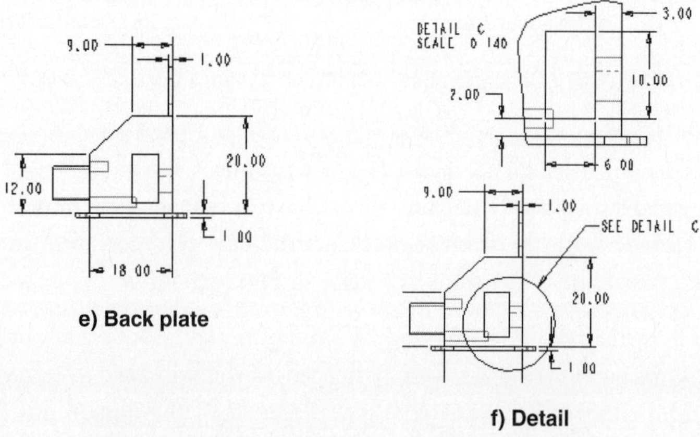

e) Back plate

f) Detail

Figure 5.45   Back plate and Detailed view of side cut.

There are two small circular and rectangular cuts on the front face that must be dimensioned. Once again, create a detailed view named "A" as seen in Figure 5.46(g). Select the two cuts, marked "g" in Figure 5.42. Place all but one dimension in the Detailed view. The depth dimensions of both cuts have to go in a side view so select the right side view.

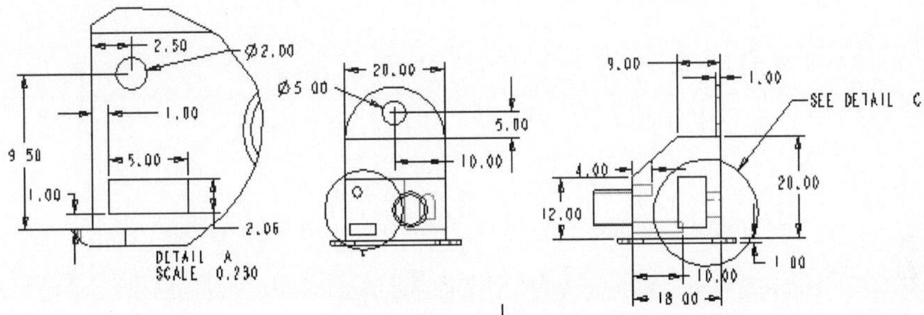

g) Front panel hole and cut

Figure 5.46   Detailed view of front hole and rectangular cuts.

As your next step, dimension the thin-walled cylinder protrusion marked "h" in Figure 5.42. However, the dimensions for this face are going to clutter our already busy Front view. We should create a second Front view. Add a second General view onto this sheet oriented in a Front view. Select the protrusion on this view and manipulate all dimensions associated with the protrusion on this view. Note that the length of the protrusion shows up on the Top view. You may have to move dimensions onto this view from the other Front view. Alternately, you could add another Front view as a projection off of one of the side, top, or bottom views. There are differences in these two approaches since the second General view is independent of the first. It can be scaled differently from the first. In this tutorial, either technique for adding the second Front view will work. Place dimensions for this protrusion on the Front and Top Views as shown in Figure 5.47.

The last feature that we need to place is the cutout on the back face. Add a Back view either by adding a new General view or a projection off of the right side. Next, create a third detailed view named "B" again with a 2:1 scale. Encircle the cutout on the back face. Once the Detailed view is completed, select the back cutout marked "f" in Figure 5.42. Place all dimensions associated with this cut onto the Detailed view.

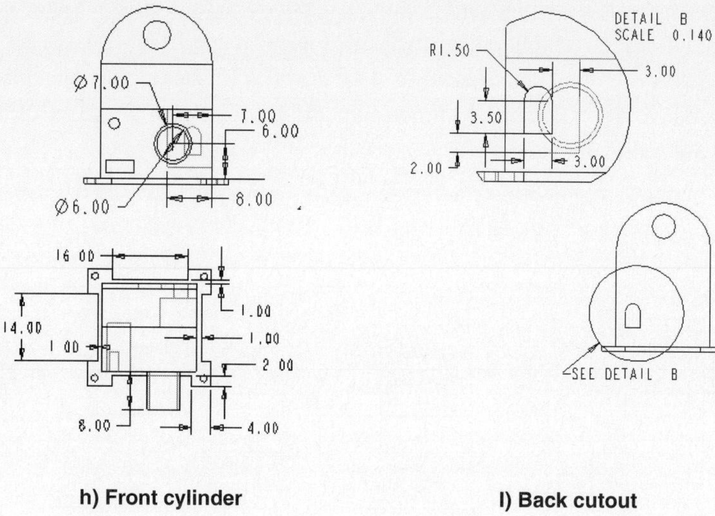

h) Front cylinder   **l) Back cutout**

Figure 5.47   Front protrusion cylinder and back cutout Detailed view.

We are done with the dimensioning. It is now time to organize our views into multiple sheets. Add two new sheets using the >Sheets >Add command. Return to sheet 1. Follow the procedure in Section 5.14.11 to move the second Front view and the Back view and its Detail B onto the second sheet. Save the drawing and you are done. You can change the size of the paper or add a border using the >Sheets > Format Menu Command.

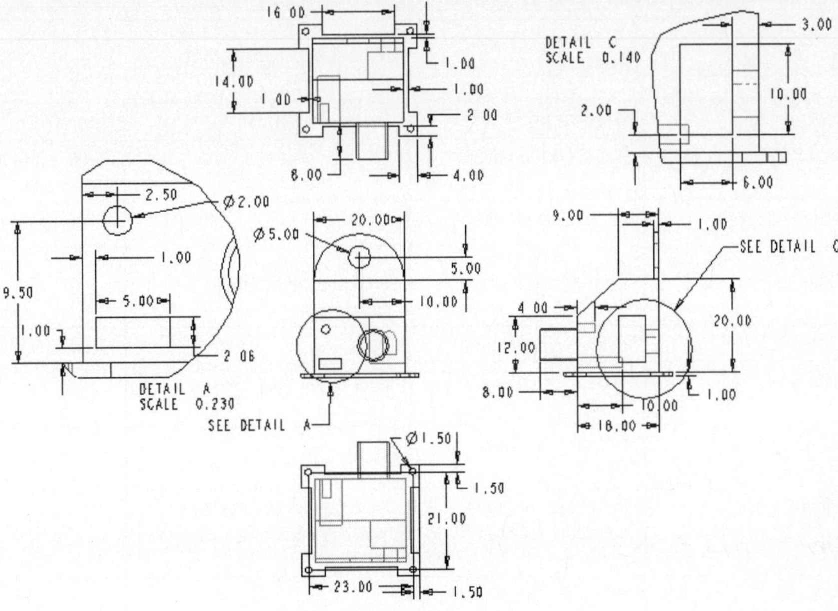

Figure 5.48 Sheet one of final drawing.

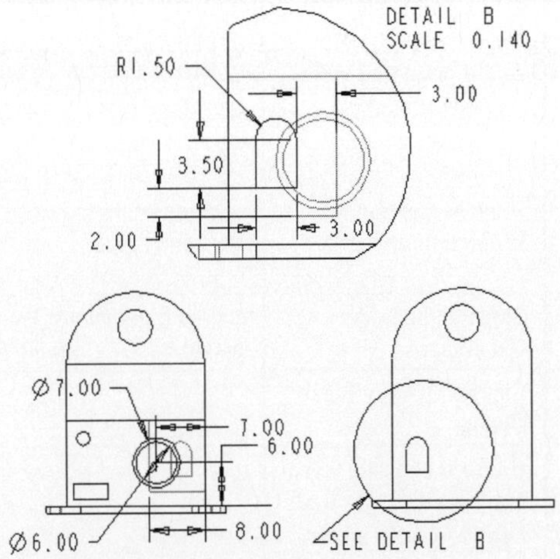

Figure 5.49 Sheet two of final drawing.

Tutorial 5.8   Dimensioning a Complicated Part

Files opened: Tut5-8.prt   **Files saved:** Tut5-8.dwg

Step	Action	Description	Further Actions	Result
1	Click PT/Modeler Icon	Run PT/Modeler		After some time, PT/Modeler on screen
2	>Mode >Misc >Show Dir	Show current directory		Message similar to "Directory searched is c:\ptc\ptprod\bin"
3	>Change Dir	Change the current directory	Type **c:\proe\tutorial\ chapter_5**	
4	>Done-Return	Leave Misc menu		Misc menu removed
5	>Mode > Drawing >Create	Create and name a drawing	Type **tut5-8** then **Enter**	
6	>Set Dwg Size | Landscape | A	Drawing is landscape size A		
7	>Views	Initialization: Model selection for the drawing	Type **Tut5-8a** then **Enter** or type **?** to select part from list	
8	>Add View | General | General | No Xsec | No Scale | Done	Add a General view		
9	Click in center of drawing	Place new view onto drawing		Part is placed onto drawing with datum planes enabled temporarily until part is oriented
10	>Names	Want to use a named view	Click on FRONT then >Done/Return	Part displayed in front view in Fig. 5.38(a)
11	>Add View >Projection | Full View | No Xsec | No Scale | Done	Add a projected view		
12	Click to right of General View in Fig. 5.43(a)	Provide location for Projection on Right	>Done/Return to return to Drawing menu	Right view displayed in Fig. 5.43(a)
13	>Drawing >Detail >Show/Erase	Show some Dimensions	Select Dimensions, Features; select base "a" as Fig 5.42	Dimensions shown
14	Click Close button	Close the Show/Erase Dialog		Dialog closes, menu returns
15	>Move, >Move Text, >Flip Arrows	On front and side view, organize dimension as Fig 5.43(a)		Dimensions organized
16	>Drawing >Detail >Show/Erase	Show some Dimensions	Select Dimensions, Features; select hole "b" as Fig 5.42	Dimensions shown
17	Click Close button	Close the Show/Erase dialog		Dialog closes, menu returns

Tutorial 5.8　Dimensioning a Complicated Part (continued)

Step	Action	Description	Further Actions	Result
18	>Switch View, >Move, >Move Text, >Flip Arrows	On front view organize dimension as Fig 5.43(b)		Dimensions organized
19	>Show/Erase	Show some Dimensions	Select Dimensions, Feature; select base plate "c" as Fig 5.42	Dimensions shown
20	Click Close button	Close the Show/Erase dialog		Dialog closes, menu returns
21	>Switch View, >Move, >Move Text, >Flip Arrows	On top and side view organize dimension as Fig 5.44(a)		Dimensions organized
22	>Show/Erase	Show some Dimensions	Select Dimensions, Features; select multiple holes in base plate "d" as Fig 5.42	Dimensions shown
23	>Switch View, >Move, >Move Text, >Flip Arrows	On front view organize dimension as Fig 5.44(d)		Dimensions organized
24	>Show/Erase	Show some Dimensions	Select Dimensions, Features; select back plate "e" as Fig 5.42	Dimensions shown
25	>Switch View, >Move, >Move Text, >Flip Arrows	On front view organize dimension as Fig 5.45e	>Done/Return	Dimensions organized
26	>Views >Add View >Detailed | Full View | No Xsec | No Scale	Add a Detailed View named C to top-right of right-side view	Follow instructions in Tutorial 5.3 to create a detailed view as Fig 5.45(f)	
27	>Drawing >Detail >Show/Erase	Show some Dimensions	Select Dimensions, Features; select side cut "f" as Fig 5.42	Dimensions shown
28	Click Close button	Close the Show/Erase dialog		Dialog closes, menu returns
29	>Switch View, >Move, >Move Text, >Flip Arrows	On detailed view organize dimension as Fig 5.45(f)		Dimensions organized
30	>Add View > Detailed | Full View | No Xsec | No Scale	Add a Detailed View named A to top-right of front view	Follow instructions in Tutorial 5.3 to create a detailed view as Fig 5.46(g)	
31	>Drawing >Detail >Show/Erase	Show some Dimensions	Select Dimensions, Features; select front hole and cut "g" as Fig 5.42	Dimensions shown
32	Click Close button	Close the Show/Erase dialog		Dialog closes, menu returns
33	>Switch View, >Move, >Move Text, >Flip Arrows	On new front view organize dimension as Fig 5.46(g)		Dimensions organized

Tutorial 5.8   Dimensioning a Complicated Part (continued)

Step	Action	Description	Further Actions	Result
34	>Views >Add View | General | Full View | No Xsec | No Scale	Add a General view to top right of drawing	>Done	
35	Click in top right of drawing	Place new view onto drawing		Part is placed onto drawing with datum planes enabled temporarily until part is oriented
36	>Names	Want to use a named view	Click on FRONT then >Done	Part displayed in front view in Fig. 5.46(g)
37	>Drawing >Detail >Show/Erase	Show some Dimensions	Select Dimensions, Features; select front protrusion "h" as Fig 5.42	Dimensions shown
38	Click Close button	Close the Show/Erase dialog		Dialog closes, menu returns
39	>Switch View, >Move, >Move Text, >Flip Arrows	On new front and top view organize dimension as Fig 5.47(h)		Dimensions organized
40	>Views >Add View | General | Full View | No Xsec | No Scale	Add a General view to top right of drawing	>Done	
41	Click in top left of drawing	Place new view onto drawing		Part is placed onto drawing with datum planes enabled temporarily until part is oriented
42	>Names	Want to use a named view	Click on BACK then >Done	Part displayed in back view in Fig. 5.47(i)
43	>Add View >Detailed | Full View | No Xsec | No Scale	Add a Detailed view named B to top-left of new back view	Follow instructions in Tutorial 5.3 to create a detailed view as Fig 5.47(i)	
44	>Drawing >Detail >Show/Erase	Show some Dimensions	Select Dimensions, Features; select back slot "i" as Fig 5.49	Dimensions shown
45	Click Close button	Close the Show/Erase Dialog		Dialog closes, menu returns
46	>Switch View, >Move, >Move Text, >Flip Arrows	On detail view organize dimension as Fig 5.47(i)	>Done/Return to return to Drawing menu	Dimensions organized
47	>Sheets>Add	Add a second sheet		Second sheet added
48	>Previous	Return to sheet 1		Back on sheet 1
49	>Switch View			
50	mLb select the second front view	Select second front view	>Done-Sel, >Done Return to end selection	
51	>Next	Go to sheet 2		Now on blank sheet two

Tutorial 5.8 Dimensioning a Complicated Part (continued)

Step	Action	Description	Further Actions	Result
52	Click in center of sheet	Place new front view		New front view on second sheet
53	>Previous	Return to sheet 1		Back on sheet 1
54	>Switch View			
55	mLb select the back view and Detail B	Select back view and Section B view	>Done-Sel, >Done Return to end selection	
56	>Next	Go to sheet 2		Now on blank sheet two
57	Click on sheet	Place both views		New front view on second sheet
58	>Drawing >View >Move	Move views as Fig 5.49		
59	>Drawing >Sheets >Previous	Go back to sheet 1		
60	>Drawing >View >Move	Move views as Fig 5.48		
61	>File >Save	Save drawing file	Type **Enter** to accept tut5-8	File tut5-8.dwg saved
62	>QuitWindow			
63	Exit	Exit program	Click Yes to confirm	PT/Modeler exited

Chapter 6

Understanding Features

This chapter dives right into the details of creating the most popular features. These include holes, cuts, protrusions, rounds, fillets, chamfers, and revolved features. Each of these features has several options that help achieve your goals. You will learn how to use many of these options.

Before we get involved in the details of these features, we will look at the topic of depth. Most of these features either remove material or add material from a sketch plane. It is necessary to specify how deep this addition or removal should proceed into the part.

The depth menu is shown in Figure 6.1. Select one of the choices, and click Done. Some of the choices—Blind, Thru Until, and Up to Pnt/Vtx—require additional information. Thru Next and Thru All do not require additional information.

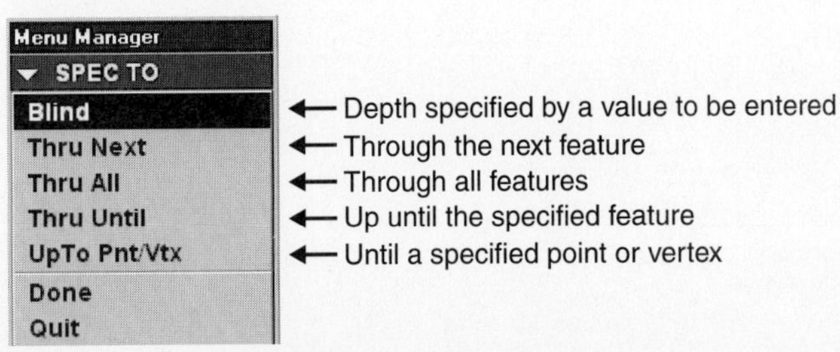

Figure 6.1 Depth menu.

Care should be taken when reordering features. What if a hole feature, A, has a Thru Next depth parameter and the next feature happens to be an protrusion B? What happens if you reorder the features such that B is placed after A in the Model Tree? What happens if you delete or suppress feature B? In each of these cases, upon the next regeneration, the hole A will search for a feature it can use as the *Next* feature instead of feature B.

6.1   Selecting a Depth

As most new features are created, it is necessary to specify a depth for the feature. In the case of a hole or cut, material will be removed up to a specified depth. In the case of an extruded protrusion, material will be added up to a specified depth. There are several ways to specify a depth, and each is described in the following sections.

In Tutorial 6.1, you will create five hole features into the side of a protrusion as shown in Figure 6.2. Each hole will be designated with a different depth attribute. It is unnecessary to have a sketch to produce a straight hole. Simply click on the side surface for the hole's face. Next click on the top-side edge for the first reference. The distance from this reference to each hole's center will be 50, 100, 150, 200, and 250 for the five holes. Lastly, you will need to click on the front-side edge for the second reference. The distance from this edge to the center of the holes will remain at 50.

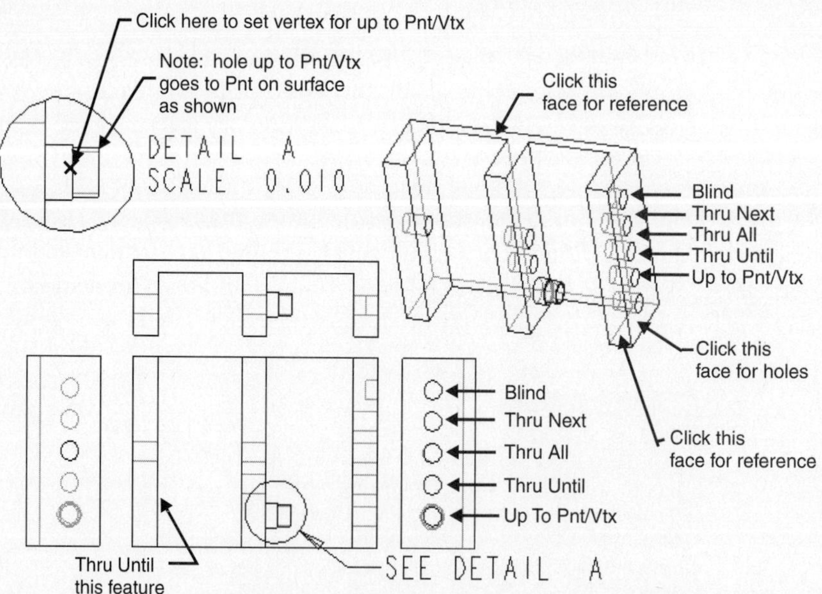

Figure 6.2   Illustrations for Tutorial 6.1.

Tutorial 6.1 Build Depth Features

Files opened: Tut6-1a.prt   **Files saved:** Tut6-1b.prt

Step	Action	Description	Further Actions	Result
1	Click PT/Modeler Icon	Run PT/Modeler		After some time, PT/Modeler on screen
2	>Mode >Misc >Show Dir	Show current directory		Message similar to "Directory searched is c:\ptc\ptprod\bin"
3	>Change Dir	Change the current directory	Type **c:\proe\tutorial\ chapter_6**	
4	>Done-Return	Leave Misc menu		Misc menu removed
5	>Mode >Part >Retrieve	Read a part	Type **tut6-1a**	Part loaded
6	>Environment	Set up the environment	Set up checks as seen in Table T6.1 Column Step 6	
7	>Done-Return			
8	>Feature >Hole	Create a hole		
9	>Straight | Done	Straight hole won't require Sketcher		
10	>Linear | Done	Linear dimensioning scheme for referencing hole		
11	Pick Side face for placing hole	Select side face in Fig. 6.2		
12	Pick top-side edge	Pick first reference for first linear dimension in Fig. 6.2	Type **50**	Want center of hole to be 50 units from top
13	Pick front-side edge	Pick second reference for second linear dimension in Fig. 6.2	Type **50**	Want center of hole to be 50 units from front
14	>One Side | Done	Hole will be extruded to one side only		
15	>Blind	Want blind depth type		
16	Type **30**	Enter diameter		Part is now ready to be previewed
17	Click Preview Type F1	View part in default view	Click OK to accept protrusion	Part should have first hole
18	>Feature >Hole	Create a hole		
19	>Straight | Done	Straight hole won't require Sketcher		
20	>Linear | Done	Linear dimensioning scheme for referencing hole		

Tutorial 6.1 Build Depth Features (continued)

Step	Action	Description	Further Actions	Result
21	Pick Side face for placing hole	Select side face in Fig. 6.2		
22	Pick top-side edge	Pick first reference for first linear dimension in Fig. 6.2	Type **100**	Want center of hole to be 100 units from top
23	Pick front-side edge	Pick second reference for second linear dimension in Fig. 6.2	Type **50**	Want center of hole to be 50 units from front
24	>One Side | Done	Hole will be extruded to one side only		
25	>Thru Next | Done	Want to go through next feature		
26	Type **30**	Enter diameter		Part is now ready to be previewed
27	Click Preview Type F1	View part in default view	Click OK to accept protrusion	Part should have second hole
28	>Feature >Hole	Create a hole		
29	>Straight | Done	Straight hole won't require Sketcher		
30	>Linear | Done	Linear dimensioning scheme for referencing hole		
31	Pick Side face for placing hole	Select side face in Fig. 6.2		
32	Pick top-side edge	Pick first reference for first linear dimension in Fig. 6.2	Type **150**	Want center of hole to be 150 units from top
33	Pick front-side edge	Pick second reference for second linear dimension in Fig. 6.2	Type **50**	Want center of hole to be 50 units from front
34	>One Side | Done	Hole will be extruded to one side only		
35	>Thru All | Done	Want hole to go through all other features in part		
36	Type **30**	Enter diameter		Part is now ready to be previewed
37	Click Preview Type F1	View part in default view	Click OK to accept protrusion	Part should have third hole
38	>Feature >Hole	Create a hole		
39	>Straight | Done	Straight hole won't require Sketcher		

Tutorial 6.1   Build Depth Features (continued)

Step	Action	Description	Further Actions	Result
40	>Linear | Done	Linear dimensioning scheme for referencing hole		
41	Pick Side face for placing hole	Select side face in Fig. 6.2		
42	Pick top-side edge	Pick first reference for first linear dimension in Fig. 6.2	Type **200**	Want center of hole to be 200 units from top
43	Pick front-side edge	Pick second reference for second linear dimension in Fig. 6.2	Type **50**	Want center of hole to be 50 units from front
44	>One Side | Done	Hole will be extruded to one side only		
45	>Thru Until | Done	Want hole to go through all features until it encounters selected feature	Then click on far protrusion face in Fig. 6.2	
46	Type **30**	Enter diameter		Part is now ready to be previewed
47	Click Preview Type F1	View part in default view	Click OK to accept protrusion	Part should have fourth hole
48	>Feature >Hole	Create a hole		
49	>Straight | Done	Straight hole won't require Sketcher		
50	>Linear | Done	Linear dimensioning scheme for referencing hole		
51	Pick Side face for placing hole	Select side face in Fig. 6.2		
52	Pick top-side edge	Pick first reference for first linear dimension in Fig. 6.2	Type **250**	Want center of hole to be 250 units from top
53	Pick front-side edge	Pick second reference for second linear dimension in Fig. 6.2.	Type **50**	Want center of hole to be 50 units from front
54	>One Side | Done	Hole will be extruded to one side only		
55	>Up to Pnt/Vtx	Want hole to extend to a specified point	>Done, then click on X in Fig. 6.2; no point is visible	
56	Type **30**	Enter diameter		Part is now ready to be previewed

Tutorial 6.1   Build Depth Features (continued)

Step	Action	Description	Further Actions	Result
57	Click Preview Type F1	View part in default view	Click OK to accept protrusion	Part should have fifth hole
58	>File>SaveAs	Save file with new name	Enter to accept [tut6-1a.prt] then type **tut6-1b.prt**	Part saved
59	>QuitWindow			
60	>Exit	Exit program	Click Yes to confirm	PT/Modeler exited

Item	Step 6
Disp DtmPln	No
Spin Center	No
Disp Pnts	Checked
Disp Axes	No
Rendering	Hidden line

Table T6.1

Environment Settings

6.1.1   Blind

The only independent depth measure is the blind depth. Here, a parameter is specified that indicates the depth. This value is measured normal to the sketching plane. After selecting blind, a query asks for the desired depth. You are required to enter a value for the depth of the feature at that time. The resulting feature has a blind depth as illustrated in Figure 6.3.

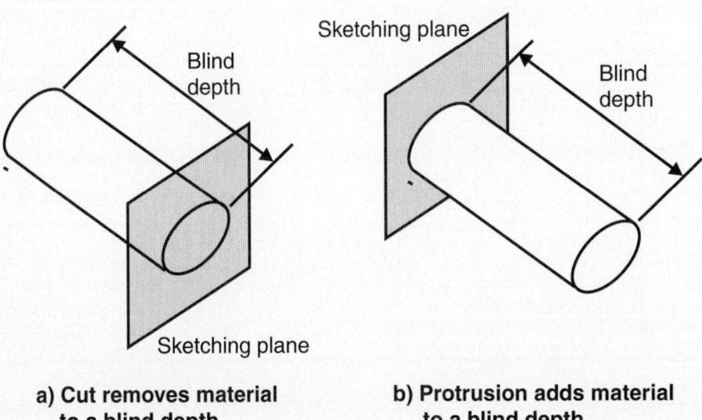

Figure 6.3   Blind depth.

Care should be taken when using the blind measure. If you want the hole to go through a feature, use the Thru Next option as opposed to selecting a blind measure that is large enough to go through that feature. Otherwise, you could end up regretting the decision when something gets modified downstream. Remember that it is easy to redefine a feature but this is no substitute for defining the feature correctly the first time.

6.1.2   Through Next

This depth type, referenced as Thru Next, takes the feature through the next surface that it encounters on its journey from the sketching plane, in its specified direction, along the normal to the sketching plane. The depth is determined by the next surface extending to the farthest extent.

6.1.3   Through All

This depth type, referred to as Thru All, takes the feature through all of the other surfaces in its direction and that are in front of it in the Model Tree. You are not required to specify any other information.

6.1.4   Through Until

This depth type, referred to as Thru Until, takes the feature through all features until it encounters the specified surface. You have to pick the feature that should be used as the limit.

6.1.5   Up to Point/Vertex

You are able to specify a point on the model. The feature under construction will extend until it hits a plane that is parallel to its sketching plane and contains the point. The feature being extended does not have to intersect the specified point directly.

6.2   Changing a Feature Using Modify, Redefine, and Reorder

In Tutorial 6.2, you have an opportunity to experiment with these depth measures using the set of holes seen in Figure 6.2. Five holes are placed into a protrusion. Each hole has a separate depth type as indicated in Figure 6.2. You will modify a feature using the Modify command, redefine a feature using the Redefine command, and lastly, reorder a feature in the Model Tree using the Reorder command.

I introduce the topics of Modify, Redefine, and Reorder in this chapter because you will use them extensively when designing features. I describe the various options for each of these in the next chapter.

6.2.1   Modify

It is very easy to modify the dimensions in a preexisting feature. Simply click the Modify menu item in the Parts menu. Click on the feature to be modified using standard picking techniques. The part is highlighted, and the dimensions are shown. You can orient the model to see the dimensions better. Click on the dimension that you wish to modify. A query is provided asking for you to change this dimension. The current dimension value is provided as a default. No changes take place in the actual model until regeneration occurs. Start the regeneration process by clicking Regenerate; this allows you to queue up changes. Once the new dimension is entered, other dimensions can be modified as well. You can select other features and modify dimensions within those features as well, before starting a regeneration.

> **NOTE:** You can cause regeneration failures by modifying dimensions improperly. In addition, you can really mess up your model. Consider changing the diameter of a hole from 1.0 to 100.0. The hole would quite likely eat your entire part.

In the case where you improperly change a value and lose sight of the model, you can (in some cases) unregenerate to get back to your known state. You can still select a feature for modification using the Model Tree, even if the feature cannot be seen.

6.2.2   Redefine

Redefining a feature provides you with access to nearly every parameter in a feature. You enter redefine from the >Feature Oper Selection in the >Part menu or from the >Resolve Feat >Quick Fix menus after a regeneration failure.

A feature dialog box is displayed as shown in Figure 6.4. All of the accessible parameter types are displayed in the top scroll-down list. You will need to select one or more of these for redefinition. Click on one to select it, and then click on the Define button to redefine that feature. All of the dialogs and menus that were used to create that aspect of the feature will be reasserted. Thus, you will be stepped through the design phase once more. If you select more than one item in the scroll-down list for redesign, you will be walked through the design process for all selected items.

You can get information about a part using the Info button; an information window is displayed. You can get reference information about a specific item in the scroll-down list by selecting an item and then clicking on Reference. Once you have followed all of the steps in the redesign, redefine menus disappear. You are left with the dialog. Click Preview to see the change. You can change the part orientation to see the changes better. When you are satisfied with the changes, click OK. If you are not satisfied, repeat the redesign process by selecting the item or items to redesign once again before clicking OK.

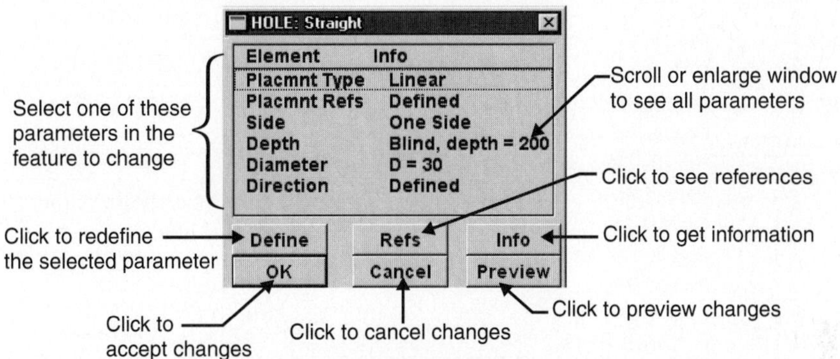

Figure 6.4   Feature dialog.

6.2.3   Reorder

Parts are constructed one feature at a time. You enter reorder from the >Feature Oper Selection in the >Part menu or from the >Resolve Feat >Quick Fix menus after a regeneration failure.

The order in which features are constructed is indicated by the order in which they were designed and reflected in the Model Tree. You can change the order of features using the Reorder menu item.

After selecting Reorder, you are requested to select the feature that you desire to move in the Feature Construction List as reflected in the Model Tree. You can select this feature using any of the standard select modes. I prefer to use the Model Tree when selecting features for the reorder operation. The menu for selecting the feature to move is shown in Figure 6.5, along with the Model Tree.

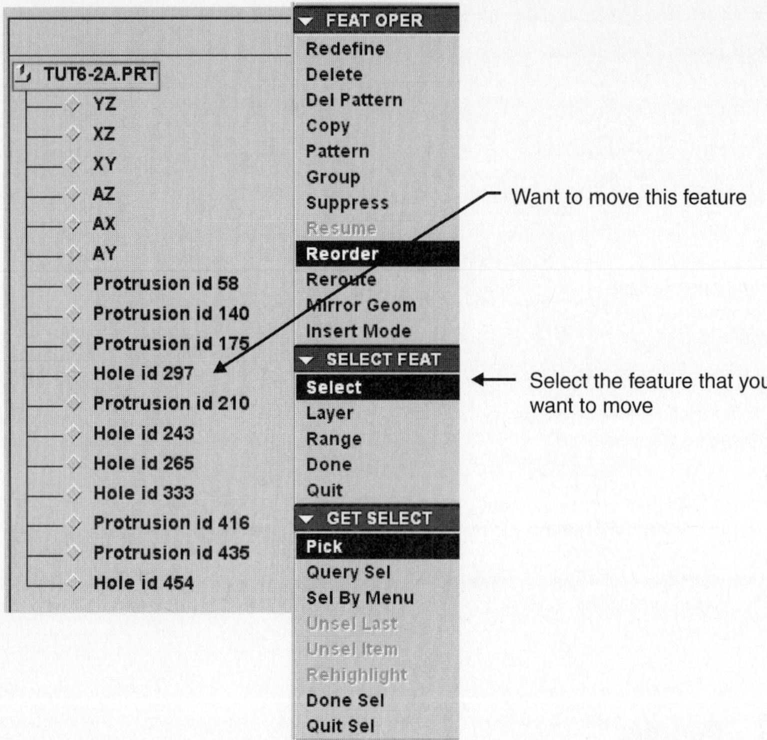

Figure 6.5   Pick a feature to place in a different location of the Model Tree.

Once selected, a message appears in the Message Window indicating the status of the reorder operation thus far. This message might indicate that the selected feature cannot be reordered. It might also indicate what locations in the Model Tree are available for this feature. Remember that parent-child relationships are all based on the parent existing before the child in the Model Tree. You cannot move a parent below a child in this list. Also remember that parent-child relationships can be quite complex. A single dimension in a feature A might be referenced to an edge of another feature B, even though those features are on opposite ends of the part. The feature B that is referenced is the parent. Consequently, you could not reorder the feature A before feature B in the Model Tree.

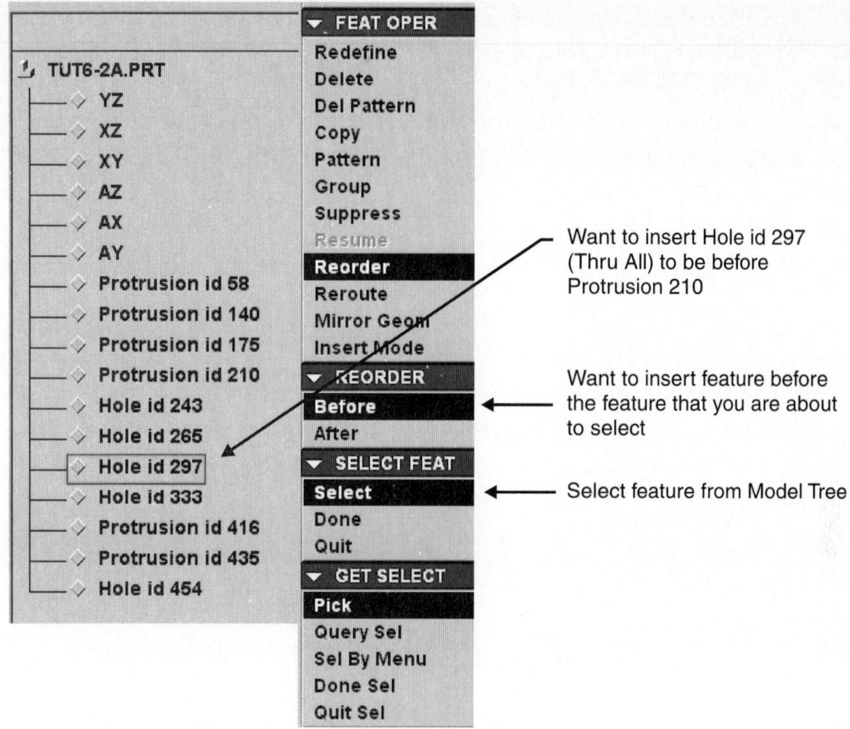

Figure 6.6   Pick a feature to use as a before-or-after reference.

6.2.4   Modifying a Part Tutorial

You will get a chance to modify, redefine, and reorder hole features in Tutorial 6.2. First, load the part represented in the drawing of Figure 6.2. You can disable the display of datum planes, axis, and spin center. Keep datum points enabled and enable the hidden line mode.

Next we will modify a feature. Click on Modify in the Parts menu. Click on the top hole marked blind in Figure 6.2. Orient the part as required and remember, it is always smart policy to use Query Select. You have selected to modify this feature. It is permissible to modify any dimensions in this Modify mode. We want to modify the blind depth of this hole. Click on the 20 dimension and type 200 to change the blind depth from 20 to 200. Click on Regenerate to see the result. Note the hole now goes part way into the center protrusion.

Next, you will redefine a feature. Click on Features Oper menu item and select Redefine. You are asked to select the feature to redesign. We are redesigning the second hole as seen in Figure 6.2. This hole feature was designed to have a Thru Until attribute. We want to redesign this hole to still have a Thru Until attribute, but this time we will change the feature at which it stops. Select Depth in the Features Dialog and click on the Define button. From here, accept Thru Until | Done again and click on the center protrusion. Click on Preview to see the changed hole. The hole used to go through the middle protrusion. Now it stops before the second protrusion. Click OK to accept the change. If another protrusion feature was added between the end and center protrusions after the hole, the hole would not go through it. However, if the new feature was added before the hole, the hole would go through the new feature.

Finally, you will reorder a feature. You will take the third hole, which resides after the three protrusions, and place it before the last protrusion in the Model Tree. Even though the third hole has a Thru All attribute, it will not penetrate the third protrusion. This occurs because the third protrusion did not exist when the hole feature was built.

Tutorial 6.2   Modify, Redefine, and Reorder Depth Features

Files opened: Tut6-2a.prt   **Files saved:** Tut6-2b.prt

Step	Action	Description	Further Actions	Result
1	Click PT/Modeler Icon	Run PT/Modeler		After some time, PT/Modeler on screen
2	>Mode >Misc >Show Dir	Show current directory		Message similar to "Directory searched is c:\ptc\ptprod\bin"
3	>Change Dir	Change the current directory	Type **c:\proe\tutorial\ chapter_6**	
4	>Done-Return	Leave Misc menu		Misc menu removed
5	>Mode >Part >Retrieve	Read a part	Type **tut6-2a**	Part loaded
6	>Environment	Set up the environment	Set up checks as seen in Table T6.2 Column Step 6	
7	>Done-Return			
8	>Part >Modify	Modify the blind depth of the first hole	Click on the first hole with blind depth in Fig. 6.2	Hole is highlighted
9	Click on 20 dimension	Select the 20 dimension to be changed	Type **200**	Changed dimension but nothing happens until regeneration
10	Regenerate	Regenerate the part		Part now shows new hole depth

Tutorial 6.2   Modify, Redefine, and Reorder Depth Features (continued)

Step	Action	Description	Further Actions	Result
11	>Feature Oper >Redefine	Want to redefine a feature	Click on second hole	Second hole highlighted
12	In Features dialog box click on Depth	Want to redefine the depth type	Click on Define button	Depth choice menu reappears
13	>Thru Until | Done	Want to go until the center protrusion	Click on center protrusion	
14	Click Preview Type F1	View part in default view	Click OK to accept protrusion	Second hole does not go through second protrusion any longer
15	>Feature Oper >Reorder	Want to reorder the third hole with Thru All	Click on third hole Feature 13 Hole id 297 in Model Tree	
16	Done Sel		>Done to get ready for insert	
17	>Before >Select >Pick	Want to place the feature before the feature about to be picked		
18	Click on Center Protrusion id 210 Feature 10 in Model Tree	Want to place the Thru All hole before the center protrusion	.	Feature is moved; note, center hole no longer goes through middle protrusion
19	>File >SaveAs	Save file with new name	Enter to accept [tut6-2a.prt] then type **tut6-2b.prt**	Part saved
20	>QuitWindow			
21	>Exit	Exit program	Click Yes to confirm	PT/Modeler exited

Item	Step 6
Disp DtmPln	No
Spin Center	No
Disp Pnts	Checked
Disp Axes	No
Rendering	Hidden line

Table T6.2   Environment Settings

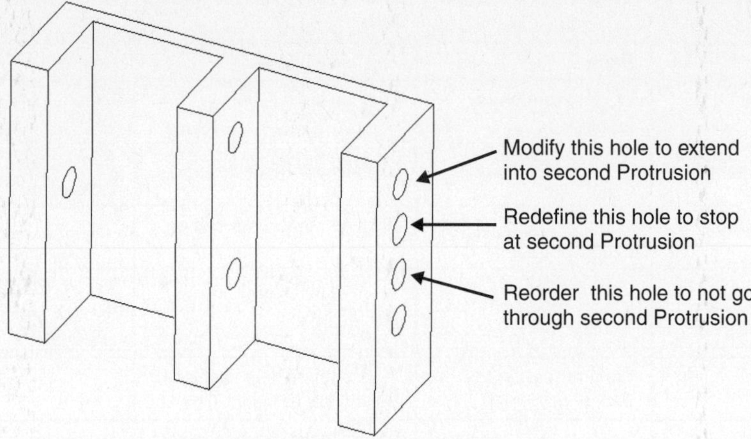

Figure 6.7   Results after Tutorial 6.2.

6.3   One-Sided or Two-Sided Attributes

During the specification of the depth of a feature, it is necessary to specify which way the feature will extend. The direction of a feature is dependent on whether the feature adds or removes material. Features that add material typically extend towards the camera. Features that remove material typically extend away from the camera. If the sketch plane is a datum plane, you can flip the direction around. Keep this in mind. Sometimes it can confuse you and you will end up looking at the sketch plane from the opposite side that you anticipated; this is illustrated in Figure 6.8. The extension sides and direction menus are shown in Figure 6.9.

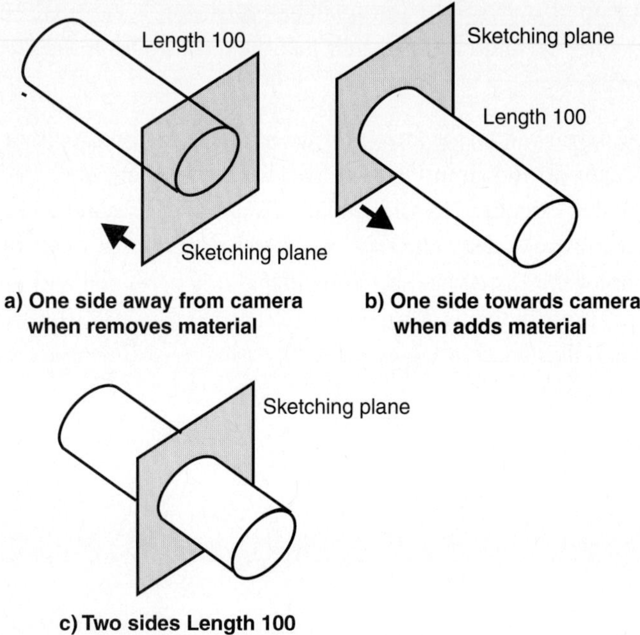

Figure 6.8   Extending in one or two directions.

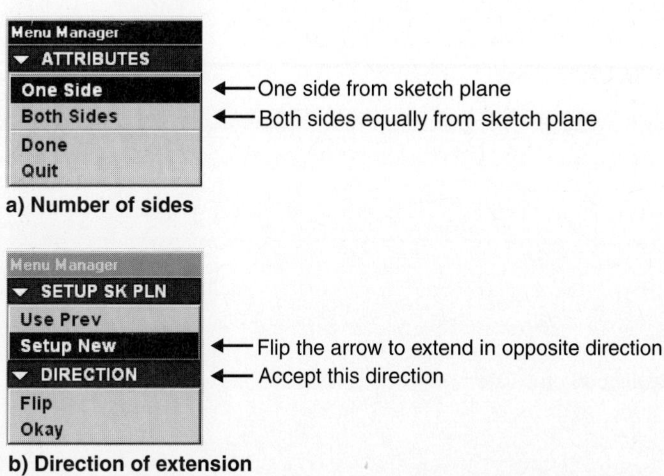

Figure 6.9   One-sided and direction menus.

If one-sided is selected, the feature will extend in the direction indicated by a direction arrow. You can choose to flip the arrow if the direction is not the desired direction. If you are specifying a blind depth, the dimension provided specifies the distance from the sketching plane to the end of the protrusion. This is the total length of the feature. If, on the other hand, you specify two-sided, the dimension that you specify is still the length of the feature. The protrusion is centered on the sketch plane. Consequently, the feature extends half the distance from the sketch plane to either end of the feature.

In Tutorial 6.3, you will create three protrusions. The first two are built on the leftmost face of the part shown in Figure 6.10. These protrusions are based on circular sections. The first extends a one-sided blind distance. The second extends the same distance, but it is two-sided. The third is a rectangle that uses a face from the center protrusion of the part as the sketching plane. It is two-sided and uses two faces from the end protrusions as Thru Until references. The part is dimensioned in Figure 6.10 and illustrated in Figure 6.11. Any remaining dimensions can be found in the Tutorial notes.

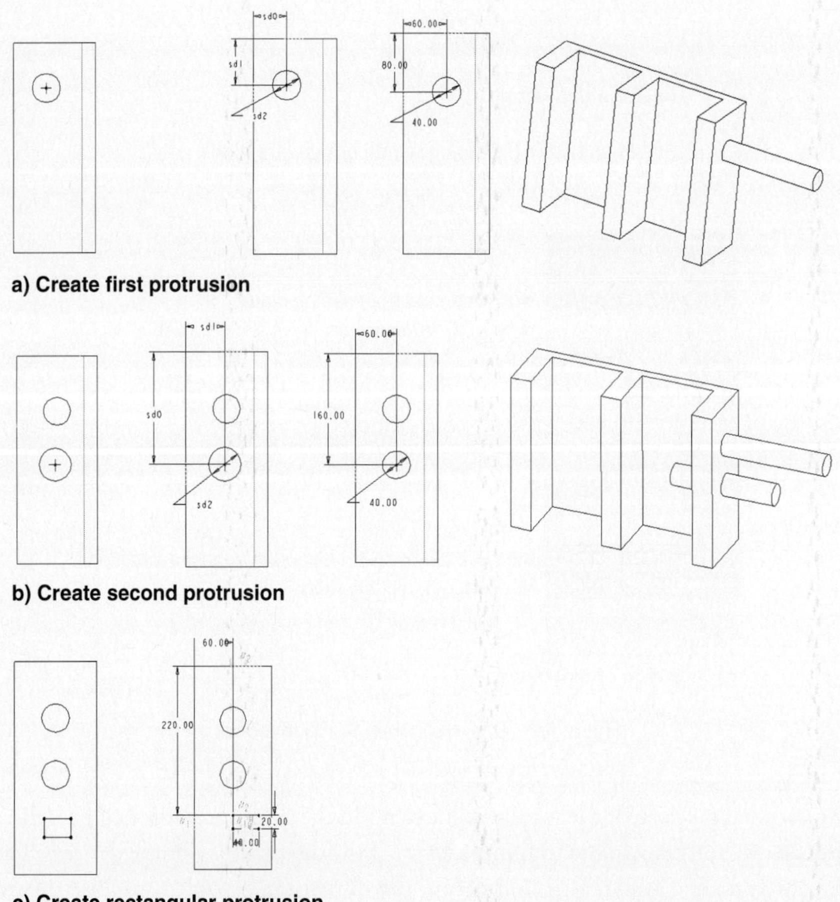

a) Create first protrusion

b) Create second protrusion

c) Create rectangular protrusion

Figure 6.10   Illustration for Tutorial 6.3, part 1.

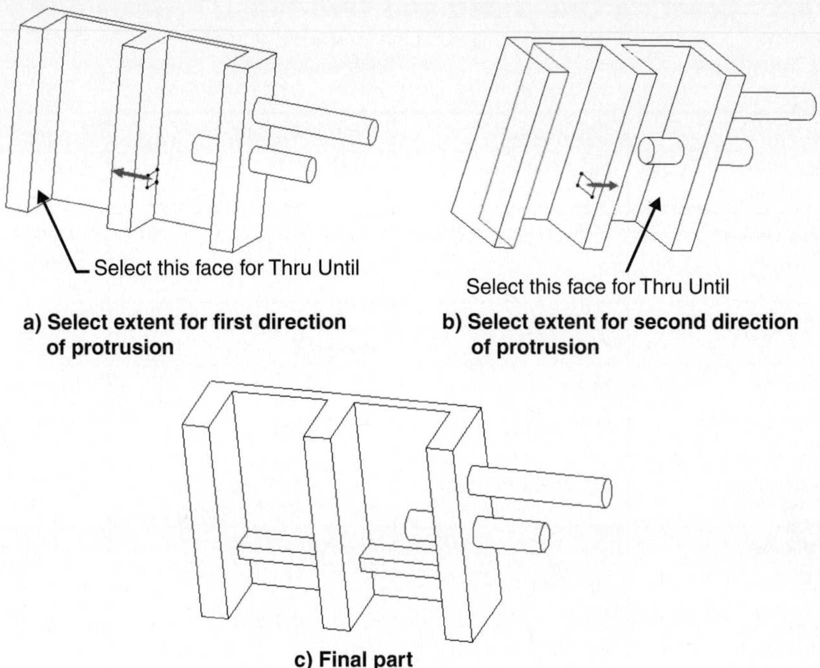

Figure 6.11 Illustration for Tutorial 6.3, part 2.

Tutorial 6.3   Creating One-Sided and Two-Sided Protrusions

Files opened: Tut6-3a.prt   **Files saved:** Tut6-3.prt

Step	Action	Description	Further Actions	Result
1	Click PT/Modeler Icon	Run PT/Modeler		After some time, PT/Modeler on screen
2	>Mode >Misc >Show Dir	Show current directory		Message similar to "Directory searched is c:\ptc\ptprod\bin"
3	>Change Dir	Change the current directory	Type **c:\proe\tutorial\ chapter_6**	
4	>Done-Return	Leave Misc menu		Misc menu removed
5	>Mode >Part >Retrieve	Read a part	Type **tut6-3a**	Part loaded
6	>Environment	Set up the environment	Set up checks as seen in Table T6.3 Column Step 6	
7	>Done-Return			
8	F1	View part in default view		Part shown in default view
9	>Feature >Protrusion >Extrude | Solid | Done	Create the first circular protrusion		
10	One-Side | Done	Want one-sided		
11	Select right side as sketching plane	Want to extend out right side	>Okay to protrusion direction	
12	> Top	Want top as reference	Click on Top	
13	Sketch >Circle | Geometry | Ctr/Point	Draw a circle as in Fig. 6.10(a)	Draw first circle, mLb on center and mLb on radius	
14	>Dimension	Dimension this circle to top	mLb on circle center, mLb on top, mMb midway to set dimension	
15	>Dimension (should already be selected)	Dimension this circle to front edge	mLb on circle center, mLb on front edge, mMb midway to set dimension	
16	>Dimension (should already be selected)	Dimension the circle diameter	mLb twice on circumference, mMb to right to set dimension	
17	>Regenerate	Regenerate the part		
18	>Modify	Modify the height dimension	mLb on vertical dimension; type **80** seen in Fig. 6.10(a)	
19	>Modify (should already be selected)	Modify the width dimension	mLb on horizontal dimension; type **60** seen in Fig. 6.10(a)	
20	>Modify (should already be selected)	Modify the diameter dimension	mLb on diameter dimension; type **40** seen in Fig. 6.10(a)	

Tutorial 6.3   Creating One-Sided and Two-Sided Protrusions (continued)

Step	Action	Description	Further Actions	Result
21	>Regenerate	Regenerate the part		Regeneration successful
22	>Done			
23	>Blind | Done	Want blind	Type **200** for depth	
24	>Preview	See the result. F1 for default view	Type **F1**, then OK	Part drawn as in Fig. 6.10(a)
25	>Feature >Protrusion >Extrude | Solid | Done	Create the second circular protrusion		
26	Both Sides | Done	Want two-sided		
27	Select right side as sketching plane	Want to extend out right side		
28	>Okay	Accept arrow direction		
29	>Top	Want top as reference	Click on Top	
30	Sketch >Circle | Geometry | Ctr/Point	Draw a circle beneath first circle as in Fig. 6.10(b)	Draw second circle, mLb on center, and mLb on radius	
31	>Dimension	Dimension this circle to top	mLb on circle center mLb on top, mMb midway to set dimension	
32	>Dimension (should already be selected)	Dimension this circle to front edge	mLb on circle center mLb on front edge, mMb midway to set dimension	
33	>Dimension (should already be selected)	Dimension the circle diameter	mLb twice on circumference, mMb to right to set dimension	
34	>Regenerate	Regenerate the part		Regeneration successful
35	>Modify	Modify the height dimension	mLb on vertical dimension; type **160** seen in Fig. 6.10(b)	
36	>Modify (should already be selected)	Modify the width dimension	mLb on horizontal dimension; type **60** seen in Fig. 6.10(b)	
37	>Modify (should already be selected)	Modify the diameter dimension	mLb on diameter dimension; type **40** seen in Fig. 6.10(b)	feature now dimensioned as desired
38	>Regenerate	Regenerate the part		Regeneration successful
39	>Done			
40	>Blind	Want blind	Type **200** for depth	
41	>Preview	See the result; F1 for default view	Type **F1**, then OK	Part drawn as in Fig. 6.10(b)
42	>Feature >Protrusion >Extrude | Solid | Done	Create the rectangular protrusion		

Tutorial 6.3   Creating One-Sided and Two-Sided Protrusions (continued)

Step	Action	Description	Further Actions	Result
43	Both Sides | Done	Want two-sided		
44	Select right side of center rib as sketching plane	Want to extend out right side of center rib as in Fig. 6.11.		
45	>Okay	Accept arrow direction		
46	> Top	Want top as reference	Click on Top	
47	Sketch >Rectangle	Draw a rectangle beneath second circle	Draw rectangle. mLb on left-top, and mLb on right-bottom	
48	>Dimension	Dimension this rectangle to top	mLb on rectangle top, mLb on top, mMb midway to set dimension	
49	>Dimension (should already be selected)	Dimension this rectangle to front edge as in Fig. 6.11	mLb on rectangle left, mLb on front edge, mMb midway to set dimension	
50	>Dimension (should already be selected)	Dimension the width as in Fig. 6.11	mLb on top, mMb above top to set dimension	
51	>Dimension (should already be selected)	Dimension the height as in Fig. 6.11	mLb on side, mMb to side of side to set dimension	
52	>Regenerate	Regenerate the part		Regeneration successful
53	>Modify	Modify the distance to top dimension	mLb on height dimension; type **220** seen in Fig. 6.10(c)	
54	>Modify (should already be selected)	Modify the distance to side dimension	mLb on width dimension; type **60** seen in Fig. 6.10(c)	
55	>Modify (should already be selected)	Modify the width dimension	mLb on width dimension; type **40** seen in Fig. 6.10(c)	
56	>Modify (should already be selected)	Modify the height dimension	mLb on height dimension; type **20** seen in Fig. 6.10(c)	Feature now dimensioned as desired
57	>Regenerate	Regenerate the part		Regeneration successful
58	>Done			
59	>Thru Until	Want to go to both surfaces		
60	Click on first face in Fig. 6.11	Select surface to extend to as in Fig. 6.11		
61	Click on second face in Fig. 6.11	Select surface to extend to as in Fig. 6.11		
62	>Preview	See the result. F1 for default view	Type **F1**, >OK	Part drawn as in Fig. 6.11

Tutorial 6.3   Creating One-Sided and Two-Sided Protrusions (continued)

Step	Action	Description	Further Actions	Result
63	>File>SaveAs	Save file with new name	Enter to accept [tut6-3a.prt] then type **tut6-3b.prt**	Part saved
64	>QuitWindow			
65	>Exit	Exit program	Click Yes to confirm	PT/Modeler exited

Item	Step 6
Disp DtmPln	No
Spin Center	No
Disp Pnts	No
Disp Axes	No
Rendering	No hidden line

Table T6.3   Environment Settings

6.4   Holes

We are all familiar with the concept of a hole. There are two kinds of holes, straight and sketched. A straight hole has a constant circular cross section and extends in a path normal to the sketching plane.

> **REMEMBER:** Holes remove material so they always extend away from the viewer. Circles can be dimensioned with one click on the circumference for a radius or two clicks for a diameter.

The cross section of a sketched hole is still a circle, but the profile need not be straight. You can draw the cross section of the circle. These two holes are illustrated in Figure 6.12.

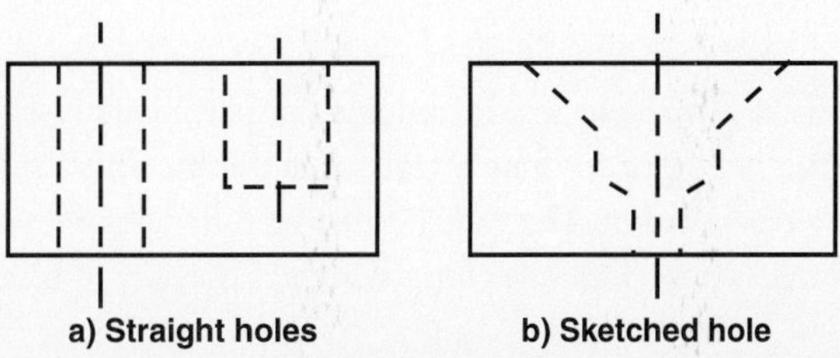

Figure 6.12   Straight and sketched holes.

6.4.1 Placement Types

There are three placement types: linear, radial, and coaxial. Thus far, we have been adding several linear holes in the tutorials of this and other chapters. A linear hole is dimensioned to two references as seen in Figure 6.13(a) using rectilinear coordinates. Radial holes are drawn in polar coordinates. A distance and an angle from a plane are required. This is shown in Figure 6.13(b). Lastly is the important coaxial option shown in Figure 6.13(c). This allows us to draw a circle constrained to the same center as a preexisting circle or arc. No dimensions other than the circle diameter or radius are provided.

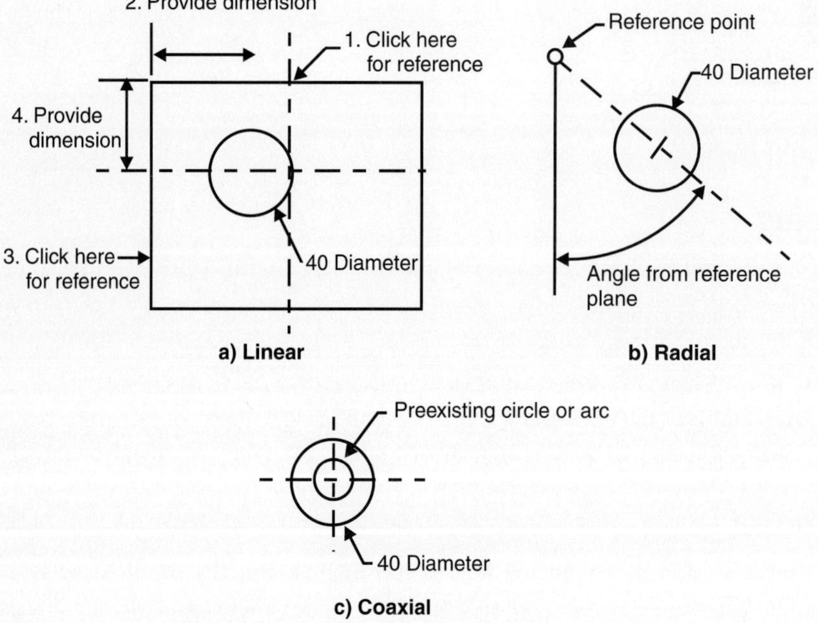

Figure 6.13   Linear, radial, and coaxial holes.

When you draw a sketched hole, a subwindow is displayed. This window is similar to the sketcher. You will need to draw a vertical centerline and a closed figure representing the hole cross section. The sketch must be fully constrained as you would dimension a normal sketch. The rules for a sketched hole are as follows.

- Cross section must have a vertical center line
- Cross section must be closed
- Dimension cross section until it is fully constrained

6.5   Rounds

Rounds are used to round off sharp edges by removing material. Rounds are also used to add material between two edges. This type of round is called the *fillet*. Rounds are pick-and-place features. Consequently, no sketch is necessary.

There are a number of ways to specify the edges that are to be rounded, as seen in Figure 6.14. One technique is the edge chain. Here you select individual edges that are to be rounded. From this edge chain mode, you can select the manner in which you want the edges selected. You can select one-by-one, a tangent chain, or a surface chain.

It is highly recommended that you add rounds late in your design. Rounds are expensive features and should be added only at the last moment. This reduces regeneration and render times. Also, you can suppress round features from the Model Tree until they are actually needed.

6.5.1   Round Menus

The two round menus are displayed in Figure 6.14. Note that the Feature dialog is always displayed. The > mark indicates the current step in the process. There are three steps. The first is to select the attributes, including whether the edge is constant or variable radius, and whether the round is an edge chain about an edge, between two surfaces, or between an edge and a surface. The second step is the References. It is necessary to select the edges and surfaces depending on the attribute. The third step is the radius of the round. An Edge Chain brings up a second menu that allows you to indicate the type of chain. This is a selection helper, and it allows you to select edges one by one, through a tangent chain or through a surface chain.

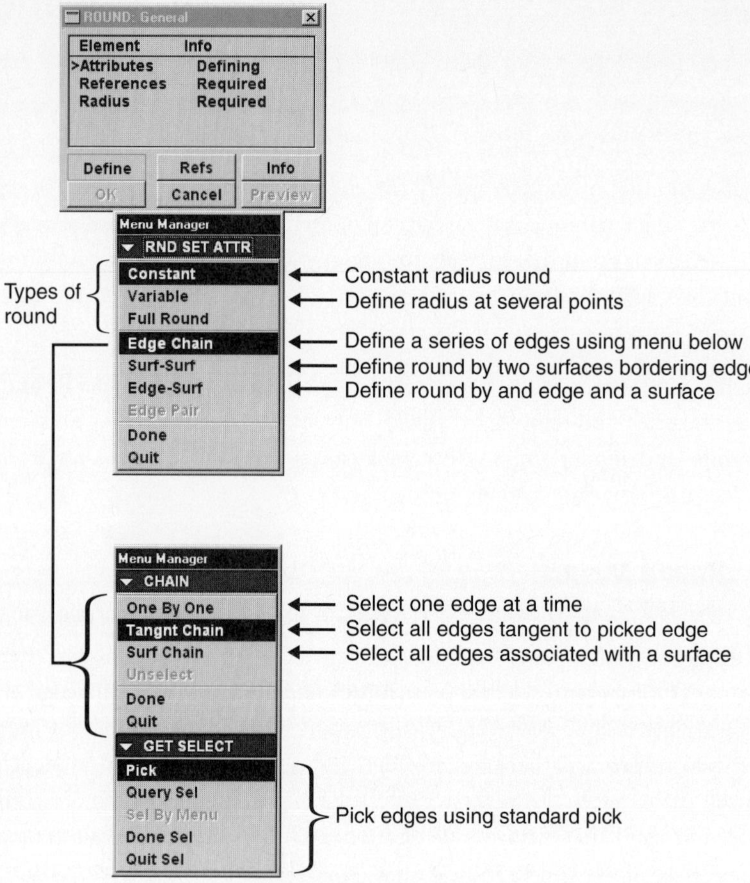

Figure 6.14   Round menus.

6.5.2 One-by-One

One-by-one requires you to select each edge. You can pick multiple edges before selecting Done-Sel.

6.5.3 Tangent Chain

When using curved surfaces, there are tangent edges that occur between separate features. For example, consider the rounded edge of Figure 6.15(a). The squared edge belonged to a feature; the round is a separate feature. Both of these features are joined with a tangent edge, as shown in Figure 6.15(b). Consequently, there are two tangent edges that connect these two features. If you pick edges using Tangent Edge, all edges that are tangent will be selected with one pick. Picking the line in Figure 6.15(c) would select all of the six edges as shown in one pick.

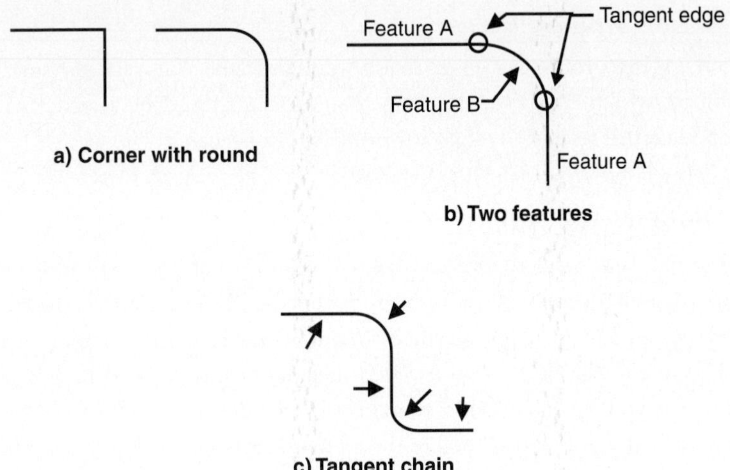

Figure 6.15   Types of rounds.

6.5.4   Surface-to-Surface Chain

When selecting edges to be rounded about a surface, you must select all or some of the edges, even when there is an ambiguity. A selection menu occurs. One edge is highlighted at a time, and you can select this edge, or move to the next. An ambiguity is shown in Figure 6.16(b). Here two surfaces are selected. These two surfaces, A and B, might both be part of a single feature, 1. A second feature, 2, splits this single edge between the two surfaces, A and B, into two parts. Selecting the two surfaces, A and B, causes an ambiguity. Do you mean the left-most edge, the right-most edge, or both? The menu of Figure 6.16(b) gives you the ability to select which edge or edges you desire.

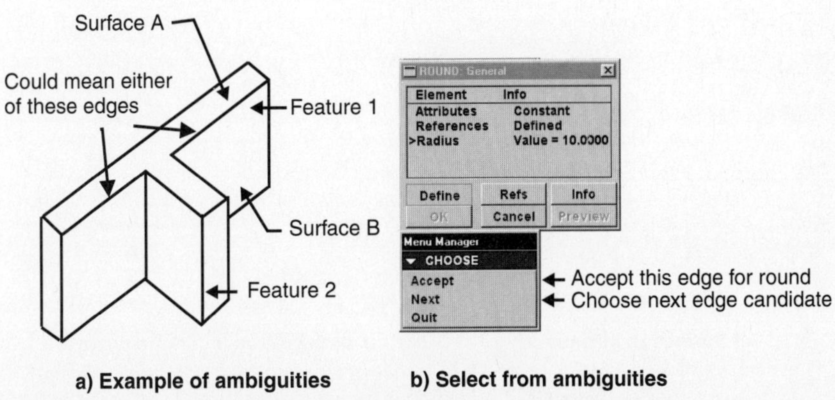

Figure 6.16   Ambiguities during edge selection.

6.5.5   Surface Chains

Surface chains help you select edges that border a surface. You pick the surface and then indicate which edges surrounding that surface should be selected. A menu choice of Select All selects all edges surrounding a surface.

6.5.6   Rounds Tutorial

In Tutorial 6.4, you get a chance to practice some rounds. You will read in a part and apply edge-chain constant radius rounds specified by edges and surfaces. Figure 6.17(a) shows an edge-to-edge specified round. You will select six edges for rounding. In Figure 6.17(b), select two surfaces that define the edge to be rounded. In Figure 6.17(c), you will again select two surfaces that define the edge to be rounded. This time an ambiguity exists. Select the right-most edge. In Figure 6.17(d), you will reorient the part to see the back side. Selecting Surface Chain | Select All, will automatically select all four of the back edges for rounding.

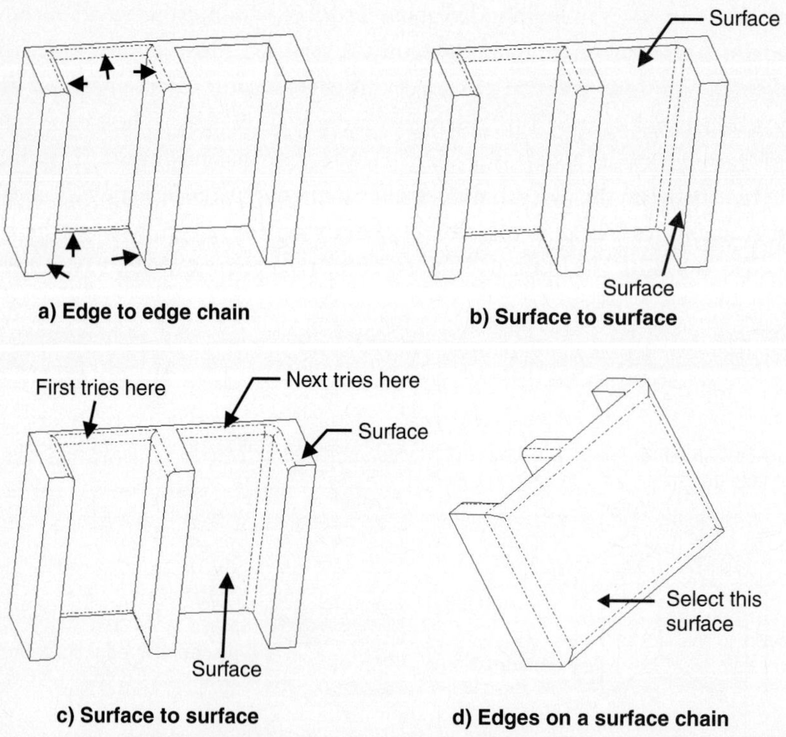

Figure 6.17   Illustration for Tutorial 6.4.

Tutorial 6.4 Creating Rounds

Files opened: Tut6-4a.prt   **Files saved:** Tut6-4b.prt

Step	Action	Description	Further Actions	Result
1	Click PT/Modeler Icon	Run PT/Modeler		After some time, PT/Modeler on screen
2	>Mode >Misc >Show Dir	Show current directory		Message similar to "Directory searched is c:\ptc\ptprod\bin"
3	>Change Dir	Change the current directory	Type **c:\proe\tutorial\ chapter_6**	
4	>Done-Return	Leave Misc menu		Misc menu removed
5	>Mode >Part >Retrieve	Read a part	Type **tut6-4a**	Part loaded
6	>Environment	Set up the environment	Set up checks as seen in Table T6.4 Column Step 6	
7	>Done-Return			
8	>Feature >Round	Create the first round as in Fig. 6.17(a)		
9	>Constant >Edge Chain	Create a constant radius round on an edge chain	>Done	
10	>One by One	Select six edges as shown in Fig. 6.17(a)	Query Sel and Accept each edge; can use mLb mMb on each edge	
11	>Done			
12	Type **5**	Enter radius		
13	Preview	View rounds	**F1** >OK	Rounds are displayed
14	>Feature >Round	Create the second round as in Fig. 6.17(b)		
15	>Constant >Surf — Surf	Create a constant radius round between two surfaces	mLb on surface, mLb on sur-face in Fig. 6.17(b)	
16	>Done			
17	Type **5**	Enter depth		
18	Preview	View rounds	**F1** >OK	Rounds are displayed
19	>Feature >Round	Create the third round New round as in Fig. 6.17(c) along inner top edge		
20	>Constant >Surf - Surf | Done	Create a constant radius round between two surfaces	mLb on surface, mLb on sur-face in Fig. 6.17(c)	

Tutorial 6.4   Creating Rounds (continued)

Step	Action	Description	Further Actions	Result
21	>Query Sel			
22	**Next** until right side edge is highlighted	Accept the right side edge in Fig. 6.17(c)	**Accept** when right side edge is highlighted	
23	Type **5**	Enter depth		
24	>Done			
25	Preview	View rounds	**F1** >OK	Rounds are displayed
26	>Feature >Round	Create the fourth round as in Fig. 6.17(d)		
27	Constant >Edge Chain	Create a constant radius round on an edge	>Done	
28	Surf Chain	Want to round all edges surrounding a surface	mLb on back in Fig. 6.17(d)	
29	>Select All	Select all edges around this surface	>Done	
30	Type **20**	Enter depth		
31	>Done			
32	Preview	View rounds	**F1** >OK	Rounds are displayed
33	>File >SaveAs	Save file with new name	Enter to accept [tut6-4a.prt] then type **tut6-4b.prt**	Part saved
34	>QuitWindow			
35	>Exit	Exit program	Click Yes to confirm	PT/Modeler exited

Item	Step 6
Disp DtmPln	No
Spin Center	No
Disp Pnts	No
Disp Axes	No
Rendering	No hidden line

TableT 6.4   Environment Settings

6.6   Edge Chamfers

Edge chamfers remove material at an edge to replace the sharp corner with a flat. Chamfers are a pick-and-place feature so it is unnecessary to provide any sketches. You can select a chamfer in one of three ways:

1. 45 × d; create a 45 degree angle and specify the dimension d
2. d1 × d1; specify both dimensions d1 and d2
3. Ang by d; specify an angle and a dimension

There are three menus associated with Chamfers. The first, illustrated in Figure 6.18(a), selects the type of chamfer as indicated by the preceding three choices. Note that the Features Dialog is shown since this is a pick-and-place feature. You select edges using the menu of Figure 6.18(b). Observe that you select multiple edges without indicating Done-Sel each edge. This is different from the picking technique used with Rounds. Once the edge selection is done, a third menu allows you to add or remove edges.

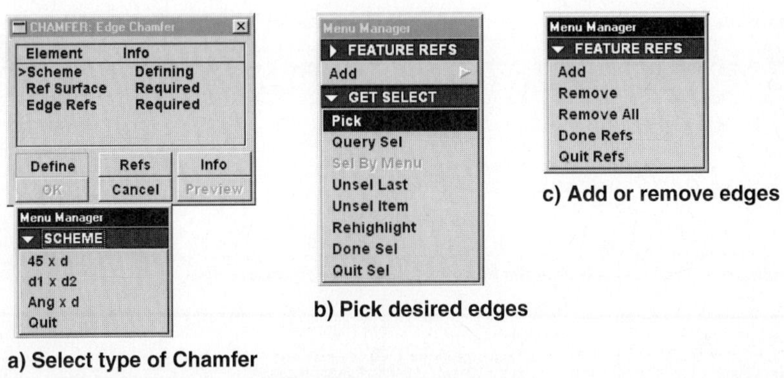

a) Select type of Chamfer

b) Pick desired edges

c) Add or remove edges

Figure 6.18   Chamfer menus.

In Tutorial 6.5 you will build some chamfers. You will read in a familiar part, and first build a 45 × d chamfer by entering the desired dimension and by selecting the surfaces on the right-most edge as indicated in Figure 6.19(a), as edges 1 and 2. The second chamfer uses the Ang × d1 option. This time you will enter the dimension followed by the angle. Select the edges 3 and 4 as in Figure 6.19(a) and build the chamfer. Third, you will build a chamfer across all edges on the top surface. There is no surface mechanism for selecting edges as there is when selecting edges for a Round. You will have to click on each of the twelve edges shown in Figure 6.19(c).

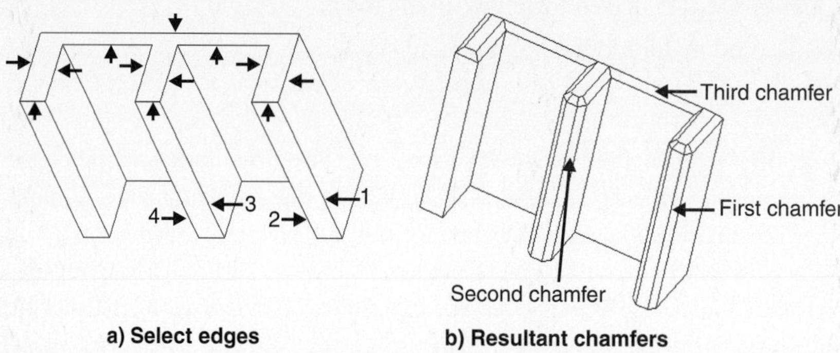

Figure 6.19   Illustration for Tutorial 6.5.

Tutorial 6.5   Creating Chamfers

Files opened: Tut6-5a.prt (E Part)   **Files saved:** Tut6-5b.prt (E part with chamfers)

Step	Action	Description	Further Actions	Result
1	Click PT/Modeler Icon	Run PT/Modeler		After some time, PT/Modeler on screen
2	>Mode >Misc >Show Dir	Show current directory		Message similar to "Directory searched is c:\ptc\ptprod\bin"
3	>Change Dir	Change the current directory	Type **c:\proe\tutorial\ chapter_6**	
4	>Done-Return	Leave Misc menu		Misc menu removed
5	>Mode >Part >Retrieve	Read a part	Type **tut6-5a**	Part loaded
6	>Environment	Set up the environment	Set up checks as seen in Table T6.5 Column Step 6	
7	>Done-Return			
8	**F1**	Get Default view		
9	>Feature >Chamfer	Create the first chamfer as in Fig. 6.19(a)		
10	> 45 x d	Create a 45 degree chamfer entering one length	>Done	
11	Type **10**	Enter dimension d	Pick edges 1 and 2 as in Fig. 6.19(a)	
12	>Done-Sel	Done with selections	>Done-Refs	
13	Preview	View chamfers	**F1** >OK	Chamfers are displayed
14	>Feature >Chamfer	Create the second chamfer as in Fig. 6.19(a)		

Tutorial 6.5   Creating Chamfers (continued)

Step	Action	Description	Further Actions	Result
15	> Angle x d	Create a chamfer entering an angle and a length	>Done	
16	Type **10** Type **30**	Enter dimension d=10 and angle = 30 degrees	Pick edges 3 and 4 as in Fig. 6.19(a)	
17	>Done-Sel	Done with selections	>Done-Refs	
18	Preview	View chamfers	**F1** >OK	Chamfers are displayed
19	>Feature >Chamfer	Create the third chamfer as in Fig. 6.19(a)		
20	> 45 x d	Create a chamfer	>Done	
21	Type **10**	Enter dimension d	Pick twelve edges on top of part as in Fig. 6.19(a)	
22	>Done-Sel	Done with selections	>Done	
23	Preview	View chamfers	**F1** >OK	Chamfers are displayed
24	>File>SaveAs	Save file with new name	Enter to accept [tut6-5a.prt] then type **tut6-5b.prt**	Part saved
25	>QuitWindow			
26	>Exit	Exit program	Click Yes to confirm	PT/Modeler exited

Item	Step 6
Disp DtmPln	No
Spin Center	No
Disp Pnts	No
Disp Axes	No
Rendering	No hidden line

Table T6.5   Environment Settings

6.7   Extruded Protrusion Feature

Extruded protrusions were described in detail in Chapter 3. Extruded protrusions are a type of extension where the section view is extended to a provided depth along a normal to the sketching plane. You can extrude a protrusion or extrude a cut. A cut is a type of extruded protrusion that removes material. Figure 6.20 illustrates an extruded protrusion.

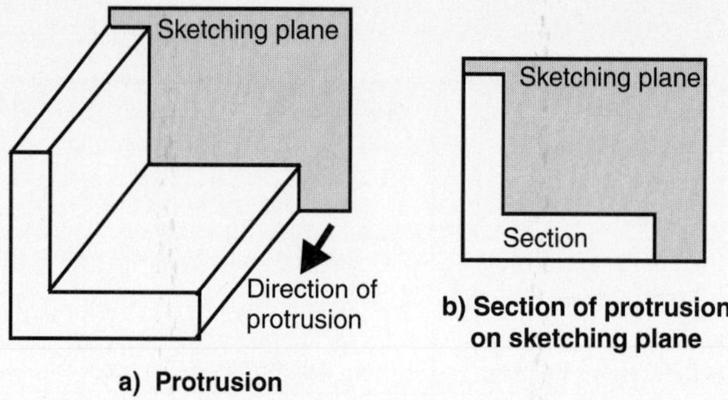

Figure 6.20   Typical protrusion.

Nearly all of the specifications for an extruded feature are done in the sketcher. We already discussed getting into the sketcher, sketching, and dimensioning, in Chapter 4.

6.7.1   Thin-Wall Protrusion

One type of protrusion not covered in Chapter 3 is a thin-wall protrusion. Up to this time, we have been designing solid protrusions. A thin-wall protrusion is a hollowed out protrusion as seen in Figure 6.21(c). A thickness measure is necessary to specify how thick the protrusion walls should be.

Tutorial 6.6 is very simple. You draw an I-beam shaped section for an protrusion on the side of our E part. You must rely on AutoDimension to provide the dimensions. Figure 6.21(a) shows the I-beam shaped section. You will draw the I to the bottom-center of the sketching surface. You will modify the dimensions provided by AutoDimension to match those of Figure 6.21(a). The first sketching plane uses the right side of the E while the second uses the left side. The second protrusion is a thin-walled protrusion. The second sketch traces over the first I feature. Make sure that hidden lines are enabled. The resultant solid is shown in Figure 6.21(b).

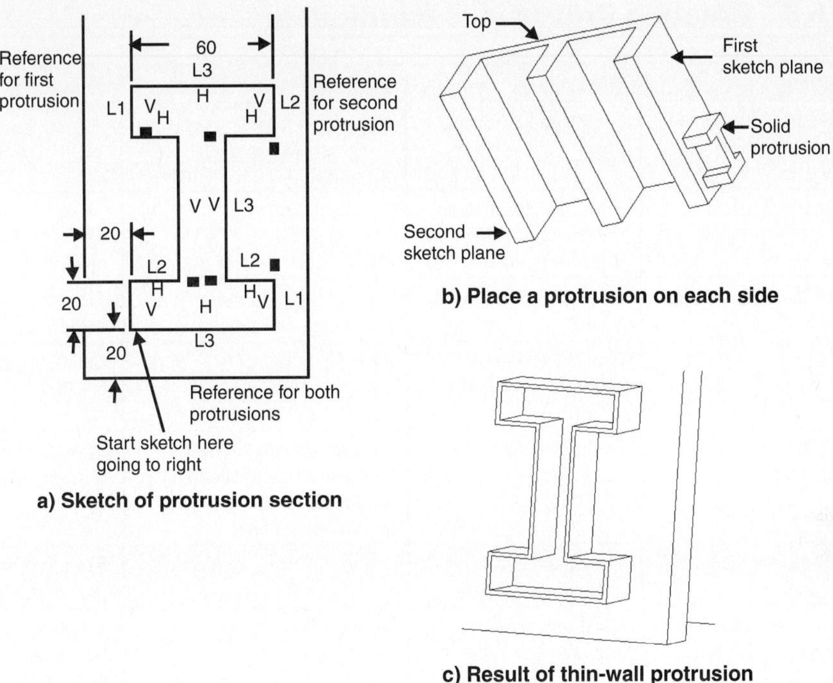

a) Sketch of protrusion section

b) Place a protrusion on each side

c) Result of thin-wall protrusion

Figure 6.21   Illustration for Tutorial 6.6.

Tutorial 6.6   Creating Protrusions

Files opened: Tut6-6a.prt   **Files saved:** Tut6-6b.prt

Step	Action	Description	Further Actions	Result
1	Click PT/Modeler Icon	Run PT/Modeler		After some time, PT/Modeler on screen
2	>Mode >Misc >Show Dir	Show current directory		Message similar to "Directory searched is c:\ptc\ptprod\bin"
3	>Change Dir	Change the current directory	Type **c:\proe\tutorial\ chapter_6**	
4	>Done-Return	Leave Misc menu		Misc menu removed
5	>Mode >Part >Retrieve	Read a part	Type **tut6-6a**	Part loaded
6	>Environment	Set up the environment	Set up checks as seen in Table T6.6 Column Step 6	
7	>Done-Return			
8	**F1** change to default view			

Tutorial 6.6   Creating Protrusions (continued)

Step	Action	Description	Further Actions	Result
9	>Feature >Protrusion | Extrude | Solid | Done	Create an extruded solid		
10	>One Side | Done	Protrusion will extend one side out of the sketching plane		
11	Pick the right side for sketching plane	Select right side in Fig. 6.21(b)	Accept arrow direction for protrusion direction	Pick face for protrusion; this is the sketching plane
12	>TOP	Pick top of part for TOP reference in Fig. 6.21(b)	Pick Top surface	Go into sketcher mode in Fig. 6.21(a)
13	>Sketch >Line | Horizontal	Sketch the I bracket in Fig. 6.21(a)	12 mLb picks ending with 1 mMb pick to end section sketch; note alternating horizontal and vertical	After last mMb, no longer drawing line
14	>AutoDimension	Have Sketcher do dimensions for you		Sketcher requests that you provide it with references
15	mLb on left edge of part mLb on bottom edge of part as shown in Fig. 6.21(a)	Need to provide references to help auto dimensioning	>Done - Sel	Message — Regeneration Successful — Part gets dimensioned in Fig. 6.21(a)
16	>Modify	Modify the dimensions	Change the dimensions in Fig. 6.21(a) using 20 and 60	
17	>Regenerate	Tell Sketcher create feature	>Done	Message — Regeneration Successful —
18	>Blind | Done	Want blind depth	Type **50**	
19	**F1** change to default view			
20	>Feature >Protrusion | Extrude | Thin | Done	Create a protrusion with a thin wall		
21	>One Side | Done	Protrusion will extend one side out of the sketching plane		
22	Pick the left side for sketching plane	Select left side in Fig. 6.21(b); have to reorient part to see left side	Accept arrow direction for protrusion direction	Pick face for protrusion; this is the sketching plane
23	>TOP	Pick top of part for TOP reference in Fig. 6.21(b)	Pick Top surface	Go into sketcher mode in Fig. 6.21(a)
24	>Sec Tools >Grid >Grid On/Off	Turn grid off to see previous sketch better		

Tutorial 6.6 Creating Protrusions (continued)

Step	Action	Description	Further Actions	Result
25	>Sketch>Line | Horizontal	Sketch the I bracket in Fig. 6.21(a) tracing over the first protrusion	12 mLb picks ending with 1 mMb pick to end section sketch; note alternating horizontal and vertical	After last mMb, no longer drawing line
26	>AutoDimension	Have sketcher do dimensions for you		Sketcher requests that you provide it with references
27	mLb on right edge of part mLb on bottom edge of part as shown in Fig. 6.21(a)	Need to provide references to help auto dimensioning	>Done - Sel	Message—Regeneration Successful—Part gets dimensioned in Fig. 6.21(a)
28	>Regenerate	Tell Sketcher create feature	>Done	Message—Regeneration Successful—
29	>Modify	Modify the dimensions	Change the dimensions in Fig. 6.21(a) using 20 and 60	
30	>Regenerate	Tell Sketcher create feature	>Done	Message—Regeneration Successful—
31	>Both	Thin feature should be created on both sides of sketched lines		
32	Type **5** then **Enter**	Respond to thickness measure for thin walls		
33	>Blind | Done	Want blind depth	Type **50**	
34	Preview	See part but don't like thickness		
35	Double click Thickness in Feature Dialog	Change the thickness measure	Type **2** then Preview, mRb on display to force redraw—note: a single mRb does a pan with no motion—quick way to redraw	
36	>Okay	Accept second protrusion		
37	>File >SaveAs	Save file with new name	Enter to accept [tut6-6a.prt] then type **tut6-6b.prt**	Part saved
38	>QuitWindow			
39	>Exit	Exit program	Click Yes to confirm	PT/Modeler exited

Item	Step 6
Disp DtmPln	No
Spin Center	No
Disp Pnts	No
Disp Axes	No
Rendering	Hidden line

Table T6.6 Environment Settings

6.8   **Open and Closed Sketches**

Some rules regulate sketching. One of these has to do with open and closed shapes. A closed shape defines a closed region. If you sketch a rectangular section for a protrusion, PT/Modeler may question you as to whether material should be added to the inside or outside of the rectangle.

An open shape does not completely separate the inside from the outside. This being true, how can you extrude an open shape? You could sketch an open-shape extruded protrusion or cut such that the missing side is aligned to a preexisting edge.

What are the consequences of open versus closed shapes? A closed shape defines its shape for all sides. An open shape defines its shape for all closed sides, but leaves the shape for the open side undefined. The sketcher is making assumptions here regarding the edge at the open side. Tutorial 6.7 will illustrate the difference.

> **REMEMBER:** When you create a new part, using the New Part macro, only datum planes and axes exist. Make sure to Enable Datum Planes and/or Axis in order to see something on the screen when you start a new part.

In Tutorial 6.7, you will design a part from scratch. You begin with an extruded shape whose section is drawn in Figure 6.22(a). Next, add a protrusion extending out the small front face as seen in Figure 6.22(b). As you can see, the sketch for this protrusion is closed. Then, you will add a protrusion that also extends out the small face as seen in Figure 6.22(c). However, this time the protrusion is open. Note there is no top section to the sketch. In this case, both top vertices of the U must be aligned to the edge. The open edge will take on the extended shape of the face on the feature to which that these vertices are aligned. As you can see, the results are quite different.

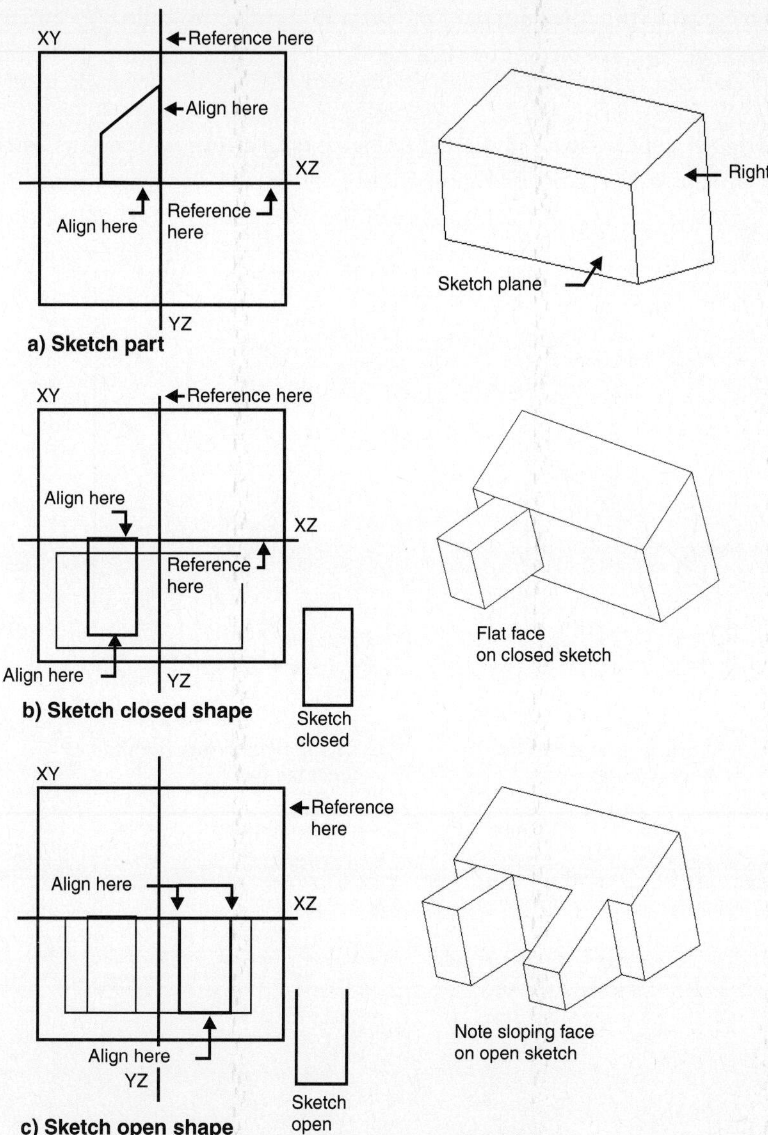

Figure 6.22   Illustration for Tutorial 6.7.

Care must be taken when borrowing attributes from other features. In this tutorial, you will modify the base part by extending the back side. This increases the slope of the front face of the base feature. During regeneration, the base piece and the second protrusion have no problems. However, the third protrusion has a big problem. The open segment borrows the slope of the face from the base feature. This face now extends into the bottom of the part causing an error called "Geometry was overlapping." You can recover by clicking >Undo Changes to return to the original part.

The original sloping face is illustrated in Figure 6.23(a). An error occurs when this slope is increased, as seen in Figure 6.23(b). Here, the slope is so great that an attempt is made to cut off the front face of the protrusion. This is not allowed.

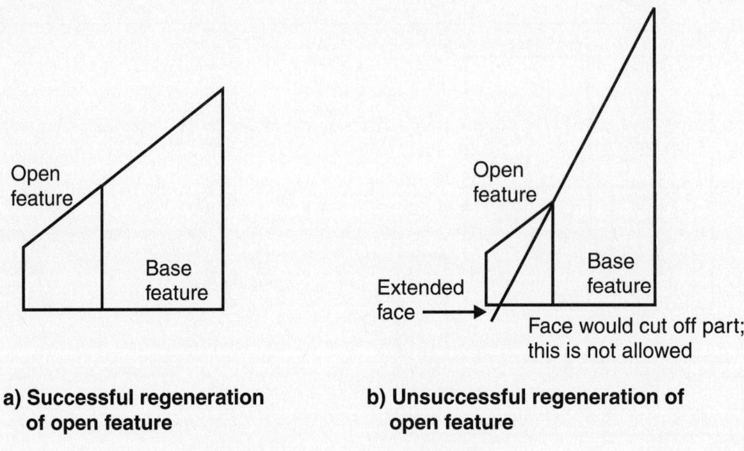

Figure 6.23   Error in regeneration.

Tutorial 6.7   Open and Closed Sketches

No files opened.   **Files saved:** Tut6-7b.prt

Step	Action	Description	Further Actions	Result
1	Click PT/Modeler Icon	Run PT/Modeler		After some time, PT/Modeler on screen
2	>Mode >Misc >Show Dir	Show current directory		Message similar to "Directory searched is c:\ptc\ptprod\bin"
3	>Change Dir	Change the current directory	Type **c:\proe\tutorial\ chapter_6**	
4	>Done-Return	Leave Misc menu		Misc menu removed
5	>Mode >Part >Retrieve	Read a part	Type **tut6-7a**	Part loaded
6	>Environment	Set up the environment	Set up checks as seen in Table T6.7 Column Step 6	
7	>Done-Return			
8	>Feature >Protrusion | Extrude | Solid	Create an extruded solid		
9	>One Side | Done	Protrusion will extend one side		
10	Pick the front lower side for sketching plane	Select front-lower side as in Fig. 6.22(a)		Pick face for protrusion; this is the sketching plane
11	>Right	Pick right face of part for Right reference in Fig. 6.22(a)	Pick Right face	Go into Sketcher mode in Fig. 6.22(a)
12	>Sketch >Rectangle	Sketch the rectangle in Fig. 6.22(b)		
13	>Align	Align top edge to top edge bottom to bottom in Fig. 6.22(b)		
14	>AutoDimension	Have Sketcher do dimensions for you		Sketcher requests that you provide it with references
15	mLb on XZ and YZ axis as shown in Fig. 6.22(b)	Need to provide references to help auto dimensioning	>Done - Sel	Part gets dimensioned
16	>Regenerate	Tell Sketcher to create feature	>Done	Message—Regeneration Successful—
17	>Modify	Modify the dimensions	Change the dimensions using 40, 80, and 60	
18	>Regenerate	Tell Sketcher to create feature	>Done	Message—Regeneration Successful—
19	>Blind	Want blind depth	Type **200**	

Tutorial 6.7   Open and Closed Sketches (continued)

Step	Action	Description	Further Actions	Result
20	Preview	See result	F1 >Okay	
21	>Feature >Protrusion | Extrude | Solid	Create an extruded solid		
22	>One Side	Protrusion will extend one side		
23	Pick the front lower side for sketching plane	Select front-lower side in Fig. 6.22(a)		Pick face for protrusion; this is the sketching plane
24	>Top	Pick top of part for TOP reference in Fig. 6.22(a)	Pick Top surface	Go into sketcher mode in Fig. 6.22(a)
25	>Sketch >Line | Vertical	Sketch the U shape in Fig. 6.22(c)		
26	>Align	Align top two vertices of U to top edge in Fig. 6.22(c)		
27	>Align	Align bottom to bottom edge in Fig. 6.22c		
28	>AutoDimension	Have Sketcher do dimensions for you		Sketcher requests that you provide it with references
29	mLb on XZ and YZ axis as shown in Fig. 6.22(b)	Need to provide references to help auto dimensioning	>Done-Sel	Part gets dimensioned
30	>Regenerate	Tell Sketcher to create feature	>Done	Message—Regeneration Successful—
31	>Modify	Modify the dimensions	Change the dimensions using 40, 80, and 60	
32	>Regenerate	Tell Sketcher to create feature	>Done	Message—Regeneration Successful—
33	>Blind	Want blind depth	Type **200**	
34	Preview	See result	F1 >Okay	
35	>Modify	Modify the base feature	Select Base Feature	
36	Click on 150 height dimension	Increase height from 150 to 250	Type **250**	
37	>Regenerate	Regenerate	Note: Errors occur and info window displayed	
38	> Undo changes	Undo the last change	>Confirm	Part saved
39	>File >SaveAs	Save file with new name	Enter to accept [tut6-7a.prt] then type **tut6-7b.prt**	
40	>QuitWindow			
41	>Exit	Exit program	Click Yes to confirm	PT/Modeler exited

Item	Step 6
Disp DtmPln	Checked
Spin Center	No
Disp Pnts	No
Disp Axes	No
Rendering	Hidden line

Table T6.7   Environment Settings

6.9   Revolved Feature

Revolved features are a second type of protrusion. These protrusions are restricted to being symmetrical about a centerline. You can specify the angle of revolution to be other than 360 degrees. This would allow hemispheres. You can select one of the preset options at 90, 180, 270, and 360 degrees or enter an angle between 0 and 360 degrees.

Once in the sketcher, you can define just about any shape that is both closed and not intersecting itself. Make sure to start with a centerline.

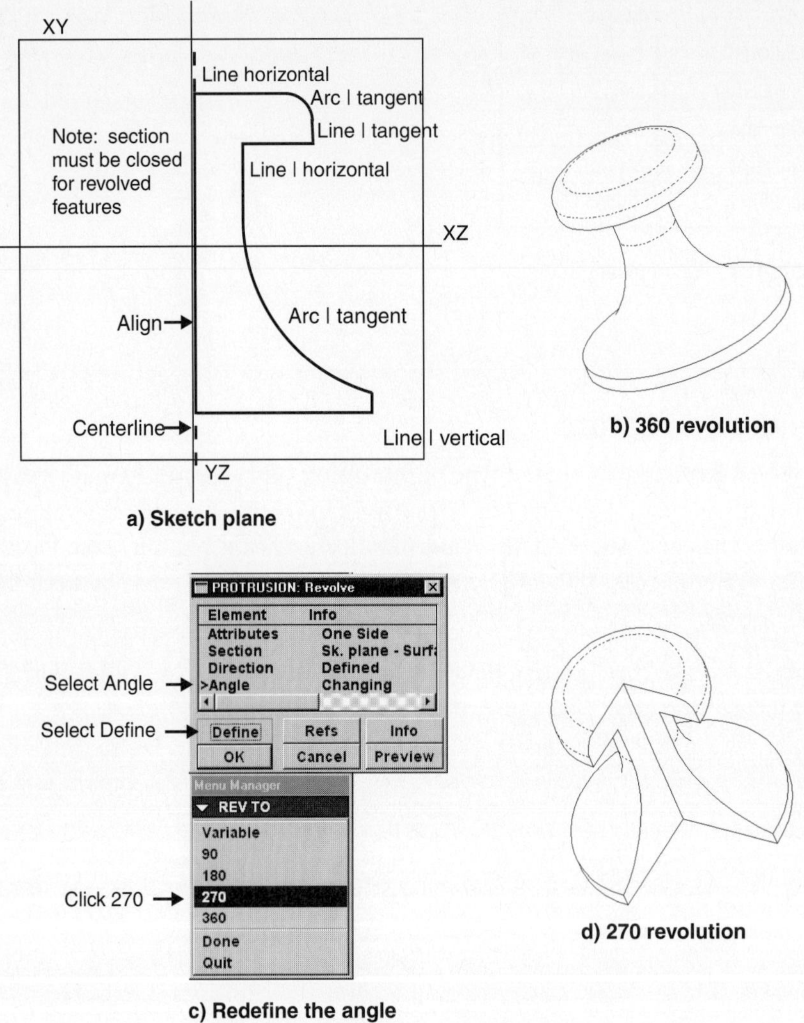

a) Sketch plane

c) Redefine the angle

Figure 6.24   Illustrations for Tutorial 6.8.

In Tutorial 6.8 you will build a sketch feature from scratch. You build a solid sketched protrusion whose sketch is shown in Figure 6.24(a). First, draw a vertical centerline using the Line | Centerline option. Align this to the YZ axis. Next, draw the shape. Do not worry about the dimensions now. Simply get the shape close to the shape in the figure. Make sure to use the sketching tools recommended. Also, make sure that the section is closed. Provide the XZ and YZ axis as references to AutoDimension. Accept the dimension and Regenerate to get the revolved feature shown in Figure 6.24(b).

Next, you will practice redefining a feature. Select Feature Oper and select the part for redefinition. The Feature Dialog appears as shown in Figure 6.24(c). Select Angle and click Define to change the angle to 270 degrees. The result is shown in Figure 6.24(d).

Tutorial 6.8   Revolved Features

No files opened.   **Files saved:** Tut6-8-360.prt
                                                                  Tut6-8-270.prt

Step	Action	Description	Further Actions	Result
1	Click PT/Modeler Icon	Run PT/Modeler		After some time, PT/Modeler on screen
2	>Mode >Misc >Show Dir	Show current directory		Message similar to "Directory searched is c:\ptc\ptprod\bin"
3	>Change Dir	Change the current directory	Type **c:\proe\tutorial\ chapter_6**	
4	>Done-Return	Leave Misc menu		Misc menu removed
5	>Mode >Part >New Part	Create a part	Type **tut6-8a** then **Enter**	Part created
6	>Environment	Set up the environment	Set up checks as seen in Table T6.8 Column Step 6	
7	>Done-Return			
8	>Feature >Protrusion | Revolved | Solid	Create a revolved solid		
9	>One Side | Done	Protrusion will extend one side		
10	Pick the XY plane for sketching plane	Select XY plane	Okay to protrusion direction	Pick face for protrusion; this is the sketching plane
11	>Top	Pick XZ plane for Top reference	Pick the XZ plane	Go into Sketcher mode in Fig. 6.24(a)
12	>Sketch >Line | Centerline	Sketch the centerline in Fig. 6.24(a)		
13	>Align	Align centerline with YZ axis in Fig. 6.24(a)		
14	>Sketch >Line | Horizontal	Draw the top of the part; draw part in Fig. 6.24(a)	mLb drag mLb for line, mMb to end	
15	>Arc | Tangent End	Draw small curve at top; do not worry about 90 degrees	mLb drag, mLb to end	
16	>Line | Tangent	Draw line going down; note this might not be vertical	mLb drag, mLb to end	

Tutorial 6.8   Revolved Features (continued)

Step	Action	Description	Further Actions	Result
17	> Line | Horizontal	Draw horizontal and vertical segments	mLb drag mLb drag mLb for lines, mMb to end	
18	>Arc | Tangent End	Draw large curve		
19	Line | Vertical	Draw Vertical, bottom, and inside vertical along centerline	mLb drag mLb drag mLb drag mLb for lines, mMb to end	
20	>Align	Align vertical line to centerline		
21	>AutoDimension	Have Sketcher do dimensions for you		Sketcher requests that you provide it with references
22	mLb on XZ and YZ axis as shown in Fig. 6.24(b)	Need to provide references to help auto dimensioning	>Done-Sel	Part gets dimensioned
23	>Regenerate	Tell Sketcher to create feature	>Done	Message—Regeneration Successful—
24	>360	Want revolution to be by 360 degrees	>Done	
25	Select Preview	Preview result	F1 select OK	
26	>File>SaveAs	Save file with new name	Enter to accept [tut6-8a.prt] then type **tut6-8-360.prt**	Part saved
27	>Feature Oper >Redefine	Want to redefine a feature	Click on the part	
28	Click on Angle in Feature dialog box	Redefine the angle	Select Define	
29	>270	Change to 270	Done	
30	Select Preview	Preview result	F1 select OK	
31	>File >SaveAs	Save file with new name	Enter to accept [tut6-8a.prt] then type **tut6-8-270.prt**	Part saved
32	>QuitWindow			
33	>Exit	Exit program	Click Yes to confirm	PT/Modeler exited

Item	Step 6
Disp DtmPln	Checked
Spin Center	No
Disp Pnts	No
Disp Axes	No
Rendering	Hidden line

Table T6.8   Environment Settings

6.10 **Cuts**

Cuts, as described in Chapter 3, are the opposite of protrusions. Cuts remove material whereas protrusions add material. You make cuts the same way that you make protrusions. You can extrude, revolve, blend, or sweep to remove material. As with protrusions, cuts can be opened or closed. There is really nothing new to describe so we will get right into the tutorial.

In Tutorial 6.9, you will load up our E part, cut an edge off of the front three protrusions, and revolve a cut. For the edge cut, you choose the right side of the part as the sketching plane. A single line is drawn from the front edge to the top edge. The ends of this line are aligned to the respective edges. The edge cut is made by a single line drawn from the front edge to the top edge as seen in Figure 6.25(a). Let AutoDimension do the work. Provide the front face and the top as references. AutoDimension constrains the edge by an angle and a distance. You will be asked to provide a direction of the cut. The arrow shown in Figure 6.25(b) points in the direction that material will be removed. Even though it may be obvious to you, the direction is totally ambiguous to the software. Either way works so you are asked to select one direction or the other.

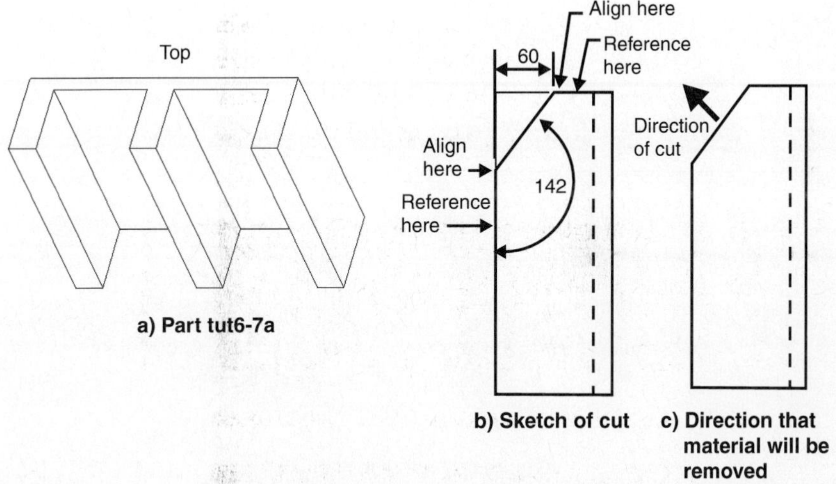

Figure 6.25   Sketch of extruded cuts.

The next step is to build a revolved cut. For this we will choose the back face of the part as the sketching plane. In the sketcher, draw a horizontal centerline and then draw a closed shape as seen in Figure 6.26. Align the vertices, select the references, and let AutoDimension work it out. After regenerating, the part looks like Figure 6.27.

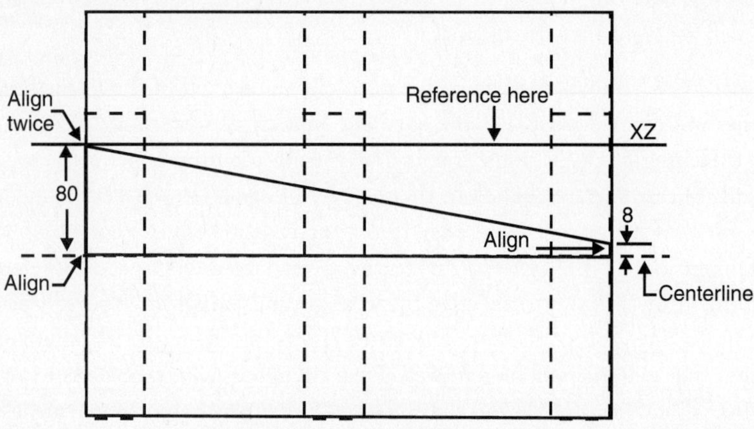

Figure 6.26   Sketch of revolved cut.

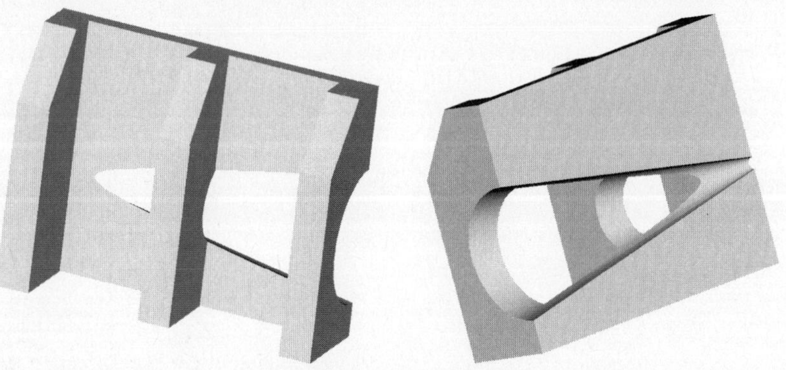

Figure 6.27   Result of cuts.

Tutorial 6.9 Cuts

Files opened: Tut6-9a.prt **Files saved:** Tut6-9b.prt

Step	Action	Description	Further Actions	Result
1	Click PT/Modeler Icon	Run PT/Modeler		After some time, PT/Modeler on screen
2	>Mode >Misc >Show Dir	Show current directory		Message similar to "Directory searched is c:\ptc\ptprod\bin"
3	>Change Dir	Change the current directory	Type **c:\proe\tutorial\ chapter_6**	
4	>Done-Return	Leave Misc menu		Misc menu removed
5	>Mode >Part >Retrieve	Read a part	Type **tut6-9a**	Part read
6	>Environment	Set up the environment	Set up checks as seen in Table T6.9 Column Step 6	
7	>Done-Return			
8	>Feature >Cut | Extrude | Solid | Done	Create an extruded solid cut		
9	>One Side | Done	Cut will extend one side		
10	Pick the right side for sketching plane	Select right side in Fig. 6.23	Okay to cut direction	Pick face for cut; this is the sketching plane
11	>Top	Pick top of part for Top reference in Fig. 6.25(a)	Pick Top surface	Go into Sketcher mode in Fig. 6.25(a)
12	>Sketch >Line | 2 point	Sketch the angled line in Fig. 6.25(b)		
13	>Align top-right vertex	Align top-right vertex once to top edge as in Fig. 6.25(b)		
14	>Align bottom-left vertex	Align bottom-left vertex to front edge as in Fig. 6.25(b)		
15	>AutoDimension	Have Sketcher do dimensions for you		Sketcher requests that you provide it with references
16	mLb on front and top edges as in Fig. 6.25(b)	Need to provide references to help auto dimensioning	>Done-Sel	Part gets dimensioned as in Fig. 6.25(c)
17	>Regenerate	Tell Sketcher to create feature	>Done	Message—Regeneration Successful—
18	>Thru All	Want to go through all three protrusions	>Done	
19	Preview	See result	F1 >Okay	

Tutorial 6.9   Cuts (continued)

Step	Action	Description	Further Actions	Result
20	>Feature >Cut | Revolved | Solid	Create a revolved solid		
21	>One Side	Protrusion will extend one side		
22	>Okay	Accept arrow direction		
23	Pick the back surface for sketching plane	Select back surface		Pick face for protrusion; this is the sketching plane
24	>Top	Pick top for Top reference	Pick the XZ plane	Go into Sketcher mode in Fig. 6.25(a)
25	>Sketch >Line | Centerline | Horizontal	Sketch the centerline in Fig. 6.26		
26	>Align	Align centerline with XZ axis in Fig. 6.26		
27	>Sketch >Line | Horizontal	Alternate horizontal, vertical to draw part in Fig. 6.26		
28	> Sketch >Line | 2-point	Draw angled line in Fig. 6.26		
29	>AutoDimension	Have Sketcher do dimensions for you		Sketcher requests that you provide it with references
30	mLb on XZ axis and on two ends and bottom as shown in Fig. 6.26	Need to provide references to help auto dimensioning	>Done-Sel	Part gets dimensioned
31	>Regenerate	Tell Sketcher to create feature	>Done	Message—Regeneration Successful—
32	>Okay to remove material direction			
33	>180	Want revolution to be by 180 degrees		
34	Select Preview	Preview result	F1 select OK	
35	>File >SaveAs	Save file with new name	Enter to accept [tut6-9a.prt] then type **tut6-9b.prt**	Part saved
36	>QuitWindow			
37	>Exit	Exit program	Click Yes to confirm	PT/Modeler exited

Item	Step 6
Disp DtmPln	Checked
Spin Center	No
Disp Pnts	No
Disp Axes	No
Rendering	Hidden line

Table T6.9   Environment Settings

6.11   **Shells**

Shells are simple but useful features that allow you to hollow out an existing feature or features. They are affectionately known as *termites*. You drop the termites into your model at a specified surface. The termites then eat their way through the model. Fortunately, these are well-behaved termites. They eat all material up to a specified thickness from the outside world.

Shells eat through the entire model beginning at a specified face. Therefore, it is extremely important that you add shells after the feature that you want shelled. If other features are connected to the feature that you want shelled, they will also get shelled (if possible).

Shells are pick-and-place features so no sketching is necessary. You will need to specify the starting face and the thickness of the shell. That is all there is to it. However, as you will see in Tutorial 6.10, shells are very sensitive. The termites will not, under any circumstances, violate their Prime Directive. They will not eat through a surface farther than the specified thickness. If they encounter a portion of material that is too thin, they will force an error.

Tutorial 6.10 will take you through the steps of building a shell. Input a part as seen in Figures 6.28(a) and 6.28(b). Create a shell by >Feature >Shell. Select first the top face in Figure 6.28(b) for the shell. Enter a thickness of 2. You can Preview and Okay the shell.

Next, try adding a second shell to one of the thinned walls as seen in Figure 6.28(c). Following the same procedure, attempt to create a two-unit thick shell. This time, an error occurs during Preview. The error indicates that the "Geometry could not be constructed." In other words, this is telling us that the shell could not be built for some reason. This is likely due to an attempted Prime Directive violation. The wall of the face selected was too thin to create another two-unit thick shell. Cancel out of this one and try again.

This time attempt to change the thickness of the shell to five. That way, the thin wall from the last failed attempt will be sufficient to handle the second shell. Use >Modify | Value and select the shell feature either through the Model Tree or by selecting the shell on the part as seen in Figure 6.28(c). Change the 2.0 thickness value to 5.0. Now, >Regenerate and another error occurs indicating a Prime Directive violation attempt. This time it is the connecting wall of the H protrusion as seen in Figure 6.28(a) that is too thin. As it is only nine units wide, there is not room for the 2 * 5.0 = 10.0+ minimum requirement for the shell. Use >Undo Changes to return to the last regenerated state.

For one last shell, select the fourth surface from Figure 6.28(b) to try and shell the H feature. Pick a thickness of three to insure that the termites can squeeze through the connecting wall. Darn, an error again. This time the problem is that the termites are going to try and eat out the entire part, not just the H feature. The wall of the base feature is only two units thick from the previous shell.

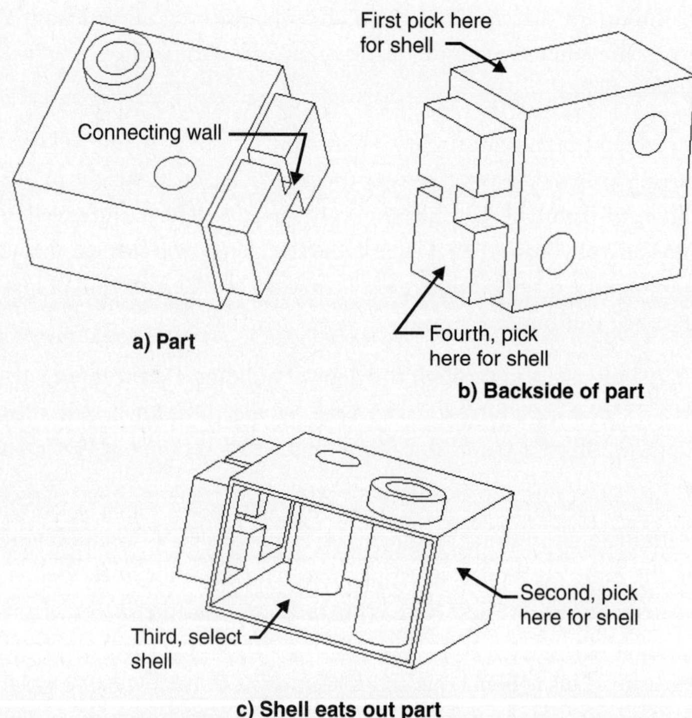

Figure 6.28   Illustrations for Tutorial 6.10.

Tutorial 6.10 Creating Shells

Files opened: Tut6-10a.prt **Files saved:** Tut6-10b.prt

Step	Action	Description	Further Actions	Result
1	Click PT/Modeler Icon	Run PT/Modeler		After some time, PT/Modeler on screen
2	>Mode >Misc >Show Dir	Show current directory		Message similar to "Directory searched is c:\ptc\ptprod\bin"
3	>Change Dir	Change the current directory	Type **c:\proe\tutorial\ chapter_6**	
4	>Done-Return	Leave Misc menu		Misc menu removed
5	>Mode >Part >Retrieve	Read a part	Type **tut6-10a**	Part loaded as in Fig. 6.28(a)
6	>Environment	Set up the environment	Set up checks as seen in Table T6.10 Column Step 6	
7	>Done-Return			
8	>Feature >Shell	Create a shell	Pick first surface as Fig. 6.28(b) >Done Sel > Done Refs	
9	Type 2	Use a thickness of 2	Preview F1 Okay	Shell is created
10	>Feature >Shell	Create a shell	Pick second surface as Fig. 6.28(c) >Done Sel > Done Refs	
11	Type 2	Use a thickness of 2	Preview	Error occurs; could not create geometry
12	Select Cancel		Confirm	
13	>Modify | Value	Change thickness of shell	Select (third) shell feature by clicking as Fig. 6.28(c)	
14	Select 2.0 thickness dimension	Change thickness to 5	>Done	
15	>Regenerate	Regenerate the part		Error occurs; could not create geometry
16	>Undo Changes		Confirm	
17	>Feature >Shell	Create a shell	Pick fourth surface as Fig. 6.28(b) >Done Sel > Done Refs	
18	Type 2	Use a thickness of 2	Preview	Error occurs; could not create geometry
19	Select Cancel		Confirm	

Tutorial 6.10   Creating Shells (continued)

Step	Action	Description	Further Actions	Result
20	>File >SaveAs	Save file with new name	Enter to accept [tut6-10a.prt] then type **tut6-10b.prt**	Part saved
21	>QuitWindow			
22	>Exit	Exit program	Click Yes to confirm	PT/Modeler exited

Item	Step 6
Disp DtmPln	No
Spin Center	No
Disp Pnts	Checked
Disp Axes	No
Rendering	Hidden line

Table T6.10   Environment Settings

6.12   Patterns

A pattern is a special kind of duplication. You will often want to replicate a feature that you have designed. It would be wasteful to recreate the feature for every duplicate instance. You would not want to sketch each and every tooth as you built a comb part. Rather, you would want to design one tooth and then pattern it.

There are many types of patterns. You can create one- or two-dimensional patterns. You can work in a rectilinear or a radial format. You can duplicate the shape of a feature by manipulating the placement dimensions. You can also change the shape by manipulating the dimensions of the shape along with the placement dimensions.

You need an original feature before you can pattern. For this reason, a pattern is not a feature, but rather a feature operation. The original, and all instances, shows up in the model tree as a single feature. You will see this in Tutorial 6.11.

6.12.1   Linear Pattern

Linear patterns are based on a rectilinear coordinate system. Patterns can be made along one or two dimensions. These two dimensions can be thought of as horizontal and vertical, or along the AX or AZ axis, or along any two orthogonal axes.

6.12.1.1   One-Directional Pattern

The simplest type of pattern is a one-dimensional pattern, where the shape of a feature is duplicated multiple times along one dimension. In this case, the placement dimension along one direction is changed. For example, the square feature in Figure 6.29(a) is duplicated four times along the horizontal direction in Figure 6.29(b). The shape of the feature remained the same. The feature was duplicated four times; another way of saying this is that the pattern contains four *instances*.

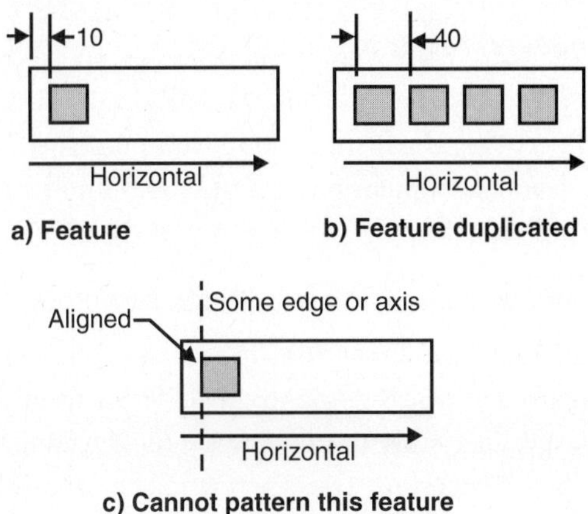

Figure 6.29   Linear pattern in one direction.

To specify a pattern, you first need to select the feature that you want to pattern. This feature is then called the *original*. You also need to provide the number of instances in the pattern. In this example, there would be four instances. This includes the original and all *duplicates*. Lastly, you must specify the dimensions that you want to manipulate during the pattern. In the case of Figure 6.29(a), we specify only one dimension to change. Somehow we must specify the horizontal direction to the software. There are many ways to specify this dimension. PT/Modeler chose the following implementation.

The square feature is referenced to the left side of the part by a 10-unit dimension, and this dimension is parallel to the horizontal direction of our desired pattern. We alert the software of our direction by selecting the 10-unit dimension. This selection tells the software that this is the direction of the pattern. Consequently, you cannot specify a direction for a pattern if no reference dimension already exists in the desired direction. This means that you cannot have an original aligned such that no reference dimension is necessary. This is indicated in Figure 6.29(c). In this case, the square feature is aligned to some edge or axis requiring no horizontal reference dimension.

> **TIP:** Be careful during the design of an original feature to include a reference dimension in the desired direction of the pattern.

Once this dimension is selected, a query asks for the increment value to be used during the duplication. This value is the distance separating the instances in the pattern. In our example, as seen in Figure 6.29(b), we type in 40, indicating that we want the square feature to be replicated every 40 units, beginning at the original and totaling four instances.

6.12.1.2   Two-Directional Pattern

You can also pattern in two dimensions in one operation. The operation is identical. However, after specifying the first direction, you must specify the second direction, including the reference dimension and the total number of instances. All of the same rules and limitations apply.

6.12.1.3   More than One Dimension in a Single Direction

You can specify more than one dimension along a single dimension. For instance, you may want to change the width of the rectangle or the height as it is duplicated. The first dimension specified must always indicate the direction of the duplication. After selecting the first dimension, you are queried for any other dimensions to change. For example, you could select the dimension that specifies the width of the square feature in Figure 6.29(a) as a second dimension. Next, it is necessary to provide the dimensional increment.

Suppose we typed 1.0. The square would become one unit wider in each instance. Technically, you do not need to move the part during the duplication. You could select the width as the first and only dimension. The feature would stay in place growing one unit for each iteration. However, I cannot think of a reason for this type of pattern.

6.12.1.4   Linear Pattern Tutorial

In Tutorial 6.11, you will build a two-dimensional pattern. A part contains a single cylindrical protrusion upon the face of a base as shown in Figure 6.30(a). The hole is dimensioned with a diameter of 33.33 and two references as shown in Figure 6.30(b). The first reference is to the left edge and the second reference is to the top edge. Both of these values are 25.

To pattern this cylinder, select >Feature Oper>Pattern and select the cylinder as the original of the pattern. Next, select the first 25 dimension as shown in Figure 6.30(c). This represents the horizontal direction and it is the first direction of our pattern. Type 50 as the increment value that will be used to separate each instance. Click >Done when requested for more dimensions.

Pay attention here. This query is requesting any more dimensions that should be manipulated during the patterning along the first direction. Do you see the difference between a dimension and a direction? We do not want any other dimensions to change during our pattern in this first direction. We want only the original duplicated every 50 units. Last, provide the number of instances including the original. In this case, enter 4. This concludes the specification of the first direction.

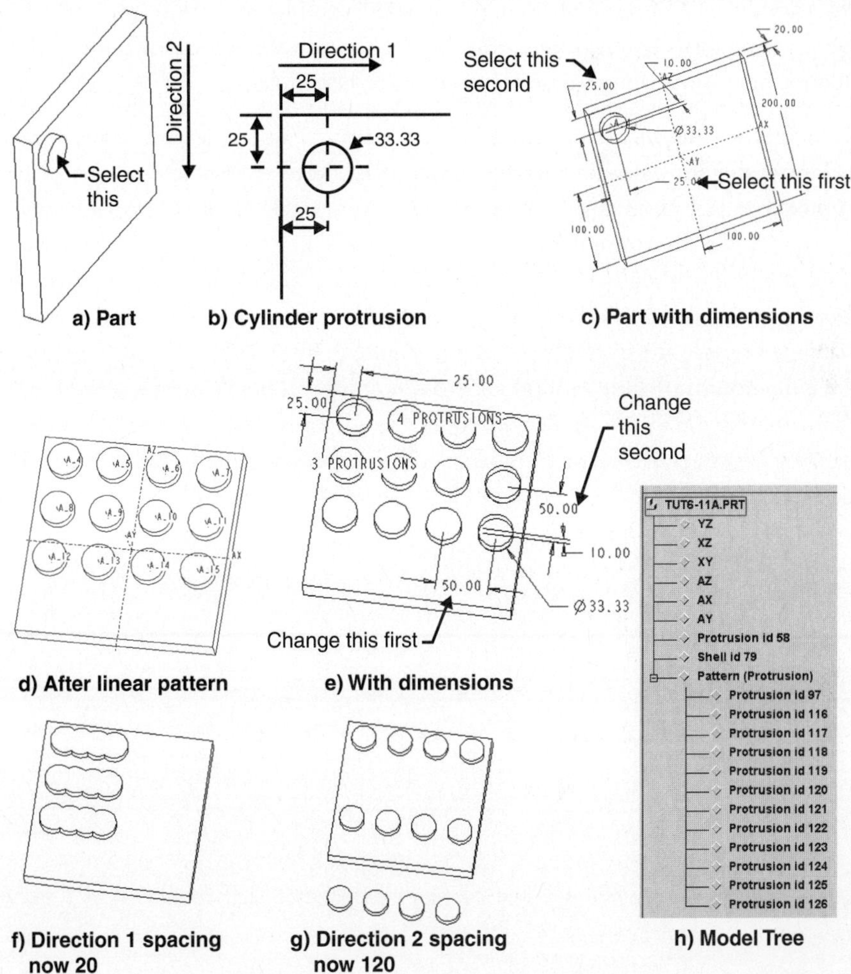

Figure 6.30   Illustrations for Tutorial 6.10.

At this time, you are asked to specify the second direction. If you wanted only a one-directional pattern, you could click >Done and the pattern would be generated. In this tutorial, you will select the second 25 dimension from Figure 6.30(c). Again, type 50 as the incremental value along the second direction. Click >Done since we want only this one dimension to change value. Finally, type 3 for the number of instances. That is it! The pattern is generated as seen in Figure 6.30(d).

What if you want to modify the pattern? It is a good idea to look at the dimensions in a pattern. Thus, click >Modify | Value and click on the top-right and bottom-left cylinders. The dimensions should look similar to Figure 6.30(e). You can rotate the part around to see the dimensions better. You can also select >Modify | Move Dim to move dimensions around the screen for better clarity.

To modify a value in the pattern, select >Modify | Value, select the pattern, and click on a dimension following the same procedure to change any pattern. Click on the dimension to change and provide a new dimension. In this tutorial, you will click on the first horizontal 50 as seen in Figure 6.30(e) and type 20. Regenerate to see the result in Figure 6.30(f). The cylinders are overlapping in the horizontal direction as expected since their diameter is 33.333. Repeat the process, this time changing the second vertical 50 as seen in Figure 6.30(e) and type 120. Regenerate to see the result in Figure 6.30(g). There is no problem here since there is no constraint that says that the model has to have contiguous features. Let us not leave the poor part in this condition; modify both dimensions back to 50 before saving the part.

Tutorial 6.11   Linear Duplication

Files opened: Tut6-11a.prt   **Files saved:** Tut6-11b.prt

Step	Action	Description	Further Actions	Result
1	Click PT/Modeler Icon	Run PT/Modeler		After some time, PT/Modeler on screen
2	>Mode >Misc >Show Dir	Show current directory		Message similar to "Directory searched is c:\ptc\ptprod\bin"
3	>Change Dir	Change the current directory	Type **c:\proe\tutorial\ chapter_6**	
4	>Done-Return	Leave Misc menu		Misc menu removed
5	>Mode >Part >Retrieve	Read a part	Type **tut6-11a**	Part loaded
6	>Environment	Set up the environment	Set up checks as seen in Table T6.11 Column Step 6	
7	>Done-Return			
8	>Feature Oper >Pattern	Create a Pattern	Pick cylinder as Fig 6.30(a) >Done	
9	>Pick 25 dimension along Direction 1	Choose first direction	Type **50** >Done	
10	Type 4	Want 4 instances		
11	>Pick 25 dimension along Direction 2	Choose second direction	Type **50** >Done	
12	Type 3	Want 3 instances		Pattern completes as Fig 6.30(d)
13	>Modify | Value	Look at dimension	Click on bottom right protrusion	
14	>Modify | Move Dim	Move the dimension for readability	mLb on dimension mLb on desired location to move	
15	>Modify | Value	Change 50 dimension in direction 1 to 20	Click on 50 as Fig 6.30(e); type **20** then **Enter**	
16	>Regenerate			Pattern seen in Fig 6.30(e)
17	>Modify | Value	Change 50 dimension in direction 2 to 120	Click on bottom right protrusion and then click on 50 as Fig 6.30(e); type **120** then **Enter**	First dimension change causes protrusions to merge and second dimension change causes some protrusions to move off of plate
18	>Regenerate			Pattern seen in Fig 6.30(f)
19	>File>SaveAs	Save file with new name	Enter to accept [tut6-11a.prt] then type **tut6-11b.prt**	Part saved
20	>QuitWindow			
21	>Exit	Exit program	Click Yes to confirm	PT/Modeler exited

Item	Step 6
Disp DtmPln	No
Spin Center	No
Disp Pnts	Checked
Disp Axes	No
Rendering	Hidden line

Table T6.11   Environment Settings

6.12.2   Radial Pattern

Two-dimensional radial patterns rely on a polar coordinate system specified by two directions. Instead of horizontal and vertical, the directions are radial and angular. When working with circles and arcs, it is often convenient to reference using angles. Figure 6.31(a) shows a square feature on a part. It is referenced to a point by a radial dimension and an angle.

Radial patterns use either of these dimensions as the direction of increment. Typically, the angle is used as opposed to the radial dimension. A one-dimensional radial pattern that uses the radial dimension is the same as a one-dimensional linear pattern.

Figure 6.31(b) shows the square being patterned six times around the 360 degrees. Each square is separated by 45 degrees. The reference dimension shown in Figure 6.31(a) is 30 degrees. What this means is that the original square is oriented on a 30 degree angle from the horizontal reference. This 30 degree angle is used as the directional reference. Its direction is used to replicate the original eight times, where every instance is separated by 45 degrees. It just so happens that 8 * 45 = 360. You could replicate the feature three times at 45 degrees such that the total arc would be only 135 degrees. You could also replicate the feature four times at 85 degrees separation, thereby causing the instances to wrap around the circle more than once. There are no restrictions as to the total number of degrees in the pattern.

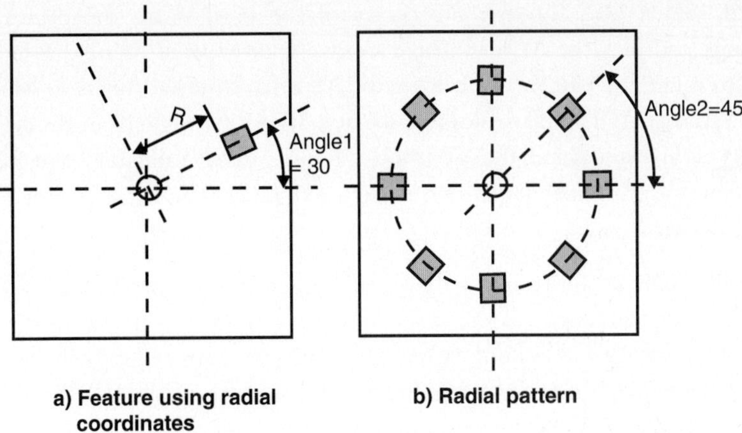

**a) Feature using radial
coordinates**

b) Radial pattern

Figure 6.31 Radial pattern in angular direction.

The mechanism is identical to a linear pattern. In fact, nowhere do you specify whether the pattern is linear or radial. You need to specify exactly the same parameters as follows.

- Pick the feature
- Pick the reference dimension
- Type the incremental distance
- Type the number of instances

6.12.3 MakeDatums

When creating a feature that is destined to be the original of a radial pattern, you must have an angular dimension. The way to accomplish this is to create a MakeDatum plane. Recall, a MakeDatum plane is a temporary datum plane specified during the feature creation process. Each radial original needs one and only one make datum plane. In Figure 6.31(a), the angular reference line would be the edge of a make datum plane. You will practice this in Tutorial 6.12.

6.12.4 Radial Pattern Tutorial

Tutorial 6.12 will show you how to build a radial pattern. This is a one-dimensional pattern that uses the angular measurement as referenced to a make datum plane. Start with loading a Pulley part. Add a cut feature specifying the top surface as the sketching plane. Note that the part has one flat side and one side with an indented center. Choose the side with the indented center and make sure to pick the topmost face as indicated in Figure 6.32(a). During the specification of the reference plane, select MakeDatum. You will constrain the MakeDatum plane such that the

AY axis, which goes through the center of the part, is on the plane. Select >Through and pick the AY axis. There are two good ways of doing this task. The first is to rotate the part so you can see the AY axis. An easier way is to select >By Menu | Axis | AY. The plane wants to be at a 30 degree angle from the XY plane so select >Angle and select the XY plane. Choose >Enter Value and type 30. This brings you into the sketcher as seen in Figure 6.32(b). The MakeDatum plane is labeled DTM1.

Sketch the circle as shown in Figure 6.32(b). Align the center to the DTM1 axis. Now the tricky dimension is the radial dimension from the AY axis to the center point. Select the AY axis as done earlier. This time you may need to break out of the 2D sketcher mode by Ctrl-Drag rotate the part. You can get back into the 2D mode by selecting >Sketch View. Dimension the radial distance to 52 and dimension the diameter of the hole to 32. Regenerate the part producing the part in Figure 6.32(c).

Select >Feature Oper>Pattern and select the cut you just made. Select the 30 dimension as shown in Figure 6.32(c) and type in 60 as the angular increment. Type in 6 instances and >Done when queried about the second direction. The pattern is built as seen in Figure 6.32(d).

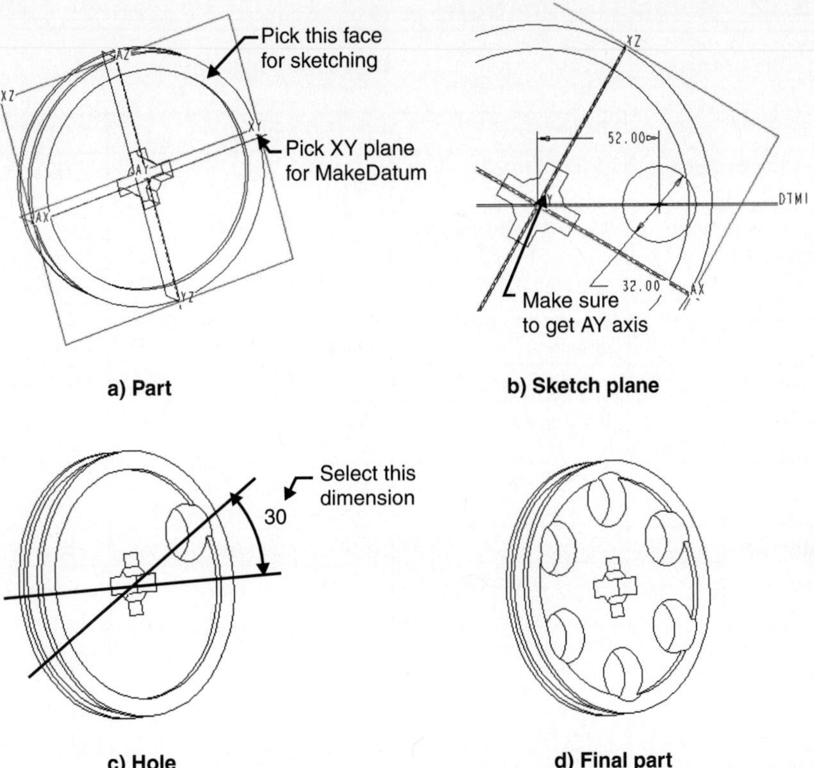

a) Part

b) Sketch plane

c) Hole

d) Final part

Figure 6.32 Illustrations for Tutorial 6.12.

Tutorial 6.12 Radial Duplication

Files opened: Tut6-12a.prt   **Files saved:** Tut6-12b.prt

Step	Action	Description	Further Actions	Result
1	Click PT/Modeler Icon	Run PT/Modeler		After some time, PT/Modeler on screen
2	>Mode >Misc >Show Dir	Show current directory		Message similar to "Directory searched is c:\ptc\ptprod\bin"
3	>Change Dir	Change the current directory	Type **c:\proe\tutorial\ chapter_6**	
4	>Done-Return	Leave Misc menu		Misc menu removed
5	>Mode >Part >Retrieve	Read a part	Type **tut6-12a**	Part loaded
6	>Environment	Set up the environment	Set up checks as seen in Table T6.12 Column Step 6	
7	>Done-Return			
8	>Feature >Cut | Extrude | Solid | Done	Create an extruded solid cut		
9	>One Side | Done	Protrusion will extend one side		
10	Pick the front face for sketching plane	Select front-outer rim in Fig. 6.32(a)	Okay to protrusion direction	Pick face for protrusion; this is the sketching plane
11	>MakeDatum	MakeDatum		
12	>Through	Want axis AY to be on plane	Select center axis AY	
13	> Angle	Want datum to be 30 degrees from XY Plane	Select XY datum plane >Done	MakeDatum is constrained; all choices are grayed
14	>Enter Value	Want to enter angle value	Type **30**	Sketch plane shown as Fig 6.32(c)
15	>Sketch>Circle	Sketch the circle in Fig. 6.32(b)		
16	>Align	Align circle center to MakeDatum in Fig. 6.32(b)		
17	>Dimension >Sel By Menu | Axis | AY	Dimension radius as Fig 6.32(b) center to AY axis		Dimension radial
18	mLb center of circle mMb to position			
19	>Slanted | >Done Sel	Specify dimension type		
20	>Modify	Modify dimension	Click on positional radius dimension; type **52** and **Enter**	

Tutorial 6.12   Radial Duplication (continued)

Step	Action	Description	Further Actions	Result
21	Click on cut diameter dimension; type **32** and **Enter**	Change cut diameter	>Done and >Okay to material removal direction	
22	>Regenerate	Tell Sketcher to create feature	>Done	Message—Regeneration Successful—
23	>Thru All	Make circle go through entire part	>Done	
24	>Preview	See part	F1 >Okay	
25	>Feature Oper >Pattern	Create a Pattern	Pick hole as Fig 6-32(c)	
26	>Pick angle dimension	Choose first direction	Type **60** >Done	
27	Type **6**	Want 6 instances	>Done	Pattern is generated as Fig 6.32(e)
28	>File >SaveAs	Save file with new name	Enter to accept [tut6-12a.prt] then type **tut6-12b.prt**	Part saved
29	>QuitWindow			
30	>Exit	Exit program	Click Yes to confirm	PT/Modeler exited

Item	Step 6
Disp DtmPln	Checked
Spin Center	No
Disp Pnts	No
Disp Axes	Checked
Rendering	Hidden line

Table T6.12   Environment Settings

6.12.5   Deleting a Pattern

You can delete the pattern by using the >Feature Oper | Delete command and selecting the pattern. This deletes the original as well as the instances. You can delete just the instances by the >Feature Oper | Delete Pattern and selecting the pattern. This will leave the original patterned feature.

6.13   Groups

At times, it is useful to organize multiple features in a group. One such example is when you want to pattern several features in one operation. You can group the features together, and then pattern the group. Groups are an operator on a Feature so they are accessed through the >Feature Oper >Groups menu. The submenu is shown in Figure 6.33.

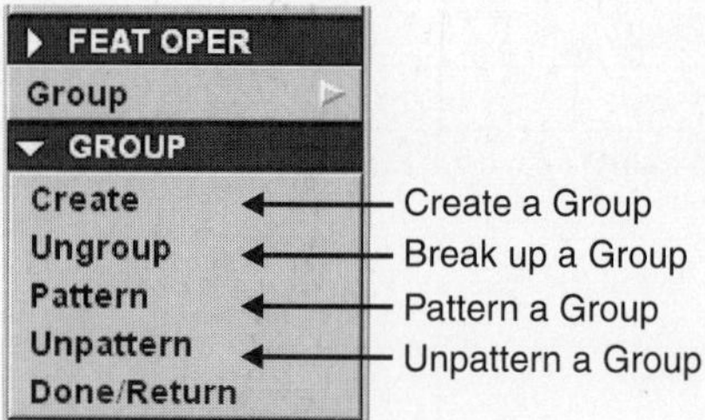

Figure 6.33   Group submenu.

It is possible to create a group using the >Create option. You are queried to enter a group name so make one up. Select all features that should be in the group and >Done Sel, >Done to exit. To ungroup a set of features, select >Ungroup and then select the group. Any feature in the group selects the group. To pattern a group, select >Pattern and follow the same instructions as in Tutorial 6.12. To unpattern a group, select >Unpattern.

Modifying a Part

There are several ways to modify a part. The simplest is the Modify command in the Features menu. Do not let the Modify command's simplicity fool you—it is a very useful tool for quickly modifying dimensions.

7.1 Modify

You can use the Modify command when viewing the 3D part or when in Sketcher mode.

7.1.1 Modify in View

Modify allows you to change the value of a dimension. The Modify menu is shown in Figure 7.1. When you select Modify, you are asked to click on a feature. All dimensions associated with the selected feature are displayed. You can select multiple features to see all of the associated dimensions. Simply click on a dimension and enter a new value in the Message window. The current dimension is always provided as a default in the prompt. Type Enter to accept the default. You can pick the dimension or datum plane using the standard pick techniques.

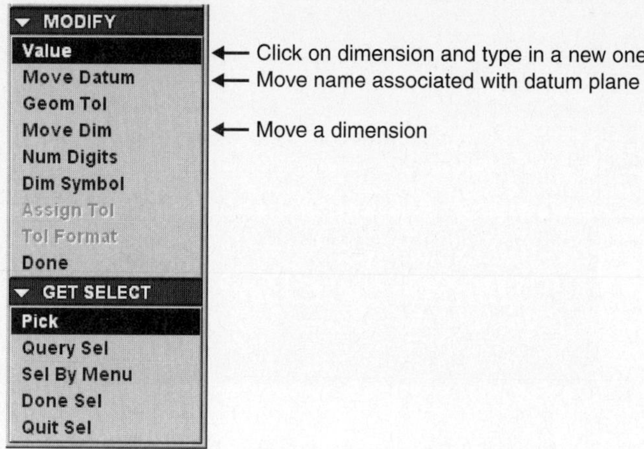

Figure 7.1   The Modify menu while viewing.

You can also move a dimension to another location on the screen using the >Move Dim menu item. This is useful when dimensions are overlapped and difficult to see. Click on the desired dimension and click again on the desired new location for the dimension. When datum planes are displayed, it can be difficult to read the datum plane name; for example, XY, YZ, XZ. Select MoveDatum. Click on the desired datum name and click again on the desired new location for the name.

7.1.2   Modify in Sketcher

The Modify command is also available within Sketcher. The menu is shown in Figure 7.2. A dimension can be modified after the section has been regenerated in Sketcher. Select >Modify. Next, select whether you want to modify an entity by typing in a value or by dragging. The >Mod Entity command allows you to change a dimensional value by clicking on the dimension and typing in a new value.

Modify

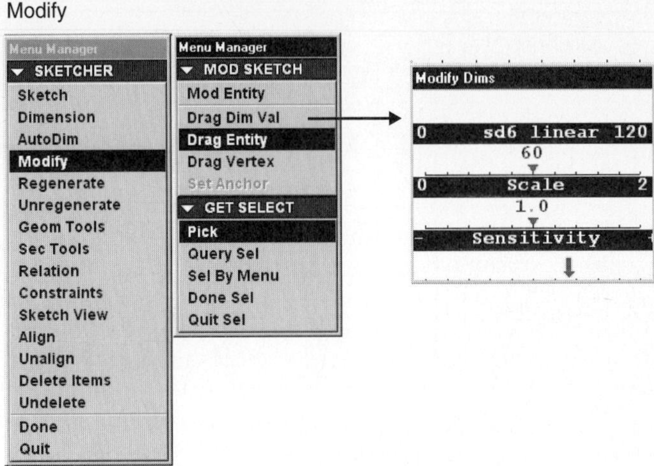

Figure 7.2   The Modify menu while sketching.

The Drag options allow you to change a dimension by dragging an entity. You can drag using a dialog, selecting a line or curve, or selecting a vertex.

Select >Drag Dim Val to use the dialog box shown in Figure 7.2. First, select the dimension to modify. Remember to click >Done-Sel after the dimension is selected. The dialog allows you to change the value using a slider. The top slider controls the actual value, and the second value controls a scale factor. You might want a part to be one and a half times larger. The last slider controls the sensitivity of the other two controls.

You can also choose to drag an entity directly. The >Drag Entity menu item allows you to move a line or curve. First, specify the dimension to modify. Next, click on the entity to modify. Drag the entity on the screen and the sketch will rubberband following the mouse, as illustrated in Figure 7.3.

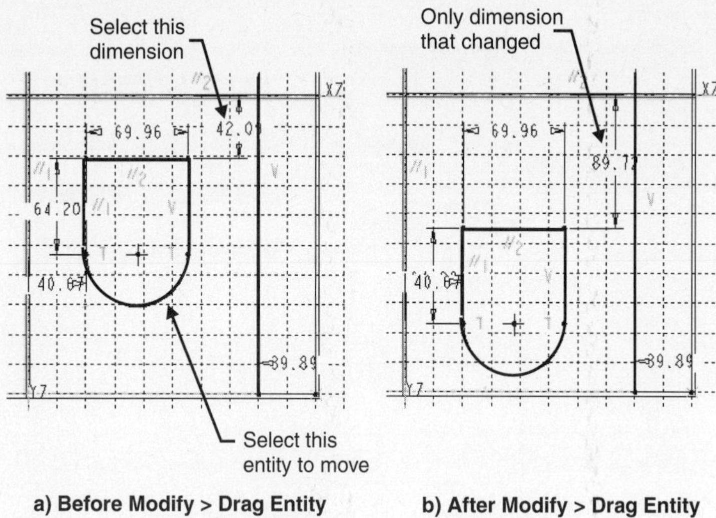

a) Before Modify > Drag Entity   **b) After Modify > Drag Entity**

Figure 7.3 The Drag Entity option.

The third option is the >Drag Vertex entity. A vertex marks the intersection of two entities. For example, a vertex may join a line and a curve. Moving the vertex will change two dimensions at the same time. It is therefore necessary to select two dimensions before >Done-Sel. When both are selected, click on the desired vertex and drag it around the screen. The sketch will rubberband following the mouse. The two selected dimensions will be modified. Selecting a different set of two dimensions produces different results, even when dragging the same vertex. This is illustrated in Figure 7.4. The same vertex is selected in Figures 7.4(a) and (c). Different pairs of dimensions are selected in each case. Dragging the same vertex is seen to produce different results in Figures 7.4(b) and 7.4(d).

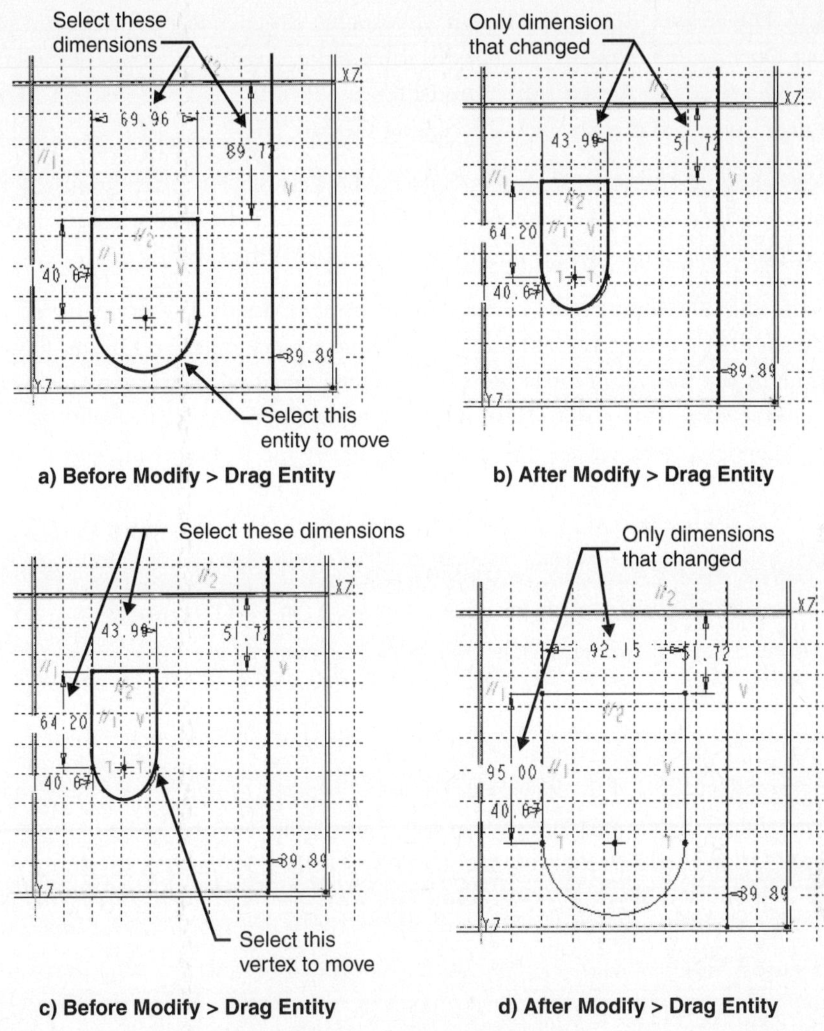

a) Before Modify > Drag Entity

b) After Modify > Drag Entity

c) Before Modify > Drag Entity

d) After Modify > Drag Entity

Figure 7.4   The Drag Vertex option.

In Tutorial 7.1 you will read in an existing part and create a cut on the front face using the top as a reference as seen in Figure 7.5(a). Design a keyhole using Rectangle to draw a rectangle, Delete to remove the top edge of the rectangle, and >Arc | Tangent to draw the 180 degree arc at the top. AutoDimension using the AX and AY axis as references. >Regenerate the part. Use >Modify | Value to change the values of the dimensions to those shown in Figure 7.5(b).

Notice how you >Regenerate before modifying the values. You should get into the habit of modifying values after regenerating. This is consistent with the Sketch,

Align, Dimension, Regenerate design philosophy. Regenerate the part again and select Done to end Sketcher. Accept the arrow indicating the direction that material will be removed; we want the material taken out of the keyhole. Select a >Thru All depth type and preview before accepting the part.

Select >Feature Oper >Redefine and select the keyhole for redefinition. In the Feature Dialog, select Section and click Define. When the menu appears, select Sketch to redefine the sketch. This brings us back into the sketcher.

Modify the 60 height of the keyhole to 80 using >Modify | Value. Change the width of the part using the >Modify | Drag Entity. Click on the 60 height dimension and select the side of the keyhole (#1) as seen in Figure 7.5(b). Drag the dimension to the value of about 80. Next, select the top arch (#2) of the keyhole and drag the dimension. Note, we are still in the Drag Entity mode. Leave it at about 70.

NOTE: Using >Drag Dim Value, >Drag Entity, or >Drag Vertex are not methods for creating accurate dimensions. Use the >Drag commands to achieve approximate results followed by >Modify Val for more accuracy.

Modify the location of the keyhole by selecting Modify | Drag Vertex. Select both the 60 and 30 dimensions that reference the part to the AY and AX axis respectively. Click (#3) on the lower-right vertex as seen in Figure 7.5(b). Drag the entire keyhole to a position about 10 away from both the AX and AY axis. Use >Modify | Value to set the dimensions as shown in Figure 7.5(c). The resultant part is shown in Figure 7.5(d).

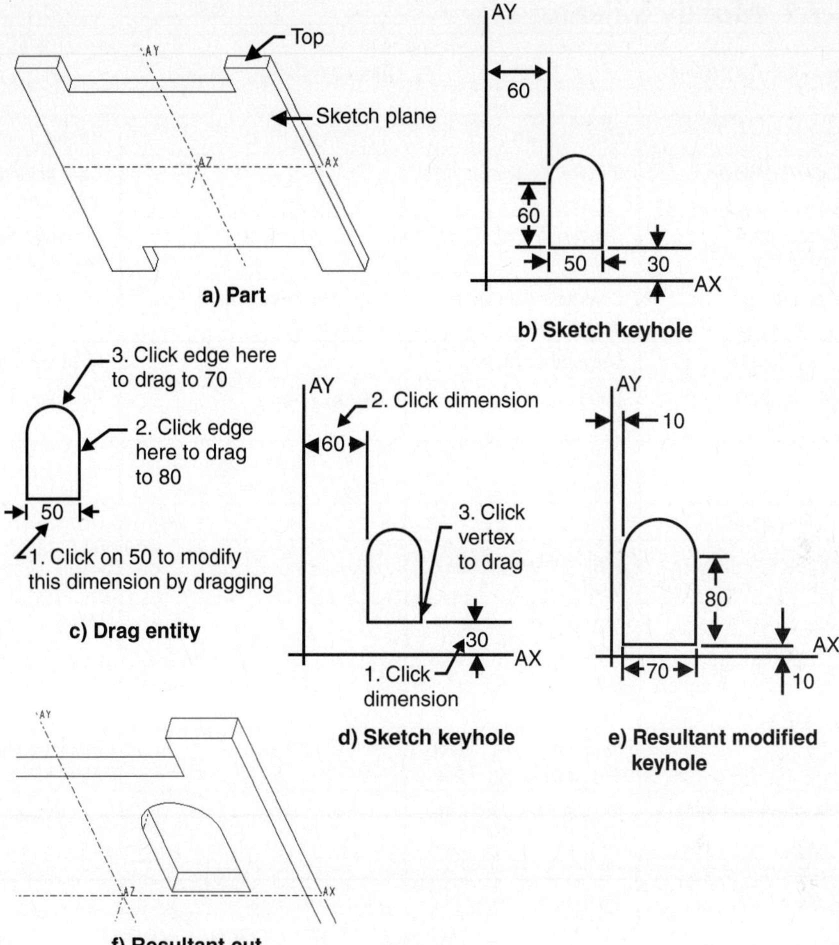

Figure 7.5   Illustration for Tutorial 7.1.

Tutorial 7.1 Modify a Feature

Files opened: Tut7-1a.prt   **Files saved:** Tut7-1b.prt

Step	Action	Description	Further Actions	Result
1	Click PT/Modeler Icon	Run PT/Modeler		After some time, PT/Modeler on screen
2	>Mode >Misc >Show Dir	Show current directory		Message similar to "Directory searched is c:\ptc\ptprod\bin"
3	>Change Dir	Change the current directory	Type **c:\proe\tutorial \chapter_7**	
4	>Done-Return	Leave Misc menu		Misc menu removed
5	>Mode >Part >Retrieve	Read a part	Type **tut7-1a**	Part read
6	>Environment	Set up the environment	Set up checks as seen in Table T7.1 Column Step 6	
7	>Done-Return			
8	>Feature >Cut >Extrude | Solid | Done	Create an extruded solid cut		
9	>One Side | Done	Cut will extend one side		
10	Pick the front face for sketching plane	Select front face in Fig. 7.5(a)	Accept arrow direction as protrusion direction	Pick face for cut; this is the sketching plane
11	>Top	Pick top of part for Top reference in Fig. 7.5(a)	Pick Top surface	Go into sketcher mode in Fig. 7.5(a)
12	>Sketch >Rectangle	Sketch a rectangle in a location of the feature in Fig. 7.5(b)		
13	>Delete Items	Delete the top line of the rectangle	mLb on top edge of rectangle then >Done-Sel or mMb	
14	>Sketch >Arc | Tangent End	Draw top arch connecting top vertices of U	mLb top of one vertical leg then mLb top of other vertical leg	
15	>AutoDimension	Have Sketcher do dimensions for you		Sketcher requests that you provide it with references
16	Select the AX and AY axis	Need to provide references to help auto dimensioning	>Done - Sel	Message – Regeneration Successful – Part gets dimensioned
17	>Modify	Change the dimensions to those shown in Figure 7.5(b)		
18	>Regenerate	Tell Sketcher to create feature		Message – Regeneration Successful –

Tutorial 7.1 Modify a Feature (continued)

Step	Action	Description	Further Actions	Result
19	>Done	Done with Sketcher	Accept direction of cut	
20	>Thru Next	Want to go through all three protrusions	>Done	
21	>OK	Accept arrow direction indicating material removal		
22	Preview	See result	F1 for default view then select Okay	
23	>Feature Oper | Redefine	Change Keyhole	Query Sel the keyhole	
24	Select Section item in Feature Dialog then Define button	Change the sketch, not the sketching plane	>Sketch in the menu	
25	>Modify	Change the keyhole height from 60 to 80	mLb on keyhole height dimension 60; type 80	
26	>Modify | Drag Entity	Change keyhole width from 50 to 80 by dragging right vertical edge	As in Fig 7.5(c), mLb on 50 width, mLb on any part of keyhole that has a component normal to selected dimension's directional sense, drag to about 80, mLb in place	
27	mLb on top arch	Change width to 70 by dragging arc edge	As in Fig 7.5(c), click on arc, drag width to about 70	
28	>Modify | Drag Vertex	Change position of arch in sketch plane; first select two dimensions	As in Fig 7.5(c), mLb on 60 and 30 references to AX and AY axis, mLb on any vertex, drag to about 10 and 10, mLb to place	
29	Click on lower-right vertex	Select vertex to drag	Drag to about 10 and 10 as seen in Fig. 7.5(e)	
30	>Modify	Change dimensions to values in Fig. 7.5(c)	Click on dimensions to change to 10, 10, 70, and 80 as in Fig 7.5(c)	
31	>Regenerate	Tell Sketcher to create feature	>Done	Message – Regeneration Successful –
32	Preview	See result	>Views > Names | Retrieve; type **TUT7-1-FRONT,** then select Okay	
33	>File >SaveAs	Save file with new name	Enter to accept [tut7-1a.prt] then type **tut7-1b.prt**	Part saved
34	QuitWindow			
35	Exit	Exit program	Click Yes to confirm	PT/Modeler exited

Item	Step 6
Disp DtmPln	Yes
Spin Center	No
Disp Pnts	Yes
Disp Axes	Yes
Rendering	No hidden line

Table T7.1 Environment Settings

7.2 Feature Operations

The Feature Operations menu, called Feature Oper, is shown in Figure 7.6. From this menu a feature can be redefined, deleted, reordered, rerouted, suppressed, resumed, or inserted at a different location in the Model Tree list. There are other important operations in this menu that will be described in later chapters.

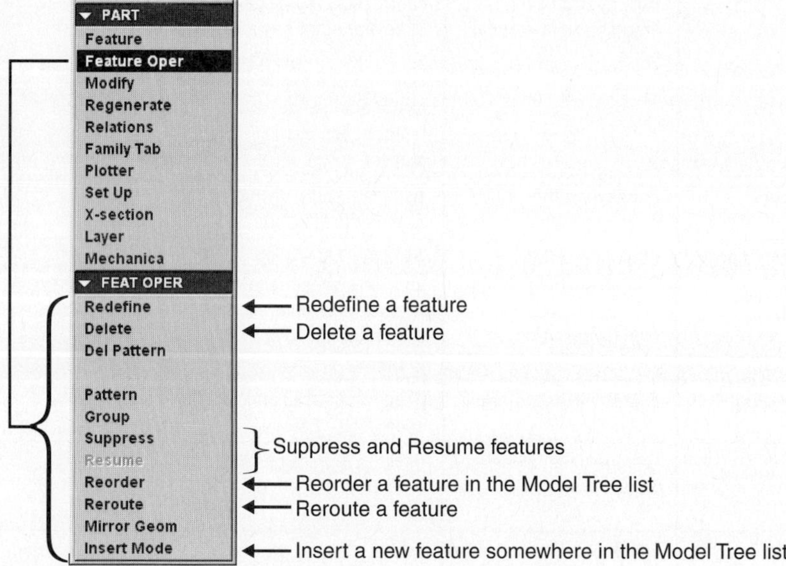

Figure 7.6 Feature Operations menu.

Redefining, Reordering, and Rerouting are ways to modify a feature. These are each discussed in later sections of this chapter. Suppressing and Resuming are useful when you wish to hide temporarily features from regeneration or display. Insert mode allows you to insert a new feature in between two existing features.

7.2.1   Suppress and Resume

As you know, a part is constructed one feature at a time, following an order as indicated in the Model Tree. The Model Tree indicates the sequential order in which features are built. At times, you might want to hide a feature or features temporarily. This is very useful when there is a lot of clutter on the screen or when you want to decrease regeneration or rendering times. Click >Suppress and then select the features to be suppressed. You can select these features from the Model Tree or from the part. Clicking >Resume brings up a submenu that allows you to resume a specific feature or all suppressed features. Any child of a suppressed feature will be suppressed.

7.2.2   Insert Mode

As new features are added into a part, each new feature is added at the end of the Model Tree construction list. At times you may want to add a feature somewhere else in the chain. This can be achieved by adding the new feature at the end of the part and then using Reorder to place this feature anywhere in the list besides the first location. However, this is sometimes very difficult. It is better to place the feature in the desired order the first time using >Insert.

There are disadvantages to this approach. For example, suppose a part consists of features A, B, C, D, and E. You want to add a feature F between features C and D. You create a new feature F and, inadvertently, select an edge from feature E as a reference. Now, you will not be able to reorder the part F to reside between C and D.

A better solution is to use >Insert Mode. After clicking >Insert Mode and Activate, you enter into an Insert Mode. Once in Insert Mode, it is necessary to specify which feature the new feature will follow. In our example, you would specify Feature C as this feature since we want F to follow C. We are now in Insert Mode, and from this point on, all features after feature C will be suppressed. You can now design feature F. Upon completion, the rendered part will show features A, B, C, and F. Clicking Insert and Cancel brings you out of Insert Mode. The rendered part then shows all features A, B, C, F, D, and E.

7.3   The Feature Edit Dialog Box

Selecting Feature Oper >Redefine brings up the Feature dialog box. The Feature dialog box, as shown in Figure 7.7, provides a concise representation of a feature. You can access nearly every parameter about the feature from this dialog. You cannot change the basic type of feature. For example, you cannot change a Cut to a Hole. You can redefine a feature using the Define menu and view information about the feature or aspect of the feature. Each element has references and the references can be highlighted one at a time using the Ref button. A submenu appears allowing you to select the next or previous reference. This is very useful when trying to understand the relationships with which an element is involved with respect to the rest of a feature.

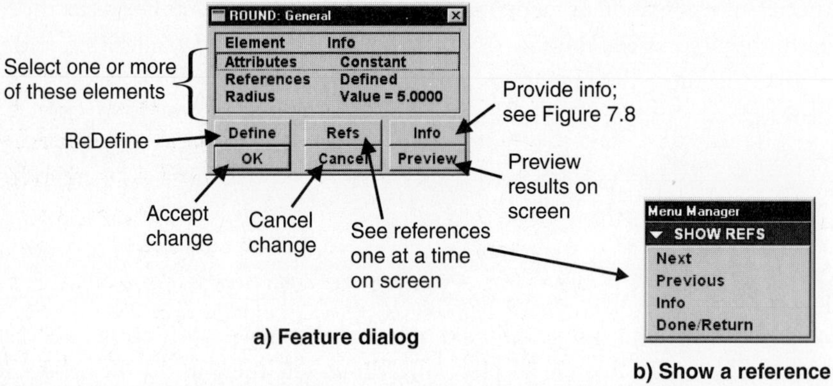

a) Feature dialog

b) Show a reference

Figure 7.7   Feature dialog box.

The elements of a feature are shown in a scrollable element list. Use the scroll bars, as seen in Figure 7.8, to see the various elements of a feature. Each type of feature has different elements. The pick-and-place features have fewer elements than the sketched features. Note also the similarity between the Cut and Extrude, reinforcing our recognition of their similarity.

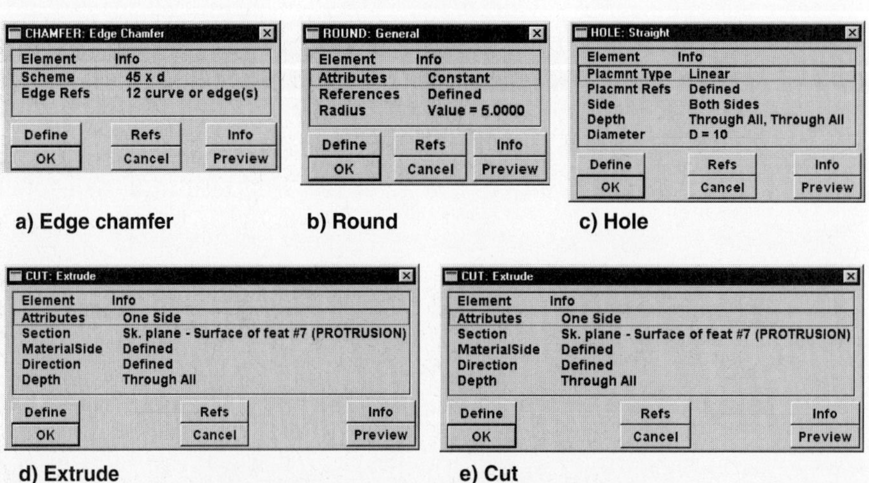

a) Edge chamfer   **b) Round**   **c) Hole**

d) Extrude   **e) Cut**

Figure 7.8   Element lists for various features.

The Info button on the Features dialog brings up an information window as seen in Figure 7.9. This window can be very useful, showing the elements of the features and the values associated with each element. The section name is provided as well as a list of all of the features dimensions. Note that the section name and the dimensions are given default names such as s2d008 or d99, d100. These names can be changed, as we discuss in later chapters.

Info Window

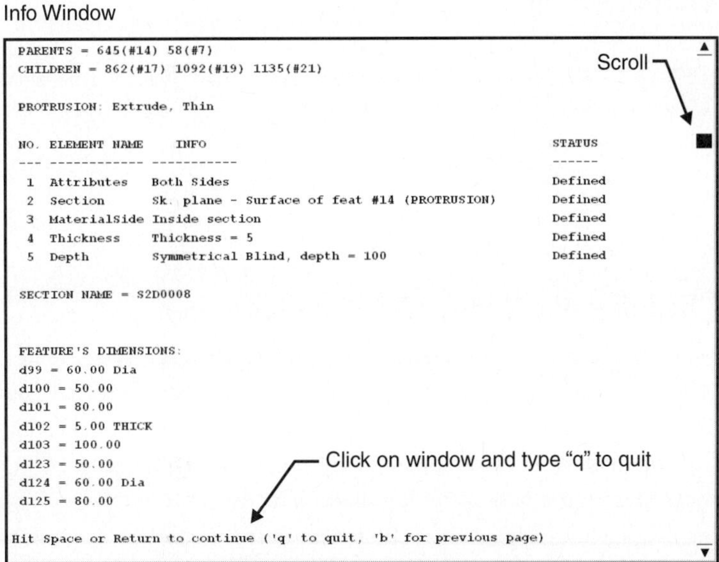

Figure 7.9   Information window.

NOTE: Always use the q command to close the Info window. Never close or minimize an Info window directly. This can cause undesirable results.

7.4   Redefine

Features that were created after the selected feature are not shown. For example, suppose you design an extruded base feature and then place four holes in the part. If you redefine the base feature, the feature will be displayed without the holes. All features after the selected feature are suppressed until the changes are accepted or cancelled from the Features dialog box.

If you have decided to change a pick-and-place feature, each element is fairly straightforward. These repeat the steps you followed when designing the part. It is a little more complicated when you redefine a sketched feature; sketched features have a Section element. This feature contains parameters regarding the sketching plane and the sketch itself. If you choose to redefine the Section element, a submenu appears allowing you to change the sketch plane, the sketch, or the scheme. This menu is shown in Figure 7.10.

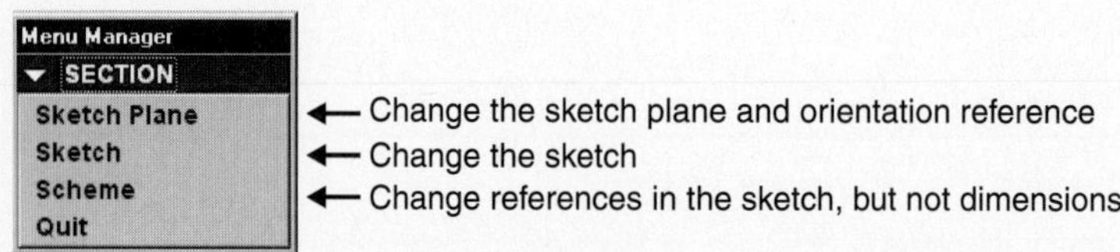

Figure 7.10   Section submenu.

7.4.1   Redefine the Section Sketch Plane

The Sketch plane allows you to reselect the sketching plane and the orientation reference. This can have major consequences. Consider the case in which your sketch is aligned to several edges in the rest of the part. Changing the sketching plane changes the orientation of these edges. Many edges may no longer exist in the new view associated with the new sketching plane. The orientation reference will determine how the sketch is displayed on the screen. It will not affect the alignment references. Perhaps the sketch may be drawn upside down or reversed left to right. However, this will not affect the alignment references because the entire part will be given this new orientation.

Consider Figure 7.11. The keyhole from the part designed in Tutorial 7.1 has been selected for redefinition. The Section element in the Features dialog is selected and the sketching plane option is selected from the menu that follows. During this redefine pass, the Top of the part is selected as the sketching plane, and the Front face of the part is selected as the Bottom reference as seen in Figure 7.11(a). The resultant sketch now looks like Figure 7.11(b). The placement of the part has caused the sketch to change since the AX and AY axes were referenced by the dimensions. The AX and AY axes were parents to the keyhole.

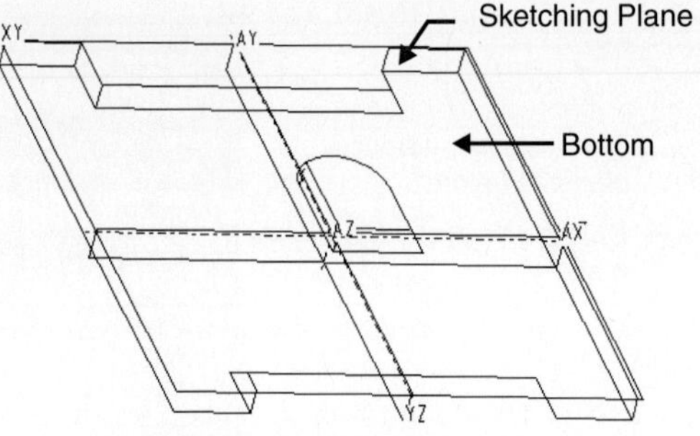

a) Redefine a new sketching plane and orientation reference

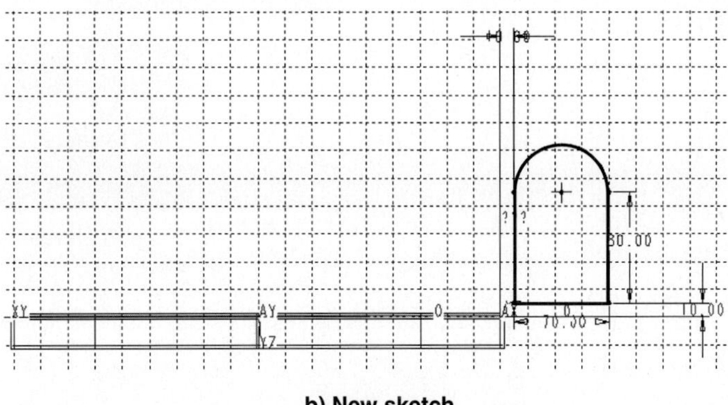

b) New sketch

Figure 7.11 Changing the sketching plane.

The submenus provided when you elect to change the sketching plane are shown in Figure 7.12. Note that both have a Same Ref menu item allowing you to keep the same reference. Other than that, the menus are identical to the sketching and reference plane selection menus used when designing a new feature.

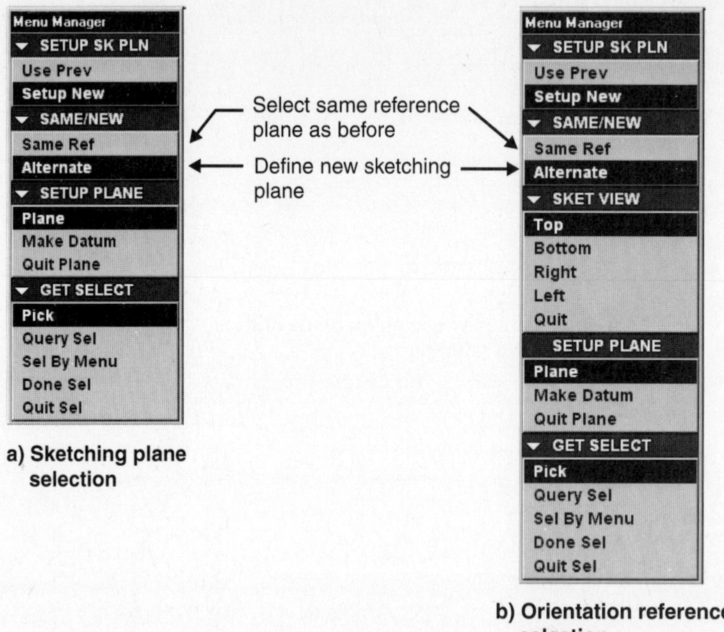

a) Sketching plane selection

b) Orientation reference selection

Figure 7.12   Selecting new sketching plane and orientation submenus.

7.4.2   Redefine the Sketch

You can change almost anything when redefining the sketch. The original sketching plane is shown with the sketch and its dimensions. You can operate on this sketch as you would on any sketch that has been regenerated. Recall that regeneration can set some of the sketcher assumptions in place. You can use the >Constraints Disable option to break an assumption.

7.4.3   Redefine the Section Scheme

This is the most limited of the menu selections. You can change how the feature is dimensioned but you cannot change the actual dimensions or add sketched entities. This option is not regularly used in practice.

7.4.4   Redefine Tutorial

In Tutorial 7.2, redefine a cylindrical protrusion feature in the part shown in Figure 7.13. The protrusions come out of a plate-shaped protrusion on the back surface of the part. The protrusions use the face of this back plate as references for their position. We want to move the cylinders up and remove the references to the back plate.

All will not go well as you will see. But relax—we will fix the problems and simultaneously get a glimpse of what is to come in Chapter 8.

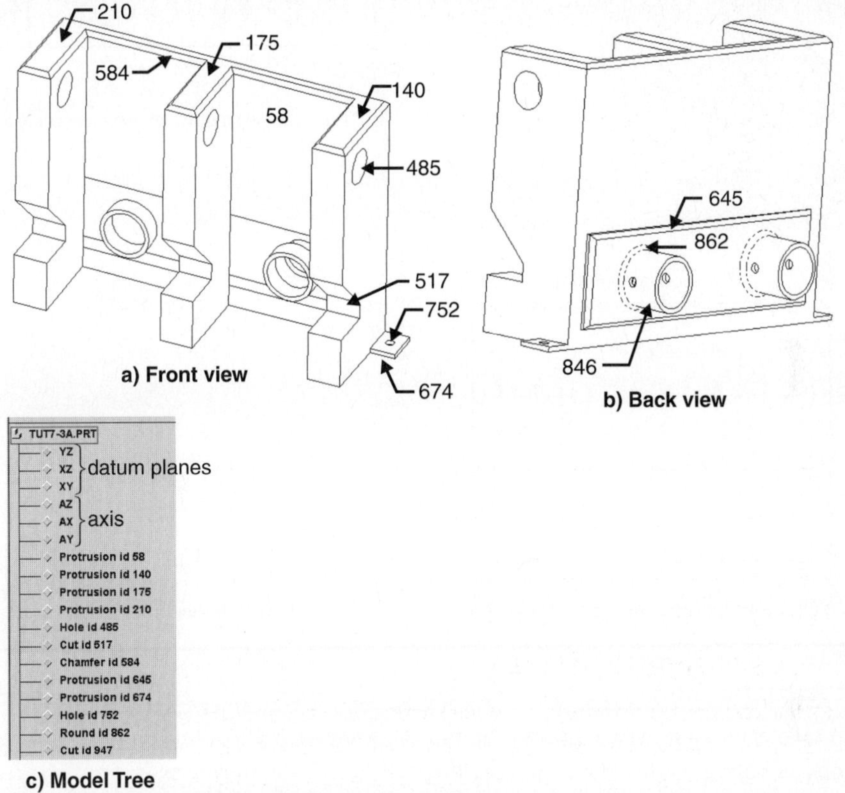

Figure 7.13   Part before redefine showing features.

You will read in a part and elect to redefine a feature using the >Feature Oper >Redefine command. Select the left-most cylinder as shown in Figure 7.14(a). Notice that both cylinders are highlighted. This is due to the fact that the right cylinder was patterned after the left cylinder. We discussed patterning in Chapter 6. The sketch, as illustrated in Figure 7.14(b), shows that the cylinders are referenced to Plate 645. Delete all four of these dimensions—50, 50, 80, and 80—and create new dimensions as seen in Figure 7.14(c). Regenerate the part. It generates correctly. You are done with Sketcher so Preview the result and select Okay. Here is where the problems start.

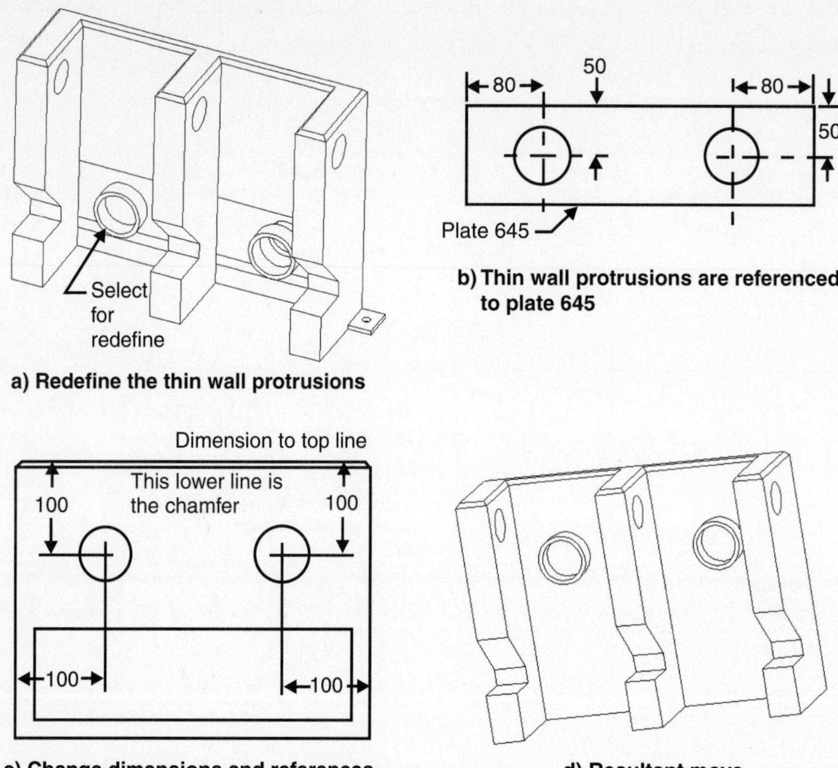

Figure 7.14   Redefine the references of the cylinders.

If the regeneration worked then why did the preview fail? An information window appears telling us that the round feature #18 failed. Recall that parts are built feature by feature. The sketcher regeneration simply regenerated the cylinder feature. The Preview forced a regeneration of the entire part. The round, as shown in Figure 7.13(b) and named 862, used a surface-to-surface reference during its design. This meant that the round was a child of the two surfaces selected. This made the round a child of the plate. We separated the cylinders from the plate, but we did not separate the round from the plate. The round is still relying on the surface of the plate, and the cylinder no longer intersects that surface. Herein lies the problem. We can take several paths; for now, we will delete the rounds. Select >Quick Fix >Delete to delete the first round. You will have to repeat this process >Quick Fix >Delete to delete the second round. Fixing regeneration problems will be discussed in detail in Chapter 8.

In Figure 7.15(b), the Feature dialog box for the round appears. Select References and select Define. This lets us specify the two face references for the round. Select the back face of the part and the side of the cylinder. It is always wise to use Query

Select. It always seems that when you use Query Select you get the correct item on the first try, but when you use Pick, you get the wrong one. This successfully regenerates the part so we can click Okay from the Feature dialog box and the round appears.

Unfortunately, only one round appears, due to the patterning that created the second round. Create a second round using the >Feature >Round. This time, specify an edge-chain so an edge will be selected instead of two surfaces. Select the desired edge as shown in Figure 7.15(a) and the second round appears.

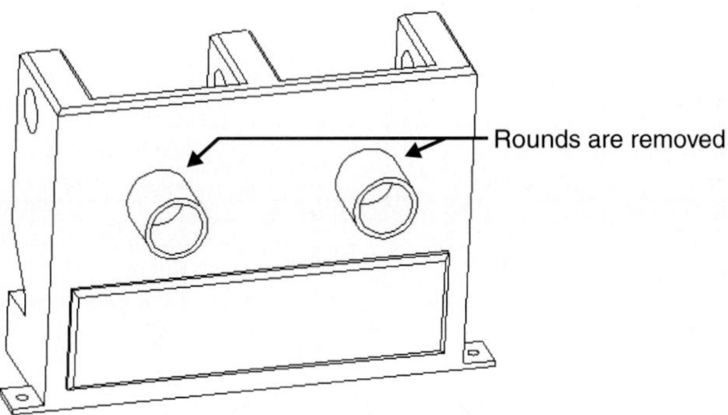

Figure 7.15   Resolve the round error.

Delete the back plate. Use the >Feature Oper | Delete option and select the back plate. Do not accept the deletion. Note that a message occurs in the Message window indicating that the highlighted children will also be deleted. Cancel the deletion. We thought that the cylinders were free and clear of all references to the back plate, but we were wrong. The cylinder still uses the back plate surface as its sketching plane. Deleting the back surface will delete the sketching plane and, consequently, will delete the cylinder.

We can rectify this by once again selecting >Feature Oper | Redefine and selecting the cylinders. Select Section and Define from the Features dialog. This time, select >Sketch Plane to change the sketching plane. The first menu allows us to select the back surface of the part as the alternate sketch plane as seen in Figure 7.15(b). We can select >Same Reference from the Orientation Reference menu to keep the same reference. This brings us into the sketcher. Since we do not need to change anything in the sketcher, simply Regenerate and Done. Preview and accept the resultant part. Note that we still have not completely succeeded in separating the cylinders from the back plate. We will return to this part in Chapter 8.

Tutorial 7.2   Redefine a Feature

Files opened: Tut7-2a.prt   **Files saved:** Tut7-2b.prt

Step	Action	Description	Further Actions	Result
1	Click PT/Modeler Icon	Run PT/Modeler		After some time, PT/Modeler on screen
2	>Mode >Misc >Show Dir	Show current directory		Message similar to "Directory searched is c:\ptc\ptprod\bin"
3	>Change Dir	Change the current directory	Type **c:\proe\tutorial\ chapter_7**	
4	>Done-Return	Leave Misc menu		Misc menu removed
5	>Mode >Part >Retrieve	Read a part	Type **tut7-2a**	Part read
6	>Environment	Set up the environment	Set up checks as seen in Table T7.2 Column Step 6	
7	>Done-Return			
8	>Feature Oper | Redefine	Redefine the Circular protrusion 846	Select left Circular protrusion from front view as marked on Figure 7.14(a)	
9	Select Section item and then Define button	Want to change the sketch	>Sketch	
10	>Delete mLb 50, mLb 50, mLb 80, mLb 80	Delete all dimensional references to plate 645	>Done-Sel	
11	Dimension circles to base plate in Fig. 7.14(b)	Reference circular protrusions to base plate		
12	Regenerate			Message – Regeneration Successful –
13	>Modify	Modify dimensions in Fig. 7.14(c)	>Change 4 new reference dimensions to 100	
14	Regenerate	See result in Fig. 7.14(d)	>Done	Message – Regeneration Successful –
15	Preview	See result	Okay	Error regenerating Round
16	>Quick Fix >Delete	Delete the rounds (Feature 18) that are causing the problem	>Confirm that you want to delete	The first round is deleted

Tutorial 7.2 Redefine a Feature (continued)

Step	Action	Description	Further Actions	Result
17	>Quick Fix >Delete	Delete the second round (Feature 18) that is still causing a problem	>Yes that you want to delete and exit from redefine	
18	>File >SaveAs	Save file with new name	Enter to accept [tut7-a.prt] then type **tut7-2b.prt**	Part saved
19	QuitWindow			
20	Exit	Exit program	Click Yes to confirm	PT/Modeler exited

Item	Step 6
Disp DtmPln	Yes
Spin Center	No
Disp Pnts	Yes
Disp Axes	Yes
Rendering	No hidden line

Table T7.2 Environment Settings

7.5 Reroute

The Reroute command allows you to change the parent-child relations of a feature, create new sketching planes and reference planes, and create new dimension references. This is an excellent tool for working out regeneration problems. Reroute gives you many of the same features as Redefine; however, you cannot change dimensional references.

Often during the reroute process, it is necessary to find new references to break parent-child relationships. You can create datum planes on the fly for this purpose. Reroute does not allow you to create new dimensions or to delete existing dimensions. You can also select an option called "Roll back the Part." This stops regeneration and display of all features that occur after the rerouted feature. It is always wise to use the "Roll back the Part" option.

In Figure 7.16(a), the reroute menu is displayed. There are two choices once >Reroute is selected. You can reroute a feature or replace a reference. Choosing Reroute Feat requests that you select the feature to be rerouted and queries whether you want to roll back the part. It brings up a second menu as shown in Figure 7.16(b) allowing you to select the sketching plane. You can choose to keep the old sketching plane or choose a new reference. If you select an alternate reference, you can make a datum plane on the fly for this purpose.

A similar menu follows, allowing you to keep the old orientation reference or select an alternate orientation reference. Finally, a comparable menu is displayed requesting that you keep the old dimensioning reference or select an alternate dimensioning reference. If you select the same reference for all three, no change will occur to the part. You are not able to change any dimensions associated with the feature.

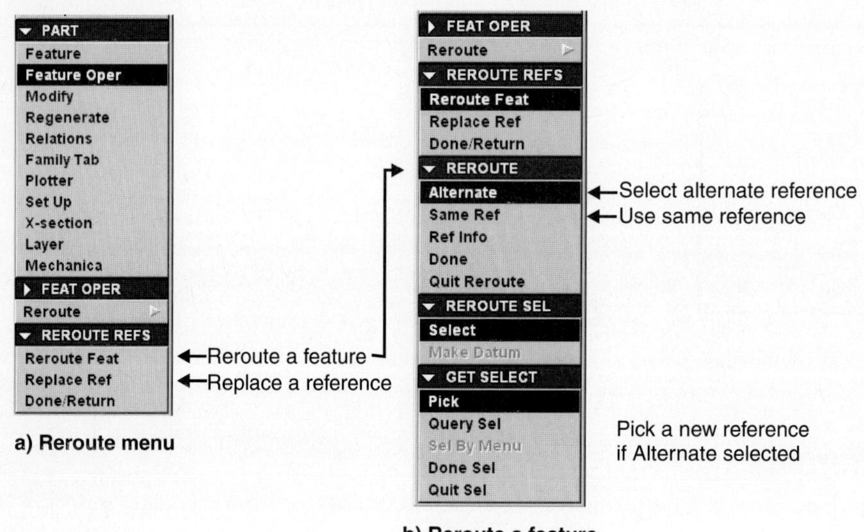

Figure 7.16   Reroute menu.

In Tutorial 7.2, we used Redefine to perform a Reroute operation. There is nothing wrong with this approach. Reroute is a more direct path towards accomplishing the same goal. In Tutorial 7.3, you will reroute the angled cut on the front protrusions. First, retrieve the part and select to reroute by >Feature Oper >Reroute. Next, select the cut feature as shown in Figure 7.17(a) and choose to roll back the part. The goal is to change the sketching plane from the outside face of the right-most protrusion to the inside face. The software displays the section sketch on the old sketching plane as seen in Figure 7.17(b). Choose an alternate reference for the sketching plane using >Alternate and click on the inner face as seen in Figure 7.17(c). You can select the Same Ref for both the orientation and the dimensional references. That is all there is to it. The part is automatically regenerated as seen in Figure 7.17(d). Note that the cut no longer occurs through the right-most protrusion since the cut is one-sided and through all. This could be changed using the Redefine command if desired.

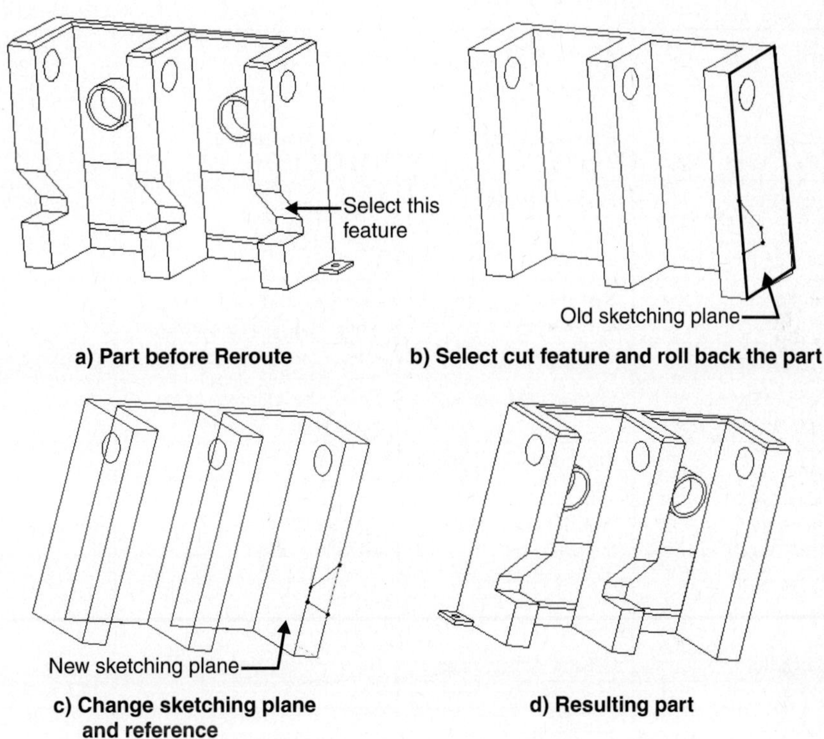

Figure 7.17   Illustrations for Tutorial 7.3.

Tutorial 7.3 Reroute a Feature

Files opened: Tut7-3a.prt   **Files saved:** Tut7-3b.prt

Step	Action	Description	Further Actions	Result
1	Click PT/Modeler Icon	Run PT/Modeler		After some time, PT/Modeler on screen
2	>Mode >Misc >Show Dir	Show current directory		Message similar to "Directory searched is c:\ptc\ptprod\bin"
3	>Change Dir	Change the current directory	Type **c:\proe\tutorial\ chapter_7**	
4	>Done-Return	Leave Misc menu		Misc menu removed
5	>Mode >Part >Retrieve	Read a part	Type **tut7-3a**	Part read
6	>Environment	Set up the environment	Set up checks as seen in Table T7.3 Column Step 6	
7	>Done-Return			
8	>Feature Oper | Reroute	Change the front cuts	Select the leftmost cut in Fig. 7.17(a)	
9	Type Y	Want to roll back the part		
10	>Alternate	Pick the inside face for the sketching plane; old plane is shown in Figure 7.17(b)	Pick the inside face in Fig. 7.17(c)	New sketching plane
11	>Same Ref	Use same reference as orientation plane		
12	>Same Ref	Use same reference as dimension plane	>Done	Part is regenerated in Fig. 7.17(d)
13	Preview	See result	>Views > Names | Retrieve; type **TUT7-3-FRONT**, then select Okay	
14	>File >SaveAs	Save file with new name	Enter to accept [tut7-a.prt] then Type **tut7-3b.prt**	Part saved
15	QuitWindow			
16	Exit	Exit program	Click Yes to confirm	PT/Modeler exited

Item	Step 6
Disp DtmPln	No
Spin Center	No
Disp Pnts	No
Disp Axes	No
Rendering	No hidden line

Table T7.3 Environment Settings

7.6   Reorder

The Reorder command provides a means of shuffling features within the Model Tree. This task is often more challenging than it might appear. As we saw in Tutorial 7.2, features are often interrelated due to dimensional references and sketching planes. Some of these relationships are purposeful and others are unintentional.

Many times, you will find yourself locked out when trying to reorder a feature due to existing parent-child relationships. If the software stops you from reordering, it is due to references. You are likely trying to move a feature before one of its references, for example, parents. The secret to successful reordering is planning. If the part was planned well, features should be able to move independently. If a reorder fails, you will likely need to reorder or even redefine the feature. This may be true for other features as well.

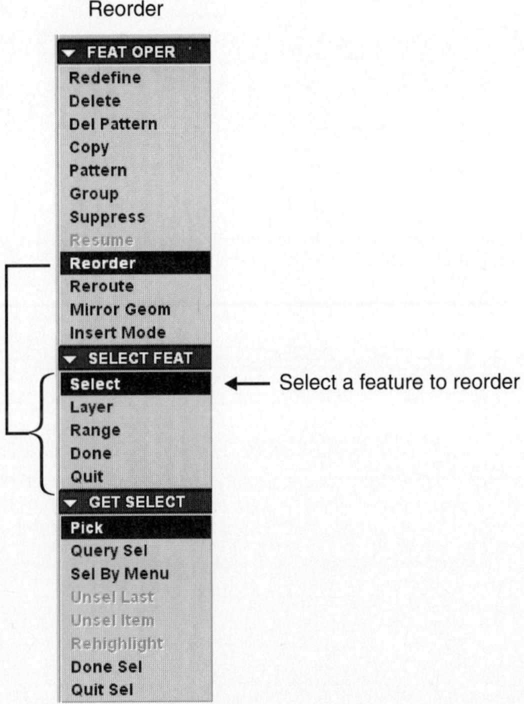

Figure 7.18   Reorder menu.

Organizing Using Layers

A successful solid model design is one that satisfies the specifications in an efficient and effective manner. The design must reflect the intent, and the model must be easy to modify. A good model is typically based upon a good structure. Layers provide an organizational tool that can help you build structure and consistency into your models.

Even simple solid models can be quite complicated. There are assemblies consisting of parts, and parts consisting of features. There are features consisting of elements, and elements consisting of parameters related to other elements. Anything you can do to help organize these many entities will work in your favor, both during the design and modification stages of development.

Layers get their name from the early animation days when drawings were made on a series of transparencies. The background was placed on one transparency sheet and each foreground character was put on its own transparency sheet. Each sheet or layer was then overlaid to create a single frame. This layer technique provided the artists with a flexible system for producing complex scenes.

Layers are equally important in three-dimensional modeling. A single command lets you show or hide all nongeometry items in a layer. This can be a very effective and easy way to reduce clutter on your screen. In addition, it is very simple to suppress and resume all items in a layer.

Layers are associated with the part, assembly, and drawing files. When you create a layer, it is added to the respective file. If you save the file, after creating a layer, the layer will remain with the part, assembly, or drawing. This occurs even if no items are placed in that layer.

8.1   What Are Layers?

Perhaps you have worked with illustration, CAD, or imaging software packages and are well aware of what a layer is and how to use one. Layers are a grouping mechanism. They enable us to create order out of randomness. They provide structure the way an element provides structure out of a group of parameters and a feature provides order to a group of elements. Layers give us many drawers to put things in.

Drawing on layers is similar to drawing on a set of transparencies. You can draw all of the dimensions on one layer, the axis on another, the protrusions on a separate layer from the rounds and chamfers. You can look at one layer at a time or enable any number of layers.

It is your job as designer to specify and use the layers. Each design is different and may well require specialized layers. However, there are many similarities among all models, and you are wise to be consistent between your models. For example, every model contains the following items that are prime candidates for layers:

- Dimensions: Parameter
- Dimensions: Driven
- Dimensions: Part reference
- Notes: Drawing
- Symbols
- Datum: Planes
- Datum: Axis
- Datum: Curves
- Datum: Points
- Features: Surface
- Features: With Axis
- Features: Rounds
- Features: Chamfers
- Features: Cuts
- Features: Protrusions

It is a very good idea to use common names for layers in all of your drawings. This way the names are easy to remember, and you are more likely to use them. Having consistent names is also important when working at the assembly level. A typical assembly has several parts displayed simultaneously. Imagine that you want to hide or display a particular layer across all parts in the assembly. Each part will need to have a layer with the same name containing the respective items. For example, if you want to hide all datum planes across all parts, each part would need a layer with the same name, say DATUM_PLANE.

Having layers and using them are two different things. You might create a list of twenty layers for a drawing and only use two or none at all. In the heat of a design, it is easy to skip the step of actually using layers. Once the layers are set up, however, they can be invaluable for your design. Only the simplest of designs work as desired the first time through, and you will often spend time troubleshooting your designs. Having layers, at that time, can really save you a lot of time. They can save much more time than is required to use them.

Layers are accessed through the Part menu as seen in Figure 8.1. There are three basic choices: Set Items, Set Display, and Setup. These are discussed in the following sections.

8.2   Setup Layers Command

Setup allows you to set up layers including creating, deleting, and renaming layers. The Layer menu is shown in Figure 8.1(a). Note the >Setup item is selected providing the create, delete, and rename options.

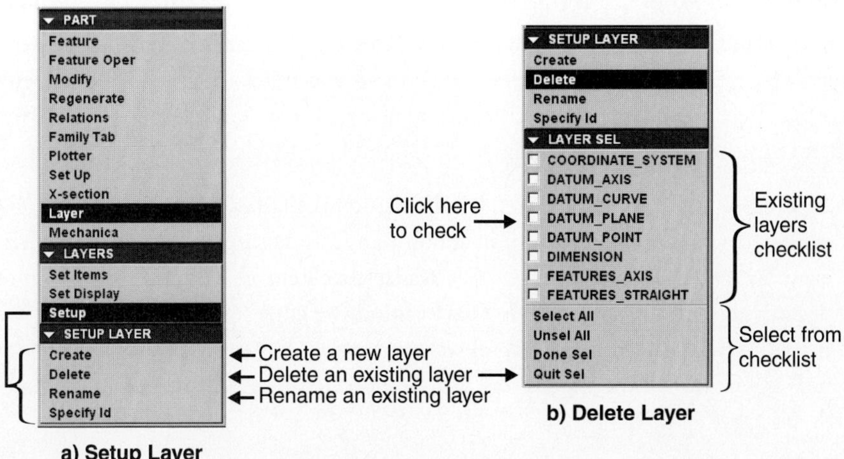

Figure 8.1   Layers menu.

8.2.1   Creating Layers

To create a layer, select Create. A query is provided in the Message Window requesting you to enter the name for the new layer. This layer will be associated with the part. However, you will need to save the part for the layer to remain with the part.

8.2.2   Deleting Layers

To delete a layer, select Delete. A checklist of all layers in the part is displayed as seen in Figure 8.1(b). You can check the layers in the checklist that you wish to delete, or you can use the selection tools at the bottom of the menu.

8.2.3   Renaming Layers

To rename a layer, select Rename. A list of all layers in the part is displayed. Select the layer name that you want to change. A query appears in the Message Window requesting that you enter the new name for the layer. The current name is displayed in the default selection of the query.

8.3   Set Items Command

Set Items allows you to work with items on layers. You can place items on layers or remove items from a layer. You can copy an item from one layer onto a different layer, leaving the item on the original layer or switch an item from one layer to another removing the item from the original layer.

Figure 8.2 illustrates this process. Assume that there are two layers set up in PT/Modeler, called Layer ONE and Layer TWO. When you create a part, all features, datums, or dimensions associated with that part are not associated with any layer. This is illustrated in Figure 8.2(a). We can add items to layer ONE in Figure 8.2(b). These items are still part of the model; they have not changed in any way other than the placement of Items A, B, D, and G into layer ONE.

In Figure 8.2(c), we repeat the step by placing Items B and D into layer TWO. For whatever reason we change our mind about item E. In Figure 8.2(d), we switch item E from layer ONE to layer TWO. We realize that item D has things in common with both layers ONE and TWO. This in mind, we copy item D from layer TWO to layer ONE. Lastly, in Figure 8.2(e) we remove item F from layer ONE. Note that item F is still part of the model. We have not deleted it. It simply is not associated with any layer.

> **NOTE:** Items in a model can reside on a single layer, more than one layer, or no layer at all.

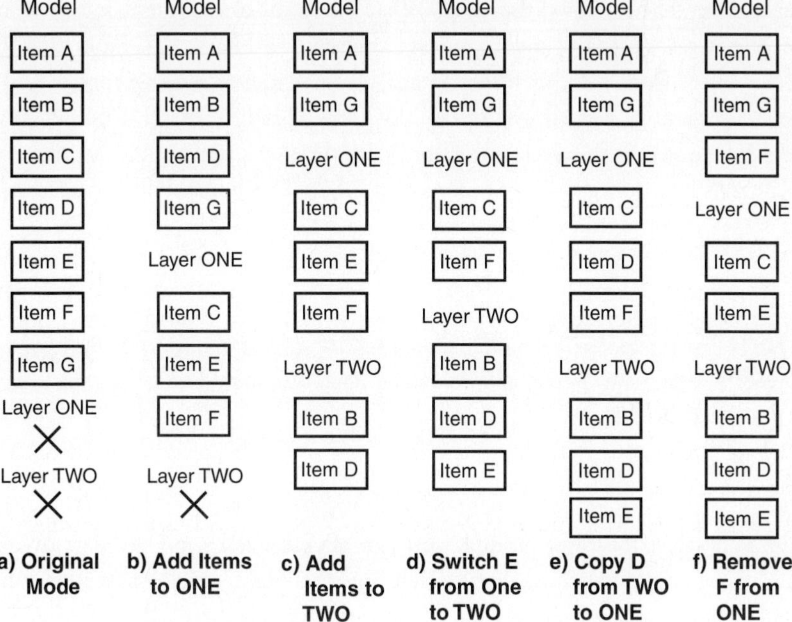

Figure 8.2   Adding, removing, and moving items example.

8.3.1   Add Items on a Layer

To add an item to a layer, select >Add Items. A checklist appears, which consists of all layers in the part as seen in Figure 8.3. Check one or more items in the checklist and select >Done Sel. Recall that >Quit Sel will exit you from the Add items selection as opposed to accepting the choices.

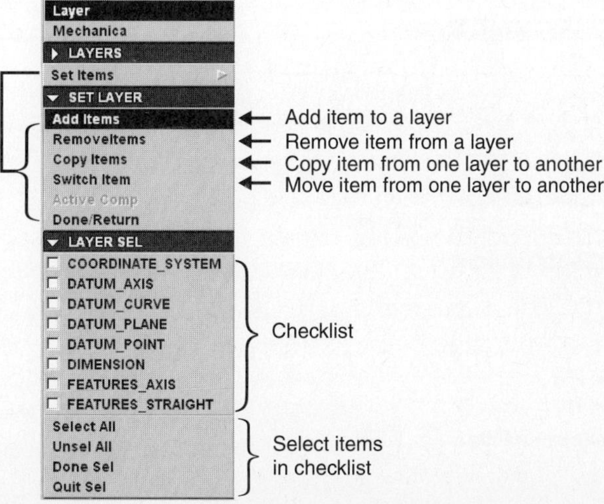

Figure 8.3   Adding, removing, and moving items menu.

Now that you have selected the layer(s) that you want to add items into, you must select the items. A second menu appears as shown in Figure 8.4. From this menu you can select from a set of filters to assist you in the selection process. You can select to pick only Features, Curves, 2D items, Text, Points, Datum Planes, or Layers. The object is to select a filter and pick the items that should be placed into the layer. When done picking, enter >Done Sel. The items will be added to the layer.

> **NOTE:** You can add a layer into a layer creating a layer hierarchy. Perhaps you want a fastener layer, and in that fastener layer you want Datum, Feature, and Dimension layers.

Before you select the filter desired, you can click on items on the part or in the Model Tree to highlight those items. Each time you make a pick a new item is highlighted. If you forget to select a filter, picking items on the display or Model Tree will cause the items to be highlighted but will NOT select them for placement into a layer. After you select a filter, each item you pick remains highlighted.

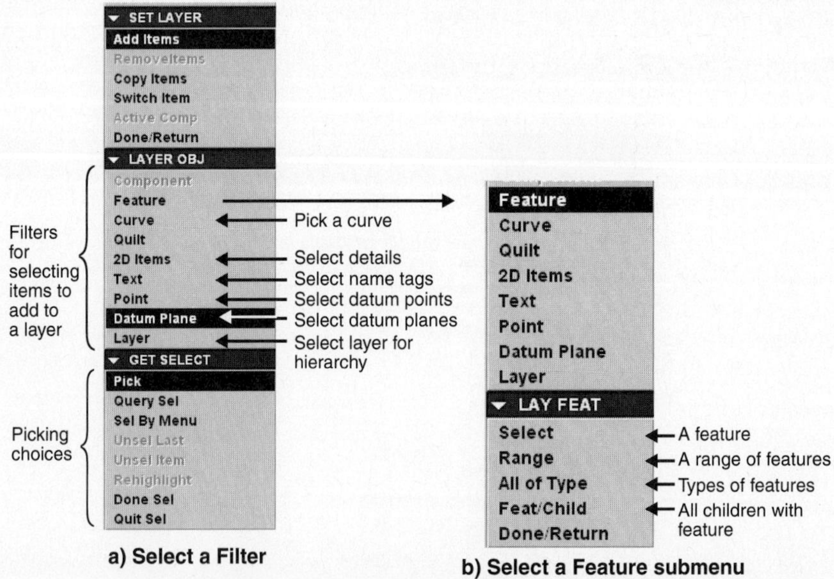

Figure 8.4   Selecting and Filtering menu.

8.3.2   Picking Items

You can select multiple items to be added to a layer. A standard pick submenu is displayed at the bottom of the menu from Figure 8.5. Selecting items for addition to a layer can be very tricky. The item that you pick will be highlighted. However the highlighting can get quite complicated when several items are selected.

> **TIP:** Use Rehighlight to remove all highlights from display. This allows you to detect the next selection easily.

It is very easy to get the wrong item using the simple Pick technique relying on the part. If you want to pick from the part, use >Query Sel. Another alternative is to use Pick, but pick from the Model Tree. This is an easy way to get the correct item since the parts are named, Cut, Protrusion, etc. A third alternative is to select the items by a menu.

As you select items, they are highlighted. If you select the wrong items, you can use >Unsel Last to remove the last item added to the select list automatically. You can also use the >Unsel Item to remove an item by selecting that item. The highlighting is removed from all Unselected items.

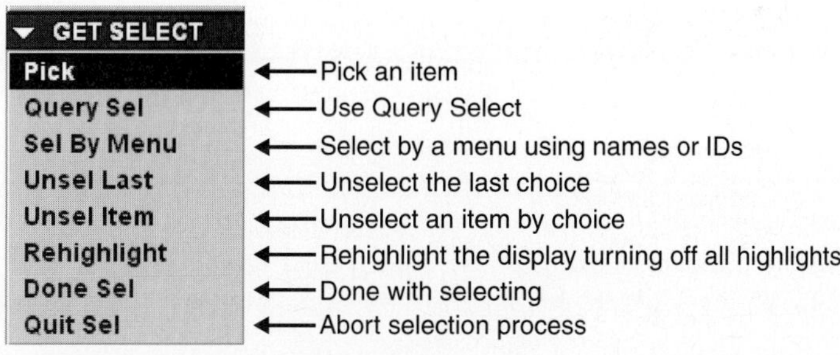

Figure 8.5   Pick menu.

8.3.3   Remove Items from Layer

Use the Remove command to remove an item from a layer. Remove items in exactly the same way as you add items. Check the appropriate layer(s) to remove items from, select the filter and pick mechanism, and pick the items to remove. Picked items are highlighted. However, there is no indication when you have selected an item to remove from a layer that did not belong to that layer in the first place. Therefore, no harm is done.

8.3.4   Copy and Switch Items between Layers

Use the >Switch command to remove an item from one layer and place it on another layer. To copy an item from one layer to another layer, also keeping the item in the original layer, use the >Copy item. In both cases, you will need to provide the name of the source layer where the item exists and the destination layer to which the item will be copied.

8.4   Set Display Command

Set Display allows you to show and blank layers. It is important to realize that not all items in a layer will be hidden from view when you blank a layer. The following items will be blanked from the display when a layer is blanked.

- Datums including planes, axes, curves, and points
- Feature axes
- Cosmetic features

The actual geometry associated with the feature is not blanked. If you do not want to see the geometry, it is necessary to suppress the feature.

The >Set Display menu is shown in Figure 8.6. There are two separate mechanisms at work here called >Display and >Blank. An item in a layer can either be displayed or blanked. At start up, the display status is set such that all layers are in a display mode. Accordingly, they are displayed.

There are two menu selections in Figure 8.6 called >Display and >Blank. If you select either, a checklist of all layers associated with the part is displayed. If you are in the >Display mode, checking a layer causes that layer to be displayed and all other nonchecked layers to be blanked. When you are in the >Blank mode, checking a layer causes that layer to be blanked and all nonchecked layers to be displayed. In the default case, no layers are checked in either the >Display or >Blank menus. Consequently, all layers are displayed.

A layer is either displayed or not displayed. The two states of Display and Blank act on the same layer but checking an item in Display does not mean that it is unchecked in Blank. There is one checklist for Display and a second checklist for Blank. Any layer checked in Display will be displayed and all other layers will not be displayed. If no layers are selected for Display, then all layers are displayed. This provides a convenient way to display one (or a few) layers while blanking all of the rest. Any layer selected in Blank will not be displayed. This provides a convenient way to blank one (or a few) layers while displaying all the rest.

> **NOTE:** Display has precedence over Blank. Therefore, if one layer is checked in both Display and Blank, that layer will be displayed.

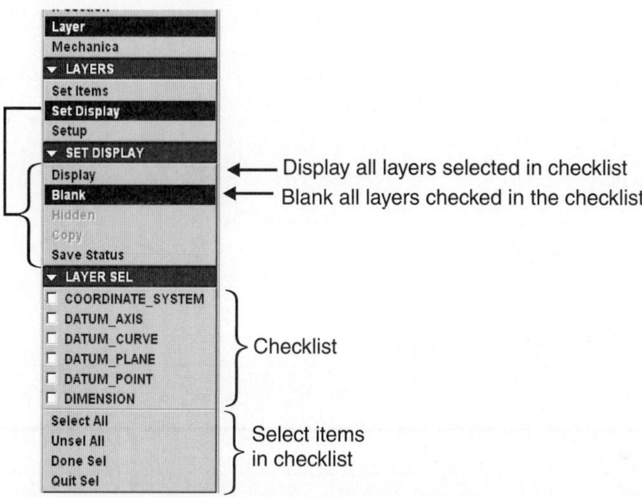

Figure 8.6   Set Display menu.

8.5   Displaying Layer Status in the Model Tree

You can view the status of a layer in the Model Tree by Selecting >Tree | Columns | Add/Remove. Select the Info heading under Available and select the Layer Status as seen in Figure 8.7(a). The resultant Model Tree is shown in Figure 8.7(b). The display or hide status of each layer is shown.

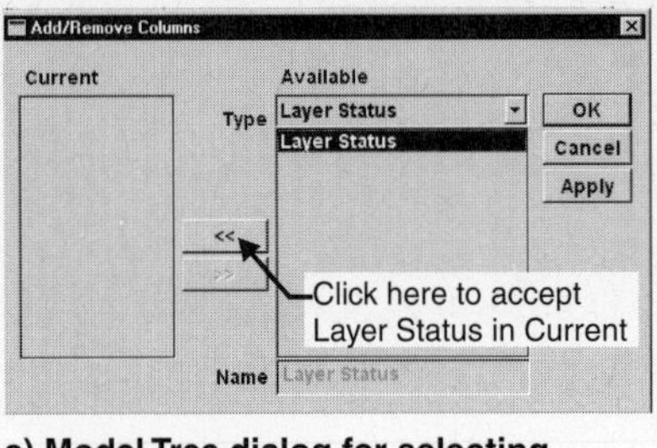

a) Model Tree dialog for selecting Layer Status

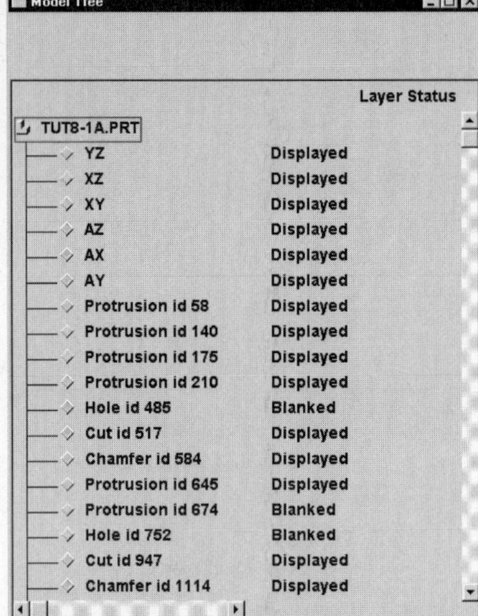

b) Model Tree with Layer Status displayed

Figure 8.7   Layer information in the Model Tree.

8.6   Items in Multiple Layers

There are some rules to consider when placing features on layers. For example, you might have a feature in two layers. What if one layer is in Display mode and the other is in Blank mode? The answer is that the Display mode has preference.

A second rule has to do with items that have multiple entities. Suppose an entire part resides in layer A while individual features of that part reside in layers C, D, and E. If the layer A is in Blank mode, all features of the part will be blanked, regardless of the status of layers C, D, and E.

8.7   Layer Tutorial

In Tutorial 8.1, you will read in an existing part that has several features as shown in Figure 8.8(a). As can be seen, it is very difficult to see the details of this part due to all of the clutter caused by the axes and datum planes. This part starts out with no predefined features. You will start by creating several layer names as seen in Figure 8.8(b).

You will be working with some patterned features in this tutorial. Pattern features are multiple instances of an existing feature organized in some manner. For example, you could create a single hole and pattern it across a surface. Note, however, that we will not be creating patterned features until Chapter 11. A patterned feature shows up as a single entry in the Model Tree, since it is one feature. There are several child features within this single entry as shown in Figure 8.8(c). To expand an entry in the Model Tree, click on the small + box to the left of the name.

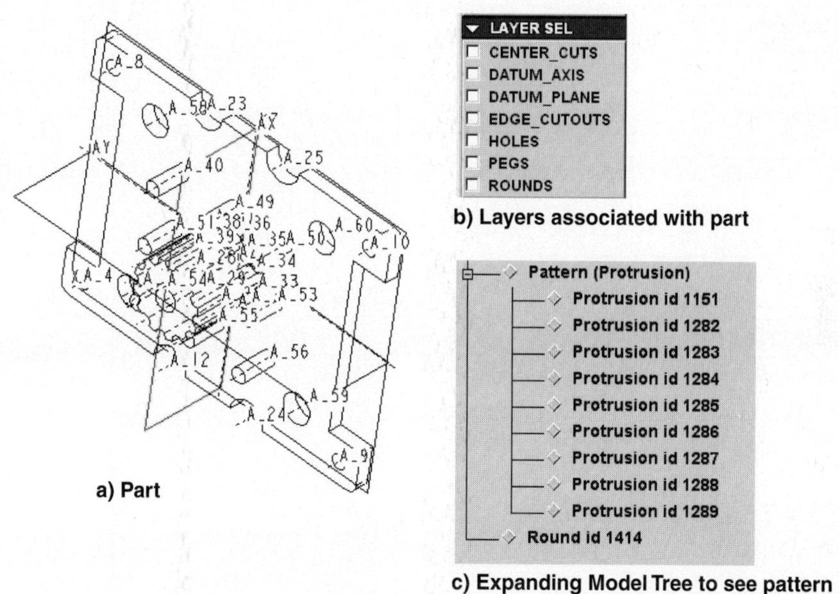

a) Part

b) Layers associated with part

c) Expanding Model Tree to see pattern

Figure 8.8   Illustrations for Tutorial 8.1, part 1.

Tutorial 8.1 Using Layers

Files opened: Tut8-1a.prt   **Files saved:** Tut8-1b.prt

Step	Action	Description	Further Actions	Result
1	Click PT/Modeler Icon	Run PT/Modeler		After some time, PT/Modeler on screen
2	Mode >Misc >Show Dir	Show current directory		Message similar to "Directory searched is c:\ptc\ptprod\bin"
3	>Change Dir	Change the current directory	Type **c:\proe\tutorial\ chapter_8**	
4	>Done-Return	Leave Misc menu		Misc menu removed
5	Mode >Part >Retrieve	Read a part	Type **tut8-1a**	Part read
6	>Environment	Set up the environment	Set up checks as seen in Table T8.1 Column Step 6	
7	>Done-Return			
8	>View	Names	Get to the named View	>BIRDS_EYE > Done/Return	
9	>Layer >Setup	Create	Create the layers	Type: CENTER_CUTS DATUM_AXIS DATUM_PLANE EDGE_CUTOUTS HOLES ROUNDS PEGS then Enter to end	
10	>Layer >Set Items >Add Items	Add items to the CENTER_CUTS layer	Check CENTER_CUTS >Done Sel	
11	>Feature	Feat/Child	Pick item 13 Pattern (Cut) in model Tree	>Done Sel >Done/Return	Note: All cuts around center get highlighted
12	>Layer >Set Display	Blank	Blank the CENTER_CUTS layer	Click on CENTER_CUTS >Done Sel	Center lines have been hidden
13	>View	Names	Get to the named View	>FRONT_LOOK	No center lines on center cuts
14	>Layer >Set Items >Add Items	Add items to the DATUM_AXIS layer	Check DATUM_AXIS >Done Sel	
15	>Feature	Pick	Pick item 4, 5, 6 in model Tree AX, AY, AZ	>Done Sel >Done/Return	
16	>Layer >Set Display	Blank	Blank the DATUM_AXIS layer	Click on DATUM_AXIS >Done Sel	CENTER_CUTS and DATUM_AXIS are both checked

Tutorial 8.1 Using Layers (continued)

Step	Action	Description	Further Actions	Result
17	>Layer >Set Items >Add Items	Add items to the DATUM_PLANE layer	Check DATUM_ PLANE >Done Sel	
18	>Feature | Pick	Pick item 1, 2, 3 in Model Tree XY, XZ, YZ	>Done Sel >Done/Return	
19	>Layer >Set Display | Blank	Blank the DATUM_PLANE layer	Click on DATUM_ PLANE >Done Sel	DATUM_ PLANE also checked
20	>Layer >Set Items >Add Items	Add items to the EDGE_CUTOUTS layer	Check EDGE_ CUTOUTS >Done Sel	
21	>Feature | Pick	Pick 4 hole cuts in side of plate associated with axes A12, A23, A24, A25	>Done Sel >Done/Return	
22	>Layer >Set Display | Blank	Blank the EDGE_ CUTOUTS layer	Click on EDGE_ CUTOUTS >Done Sel	EDGE_CUTOUTS also checked
23	>Layer >Set Items >Add Items	Add items to the HOLES layer	Check HOLES >Done Sel	
24	>Feature | Feat/Child	Pick Pattern (Hole) #8, #9, #10, and #11 in Model Tree		
25		Pick Cut id 203 #9 in Model Tree	>Done Sel >Done/Return	
26	>Layer >Set Display | Blank	Blank the HOLES layer	Click on HOLES >Done Sel	HOLES also checked
27	>Layer >Set Items >Add Items	Add items to the ROUNDS layer	Check ROUNDS >Done Sel	
28	>Layer >Set Items >Add Items	Add items to the PEGS layer	Check PEGS >Done Sel	
29	>Feature | Feat/Child	Pick Pattern (Protrusion) #14 in Model Tree		
30	>Layer >Set Display | Blank	Blank the PEGS layer	Click on PEGS >Done Sel	PEGS also checked
31	>Layer > Set Items >Remove Items	Remove items from the PEGS layer	Check PEGS >Done Sel	
32	>Remove All	Remove everything in that layer	Type Y for yes response of query to purge	Protrusion axes are displayed again
33	>Layer >Set Items >Add Items	Add items back to the PEGS layer	Check PEGS >Done Sel	

Tutorial 8.1 Using Layers (continued)

Step	Action	Description	Further Actions	Result
34	>Feature | Feat/Child	Pick Pattern (Protrusion) #14 in Model Tree		Protrusion axes once again are hidden
35	>Layer >Set Display | Blank	Redisplay all layers	> UnSel All >Done Sel	All layers unselected for display; all axes return since none are blanked any longer
36	>Layer >Set Display | Blank	Blank the EDGE_CUTOUTS layer	Click on PEGS >Done Sel	EDGE_CUTOUTS are blanked
37	>Layer >Set Display | Display	Display the EDGE_CUTOUTS layer, blanking all the rest	Check the EDGE_CUTOUTS >Done Sel	Only EDGE_CUTOUTS layer is displayed
38	>File >SaveAs	Save file with new name	Enter to accept [tut8 1a.prt] then type **tut8-1b.prt**	Part saved
39	QuitWindow			
40	Exit	Exit program	Click Yes to confirm	PT/Products exited

Item	Step 6
Disp DtmPln	Checked
Spin Center	No
Disp Pnts	Checked
Disp Axes	Checked
Rendering	No hidden line

Table T8.1   Environment Settings

First you will create two layers. Next, you will add entities from the model into these layers. Add entities to each of the layers, one at a time. After adding to a layer, you will Blank that layer observing that the datum planes, datum axes, and axes associated with the Features are removed. Next, you will use the UnSel all to remove all Blanking checks. All layers are once again displayed. At this point, you will select to Display a single layer by checking that layer in the Display checklist. All other layers are blanked.

In Figure 8.9(a), the part is shown with all layers blanked. I have indicated each feature's number in the Model Tree. Figure 8.9(b) illustrates the part with just the PEGS layer displayed.

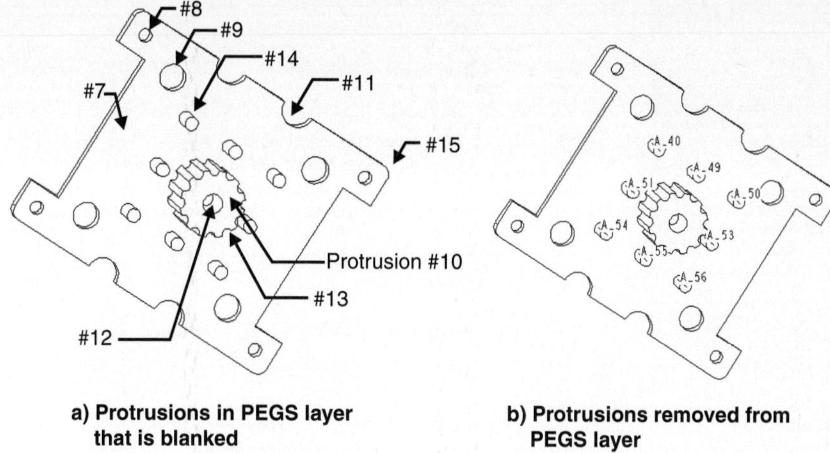

**a) Protrusions in PEGS layer
that is blanked**

**b) Protrusions removed from
PEGS layer**

Figure 8.9   Illustrations for Tutorial 8.1, part 2.

Experiment at the end of the Tutorial until you are completely comfortable with the
Display and Blank options.

8.8   Acquiring Information about Layers

You can get valuable information about layers using the >Layer | Info command
found in the >Main >Info menu. You can request an information window that contains all relevant information about a layer or you can request to highlight all items
in a feature, one at a time, or all at the same time.

8.8.1   Layer Display Status

You can acquire information about the display status or the items in a layer as
shown in the menu of Figure 8.10(a). The submenu checklist provides access to all
of the current layers associated with this part. You can select any number of the layers for display in the information window as shown in Figure 8.10(b). The information window contains the part name and information about the checked layers
in the menu checklist. Each layer has its status, either displayed or blanked, as well
as a list of all features in the layer.

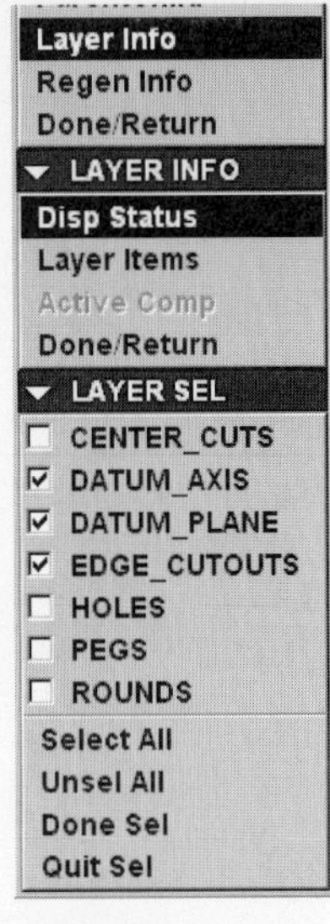

a) Layer Info menu

```
********* Layer DATUM_AXIS Information *********
    CURRENT LAYER OPERATION =        NORMAL

    SAVE LAYER OPERATION =        NORMAL

    LAYER CONTAINS:
        3  TUT8-1B  FEATURES
                DATUM AXIS NUMBER 4, INTERNAL ID 7
                DATUM AXIS NUMBER 5, INTERNAL ID 11
                DATUM AXIS NUMBER 6, INTERNAL ID 15

********* Layer DATUM_PLANE Information *********
    CURRENT LAYER OPERATION =        BLANK

    SAVE LAYER OPERATION =        NORMAL

    LAYER CONTAINS:
        3  TUT8-1B  FEATURES
                DATUM PLANE NUMBER 1, INTERNAL ID 1
                DATUM PLANE NUMBER 2, INTERNAL ID 3
                DATUM PLANE NUMBER 3, INTERNAL ID 5

********* Layer EDGE_CUTOUTS Information *********
    CURRENT LAYER OPERATION =        NORMAL

    SAVE LAYER OPERATION =        NORMAL

    LAYER CONTAINS:
        4  TUT8-1B  FEATURES
                HOLE NUMBER 14, INTERNAL ID 409
                HOLE NUMBER 15, INTERNAL ID 656
```

**b) Information window showing display status
of layers**

Figure 8.10   Layer information display status.

8.8.2   Items in a layer

You will often want a visual display of what features are in a layer. This is accomplished using the >Layer Items menu selection. The menu is shown in Figure 8.12. Once a layer is selected from the layer checklist as shown in Figure 8.10(a), all items in that layer are highlighted on the screen. You can choose to see one at a time using the >Next and >Previous commands. You can also choose to see all of them at the same time using the >Show All option.

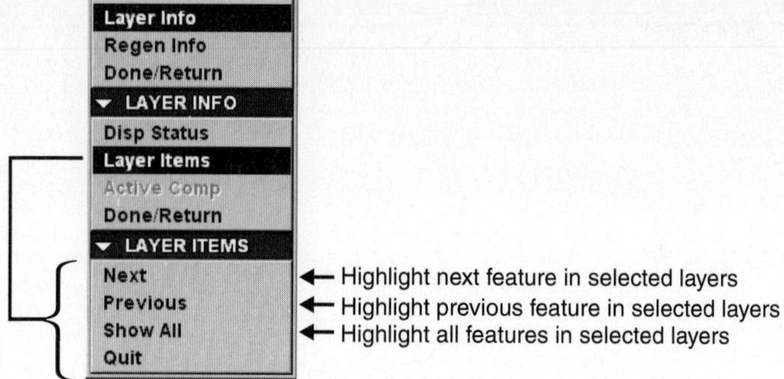

Figure 8.11   Layer information layer items.

Chapter 9

Troubleshooting Your Model

In this chapter we will look at different techniques that you can use to get your models working correctly. Few of us can design a model on the first try and get it correct. In fact, solid modeling is meant to be used at the design and conceptualization stages as opposed to the documentation stage after the design is locked into production.

First we will look at different ways to access information about your model and the PT/Modeler environment using the Info Menu and the Model Tree. You will learn to acquire and understand information provided about features, the model, parent-child relationships, and layers.

Next we will look at the regeneration process. If an error is going to occur, it will occur during the regeneration process, either at the feature, part, or assembly level. You will have to deal with these errors by tracking down the source of the error and fixing the problem. In this process you will acquire information about the part and features involved in the problem. Eventually, you will have to find the source of the problem. Feature A might fail during a part-wide regeneration, not because there is a problem with the feature A, but because there is a problem with another feature, B. In some way, feature A references feature B. You will have to sort out the symptoms from the problems.

We will look at the Resolve Features and Investigate Menus along with the Failure Diagnostics and Display Information windows. Before we begin, I want to introduce you to the parts we will be using in this chapter.

Troubleshooting is not just for fixing problems. It is also an important tool for testing your part. Many of you are familiar with some of the concepts involved in testing. Basically, you try to break your design. Save your design in a safe place and then manipulate it to see how it performs. Perhaps you attempt to delete a feature that no other feature should reference. If a regeneration error occurs, then you know that the design intent was not satisfied.

Being a good troubleshooter is a valuable asset to any designer. You will be able to find errors before they propagate into designs. Keep in mind, however, that being able to fix errors is not a good substitute for designing the part correctly in the first place. Some errors or changes are inevitable; however, sloppiness is a bad habit. Take time to plan your designs and to check each feature at every step. The earlier you catch an error, the easier it will be to fix.

You will use these troubleshooting techniques extensively when you make changes. Perhaps you designed the part correctly and everything is in its proper place. Now, a change request comes in and you need to add or remove something. In software design, every two changes you make will likely generate an error somewhere else in the product. If you have done your conceptualization well, these errors should be minimal. They should, at least, be localized to the immediate region of the original change.

9.1   Part Used in this Chapter

The Model Tree of a part we will use in this chapter is illustrated in Figure 9.1(a). We will be looking at features #7 through #14 as listed in Table 9.1. Note that each of these has an Order number and an ID associated with them as seen in the Model Tree and repeated in Table 9.1. Sometimes you will refer to a feature by its order number and other times you will refer to it by its ID number. Displaying ID numbers in the Model Tree was discussed in chapter 1.

Order Number	ID #
7	58
8	79
9	112
10	188
11	Datum
12	229
13	406
14	519

Table 9.1 Feature Numbers
and ID Numbers for Part

The part itself is shown in Figure 9.1(b). It is created from a base feature that is a cube protrusion 7 (#58). A cut 8 (#79) is made out of one corner. A second cut 9 (#112) is made in another side and a third cut 10 (#188) is made out of the top corner. A datum plane is created that cut number 12 (#229) is defined upon. One more cut 13 (#406) is made into the face of the cut 12 and a protrusion 14 (#509) extends from a face of the original cube.

Warning! There are some time bombs lurking in this part. Their fuse is set to go off during the tutorial at the end of the chapter. We will work together to fix this part.

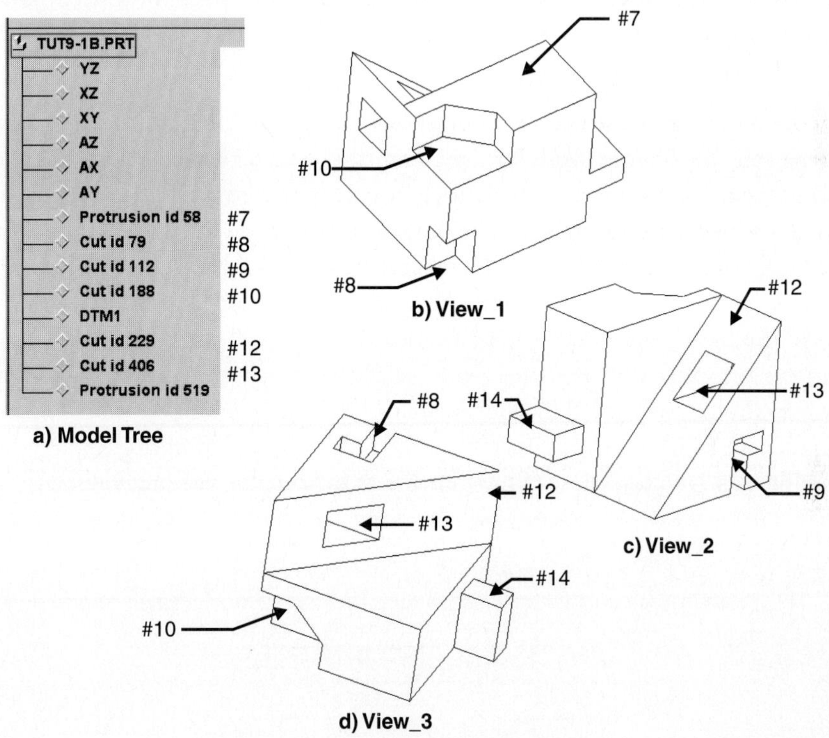

Figure 9.1   Model used in this chapter.

9.2   Getting Information about the Model

To effectively troubleshoot, you will need to gather as much relevant information as possible. PT/Modeler anticipates this fact and provides ready access through the Info Menu. You are going to have ready reference to your model. This can be accomplished in the form of a printout where you flag the different features and the Model Tree as I did in Figure 9.1. I rely on a screen grab utility to grab some 3D views of the model and the Model Tree. I document the model and print it out. These steps take time, but the end result is a tremendous savings of time.

You will often find yourself in the middle of a step when you are requested to pick some feature. You had better know what feature you are selecting, or else you will be really creating new problems for your design. You can rely to a certain degree on the highlighting capability in PT/Modeler to refresh your memory on which features in the Model Tree refer to which features in the part. Was that hole feature 58 or 406 on the top of the part? It can be difficult to remember. Worse yet, while hunting down the correct feature number, it is very easy to lose your concentration and forget what you were doing in the first place. This may leave you alone with a query that has to be answered.

You will notice that there are two numbers associated with every feature: the Order Number and the Feature Identification Number. The Order Number is the position in the feature list as shown in the Model Tree. This number indicates the order in which the feature was created and the order in which it will be built during regeneration. The Feature Identification Number is a unique number that identifies a feature within a part. The Order Number may change as features are reordered in the Model Tree List. The Feature Identification Number will not change. The two numbers are often differentiated with parenthesis and # prefix. For example "Feature Protrusion 8 (#19)." Unfortunately, there is no convention. You will have to figure out which number, either #8 or (19) is the Order Number or the Feature Identification Number. Most of the time the #s indicate the Feature Number.

> **TIP:** The sequence numbers are sequential. This can be useful when referring to a feature by number.

9.2.1   Information Windows

Many of the items in this list will bring up information windows. Information windows are child windows and do not go away by themselves. If you click on your main graphics window, you will likely hide the information window; however, the information window is still present as indicated by the icon in the Windows Task Bar. You may want to keep these around for later reference, or they just might add to the confusion. These windows are not updated automatically so an old information window might not accurately reflect the current state of the model. To delete an information window it is necessary to click in the window or click on the icon in the Task Bar. This brings the information window to the front and you can type q for quit. Remember not to close the Info window directly.

The information window might contain more information that can fit on a single page. Use the scroll bars to scroll the window. The scroll bars are not standard windows scroll bars. To scroll a window, click in the scroll bar area and the window will reposition to the relative location of the click. You cannot drag scroll bars in this application. You can also click on the up and down arrow keys to scroll a line at a time.

One last point: You can resize the window to suit your needs by dragging on a corner of the window as you would in other Windows applications.

> **NOTE:** You can have only four Info windows open at a time. Attempting to open a fifth Info window will generate an error message.

9.2.2   The Info Menu

The Info Menu contains several options for accessing information. I will describe those items that are covered in the scope of this book. The Info menu is shown in Figure 9.2. The following topics are based on the items from this menu.

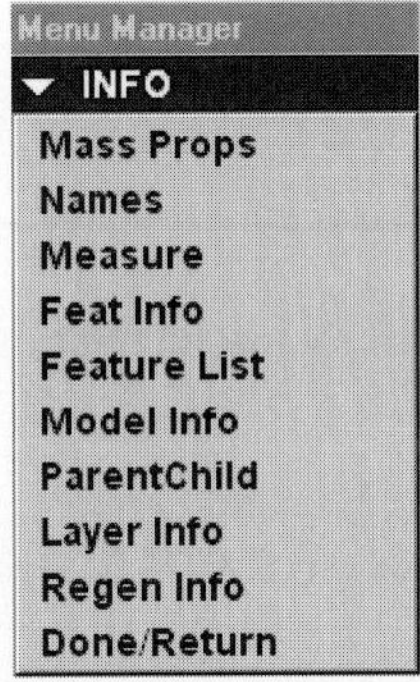

Figure 9.2   Info menu.

9.2.2.1   Names

The >Names menu item provides an information window that shows all active Parts, Assemblies, Drawings, and Sections in the current session.

9.2.2.2   Feat Info

The >Feat Info menu item provides information about a selected feature. This information includes the following:

- Part name
- Feature number

- Internal Feature number
- Parents and children
- Type of Feature
- Element list as found in the Feature dialog box
- Section name
- Layers
- Feature dimensions

A Feature Identification window of the feature 14 (#519) of the part shown in Figure 9.1 is provided in Figure 9.3. As you can see, there is a lot of information packed into this page. You can keep Feat Info selected and pick different features to get multiple windows describing different features in your part.

```
PART NAME = TUT9-1B


FEATURE NUMBER        14
INTERNAL FEATURE ID   519
PARENTS = 58(#7)  406(#13)


PROTRUSION: Extrude

NO. ELEMENT NAME      INFO                                        STATUS
--- ------------ -----------                                     ------
 1  Attributes    One Side                                       Defined
 2  Section       Sk. plane - Surface of feat #7 (PROTRUSION)    Defined
 3  MaterialSide                                                 Defined
 4  Direction                                                    Defined
 5  Depth         Blind, depth = 60                              Defined


SECTION NAME = S2D0002
OPEN SECTION


FEATURE'S DIMENSIONS:
d80 = 60.00
d83 = 50.00
```

Figure 9.3   Sample Feature Identification window.

9.2.2.3   Feature List

The >Feature List provides you with a concise list of the different features in the part. This improves upon the information in the Model Tree, providing an excellent bird's eye view of your part. Included in this Information window is the following:

- Order number
- ID number

- Name
- Type of Feature
- Suppression order
- Regeneration status

A Feature list of the part in Figure 9.1 is shown in Figure 9.4. Note the suppressed feature number #494 between order numbers 13 and 14. I think that this is one of those time bombs I told you about. This information window shows you that there is a suppressed feature that would not show up in the Model Tree. Already, you have found use for this handy Feature list—it is one of your most powerful and useful tools.

```
MODEL NAME          : TUT9-1B
FEATURE LINK LIST:
*******************

Num   ID        Name      Type                Sup Order     Regen Status

0001  000001 YZ           DATUM PLANE                       Regenerated
0002  000003 XZ           DATUM PLANE                       Regenerated
0003  000005 XY           DATUM PLANE                       Regenerated
0004  000007 AZ           DATUM AXIS                        Regenerated
0005  000011 AX           DATUM AXIS                        Regenerated
0006  000015 AY           DATUM AXIS                        Regenerated
0007  000058             PROTRUSION                         Regenerated
0008  000079             CUT                                Regenerated
0009  000112             CUT                                Regenerated
0010  000188             CUT                                Regenerated
0011  000227 DTM1         DATUM PLANE                       Regenerated
0012  000229             CUT                                Regenerated
0013  000406             CUT                                Regenerated
      000494             CUT                 2              Suppressed
0014  000519             PROTRUSION                         Regenerated
```

Figure 9.4   Sample Feature list window.

9.2.2.4   Model Info

The >Model Info window provides a series of feature information data as if you had clicked >Feat Info for every feature in the model. A single information window then provides detailed information of all features in the model. Each feature is described the same as in the >Feat Info window. You will need to scroll this window to see all of the information about each feature. A sample showing the first feature is provided in Figure 9.5.

```
PART TUT9-1B


LENGTH UNIT: INCH


FEATURES:


FEATURE NUMBER        1
INTERNAL FEATURE ID   1
CHILDREN = 7(#4)  15(#6)  58(#7)  79(#8)  112(#9)  188(#10)  227(#11)  229(#12)
           406(#13)  494(*)  519(#14)
TYPE = DATUM PLANE
NAME = YZ
```

> OTHER FEATURES DESCRIBED IN THE MODEL INFO WINDOW ARE NOT SHOWN IN THIS FIGURE

Figure 9.5   Sample Model Info window.

9.2.2.5   ParentChild

The submenu shown in Figure 9.6 illustrates the ParentChild options. You can elect to see the Parents of a selected feature, see the Children of a selected feature, all References of a selected feature, or references of all of the children of a selected feature.

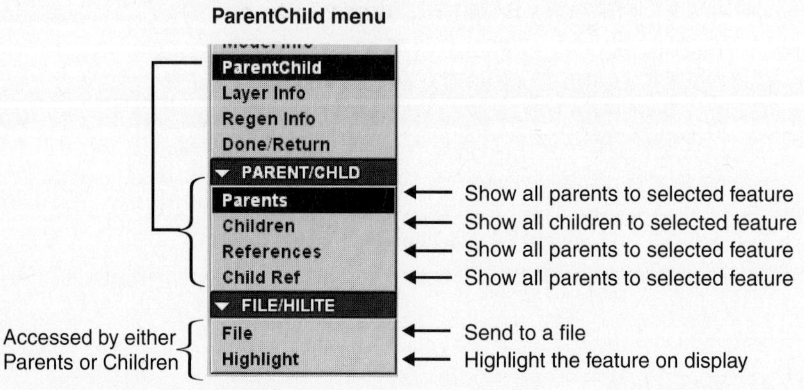

Figure 9.6   ParentChild submenu.

Selecting either Parents or Children provides an additional option. You can elect to send the output to a file or to the screen in the form of highlights.

9.2.2.6   Parents and Children

The >ParentChild option provides you with information regarding the parent and child relationships of a selected feature. Figure 9.7(a) shows the information window that appears when you request the >ParentChild>Parents | File option. The submenu shown in Figure 9.7(b) shows the information window that appears when you request the >ParentChild>Children | File option and select Feature 8. As you can see, the file indicates the selected feature, all of the parents or children, and the file name.

```
PARENT FEATURE IDS OF FEATURE ID 58(#7) :    CHILD FEATURE IDS OF FEATURE ID 79(#8) :

PARENTS = 11(#5) 15(#6) 3(#2) 5(#3)          CHILDREN = 112(#9) 188(#10)

FILENAME = par58.inf.2                        FILENAME = chld79.inf.1
```

a) Parent file for feature 58   **b) Child file for feature 79**

Figure 9.7   Sample Parents and Children files.

9.2.2.7   References

The >References provides a sequential display of all references made by a part. These include the sketching plane, the sketcher reference, and all section dimensioning references (one at a time). The references are highlighted on the screen and a single line message occurs in the Message window similar to the following:

```
Showing sketching plane reference (#1)
of CUT (#8, id 79).
```

A submenu is provided as seen in Figure 9.8 allowing you to select the feature of interest.

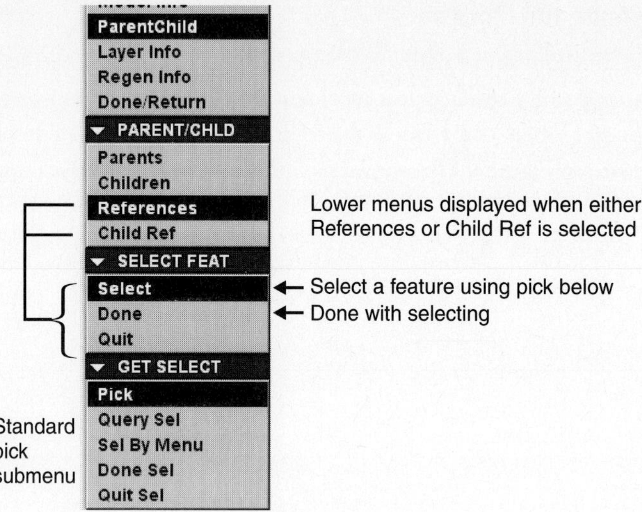

Figure 9.8   References menu.

9.2.2.8   Child Ref

The >Child Ref provides information about a selected feature. The information
provided illustrates all of the items in this feature that are referenced by other features. These items might be a face, edge, vertex, etc. Since the other features are referencing something about this feature, the other features are children. The display
is quite effective. The referenced item in the selected feature is highlighted in pur-
ple on the display, and all children that reference this feature are shown in blue. The
menu of Figure 9.9 shows that you can select the >Next or >Previous reference. The
highlighted information is also provided in a single line fashion, one feature at a
time, in the Message window. Sample lines are shown here.

```
Showing reference No. 1 out of 8 and its children.
There is no DIRECT child for this feature. Select
    again.
```

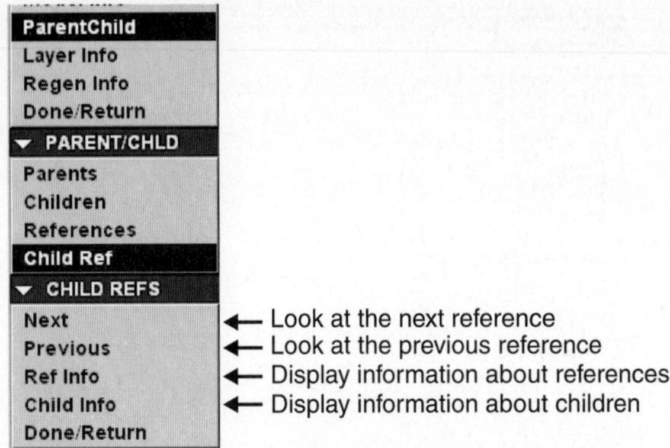

Figure 9.9   ParentChild | Child Ref selection submenu.

As seen in Figure 9.9, you can also select the >Ref Info to see information about the current reference. A sample Reference Information screen is shown in Figure 9.10. This display provides information as listed in Table 9.2.

Topic	Description
Item being referenced	Edge, plane, etc.
Item status	Whether it is part of the geometry
Number of children	
Reference owner	Name and type
Feature (referenced by child) sequence number	Number in sequence (7 of 9)
Feature ID	Unique Feature number
Parents	Feature number and ID of children
Children	Feature number and ID of children
Type of Feature	Protrusion, Hole, Cut, etc.

Table 9.2   Reference Information for ParentChild | Child Reference

```
|*****************************|
       REFERENCE INFORMATION
|*****************************|
    Reference No.8 out of 9


Reference:
    TYPE    : EDGE


Status    : not in geometry


Number of the children : 1


Reference owner:
 Model    :
    NAME    : TUT9-1B
    TYPE    : PART
 Feature  :


    FEATURE NUMBER        7
    INTERNAL FEATURE ID   58
    PARENTS = 11(#5) 15(#6) 3(#2) 5(#3)
    CHILDREN = 79(#8) 112(#9) 188(#10) 229(#12) 406(#13) 494(*) 519(#14)


 PROTRUSION: Extrude
```

Figure 9.10   Reference Information window.

As a last option, you can select to see an information window about the children associated with a reference. This Information window provides all of the Feature information about each of the Features in the model that are children to the selected Feature.

9.2.3   Getting Information Tutorial

In Tutorial 9.1, you will load the part illustrated in Figure 9.1. Place the part into the VIEW_3 orientation as shown in Figure 9.1(d). Next, select Names from the Info menu. This is not the same >Names as used in Named Views. An information appears showing that this is part TUT9-1A and that there are no active assemblies, drawings, or sections. Next, click on Feat Info and select Feature 14 as seen in Figure 9.1. This brings up an information window for Feature 14 ID #519.

> **TIP:** You can keep information windows open or you can close them by clicking in the window and typing "q". Remember, you may have to scroll down to see more information than fits on the current screen.

Look at the information presented. All of the elements are described including the section, material side, direction, and depth. Note that this feature has two dimensions called d80, d83, d84, and d85. These are the internal symbolic names for the sketch dimensions that completely constrain this feature.

Click on the Feature List option. In another information window, 14 sequential features are presented. These indicate the order in which the features will be constructed. Note that Feature 14 is the last feature in the list, and that the suppressed feature #494 is also shown.

To see feature information for all of the features in the model click >Model Info. The Model information window appears. Scroll down to the end of the list to see the feature information for Feature 14. This is the identical information that was obtained from the >Feat Info selection of Feature 14.

Next, we will look at parent-child relationships. First we will look at the parents of Feature 14 highlighted on the screen, in the reference color. Quite a number of lines are highlighted so it is a little difficult to tell which features were parents to Feature 14. Try it again, this time with >ParentChild | Parents | File option. The information window shows us that Feature 14 has two parents, Feature 7 and Feature 13. Referring back to Figure 9.1, we see that Feature 7 is the base feature and Feature 13 is the cut. It is easy to imagine that the base feature is a parent but why is the cut a parent to Feature 14? We will have to analyze this further.

Selecting > ParentChild | References and selecting Feature 14, once again will show us each reference, one at a time. The first reference is the sketching plane as highlighted on the display. Click >Next and we see the culprit. The right-most edge of the cut is highlighted and the message indicates that this edge was used as the horizontal sketcher reference. What does that mean?

When entering into the sketcher, we selected a horizontal edge as the orientation reference; this was not a very good choice. If this cut moves or is resized, Feature 14 will also change. We will return to this Feature and fix this problem in a later tutorial.

For now, click >Next again to see the base of the feature also being used as a dimensional reference. Clicking >Next one more time shows us the far side of the base feature also being used as a dimensional reference. Neither of these base features will cause trouble at this time. Continue by looking at the Children of Feature 14.

Click >ParentChild | Children | File and select Feature 14 again. A message indicates that there are no children for Feature 14. Try clicking on Feature #8. To do this, you could select >View >Names | VIEW_1. However, this would lose our place. Instead just View Spin (mMb drag) the image to rotate it so that Feature 8 comes into view. Alternately, you can easily select Feature 8 from the Model Tree.

Pick Feature 8 and the information window tells us that this feature has two children, Feature 9 and Feature 10. Now Feature 9 and 10 are both cutouts on different faces. We had better look at the references for Feature 8 to determine why these two cuts, 9 and 10, are referencing Feature 8.

Click >ParentChild | References and select Feature 14. Remember that >References shows us all of the references that a Feature requires. Since we learned that Feature 13 was a parent of Feature 14, we will want to see all references made by Feature 14. The first reference is the sketching plane as expected. The second reference is the reference to Feature #13 that we determined previously. The third and fourth references are faces of the base feature. Notice, no reference pointed us to Feature 8, the parent. How then can Feature 8 be a parent of Feature 14? The answer probably lies in a sketcher assumption. Perhaps an edge or vertex of Feature 14 was aligned to Feature 8. We will check this out in a later tutorial.

One more thing to check: Let's look at layers. Click >Layer Info | Disp Status. This shows us that the layers present in this part are as seen in Table 9.3.

Layer	Features in this layer
BASE	7
CUTS	8, 9, and 13
DATUM_AXIS	4, 5, and 6
DATUM_PLANE	1, 2, 3, and 11
PROTRUSIONS	14

Table 9.3   Layers in Part for Tutorial 9.1

This information window also shows us that all layers are currently displayed as indicated by the CURRENT LAYER OPERATION = NORMAL status as opposed to BLANKED.

Tutorial 9.1 Getting Information from a Model

Files opened: Tut9-1a.prt   **No files saved.**

Step	Action	Description	Further Actions	Result
1	Click PT/Modeler Icon	Run PT/Modeler		After some time, PT/Modeler on screen
2	Mode >Misc >Show Dir	Show current directory		Message similar to "Directory searched is c:\ptc\ptprod\bin"
3	>Change Dir	Change the current directory	Type **c:\proe\tutorial\ chapter_9**	
4	>Done-Return	Leave Misc menu		Misc menu removed
5	Mode > Part >Retrieve	Read a part	Type **tut9-1a**	Part read
6	>Environment	Set up the environment	Set up checks as seen in Table T9.1 Column Step 6	
7	>Done-Return			
8	>View | Names	Get to the named View	>VIEW_3 | Done/Return	
9	>Info >Names	See what is currently active	Type **q** to remove info window	Info window displayed shows that part TUT9-1A is present
10	>Info >Feat Info	Get information on a Feature	Select Feature 14	Info window displayed shows Feature 14
11	>Info >Feat List	Get list of all features in part		Info window displays a list of all features and their current state
12	>Info >Model Info	Get information on all features in part		Info window displays info on all features
13	>ParentChild | Parents | Highlight	Highlight all Parents on screen of selected feature	Select Feature 14	Parents highlighted but screen is full of highlights
14	>ParentChild | Parents | File	Send info on all Parents to file and info window	Select Feature 14	Info window clearly shows parents
15	>ParentChild | References	Check out the references made by a feature one at a time	Select Feature 14	
16	>Next until all are viewed	See each reference in sequence; one refers to Feature 8	>Done	Each reference is highlighted and information provided in the message window

Step	Action	Description	Further Actions	Result
17	>ParentChild | Children | File	See all children to find reference to Feature 8	Select Feature 14	
18	>Next until all are viewed	See each reference in sequence	>Done	Each reference is highlighted and information provided in message window; none refer to Feature 8
19	>Layer Info | Disp Status	See information of layers	>Select All | Done	Info provided on each layer and what features reside in each layer
20	QuitWindow			
21	Exit	Exit program	Click Yes to confirm	PT/Products exited

Item	Step 6
Disp DtmPln	Checked
Spin Center	No
Disp Pnts	Checked
Disp Axes	Checked
Rendering	No hidden line

Table T9.1   Environment Settings

9.3   The Regenerating Process

Regeneration is the time when PT/Modeler has a look at your input and tries to make a successful model. Remember that success is not based on whether the part solves your need, but rather whether all of the rules that dictate how a model can be made are satisfied. For example, suppose that you dimensioned a hole incorrectly. Perhaps you specified a radius when you thought you were specifying a diameter. The consequence might be that a protrusion feature gets totally swallowed by the hole. This is not a problem as far as PT/Modeler is concerned. All of PT/Modeler's rules are satisfied. It may be a big problem for your part.

All errors are flagged during regeneration. You can enter a hundred dimensions and alignments that seem okay. It isn't until a regeneration cycle that PT/Modeler will test the new information. There are two phases of regeneration. The first has to do with regenerating a sketch associated with a feature. The second involves regenerating the entire Model, based on new information about one or more features.

Let us look at a mistake that does generate a regeneration error. What if you have a feature A that references an earlier feature B for a dimension? Suppose you delete feature B. How is PT/Modeler going to reference feature A? It cannot figure out which reference should replace the missing item in the now failed feature B. Consequently a regeneration error occurs.

A second example of a regeneration error would occur when the following takes place. A protrusion A is based on a sketching plane that is a face of a feature B. Feature B subsequently is modified and the referenced face is removed. In Sketcher, the modification to feature B goes well and the feature regenerates correctly. However, when you go to preview the part, PT/Modeler performs a part-wide regeneration and finds that the later feature B no longer has a section plane. Once again, PT/Modeler has no crystal ball and consequently, a regeneration error is generated.

9.3.1   Single Stepping through Regeneration

So far, we have looked at regeneration as a single operation. We click >Regenerate and the part regenerates. We know, however, that a part is built one feature at a time. This is another way of saying that the part is regenerated one feature at a time. This attribute can really work in our favor. There is a command, through the >Info >Regen Info menu, where you can view the regeneration process, one feature at a time.

After selecting >Info >Regen Info, the submenu in Figure 9.11 appears. This menu is used to specify the starting feature for the regeneration single stepping. You can request that the single stepping begin at the first feature in the part, or at any specified feature. Perhaps the feature of interest is number 93 and you would rather not spend the time single stepping through features 1 through 92. In this case you can select feature 93 as the starting feature using the >Specify option. You would need to specify which feature you desire as the starting feature using a standard pick operation in the model or Model Tree. Alternatively, you could use the >Sel by Menu to select Number 93.

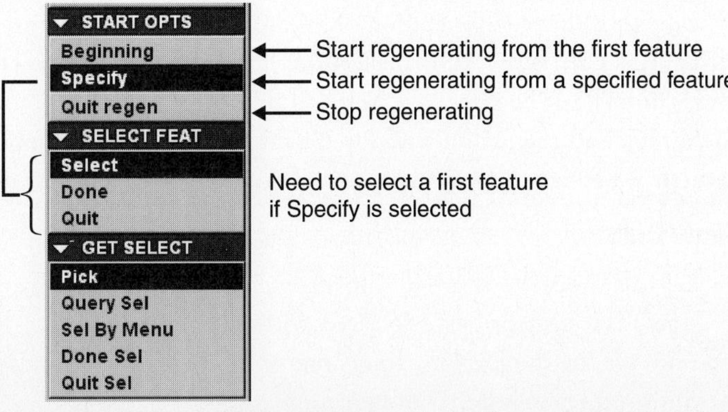

Figure 9.11   Regen Info menu.

Once the starting feature is specified, the menu of Figure 9.12 is displayed. The Regen Info command only appears when the MAIN menu is showing. The software is ready to begin single stepping through the features. By clicking >Continue once, you cause a regeneration preview as if you had clicked preview in the Features Dialog. The new feature is highlighted but not yet placed into the part. Clicking >Continue again places the feature into the part as if you had clicked Okay in the Features Dialog.

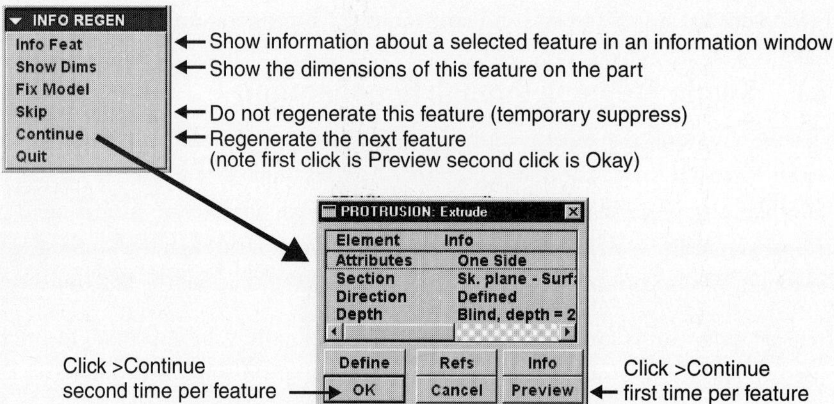

Figure 9.12   Single step regeneration control menu.

On the screen, you will see the part being regenerated one feature at a time. You can click continue through the entire part. A message will appear in the Message window indicating the feature you are currently regenerating.

9.3.1.1   Skip

You can also choose to skip the generation of a feature using the >Skip menu item. This is NOT equivalent to suppressing the feature. The skipped feature will be regenerated; however, it will not be displayed. You will be asked "How many features do you want to skip [0]?" You can select 1 to skip the next feature or any number to skip multiple features. When you >Continue again, all skipped features will be displayed.

9.3.1.2   Show Dims

At any time you can choose to show all dimensions associated with a feature using the >Show Dims. The dimensions associated with current feature are displayed. Although you can see the dimensions, you cannot modify them from this mode of operation as you would using the >Modify command.

9.3.1.3   Info Feat

At any time you can choose to bring up a Feature Information window using the >Info Feat. The information window is identical to the Feature Identification window displayed in Figure 9.3.

9.4   Troubleshooting Regeneration Errors in the Sketcher

We are ready to troubleshoot regeneration errors. You cannot leave a regeneration error for later. The system will stop and you cannot save a part file that has a regeneration error. Let us begin with solving regeneration errors at the feature level within Sketcher, then we will move on to solving regeneration errors at the part level.

Remember, regeneration errors do not necessarily include design errors. A regeneration might finish successfully, but create a totally wrong part due to assumptions. You will have to learn to correct the Sketcher assumptions when they are not consistent with your design intent. This is described in Chapter 4.

Regeneration errors are highlighted in Sketcher with red circles. These are affectionately called the *measles*. There are four basic causes of regeneration errors in Sketcher as listed below:

- Under-dimensioned errors
- Over-constrained errors
- Unintended segments
- Inappropriate segments

9.4.1   Under-Dimensioned Errors

This error occurs when you have not sufficiently constrained the part. The line, arc, or vertex that is lacking a dimension or reference is highlighted in red. Perhaps the sketcher does not know where an edge should be placed or the length of a side. Perhaps an arc has no radius or its center has no coordinates. Often, you might expect that the sketcher would assume that a side was the same length as another side and therefore did not need a dimension. Other times you might think that a center point is at the intersection of two axes, when it was never aligned there. All of these things cause under-dimensioning. Often, you can fix these problems easily by performing one of the following operations.

- Add dimensions
- Override Sketcher assumptions
- Align lines, endpoints, edges, and center points to model

9.4.2   Over-Constrained Errors

Ideally, you will have neither too few nor too many dimensions. Redundant dimensions are highlighted in red. You can easily delete them, however, this might not be your intent. Perhaps you wanted to dimension a side of a rectangle, only to find that Sketcher had assumed that the side was the same as a rectangle beneath it. Often, the problem might be caused by not understanding the rules in geometry. I have often thought that a side needed a dimension only to have Sketcher show me that it could calculate that side based on other dimensions and some basic trigonometry and geometry. If you get an over-constrained warning, first make sure that the cause is not an assumption. It is possible to override the assumptions; this is discussed fully in Section 9.10. Then, look at the other dimensions and see if you could calculate the redundant dimension from the others. Two basic operations that will fix over-constrained errors follow:

- Remove dimensions
- Override assumptions (as discussed in Section 9.10)

NOTE: Over dimensioning does not cause a regeneration error. Rather, it provides a stern warning. You can choose to ignore the warning and accept the regeneration, keeping the extra dimensions.

9.4.3   Unintended Segments

Two regeneration error messages that often pop up usually indicate that there is something in the drawing that was not intended. These two error messages are shown in Table 9.4.

Error Message	Likely Cause
Segment too small	A line segment was drawn inadvertently
Zero length segments	Segment has zero length perhaps due to zoom factor

Table 9.4   Unintended Segment Errors

The cause here is usually that an inadvertent line segment or part of an arc was drawn. For instance, you might provide one too many clicks when drawing a line chain. The result is a tiny line segment that is too small to see readily. Not noticing it, you dimension the rest of the part, and one of the messages from Table 9.4 shows up and a little red dot appears on the screen. You can usually just delete the dot and the problem goes away. Other times, you might need to zoom into the area of the error to find what is causing the problem.

9.4.4   Inappropriate Segments

The last error discussed is the Inappropriate Segment error. This error occurs when you have not followed the rules of a feature. For example, perhaps a cut feature is being specified inside a part and the section is not closed. Another example that would generate this error is a revolved feature that has no center line.

9.4.5   Getting Back to a Known State

At times, following a regeneration error, you will want to return to a known state as opposed to trying to deal with the problem. You can rely on a backup file or >Undo Changes to get back to the state before the regeneration.

9.5   Redefining

You can redefine almost anything in a feature using the >Redefine menu selection from the >Feature Operator menu selection. You can also redefine using the Define button on the Features dialog. When a regeneration error occurs during Preview, you can select, among other things, to redefine the sketch plane, the sketch, or the scheme using the Section option. The flow chart for Define is shown in Figure 9.13. Selecting Define after selecting the feature element Section will bring you back into the sketcher.

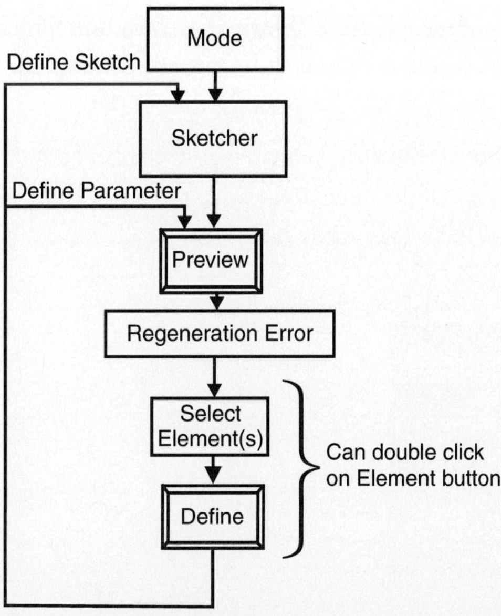

Figure 9.13   Define Flow Chart.

The Define button on the Feature Dialog is shown in Figure 9.14 after Section has been selected. You could have also chosen a parallel sketching plane or the scheme of referencing.

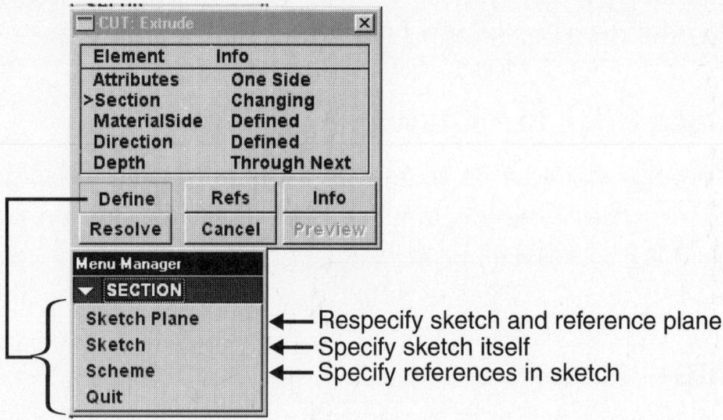

Figure 9.14   Selecting Section and Define from the Features dialog.

9.6   Troubleshooting Regeneration Problems in the Resolve Environment

When a regeneration error occurs during Preview after sketching, the Features Dialog box presents a Resolve button. When you click Resolve, a Failure Diagnostics window appears. In this window are the name of the failed part, the reason for the failure, and two options called Overview and Feature Info. Selecting >Feature Info brings up the Feature Information window, which provides valuable information about a feature. Selecting >Overview brings up some tips on the Resolve process, all of which are discussed in this section.

Selecting this Resolve button brings up a menu as seen in Figure 9.15. From this menu you can select to Undo all changes since the last regeneration, investigate the part, or perform a >Quick Fix on the failed feature.

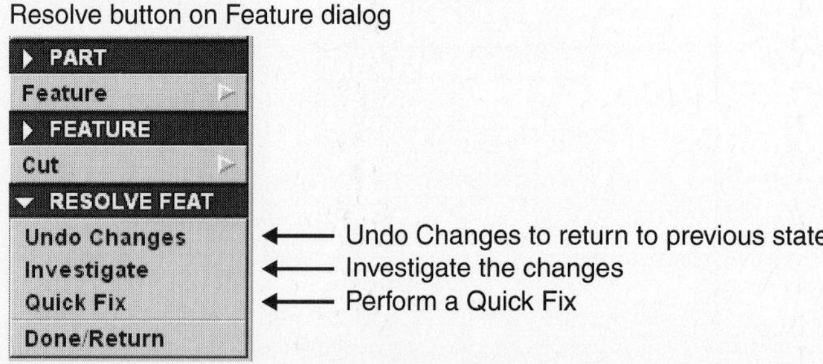

Figure 9.15   Resolve button.

I want to show you, in one place, what we are facing as we discuss the trouble-shooting paths available to us. Figure 9.16 illustrates the many paths. I will discuss each of these paths in the sections that follow. From this figure, you can see each choice available to you. It is important to know where you came from, what operation you are about to perform, and where the operation will lead you. This flow chart provides a concise look at the big picture. Let us take it one step at a time.

As someone once said, "The beginning is as good a place to start as any." Following this advice, we will start at the top of our flow chart. The Feature menu provides us with the opportunity to design a sketched feature. In so doing, we end up in Sketcher. When we have finished sketching, we attempt a Preview to incorporate the new feature into the rest of the part. If there is a Regeneration error, we have two choices. We can select an element from the Features Dialog or we can choose to Resolve the problem.

If we click Resolve, we are provided with a Failure Diagnostic Window that provides us with some early clues regarding the problem and a choice of three other paths. The first attempts to Undo our changes by reverting to the last successful regeneration. If Undo works, we are back in the Feature state because the problem, along with the new feature, has been eliminated. The new feature has likely been eliminated as well.

The second path is called the Quick Fix. From here, we can select to Redefine or Reroute the part (which likely brings us back into Sketcher) or we can Suppress, Clip Suppress, or Delete the offending feature (which brings us back into mode).

The third path allows us to Investigate the problem. Note that the Investigate path always leads us back to the Resolve state. We cannot fix a problem from Investigate. We can only analyze the problem from this choice. As we can see, there are a number of investigation techniques available to us. From Investigate, we can List all Changes, Show all References that are used by the offending feature, Roll back the Model, or view the Failed Geometry.

If we choose to view the Failed Geometry, we can bring up a Feature Information Window, an Item Information Window, or hide the offending item from the display.

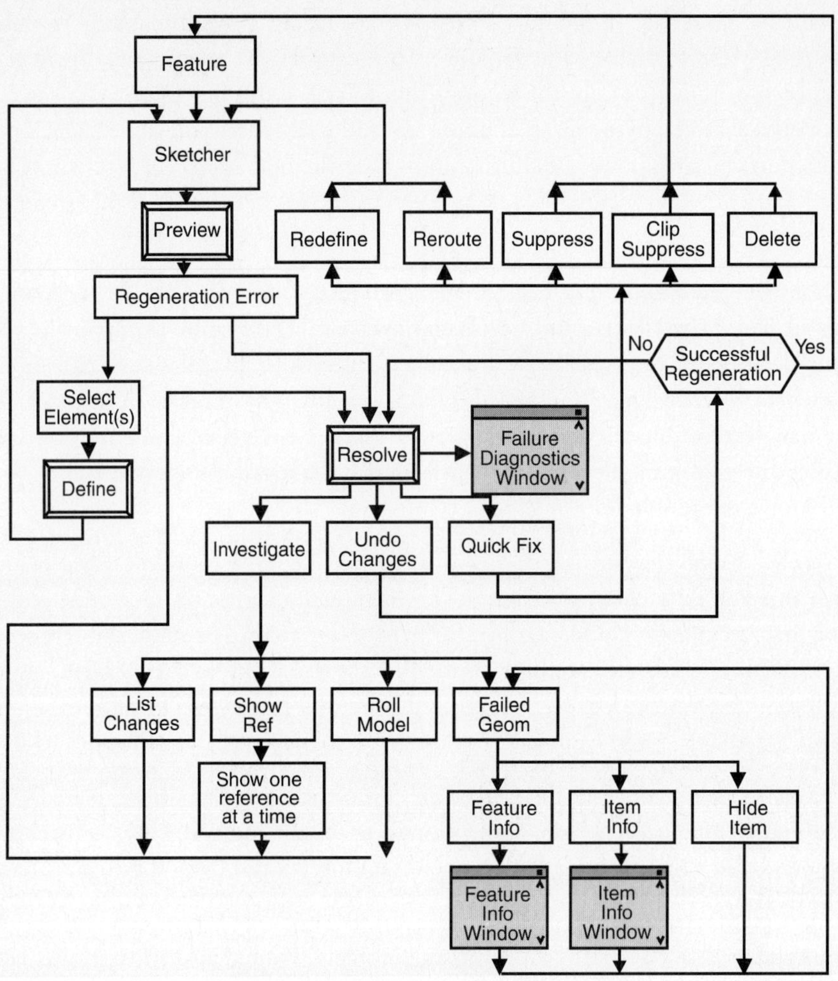

Figure 9.16   Troubleshooting flow chart.

9.6.1   Undo Changes

Undo all changes since last successful regeneration. If the cause of the problem had to do with a new feature being built and the problem was caught at the Preview stage, then the Undo Changes option will simply abort the new feature and regenerate the part from the point before the new feature was created. This may or may not fix the problem. Figure 9.17 provides the flow chart of Undo Changes. As we can see, if the error can be undone, although not fixed, then you are returned to the Mode command, more than likely, at a point before you designed the offending feature. If Undo fails, you are back at the Resolve state.

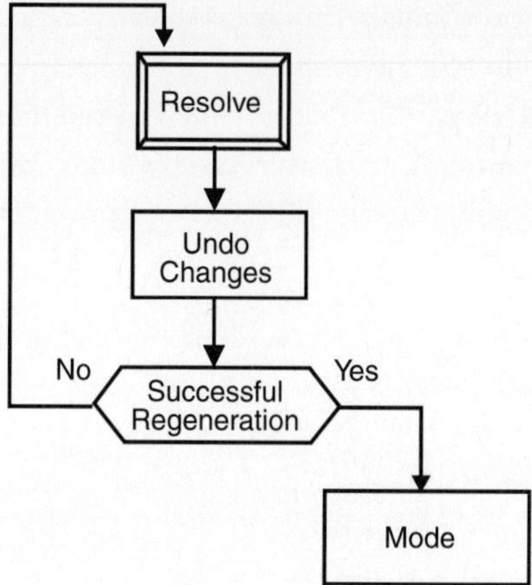

Figure 9.17   Undo Changes flow chart.

9.6.2   Investigate

The Investigate menu is shown in Figure 9.18. From this menu you can choose to investigate the working model, or a backup file of the model. The backup model can come from two places. In the Environment menu, a Regen Backup checkbox is provided. If checked, a temporary backup file is saved to disk before each regeneration. This backup file is used by the Investigate menu if Backup model is selected. If the Regen Backup checkbox is not checked, then the last part version saved to the hard disk is used as the backup file. For example, if you are working on part TUT9-1a.4 when the error occurs and you select Backup Model from the Investigate menu, then the file TUT9-1a.3 will be used (presuming that it exists in the working directory).

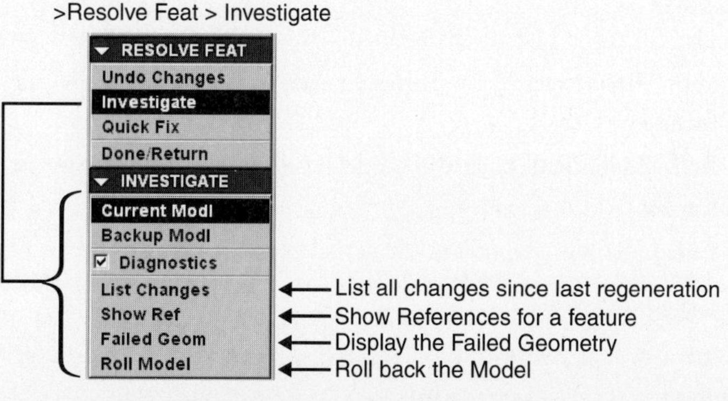

Figure 9.18   The Investigate menu.

The Feature Diagnostics window can be displayed or hidden by checking the Diagnostics check box in the Investigate menu. The Investigate menu does not allow you to fix any problems. No matter which of the many paths you take from the Investigate menu, you end up at the Resolve state. Hopefully, the Investigate tutorial has enlightened you as to the cause of your problem. Figure 9.19 illustrates the Investigate pathways.

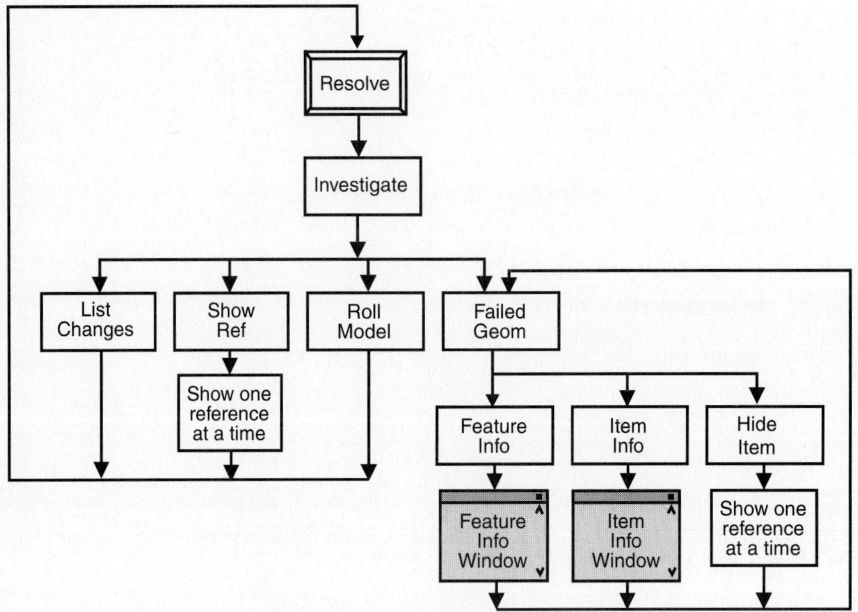

Figure 9.19   Investigate flow chart.

From Investigate, you can perform the following analysis:

- List Changes: List all changes since the last successful regeneration
- Show References: Step through each reference used by the offending feature
- Roll Model: Roll back the model so it regenerates only up to a specified feature
- Failed Geometry: Look at the actual geometry that failed

9.6.2.1   List Changes

If there were any changes since the last successful regeneration, besides the feature in question, then they will be displayed in an information window.

9.6.2.2   Show Ref

The >Show Ref command allows you to step through all of the references made by the part in question. You can step through each reference one at a time using the Next or Previous menu selections. You can also bring up an Information Window about the reference containing the information shown in Table 9.5.

Topic	Description
Reference number in the sequence of references	1 out of 4
Reference type	Plane, edge, etc.
Reference owner	Name and type, for owner
Feature number	Sequence number
Feature ID number	Unique number
All parents	Feature number and ID of each
All children	Feature number and ID of each

Table 9.5   Information about a Reference

9.6.2.3   Failed Geometry

The geometry of a feature could be the source of the problem. Clicking >Failed Geometry highlighted the part with the geometry that failed. If vertices are involved, they will be also highlighted with crossed circles indicating a problem area. The Failed Geometry flow chart was displayed in Figure 9.16. The menu is displayed in Figure 9.20. From Failed Geometry you can select from the following:

- Select Desired Geometry: Step through items in Geometry to choose desired display
- Feature Info: Display a Feature Information window
- Item Info: Display a Item Information window
- Hide Item: Hide the item

If there are more than one items in the failed geometry, you can cycle through them or display all failed items at the same time. You can request a Feature Information window describing the failed feature or an Item information window that provides a synopsis of the problem and a suggestion at a solution.

>Resolve Feat > Investigate > Failed Geometry

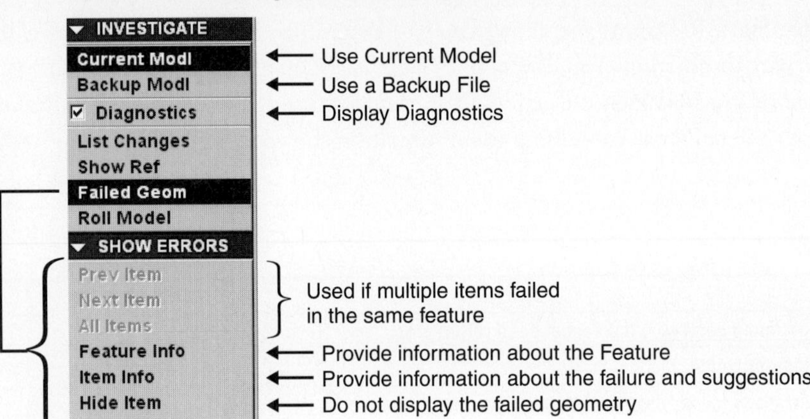

Figure 9.20 Failed Geometry menu.

The display of the failed geometry can be quite useful. In the upcoming tutorial, you will create an open cut that will cause an error. Selecting Failed Geometry provided the display in Figure 9.21. It is quite easy to see what is going on here. Knowing that the feature causing the error is a Cut from the Feature Information window, combined with this display, provides some pretty good clues as to the source of the problem. You can keep the highlighted failed geometry on the screen while working on the part. You can hide the displayed geometry by selecting the Hide Item menu item.

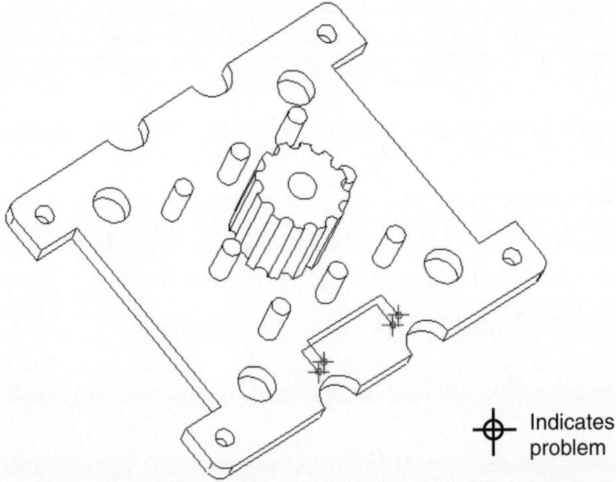

Figure 9.21 Failed Geometry displayed on the 3D part.

9.6.2.4 Roll Model

Rolling back the model requests that the regeneration begin at the first feature and go through until either the failed feature, the feature immediately before the failed feature, or a specified feature. The Roll Model menu is shown in Figure 9.22. Specifying different features can provide you with some insight into which features were generated at what time in the model. This can be very useful in isolating the part of the feature sequence where the error occurred.

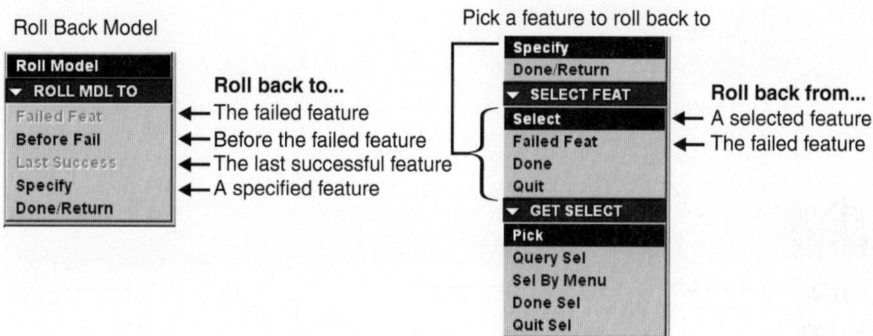

Figure 9.22 Roll back the model menus.

9.6.3 Quick Fix

From the Resolve menu you can select to perform a quick fix. The Quick Fix menu is shown in Figure 9.23. From this menu you can Redefine, Reroute, Suppress, Clip Suppress, or Delete a feature.

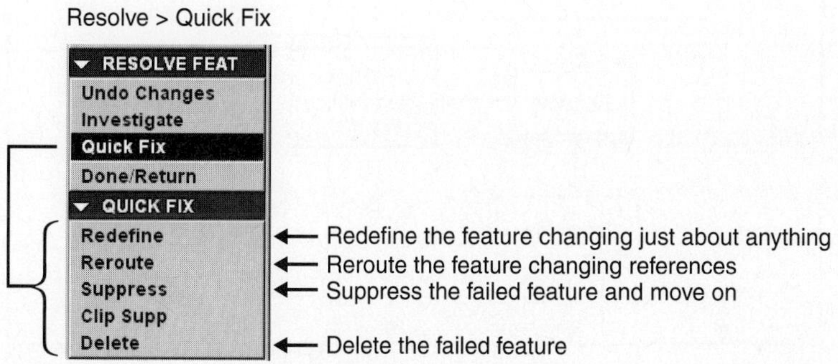

Figure 9.23 The quick fix.

A quick fix addresses the regeneration error by allowing manipulation of only the failed feature. Each of these choices brings you back into the Mode menu assuming that the change was successful. Otherwise, it brings you back to the

Resolve state as shown in Figure 9.24. Note that the Redefine and Reroute likely bring you back into the sketcher for another try at fixing the feature. The Suppress, Clip Suppress functions put the offending feature on hold. Nothing has been fixed yet. The offending feature is simply going to be ignored until someone fixes it, or until someone unwittingly hits Resume. Delete is a final act of desperation. Get that feature out of here! These options are summarized below.

- Redefine: Change most anything about the feature
- Reroute: Change references
- Suppress: Suppress the failed feature from regeneration
- Clip Suppress: Suppress the failed feature and all features that follow it from regeneration
- Delete: Delete the feature

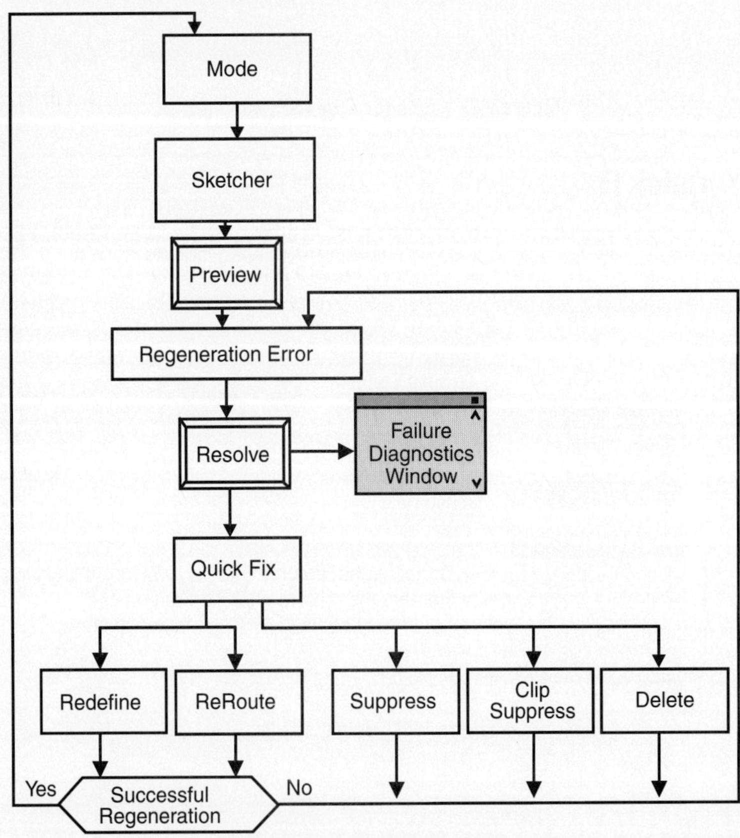

Figure 9.24 Quick fix flow chart.

9.7   **Troubleshooting Regeneration Errors from Sketcher**

In the second tutorial, you will read in an existing as part shown in Figure 9.25(a). Create a Cut as an Extruded Solid choosing the sketch plane and reference as shown in Figure 9.25. Add an open cut at the bottom center as shown in Figure 9.25(b). You can accomplish this by using the >Line Vertical Tool drawing the three lines of the upside-down U. You can also use the Rectangle tool and delete the bottom edge. Either way, you have created an open sketch. This violates the rules regarding closed cuts. Sketcher would have no way of knowing where to stop removing material. Material will be removed from the inside of the three lines and would continue removing material because the section is not closed.

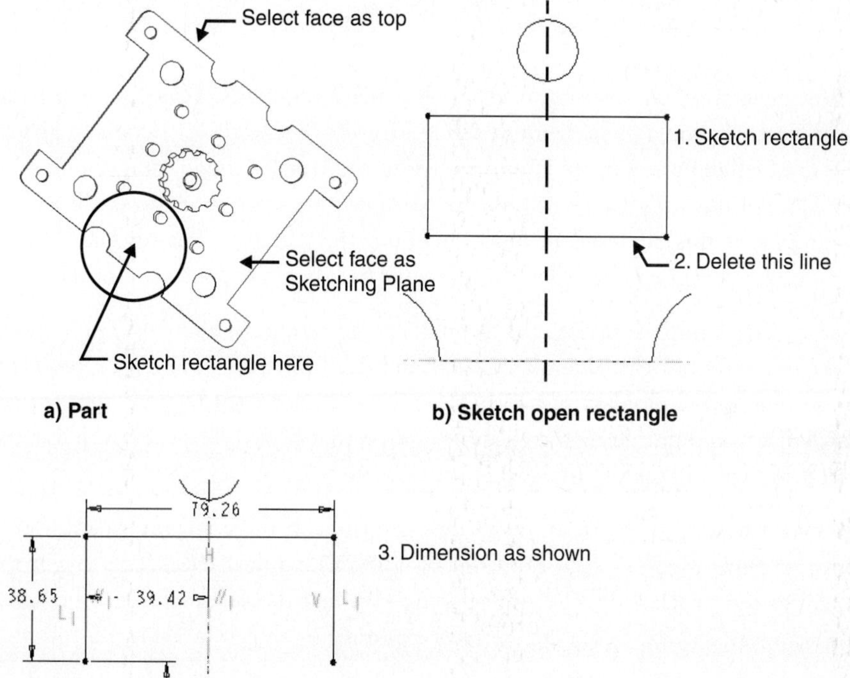

Figure 9.25   Draw a rectangle and remove bottom edge.

Dimension the cut as shown in Figure 9.25(c). Do not worry about the dimension values. Just get them close to the values shown. Be careful to avoid any alignment assumptions. The open cut will regenerate at the sketch level, but will fail at the

Preview level when it is incorporated into the rest of the part. An error message "Error: Could not intersect part with feature" occurs in the Message Box. This message is indicating that it was not possible to incorporate the feature into the part due to some unmentioned intersection problem. Now, in this simple example, we know that the problem is due to the open cut. Our goal here is to step through some of the menu options for troubleshooting. This simple tutorial will serve our purposes.

NOTE: Please bear with me here. Troubleshooting regeneration errors is probably the single most complicated task in Solid Modeling. There are many different avenues that you can follow. I am leading you down a few in this tutorial. It will be up to you to experiment with other paths as you encounter your own, unexpected errors.

The regeneration error leaves us at the Features Dialog box. There are two paths from here. We could go back and redefine a feature by selecting >Section and clicking the Define button or we could enter into the Resolve mode using the Resolve button. For this tutorial, we will use the Resolve route, even though we will end up right back at this point again to get back into the sketcher. This tutorial is like a loop trail. We will end up where we started. The adventure is in the process.

Select Resolve from the Feature Dialog box. A menu appears allowing you to Undo the changes, Investigate the model to try and determine the cause of the problem, or go right at the problem using Quick Fix. We do not want to undo the changes since that would just delete the work we just did that caused the problem in the first place. We will choose the Investigate route to see what we can solve.

You want to keep the current model. You can turn off the Error Information window by removing the check from the Diagnostics window check box. Begin the investigation by selecting to see the references of the failed feature using >Show Ref. You can select >Next to see each reference in order as shown in Table 9.6.

Reference Number	Description	Used as
1	Face of the part	Sketching plane
2	Top of the part	Horizontal reference (TOP)
3	Bottom edge	Dimension reference
4	Centerline	Dimension reference

Table 9.6   References of new feature

All of these references looked okay, and in fact were okay. If any unusual references were made during the specification of the feature they would have showed up at this stage. Click >Done/Return to end the Show References. Next, we will take a look at the failed geometry using the >Failed Geometry selection. Click on >Feature Info to see a complete description of the feature in question. Click on >Item Info to get some hints about the particular items in the sketch, in this case the three lines and two unconnected vertices.

We will roll back the part using >Roll Back to the feature before the error, which in this case happens to be the entire part except the last open-ended feature. We could have specified any feature at this stage for the roll back. This is an excellent way to see the consequence of certain features.

From here, we are back in the Investigate menu, so we will fix the part. The problem is in the sketch so select >Quick Fix >Redefine >Section >Define >Sketch >Sketch View. Connect the open vertices with a line and regenerate the part. This time the Preview works fine and you can accept and save the result. The resulting part is shown in Figure 9.26.

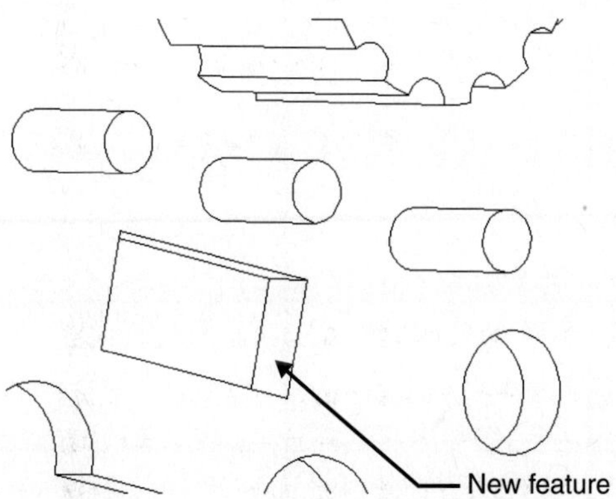

Figure 9.26   Final result after resolving the error.

Tutorial 9.2   Troubleshooting Regeneration Errors in Sketcher

Files opened: Tut9-2a.prt   **Files saved:** Tut9-2b.prt

Step	Action	Description	Further Actions	Result
1	Click PT/Modeler Icon	Run PT/Modeler		After some time, PT/Modeler on screen
2	Mode >Misc >Show Dir	Show current directory		Message similar to "Directory searched is c:\ptc\ptprod\bin"
3	>Change Dir	Change the current directory	Type **c:\proe\tutorial\chapter_9**	
4	>Done-Return	Leave Misc menu		Misc menu removed
5	Mode >Part >Retrieve	Read a part	Type **tut9-2a**	Part read
6	>Environment	Set up the environment	Set up checks as seen in Table T9.2 Column Step 6	
7	>Done-Return			
8	>View	Names	Get to the named View	>VIEW_3	
9	>Feature >Cut	Extrude	Solid	Done	Create an extruded solid cut		
10	>One Side	Done	Cut will extend one side out of the sketching plane		
11	Pick front face as the sketching plane	Select front face in Fig. 9.25(a)	> Okay for Cut direction	
12	>Top	Pick top of part for Top reference to sketching plane in Fig. 9.25(a)	Pick top face	Go into Sketcher mode in Fig. 9.25(b)
13	>Sketch>Rectangle	Draw a rectangle as shown in Figure 9.25(b)		
14	>Delete Items	Delete lower line in rectangle in Fig. 9.25(b)	mLb on lower rectangle edge, mMb to accept delete	
15	>Dimension	Dimension part as shown in Figure 9.25(c); don't worry about actual dimension values		
16	>Regenerate	Tell Sketcher to regenerate	>Done	Warning received "Unattached CUT was detected"

Tutorial 9.2   Troubleshooting Regeneration Errors in Sketcher (continued)

Step	Action	Description	Further Actions	Result
17	>Okay for direction of cut	Accept direction of cut		
18	>Thru Next	Choose depth	>Done	Part is now ready to be previewed
19	Click Preview	Error occurs "Could not intersect part with feature"	Type **F1**	Check part in Default view
20	>Resolve	Enter Resolve mode		
21	>Investigate | Current Model	Investigate the problem		
22	Uncheck Diagnostics	Remove Error Info Window		
23	>Show Ref	Show references one at a time	>Next until all references are seen	Each reference highlighted
24	>Done/Return	End Show Ref		Back to Investigate
25	>Failed Feature Geometry	Look at the geometry		
26	>View | Names	Get to the named View	>VIEW_3	See view in 3D
27	>Feature Info	See Feature Information window	Q to close window	
28	>Item Info	Message reminds us to intersect geometry	Q to close window	Message "Redefine the feature so that it intersects the part"
29	>Roll Model	Roll back the part	> Before Fail | Done/Return	
30	>Quick Fix > Redefine | Confirm	Fix the part using redefine		Brings us to the sketching plane
31	Click Section Click Define	Select to redefine a section	>Sketch	Enter Sketcher
32	>Sketch >Line | horizontal	Connect the open bottom	mLb mLb mMb to draw a single horizontal line	
33	>Regenerate	Regenerate the feature	>Done	Regeneration successful
34	>Preview	See the cut	F1 >Okay	Feature defined successfully as in Fig. 9.26
35	>File>SaveAs	Save file with new name	Enter to accept [tut9-2a.prt] then type **tut9-2b.prt**	Part saved
36	QuitWindow			
37	Exit	Exit program	Click Yes to confirm	PT/Products exited

Item	Step 6
Disp DtmPln	Checked
Spin Center	No
Disp Pnts	Checked
Disp Axes	Checked
Rendering	No hidden line

Table T9.2   Environment Settings

9.8   Troubleshooting Regeneration Errors at the Part Level: Tutorial 9.3

We are going to look at the part displayed in Figure 9.1. Recall that we determined that two troublesome references showed up during our investigation of this part. The first had to do with a reference made by Feature 14. For some reason, it was referencing Feature 8. We are going to trace this one down and change this unwanted reference. Second, we found that Feature 14 referenced Feature 13. This was also undesired and we will change that as well. Let us investigate these two problems and find a solution.

You will read in a part and go immediately to the Info menu since we desire some information. We are currently running with an operational part. There are no current regeneration errors. Select >ParentChild >Parents | File to see a list of parents and select Feature 9. An information window shows us the parents as seen in Table 9.7. The two axes and the base feature seem appropriate choices. However, Feature 8 is a cut and should not be a parent of Feature 9.

Feature	Description	Conclusion
5	AX axis	OK
6	AY axis	OK
7	Base feature	OK
8	Cut	Problem

Table 9.7   Parents of Feature 9

Next, we will look at the references made by Feature 9 using the >ParentChild | References | File. Stepping through each reference one at a time using the >Next command we arrive at Table 9.8. As can be seen, we are using an edge and a face of Feature 8.

Reference	Usage	Conclusion
Face of base	Sketch plane	OK
Top of base	Horizontal reference	OK
Edge of feature 8	Dimension	Problem
Face of feature 8	Dimension	Problem
AY axis	Dimension	OK
AX axis	Dimension	OK
Bottom edge of base	Dimension	OK
Bottom face of base	Dimension	OK

Table 9.8   References Feature 9

It is time to fix Feature 8. Since a dimensional reference is made, we will go into the sketcher using >Feature Oper > Redefine and selecting Feature 9. The sketch plane and the horizontal reference seem fine so we will go directly to the sketcher by selecting >Sketch from the menu that is provided.

Once in Sketcher, we see our cut section, but we do not see much else. Make sure hidden line is selected using >Environment > Hidden Line. We have hidden line selected but we do not see any hidden lines as seen in Figure 9.27(a). Use the 3D view spin to rotate the part slowly so that you do not lose your reference. This is accomplished using the Ctrl-mMb drag. Now the problem becomes apparent. Feature 8 is hiding behind Feature 9 as shown in Figure 9.27(b). Due to the lack of dimensions in Figure 9.27(a), we can conclude that Sketcher is creating assumed alignments to Feature 8. We will need to break these alignments. I have added a number of dimensions to the figure to refresh your memory. These extra dimensions are labeled with an asterisk (*).

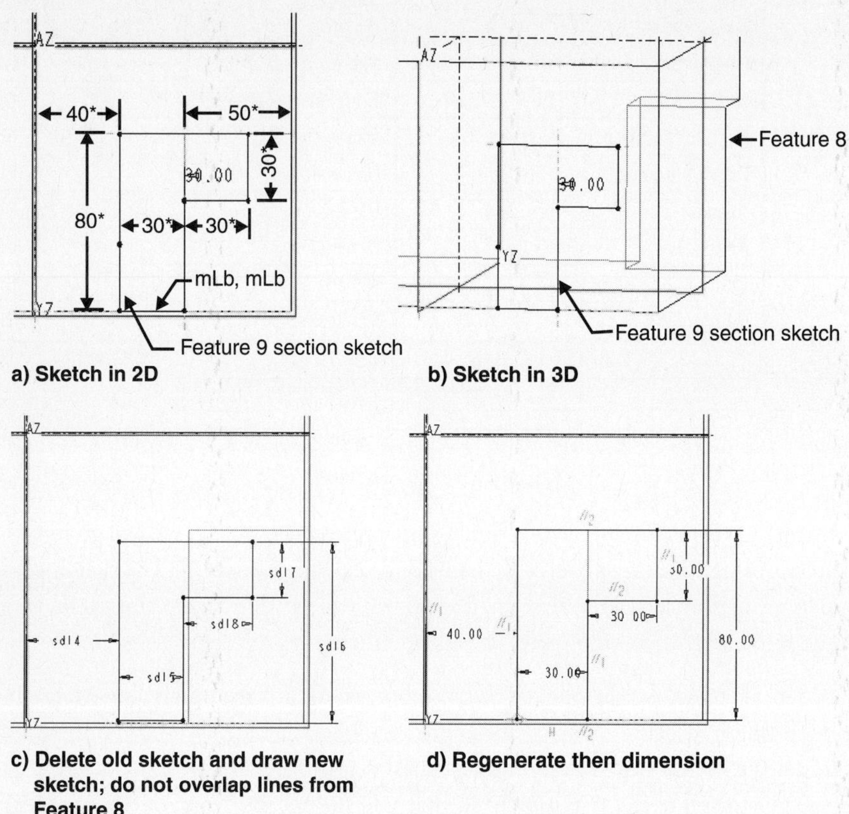

Figure 9.27   Sketch of Feature 9.

Some assumptions are very difficult to break in Sketcher. The overlapping lines aligned to Feature 8 cannot be moved by providing dimensions. Any additional dimensions will over-constrain the part and cause a regeneration failure. One way to proceed is simply to delete the entire sketch and start over. Use >Delete Item | Select >Many to draw a rectangle around all of the parts and perform the delete. Another approach would be to move the lines out of alignment rather than deleting the entire sketch. This would maintain all references to any children.

Next, use >Line | Vertical to draw the line. Recall that each segment ends with a mLb and the next segment drawn shifts between horizontal and vertical. Make sure to draw the shape so that the lines do not overlap the lines from Feature 8. Dimension the part as seen in Figure 9.28(c). Regenerate and >Modify the dimensions to the desired values as seen in Figure 9.28(d). Regenerate and accept the new feature with Okay.

Now, we will check our work. Return to >Info > ParentChild | Parents | File. The info window shows us that only Features 5, 6, and 7 are parents. We have been successful.

The same exact procedure should be followed for Feature 14 that references Feature 13. In this case, the parents, seen by Info>ParentChild | Parents | File, of Feature 14 are Feature 7 (the base part) and Feature 13 (a Cut). We want to remove the reference to Feature 13. The references, seen by Info>ParentChild | References, indicate that the horizontal sketching plane uses Feature 13. To change this we will need to >Feature Oper >Redefine, and select Feature 14. From the Feature Dialog select Section, Define and Sketch Plane from the menu.

You can select the highlighted face on the base for the sketching plane. An easier way, since we are keeping the same sketching plane, is to select >Same Ref from the menu, as shown in Figure 9.28(a). This brings us to the sketch Reference. We want to change this reference, but we need to change it carefully. Instead of using the highlighted face from Feature 14, select >Alternate | Top | Plane and this time select the top face of the base feature as opposed to the top face of the Cut Feature 13. This is shown in Figure 9.28(a) and the resulting sketch is shown in Figure 9.28(b). If the sketch does not look like Figure 9.28(b), Cancel out and begin the Redefine process over until you do it correctly. Once you have the correct orientation, you can >Regenerate the part since the sketch is fine. Preview and accept the new Feature with Okay.

Test the Feature by selecting >Info > ParentChild | Parents | File. The info window shows us that only Feature 7, the base, is a parent. We have been successful once again. Save the part.

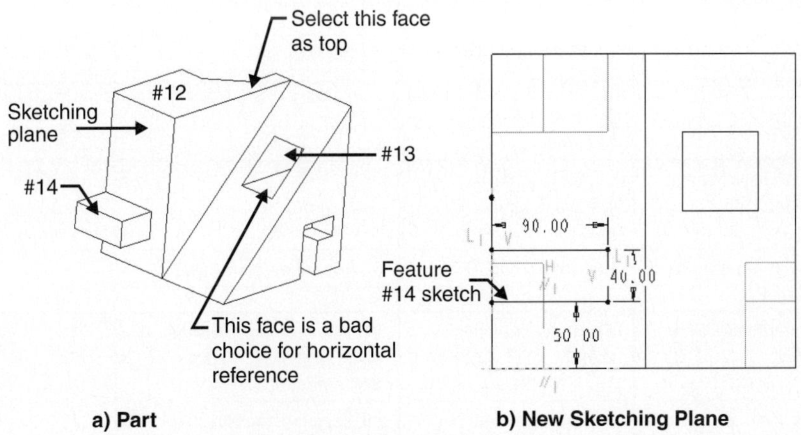

Figure 9.28   Illustrations for Feature 14.

Tutorial 9.3 Troubleshooting Regeneration Errors at the Part Level

Files opened: Tut9-3a.prt   **Files saved:** Tut9-3b.prt

Step	Action	Description	Further Actions	Result
1	Click PT/Modeler Icon	Run PT/Modeler		After some time, PT/Modeler on screen
2	Mode >Misc >Show Dir	Show current directory		Message similar to "Directory searched is c:\ptc\ptprod\bin"
3	>Change Dir	Change the current directory	Type **c:\proe\tutorial\ chapter_9**	
4	>Done-Return	Leave Misc menu		Misc menu removed
5	Mode >Part >Retrieve	Read a part	Type **tut9-3a**	Part read
6	>Environment	Set up the environment	Set up checks as seen in Table T9.3 Column Step 6	
7	>Done-Return			
8	>View | Names	Get to the named View	>VIEW_3 | Done-Return	
9	>Info > ParentChild | Parents | File	Get a list of parents of Feature 9	Select Feature 9 in Fig. 9.1; type "Q" when done	Info window shows Feature 9 (5, 6, 7, 8)
10	>Info > ParentChild | References Select Feature 9	Look at references one at a time	> Next through all references	References highlighted one at at time; message indicates source of reference
11	>Done	Exit Info	Type "Q" to remove window	
12	>Feature Oper >Redefine	Redefine Feature 9	Select Feature 9	
13	Select Section in Feature Dialog	Want to change the section	Select Define	
14	>Sketch	Go directly into Sketcher		
15	>Main >Environment > Hidden Line	Check to make sure we are in hidden line mode		
16	Ctrl — mMb drag to see 3D view	Look at part in 3D	>Sketch View to return to 2D view	
17	>Delete Items | Pick Many	Delete all lines in sketch	Draw a rectangle around all lines in sketch >Done-Sel to accept	
18	Line | Vertical	Redraw figure as in Fig. 9.27(a) however, do not overlap Feature 8	mLb around section shape mMb when done	

Tutorial 9.3   Troubleshooting Regeneration Errors (continued)

Step	Action	Description	Further Actions	Result
19	>Align	Align lower edge to bottom edge of existing part	mLB on bottom edge of sketch and mLB on bottom edge of preexisting part as in Fig. 9.27(a)	
20	>Dimension	Dimension as shown in Figure 9.27(c)	>Regenerate	Regeneration Successful
21	>Modify	Change all dimensions as shown in Figure 9.27(c)	>Regenerate	Regeneration Successful
22	>Done | Okay	Done with Sketcher		
23	>Info > ParentChild | Parents | File	See parent/child relations	Select Feature 9 Q to close info window	Info window displayed; only Features 5, 6, and 7 are Parents
24	>Info > ParentChild | Parents | File	Get a list of parents of Feature 14	Select Feature 14 in Fig. 9.29(a), click Q when done	Info window displayed; only Features 7 and 13 are Parents
25	>Info > ParentChild | References	Look at references one at a time	Select Feature 14 > Next through all references	References highlighted one at at time; message indicates source of reference
26	>Done	Exit Info		
27	>Feature Oper > Redefine	Redefine Feature 14	Select Feature 14	
28	Select Section in Feature Dialog	Want to change the section	Select Define	
29	>Sketch Plane	Want to change the references		
30	>Same Ref	Accept same sketching plane		
31	>Alternate | Top	Select a new reference	Select the top of the base in Fig. 9.28(a)	
32	>Regenerate	Accept original sketch as shown in Figure 9.28(b)	>Done	Regeneration Successful
33	>Preview	See the cut	F1 >Okay	Accept the new feature
34	>File >SaveAs	Save file with new name	Enter to accept [tut9-3a.prt] then type **tut9-3b.prt**	Part saved
35	QuitWindow			
36	Exit	Exit program	Click Yes to confirm	PT/Products exited

Item	Step 6
Disp DtmPln	Checked
Spin Center	No
Disp Pnts	Checked
Disp Axes	Checked
Rendering	Hidden line

Table T9.3   Environment Settings

9.9   One Last Fix: Tutorial 9.4

Now, it is time to unleash the time bomb. We have a suppressed feature that is going to cause a regeneration error. This error occurred earlier, and during troubleshooting I requested that the feature be suppressed. We Resume the suppressed feature using the >Feature Oper >Resume | All. This forces a regeneration causing a Failure Diagnostics window to appear and a regeneration error. The messages indicate that Feature 15 had an error and that it could not intersect part with feature.

You will have to be careful here. Our newly resumed feature is a Cut named Feature 14 with an ID #494. The Resume operation has added a new feature. The Protrusion that used to be Feature 14 is now Feature 15. This newly numbered feature is shown in the Model Tree of Figure 9.29(a) and in the pre-Resume view in Figure 9. 29(b). NOTE: This is a view before the Resume. The view after the Resume is shown in Figure 9.29(c). You could return to the pre-Resume view by suppressing the new cut Feature 14 again. But that would not be very constructive. We need to find the problem. The new part, regenerated up to the failed feature, is shown in Figure 9.29(c).

Select >Investigate and >Show Ref to see the references for the failed Protrusion Feature 15. Stepping through the references, we see the sketching plane, which is now severely clipped, the Top orientation reference, and the left side and bottom of the base part. Some clues are here, having to do with the bottom and left side of the base part. These are both in the vicinity of the failed feature.

At this time, I suggest going into >Quick Fix, selecting >Redefine. The sketching plane and orientation reference seemed okay. Even though the sketching plane was clipped, it was still present and a plane could be derived from what was left. Recall that the sketch does not need to overlap the actual face selected to be the sketching plane.

We will select Section and Define selecting the sketch. From the sketch, shown in Figure 9.29(d), we can see two problems. One, we have an open segment. Open segments are allowed in Protrusions, however, the open segment has to intersect fully with the part. Otherwise, matter will flow out the gap filling the entire model. Close the segment with a vertical line. The second problem is a line that goes nowhere. Delete the line as indicated in Figure 9.29(d). Regenerate the part and exit Sketcher. Okay the new feature.

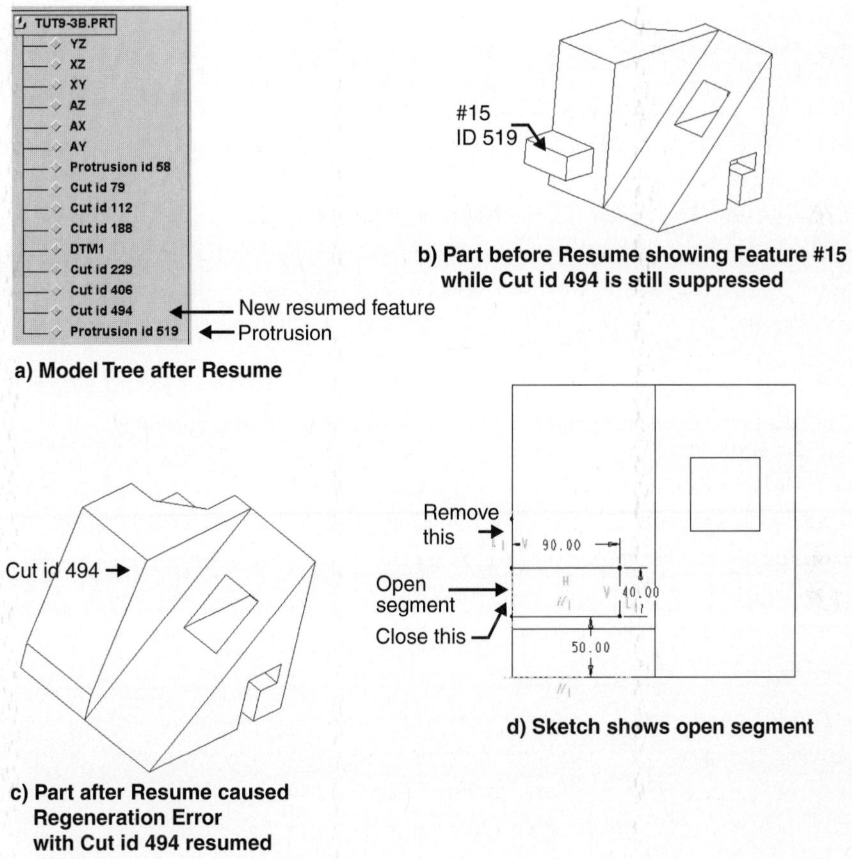

a) Model Tree after Resume

b) Part before Resume showing Feature #15 while Cut id 494 is still suppressed

c) Part after Resume caused Regeneration Error with Cut id 494 resumed

d) Sketch shows open segment

Figure 9.29   Resumed feature.

A message occurs indicating that the "Failure has been resolved, do you want to exit Resolve Feature mode?" That is exactly what we wanted to see. Type Y. We are done—or are we? This is a perfect example of why we need to check our work constantly. Look at Figure 9.30(a). The sketching plane has been clipped by the cut

Feature 14. Our protrusion Feature 15 now hangs in space. There is nothing wrong with this from the regeneration's perspective but we want to change it.

Redefine the Feature 15 using the >Feature Oper >Redefine. Select the Attributes and Define, this time choosing both sides. For now, select Blind with a distance of 30. We are trapped into a Blind distance measure here. We would like the protrusion to go to the next surface towards the part and blind away from the part, but this is not allowed. Select Preview and Okay the result as shown in Figure 9.30(b).

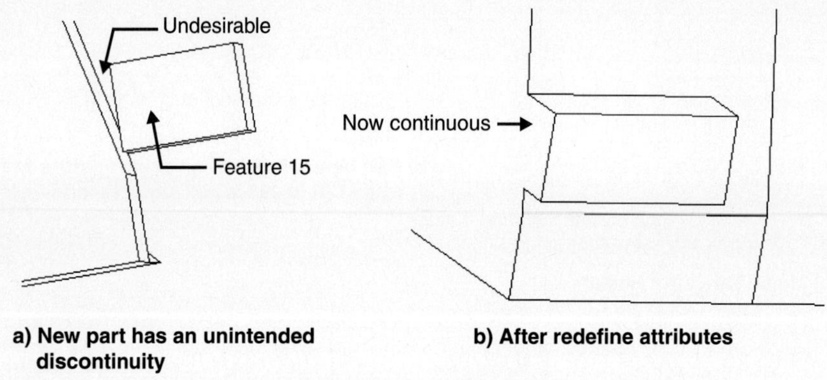

Figure 9.30   One last fix.

Tutorial 9.4   Resume a Suppressed Feature

Files opened: Tut9-4a.prt   **Files saved:** Tut9-4b.prt

Step	Action	Description	Further Actions	Result
1	Click PT/Modeler Icon	Run PT/Modeler		After some time, PT/Modeler on screen
2	Mode > Misc >Show Dir	Show current directory		Message similar to "Directory searched is c:\ptc\ptprod\bin"
3	>Change Dir	Change the current directory	Type **c:\proe\tutorial\ chapter_9**	
4	>Done-Return	Leave Misc menu		Misc menu removed
5	Mode > Part >Retrieve	Read a part	Type **tut9-4a**	Part read
6	>Environment	Set up the environment	Set up checks as seen in Table T9.4 Column Step 6	
7	>Done-Return			
8	>View | Names	Get to the named View	>VIEW_3	
9	>Feature Oper | Resume | All | Done	Resume all features in part		Failure Diagnostics window indicates that Feature 15 had an error
10	>Investigate	Look into the problem by seeing references	>Show Ref	
11	>Next through references	See references all refer to base part; sketching plane, orientation reference, side, and top	>Done/Return	
12	>Quick Fix	Try and fix the problem	>Redefine	
13	Select Section	Redefine the section	Select Define	
14	>Sketch	Select to redefine the sketch		Sketch view shows bad line and open segment
15	>Delete Item	Delete the unintended line	Select Line in Fig. 9.29(d)	
16	>Sketch >Line | Vertical	Close the segment	mLb mLb mMB a line to close segment in Fig. 9.29(d)	
17	>Regenerate		>Done	Regeneration successful
18	>Preview	Try a part wide regeneration	F1	Part regenerated successfully but there is an undesirable gap in Fig. 9.30(a)

Tutorial 9.4   Resume a Suppressed Feature (continued)

Step	Action	Description	Further Actions	Result
19	Select Attributes	Redefine the Feature 15 again	Define	
20	>Both Sides | Done	Change from one-sided to two-sided		
21	>Blind | Done	Use a blind extension	Type **30**	
22	>Preview	Try a part wide regeneration	F1 Okay	Part regenerated successfully in Fig. 9.30(b)
23	>Yes	Yes to leave Resolve mode		
24	>File >SaveAs	Save file with new name	Enter to accept [tut9-4a.prt] then type **tut9-4b.prt**	Part saved
25	QuitWindow			
26	Exit	Exit program	Click Yes to confirm	PT/Products exited

Item	Step 6
Disp DtmPln	Checked
Spin Center	No
Disp Pnts	Checked
Disp Axes	Checked
Rendering	Hidden line

Table T9.4   Environment Settings

9.10   Override Assumptions

At times, you might desire to override a sketcher assumption. For example, the sketcher might assume that a line is horizontal, vertical, or parallel to another line. This might not be consistent with your design intent. You can override these assumptions.

Assumptions are displayed by default using a set of symbols including H for horizontal, V for vertical, || for parallel. Figure 9.31(a) shows a rectangle where the right-most edge is assumed to be vertical and is marked with a V. When overwritten, a universal No symbol is placed over the assumption as shown in Figure 9.31(b). This likely will require additional dimensions since the assumption was providing dimensional information.

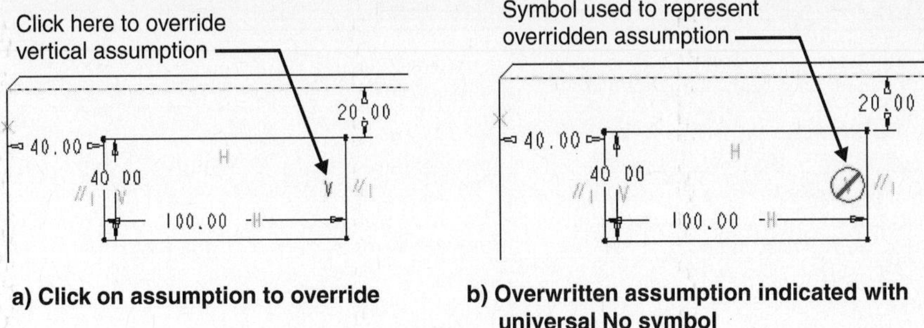

a) Click on assumption to override   **b) Overwritten assumption indicated with universal No symbol**

Figure 9.31   Overriding an assumption.

From the sketcher menu, you can select the >Constraints item to display the Constraints submenu as shown in Figure 9.32. To override an assumption, select >Disable. Next, select the assumptions in the sketcher view by clicking on the constraint symbol. The constraint symbols are displayed when the Display checkbox is checked. You can remove the constraint symbols from the display by removing the check from this box. It is also possible to reenable a previously disabled constraint. This is accomplished by selecting the >Enable item and clicking on the disabled constraint symbol.

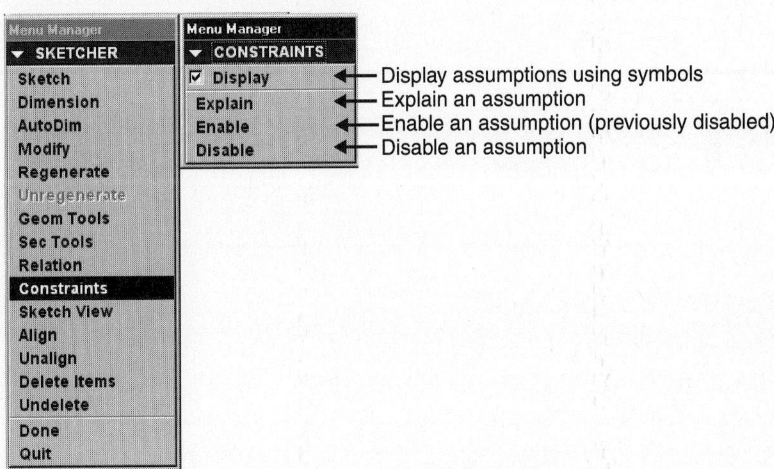

Figure 9.32   Constraints Override menu.

Making an Assembly

A design often includes more than one part that is somehow connected to others. A *part* is a collection of features. An *assembly* is a collection of parts, built one part (component) at a time. As you bring a component into an assembly, it is necessary to orient the new component with respect to the assembly. Assemblies may also contain subassemblies. Either a part or a subassembly is called a *component.*

10.1 Constraining Parts in Three Dimensions

Positioning a part in three dimensions is about as tricky as docking the space shuttle with a space station. Not only are the positions of both objects critical, the orientation of both is equally important. There are six degrees of freedom that fully constrain a three-dimensional object in a three-dimensional space.

10.1.1 Six Degrees of Freedom

The first three degrees of freedom are simple ones. These three describe the translation in the assembly coordinate system. We will call this cx, cy, and cz as seen in Figure 10.1(a). The later three are the angular components, commonly called pitch, roll, and yaw. We will call them rx, ry, and rz, indicating the rotation about the AX, AY, and AZ axis. These three represent the degree of rotation about each of the axes, and are demonstrated in Figure 10.1(b).

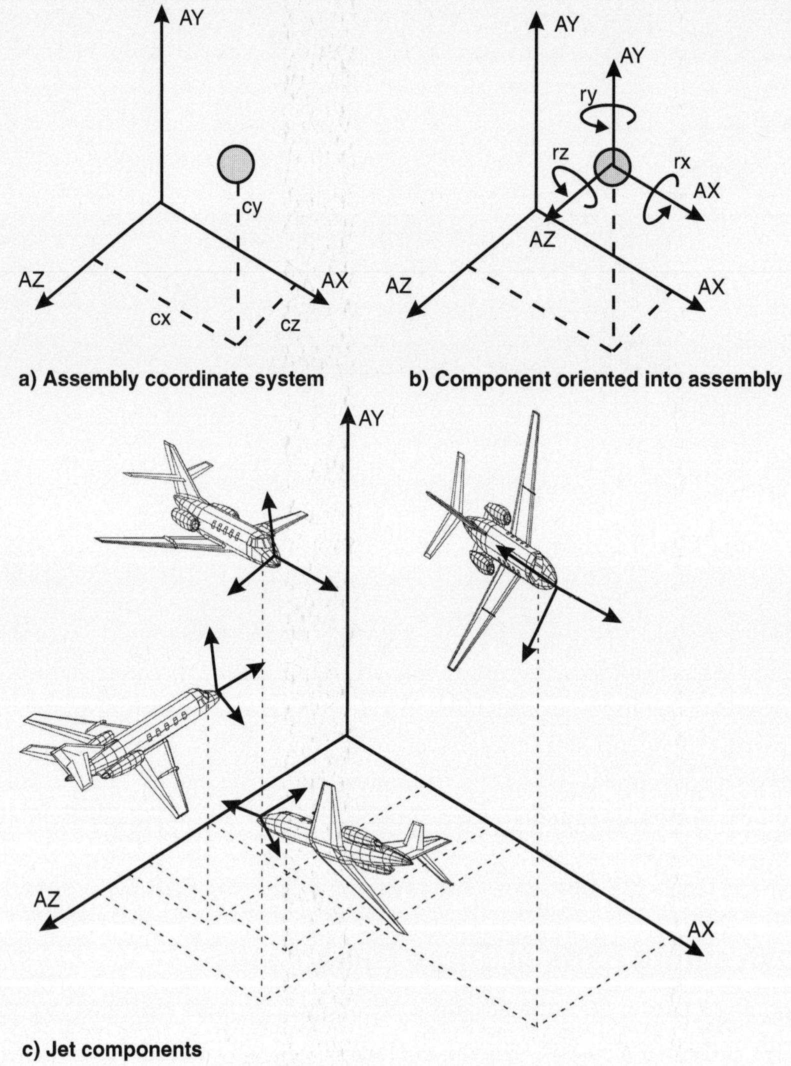

Figure 10.1   Six degrees of freedom.

The example shown in Figure 10.1(c) illustrates several jet airplanes, each oriented at a different cx, cy, and cz translation, and each with different rx, ry, and rz orientation angles. As air traffic controllers know all too well, the position of an aircraft does not tell the whole story.

Positioning a component into an assembly requires specification of these six degrees of freedom. For some components, each is critical. For other components, some may be unimportant. Take the sphere object in Figure 10.2(a). It really would not matter what any of the three rotational components were as far as the display of the object is concerned. Similarly, a cylinder might not be concerned about the rotation with regard to its long axis as shown in Figure 10.2(b). However, a cylinder with a keyhole might depend on the orientation of the rx rotation as seen in Figure 10.2(c). The cylinder of Figure 10.2(b) might have identical ends. Consequently, it might not matter which end was facing in either direction along the AX axis. The cylinder of Figure 10.2(d) has a different end, and it might matter which side faced in the direction of the positive AX axis.

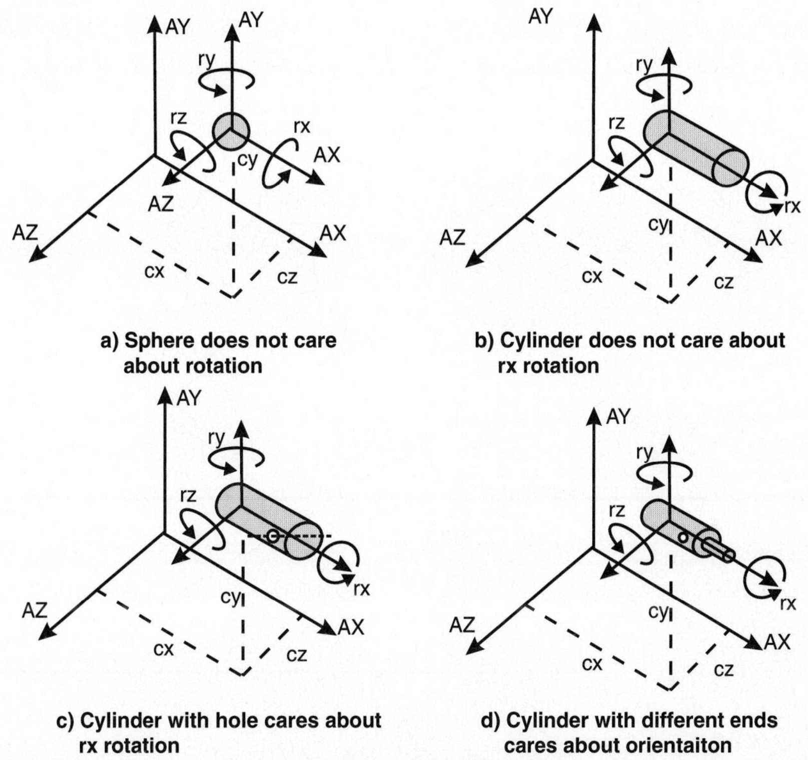

Figure 10.2   Six degrees of freedom.

10.1.2   Constraining a Part

As you place components into an assembly, you are asked to constrain the part. A fully constrained component is one that has all six degrees of freedom specified. That is, a translation is provided for each of the AX, AY, and AZ axes and an angle is provided for every one of the rx, ry, and rz rotational angles.

A component is partially constrained if any of the six degrees of freedom are unspecified. In Figure 10.3(a), the component B is partially constrained with respect to A since the az translation along the AZ axis is not specified. The component B can slide along an axis parallel to the AZ axis since no az translation is provided.

Similarly, In Figure 10.3(b), the component B is partially constrained with respect to A since the ay translation along the AY axis is not specified. The component B can slide along an axis parallel to the AY axis since no ay translation is provided.

In Figure 10.3(c), the component B is partially constrained with respect to A since the rx rotation along an axis parallel to the AX axis is not specified. The component B can rotate about an axis parallel to the AX axis since no rx dimension is provided.

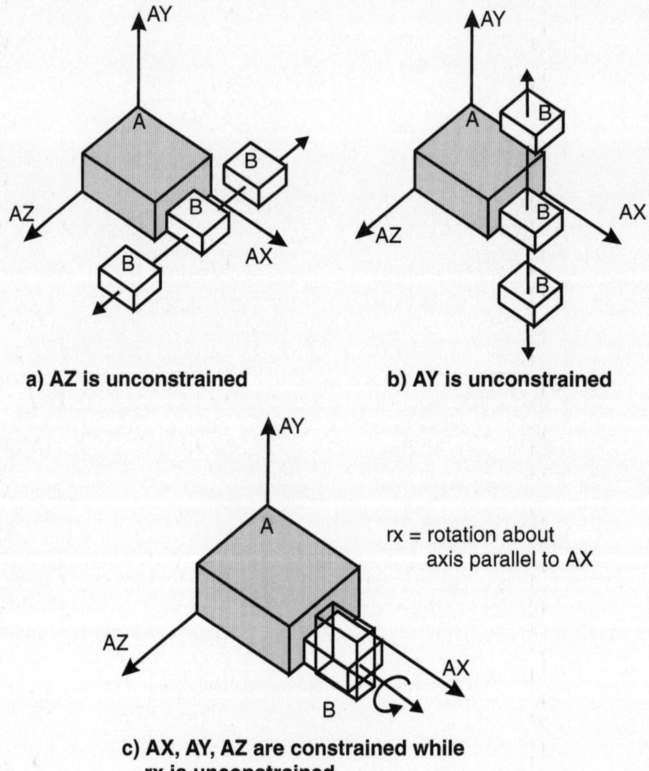

Figure 10.3   Constraining a part.

10.2 Assembly Datum Planes

As is the case with a part, it is a very good idea to begin an assembly with a set of default datum planes. You would need three datum planes to constrain parts in the three-dimensional space. Each datum plane has a translation origin at 0.0, and rotational component of 0.0 degrees.

The first component placed in an assembly determines the coordinate system of the assembly. It is unwise to choose a geometry component (a part or subassembly) as the first component. At some point you might want to reorder the components. You would have a difficult time changing the first (base) component.

10.3   Creating an Assembly

Before we discuss constraining parts, let us create a new assembly just to get our feet wet. You create a new assembly by selecting >Mode >Assembly >Create and typing in an assembly name. Name this one Tut10-1. Each assembly gets an .ASM file extension. The Assembly menu is shown in Figure 10.4(a). Once created, a Model Tree is displayed that contains an empty assembly.

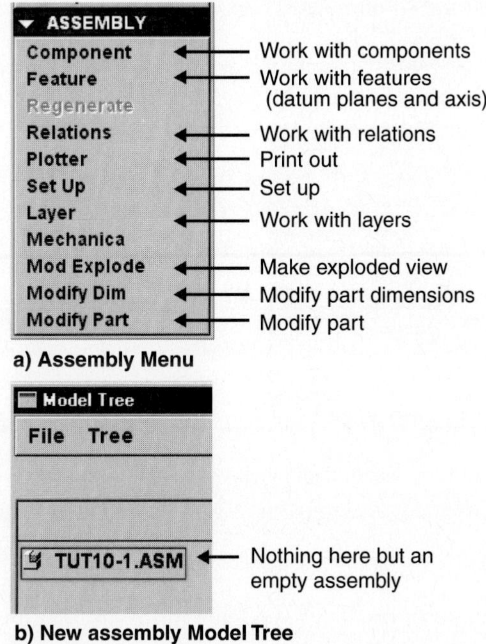

Figure 10.4   Assembly menu and Model Tree.

From the >Assembly menu, you can work with components, features, relations, and layers. You can modify parts within an assembly through >Modify Part or >Modify Dimension and then >Regenerate the part that has been modified. Assemblies are groups of parts. You do not regenerate an assembly; rather, you regenerate a part or parts within an assembly. You can also create assembly level relations that dictate how parts work together. The Mod Explode performs an exploded assembly view.

Figure 10.5(a) shows the >FEATURE submenu. From this menu you can create Datum Planes and Datum Axis, delete features, suppress a feature or redefine a feature. The >ASSEM SETUP menu is shown in Figure 10.5(b). From this menu you can change the Datum Plane or Axis name.

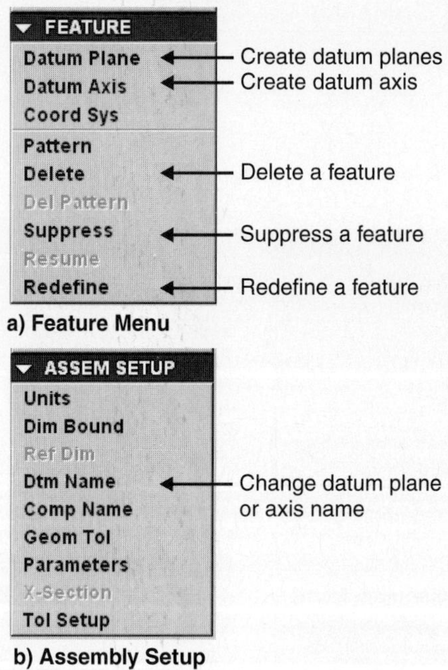

Figure 10.5   Feature menu and Assembly Setup menu.

Tutorial 10.1 is a simple tutorial. All you must do is add datum planes and axes before saving the file. To accomplish this, choose >Feature >Datum Plane. This adds the three datum planes. We should rename these datum planes to be consistent with our part datum plane names. We do want, however, to distinguish them from the part level Coordinate systems so we will name them ASXY, ASXZ, and ASYZ (AS for assembly). Choose >Setup >Dtm Name. Select each of the three datums and rename them as seen in Figure 10.6. Next select >Feature >Datum Axis. Choose >Two Plane as the means for specifying the axes. Select the XY and YZ planes to place the first axis. Select the XY and XZ planes to place the second axis. Select the

XZ and YZ planes to place the third axis. Next, go back to >Setup >Dtm Name and select the three axes, naming them ASAY, ASAX, and ASAZ respectively, as seen in Figure 10.6. Renaming the axis makes it a little easier to distinguish the different axes when working with assemblies and subassemblies. That is all for this first tutorial; save the file and exit.

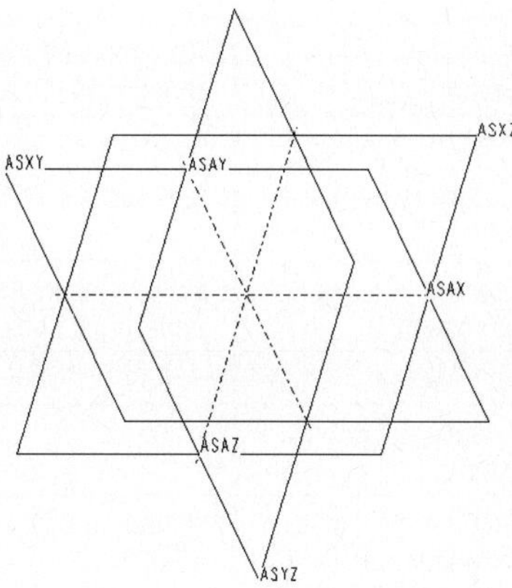

Figure 10.6   Default datum planes.

Tutorial 10.1   Creating an Assembly

No files opened.   **Files saved:** Tut10-1.asm

Step	Action	Description	Further Actions	Result
1	Click PT/Modeler Icon	Run PT/Modeler		After some time, PT/Modeler on screen
2	>Mode >Misc >Show Dir	Show current directory		Message similar to "Directory searched is c:\ptc\ptprod\bin"
3	>Change Dir	Change the current directory	Type **c:\proe\tutorial\ chapter_10**	
4	>Done-Return	Leave Misc menu		Misc menu removed
5	>Mode > Assembly >Create	Create an assembly	Type **tut10-1**	Assembly created
6	>Environment	Set up the environment	Set up checks as seen in Table T10.2 Column Step 6	
7	>Done-Return			
8	>Assembly >Feature >Datum Plane	Set up default datum planes		
9	>Assembly >Setup >Dtm Name	Select datum planes and change names as Fig. 10.6	Change to ASXY, ASXZ, ASYZ	
10	>Assembly >Feature >Datum Axis >Two Plane	Set up datum axis as intersection of two planes	Select XY — XZ, select XY— YZ, select YZ — XZ	
11	>Assembly >Setup >Dtm Name	Select datum axis and change names as Fig. 10.6	Select axis and change to ASAX, ASAZ, ASAY	
12	>File >Save	Save file	Save **tut10-1**	
13	QuitWindow			
14	Exit	Exit program	Click Yes to confirm	PT/Modeler exited

Item	Step 6
Disp DtmPln	Checked
Spin Center	No
Disp Pnts	No
Disp Axes	Checked
Rendering	No hidden line

Table T10.1   Environment Settings

10.4   Placing the First Component

Before we look at how to constrain parts into an assembly, I want you to assemble a first component. After doing it once, we will look at the details. The first geometry component, whether it is a part or assembly, has the same significance as the first feature of a part. The first component should encompass as much of the part as possible. As an example, an engine block would make a good first component for an assembly, as opposed to a fan belt. This is not a hard and fast rule, though. Consider the case of an axle with two wheels on either end. Based on your design intent, the axle might not be a good choice for the first component.

The selection of the first component is also based on the way that PT/Modeler helps you to constrain parts. This is the topic of a later section.

There is a technique, although a bit laborious, that aligns the first part to the datums. This involves aligning each of the datum planes in the component, XY, XZ, and YZ, to the respective Datum Planes in the assembly, ASXY, ASXZ, and ASYZ. Recall that each datum has two sides, yellow for positive and red for negative. You will align all yellow sides of the part's datum planes to all yellow sides of the assembly's datum planes. You could have chosen all red sides for the same result. Alternately, you could perform a flip operation by assigning a red to a yellow side (or vice versa). Finally, you could perform a 90 degree rotation in any dimension by assigning the part's datum planes to a different assembly datum plane. For example, assigning XY to ASYZ would orient the part differently from XY to ASXY or XY to ASXZ.

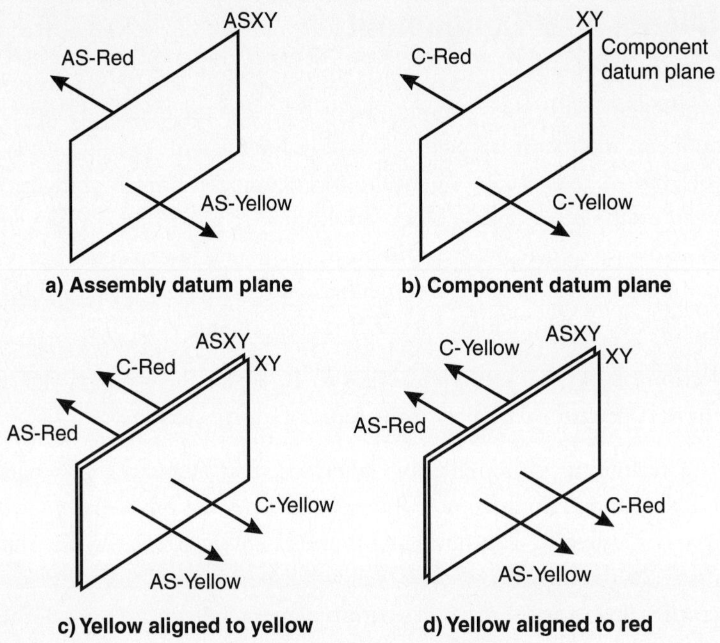

Figure 10.7   Default datum planes.

Alignment of datum planes requires the extra step of specifying the direction. This is not required when specifying a face of an object because faces have only one side. The alignment process is very simple to understand. It is similar to taking two playing cards and placing them one on top of the other. Aligning the faces means that both faces point in the same direction. Aligning a face to a back means that one card's face points in the opposite direction from the other card's face. Remember, datum planes have no depth—they are pure two-dimensional objects. This is illustrated in Figure 10.7.

The procedure to align the part to the assembly datum planes is shown in Table 10.1. As we can see, naming all datum planes consistently is extremely helpful during alignment.

Step	Constraint	Pick on Part	Side	Pick on Assembly	Side
1	>Align	XY	>Yellow	ASXY	>Yellow
2	>Align	XZ	>Yellow	ASXZ	>Yellow
3	>Align	YZ	>Yellow	ASYZ	>Yellow
4	>Done				

Table 10.1   Aligning the First Part to the Datum Planes

In Tutorial 10.2, you will read in the assembly similar to the file created in Tutorial 10.1. I have created a new file named Tut10-2a.asm for this purpose. This contains all of the datum planes. Make sure that the zoom factor is sufficiently zoomed out so that you can place the part such that it does not touch the datums. This way you will have an easy time selecting the datum planes for both the part and assembly. This is illustrated in Figure 10.8(a). Next, select >Component >Assemble to add a component to the assembly. Type in Gear_A as the part to add to the assembly. Move the mouse above and to the right of the datums and the gear is brought along with the mouse as shown in Figure 10.8(b). Click to place the view. Follow the procedure in Table 10.1 to fully constrain the gear. Once finished, save the assembly file using >Save As and name it Tut10-2b. The final alignment is shown in Figure 10.8(c).

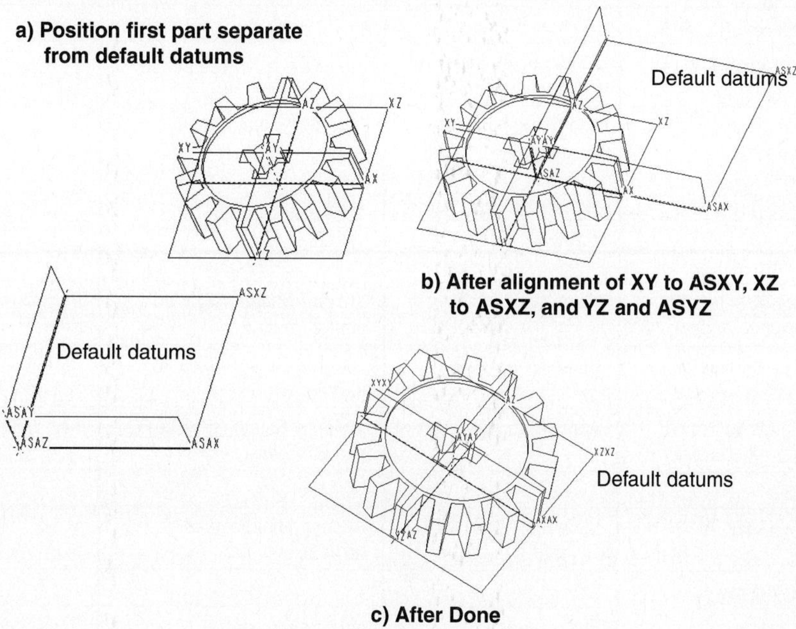

Figure 10.8   Illustration for Tutorial 10.2.

Tutorial 10.2 Placing a First Part

Files opened: Tut10-2a.asm   **Files saved:** Tut10-2b.asm
Big_Gear.prt

Step	Action	Description	Further Actions	Result
1	Click PT/Modeler Icon	Run PT/Modeler		After some time, PT/Modeler on screen
2	>Mode > Misc >Show Dir	Show current directory		Message similar to "Directory searched is c:\ptc\ptprod\bin"
3	>Change Dir	Change the current directory	Type **c:\proe\tutorial\ chapter_10**	
4	>Done-Return	Leave Misc menu		Misc menu removed
5	>Mode >Assembly >Retrieve	Retrieve an Assembly	Type **tut10-2a**	Assembly created
6	>Environment	Set up the environment	Set up checks as seen in Table T10.2 Column Step 6	
7	>Done-Return			
8	Ctrl Drag mLb up	Zoom out leaving room on the screen		
9	>Assembly >Component >Assemble	Add a component to the assembly	Type **Big_Gear**	
10	Move mouse above and to right of datums	Place part away from datums	mLb to place part	
11	>Align & Select XY on part & >Yellow	Align XY to ASXY	>Align & Select ASXY on part & >Yellow	Part aligned to ASXY
12	>Align & Select XZ on part & >Yellow	Align XZ to ASXZ	>Align & Select ASXZ on part & >Yellow	Part aligned to ASXZ
13	>Align & Select YZ on part & >Yellow	Align YZ to ASYZ	>Align & Select ASYZ on part & >Yellow	Part aligned to ASYZ
14	>Done			
15	>File >Save As	Save file	Accept tut10-2a, type **tut10-2b**	
16	QuitWindow			
17	Exit	Exit program	Click Yes to confirm	PT/Modeler exited

Item	Step 6
Disp DtmPln	Checked
Spin Center	No
Disp Pnts	No
Disp Axes	Checked
Rendering	No hidden line

Table T10.2 Environment Settings

10.5   **Saving an Assembly**

Saving an assembly can become a little complicated. Each assembly stores all of the components that it contains. You can modify a component within an assembly and this can create some problems. Suppose that you have an assembly named FIRST_ASSEM. In this assembly you place a component FIRST_COMPONENT. You save this assembly using the >File >Save command. Now suppose you want to save this assembly to another name, for example, SECOND_ASSEM using the >File >Save As command. You will be queried, indicating that you have a potential problem. The problem concerns the files in the working folder. A component named FIRST_COMPONENT already exists in this folder from the first save of FIRST_ASSEM. Using the >Save As command wants to save the FIRST_COMPONENT again. However, PT/Modeler understands that at some later time you might change some feature of FIRST_COMPONENT in one of your assemblies. If you do and both assemblies, FIRST_ASSEM and SECOND_ASSEM, use FIRST_COMPONENT, then the part will also change in the other assembly.

Heading off a potential problem, PT/Modeler will attempt to rename the component file during the second change to FIRST_COMPONENT. During the >File Save As, a Table Editor comes on the screen showing a spreadsheet of components in the assembly. You will see the FIRST_COMPONENT indicated there. You can change the name if you so desire.

If you save yet another assembly that uses FIRST_COMPONENT, an error will occur because the file FIRST_COMPONENT already exists in the folder. You are forced to change the name in the Table Editor.

> **TIP:** It is best to keep each assembly and all of its components in a separate folder if you plan on changing components.

The menu that appears when you perform a >Save As is shown in Figure 10.9. You can simply select >Done if you do not plan on changing the component. The components are renamed in this instance. However, be careful. If you modify a component, the component will be saved regardless of the components selected. They will be saved to the same name. Alternately, you can select any of the components through the check boxes or select all of the components.

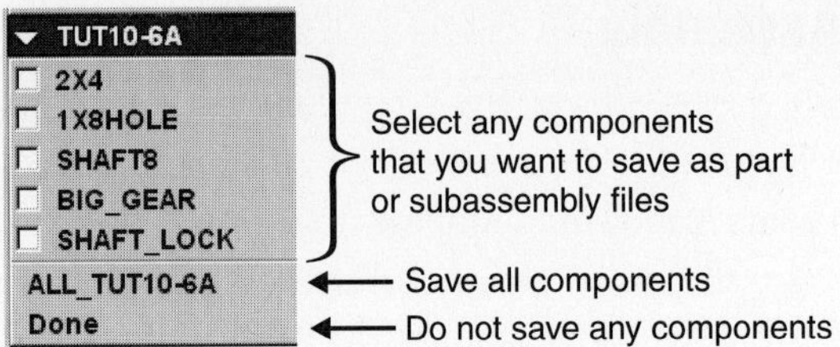

Figure 10.9   Save components with Assembly menu.

10.6   Selecting a Face, an Edge, or a Point

Before we begin with the placement discussion, be careful that you can place faces, edges, or points. If you select a face and you see a circle and cross hairs, the software has assumed that you want to constrain to a point. We will not be constraining to points in this chapter. Should you see a point highlight when you try to select a plane, begin the constraint again and select the face in a slightly different location to break the point assumption.

At times, you will get so confused that it is best to >Quit and replace the part from the >Assemble >Component level. The part you were placing is deleted and you can begin again.

After creating a constraint, the software will reposition the new part. At times, this repositioning might make it very difficult to select a face for a later constraint. It is best to Quit and reorder your constraints.

10.7   Overriding Constraints

You will often get into a situation where you have selected the wrong constraint or do not know what constraints are active. You can override a constraint by picking another restraint that conflicts. For example, suppose you first align the top face of a new part to the assembly's top face. Next, you align the top face of the part to the assembly front face. The system will query you indicating that you are about ready to override a constraint. You can confirm or cancel the new constraint.

There is nothing wrong with overwriting a constraint. You may enter the wrong offset value or enter an align, but really want an align offset. Simply redo the constraint and allow the override. Alternatively, you can click on the constraint in the component placement box and delete it.

10.8   Placing Components in the Assembly

There are several ways to constrain a new part into an assembly. Fortunately, you do not have to specify ax, ay, and az translations and rx, ry, and rz rotations. That would be very painful. The technique employed to place components takes advantage of the fact that components attach, in some manner, to each other. Therefore, you can place components into an assembly using surfaces of preexisting components. This makes the task a lot simpler. For example, you could specify the following:

- Make this new surface be coplanar with that existing surface (Align)
- Make this new face flat up against that face (Mate)
- Make this axis of this new part be co-axial with that axis on that existing part (Insert)
- Make this new face point in the same direction as that face (Orient)

You will use these four commands—Align, Mate, Insert, and Orient—to constrain the new component into the assembly. Mix and match these commands to reach the final goal of specifying each of the six degrees of freedom.

This process is very similar to picking a view using >Orientation. There you selected either TOP or BOTTOM, LEFT or RIGHT, FRONT or BACK to orient a part. In that case, you were orienting a part by constraining its three degrees of freedom rx, ry, and rz rotation angles. You did not need to worry about the positional translations ax, ay, and az since the part did not have to connect to any other parts.

It will take you considerable practice to master these commands. It is not that the commands are difficult; each is very simple as you will see. The difficult part is visualizing in three dimensions.

10.8.1   Align

The Align command forces two selected faces or planes to become coplanar. That is, each points in the same direction. Use Align when you want surfaces to line up. Align all of the front faces of tile to tile a wall. Note, alignment does not mean touching.

Following are several examples of an Align operation. Two blocks, big and small, are seen in Figure 10.10(a). The faces big A and small A are aligned in Figure 10.10(b). Observe that the two side faces happen to be coplanar. Perhaps the bottom faces are also aligned. In Figure 10.10(c), small B is aligned to big A. Small B in both boxes are aligned to big A in Figure 10.10(d). In Figure 10.10(e), the small B and big A alignment is broken, and the small C is aligned to big C. In Figure 10.10(f), big B is aligned to small D.

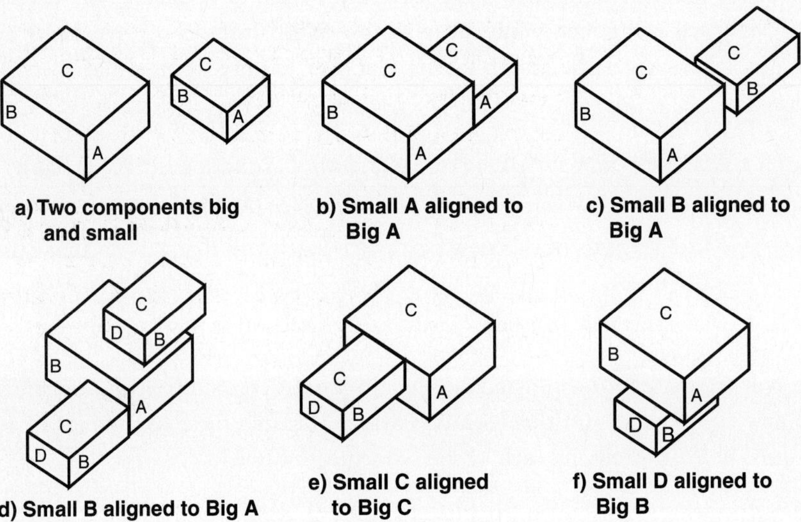

Figure 10.10   Aligning two faces.

10.8.2   Align Offset

There are times when you want two faces to point in the same direction, but not to be coplanar. This is demonstrated in Figure 10.11(a) where the A face of the small block is 10 positive units along the normal from the big Face A. The offset can be positive, as seen in Figure 10.11(a), or negative as you can observe in Figure 10.11(b). Positive is measured along the direction of the surface normal of the face being aligned to, in this case, the Big A. To repeat, Align Offset faces are not coplanar. However, the distance is specified in the constraint.

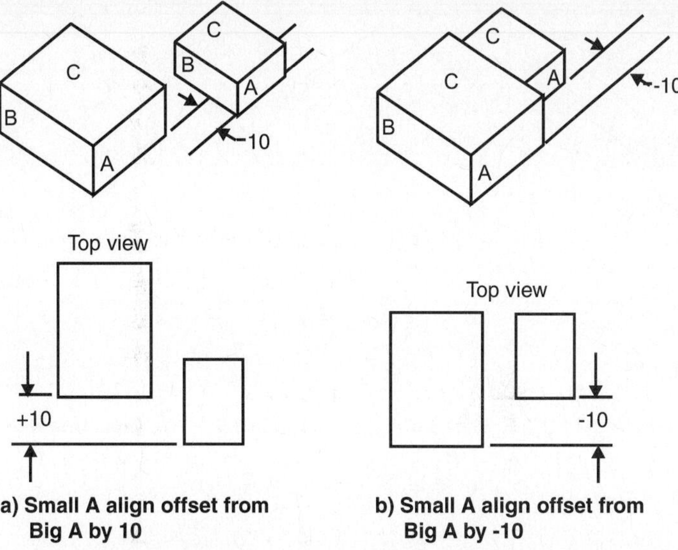

a) Small A align offset from Big A by 10

b) Small A align offset from Big A by -10

Figure 10.11   Offset aligning two faces.

10.8.3   Mate

Mate is the exact opposite of Alignment. When mating two surfaces, the faces point toward each other while both faces remain coplanar. You would mate two wood surfaces to glue them but not necessarily with edges coincident.

In Figure 10.12(a), small face E is mated to big Face E. The two faces point in opposite directions and are coplanar. In Figure 10.12(b), the small face E is mated to the Big face A. They are not touching, but both are coplanar and point in opposite directions. In Figure 10.12(c), small G is mated to big B. They are partially touching.

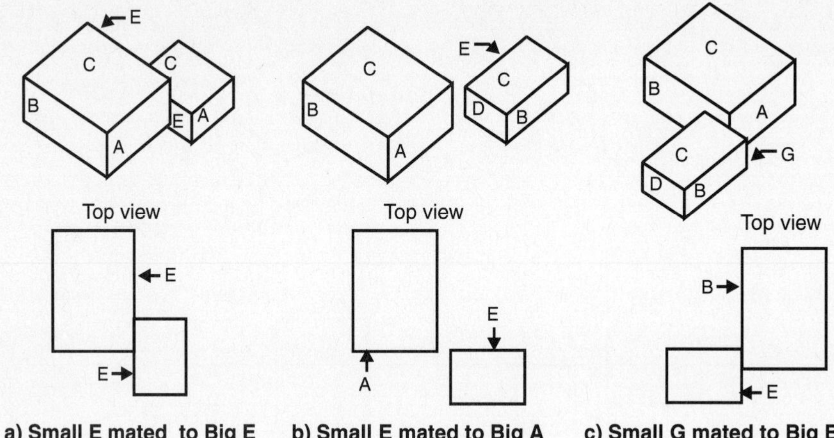

a) Small E mated to Big E   b) Small E mated to Big A   c) Small G mated to Big B

Figure 10.12   Mating two faces.

10.8.4   Mate Offset

Mate Offset is the exact opposite of Align Offset. Mate Offset is used when you want two faces to point in opposite directions but not line up in a 3D space. The offset can be positive, as seen in Figure 10.13(a), or negative as seen in Figure 10.13(b). Positive is measured along the direction of the surface normal of the face being aligned to, in this case, the Big A. As you can see, Mate Offset faces are not coplanar.

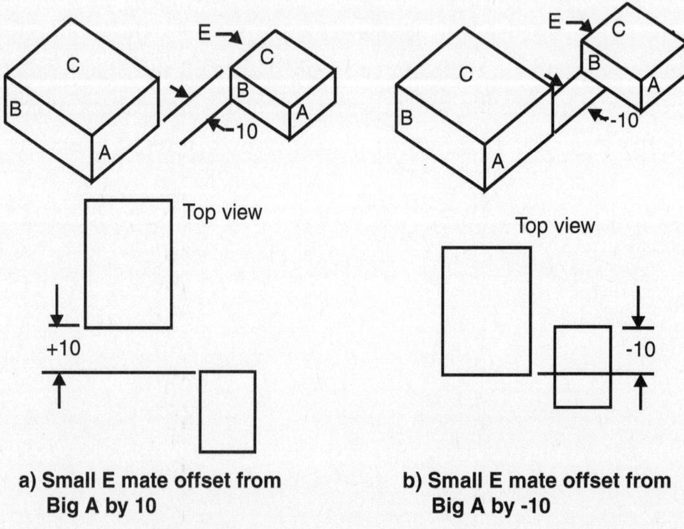

a) Small E mate offset from   b) Small E mate offset from
Big A by 10   Big A by -10

Figure 10.13   Offset Mating two faces.

10.8.5   Mate and Align Tutorial

The basic shape of the blocks that you will be using in this tutorial is shown in Figure 10.14(a). Refer to this figure to see the top, side, or bottom of a part.

In Tutorial 10.3 you will start by reading in a preexisting assembly that contains a 2x4 edge part and place a 2x4 part command. This is shown in Figure 10.14(b).

As seen in Figure 10.14(b), first, align the top of the 2x4 part to the top of the existing 2x4 edge part as indicated by align1. Next, mate the sides of the parts, indicated by mate1. Lastly, align the fronts of the parts, indicated by align2. This constrains the part. Select >Done to finish. The resultant assembly is shown in Figure 10.14(c).

Next, use >Assemble to read in a 2x8 part. We want to position this part on top of the 2x4 part. First, mate the bottom of the 2x8 part with the top of the 2x4 edge part. This is accomplished by >Mate, selecting the bottom of the 2x8 and selecting the top of the 2x4 edge. This is an important first step because, if you perform the other two alignments first, the bottom of the 2x8 block will be difficult to reach, so use the Query Sel. When selecting the top face, it does not matter which 2x4 you chose because both faces are coplanar. Continuing on, align the fronts of the parts as shown in Figure 10.14(d).

Now we want to position the 2x8 such that it connects to both of the 2x4 parts. To accomplish this task, we will use the >Align Offset command. Select both side faces marked by offalign in Figure 10.14(d). An arrow shows the direction of the alignment. If the arrow points into the part, as shown in Figure 10.14(e), type 50. We are entering 50 because that is the width of one row of bumps. If the arrow points away from the part, enter −50. The arrow indicates the direction of the offset. If the arrow points in, then a positive offset means that the new face will be farther in to the assembly in the direction of the arrow. You can never be sure which way the arrows will point, so look at each one.

> **TIP:** The number 50 is an important offset number to remember with these blocks. One row of bumps is 50 units. A block with two rows would be 100 units wide, and so on.

The three constraints satisfy the placement and you can select >Done. The resultant assembly is shown in Figure 10.14(f). The last part we will add is another 2x4 edge part. Use >Assemble to load the part. Mate the bottom of the new 2x4 edge to the top of the 2x8 and then align the front faces as shown in Figures 10.14(g) and (h). Use an offset align to position the side of the 2x4 edge 50 units out from the side of the 2x8. This could have been accomplished using an align to the lower 2x4 edge.

However, I want you to practice using the trickier >Align Offset. The final part is shown in Figure 10.14(i). Save the assembly.

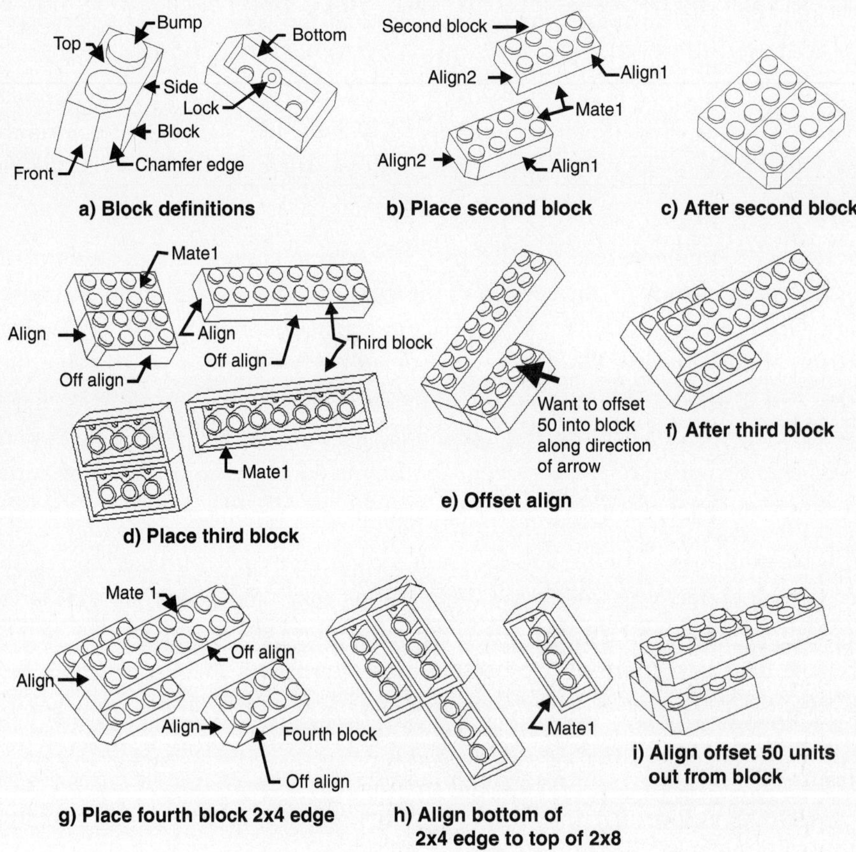

Figure 10.14 Illustration for Tutorial 10.3.

Tutorial 10.3   Aligning and Mating

Files opened: Tut10-3a.asm
      2x8.prt
      2x4edge.prt

Files saved: Tut10-3b.asm

Step	Action	Description	Further Actions	Result
1	Click PT/Modeler Icon	Run PT/Modeler		After some time, PT/Modeler on screen
2	>Mode >Misc >Show Dir	Show current directory		Message similar to "Directory searched is c:\ptc\ptprod\bin"
3	>Change Dir	Change the current directory	Type **c:\proe\tutorial\ chapter_10**	
4	>Done-Return	Leave Misc menu		Misc menu removed
5	>Mode >Assembly >Retrieve	Retrieve an assembly	Type **tut10-3a**	Assembly created
6	>Environment	Set up the environment	Set up checks as seen in Table T10.3 Column Step 6	
7	>Done-Return			
8	Ctrl Drag mLb up	Zoom out leaving room on the screen		
9	>Assembly >Component >Assemble	Add a component to the assembly	Type **2x4 edge**	
10	Move mouse above and to right of datums	Place part away from datums	mLb to place part	
11	>Align & select top of 2x4	Put new part to side of old part	Select top of 2x4 edge as in Fig. 10.14(a)	Tops aligned
12	>Align & select side of 2x4	Align side	Select side of 2x4 edge as in Fig. 10.14(a)	Part aligned to side
13	>Align & select front of 2x4	Align front	Select front of 2x4 edge as in Fig. 10.14(a)	Part fully constrained in Figure 10.14(c)
14	>Done			
15	>Component >Assemble	Add a component to the assembly	Type **2x8**	
16	Move mouse above and to right of datums	Place part away from datums	mLb to place part	
17	>Mate & select bottom of 2x8	Put new part on top of old part	Select top of 2x4 edge or 2x4 as in Fig. 10.14(d)	Tops aligned
18	>Align & select front of 2x8	Align fronts	Select front of 2x4 edge as in Fig. 10.14(d)	Part aligned to front
19	>Align Offset & select side of 2x8	Align offset side	Select side of 2x4 edge as in Fig. 10.14(d)	

Tutorial 10.3   Aligning and Mating (continued)

Step	Action	Description	Further Actions	Result
20	Type 50 if arrow points in, −50 if arrow points out	Want new face to be 50 units in from old face		Part fully constrained in Figure 10.14(f)
21	>Done			
22	>Component >Assemble	Add a component to the assembly	Type **2x4 edge**	
23	Move mouse above and to right of datums	Place part away from datums	mLb to place part	
24	>Mate & select bottom of 2x4edge	Put new part on top of old part	Select top of 2x8	Tops aligned
25	>Align & select front of 2x4edge	Align fronts	Select front of 2x8	Part aligned to front
26	>Align Offset & select side of 2x4edge	Align offset side	Select side of 2x8	
27	Type 50 if arrow points out, −50 if arrow points in	Want new face to be 50 units out from old face		Part fully constrained in Figure 10.14(i)
28	>Done			
29	>File >Save As	Save file	Accept tut10-3a, type **tut10-3b**	
30	QuitWindow			
31	Exit	Exit program	Click Yes to confirm	PT/Modeler exited

Item	Step 6
Disp DtmPln	No
Spin Center	No
Disp Pnts	No
Disp Axes	No
Rendering	No hidden line

Table T10.3   Environment Settings

10.8.6   Orient

Orient is similar to an align offset but without a specified amount of offset. It specifies that two surfaces are parallel and face the same direction. No information is specified regarding the distance between these surfaces. In Figure 10.15(a), faces big C and small C can be oriented such that the faces are parallel. In Figure 10.15(b), a partial revolved protrusion has a face A that can be readily oriented to the top face

B of the block. This is a very useful feature when you want to orient two partially revolved features. An excellent example of using Orient, as contrasted to Align, is demonstrated in Tutorial 10.7.

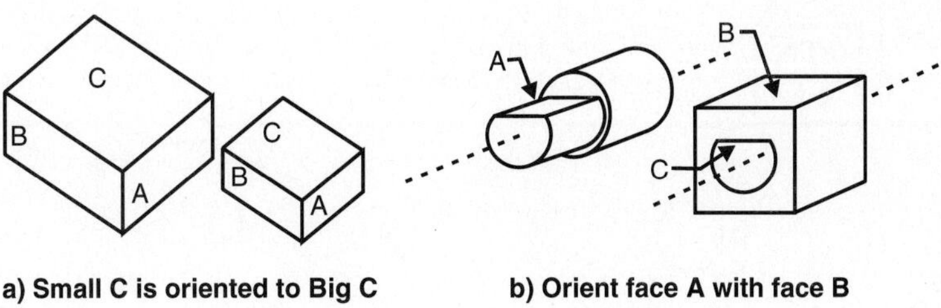

a) Small C is oriented to Big C   **b) Orient face A with face B**

Figure 10.15   Orient two faces.

10.8.7   Insert

Insert makes two axes of revolution coaxial. You always select rounded surfaces when using Insert. This is most commonly used to insert a shaft into a hole as seen in Figure 10.16(a). The two objects might be partially revolved as seen in Figure 10.16(b). Insert is often combined with Orient during placement of revolved parts. In Figure 10.16(b), we want to insert the shaft into the cube. To accomplish this, use Insert and select A_1 and A_2. This makes A_1 and A_2 coaxial. However, this does not determine whether the flat section of the shaft is oriented to the flat opening in the hole. Using Orient on both faces A and B performs this task nicely. A datum plane could be constructed if no face was parallel to the flat face in the hole. As a last constraint, Mate faces C and D to fully constrain the two parts.

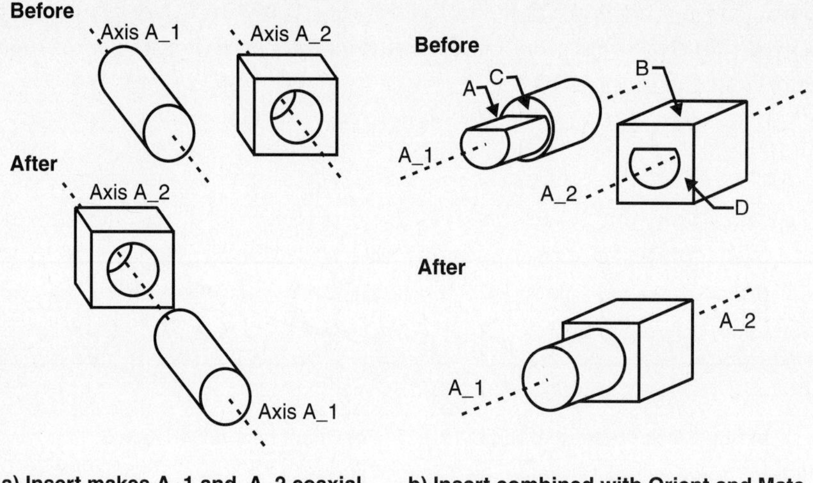

Figure 10.16   Insert two faces.

10.8.8   Orient and Insert Tutorial

Let's begin Tutorial 10.4 by reading in the preexisting assembly tut10-4a. This assembly consists of a single 2x4 component. Load a 1x8 hole part. The details of this part are shown in Figures 10.17(a) and (b). Mate the bottom of the 1x8 hole to the top of the 2x4. Align the end of the 1x8 hole with the side face of the 2x4 marked align1. Align the side with holes, align2, in the 1x8 with the edge face or the 2x4 marked align2. This constrains the part as seen in Figure 10.17(c).

Next, load another 2x4 using the >Assemble command. This time mate the top surface of the new 2x4 to the bottom surface of the 1x8 with holes. Align the side of the 2x4 to the small end of the 1x8. Align the front of the 2x4 with the side with holes of the 1x8. The result is shown in Figure 10.17(d).

Now comes the fun part. Load the part shaft8 using >Assemble. Note the detail of the shaft in Figure 10.17(e). The shaft consists of a section that has a revolved surface, a circle, with four protrusions out the sides. We will be assembling this part into the third hole as marked in Figure 10.17(d). First, offset align the end of the shaft with the surface of the 1x8 holes as seen in Figure 10.17(e). If the arrow points out, as in Figure 10.17(f), this indicates that the end of the shaft will protrude from the 1x8 holes face. This is what we want; therefore, enter 60. If the arrow points in the opposite direction, enter –60. Now, use the >Insert command. Carefully select the revolved surface portion of the shaft as seen in Figure 10.17(e). Next, select the inside surface of the third hole from the left. This inserts the shaft. We have not constrained the rotation about the shaft axis. What happens? Well, the default orientation of the shaft has the AY axis pointing upwards. This will be accepted and is fine for now. Later we will see that we do not want to accept the default orientation, and we will constrain the rotation by using the Orient command. Now fully constrained, the shaft is shown in Figure 10.17(g).

At this time we will place a gear on the shaft. Use >Assemble to bring in the part big_gear as seen in Figure 10.17(h). Note the same cut-out pattern. The surface of revolution is the inner curve. Use this for the insert operation along with the same circular surface on the shaft. The flat edge of the protruding cut will be used to orient the part to the same flat edge on the shaft. First, >Insert the revolved surface of the gear onto the revolved surface of the shaft. Next, >Orient the flat surface of the gear cut-out to the flat edge of the shaft.

As you provide a constraint, the software will reposition the new part to reflect the new constraint. In this instance, the first two constraints place the gear on the shaft but on the wrong side of the 1x8 as seen in Figure 10.17(i). This is not a problem. The next constraint will place it correctly. Align offset the face of the gear with the end of the shaft. We want the gear to be situated 25 units in on the shaft. This constrains the gear on the shaft as seen in Figure 10.17(j).

The last part is named shaft_lock as seen in Figure 10.17(k). Use >Assemble to bring this into the assembly. Once again, orient the flat surface of the shaft cut-out with the flat surface of the shaft and insert the revolved surface of the cut-out onto the revolved surface of the shaft. Finally, align any of the protruding faces of the shaft_lock onto the outside surface of the gear. This constrains the part as done in Figure 10.17(l).

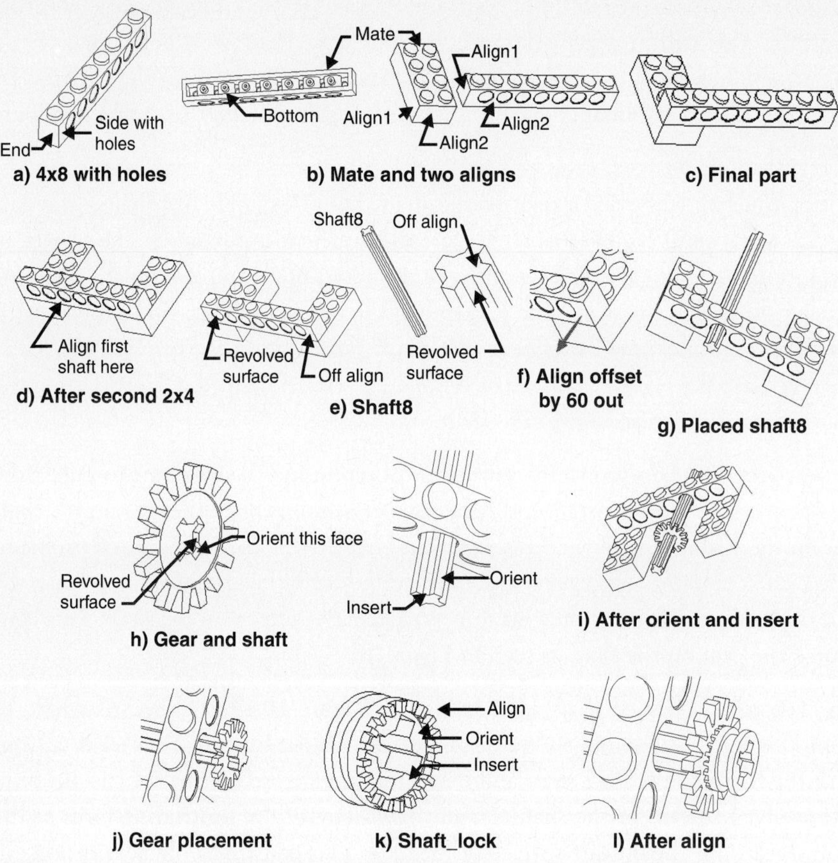

Figure 10.17 Illustration for Tutorial 10.4.

Tutorial 10.4   Orienting and Inserting a Part

Files opened: Tut10-4a.asm
                    1x8 hole
                    2x4
                    shaft8
                    big_gear
                    shaft_lock

Files saved: Tut10-4b.asm

Step	Action	Description	Further Actions	Result
1	Click PT/Modeler Icon	Run PT/Modeler		After some time, PT/Modeler on screen
2	>Mode >Misc >Show Dir	Show current directory		Message similar to "Directory searched is c:\ptc\ptprod\bin"
3	>Change Dir	Change the current directory	Type **c:\proe\tutorial\chapter_10**	
4	>Done-Return	Leave Misc menu		Misc menu removed
5	>Mode >Assembly >Retrieve	Retrieve an assembly	Type **tut10-4a**	Assembly created
6	>Environment	Set up the environment	Set up checks as seen in Table T10.4 Column Step 6	
7	>Done-Return			
8	>Assembly >Component >Assemble	Add a component to the assembly	Type **1x8hole**	
9	Move mouse above and to right of datums	Place part away from datums	mLb to place part	
10	>Mate & select bottom of 1x8 hole	Put new part on top of old part	Select top of 2x4 in Fig.10.17(b)	Tops aligned
11	>Align & select side of 1x8 hole	Align end of 1x8 hole with side of 2x4	Select side of 2x4 marked align1 in Fig.10.17(b)	Part aligned to side
12	>Align & select front of 1x8 hole	Align side of 1x8 hole with end of 2x4	Select end of 2x4 marked align2 in Fig.10.17(b)	Part fully constrained in Fig. 10.17(c)
13	>Done			
14	>Component >Assemble	Add a component to the assembly	Type **2x4**	
15	Move mouse above and to right of datums	Place part away from datums	mLb to place part	
16	>Mate & select top of 2x4	Put new part on top of old part	Select bottom of 2x8 hole in Fig.10.17(d)	
17	>Align & select side of 2x4	Align side	Select open end of 2x8 hole in Fig.10.17(d)	Part aligned to side
18	>Align & select front of 2x4	Align fronts	Select side with holes of 2x8 hole in Fig.10.17(d)	Part fully constrained in Figure 10.17d

Tutorial 10.4   Orienting and Inserting a Part (continued)

Step	Action	Description	Further Actions	Result
19	>Done			
20	>Component >Assemble	Add a component to the assembly	Type **shaft8**	
21	Move mouse above and to right of datums	Place part away from datums	mLb to place part	
22	>Align Offset & select end of shaft	Align shaft end	Select side with holes of 2x8 in Fig.10.17(e)	
23	Type 60 if arrow points out, −60 if arrow points in	Want shaft to extend 60 units out from face in Fig.10.17(f)		
24	>Insert & select revolved surface of shaft	Insert	Select third hole from left in Fig.10.17(g)	Shaft in hole
25	>Done			
26	>Component >Assemble	Add a component to the assembly	Type **big_gear**	
27	Move mouse above and to right of datums	Place part away from datums	mLb to place part	
28	>Insert & select revolved face on gear	Insert gear on shaft	Select revolved face on shaft in Fig.10.17(i)	
29	>Orient & select flat face on gear	Orient gear on shaft	Select flat face on shaft in Fig.10.17(i)	
30	>Align Offset & select face of gear	Align shaft end	Select face of shaft in Fig.10.17(i)	
31	Type 25 if arrow points out, −25 if arrow points in	Want gear to extend 25 units onto shaft		
32	>Done			Part seen in Fig. 10.17j.
33	>Component >Assemble	Add a component to the assembly	Type **shaft_lock**	
34	Move mouse above and to right of datums	Place part away from datums	mLb to place part	
35	>Mate & select outer face of teeth	Mate shaft_lock to gear	Select outer face of gear in Fig. 10.17(k)	
36	>Orient & select flat face on shaft_lock	Orient shaft_lock on shaft	Select flat face on shaft in Fig. 10.17(k)	
37	>Insert & select centerline of shaft_lock	Align shaft and shaft_lock	Select centerline of shaft in Fig. 10.17(k)	

Tutorial 10.4   Orienting and Inserting a Part (continued)

Step	Action	Description	Further Actions	Result
38	>Done			Part seen in Fig. 10.17(I)
39	>File >Save As	Save file	Accept tut10-4a, type **tut10-4b**	
40	QuitWindow			
41	Exit	Exit program	Click Yes to confirm	PT/Modeler exited

Item	Step 6
Disp DtmPln	No
Spin Center	No
Disp Pnts	No
Disp Axes	No
Rendering	No hidden line

Table T10. 4   Environment Settings

10.9   Redefining Constraints

It is very easy to make mistakes while constraining components in assemblies. These mistakes might be due to poor planing or just due to picking a wrong face. It is worthwhile to spend some time looking at how to fix a mistake. In the >Component menu shown in Figure 10.5(a), you will find a Redefine command. From this menu, you can redefine the set of constraints that place a component. The Redefine menu is shown in Figure 10.18(a). From this menu, you can add, delete, or redo a constraint.

When you select >Redefine, you are requested to select the component in the assembly that you wish to redefine. Once selected, a Component Placement window is displayed as seen in Figure 10.18(b). This window provides the Type of placement constraint for each constraint associated with the component. In Figure 10.18(b), you can see that the first constraint is an Orient, the second is an Insert, and the third is a Mate Offset. You have to select one of these constraints in order to perform a delete or redo. Select the constraint by clicking on it in the Component Placement window.

Suppose that you want to redo a constraint. Select the Redo item. Another menu appears with a set of checkboxes. This menu is shown in Figure 10.18(c). From here you can select the Type check box. By checking Type, you are able to reselect the *type* of constraint, that is, mate, align, insert. If you select Mate Offset or Align Offset, you will be asked to enter the new offset. Take note; the default value provided in the Offset query is always [0.00] and not the old value. You can see the old value in the Component Placement Window. Once specified the component is reconstrained and you can Cancel or Confirm the change.

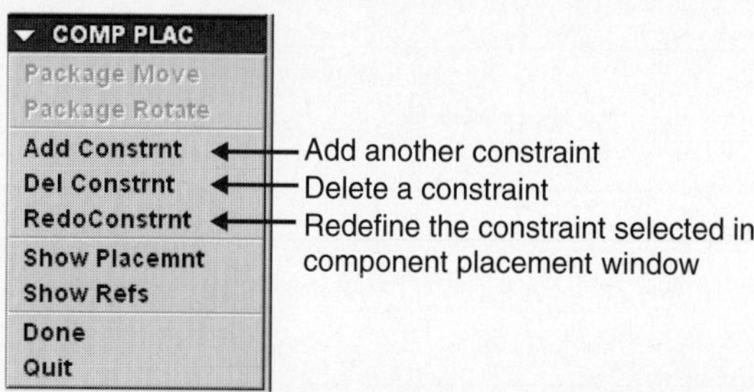

a) Constraint redefinition options for constraint selected above

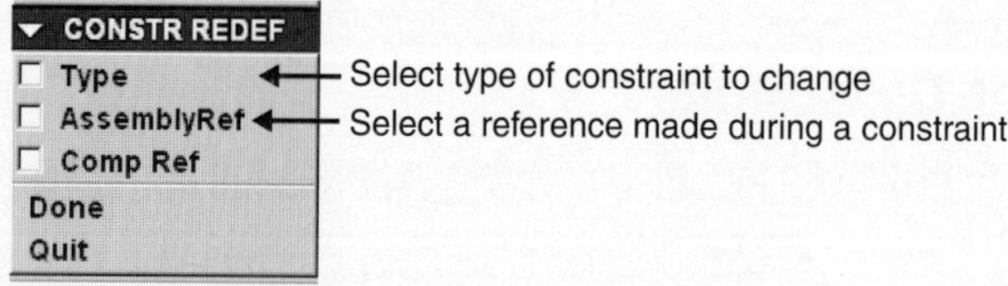

b) Component placement window

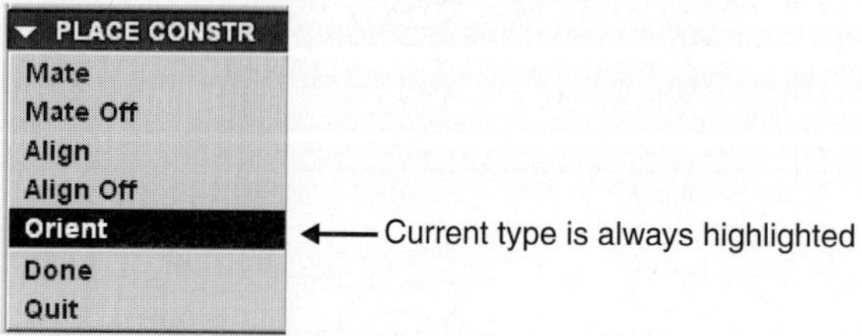

c) Action to take if Redo Constrnt selected above

d) Redefine the type of constraint

Figure 10.18   Component Placement window and Redefine menus.

10.9.1   Redefine Tutorial

In Tutorial 10.5, we will fix a problem that we created by placing the gear too close to the end of the shaft. If you look at Figure 10.17(l), you can see that the shaft_lock is only partially engaging the shaft. The shaft_lock is aligned to the gear; consequently, we need to move the gear farther up onto the shaft. The gear was constrained to the 4x8_with_holes using a Mate Offset. The offset value determines the distance from the end of the shaft. Originally this was specified as –25. We will change it to –35. At that location, the shaft_lock will fit perfectly.

> **NOTE:** This is only an example demonstrating how to redefine a constraint. It would have been better practice to place the shaft_lock onto the shaft before placing the gear if we knew that we wanted the shaft_lock to align perfectly with the end of the shaft. There is no physical constraint here. We could put the shaft in the 1x8, put the shaft lock on the shaft, and put the gear in between the two.

Start the tutorial by loading Tut10-5a. This contains the output from Tutorial 10.4. Select >Component >Redefine and select the gear component. A Component Placement window appears providing the types of constraints preformed for the selected gear component. Select the #3 Mate Offset constraint; it is highlighted.

From the next menu, select >Redo Constraint and check the Type box. This allows you to respecify the type of constraint and, in this case, the offset value. The >Mate Offset item is highlighted since it was the type of constraint. Keep this, selecting >Done. A query requests the new offset value. Enter –35 and >Done again. Confirm the change, observe the change, and save the assembly as Tut10-5b. Notice that by moving the gear, the shaft_lock also moved to its new position. This is caused by the alignment of the shaft_lock to the gear_face. This is one of the most powerful features of the PT/Modeler software.

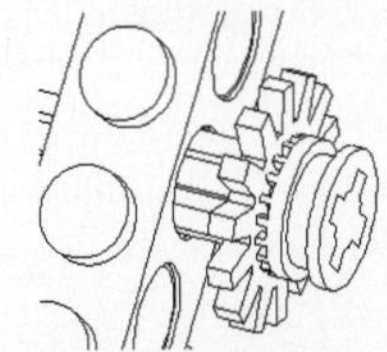

Figure 10.19   Illustration for Tutorial 10.5.

Tutorial 10.5 Redefining a Constraint

Files opened: Tut10-5a.asm
unit_straight
unit_corner

Files saved: Tut10-5b.asm
unit_corner_length
unit_half_plan

Step	Action	Description	Further Actions	Result
1	Click PT/Modeler Icon	Run PT/Modeler		After some time, PT/Modeler on screen
2	>Mode >Misc >Show Dir	Show current directory		Message similar to "Directory searched is c:\ptc\ptprod\bin"
3	>Change Dir	Change the current directory	Type **c:\proe\tutorial\ chapter_10**	
4	>Done-Return	Leave Misc menu		Misc menu removed
5	>Mode >Assembly > Retrieve	Retrieve an assembly	Type **tut10-5a**	Assembly created
6	>Environment	Set up the environment	Set up checks as seen in Table T10.5 Column Step 6	
7	>Done-Return			
8	>Assembly >Component >Redefine	Redefine the gear mate offset constraint	Select the gear part	Component Placement window appears showing constraints
9	Click on 3 Mate Offset	Select the mate offset		Constraint #3 is highlighted with a box
10	>Redo Constraint	Want to redo the constraint	Check Type checkbox >Done	
11	Keep Type at Mate Offset	Mate offset is okay	>Done	
12	Type **–35**	Change offset to –35	>Done	Part gets reconstrained in assembly
13	>File >Save As	Save file	**Enter** to accept tut10-5a, type **tut10-5b**	
14	QuitWindow			
15	Exit	Exit program	Click Yes to confirm	PT/Modeler exited

Item	Step 6
Disp DtmPln	No
Spin Center	No
Disp Pnts	No
Disp Axes	No
Rendering	No hidden line

Table T10.5 Environment Settings

10.10 Subassemblies

A component placed into an assembly can be a part or a subassembly. Subassemblies are placed into assemblies in exactly the same way that you place parts. As you create an assembly, you can perform >Save As to save the state of the assembly, and go on to reload this back into the assembly as a subassembly. This is illustrated in the next tutorial.

10.10.1 Building Block Tutorial

In Tutorial 10.6, you will build three layers of a wall using 2x4 blocks. Start with a blank assembly, Tut10-6a, that contains named datum planes. Remember that all new assemblies should have default datum planes as the first component. Read in the unit_length.asm subassembly using >Component >Assemble as seen in Figure 10.20(a) and align all datum planes. Note that both the tut10-6a assembly and the unit_length assembly now have ASXY, ASXZ, and ASYZ datum plane names.

Next, read in the unit_corner.asm subassembly using >Assemble as seen in Figure 10.20(b). Perform three aligns marked align1, align2, and align3 as illustrated in Figures 10.20(a) and (b). This produces the assembly in Figure 10.20(c). Use >Save As to save this to unit_corner_length. Make sure to select >Done since we do not have to save any of the individual parts as separate files. We will not be altering any of the parts.

Read in the unit_corner_length.asm subassembly that you have just created using >Component >Assemble. Perform a mate1, align2, and align3 as illustrated in Figure 10.20(d). This produces the assembly in Figure 10.20(e). Use >Save As to save this to unit_half_plan.

Now, repeat this process one more time. Read in the unit_half_plan.asm subassembly that you just saved using >Component >Assemble. Perform a mate1, align2, and align3 as illustrated in Figure 10.20(f). This produces the final assembly in Figure 10.20(g). Use >Save As to save this to tut10-6b.

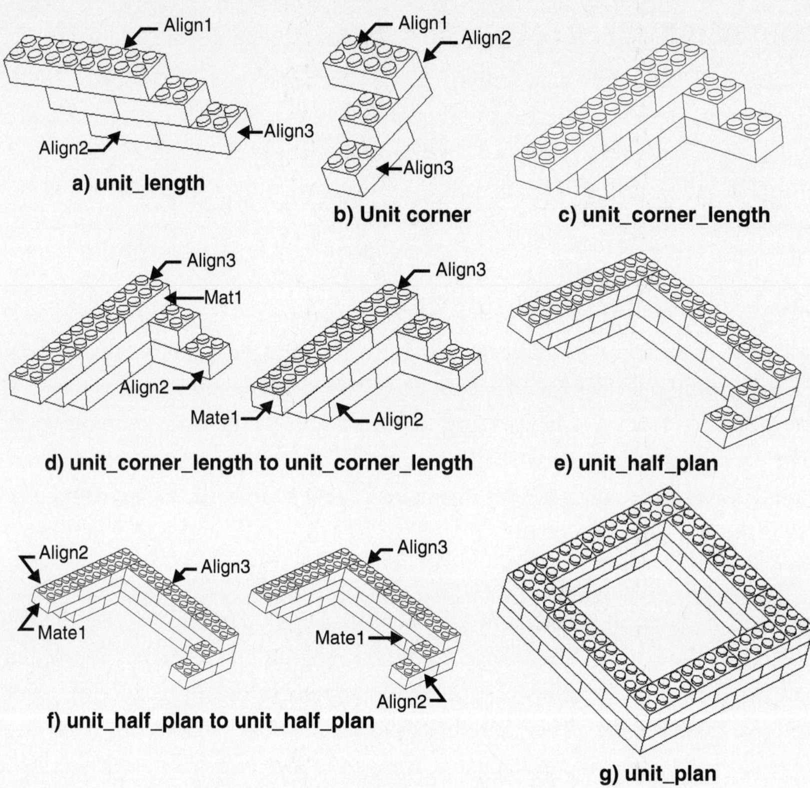

Figure 10.20 Illustrations for Tutorial 10.6.

Tutorial 10.6 Building a Subassembly

Files opened: Tut10-6a.asm
unit_length.asm
unit_corner.asm

Files saved: unit_corner_length
unit_half_plan
Tut10-6b.asm

Step	Action	Description	Further Actions	Result
1	Click PT/Modeler Icon	Run PT/Modeler		After some time, PT/Modeler on screen
2	>Mode >Misc >Show Dir	Show current directory		Message similar to "Directory searched is c:\ptc\ptprod\bin"
3	>Change Dir	Change the current directory	Type **c:\proe\tutorial\ chapter_10**	
4	>Done-Return	Leave Misc menu		Misc menu removed
5	>Mode >Assembly >Retrieve	Retrieve an assembly	Type **tut10-6a**	Assembly created
6	>Environment	Set up the environment	Set up checks in Table T10.6 Column Step 6	
7	>Done-Return			
8	>Component >Assemble	Add a subassembly	Type **unit_straight** then click to place component	Make sure to check Disp Dtm Plane in >Environment
9	>Align & select ASAX datum plane of assembly then >Yellow	Align datums of assembly to datums of unit_straight component	Select ASXY of unit_straight component then >Yellow	
10	>Align & select ASXZ datum plane of assembly then >Yellow	Align datums of assembly to datums of unit_straight component	Select ASXZ of unit_straight component then >Yellow	
11	>Align & select ASYZ datum plane of assembly then >Yellow	Align datums of assembly to datums of unit_straight component	Select ASYZ of unit_straight component then >Yellow	
12	>Done			Unit_length aligned to datum planes
13	>Environment	Set up the environment	Set up checks in Table T10.6 Column Step 13	Make sure to uncheck Disp Dtm Plane in >Environment
14	>Component >Assemble	Add a subassembly	Type **unit_corner**	
15	> Align & select end of unit_corner	Align1 as Figs. 10.20(a), (b)	Select inner side of top block	Units mated
16	>Align & select side of unit_corner	Align2 as Figs. 10.20(a), (b)	Select side of unit_corner	Part aligned to side
17	>Align & select top of unit_corner	Align3 as Figs. 10.20(a), (b)	Select top of unit_corner	Part fully constrained in Figure 10.20(c)
18	>Done			

Tutorial 10.6 Building a Subassembly (continued)

Step	Action	Description	Further Actions	Result
19	>File >Save As	Save this	Enter to accept [tut10-6a], type **unit_corner_length**	
20	Check ALL_TUT10-6A	Save entire assembly	>Done	
21	>Component >Assemble	Add a subassembly	Type **unit_corner_length**	
22	>Mate & select end of unit_corner_length	Mate 1 as Fig 10.20(d)	Select inner side of top block of unit_corner_length	Units mated
23	>Align & select side of unit_corner_length	Align2 as Fig 10.20(d)	Select side of unit_corner_length	Part aligned to side
24	>Align & select top of unit_corner_length	Align3 as Fig 10.20(d)	Select top of unit_corner_length	Part fully constrained in Figure 10.20(e)
25	>Done			
26	>File >Save As	Save this	Enter to accept [tut10-6a], type **unit_half_plan** then >Done	
27	>Component >Assemble	Add a subassembly	Type **unit_half_plan**	
28	>Mate & select end of unit_half_plan	Mate 1 as Fig 10.20(f)	Select inner side of top block of unit_half_plan	Units mated
29	>Align & select side of unit_half_plan	Align2 as Fig 10.20(f)	Select side of unit_half_plan	Part aligned to side
30	>Align & select top of unit_half_plan	Align3 as Fig 10.20(f)	Select top of unit_half_plan	Part fully constrained in Figure 10.20(g)
31	>Done			
32	>File >Save As	Save this as tut10-6b	Enter to accept [tut10-6a], type **tut10-6b** then >Done	
33	QuitWindow			
34	Exit	Exit program	Click Yes to confirm	PT/Modeler exited

Item	Step 6	Step 13
Disp DtmPln	Checked	No
Spin Center	No	No
Disp Pnts	No	No
Disp Axes	No	No
Rendering	No hidden line	No hidden line

Table T10.6   Environment Settings

10.10.2   Gear Shaft Tutorial

In Tutorial 10.7, you will be adding a subassembly that consists of a shaft, gear, and shaft lock, to a subassembly that contains some blocks, a shaft, gear, and shaft lock. This is seen in Figure 10.21(a) and Figure 10.21(b). The goal of this tutorial is to insert the second shaft into the first subassembly such that the gears mesh.

Start by loading the subassembly, Tut10-7a. Read in the gear_shaft subassembly using >Component >Assemble. First, align the front faces of both gears as align1 in Figures 10.21(a) and (b). Next, insert the shaft using the revolved surface of the shaft and the hole indicated by insert2 in Figures 10.21(a) and (b). We now have what looks like a meaningful relationship. But there is a problem: the teeth of the two gears collide as can be seen in Figure 10.21(c). We will solve this problem using the Orient constraint.

Figure 10.21(d) shows that the big_gear part has a datum plane called DTM2. This datum plane was designed specifically for the purpose of meshing this gear. There are 16 teeth to this gear; therefore, every tooth is separated by 360/16 = 22.5 degrees. If both of the gears are aligned such that their YZ axis is vertical, the teeth will collide since both use the same big_gear part; thus, a new plane is necessary. The datum DTM2 was designed to be at an angle of 11.25 degrees from the YZ plane and centered between two teeth.

As the third constraint, >Orient the DTM2 plane to the horizontal face of the subassembly. This produces the final assembly in Figure 10.21(e). As you can see, the teeth mesh perfectly. Picking DTM2 is not as easy as it might seem. There are a good number of datum planes so when they are enabled for display, it can be tricky to Query Sel DTM2. A better technique is to use the >Sel by Menu command. By choosing >Sel by Menu, you are instructing the software to find a plane to orient. The next submenu that appears requests that you select the component that contains this plane. Click on the gear_shaft component. Next, respond with >Datum to limit the choices to a datum plane, >Name, to choose the datum plane by name, and finally DTM2. Accept the yellow side. At this point, pick a horizontal face on the main subassembly. Choose any horizontal face as seen in Figure 10.7(a). Use >Save As to save this to tut10-7b.

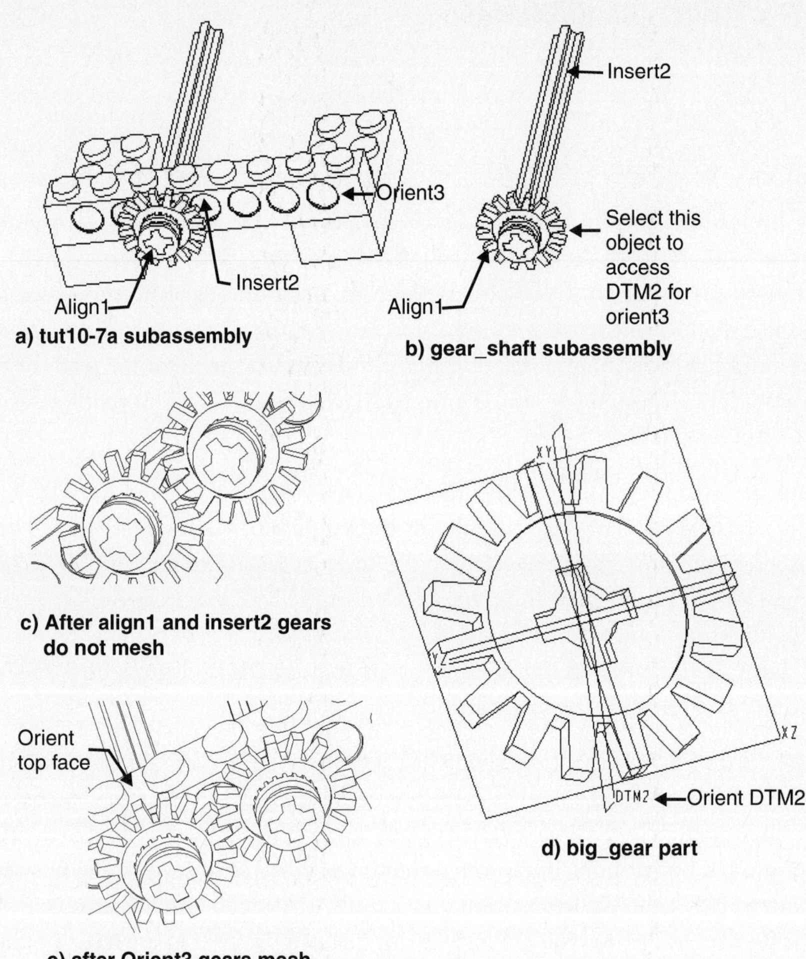

Figure 10.21 Illustrations for Tutorial 10.6.

Tutorial 10.7 Building a Subassembly

Files opened: Tut10-7a.asm   **Files saved:** Tut10-7b.asm
gear-shaft.asm

Step	Action	Description	Further Actions	Result
1	Click PT/Modeler Icon	Run PT/Modeler		After some time, PT/Modeler on screen
2	>Mode >Misc >Show Dir	Show current directory		Message similar to "Directory searched is c:\ptc\ptprod\bin"
3	>Change Dir	Change the current directory	Type **c:\proe\tutorial\ chapter_10**	
4	>Done-Return	Leave Misc menu		Misc menu removed
5	>Mode >Assembly >Retrieve	Retrieve an assembly	Type **tut10-7a**	Assembly created
6	>Environment	Set up the environment	Set up checks as seen in Table T10.7 Column Step 6	
7	>Done-Return			
8	>Component >Assemble	Add a subassembly	Type **gear_shaft**	
9	>Align & select front face of gear in gear_shaft	Align 1 as Figs. 10.21(a), (b)	Select front face of gear in assembly	Units mated
10	>Insert & select revolved surface of shaft in gear_shaft	Insert2 as Figs. 10.21(a), (b)	Select revolved surface of hole in assembly	Part aligned to side but gears mesh as in Fig. 10.21(c)
11	>Orient >Sel by Menu	Want to select the DTM2 plane of the gear in gear_shaft	Pick the gear in the gear_shaft component	
12	>Datum >Name	Select a datum by name and accept yellow side	>DTM2 | Yellow	The DTM2 is a feature of the gear; you have to select the gear to get the DTM2 plane
13	Select vertical face of a block in the subassembly	Select orient3 face as Fig 10.21(a)		
14	>Done			
15	>File >Save As	Save this as tut10-7b	Enter to accept [tut10-7a], type **tut10-7b** then >Done	
16	QuitWindow			
17	Exit	Exit program	Click Yes to confirm	PT/Modeler exited

Item	Step 6
Disp DtmPln	No
Spin Center	No
Disp Pnts	No
Disp Axes	No
Rendering	No hidden line

Table 10.7   Environment Settings

10.11 Viewing Assemblies in Color

In Chapter 2 you worked with colors. There you learned how to set up colors in the User Color table. You accessed these colors through the >View >Cosmetic >Appearances menu. This menu is shown in Figure 10.22.

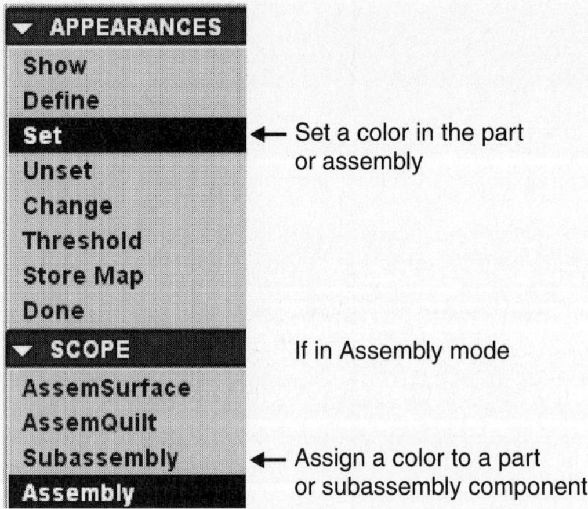

Figure 10.22   Color Assembly menu.

You can assign colors to different components within an assembly using the colors that you have specified in the user color set. If you are in the Assembly Mode, a submenu at the bottom of Figure 10.22 requests that you select the type of item to color. Select Subassembly to color either a part or a subassembly.

The procedure for assigning a color to a component is as follows:

- Select >View >Cosmetic >Appearances to get the color menu
- Select >Set brings up the User Color Table
- Pick the color from the User Color Table
- If in Assembly mode, select the type of component to color from the menu

- Select the component that you wish to have assigned the color
- Done

An important check box exists in the Environment menu. This check box globally enables or disables colors in the display of the assembly or part. Check this box to display colors, and uncheck it to ignore the colors.

Select >Shade Display to see the part shaded in the specified color. Otherwise, the outlines of the components will be displayed in the selected colors.

10.11.1   The color.map File

Color files can be stored in the color.map file. I have placed a file in the TUT directory. This directory is in the search directory path of the software and is loaded each time the program runs.

10.11.2   Tutorial on Coloring an Assembly

In Tutorial 10.8, you will color an assembly. Start by loading the Tut10-8a assembly. Next, select >View >Cosmetic >Appearances. From here you will need to define a set of colors. Follow the procedure in Chapter 2 to define a set of colors. For this tutorial, define red, green, blue, magenta, cyan, yellow, and at least three others of your choice.

We will be displaying the model in No Hidden Line mode. You should see the lines drawn in the selected colors for the selected parts. Select >Set to select a color to map to a block. Select the red color by clicking on the red box in the User Color window. Next, choose >Subassembly in the window. This is used to assign the color to either a subassembly or to a part. Click on the back 8x8 hole block as shown in Figure 10.23(a). Select >Done Sel and note that the 8x8 hole is drawn in red.

Next, select >Set again and choose the blue color. Select >Subassembly but this time select the front 8x8 hole as seen in Figure 10.23(a). After >Done Sel, note that the entire subassembly is displayed in blue. You cannot change the color of an individual component in a subassembly. What to do?

You can color the components of that subassembly at its assembly level. For example, the subassembly with the gears was the file tut10-7b.asm. You could go back to the >Mode menu, select >Assembly >Retrieve and request the tut10-7b.asm subassembly. From here you can color each block independently. But this tut10-7b assembly also contains a gear_shaft assembly. You would need to go back to this assembly and color these parts as well. This is left up to you.

Repeat this process for green and blue until all of the blocks are colored. Use your own colors for the shafts and pulleys. Leave the shaft locks in gray.

Turn on shading using >Environment >Shading | Done. The parts are shaded in the selected colors. Now, turn off colors through Colors check box in the Environment menu. The parts revert back to black and white. Save this file as Tut10-8b.

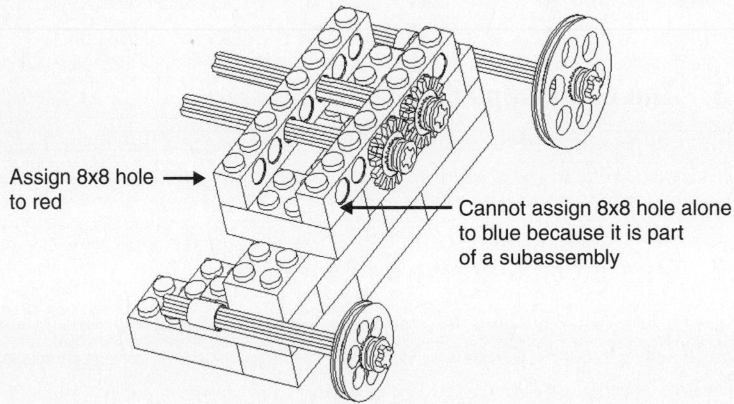

Figure 10.23   Illustration for Tutorial 10.8.

Tutorial 10.8   Coloring an Assembly

Files opened: Tut10-8a.asm   **Files saved:** Tut10-8b.asm

Step	Action	Description	Further Actions	Result
1	Click PT/Modeler Icon	Run PT/Modeler		After some time, PT/Modeler on screen
2	>Mode >Misc >Show Dir	Show current directory		Message similar to "Directory searched is c:\ptc\ptprod\bin"
3	>Change Dir	Change the current directory	Type **c:\proe\tutorial\ chapter_10**	
4	>Done-Return	Leave Misc menu		Misc menu removed
5	>Mode >Assembly >Retrieve	Retrieve an assembly	Type **tut10-8a**	Assembly created
6	>Environment	Set up the environment	Set up checks as seen in Table T10.8 Column Step 6	
7	>Done-Return			
8	>View >Cosmetic >Appearances >Define	Define a color by clicking on the top color swatch in Appearance editor	Click on the Colors box	Color Editor dialog appears
9	Create a red color	Move sliders in color editor, red up, green and blue down	>Okay then >Add in the Appearance editor	
10	>View >Cosmetic >Appearances >Define	Define a color by clicking on the top color swatch in Appearance editor	Click on the Colors box	Color Editor dialog appears
11	Create a green color	Move sliders in color editor, green up, red and blue down	>Okay then >Add in the Appearance editor	
12	>View >Cosmetic >Appearances >Define	Define a color by clicking on the top color swatch in Appearance editor	Click on the Colors box	Color Editor dialog appears
13	Create a blue color	Move sliders in color editor; blue up, green and red down	>Okay then >Add in the Appearance editor	
14	Repeat for yellow, cyan, magenta, others		>Cancel to leave appearance editor	
15	>Set	Assign red to the back 1x8 hole block	Click on the red box in the User Colors; >Subassembly then click on back 1x8 then Done-Sel	Just the 1x8 colors in red

Tutorial 10.8   Coloring an Assembly (continued)

Step	Action	Description	Further Actions	Result
16	>Set	Assign blue to the front 1x8 hole block	Click on the blue box in the User Colors; >Subassembly then click on the front 1x8 then Done-Sel	Note the entire subassembly colors in blue
17	>Set	Assign green to a few blocks	Click on the green box in the User Colors; >Subassembly then click on several blocks then Done-Sel	
18	Repeat for other colors until all blocks are colored			
19	>Set	Assign your own color to the shafts	Click on a box in the User Colors; >Subassembly then click on the shafts then Done-Sel	
20	>Set	Assign your own color to the pulleys	Click on a box in the User Colors; >Subassembly then click on the pulleys then Done-Sel	
21	>Done			
22	>Environment	Change to shading	>Shade	Blocks show up shaded in selected colors
23	>Environment	Turn off colors	Uncheck the Colors box	
24	>File >Save As	Save this as tut10-8b	Enter to accept [tut10-8a], type **tut10-8b** then >Done	
25	QuitWindow			
26	Exit	Exit program	Click Yes to confirm	PT/Modeler exited

Item	Step 6
Disp DtmPln	No
Spin Center	No
Disp Pnts	No
Disp Axes	No
Rendering	No hidden line

Table T10.8   Environment Settings

10.12 Assembly Layers

Chapter Eight described how to use layers effectively to organize your features. This time you will be using layers to organize your components. Assembly layers are more powerful than feature layers. All items in an assembly layer are affected by commands; for example, Suppress, Resume, and Delete. Recall that in feature layers, performing a Blank only blanks the axis, datum planes, and text, not the feature itself. This is not the case with assembly layers. If you suppress a layer, all items on that layer will be suppressed. This is a very useful feature; you will rely on it extensively when building assemblies.

Layers are hierarchical. The assembly layer sits above all component layers. A subassembly layer would sit above all the layers in the components of the subassembly. If you suppress a layer at the assembly level, all items in that layer will be suppressed. However, for an item in a component to be suppressed, it must belong to the same layer, which means it needs the same layer name. It should now become apparent why naming layers consistently is so important.

Using layers in assemblies can be quite complicated, especially where subassemblies are concerned. In the following tutorial, I will introduce you to some basic techniques that you can use with layers.

10.12.1 Tutorial on Using Layers in an Assembly

In Tutorial 10.9, you will read in the assembly tut10-9a. There are no layers at the top level so we will create two layers named Shaft and Pulley. Select >Layer >Assembly >Top Level >Setup >Create and type in the names Shaft and Pulley. Type Enter to finish. We now have two layers at the top level of the assembly named Shaft and Pulley.

Next, set items to these layers. Select >Set Items >Add items and check the Shaft check box ending with Done-Sel. Select >Component >Individual and then select the two outside shafts. Do not select the inside shafts at this time since they are parts of subassemblies. Refer to the help file for working your way through the layer hierarchy. End selection with >Done-Sel and >Done-Return. Repeat this process for the pulleys.

Now, blank the shafts. Select >Set Display >Blank and check the Pulley layer ending with Done-Sel. Type F2 to redraw the display and note that the pulleys are missing. Select >Set Display >Blank and uncheck the Pulley layer ending with Done-Sel. Type F2 to redraw the display and note that the pulleys are back again.

At this time, display only the pulleys. Select >Set Display >Display and check the Pulley layer ending with Done-Sel. Type F2 to repaint the display and note that only the pulleys are displayed. Select >Set Display >Display and uncheck the Pulley layer ending with Done-Sel.

Repeat this process for the shafts. Save the file as Tut10-9b.

Tutorial 10.9   Using Layers in Assemblies

Files opened: Tut10-9a.asm   **Files saved:** Tut10-9b.asm

Step	Action	Description	Further Actions	Result
1	Click PT/Modeler Icon	Run PT/Modeler		After some time, PT/Modeler on screen
2	>Mode >Misc >Show Dir	Show current directory		Message similar to "Directory searched is c:\ptc\ptprod\bin"
3	>Change Dir	Change the current directory	Type **c:\proe\tutorial\ chapter_10**	
4	>Done-Return	Leave Misc menu		Misc menu removed
5	>Mode >Assembly >Retrieve	Retrieve an assembly	Type **tut10-9a**	Assembly created
6	>Environment	Set up the environment	Set up checks as seen in Table T10.9 Column Step 6	
7	>Done-Return			
8	>Layer >Assembly >Top Level	Create layers Shaft and Pulley at top level		
9	>Setup >Create		Type **shaft**, type **pulley**, and **Enter** to finish	Shaft layer and pulley layer are created
10	>Set Items	Want to set items into layers		
11	>Add Items	Want to add items into layers	Check **shaft** check box then >Done-Sel	
12	>Component | Individual	Add items to shaft		
13	Select the two shafts		>Done-Return	
14	>Set Items	Want to set items into layers		
15	>Add Items	Want to add items into layers	Check **pulley** check box then >Done-Sel	
16	>Component | Individual	Add items to pulley		
17	Select the two pulleys		>Done-Return	
18	>Layers >Set Display | Blank	Blank the pulleys	Check pulley check box and >Done Sel	

Tutorial 10.9   Using Layers in Assemblies (continued)

Step	Action	Description	Further Actions	Result
19	F2 to repaint display		May have to Ctrl-mMB click to redraw screen	Pulleys are blanked
20	>Set Display > Blank	Unblank the pulleys	Uncheck pulley check box and >Done Sel	
21	F2 to redisplay		May have to Ctrl-mMB click to redraw screen	Pulleys are displayed
22	>Set Display > Display	Display only the pulleys	Check pulley check box and >Done Sel	
23	F2 to redisplay		May have to Ctrl-mMB click to redraw screen	Only pulleys are displayed
24	>Set Display > Display	Display everything	Uncheck pulley check box and >Done Sel	
25	F2 to redisplay	Only pulleys are displayed	May have to Ctrl-mMB click to redraw screen	All displayed
26	>File >Save As	Save this as tut10-9b	Enter to accept [tut10-9a], type **tut10-9b** then >Done	
27	QuitWindow			
28	Exit	Exit program	Click Yes to confirm	PT/Modeler exited

Item	Step 6
Disp DtmPln	No
Spin Center	No
Disp Pnts	No
Disp Axes	No
Rendering	No hidden line

Table T10.9   Environment Settings

10.13 Exploding an Assembly

I am sure you are acquainted with what an exploded assembly looks like.
Exploding an assembly is a viewing operation. It has nothing at all to do with the
data in the assembly. It is merely a way of viewing the assembly similar to a rotation or zoom. You can create exploded assemblies using the >View >Cosmetic
>Explode command.

Components explode in the direction of their placement constraints. A shaft and
hole will separate along the direction of the axis. Two mated or aligned surfaces will
separate along the normal of the two surfaces.

The Explode command separates all components by a fixed distance. You can change the distance between components using the Mod Explode command. Next, select a component. All explode dimensions associated with that component are displayed. You can select any of these dimensions and modify them as you would change any dimensional value using the Modify command.

10.13.1   Tutorial 10.10, Exploding an Assembly

Load the File Tut10-10. You have viewed this assembly before. It is seen in Figure 10.24(a). Select the >View >Cosmetic >Explode command. The assembly explodes as seen in Figure 10.24(b). Perhaps this is not what you had in mind. Select the >Assembly >Mod Explode command. A submenu is displayed as seen in Figure 10.24(c). Select >Move. Now you can click on a component in the assembly and click on a new location to place the assembly. You do not have to worry about locating the component at the exact location along the axis of explosion. The software will do this for you. Just click about where you would like to see the new component. Select the shaft lock, and then select a position off of the end of the shaft. Select the gear and place it between the shaft and the shaft lock as shown in Figure 10.24(d).

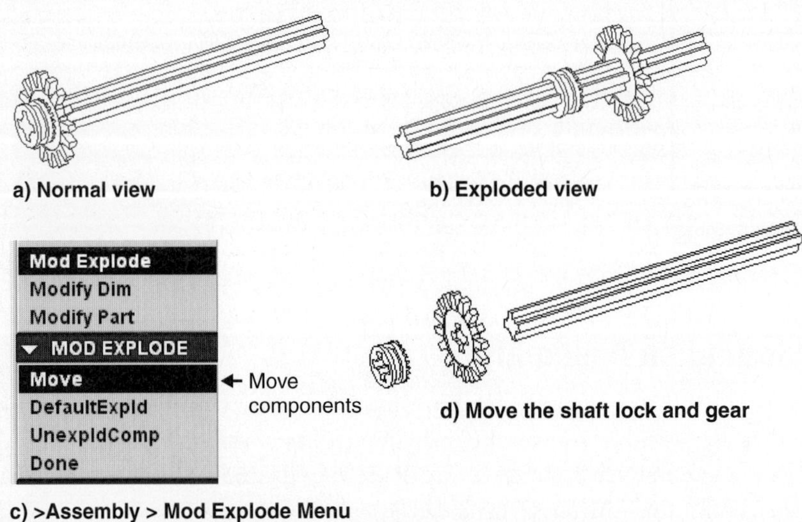

Figure 10.24   Illustration for Tutorial 10.10.

Tutorial 10.10   Exploding an Assembly

Files opened: Tut10-10a.asm   **No files saved.**

Step	Action	Description	Further Actions	Result
1	Click PT/Modeler Icon	Run PT/Modeler		After some time, PT/Modeler on screen
2	>Mode >Misc >Show Dir	Show current directory		Message similar to "Directory searched is c:\ptc\ptprod\bin"
3	>Change Dir	Change the current directory	Type **c:\proe\tutorial\ chapter_10**	
4	>Done-Return	Leave Misc menu		Misc menu removed
5	>Mode >Assembly >Retrieve	Retrieve an assembly	Type **tut10-10a**	Assembly created
6	>Environment	Set up the environment	Set up checks inTable T10.10 Column Step 6	
7	>Done-Return			
8	>View >Cosmetic >Explode	Explode the view as Fig. 10.24(b)		
9	>Assembly >Mod Explode	Move the components	>Move	
10	mLb on shaft lock	Move shaft lock	mLb on new location	
11	mLb on gear	Move gear	mLb on new location	
12	QuitWindow			
13	Exit	Exit program	Click Yes to confirm	PT/Modeler exited

Item	Step 6
Disp DtmPln	No
Spin Center	No
Disp Pnts	No
Disp Axes	No
Rendering	No hidden line

Table T10.10   Environment Settings

Chapter 11

Working with Relations

PT/Modeler provides a way to specify the dimensions of a feature, part, or assembly by using equations instead of hard-coded values. These equations are called *relations*. We are used to hard-coding dimensional values. We have assigned a length to 200, a diameter to 50, and so forth as shown in Figure 11.1.

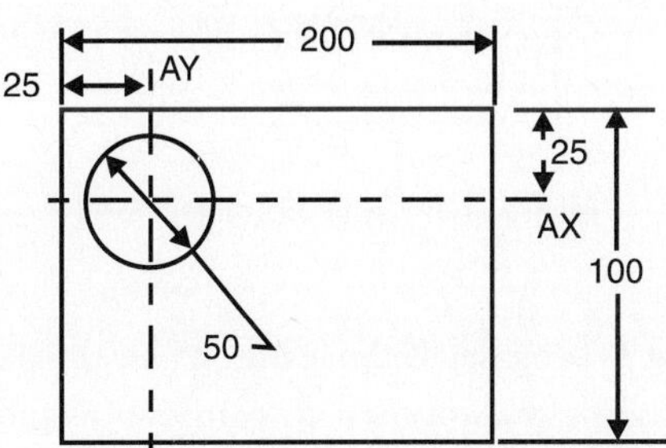

Figure 11.1 Hard-coding dimensions.

We have also seen the sketcher assign symbols as dimensions, such as sd4 or sd19, before a regeneration. These symbols are then changed to dimensional values during regeneration. Afterwards, we have modified these values to other dimensional values. PT/Modeler keeps symbols for each dimension: Sketcher symbols use the code sd#; part level symbols use the code d#. An example in Sketcher is shown in Figure 11.2.

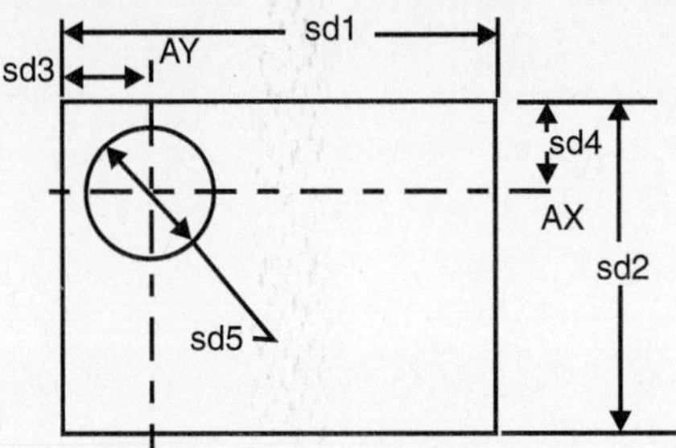

Figure 11.2   Sketcher symbols.

In this chapter, we will look at assigning relations to these dimensions. The advantages are obvious to anyone who has studied algebra. Dimensions specified with relations can easily be manipulated. They can be put into equations. A model dimensioned with relations is flexible and easy to understand. Relations are at their best when their names are descriptive. This is illustrated in Figure 11.3 where the names have been changed from their more cryptic form to a descriptive one.

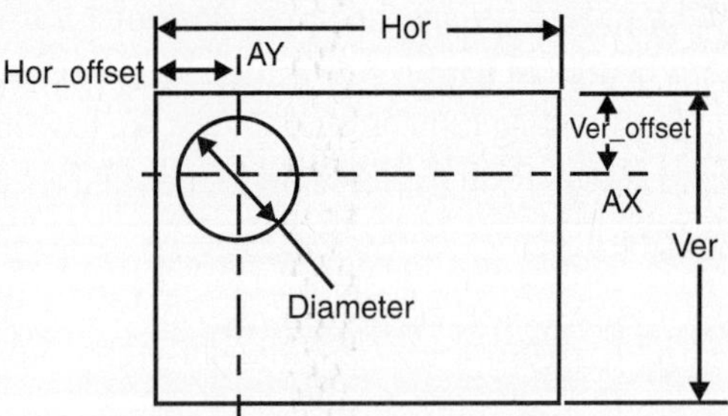

Figure 11.3   Symbolic dimensions.

Relations can be added to a model at the feature level, the part level, or the assembly level. We will be dealing exclusively with part-level relations in this chapter.

11.1   Creating and Modifying a Relation

Once the dimensions are in symbolic form, they can be built into relations. PT/Modeler keeps a symbol and a value for each dimension. In Figure 11.3, the symbolic name for the horizontal side is Hor. In Figure 11.1, the value associated with this symbol is 200. Both are true. When we set Hor = 100, the symbol name is still Hor and its value is now 100. Regenerating would produce a part that had a side of 100. No need to redo the sketch. Just modify the Hor = 100 dimension and it is all done for you!

Relations can be created and manipulated using the Relations menu shown in Figure 11.4. There are two ways of adding a relation. One way is to type it in, a line at a time, using the >Add Rel command. A second way is to type in the relations using Notepad or the Pro/Table Editor through the >Edit Rel command. I prefer using Notepad since you can see the entire relations file, as opposed to seeing only one line at a time. From the Relations menu you can also show the current relations in an information window. The information window shows the relations and the calculated values. Lastly, you can switch the view from values to symbols. This is very important.

NOTE: Using the Pro/Table Editor or NotePad does not provide the checking that >Add Relation provides. Each line entered using >Add Relation is checked as it is typed to see if the relation is valid.

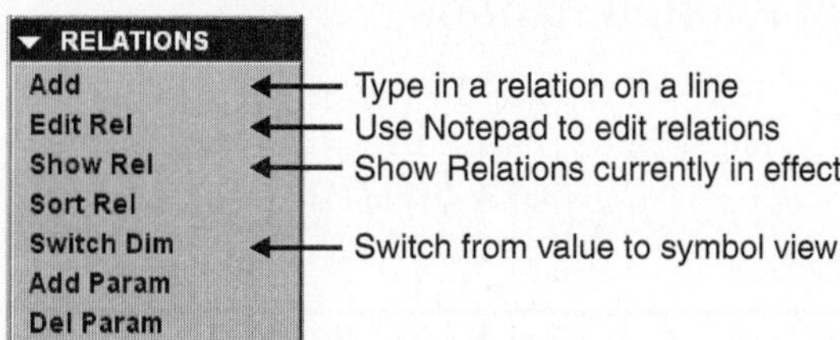

Figure 11.4   Relations menu.

Relations are equations. You enter one per line. I will use the symbol ➡ to represent the end of a line or typing the Enter key. You might type Hor_offset = 20➡ or Hor_offset = 40➡.

11.2   Create a New Variable Name

You can also create a new variable name, such as *standard*. In this case you might type Standard = 50 ➡ Hor_offset = Standard ➡ and Ver_offset = Standard ➡. This simple step would change the position of the corner of the rectangle with respect to the AX and AY axis.

NOTE: Relations >Edit Rel may bring up Notepad by using a DOS window. If it does, make sure that you Save and Exit Notepad using the Notepad menu or button commands. This will close the DOS window as well.

You can also change the value of a dimensional symbol using the Modify | Value command. Remember that changing a value, either through the Relations or Modify commands, requires a regeneration.

11.3   Naming Conventions

You can use just about any name you want for a symbol in a relation. Follow the few rules shown below:

- Symbol names must begin with a letter
- Names cannot contain nonalphanumeric characters such as !, @, #, $, etc.
- Do not use the reserved names PI, G, C1, C2, C3, C4
- Do not use names d#, kd#, rd#, sd#, tm#, tp#, or tpm#; these are reserved for dimensions
- Do not use any spaces inside a name; use underscores instead
- Make your names clear, descriptive, and consistent

11.4   Changing Dimension Names

You can change a dimension name at any time. Use the >Modify >Dim Symbol command. Click on the dimension name that you wish to change and type in a new name. You cannot enter a name that is already defined. When you just press Enter, the same name is kept.

Relations files are back-annotating. Using the >Modify >Dim Symbol, the old name is changed to a new name. Back-annotating means that if you change a dimension name using this command, all references to the old name in the Relation file will also be changed automatically to the new name.

11.5   A First Relation

In Tutorial 11.1, we will start by creating a rectangular protrusion centered on the AX and AY axis (but not aligned there) of depth 100. You will sketch and dimension the rectangle as seen in Figure 11.5(a). From here we will enter the >Relations menu to show the relationships. So far, all we have are dimensions. When we click >Relations >Switch Dim, these dimension values are shown as symbols as shown in Figure 11.5(b). Clicking Relations >Switch Dim again causes the values to appear once more.

We will use these symbols to specify the part in a Relations file. Before we begin, let us change the names of these symbols, from d3 and d5 type names to descriptive names. To do this we will use the Modify >Dim Symbols as seen in Figure 11.5(c). You can also use the >Move Dim command to move a dimension to a place where it will be more readable. This does not change the dimension references, it merely moves the dimension for documentation clarity. Click on each dimension and type the new names as seen in Figure 11.5(d).

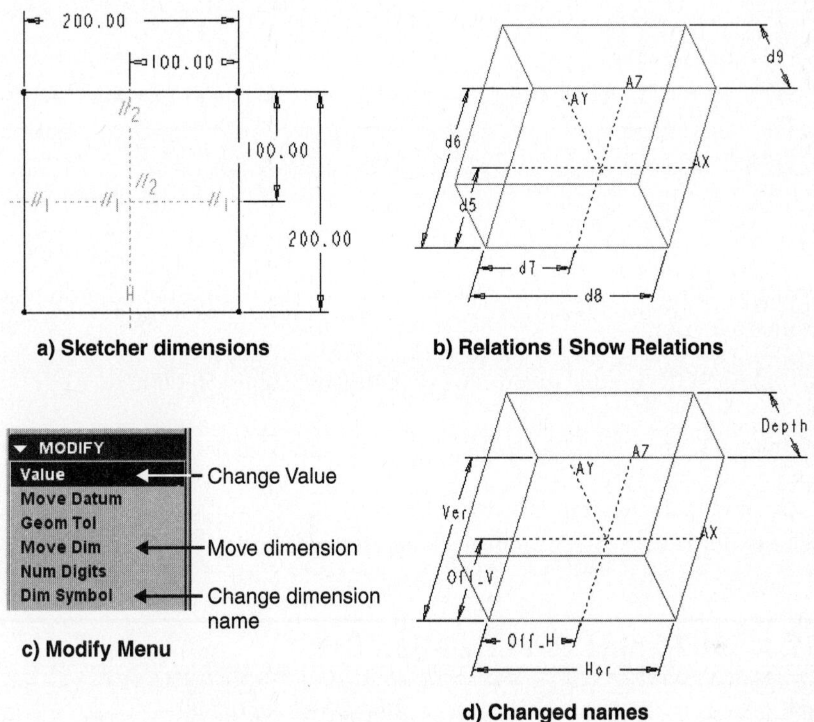

Figure 11.5   Illustrations for Tutorial 11.1 base part.

We are ready to enter our first relation. There are two ways that this can be accomplished. For now, let us edit using the >Edit Rel command. An empty file is opened in Notepad. It is empty because you have not yet entered any relations. Type in the following relations:

Relations 11.1: A first relation
/* standard is a size constant
standard = 50

/* offsets from back-left corner are fixed to standard
OFF_H = standard
OFF_V = standard

Note that the lines that begin with a /* symbol are comment lines and do not enter into the relation. Save and Exit from Notepad. Click >Show Rel to view the relations. Next, select >Modify | Value and click on the Hor symbol. Note that the value [100] is shown as the current value in the message query. Type in 200. We have changed the model so >Regenerate. We can see that the change occurred. Click >Relations and click on the part. To see the new values, switch dimensions again using Select >Switch Dim.

Nobody is perfect, so let us create an error. Change the line as follows: OFF_H = -standard. This attempts to create a negative dimension. Since negative numbers are not allowed, an error message is provided in the message box saying:

> The Relations contains errors. Re-edit?

Selecting yes brings us back into Notepad or Pro/Table to find the following message after our error.

> /* ERROR: Invalid attempt to assign negative value -50.0000 to 'd13'.

Change back to OFF_H = standard again.

This demonstrates how errors work. They are not very difficult to fix; just look closely at your code and any problem should be evident.

Tutorial 11.1   Building a First Relation Set

No files opened.   **Files saved:** Tut11-1.prt

Step	Action	Description	Further Actions	Result
1	Click PT/Modeler Icon	Run PT/Modeler		After some time, PT/Modeler on screen
2	>Mode >Misc >Show Dir	Show current directory		Message similar to "Directory searched is c:\ptc\ptprod\bin"
3	>Change Dir	Change the current directory	Type **c:\proe\tutorial\ chapter_11**	
4	>Done-Return	Leave Misc menu		Misc menu removed
5	>Mode >NewPart	Create a new part	Type **tut11-1**	Part created
6	>Environment	Set up the environment	Set up checks as seen in Table T11.1 Column Step 6	
7	>Done-Return			
8	>Feature >Protrusion	Extrude	Solid	Done	Create an extruded solid Protrusion		

Tutorial 11.1   Building a First Relation Set (continued)

Step	Action	Description	Further Actions	Result
9	>One Side | Done	Protrusion will extend one side out of the sketching plane		
10	Pick XZ datum plane	Select sketch plane		
11	>Okay	Okay to select direction of arrow		Go into Sketcher mode
12	>TOP	Pick XY as Top reference	Pick XY	Go into Sketcher mode
13	>Sketch>Rectangle	Draw a rectangle as Fig. 11.5(a)	Sketch rectangle in Fig. 11.5(a)	Rectangle centered on datum plane
14	>Dimension	Dimension as Fig. 11.5(a)		
15	>Regenerate		>Done	Regeneration successful
16	>Blind	Specify the depth	Type **60**	
17	Preview	See part	F1 then Okay	
18	>Feature >Relations		mLb on part	See dimensions
19	>Modify >Dim Symbol	Change to new names as Figure 11.5(d)		
20	>Relations >Edit Relations	Create relations	Type in Relations 11.1 into Notepad	Notepad comes up; type in relations then save/exit
21	>Modify >Value	Change Hor to 400	Click on Hor, type **400**	
22	>Regenerate	See result		Regeneration successful
23	>Relations >Edit Rel	Create a purposeful error	Change to Off_H = -100 then exit/save	Error shown in message window
24	**Enter** to re-edit		Change back to Off_H = 100 then exit/save	Notepad comes up; type in relations then save/exit
25	>File >Save	Save file	Save **tut11-1**	
26	>QuitWindow			
27	Exit	Exit program	Click Yes to confirm	PT/Modeler exited

Item	Step 6
Disp DtmPln	Checked
Spin Center	No
Disp Pnts	No
Disp Axes	Checked
Rendering	No hidden line

Table T11.1   Environment Settings

11.6 Adding More Relations

In Tutorial 11.2, you will add a cylindrical protrusion to our block. We will call this protrusion a *bump*. Once we have created a bump, we shell out the part.

The part should be dimensioned so that Hor = 100, Ver = 100 and Depth = 60 before we begin. Use Modify >Value to provide these dimensions.

Now we are ready to add our protrusion. Add an extruded solid protrusion as shown in Figure 11.6(a) using the top face as the sketching plane and the bottom face as the Bottom reference. Sketch a circle and dimension as seen in Figure 11.6(b). Regenerate and select a Blind depth of 11. Okay the protrusion.

Next, we want to add our protrusion to the Relations. It does not matter whether any or all of the dimensions associated with the protrusion are in the Relations. The protrusion feature will still regenerate. When you want to change one or more dimensions of the protrusion feature using relations, the values have to be included in the relations for the part.

Selecting >Relations and clicking on the base part provides the dimensional parameters as seen in Figure 11.6(c). Clicking on the bump feature provides the dimensions as shown in Figure 11.6(d). Note that the new dimensions have been assigned the default d# names. Before we use these values, we will change their names to something more descriptive. Since this is a bump feature we will use bump_off_H, bump_off_V for the bump offsets. These two dimensions represent the distance from the edge of the part to the center of the circle section. Note that I have not used the AX and AY axis for the references. I am calling the depth of the bump bump_depth and the diameter bump_diameter.

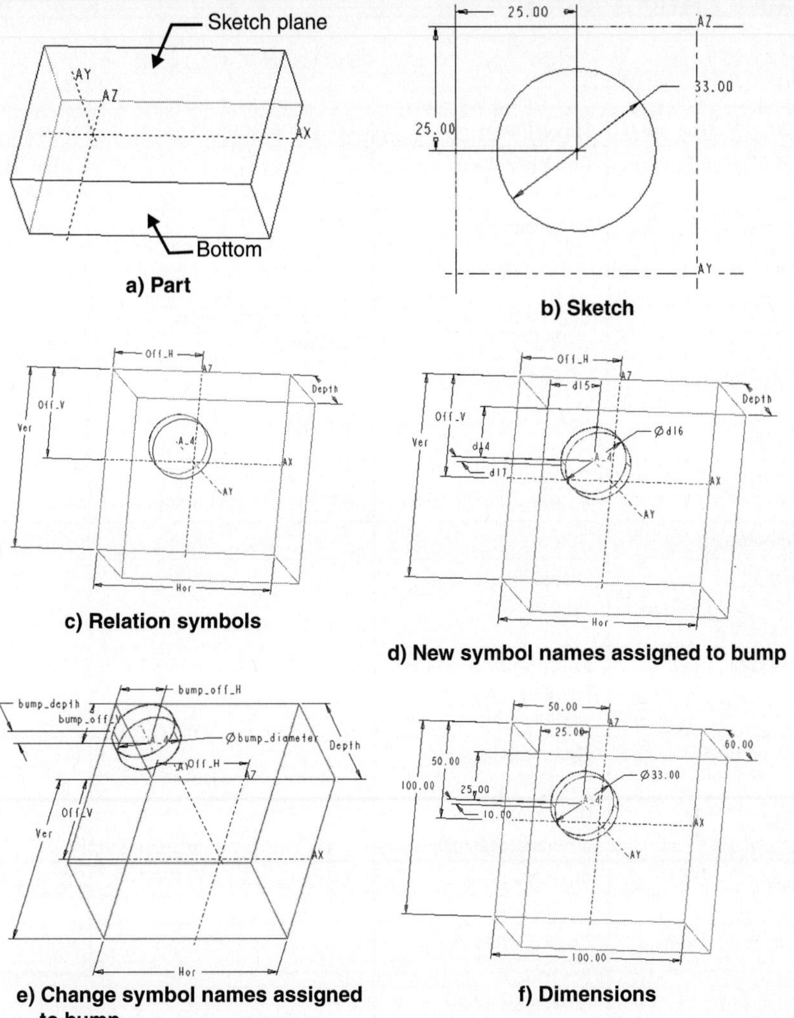

a) Part

b) Sketch

c) Relation symbols

d) New symbol names assigned to bump

**e) Change symbol names assigned
to bump**

f) Dimensions

Figure 11.6   Illustrations for Tutorial 11.2.

Tutorial 11.2   Add a Bump

Files opened: Tut11-2a.prt   **Files saved:** Tut11-2b.prt

Step	Action	Description	Further Actions	Result
1	Click PT/Modeler Icon	Run PT/Modeler		After some time, PT/Modeler on screen
2	>Mode > Misc > Show Dir	Show current directory		Message similar to "Directory searched is c:\ptc\ptprod\bin"
3	>Change Dir	Change the current directory	Type **c:\proe\tutorial\ chapter_11**	
4	>Done-Return	Leave Misc menu		Misc menu removed
5	>Mode >Part >Retrieve	Read a part	Type **tut11-2a**	Part read
6	>Environment	Set up the environment	Set up checks as seen in Table T11.2 Column Step 6	
7	>Done-Return			
8	>Feature >Protrusion | Extrude | Solid | Done	Create an extruded solid cylinder		
9	>One Side | Done	Protrusion will extend one side out of the sketching plane		
10	Pick top face of base	Select top face as Fig. 11.6(a)		
11	>Okay	Okay to select direction of arrow		Go into Sketcher mode
12	>Bottom	Pick XY as Bottom reference	Pick bottom face as Fig. 11.6(a)	Go into Sketcher mode
13	>Sketch >Circle	Draw a circle as Fig. 11.6(b)		
14	>Dimension	Dimension as Fig. 11.6(b)		
15	>Regenerate		>Done	Regeneration successful
16	>Blind | Done	Enter depth	Type **100**	
17	Preview	See part	F1 then Okay	
18	>Feature >Relations	See relations menu	mLb on base	
19	>Modify | Value	Change Depth to 60, Hor to 100, Ver to 100	mLb Depth type 60, mLb Hor type 100, mLb Ver type 100	
20	>Regenerate	Regenerate to see changes		
21	>Feature >Relations	See relations	mLb on bump	

Tutorial 11.2   Add a Bump (continued)

Step	Action	Description	Further Actions	Result
22	>Modify >Mod Dim Symbol	Change to new names as Figure 11.6(e)		
23	>File >Save As	Save file	Save **tut11-2b**	
24	>QuitWindow			
25	Exit	Exit program	Click Yes to confirm	PT/Modeler exited

Item	Step 6
Disp DtmPln	No
Spin Center	No
Disp Pnts	No
Disp Axes	Checked
Rendering	No hidden line

Table T11.2   Environment Settings

11.7   Creating Pattern Relations

In Tutorial 11.3, you will create a pattern out of our bump. You will then create a set of relations from this pattern. As you will soon see, it is possible to make a relation out of the duplicate count of a pattern.

First, select >Feature Oper >Pattern and select the bump. Choose the horizontal bump offset, bump_off_H, as the first dimension and set it to 50. There are no more dimensions to pattern in this direction so select >Done. Enter 2 as the number of instances. Choose the vertical bump offset, bump_off_V, as the second dimension, select >Done and set it to 50. There are no more dimensions to pattern in this direction. Enter 2 as the number of instances.

Now, we will add these bump dimensions to our dimension list as seen in Relations 11.2. You only need to add the new lines since the other lines are already present in the file. Access the file through >Relations>Edit Rel and type the new lines using Notepad.

Relations 11.2: Adding Pattern relationships
/* standard is a size constant
standard = 50

/* bump pattern repeat counts
bump_pat_repeat_H = P0
bump_pat_repeat_V = P1

```
/* offsets from back-left corner are fixed to standard
OFF_H = standard
OFF_V = standard

/* bump dimensions
bump_off_H = standard/2
bump_off_V = standard/2
bump_depth = 10

/* bump pattern dimensions
bump_pat_off_H = standard
bump_pat_off_V = standard

/* bump pattern repeat counts
bump_pat_repeat_H = 2
bump_pat_repeat_V = 2

/* restore the pattern counts before leaving the relations
P0 = bump_pat_repeat_H
P1 = bump_pat_repeat_V
```

Let us spend a little time looking at this relations file. First of all, as you can observe, I am assigning several values to be standard or standard/2. The reason for this has to do with the particular part that I am designing.

What is the effect of setting bump_depth to 10 in this file? It is already set to 10 in the model. Why is this necessary? Actually it is not necessary. However, by setting it to 10, a user cannot change the value using the >Modify | Value command. An error will occur if this is attempted. This holds true for the other relations also.

Notice the occurrence of P0 and P1 from Figure 11.7(b). These are the PT/Modeler repeat counts for the two dimensions involved in the pattern. They are labeled P0 PROTRUSIONS and P1 PROTRUSIONS in Figure 11.7(b). These are dimensions and are thus available for relations. However, the P# code can either be modified or put into a relation and cannot be changed. For that reason, I have chosen to set up two new dimension names called bump_pat_repeat_H, and bump_pat_repeat_V. I set them to the P0 and P1 values. I did this for only one reason. Later on in the code, when we start using these dimensions, it will be difficult to remember what P0 or P1 represent. As we add other P# dimensions, this will become even more unclear. This is one of the most frequent sources of errors when setting up relations.

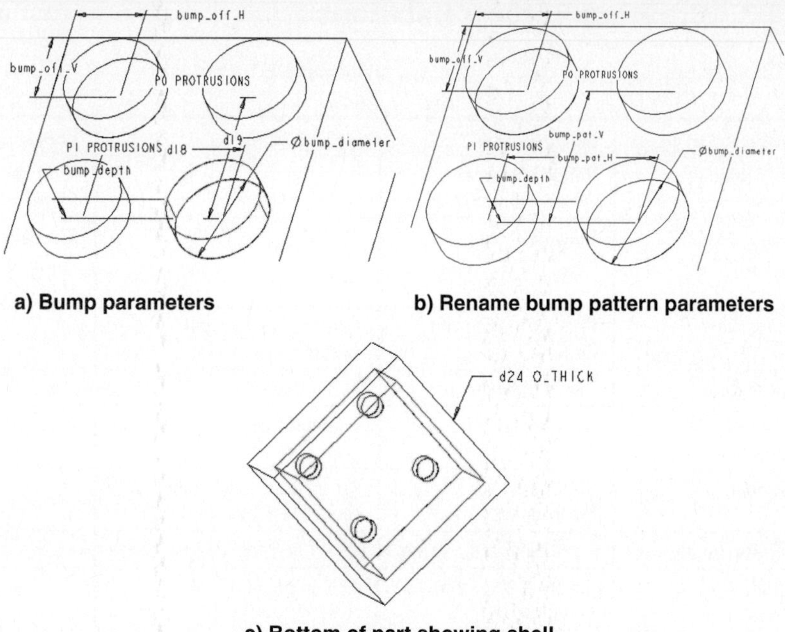

a) Bump parameters   **b) Rename bump pattern parameters**

c) Bottom of part showing shell

Figure 11.7   Illustrations for Tutorial 11.3.

By setting bump_pat_repeat_H equal to P0, we have created a new local variable bump_pat_repeat_H and have set it equal to P0. If we later set bump_pat_repeat_H to 20, this would have no affect on P0. They are two different dimensions. It is necessary to restore the repeat counts P0 and P1 with the values we will be loading into our local variables. This is accomplished at the end of the file.

Thus far, we have done little with our relations. It will start warming up in the next tutorial and then really will get interesting in Tutorial 11.5. Before we end this tutorial, let's add a Shell feature. Select Features >Shell. The shell will begin on the bottom face of the base, so drag rotate the part around to see the back. Pick this surface when requested and >Done Ref. Enter a shell thickness of 2.

As you may have suspected, we are going to rename this d# dimension to the name shell_thick. We want to set this value in our relations but we will do that in the next tutorial.

Tutorial 11.3   Creating Pattern Relations

Files opened: Tut11-3a.prt   **Files saved:** Tut11-3b.prt

Step	Action	Description	Further Actions	Result
1	Click PT/Modeler Icon	Run PT/Modeler		After some time, PT/Modeler on screen
2	>Mode >Misc >Show Dir	Show current directory		Message similar to "Directory searched is c:\ptc\ptprod\bin"
3	>Change Dir	Change the current directory	Type **c:\proe\tutorial\ chapter_11**	
4	>Done-Return	Leave Misc menu		Misc menu removed
5	>Mode >Part >Retrieve	Read a part	Type **tut11-3a**	Part read
6	>Environment	Set up the environment	Set up checks as seen in Table T11.3 Column Step 6	
7	>Done-Return			
8	>Feature Oper >Pattern	Create a 2D pattern of bump	mLb on bump	
9	>Modify >Relations >Switch Dims	Change value dimensions to symbol dimensions		
10	Select bump_off_H (in AX direction) displayed as 25	Select first direction dimension for pattern	Type **50** for increment, >Done; type **2** for number of instances	
11	Select bump_off_V (in AY direction) displayed as 25	Select first direction dimension for pattern	Type **50** for increment, >Done; type **2** for number of instances	Part regenerates with pattern
12	Modify > Dim Symbol	Change the names	Select bump pattern in lower-right corner	Note: your dimension names may vary; see Figure 11.7(a)
13	Select AX direction, type **bump_pat_H**; select AY direction, type **bump_pat_V**	Change 50 (in AX) to bump_pat_H, change 50 (in AY) to bump_pat_H		
14	>Relations >Edit Rel	Edit the relations file as Relations 11.2	Enter new data as in Relations 11.2 in text; >Save/Quit	
15	>Feature >Shell	Make a shell	Select bottom of base; >Done-Sel and >Done Refs	
16	Type **2** for thickness	Enter thickness	Preview F1 done	Shell is created
17	Modify >Dim Symbol	Select shell	Select d# symbol and change to **shell_thick**, then **Enter** and >Done	Change thickness name

Tutorial 11.3   Creating Pattern Relations (continued)

Step	Action	Description	Further Actions	Result
18	>File >Save As	Save file	Save **tut11-3b**	
19	>QuitWindow			
20	Exit	Exit program	Click Yes to confirm	PT/Modeler exited

Item	Step 6
Disp DtmPln	No
Spin Center	No
Disp Pnts	No
Disp Axes	Checked
Rendering	No hidden line

Table T11.3   Environment Settings

11.8   Mathematical Operators and Functions

When using mathematics, you can use the operators seen in Table 11.1. For example, A = B^2 would be A equals B squared.

Operator	Description
=	Equals
+	Addition
-	Subtraction
/	Division
*	Multiplication
^	Exponent
()	Grouping

Table 11.1   Mathematical Operators

You can also make sophisticated mathematical operations using the functions shown in Table 11.2.

Function	Description	Function	Description
COS()	Cosine	Sinh()	Hyperbolic sine
SIN()	Sine	Tanh()	Hyperbolic tangent
TAN()	Tangent	Log()	Base 10 log
SQRT()	Square root	Ln()	Natural log
ASIN()	Arc sine	Exp()	e raised to the power of
ACOS()	Arc cosine	Abs()	Absolute
ATAN()	Arc tangent	Ceil()	Smallest integer not less than
COSH()	Hyperbolic cosine	Floor()	Largest integer not greater than

Table 11.2   Mathematical Functions

11.9 Using Mathematics in Relations

In Tutorial 11.4, we will use a little mathematics to design our part and show how useful relations can be. First, let us address our shell from the previous tutorial. Perhaps you have guessed what we are building here. It is a Lego ® type piece. The bottom of the piece is going to lock to the top of another piece. To do this, the inside of the shell has to fit tightly onto the outside of the bumps. We will ignore tolerances in this tutorial.

The geometry is pretty simple here. The thickness of the shell has to be equal to the difference between the bump_off_V and the bump radius. All we have is bump_diameter so bump_diameter /2 will do just fine. We enter the new relation seen in Relation 11.3 into our relation file.

Relation 11.3: Add this to the end of the relation file

    /* set up the shell thickness to mate with the bump
    Shell_thick = bump_off_V - bump_diameter /2

The fit on the outside of the bumps will not be sufficient to hold the blocks together. We will also need a fit on the inside of the bumps.

We will add our new inner protrusion. We will call it *lock*. This lock is a cylinder that uses the bottom surface of the shell as the sketch plane. This is shown in Figure 11.8(b). The shell will use a Blind depth that we will set to 58, two less than the depth of the base. This will extend nearly to the bottom of the part. We do not want the lock to interfere with the part base. However, we also do not want this rather arbitrary depth either. What if we want to change the depth of the part? Then we would either be too short or too long. This is a perfect application for a relation.

Select the inside bottom face of the shell as the sketch plane and the surface indicated in Figure 11.8(c) as Top. Dimension the sketch as shown in this figure.

Make sure that you do not allow sketcher to align the part to the AX, AY axis. Since this lock is going to touch the clips, it is tempting to draw the circle that is tangent to the circles. Do not do this. We do not want any alignments. We want dimensions as shown. Regenerate, select a depth of 58, and accept the changes.

Now, we need to add this all to our relations. Change the d# names as seen in Figure 11.8(d) to the names shown in Figure 11.8(e). We are consistent here using the lock_off_H, lock_off_V, lock_diameter, and lock_depth. Edit the relations file and add the relations seen in Relation 11.5.

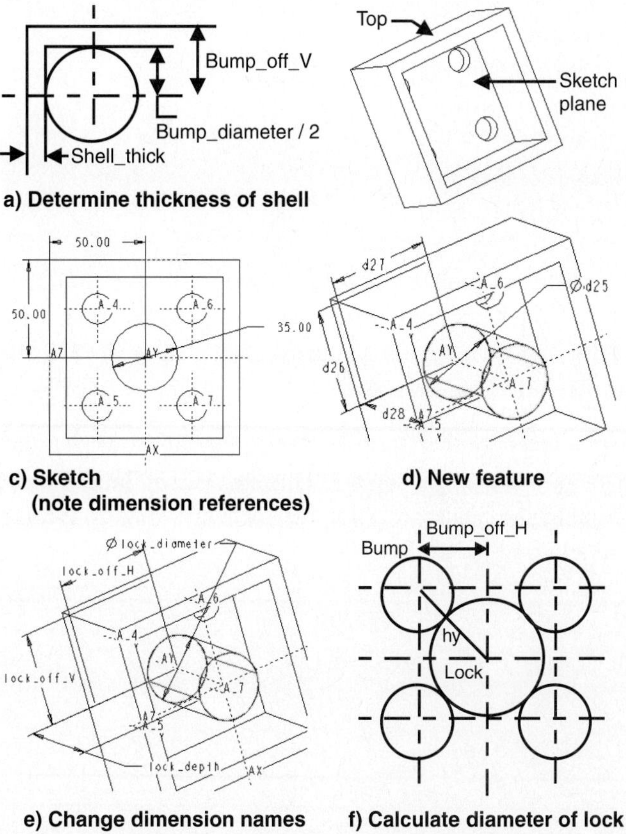

Figure 11.8   Illustrations for Tutorial 11.4.

Next, we will determine the actual diameter of the lock. We need a little trigonometry here in reference to Figure 11.8(f). Let us call the distance between the center of the lock and the center of the bump *hy*. Now hy is the hypotenuse of the triangle where each side is bump_off_H. We could use Pythagorean Theorem and enter

$$Hy = SQRT(\, (bump\_off\_H * bump\_off\_H) + (bump\_off\_H * bump\_off\_H) \,)$$

This would work since SQRT is supported. We will use the simplification to reduce calculation time.

$$hy = 1.414 * bump\_off\_H$$

The radius of lock is equal to hy – (bump_diameter/2). The diameter of the lock is twice this, leading us to the equation found in Relation 11.4. Since we are in the relations file, you might as well fix the depth of the lock as well. Recall we want it to be a little less than the depth of the base.

Relation 11.4: Add this to the end of the relation file

```
/* hypotenuse
hy = 1.414 * bump_off_H
/* diameter
lock_diameter = 2 * (hy – (bump_diameter/2))
/* fix depth of lock
LOCK_DEPTH = DEPTH – 2
```

Regenerate the part and look at the part normal to the back surface with hidden lines enabled. You will see that we have a perfect fit. Try and change the lock diameter using Modify | Value. An error message alerts you to the fact that this is not allowed since the dimension is driven.

I want you to suppress the shell for now. As you develop your relations files, a mistake later on could cause the shell to fail. This way, we will be able to work with our part while keeping the placeholder for the shell. Do this by using the >Feature >Suppress and selecting the shell.

Tutorial 11.4   Using Mathematics in Relations

Files opened: Tut11-4a.prt   **Files saved:** Tut11-4b.prt

Step	Action	Description	Further Actions	Result
1	Click PT/Modeler Icon	Run PT/Modeler		After some time, PT/Modeler on screen
2	>Mode > Misc >Show Dir	Show current directory		Message similar to "Directory searched is c:\ptc\ptprod\bin"
3	>Change Dir	Change the current directory	Type **c:\proe\tutorial\ chapter_11**	
4	>Done-Return	Leave Misc menu		Misc menu removed
5	>Mode >Part >Retrieve	Read a part	Type **tut11-4a**	Part read
6	>Environment	Set up the environment	Set up checks as seen in Table T11.4 Column Step 6	
7	>Done-Return			
8	>Feature>Relation	Set up the relation	Type line as seen in Relation 11.3; Save/Exit	
9	>Regenerate	Regenerate the part		Regeneration successful
10	>Modify | Value	Check out the new value	mLb on shell in Model Tree	
11	>Relations | Switch Dim	Switch to see the actual value		Value shows up as 8.5
12	>Feature >Protrusion | Extrude | Solid | Done	Create an extruded solid cylinder		
13	>One Side | Done	Cut will extend one side out of the sketching plane		
14	Pick top inside face of shell	Select shell face as Fig. 11.8(b)		
15	>Okay	Accept direction		
16	>Top	Pick face as Top as Fig. 11.8(b)	Pick bottom face as Fig. 11.6(a)	Go into Sketcher mode
17	>Sketch >Circle	Draw a circle as Fig. 11.8(c)		Draw a circle
18	>Dimension	Dimension as Fig. 11.8(c)		Note: Dimension references; do NOT align to AX, AY axis
19	>Regenerate		>Done	Regeneration successful
20	>Blind	Specify the depth	Type **58**	
21	Preview	See part	F1 then Okay	

Tutorial 11.4   Using Mathematics in Relations (continued)

Step	Action	Description	Further Actions	Result
22	>Feature>Relations Select lock	Change the names		Symbol names as Fig. 11.8(d)
23	Modify >Dim Symbol	Select dimension name	Select d# symbols and change to Fig. 11.8(e)	Change name
24	>Relations>Edit Rel	Edit the relations file as Relations 11.4	Enter new data as in Relations 11.5; Save/Quit	
25	>Regenerate			Regeneration successful
26	>Modify | Value	Try and change lock_diameter	Click on lock feature and lock_diameter	Error message: Can't change a driven dimension
27	Feature Oper >Suppress	Suppress the shell feature	mLb on shell in Model Tree > Done	Shell and lock disappear
28	>File >Save As	Save file	Save **tut11-4b**	
29	>QuitWindow			
30	Exit	Exit program	Click Yes to confirm	PT/Modeler exited

Item	Step 6
Disp DtmPln	No
Spin Center	No
Disp Pnts	No
Disp Axes	Checked
Rendering	Hidden line

Table T11.4   Environment Settings

11.10 The IF ELSE Conditionals

Before we begin, we need to look at the IF statement. You can formulate an IF statement where you indicate "perform these relations if condition is true." You proceed and follow the statements with the IF statement and the ENDIF statement as follows:

```
IF (condition is TRUE)
    Relation
    Relation
ENDIF
```

A second form of this is the IF-ELSE statement as follows:

```
IF (condition is TRUE)
    Relation
    Relation
ELSE
```

```
        Relation
        Relation
    ENDIF
```

The conditions utilize the comparison operators as shown in Table 11.3. We will be using only the Equal to conditional in this tutorial. Note that there are two equal signs signifying that a conditional statement is checking if one item is equal to another item.

Operator	Description
==	Equal to
>	Greater than
>=	Greater than or equal to
!=	Not equal to
>	Less than
<=	Less than or equal to
|	Or logical operator
&	And logical operator
!	Not

Table 11.3   Conditional Expressions

11.11 Conditional Statements in Relations

In Tutorial 11.5, you will add a set of conditional statements to handle the case when desiring a pattern with only one unit. This tutorial will complete our part. I have done some work on the part since our last tutorial. I patterned the lock protrusion on the back of the part, providing relations for all dimensions. Basically, I mimicked the steps in Tutorial 11.3. The Relations file is shown in Relation 11.5. I have structured the file in the following ways.

1. I have provided a prefix and suffix. The prefix sets up the local dimensions and constant dimensions.
2. The main body contains the code.
3. The suffix copies all local dimensions back to global dimensions.

When you run the tutorial, you will see that the part has patterned bumps and pattern locks as shown in Figure 11.9(a). Note that the locks are in between the bumps. Consequently, there is one more patterned instance of bumps than there is for locks. I have taken advantage of this by making the lock repeat count dependent on the bump repeat count as follows:

```
lock_pat_repeat_H = bump_pat_repeat_H - 1
lock_pat_repeat_V = bump_pat_repeat_V - 1
```

Looking at Figure 11.9(b), we begin to see the pattern. We have a standard block length that contains one bump. This standard can be duplicated in either direction, making blocks that are 1 by 2, 2 by 2, 2 by 4, or 4 by 4, etc. The size of the part, as indicated by Hor and Ver, determines the number of bumps and locks. The size should always be a multiple of standard. If there are at least 2 by 2 bumps, then there can also be a lock. A block that is one standard wide is shown in Figure 11.9(c). Note that the size of the lock is smaller to accommodate the shorter distance between the bumps. I took the liberty of tying the diameter of the bump to two-thirds of the standard size. Figure 11.9(d) shows the dimension names for the patterned locks.

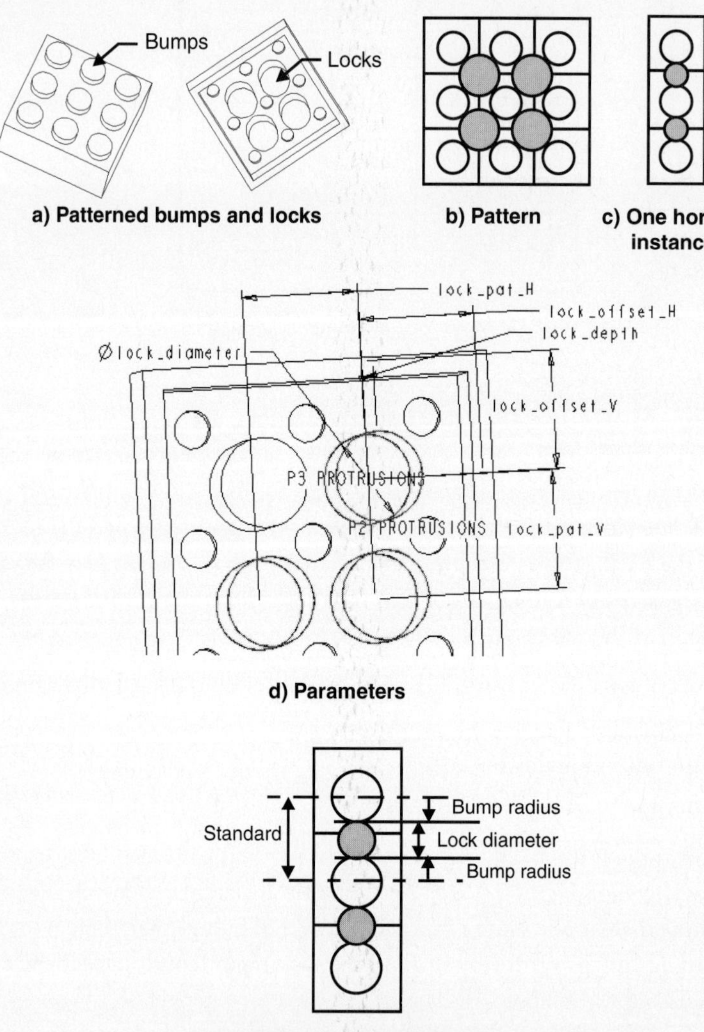

Figure 11.9   Illustrations for Tutorial 11.5.

We now have a way of driving the entire design of the block by two dimensions, the Hor and Ver of the base.

Relation 11.5: Relation File entering Tutorial 11.5

```
/* ************** setup dimensions at entry *************
/* standard is a size constant
standard = 50
BUMP_DEPTH = 10
Lock_less_depth = 2

/* dimension bump circle diameter to be 1/3 of size
BUMP_DIAMETER = (standard *2)/ 3

/* bump pattern repeat counts
bump_pat_repeat_H = P0
bump_pat_repeat_V = P1

/* lock pattern repeat counts
lock_pat_repeat_H = P3
lock_pat_repeat_V = P2

/* offsets from back-left corner are fixed to standard
OFF_H = standard
OFF_V = standard

/* bump dimensions
BUMP_OFF_H = standard/2
BUMP_OFF_V = standard/2

/* bump pattern dimensions
bump_pat_off_H = standard
bump_pat_off_V = standard

/* ********************** setup repeat counts
/* bump pattern repeat counts
bump_pat_repeat_H = HOR / standard
bump_pat_repeat_V = VER / standard

/* thickness of shell
SHELL_THICK = BUMP_OFF_H - BUMP_DIAMETER/2

/* lock pattern dimensions
LOCK_OFF_V = standard
LOCK_OFF_H = standard

/* determine the lock diameter
/* hypotenuse
```

```
hy = 1.414 * BUMP_OFF_H

/* diameter
LOCK_DIAMETER = 2 * (hy - (BUMP_DIAMETER/2))

/* fix depth of lock
LOCK_DEPTH = DEPTH - Lock_less_depth

/* ******* handle the case when the Hor is only one standard size *******
IF BUMP_PAT_REPEAT_H == 1
/* H repeat count for locks
LOCK_PAT_REPEAT_H = 1
/* H distance from lock center to center axis
LOCK_OFF_H = standard / 2
ELSE
/* H repeat count for locks
LOCK_PAT_REPEAT_H = BUMP_PAT_REPEAT_H -1
/* H distance from lock center to center axis
LOCK_OFF_H = standard
ENDIF

/* ******* handle the case when the Ver is only one standard size ********
IF BUMP_PAT_REPEAT_V == 1
/* V repeat count for locks
LOCK_PAT_REPEAT_V = 1
/* V distance from bump center to center axis
LOCK_OFF_V = standard / 2
ELSE
/* V repeat count for locks
LOCK_PAT_REPEAT_V = BUMP_PAT_REPEAT_V-1
/* V distance from bump center to center axis
LOCK_OFF_V = standard
ENDIF

/* handle the lock diameter when either dimension is one standard size
IF ((BUMP_PAT_REPEAT_H==1) | (BUMP_PAT_REPEAT_V==1))
LOCK_DIAMETER = standard - BUMP_DIAMETER
ENDIF

/* ************* restore dimensions before exit *************
/* reset the bump pattern repeat counts
P0 = bump_pat_repeat_H
P1 = bump_pat_repeat_V
```

/* reset the lock pattern repeat counts
P3 = lock_pat_repeat_H
P2 = lock_pat_repeat_V

In Tutorial 11.5, you will first tie the repeat count to the Hor and Ver of the block. Together we will then deal with the problem case that occurs when either the Hor or Ver are one standard unit.

First things first. We can determine the number of instances of the bump as follows:

bump_pat_repeat_H = Hor / standard
bump_pat_repeat_V = Ver / standard

That is simple enough. But what happens when either is equal to 1? Determining the dependent lock repeat counts would be set to 0 and patterns do not like that. We also have two other problems. The first is the size of the lock. The lock now has to sit inline with the bumps leaving less space between the bumps. The lock has to be smaller, as seen in Figure 11.9(c). Secondly, the horizontal offset of the lock has to be the same as the horizontal offset of the bumps.

Tutorial 11.5 Adding Conditionals to the Relations

Files opened: Tut11-5a.prt   **Files saved:** Tut11-5b.prt

Step	Action	Description	Further Actions	Result
1	Click PT/Modeler Icon	Run PT/Modeler		After some time, PT/Modeler on screen
2	>Mode >Misc >Show Dir	Show current directory		Message similar to "Directory searched is c:\ptc\ptprod\bin"
3	>Change Dir	Change the current directory	Type **c:\proe\tutorial\ chapter_11**	
4	>Done-Return	Leave Misc menu		Misc menu removed
5	>Mode >Part >Retrieve	Read a part	Type **tut11-5a**	Part read
6	>Environment	Set up the environment	Set up checks as seen in Table T11.5 Column Step 6	
7	>Done-Return			
8	>Feature >Relation	Set up the relation	Type line as seen in Relation 11.5; Save/Exit	
9	>Regenerate	Regenerate the part		Regeneration successful
10	>Modify | Value	Change the Hor value	Click on base	
11	Click on Hor	Change Hor	Type **200**	
12	Click on Ver	Change Ver	Type **100**	
13	>Regenerate		>Done	Create a 4 by 2 piece
14	>Modify | Value	Change the Hor value	Click on base	
15	Click on Hor	Change Hor	Type **50**	
16	Click on Ver	Change Ver	Type **100**	
17	>Regenerate		>Done	Create a 1 by 2 piece
18	>Modify | Value	Change the Hor value	Click on base	
19	Click on Hor	Change Hor	Type **150**	
20	Click on Ver	Change Ver	Type **50**	
21	>Regenerate		>Done	Create a 3 by 1 piece
22	>Modify | Value	Change the Hor value	Click on base	
23	Click on Hor	Change Hor	Type **450**	
24	Click on Ver	Change Ver	Type **300**	
25	>Regenerate		>Done	Create a 9 by 6 piece
26	>File >Save As	Save file	Save **tut11-5b**	
27	>QuitWindow			
28	Exit	Exit program	Click Yes to confirm	PT/Modeler exited

Item	Step 6
Disp DtmPln	No
Spin Center	No
Disp Pnts	No
Disp Axes	No
Rendering	No hidden line

Table T11.5   Environment Settings

The following equalities have to be added before we restore our global variables at the end of the file. These equalities check for a single bump in either the horizontal or vertical dimension. The two cases are identical so I will discuss only the horizontal.

When there is one horizontal bump, there has to be one horizontal lock. Otherwise, there is one less lock than bump. When there is one horizontal bump, the offset of the lock is half of its normal size. This puts it colinear with the bumps. Lastly, if there is either one horizontal or vertical bump, the diameter of the lock has to be decreased to the standard distance - 2*bump radius. However, 2*bump radius is equal to bump diameter. This is shown in Figure 11.9(e).

Relation 11.6: Equalities

```
/* ******* handle the case when the Hor is only one standard size *******
IF BUMP_PAT_REPEAT_H == 1
/* H repeat count for locks
LOCK_PAT_REPEAT_H = 1
/* H distance from lock center to center axis
LOCK_OFF_H = standard / 2
ELSE
/* H repeat count for locks
LOCK_PAT_REPEAT_H = BUMP_PAT_REPEAT_H -1
/* H distance from lock center to center axis
LOCK_OFF_H = standard
ENDIF

/* ******* handle the case when the Ver is only one standard size ********
IF BUMP_PAT_REPEAT_V == 1
/* V repeat count for locks
LOCK_PAT_REPEAT_V = 1
/* V distance from bump center to center axis
LOCK_OFF_V = standard / 2
ELSE
```

```
/* V repeat count for locks
LOCK_PAT_REPEAT_V = BUMP_PAT_REPEAT_V-1
/* V distance from bump center to center axis
LOCK_OFF_V = standard
ENDIF

/* handle the lock diameter when either dimension is one standard size
IF ((BUMP_PAT_REPEAT_H==1) | (BUMP_PAT_REPEAT_V==1))
LOCK_DIAMETER = standard - BUMP_DIAMETER
ENDIF
```

The part is now complete. You can generate any block (other than 1 by 1) using this relation set. Suppose you wanted a 2 by 4. You would simply select Modify >Value click on Hor and type 2, then click on Ver and type 4. All that is left is to force a Regeneration. Try setting Hor and Ver to several different values and regenerate to see the results.

Appendix A

Configuration Files

A menu file is provided named MENU_DEF.PRO. This file provides an additional menu item called >New Part. If the MENU_DEF.PRO file provided is loaded into the `<install dir>/text` directory, this >New Part menu item will appear in the >MODE menu. Selecting this >New Part creates a new part based on a template that contains a set of XY, XZ, and YZ datum planes and AX, AY, and AZ axes. This relies on a file named START.PRT which must be placed into search path. A directory is placed into the search path using the SEARCH_PATH statement in the CONFIG.PRO file as shown in the sample CONFIG.PRO file provided.

```
@setbutton MODE New#Part "#part;#retrieve;start;#file;
     #save as;;temp;\
#erase;#confirm;#part;#retrieve;temp;#file;#rename;\
#done-return" "Tutorial: Start a new part"
```

The CONFIG.PRO file that I use follows. Note the use of the F1 keys.

```
menu_horizontal_hint right
PROMPT_ON_EXIT NO
FEATURE_CREATE_AUTO_BEGIN YES
FEATURE_CREATE_AUTO_OK NO

set_menuitem_font -Ariel-6-400-0
```

```
! ************* SCREEN SETTINGS ************
menu_horizontal_hint right
INFO_OUTPUT_MODE SCREEN
VISIBLE_MESSAGE_LINES 3
WINDOW_SCALE 1
TREE_PLACEMENT LEFT


! ************* VIEW DISPLAY SETTINGS ********
! GRAPHICS gl
GRAPHICS opengl
DISPLAY HIDDENVIS
TANGENT_EDGE_DISPLAY PHANTOM
SPIN_CONTROL DRAG
DIM_OFFSCREEN_LIMIT 1.1
SKETCHER_ANIMATED_MODIFY YES


! ************* DRAWING OPTIONS ********
ALLOW_MOVE_ATTACH_IN_DTL_MOVE YES
HIGHLIGHT_NEW_DIMS YES


! ************* map keys ************

mapkey $f1 #view;#default;#done-return
mapkey $f2 #view;#repaint;#done-return
mapkey $f3 #view;#default;#cosmetic;#shade;#display;#done-
     return
mapkey $f4 #view;#names;retrieve
mapkey $f5 #file;#save;#done-return
mapkey $f6 #regenerate;#automatic;#done
mapkey $f7 #environment;#no hiddenline;#done-return
mapkey $f8 #environment;#hiddenline;#done-return


mapkey zout #view;#pan/zoom;#zoom out;#done-return
mapkey zreset #view;#pan/zoom;#reset;#done-return
mapkey zin #view;#pan/zoom;#zoom in
```

Two sets of directories are provided with the tutorials. One set, named Chapter 1 through Chapter 11 in the TUT directory, contains the tutorial exercises. All of the files that you need are located in these directories. A second set, named Chapter 1 through Chapter 11 in the TUTA directory, contains answers to the tutorial exercises.

Appendix B

Useful References

Web Sites: General

Site	Address
Parametric Technologies	http://www.ptc.com/
PT/Products	http://www.ptc.com/PTProducts/
Pro/E the Magazine	http://www.proe.com/
SoftStore Book Store	http://www.softstore.com/catalog/
Pro/E Job Network	http://www.pejn.com/
Pro/E Web Ring	http://www.geocities.com/SiliconValley/Pines/3052/proering.html/
Pro User Group	http://www.prouser.org/
Central Texas User Group	http://www.centex-prouser.org/
Northern Ohio User Group	http://www.zh.com/~nopug/
Pro/E Web Ring	http://www.webring.org/cgi-bin/webring?ring=proering;list/

Web Sites: Tutorials

Site	Address
Rensselaer Polytechnic Institute	http://www.rpi.edu/Computing/Docs/Memos/PROENG
NorthWestern University	http://www.mech.nwu.edu/proe/toc.htm
Georgia Institute of Technology	http://rpmi.marc.gatech.edu/~tutorial/proe_intro.html
University of Alberta	http://faramir.mece.ualberta.ca/staff/toogood/me265/proeng

INSIDE Pro/ENGINEER 2E
The Professional User's Guide to Designing with Pro/ENGINEER
By: James Utz and W. Robert Cox, P.E.

INSIDE Pro/ENGINEER 3E
Revised Edition
Revised by Dennis Steffen
By: James Utz and W. Robert Cox, P.E.

INSIDE Pro/ENGINEER, 4E
Written to Release 18
By: Dennis Steffen

INSIDE Pro/JR.
By: OnWord Press Development Team with Guy Edkins and David Talbott

Pro/ENGINEER Exercise Book 2E
By: Bill Paul, P.E.

Pro/ENGINEER Tips and Techniques
By: Tim McLellan and Fred Karam

Pro/ENGINEER in Practice
Written to Release 19
By: David Bigelow

Thinking Pro/ENGINEER
Mastering Design Methodology
By: David Bigelow

Index